Rethinking Anti-Americanism

The History of an Exceptional Concept in American Foreign Relations

"Anti-Americanism" is an unusual expression; although stereotypes and hostility exist toward every nation, we do not hear of "anti-Italianism" or "anti-Brazilianism." Only Americans have elevated such sentiment to the level of a worldview, an explanatory factor so significant as to merit a name – an "ism" – usually reserved for comprehensive ideological systems or ingrained prejudice. This book challenges the scholarly consensus that blames criticism of the United States on foreigners' irrational resistance to democracy and modernity. Tracing 200 years of the concept of anti-Americanism, this book argues that it has constricted political discourse about social reform and U.S. foreign policy, from the War of 1812 and the Mexican War to the Cold War, from Guatemala and Vietnam to Iraq. Research in nine countries in five languages, with attention to diplomacy, culture, migration, and the circulation of ideas, shows that the myth of anti-Americanism has often damaged the national interest.

D1599139

Rethinking Anti-Americanism

The History of an Exceptional Concept in American Foreign Relations

MAX PAUL FRIEDMAN

American University

CAMBRIDGE
UNIVERSITY PRESS

CAMBRIDGE UNIVERSITY PRESS
Cambridge, New York, Melbourne, Madrid, Cape Town,
Singapore, São Paulo, Delhi, Mexico City

Cambridge University Press
32 Avenue of the Americas, New York, NY 10013-2473, USA

www.cambridge.org
Information on this title: www.cambridge.org/9780521683425

© Max Paul Friedman 2012

This publication is in copyright. Subject to statutory exception
and to the provisions of relevant collective licensing agreements,
no reproduction of any part may take place without the written
permission of Cambridge University Press.

First published 2012

Printed in the United States of America

A catalog record for this publication is available from the British Library.

Library of Congress Cataloging in Publication Data

Friedman, Max Paul.
Rethinking anti-Americanism : the history of an exceptional concept in American foreign
relations / Max Paul Friedman.
　　p.　cm.
Includes index.
ISBN 978-0-521-86491-6 (hardback)
1. Anti-Americanism – History.　2. United States – Foreign public opinion.　3. United States –
Relations.　I. Title.
E183.7.F78　2012
327.73–dc23　　　2012001481

ISBN 978-0-521-86491-6 Hardback
ISBN 978-0-521-68342-5 Paperback

Cambridge University Press has no responsibility for the persistence or accuracy of URLs for
external or third-party Internet Web sites referred to in this publication and does not guarantee
that any content on such Web sites is, or will remain, accurate or appropriate.

for Katharina

Certain truths can reach the ears of Americans only from foreigners or from experience.

– Alexis de Tocqueville

Contents

Acknowledgments		*page* ix
Abbreviations		xiii
	Introduction: The Myth of Anti-Americanism	1
1	History of a Concept	19
2	Americanism and Anti-Americanism	52
3	The Specter Haunting Europe: Anti-Americanism and the Cold War	87
4	Bad Neighborhood: Anti-Americanism and Latin America	123
5	Myth and Consequences: De Gaulle, Anti-Americanism, and Vietnam	157
6	Anti-Americanism in the Age of Protest	190
	Epilogue: The Anti-American Century?	224
Notes		243
Sources		315
About the Author		339
Index		341

Acknowledgments

The field of U.S. foreign relations history has become a big tent, welcoming scholars who are interested in diplomacy and state power, domestic politics and national ideology, language and culture, sources in Washington and sources from abroad. The subject of this book also seemed to demand multiple lines of inquiry, ranging across military intervention and migration, bureaucratic politics and poetry, street demonstrations and diplomacy. My appreciation goes to all my colleagues in the Society for Historians of American Foreign Relations who have pursued a wide range of methodologies in the study of America's complex interactions with the world.

The research undertaken for this book would not have been possible without the generous support of organizations that saw the need for a fresh look at a familiar topic. I thank the Alexander von Humboldt Foundation, the German Historical Institute, the Society for Historians of American Foreign Relations, the Dwight D. Eisenhower Library Foundation, the John F. Kennedy Library Foundation, the Lyndon B. Johnson Library Foundation, American University's College of Arts and Sciences and Department of History, and Florida State University's Committee on Faculty Research Support. I am obliged to the journals that published some of my findings, including topics only summarized in this book: *Atlantic Studies* (on Sartre's transnationalism, in Chapter 3), the *Bulletin of the German Historical Institute* (an early précis), *Diplomacy & Statecraft* (for more on the Caracas summit in Chapter 4), *Diplomatic History* (an overview of the foreign policy dilemma), and the *Journal of Social History* (an expanded treatment of the migrant folklore presented in Chapter 1). I thank the Verlag Klaus Wagenbach for permission to translate and reprint the verses from Erich Fried in Chapter 6.

To historians, archivists are the keepers of the keys. I have depended greatly on their knowledge and professionalism, especially when they were willing to let me use uncatalogued collections or facilitated freedom of information requests in the United States and overseas. For their many kindnesses, I thank Michelle DeMartino, Sharon Kelly, and Stephen Plotkin at the John F. Kennedy Library in Boston; Regina Greenwell at the Lyndon Baines Johnson Library in Austin; Valoise Armstrong at the Dwight D. Eisenhower Library in Abilene and Marty McGann at the National Archives in College Park; Marilyn Milliken at the Roper Center for Public Opinion Research in Storrs; Knud Piening at the Politisches Archiv des Auswärtigen Amtes, Christine Hammann at the Stiftung Wissenschaft und Politik, and Siegward Lönnendonker at the Freie-Universität's archive of social movements, all in Berlin; Heidi Dorn at the Zentralarchiv für Empirische Sozialforschung in Cologne; Stefania Ruggeri at the Archivio Storico Diplomatico of the Ministero degli Affari Esteri in Rome; Dominique Parcollet at the Archives d'Histoire Contemporaine, Françoise Watel and Eric Trouilleux at the Ministère des Affaires Etrangères, and Agnès Callu at the Archives Nationales in Paris; Andrew Murphy and Bill Brooke of the National Archives (United Kingdom) in Kew; Leticia Luna and Jorge Fuentes at the Archivo Histórico Genaro Estrada of the Secretaría de Relaciones Exteriores in Mexico City; Álvaro Corbacho Casas and Sylvia Belli y Latina at the Archivo Histórico-Diplomático del Ministerio de Relaciones Exteriores in Montevideo; Ministro Carlos Dellepiane, Javier Lafont, and especially Carmen Rebagliati at the Archivo del Ministerio de Relaciones Exteriores y Culto in Buenos Aires; and Sandra Gutiérrez of the Archivo General Histórico at the Ministerio de Relaciones Exteriores and Marcela Cavada Ramírez, Director of the Archivo Nacional de la Administración Central del Estado, in Santiago.

Countless colleagues and friends have contributed to this book by sharing their ideas and specialized knowledge. I would like to single out those who took the time to read portions of the manuscript: Michael Brenner, Matt Childs, Mike Creswell, Roger Daniels, David Engerman, the late Jon Gjerde, Jennifer Hosek, Lisa Leff, Richard Lock-Pullan, Eric Lohr, Darrin McMahon, Dirk Moses, Brendon O'Connor, Roger Peace, Tom Schoonover, and Suzanne Sinke. Carolyn Eisenberg heroically read the longest draft and pointed out the path to fewer trees and more forest. For thoughtful conversation, suggestions, and criticisms, I thank Mustafa Aksakal, Patrick Barr-Melej, Bob Beisner, Eva Boesenberg, Richard Breitman, Phil Brenner, Jim Cane-Carrasco, Daniel Cohn-Bendit, Frank Costigliola, Belinda Davis, Christiane Eilders, David W. Ellwood, Eileen Findlay, Edith Friedman, Elisabeth Jay Friedman, Roberto García Ferreira, Jessica C. E. Gienow-Hecht, Pierre Guerlain, Jürgen Habermas, Michaela Hampf, Marcel Hawiger, Seymour Hersh, William Hitchcock, Kathryn Jay, Ines and Gerd Kaiser, Alan Kraut, Peter Kuznick, Nelson Lichtenstein, Allan Lichtman, Alan McPherson, Steven Miner, Leandro Morgenfeld, Shoon Murray, Jacques Portes, Stefan Rinke, Philippe Roger, Peter Starr, Ilka-Maria and Klaus Vester, and Heidrun Wimmersberg. I am continually inspired by the enthusiasm of my students at American University.

I have been blessed with department chairs, Tom Zeiler, Neil Jumonville, Pam Nadell, and the late Bob Griffith, who were wonderful community builders. Norbert Finzsch provided incisive critiques, friendship, and a collegial place to work at the Universität zu Köln. For their indispensable research assistance I thank Andrew Barron, Aaron Bell, Rod Coeller, Matthew Pembleton, and Jennifer Pratt, and Christopher Griffin, who also expertly prepared the index. Assen Assenov, Director of the Social Science Research Laboratory, cheerfully assisted with the processing of survey data. I thank Elena Servi and Jim Murphy for their help on fine points of language and linguistics. My editor extraordinaire, Lew Bateman, has supported this book at every stage of its development. I appreciate the thoughtfulness with which the anonymous referees selected by Cambridge University Press read the initial proposal and helped to improve the manuscript, especially in making it less damned thick. My deepest gratitude goes to my closest reader, Martin B. Friedman, whose gentle instruction and quiet praise have always been the most prized reward for all my scribbles.

Katharina Vester has put up with this book for almost as long as she has put up with me, and longer than it took us to bridge the Atlantic. Under her influence the book and I are in much better shape. Of what this means to me, you can have only the quietest glimmering.

Abbreviations

AA	Auswärtiges Amt
AAPD	*Akten zur Auswärtigen Politik der Bundesrepublik Deutschland*
ACS	Archivio Centrale dello Stato, Rome
AGHMRE	Archivo General Histórico del Ministerio de Relaciones Exteriores, Santiago
AGN	Archivo General de la Nación, Mexico City
AHDMRE	Archivo Histórico-Diplomático del Ministerio de Relaciones Exteriores, Montevideo
AHGE	Archivo Histórico Genaro Estrada, Secretaría de Relaciones Exteriores, Mexico City
AMREC	Archivo del Ministerio de Relaciones Exteriores y Culto, Buenos Aires
AN	Archives Nationales, Paris
APOSB	Archiv der Ausserparlamentarischen Opposition und Sozialen Bewegungen, Berlin
ARNAD	Archivo Nacional de la Administración Central del Estado, Santiago
ASDMAE	Archivio Storico Diplomatico, Ministero degli Affari Esteri, Rome
CF	Country Files
CHEVS	Archives d'Histoire Contemporaine, Centre d'Histoire de Sciences Po, Paris (formerly Centre d'Histoire de l'Europe du Vingtième Siècle)
CIA-FOIA	Central Intelligence Agency Declassified Documents Electronic Reading Room
ConsulMex	Consulate of Mexico
CREST	Central Intelligence Agency Records Search Tool at NARA
DDEL	Dwight D. Eisenhower Presidential Library, Abilene, Kansas
DDF	*Documents Diplomatiques Français*

DDRS	Declassified Documents Reference System Database
DELARGENU	Delegation of Argentina to the United Nations
DIVO	Deutsches Institut für Volksumfragen (German Institute for Population Surveys)
DoS	Department of State
FM	Foreign Minister
FO	Foreign Office
FOIA	Freedom of Information Act
FRUS	*Foreign Relations of the United States*
HICOG	High Commission for Germany
IFOP	Institut Français d'Opinion Publique
IfZ	Institut für Zeitgeschichte, Munich
ItAmbPeru	Ambasciata d'Italia a Peru
ItAmbVen	Ambasciata d'Italia a Venezuela, etc.
JFKL	John F. Kennedy Presidential Library, Boston, Massachusetts
LAPC	Latin America Policy Committee
LBJL	Lyndon B. Johnson Presidential Library, Austin, Texas
LC	Library of Congress, Washington, DC
MAE	Ministère des Affaires Étrangères, Paris
MRE	Ministerio de Relaciones Exteriores
NA-K	National Archives, Kew, UK (formerly Public Record Office)
NARA	National Archives, College Park, Maryland
NSC	National Security Council
NSF	National Security Files
OCB	Operations Coordinating Board
OMGUS	Office of the Military Government, United States
PAAA	Politisches Archiv des Auswärtigen Amtes, Berlin
POF	President's Office Files
PREM	Records of the Prime Minister's Office
PSB	Psychological Strategy Board
PSF	President's Subject Files
RC	Roper Center Public Opinion Archives, Storrs, Connecticut
SecState	Secretary of State
SRE	Secretaria de Relaciones Exteriores
SWP	Stiftung Wissenschaft und Politik, Berlin
USIA	United States Information Agency
USIS	United States Information Service
ZES	Zentralarchiv für Empirische Sozialforschung, Cologne

Introduction

The Myth of Anti-Americanism

"Why Do They Dislike Us?" asked the *New York Times*. The year was 1913, the "they" were Canadians, and the *Times* thought it had the answer: "unreasoning animosity" and "jealousy."[1] It was not the first time the paper tried to explain to its baffled readers why there was resentment abroad toward what many considered "the best country in the world."[2] In 1899, the *Times* editorial "Why They Hate Us" asserted that foreign hostility lay in "envy" of our "political and social and industrial success."[3] The question would be asked again and again in the course of the twentieth century, and each time, the riddle was solved with the reassuring proclamation of foreign vice and American virtue.

Flash forward a century to a moment of national anguish. The horrifying attacks of September 11 were unprecedented in this country. Less new were the questions that followed. "Why do they hate us?" asked President George W. Bush in an address to Congress, the nation, and the world. He immediately provided his own answer: "they hate our freedoms."[4] This was followed by a wave of investigations – official, journalistic, and scholarly – into the distressing phenomenon of anti-Americanism. Since that calamitous day in 2001, more than 6000 newspaper articles have referred to "anti-Americanism."[5] A sampling of their headlines reads "Why the World Loves to Hate America," "Anti-Americanism Is One 'Ism' That Thrives," "An Irrational Hatred," "Hating America, Hating Humanity."[6] The consensus that emerged largely reaffirmed what Americans have heard for a hundred years: foreigners are irrational and ill-informed about the best country in the world.

The twenty-first century has brought a new urgency to the need to understand anti-Americanism, but for the most part, recent discussion has brought repetitions of misconceptions that we do not realize are repetitions because we have lacked a history of the concept. Taking the term *anti-American* at face value, many have gone straight to asking why certain groups or individuals have resented or opposed the United States, finding the answer in psychopathology, malevolence, and ignorance, "an irrational dynamic ... that springs from the need of human beings to explain and reduce responsibility for the misfortunes in their lives."[7] We learn that anti-Americanism is "entrenched in the world's psyche" because foreigners resist modernity or dislike democracy.[8] We have not stopped to consider that the term itself is embedded in the American past, and that studying its history is essential to understanding its meaning – and to revealing the circular effect it has produced in constricting American thinking about the world. This book demonstrates how frequently the concept of "anti-Americanism" has produced analytical failures about conditions abroad, contributing to ineffective policy decisions that have in turn increased hostility toward the United States.

"Anti-Americanism" is a phrase so unusual, so exceptional, as to cry out for examination. We do not often speak of "anti-Germanism" or "anti-Mexicanism," even though hostility and historical grievances exist against every nation. When other countries are resented or hated, we do not elevate that hatred to the level of an ideology, or seek its cause in deep-seated psychology, or in opposition to first principles like freedom and democracy. Of course there is plenty of disparagement of the United States to be found around the world – national prejudices are an international sport – but why has this been turned into an "ism" in the case of only one country? When foreigners made fun of Italy's former Prime Minister Silvio Berlusconi, Italians did not launch inquiries into the outbreak of anti-Italianism. When Brazilians clash with Argentines over water rights or regional leadership, they do not assume that the true cause of conflict must lie in anti-Brazilianism or anti-Argentinism. The few vaguely comparable locutions that do exist have developed out of totalitarian or imperialist ideology, giving Americans some strange linguistic bedfellows. Defenders of the British Empire turned to "Anglophobia" to explain why their civilizing mission somehow met with opposition from the colonized, whereas imperial Russia, "defender of the Slavs," saw "Russophobia" among peoples who stubbornly resisted its iron rule. Nazis called their opponents *undeutsch*, or un-German, while dissidents in the USSR were accused of "anti-Sovietism" for deviating from sanctioned doctrine. "Power tends to confuse itself with virtue," in the words of Senator J. William Fulbright, making opposition to power a perplexing phenomenon to those exercising it.[9] That a democracy would take up the language of empire is a sign that something needs explaining.

We Americans are not accustomed to thinking of our country as another in a long line of empires, and it does differ in important ways from the empires of the past. Yet we have developed in "anti-Americanism" a word as transcendent as our nation's sense of mission, assuming that it is the goodness inherent in America that inexplicably encounters resistance abroad. This book differs from all other studies of anti-Americanism by investigating the concept itself: how it developed, which meanings it has acquired over time, and what function it has served in American politics and foreign policy. The surprising discovery is that our thinking about anti-Americanism has repeatedly led to mistaken interpretations of the behavior of people and states, with results that were not in America's own interest. Rather than asking "Why do they hate us? Why is there so much anti-Americanism?" we may begin by asking, "Why this unique concept for America? And what has it done to us and to our relations with the world?"

The Myth

Myth-making and stereotypes have been the stock-in-trade of "anti-Americans" across the centuries, from the claim of eighteenth-century degeneracy theorists Cornelius de Pauw and the Comte de Buffon that America's inhospitable climate must inevitably stunt the growth of its people and animals to the post-2001 rumor that the attacks of September 11 were a Bush administration conspiracy. Such "anti-American myths" have been thoroughly dissected by a growing cohort of committed defenders who have come to be known as the "anti-anti-Americans."[10] Their torchbearer is Paul Hollander, a refugee from Hungary who settled into a long academic career in the United States.[11] Hollander joins other scholars who think that opposition to the United States is a symptom of psychological or moral weakness. "Primordial emotions such as envy, resentment, and self-loathing," writes Victor Davis Hanson, "explain why the world's elites damn Americans for who they are and what they represent rather than what they actually do."[12] Because "the United States sets a higher moral standard," asserts Russell Berman, "anti-Americanism is the expression of a desire to avoid the moral order."[13]

Other anti-anti-American scholars have compiled lengthy accounts of foreigners who have written or said mean-spirited and often absurd things about America and Americans, depicting a rogues' gallery of notorious "anti-Americans," and convincingly demonstrating that there has been a great deal of biased sentiment directed at this country over the years.[14] This book does not repeat their labors. Rather than cataloguing the recurrent themes in anti-American myths, the chapters that follow address what I call the myth of anti-Americanism: the conviction that criticism the United States encounters at home is produced by disloyal citizens, and opposition it meets abroad springs principally from malevolence, anti-democratic sentiment, or psychological pathologies among foreigners.

Myths are stories we tell ourselves to explain the world's workings and to give meaning to events. Anthropologist Claude Lévi-Strauss used the word *myth* not as a synonym for falsehood but to mean a story that, together with other stories, provides the basis of what a culture believes to be true.[15] He noticed, among other things, that myths tend to divide the world into binary opposites: good versus evil or insider versus outsider. Roland Barthes, whose ideas influenced Philippe Roger's exemplary study of French anti-Americanism, argued that myths are "naturalized" through frequency of repetition by a process of "sedimentation" until they are taken for granted as common sense (*doxa*).[16] The process has important political implications, because myths that achieve the level of self-evident truth can sustain political orthodoxy and exclude alternative views without having to be proved or defended.

To say that there is a myth of anti-Americanism is not to say that anti-American sentiment does not exist. Blanket prejudice plays a distorting role in international affairs, by depriving its practitioners of a sober assessment of another country's intentions and behavior. When some foreign leaders explain U.S. policies by saying Americans are power-mad or godless materialists, they choose simplifying stereotypes no more useful than to say that Italians are disorganized, or Germans are rigid, or Asians are inscrutable. When some protestors see the endlessly complex phenomena that fall under the rubric of globalization as nothing but an American plot, or when they ascribe all unwelcome political change in their own countries to a superhuman Central Intelligence Agency as if it were the only actor on the international stage, they mislead themselves and undermine their own effectiveness in opposing policies to which they object.

If anti-American myths have offered some foreigners an unproductive way to explain the relative decline of their own societies in the face of growing American power, the myth of anti-Americanism has also had a damaging effect. In the United States, it has worked its own logic in a comparable process of sedimentation through repetition, and it now risks hardening into a scholarly consensus that has had profound and regrettable effects on policy makers and the American public. I have undertaken to write this book because those who are unaware of the history of the term – who, for example, erroneously believe that it originated in 1901, off by more than a hundred years – contribute to its proliferation as an explanatory category even though it does less to illuminate than to obscure.

The main function of the myth of anti-Americanism in the United States, and the central concern of this book, has been the constriction of political discourse about U.S. society and especially about U.S. foreign relations, as the concept stands between American policy makers and their ability to draw upon potentially useful information from abroad, or to improve their policies by knowing more about the world for which the policies are made. One recent example should make this clear.

In 2002, France's President Jacques Chirac warned the United States against invading Iraq, basing his advice in part on French – and his own – experience fighting in Algeria. The reaction was fierce and swift: Americans launched a boycott of French goods, burned French flags, and poured French wine down the drain. The Congressional cafeteria revised its menu to offer Freedom Fries and Freedom Dressing. Members of Congress gave speeches saying the bodies of dead American soldiers buried in Normandy should be dug up and brought home, because French soil was no longer fit to be the last resting place of American heroes. Meanwhile, the largest worldwide demonstration in the history of humankind saw millions of people around the globe urge the United States not to begin a war whose necessity was hotly contested. Ignoring this outpouring of "anti-Americanism," most Americans united behind their president's decision as he ordered U.S. troops to march off into the worst American foreign policy debacle of the early twenty-first century.[17]

To an historian, the episode was eerily familiar. In the 1960s, France's President Charles de Gaulle warned the United States against military intervention in Vietnam, basing his advice in part on French experience fighting in Indochina, predicting that a war would last ten years and end in American defeat. When he continued to speak against the war and opposed other U.S. policies, Americans launched a boycott of French goods, burned French flags, and poured French wine down the drain. Members of Congress gave speeches saying the bodies of dead American soldiers buried in Normandy should be dug up and brought home, because French soil was no longer fit to be the last resting place of American heroes. Antiwar demonstrations around the world were labeled anti-American events. Government officials pronounced de Gaulle's "anti-Americanism" to be "a compulsive obsession" and ordered U.S. troops to march off into the worst American foreign policy debacle of the twentieth century.[18]

Decades later, a remorseful Defense Secretary Robert McNamara lamented that he had not paid more attention to de Gaulle's warnings, just as many Americans have come to rue the decision to invade and occupy Iraq.[19] The French have no monopoly on wisdom; each French president had an ambitious agenda of promoting France's interests, sometimes in competition with American ones. But the belief that French policies were driven chiefly by "anti-Americanism," rather than coming from French perspectives that should be judged on their merits, precluded a sober assessment of alternatives.

Definitions

This function of the myth of anti-Americanism – its ability to seriously mislead those who employ it – has been neglected in the scholarly literature and is largely absent from discussion in government and the media. The term *anti-Americanism* is variously defined as an ideology, a cultural prejudice, a form of resistance, a threat, or as opposition to democracy, the rejection of modernity, or neurotic envy of American success.[20] Most scholars agree that criticism of the United States in itself is not necessarily anti-Americanism, and they specify that at least two elements are necessary to make it so: *particularized* hostility toward the United States (more than toward other countries), and *generalized* hatred of the United States (in most if not all its aspects). Foreigners move from criticism to anti-Americanism when they are unfairly selective in focusing on the deficiencies of the United States instead of other societies, especially their own: they become "obsessive."[21] Theirs must be a totalizing view: "Anti-Americanism is a systematic opposition to America as a whole," says Ivan Krastev.[22] It implies "an across-the-board abhorrence of American politics, culture and people," writes Brendon O'Connor.[23] Anti-Americanism is a "rejection of America as a totality," says Peter Krause; "a generalized and comprehensive normative dislike of America and things American," says Andrei Markovits.[24] Barry Rubin and Judith Colp Rubin assert that anti-Americanism

views the United States as "completely and inevitably evil."²⁵ The twin
requirements of particularized and generalized hatred of the United States –
hating the country more than any other, and hating everything about it – have
the appeal of consistency and would warrant classifying anti-Americanism as
both ideology and prejudice.

If we accept this definition, however, there will be few portraits left hanging on the walls of the rogues' gallery. For it is the rare critic of the United
States who is not also a critic of his or her own society, aside from state-
employed ideologues and far-right national chauvinists. The most frequently
cited "anti-Americans" saw both the mote in their neighbor's eye and the beam
in their own. The philosopher Jean-Paul Sartre, often depicted as the preeminent anti-American in France, was an early critic of French complicity in the
Holocaust at a time when his compatriots preferred to pretend that the whole
nation had resisted the Nazis. He also spoke fervently against French control
of Indochina and Algeria and attacked French and American racism alike.²⁶
The leading Mexican writer Carlos Fuentes, labeled "anti-American" by the
State Department, grew prominent through decades of social criticism and frequent denunciations of Mexico's state repression and corruption.²⁷ Among the
best-known postwar German intellectuals routinely dubbed "anti-American,"
Heinrich Böll, Hans Magnus Enzensberger, Günter Grass, and others may have
criticized U.S. military actions, but all of them spent far more time and ink criticizing aspects of their own society that they saw as undemocratic or inhumane,
from the reintegration of former Nazis into the West German government to
the turn to violence by the radical fringe of the student movement.²⁸ All of these
figures praised aspects of American society that they approved of or admired.
To analyze their thinking as obsessive anti-Americanism reverses the process
actually at work: their criticism of the United States was an effect, not a cause,
of their beliefs, which were diverse and evolving (and debatable) but stemmed
from an intense commitment to engagement with the problems of their own
societies.

There have been attempts to develop a less partisan application of the term.
Some scholars have understood "anti-Americanism" as a synonym for opposition to U.S. power. In his sophisticated research on U.S.–Latin American
relations, Alan McPherson uses "anti-Americanism" to describe "a collection
of mass-based anti-U.S. strategies . . . an idealistic but confused resistance to
idealistic but confused U.S. foreign policies."²⁹ This is a sensible definition in
the context of his scholarship, as is Richard Kuisel's use of "anti-Americanism"
to describe French cultural defensiveness, but public discourse and officialdom
have been immune to the more careful usage in these academic texts.³⁰ The
term has not shed the powerful pejorative connotations it acquired over two
centuries of use as an epithet suggesting irrational prejudice and illegitimate
slander.

Having read various thoughtful definitions of anti-Americanism, I have chosen not to argue for the superiority of one or another formula but to histori-
cize the problem by taking a cue from Quentin Skinner, J.G.A. Pocock, and

Reinhardt Koselleck, early proponents of speech-act theory and the history of concepts, who urged scholars to move away from arguments over parsing definitions of "essentially contested concepts" and recognize that their meaning inheres in the way that they are used over time.[31] This book therefore traces how the term "anti-Americanism" has been used historically and how it has come to have a specific and, in my view, pernicious form of discursive power. Its effect may be the inevitable consequence of an abiding faith in American exceptionalism, the belief that the United States is intrinsically superior to other countries. If the United States is a city upon a hill, a model to the world, and its actions intended to spread the benefits of freedom and democracy, then to oppose it must be irrational or nefarious.[32] If the American way represents progress – indeed, as modernization theory in the 1950s and 1960s and neoliberalism in the 1990s and early 2000s argued, it is the only route to progress – then to oppose the United States must be perverse: in the view of modernization theorist Lucian Pye, anti-Americanism emerged from "a constellation of psychological insecurities and inhibitions."[33] As long as American exceptionalism is central to the American creed, a belief in anti-Americanism as the motor behind foreign opposition is the logical corollary to that exceptionalist stance.

"Anti-American" Americans

If American nationalists look abroad and see a worrisome tide of anti-Americanism posing a threat to their survival, criticism from their fellow Americans seems even more sinister, a stab in the back by treasonous compatriots. This is the main argument of Paul Hollander's influential jeremiad against an "adversary culture" he sees undermining America from within. To judge from his examples, all sorts of Americans exhibit anti-Americanism: environmentalists, feminists, voters who supported a black presidential candidate, Catholic advocates for the poor, even supporters of rights for the disabled.[34]

Hollander's vision of an authentic, harmonious America rallying around politically conservative ideas is perhaps more sharply drawn than that of other anti-anti-Americans, but it exemplifies a tendency among those most outraged over anti-Americanism to eliminate from their idea of America so much of what is characteristic of the place. The United States is notable above all for its extraordinary diversity – its population drawn from around the world, its polity founded on a tradition of dissent. This truth does not sit well with some of America's self-appointed defenders, which is why they sometimes find themselves in the ironic position of identifying criticism of authority at home with rejection of the idea of America, when the idea of America began with a challenge to authority. As for foreigners, they must never speak a discouraging word. Thus we encounter the curious effect of seeing European and Latin American writers labeled "anti-American" for calling attention to the mistreatment of African Americans, as if it could not be pro-American to defend the rights of Americans when those Americans are black. Students in Paris, Frankfurt, or Mexico City are called "anti-American demonstrators" when they put into practice ideas and tactics knowingly borrowed from an American tradition running from Henry David Thoreau to Martin Luther King, Jr.[35] Members of Congress have gone went so far as to call Dr. King, whom the country honors each year with a national holiday and whose statue on the National Mall is larger than Lincoln's, "anti-American." That vision of true Americanism is a narrow one indeed.[36]

Some scholars join George W. Bush in asserting that behind critical utterances about America lies a deeper hostility toward freedom. Jean-François Revel calls anti-Americanism "hatred of democracy."[37] Stephen Haseler says anti-American criticisms are "criticisms of democracy itself."[38] Dan Diner argues that German attitudes toward America are a litmus test for whether Germany belongs to "'Western' civilization based on the foundation of individual freedom and democracy."[39] We do have examples of anti-democratic hostility directed against the United States, especially from nineteenth-century monarchists, twentieth-century fascists and state communists, and twenty-first-century followers of al-Qaeda. But much of what winds up catalogued as anti-Americanism is the opposite of anti-democratic. Heinrich Heine, whose sarcastic comments about America appear in many books on anti-Americanism, dedicated himself to the movement for democracy in Europe and paid for it with half a lifetime spent in French exile. When Latin Americans seeking social and political progress were thwarted by direct U.S. military intervention in their countries or indirect U.S. support for anti-democratic regimes, they wanted more of the democracy the United States champions, not less.[40] Majorities of the same Middle Eastern publics who tell pollsters that they do not like the United States also say that they favor democracy.[41] These are not disagreements over first principles, but over how best to bring them to fulfillment.

America as a Concept

Those quick to condemn "anti-Americanism" abroad often have in mind a particular meaning of "Americanism" that represents freedom, democracy, and progress. But there is no consensus on what Americanism is, because "America" as a concept is not stable. Even before the founding of the United States, "America" was a contested place in the European imagination, representing to some an earthly space for the mythical paradise in the West: the Elysian Fields, Eden, Atlantis. Thomas More's *Utopia* (1516) and Francis Bacon's *New Atlantis* (1627) were set in the New World.[42] But to others, it was a dystopia. After 1776, aristocrats looked with horror upon a political system that they believed was based on mob rule, whereas true democrats might find inspiration there even as they condemned a version of human freedom that allowed for human slavery. In the later nineteenth century, both left and right cast America as a materialistic Mammon, an industrial Moloch whose machinery would crush spiritual or communal values, the exemplar and source of much that was wrong with the modern world. These tropes appear in travel literature, political commentary, and fiction, and they proved remarkably enduring – in part because they drew upon observable aspects of U.S. society. In the twentieth century, the left also deplored the power of finance capital, the Taylorist regimentation of labor, and military adventurism abroad. The right abhorred what it saw as the tendency toward social leveling, a mass culture that appealed to plebian tastes, an emasculated male population lacking a martial tradition and dominated by women who, in gaining political power, had lost their femininity. Above all, rightists recoiled at what they saw as rampant racial mixing in a country whose vulgar music (jazz) was black and whose economic power (Wall Street) was in Jewish hands.[43] In Latin America, the appropriation of the term *America* itself by the northern half of the hemisphere was contested. José Martí wrote defiantly of *Nuestra América*, "our America." In 1901, José Enrique Rodó drew on Shakespeare's *Tempest* when he wrote the most popular book of his era, comparing South America to a spiritual Ariel, guardian of Mediterranean culture, who challenges the soulless, materialistic Caliban of the North.[44] Most important, to the apprehensive critics America represented the likely future for their own societies, a prospect that was a source of hope when positive aspects were stressed, but not for those who saw American society taking the shape of their own fears. These symbolic meanings of America overlapped in complex ways, as Figure 1 demonstrates.

That America looms large in discussions abroad reflects its role as a site for the projection of ideas, a dream factory long before the establishment of Hollywood. For two centuries, "America" has often served in other countries as a symbol in internal political disputes about capitalism, technology, urbanization, immigration, gender roles, youth culture, and other issues in societies undergoing change, especially when they are destabilized by the industrializing process. As the first modern democratic republic and an early industrializer, America could seem to be blazing a path for other societies to follow, and so discourse about the United States often represents a position in a debate about one's own world and how it should change.[45] This was true in the nineteenth century, and it is still true today, as arguments over social policy and government regulation are often articulated for or against "the American model" or "American conditions" – *amerikanische Verhältnisse, condizione americane, el modelo norteamericano, le modèle anglo-saxon*. (The French phrase combines the British and American models into one, thereby conflating two countries divided by a common tongue but often united by shared ideas on political economy – and simultaneously transferring the accumulated baggage of a thousand-year rivalry with the British onto their descendants across the Pond.)

These debates are principally about the relationship of the government to the market and to private life, using America as shorthand. "American conditions" usually refers to low taxes, weak labor unions, lightly regulated corporations, market-based health care and education, and so on, in the way that "Rhenish capitalism" or "Scandinavian socialism" can be shorthand for other models that involve more government intervention to guide development and protect workers, families, and the environment. In other words, "America" has

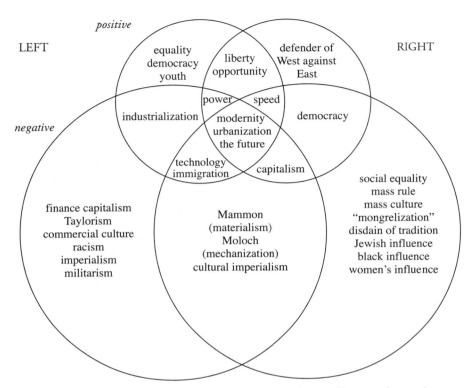

FIGURE 1. America as a concept. Here I use a Venn diagram to illustrate the overlapping attributes associated with the United States as they are viewed positively or negatively – or ambivalently – by left and right abroad. Because "America" and "Americanism" can have such diverse meanings, there is no necessary correlation between a given principle and a "pro-American" or "anti-American" stance, nor is approval of American policy or social attributes necessarily an indicator of a democratic or progressive orientation.

polyvalent meanings, and its appearance in political or cultural debates abroad is not necessarily a sign that anti-democratic anti-Americanism is at work, any more than praise for American ways is a reliable indicator of a fundamental pro-democratic position.

The anti-anti-Americans noted this function of America as a symbol in foreign debates. "A large portion of all critiques of the United States and American society are as much critiques of modernity as they are of American foreign policy or economic rapaciousness," writes Hollander.[46] Indeed, the conflation of modernity with the United States makes some sense, because the United States underwent most of these developments earlier or more substantially or visibly than other countries, and the U.S. government often promoted policies that provided incentives or exerted pressures on other countries to follow suit.

The equivalence claim in the modernity thesis – the United States is modern; ergo, anti-Americanism stems from opposition to modernity – is where the logic breaks down. There are highly modern aspects of American society, such as rapid innovation in technology, communication, literature, and the arts, or the integration of immigrants into the national community, and the participation of women in the paid labor force. By some measures, however, the United States was and is less modern than, for example, some Western European countries: it took longer to adopt a system of social welfare, engages in harsher punishment for criminals (including the death penalty and the world's highest incarceration rates), has been slower to adopt environmental and workplace protections, and has fewer women in high elective office. The United States has also often been more reluctant to adopt treaties and join supranational institutions intended to reduce the frequency and brutality of armed conflict, and in the twenty-first century it officially reintroduced routine physical abuse of some prisoners suspected of politically motivated crimes. Whatever their political or policy merits, these attributes do not make American society more modern than its counterparts. Not only are Americans less secular than comparable societies – religion is "very important" to 59 percent of Americans, but only 21 percent of Germans and 11 percent of the French – but they are also less committed to free trade, a central element of capitalist modernity.[47] In a recent survey of 24 countries, Americans came in 24th among nationalities that agreed with the statement, "Growing trade ties between countries are very good or somewhat good for your country." Germans, French, Russians, Chinese, Lebanese, Brazilians, and Poles all support increased international trade by majorities of 80 percent or more, whereas for Americans, the figure is about half. If Americans are the least supportive of international trade, this certainly clouds the notion that "anti-Americanism" is an objection to economic globalization or capitalist modernity – unless Americans are the most anti-American of the lot.[48] In the modern world, societies have embraced varied approaches to the pursuit of happiness; Americans are not the only people to have found avenues for pursuing scientific advancement, human rights, social equality, and material gain. Hollander might think that "Americanization is the major, perhaps the only, widespread form of modernization," but in the real world, there are many modernities.[49]

Anti-Americanism Is Anti-Semitism?

The imagery accompanying some protest of U.S. policies in the Middle East has revived the question of anti-Americanism's links to anti-Semitism. Ever since Max Horkheimer observed in 1967 that "everywhere where one finds anti-Americanism, anti-Semitism also flourishes," anti-anti-Americans have emphasized the connections between the two. There are striking similarities in the ugly charges that both Americans and Jews are rootless, money-grubbing, uncannily powerful bearers of modernity who threaten traditional societies and seek to dominate the world. Much was made of the Jewish origin of advisers to presidents Franklin D. Roosevelt and George W. Bush, as if Jews somehow manipulated the American government from behind the scenes. One can hear, in attacks on the outsized influence of New York investment banks in the international financial system, echoes of conspiracy theories about Jewish banking families secretly controlling world affairs. As Horkheimer put it, "the general malaise caused by cultural decline seeks a scapegoat. . . . It finds the Americans and, in America itself, once again the Jews, who supposedly rule America."[50]

But this observation can be carried too far, as in the assertion that "the growing hatred of America is but another form of Judeophobia," or that "anti-Americanism can even be understood as a further stage in the secularized hostility towards Jews."[51] To claim that anti-Americanism is but a veiled anti-Semitism has the intended effect of de-legitimizing any critiques of the United States. Enlightened circles in the West rightly no longer tolerate any point on the continuum of prejudice that begins with stereotypes and hostile jokes about Jews, develops into criticism and hatred, and culminates in mass murder: any anti-Semitism, we have come to believe, could lead to another Holocaust. If anti-Semitism and anti-Americanism are understood as parallel prejudices, then it becomes unacceptable to engage in any kind of criticism or stereotype of Americans, because that could be the entry point on a continuum that culminates in fanatical hatred and mass murder: any anti-Americanism, such logic would imply, might lead to another 9/11 or worse.

This would be a powerful admonition to America's critics anywhere, were it not for a basic structural difference between the two forms of prejudice that makes the equivalence fundamentally flawed. It is never legitimate to hold "the Jews" responsible for anything, because there is no such collectivity that behaves as a unit. There is a country called Israel and known as "the Jewish state," but in spite of what some Zionists or anti-Zionists might think, the Jews of the world are not in fact acting in concert through that state. There is no such thing as a monolithic entity called "the Jews" who together carry out acts of any kind. To say that they do is to indulge in the anti-Semitism familiar from such phrases as "the Jews control Hollywood" or "the Jews killed Christ."[52]

There is, however, a collectivity called "the Americans," who jointly elect their leaders and fund their nation's activities through their tax payments. This basic aspect of citizenship under the nation-state system is not an argument for holding individual Americans responsible for any particular U.S. government policy, but to say that "the Americans are occupying Iraq" is qualitatively different from saying "the Jews are occupying the West Bank." To criticize "the Americans" for, say, producing high rates of environmental pollution might be shorthand, but it is legitimate shorthand in informal discourse on international affairs and need no more convey a sentiment of "anti-Americanism" than to criticize "the Chinese" for the same thing would indicate anti-Sinism. To criticize "the Jews" for anything, however, is always illegitimate – and an indication of anti-Semitic prejudice. Thus the apparent parallel between anti-Americanism and anti-Semitism breaks down. The notion that opposition to U.S. policy (or to Israeli policy, for that matter) can be traced principally to irrational enmity and prejudice carries the danger of misdiagnosis – and of stifling a needed discussion of policy alternatives.

Rethinking Anti-Americanism

The concept of anti-Americanism has evolved over time, as has its impact. This book traces the history of its development. Research in the archives and libraries of nine countries in five languages allows some familiar episodes to appear in a new light, showing that the assumption that anti-American prejudice explains foreign criticism or opposition to U.S. policy has constricted discussion and harmed U.S. interests. The myth of anti-Americanism has inhibited the ability of policy makers to see beyond their faith in the superiority of American thinking, thereby retarding progressive reform and encouraging foreign adventurism.

This study does not attempt a comprehensive, global history of "anti-Americanism." It focuses on Western Europe and Latin America, two regions long understood as the most vital areas of U.S. interest, where an American presence in the form of political ascendancy, trade ties, military power, and cultural influence has been the longest lived. For that reason, they have also generated the greatest volume of commentary on the United States. As regions with a shared cultural tradition firmly located in "the West" or "the Free World" – as contested as those expressions may be – they have posed a dilemma that has perplexed Americans for generations: Why has so much conflict arisen where common values and shared interests seem to exist? It is not difficult to explain hostile discourse in the Soviet Union or the People's Republic of China during the Cold War. The epistemological challenge for this book is not to understand officially sponsored ideological anti-American doctrine by rivals of the United States, which is self-explanatory, but to understand why many Americans have seen "anti-Americanism" where they expected to find compliance and gratitude.

Derogatory stereotypes, criticism, and opposition have been directed against every nation, and perhaps most frequently against powerful countries that make their presence widely felt. In that regard America is no exception. What is unusual is that Americans have elevated such routine sentiment when directed against ourselves to the level of a worldview freighted with symbolic import, an explanatory factor so encompassing in its significance as to merit a name – an "ism" – usually reserved for comprehensive ideological systems or ingrained prejudice. This curious state of affairs did not arise overnight. It has a history of its own.

Chapter 1, "History of a Concept," reveals the evolution of the terms "anti-American" and "anti-Americanism" from the earliest recorded usage in the eighteenth century through recurrent nineteenth-century struggles between nationalists and cosmopolitans, racial supremacists and abolitionists, hawks and doves, each of whom sought to deploy the term to take advantage of its impressive rhetorical power. "Anti-Americanism" was used to slander Americans as disloyal for questioning the drive to war against Britain in 1812 and Mexico in 1846, as well as to ridicule Latin Americans angered by U.S. encroachment on their independence. Foreign critics often derided as elitists who disdained democracy are shown here in a new light, from Frances

Trollope and Charles Dickens to Heinrich Heine and Francisco Bilbao: passionately devoted to human rights and democratic reform, they have been routinely mischaracterized and their life's work misunderstood through the anti-American label. This chapter engages the arguments of intellectual historians by reconsidering the writings of "anti-American" elites, and those of cultural historians by drawing on underutilized linguistic sources to call into question the conventional claim that the United States appeared to "pro-American" masses abroad principally as a promised land of freedom.

The second chapter, "Americanism and Anti-Americanism," examines how the concept of anti-Americanism flourished in the first half of the twentieth century as a category of analysis widely used – and misused – by journalists, scholars, and government officials. The political contention over its meaning ended in a rightist victory, and the term became a club wielded to silence the left with charges of disloyalty against domestic critics on the one hand, and with the ascription of irrationality to uncooperative foreigners on the other. Just as American nationalists sought to monopolize the concept of "100% Americanism" to exclude immigrants and socialists from the national community, the term "anti-Americanism" had the effect of associating traitorous qualities with political dissent, social reform, and transnational identities at home, and of depicting as unreasonable the national interests of foreigners in disputes with the United States. The first great social revolution of the twentieth century, in Mexico, prompted a flurry of dispatches and publications by Americans in and out of government attributing Mexican violence to an "anti-Americanism" rooted in passion rather than reason. Intellectuals came in for the same treatment, such as Great Britain's George Bernard Shaw and Austria's Stefan Zweig, although analysis of their writings demonstrates that anti-Americanism had little if anything to do with their thinking. The anti-American label that was applied to the globalization of protest over the execution of the anarchists Sacco and Vanzetti is called into question through a comparison to similar global outrage over the persecution of Alfred Dreyfus in France, showing that both reflected the birth of a transnational movement for human rights rather than any obsessive hostility against America. Just how unreliable is the concept of "anti-Americanism" can be seen in what should be the most extreme case of the twentieth century: Adolf Hitler came to express hateful stereotypes of Americans quite late, after years as an enthusiast of American technology and fan of its restrictive immigration policy who idolized Henry Ford and admired Walt Disney. His embrace of some aspects of America did not prevent him from launching a war against the United States; his equally ill-informed negative views were a product of his belligerent agenda, not its cause.

The third chapter, "The Specter Haunting Europe: Anti-Americanism and the Cold War," shows how the Cold War magnified the discursive power of "anti-Americanism" by embedding it in a global clash between the superpowers in which individual people, countries, and national movements were all expected to choose a side. If domestic critics or social reformers had suffered from being described as "anti-American" before, now the charge was exacerbated, tinged with a specific kind of disloyalty linked to a foe assumed to be engaged in subversion to undermine the United States from within. The national security state created after 1947 institutionalized the concept of anti-Americanism, as it was measured, analyzed, and addressed through policy initiatives. The confluence of academic investigation, scientific polling, and government investment in public diplomacy helped to push anti-Americanism to the forefront of Cold War concerns, even as the basic conceptual weakness of the term went largely unnoticed. Its distorting effects interfered with U.S. perceptions of foreign behavior as well as U.S. foreign policy. Careful reading of polling methods and data refutes claims of a massive increase in anti-Americanism in this period, even in France, where Americans remained far more popular than is conventionally assumed. The centrality of McCarthyism and race relations in global perceptions of the United States highlights the contradiction inherent in the claim that foreign critics were infected by an "anti-Americanism" that came from uneasiness over democracy, because many were calling for a fulfillment of America's democratic promise by supporting the movements for civil liberties and civil rights. An examination of Jean-Paul Sartre's writings on America challenges his reputation as an anti-American *par excellence*. The chapter concludes with the private qualms of staffers at the United States Information Agency, whose internal self-study showed that some professional anti-anti-Americans who held government posts could recognize the contradictions of the concept of anti-Americanism.

Chapter 4, "Bad Neighborhood: Anti-Americanism and Latin America," explores the impact of the official U.S. division of the world, beginning with the Truman administration, not only into communists and anti-communists but also into pro-Americans and anti-Americans – the latter category encompassing noncommunist nationalist movements apparently afflicted by an irrational reluctance to follow America's lead. U.S. officials, the media, and scholars might worry endlessly over Latin American "anti-Americanism," attributing it to ignorance, emotionalism, and envy, but evidence from Latin American policies, written texts, survey data, and diplomatic records shows very little resemblance between that caricature and reality. This is sketched through a detailed examination of U.S. policy toward Guatemala, the country in the region of greatest concern to American officials during the early Cold War. Documents from British, German, Italian, and Latin American archives show that governments sympathetic to the United States did not share U.S. assessments of the Guatemalan government as Communist and anti-American. The CIA-sponsored 1954 coup against that country's elected president was condemned from Western Europe to Asia to the Middle East, damaging U.S. prestige and producing the very kind of hostility it had been designed to counteract. The Kennedy administration subsequently acknowledged that reformist former president Juan José Arévalo was not a Communist, but explicitly labeled him an "anti-American" despite evidence to the contrary, and on that basis supported a second overthrow of the Guatemalan government to keep him from returning to office in 1963. The Eisenhower and Kennedy administrations failed to perceive that what they attacked as anti-Americanism in Latin America had other motives and objectives, and when their interventionist policies drew global criticism, they turned to the same misleading concept to discount world opinion and failed to call their own basic assumptions into question – even when such a rethinking of the notion of "anti-Americanism" might have produced policies more in line with the long-term interests of the United States.

Chapter 5, "Myth and Consequences: De Gaulle, Anti-Americanism, and Vietnam," yields new insights into the textbook case of an important Western leader whose policies seemed to be driven by anti-Americanism. U.S. intelligence and diplomatic officials explained French policies, and French President Charles de Gaulle's own agenda, using the language of mental illness popularized by the postwar growth of interest in psychology. His outspoken opposition to the Vietnam War was laid to his alleged predisposition to hate the United States for personal, cultural, and psychological reasons. This chapter refutes the conventional wisdom by showing that de Gaulle's policies reflected dispassionate French assessments of French and Western interests, and that his conflicts with the United States were offset by tangible and largely unrecognized support on crucial security issues. Archival materials in France, Great Britain, and Germany reveal that his lengthy effort to dissuade the Americans from intervening militarily in Vietnam began as a confidential, cautionary message repeated diplomatically and privately for several years before he finally took his criticism public. His view that a war in Vietnam could not be successful and would be counterproductive was shared throughout the French diplomatic corps by the best-informed Western officials on Southeast Asia, who accurately predicted when and why the American effort would fail, and tried to warn against it – only to be upbraided in Washington for their "anti-Americanism." Bernard Fall, a Franco-American journalist widely regarded today as one of the most insightful analysts of the Vietnam War and of counterinsurgency, was accused at the time of "anti-Americanism" and investigated by the FBI for his articulation of French skepticism about the war's progress. De Gaulle's views were shared – in private – by top officials in West Germany and Great Britain, but their awareness that the Kennedy and Johnson administrations were intolerant of foreign criticism led them to keep their doubts mostly to themselves and present a publicly "pro-American" face of rhetorical support for U.S. policy in Vietnam. This case shows that the "anti-American" French provided the best advice, while the "pro-American" allies, who placed a premium on the appearance of solidarity, helped American policy makers to do great damage to the United States. The concept of anti-Americanism, by closing off alternative viewpoints, contributed to one of the worst foreign policy failures in U.S. history.

Chapter 6, "Anti-Americanism in the Age of Protest," challenges the depiction of the mass international antiwar movements of the 1960s and 1980s as expressions of "anti-Americanism." Protestors in Europe who took to the streets to denounce the Vietnam War or the deployment of nuclear missiles were the most culturally and politically Americanized generations in history. They drew consciously upon American traditions of civil disobedience, enthusiastically adopted American styles of dress, and craved American popular culture, making explicit connections to contemporary American social movements. This transnational protest culture can be called "anti-American" only under the most conservative definition of Americanism that excludes racial minorities, a dissenting tradition, and the left in general from a monolithic America that must be either embraced or rejected in toto. The German New Left, often characterized as driven by an anti-Americanism that emerged out of German ambivalence over its place in a democratic West and the transference of guilt over its Nazi past, is reexamined in the light of its "gray literature" of pamphlets and petitions as well as the writings of some of its leading participants. The movement, the intellectuals who inspired it, and German society as a whole are shown to be far more diverse and less anti-American than is conventionally believed. Indeed, Germans who protested the Vietnam War were often among the country's most committed democrats, who were vigilant for any signs that fascist tendencies might be reviving, and who helped advance the democratization and Americanization of German society. The anti-nuclear movement of the 1980s, similarly misunderstood as the unleashing of underlying anti-Americanism, is shown to have been a transient response to newly belligerent rhetoric and policies of the first Reagan administration. The end of the Cold War was followed by a wave of publications on anti-Americanism, many of which reinforced old myths and introduced new ones, just as understanding the nature and causes of anti-Americanism was about to become a question of urgent necessity in the twenty-first century.

The Epilogue challenges the renewed myth-making that arose in the aftermath of the terrorist attacks of September 11, 2001, and international controversy over the war in Iraq. Analysis of official and public opinion surrounding these events shows that even when discussing horrific violence by terrorists filled with hatred for America, unreflecting use of the concept of anti-Americanism in cases where it is inappropriate has contributed to bad policy outcomes for the United States. The intensification of radical rhetoric and violence directed against civilians should strengthen efforts at understanding and addressing, rather than conflating and misinterpreting, the diverse array of movements that can otherwise appear to be building into a tsunami of anti-Americanism. Just as the idea of a single, monolithic force of "global Communism" proved unhelpful to American strategy during the Cold War, frightening ourselves with the specter of an anti-American world is neither useful nor effective.

This book, then, focuses not on obsessive anti-Americanism among foreigners, which remains a marginal position, but on the obsession with anti-Americanism among some Americans. Studying political conditions abroad through the prism of anti-Americanism risks becoming an exercise in international navel-gazing: it focuses not on understanding foreign societies but on how America is perceived in them, approaching the question with assumptions that preclude taking foreigners seriously. Interpreting international affairs by assigning foreigners to pro- and anti-American categories will remain a monologue before the world as a mirror, to which the only acceptable response must always be that America is the fairest of them all. That kind of thinking produces excellent fairy tales, but fairy tales do not well serve the national interest.

I

History of a Concept

> This is not the Republic I came to see. This is not the Republic of my imagination.
> – Charles Dickens[1]

There are two ways to write about the history of anti-Americanism. Until now, many scholars – the "anti-anti-Americans" – have taken the term at face value and assembled catalogues of published statements exhibiting animosity toward the United States. These histories often convey the impression of continuity, consistency, and consensus, so that in effect they present a single, transnational tradition of anti-Americanism. From Enlightenment philosophers deriding the New World's climate to Latin American nationalists blaming U.S. imperialism for all their countries' ills, we are invited to contemplate an apparently unbroken chain of irrational hostility, an enduring ideological mind-set with a long pedigree. Anti-Americanism, in the conventional approach, is understood as an obsessive and particular hatred of the United States, expressed in exaggerated language and traceable to a fundamental hostility toward democracy, freedom, and modernity.

This chapter differs. Instead of presenting a history of anti-Americanism as if the existence of such a phenomenon were self-evident, it places that assumption under the microscope and examines how the concept of anti-Americanism arose and evolved into a credo of unusual power. This chapter does not deny, by any means, that many people in many lands at many times have said or written ill-informed, derogatory, and even false and defamatory things about the United States. It does, however, ask us to rethink the imposition of the distorting lens that we call anti-Americanism, because the term itself is burdened with unhelpful myths.

One of the most enduring myths of anti-Americanism is that ever since the country came into being, foreign elites have been anti-American, whereas ordinary people have not. The frequency of cultural complaint in the writings of foreign visitors to the young United States has led scholars to make broad assertions. "Antipathy toward the United States has been endemic among European intellectuals... since the founding of the republic."[2] European elites "have consistently been anti-American since 1776."[3] For Latin American elites, anti-Americanism has been "a matter of identity... almost from the beginning."[4] This elite hostility, we are told, stood in sharp contrast to the enthusiasm for America that ordinary people expressed through mass migration, as they "voted with their feet" in favor of the democratic country slandered by the upper classes.[5] Late eighteenth- and nineteenth-century anti-Americanism thus has been ascribed to aristocratic resentment of America's democratic ways, aversion to a land whose political system and culture reflect the importance of the many rather than the influence of a select few. In the words of a standard account, "European skepticism about the total democratic experiment in the new world is the real seedbed of anti-Americanism."[6]

The problem with this conventional tale is that it is based on partial and impressionistic readings of a few classic texts, excerpted and repeated. Many books on anti-Americanism stand on the shoulders of Antonello Gerbi's 780-page mid-century study of early European views of the New World, the source – sometimes unacknowledged – of recurrent quotations from famous authors.[7] Again and again, Charles Dickens, Frances Trollope, Heinrich Heine, Francisco Bilbao, and a chorus of critics are trotted out to deliver their now-familiar lines about American coarseness and materialism. The offending excerpts are disconnected from the wider work, and the authors appear in caricature, without reference to their lifelong political allegiances and engagements. After the negative consensus among the elite is established in this fashion, the corresponding positive consensus among the masses is asserted on the basis of even less empirical evidence. To be sure, there is no shortage of expressions of cultural disdain by privileged foreign observers, and many immigrants were indeed grateful to their adopted country. It may come as a surprise, however, that among the most frequently invoked "anti-American" elites allegedly wielding their quills against the project of democratic freedom were some of the century's most prominent advocates of democracy and social reform, whereas the broad masses of immigrants often expressed ambivalence and disappointment, recorded in their letters and folk expressions analyzed later in this chapter.

Ironically, the myth of anti-Americanism serves to denigrate the importance and legitimacy of social criticism that was aimed at fostering greater democratic practice, while it consigns the lived experience of non-elites to "the enormous condescension of posterity."[8] This chapter questions both of these overly simplified assumptions – elite hostility and mass appeal – and refutes the argument that behind cultural anti-Americanism lurked above all a hostility to democracy.

Origins

Before subjecting some of the canon of alleged anti-American writing to closer scrutiny, we can learn something of the history of the concept itself, which is much older than is generally believed. We are told that the term *anti-Americanism* first came into use in the twentieth century.[9] In fact, it dates back at least to 1767, and together with the adjective *anti-American* was used – and contested – frequently throughout the nineteenth century. The initial, neutral definition of being opposed to America or Americans, comparable to anti-French or anti-Russian sentiment, evolved to acquire a deeper, dual meaning: domestically, the term carried the implication of disloyalty and betrayal, used to delegitimize opponents of war and expansion; internationally, it implied an irrational, often culturally based, hatred of American democracy. These associations have clung to the word right up to our own time, giving it a special rhetorical power that enables the concept of anti-Americanism to cause two kinds of damage, stifling dissent at home while distorting Americans' perceptions of the motives and intentions of foreign critics.

Recovering the history of the concept of "anti-Americanism" helps to explain how it acquired its particular power. Although its earliest uses mostly have gone undetected until now, we can find the word being used even before there was a United States of America. At first, *anti-American* meant simply opposed to the interests of the residents of Britain's North American colonies, or opposed to their aspirations for independence. The *Boston Evening-Post* attacked an anonymous advocate of the Stamp Act for his "Anti americanism" in 1767, because he took London's side in a quarrel over taxation.[10] In 1773, a Boston letter writer condemned "the anti-American doctrine" of Parliamentary supremacy over colonials' wishes.[11] Josiah Martin, Royal Governor of North Carolina Province, addressed the provincial assembly in "a high flying, abusive, anti-American speech" in 1775, unsuccessfully urging them not to send delegates to the revolutionary Continental Congress.[12] That same year, Earl Camden, a member of the House of Lords sympathetic to American protests against taxation without representation, despaired that "the landed interest [in Britain] is almost altogether anti-American."[13]

Once the War for Independence began, the term *anti-American* referred, logically enough, to those who sided with Great Britain against the rebellious colonies. The biweekly *Courier de l'Europe*, an advocate of French intervention on the side of the revolutionaries, used the term *les anti-Américains* to refer to British royalists.[14] Benjamin Franklin's collected correspondence contains multiple uses of "anti American" by various writers referring to opponents of the Revolution.[15] This usage continued after the war was over. John Adams, Benjamin Franklin, John Jay, and Gouverneur Morris all used "the anti-American party" as shorthand to refer to factions in London opposed to reconciliation with the new republic.[16]

Soon, however, those using the term veered from its initial narrow and unexceptional sense of mere opposition and deepened its meaning. Among the most prominent figures to do so was Thomas Jefferson, who, by using "pure Americanism" as a synonym for loyalty, made "anti-Americanism" imply the opposite, that is, disloyalty to the United States.[17] As tensions rose during the "quasi-war" with France at the end of the eighteenth century, the draconian Alien and Sedition Acts aimed to silence dissent and control the activities of foreign residents, and the hunt for traitors was on. In 1798, the Massachusetts *Windham Herald* blurred the line between foreignness and disloyalty, calling for a Constitutional amendment barring foreign-born citizens from serving in Congress "to purge that body of their impure Anti-American intriguers."[18] The same year, the *Albany Centinel* attacked the "Anti American abominations" contained in a petition from Bernard Magnien to the House of Representatives warning that a war with France was needless and full of hazards to American democracy. Magnien, a native of France, had fought on the American side in the Revolution, rising to the rank of colonel, and would go on to command a company of militia defending Norfolk in the War of 1812. His petition, presented on behalf of his company of grenadiers, did not attack the government of the United States or take the side of France, but invoked the duty of American citizens to defend their Constitution, to convey their opinions to their elected representatives, and to be on guard against the danger posed by a standing army.[19] Nonetheless, this decorated veteran of the American Revolution could still be accused of "anti-Americanism" for opposing a military conflict that he deemed not in the best interests of the country he had adopted as his own.

Once the second war against Britain began, citizens who demonstrated against it were attacked for their "anti-Americanism" in New Jersey and Maine.[20] The Federalist Party convention at Hartford in 1815 denounced the war and was promptly castigated by the Republican press as the "anti-American Party."[21] New England merchants were likewise dubbed "anti-American," not only for dealing in British imports (rather than supporting American manufacturing) but also for thereby allegedly endangering the independence of the young republic.[22]

The notion that dissidents betray their nation by calling attention to its faults and therefore should be excluded from it is, unfortunately, a tradition in America that can be traced back to the Puritans. Critics in Denmark and Italy are not routinely labeled "un-Danish" or "anti-Italian" for expressing their political views. They may draw other epithets, sometimes ugly ones. But to urge political change is not to be a traitor in countries that tolerate a broad spectrum of opinion. The rare exceptions of a term parallel to the labeling of Americans as "anti-American" in other countries' domestic politics demonstrate that the "anti-national" construction, although deployed by champions of America's democracy, is anything but democratic. Consider the company we keep when we claim that Americans are anti-American. The leader of the Federation of Chilean Students, Daniel Schweitzer, was exiled by the military dictatorship of Carlos Ibáñez in the 1920s for being *anti-chileno* after he urged a return to constitutional government.[23] The collaborationist head of Vichy France, Maréchal Philippe Pétain, and the French proto-fascist leader Charles Maurras claimed a conspiracy of Jews, Bolsheviks, foreigners, and Freemasons formed *les forces de l'anti-France* – a term taken up by the contemporary neo-fascist Jean-Marie Le Pen.[24] Fidel Castro's followers attacked former revolutionary comrades who deviated from the new orthodoxy as *ex-cubanos*.[25] One of the loudest voices crusading against "anti-Russianism" belongs to the anti-Semitic mathematician Igor Shafarevich, whose notorious essay "Russophobia" was "for Russian national chauvinists of the 1990s what the *Protocols of the Elders of Zion* had been a century earlier."[26] The Nazis burned books by *undeutsch* (un-German) writers, then fulfilled Heinrich Heine's prophecy that when one begins by burning books, one ends up burning human beings. Knowledge of that past has led to the disappearance of the term from postwar German democratic politics.

Curiously, Americans very early began using a linguistic construction that elsewhere is largely the province of authoritarian leaders and the ethno-nationalist far right. This discomforting observation should call our attention to a similarity and a difference. Historically, the cry of "anti-Americanism" has come especially from the most conservative part of the political spectrum. But in another sense, we are seeing how America truly can be exceptional. Because national identity in the United States is linked to a set of values rather than a myth of ethnic origin as in many other countries, opposition to those values could be more readily labeled as hostility toward the nation itself.

At first, just which values were most American, and their violation therefore anti-American, was a matter of dispute. Supporters of democratic government and social justice tried to appropriate the term. The *New York Sentinel and Working Man's Advocate* found the widening class distinctions in U.S. society to be "anti-American," and, joined by *The Catholic Telegraph*, the *Advocate* regularly chided nativists for their "Anti-American principles" of excluding naturalized citizens from political participation.[27] In 1830, Scottish-born social reformer Frances Wright argued that American speculators and corrupt politicians had produced "anti-American institutions" by making the banks, courts, and legislatures serve the interests of the rich.[28] James Fenimore Cooper faulted his affluent compatriots for being "Anti-American" when they expressed nostalgia for a pre-revolutionary aristocratic order. (In a sign of the ongoing struggle over the term's meaning, Cooper himself, sometimes described as the first authentic American novelist for his *The Last of the Mohicans*, was accused of writing "anti-American" books whose depiction of violence on the frontier damaged America's image abroad.)[29]

The power of the term could be both recognized and ridiculed. "An American Patriot" in 1837 signed a satirical letter claiming to be "opposed to all foreigners, and especially the Irish," because Irish immigrants are "clownish and anti-American – and the proof of this proposition is the fact that they adhere obstinately" to their own accents: "If you ask one of them to say 'peas,' he will pronounce the word 'pays,' as if in open mockery of our free institutions." The satirist concluded with praise for "the patriotic services of the Boston lads" who had recently run riot and burned down Irish homes.[30] The point of the satire was to highlight the inherent contradiction of fusing Americanism and intolerance – or of linking foreignness to anti-Americanism in a land of immigrants.

The connotation of treason inherent in the charge of "anti-Americanism," and thus the danger that the formulation posed to American democracy, were both apparent for almost as long as the term has been in use. Early objectors recognized – and decried – its potential as an instrument for silencing dissent. In 1811, controversy broke out over the right of American author Robert Walsh to criticize the policy of the U.S. government. That year, Walsh had launched the first quarterly journal in the United States, *The American Review of History and Politicks*, to oppose President James Madison's confrontational stance toward Great Britain, which seemed likely to lead to war. Madison's restrictions on trade with Britain hurt American interests and aligned the United States with the tyrant Napoleon, Walsh argued; the president was antagonizing a natural ally of the United States.[31]

In the heated political atmosphere leading up to the War of 1812, while the Royal Navy was kidnapping American sailors on the high seas and American "War Hawks" talked openly of seizing Canada, Walsh drew fierce denunciations for his "anti-Americanism."[32] At this point Samuel Ewing, editor of *The Select Reviews of Literature and Spirit of Foreign Magazines*, stepped in to defend Walsh's right to dissent in the strongest terms:

> Is it any evidence of the want of American feelings in Mr. W. that he does not approve of the ruling administration? On the contrary, would he have the feelings of an American if he did not express himself decidedly and independently upon their conduct? Is not this the first and most valued right of the citizen of every free government?[33]

The "charge of *anti-Americanism*," according to the *Select Reviews*, overlooked Walsh's "rational respect for the American people, their character, power, and resources." If Walsh was wrong on policy, the article concluded, "it is his judgment and not his patriotism that should meet condemnation."[34]

Here was an early, full-throated protest against the inaccuracy and malignancy of the anti-American label. For all Walsh's criticisms of Madison (with whom he maintained an active correspondence), he hardly fit the profile of an America-hater. A Hamiltonian federalist and Burkean conservative, Walsh was a strong proponent of free trade who praised "the genius of commerce" and believed the United States had a mission to spread republican government abroad.[35] Thomas Jefferson considered him "one of the two best writers in America," and John Quincy Adams called him "the first internationally recognized American author"; he would later be commissioned U.S. Consul General in Paris.[36] Both the critic Walsh and his advocate Ewing took seriously that core American value embodied in the guarantee of the right to free speech, which the Founders decided to make first among the Amendments to the Constitution, thereby placing dissent at the center of American democracy.

The charge of "anti-Americanism" aimed at Walsh, then, like so many more to come, was not a descriptive or explanatory term but a discursive weapon designed to impugn his patriotism in order to discredit a challenge to presidential decision making on foreign policy. Given the ferocious language wielded by opposing sides in the run-up to the War of 1812, this would not in itself be remarkable were it not for the fact that the term would flourish over the next two centuries as a particularly potent and distorting accusation leveled against domestic and foreign critics of U.S. policies.

Opponents of the extension of slavery and of war with Mexico soon received the same treatment. The debate over territorial disputes in the 1840s, such as the annexation of Texas and the James Polk administration's contention that Mexico posed a threat that called for war, was as heated as that over the calls for war with Iraq in 2003; it was accompanied by comparable skepticism toward presidential claims – and by charges of disloyalty made against the skeptics. Critics of the proposed annexation of Texas in 1844 quickly found themselves stigmatized as "disloyal, anti-national, anti-American" for distrusting the administration's case against Mexico and predicting that it would lead to needless bloodshed.[37] The *Democratic Review* fulminated against the "unpatriotic moral treason" of the opponents of annexation: "this traitorous anti-Americanism has been dealt with all too leniently."[38] Among the "anti-Americans" guilty of "moral treason" were, presumably, almost half the members of the Senate who voted against annexation, and leading opponents of the ensuing war with Mexico such as John Quincy Adams and a young Congressman from Illinois named Abraham Lincoln. Anti-Americans all? The Massachusetts *Pittsfield Sun* denounced anti-war Whigs for their "Anti-Americanism."[39] Henry Clay drew the epithet when he spoke out against the attack on Mexico.[40] Even Mexicans who opposed an unfavorable settlement of boundary disputes with the United States were dubbed not "pro-Mexican" but "anti-American," a term suggesting that inveterate hostility and emotionalism rather than patriotism or national self-interest was the motive behind Mexican behavior.[41]

The end of the Mexican war did not bring an end to the practice of stigmatization by the right. A Tennessee editor labeled Senator John C. Frémont, a decorated veteran and the first national presidential candidate to oppose slavery, "anti-American" for his abolitionist views.[42] By mid-century, congressional proponents of easier naturalization for immigrants were accused of "anti-Americanism,"[43] and educational reformers had to endure the label for suggesting that foreign school systems might offer useful models for the United States.[44] Even before the Civil War, then, the term's implication of disloyalty served as a club to quash dissent, to encourage a martial form of nationalism, and to discourage looking abroad for possible solutions to America's social problems.

Anti-Americanism as Cultural Disdain

In the course of the nineteenth century, the term also came to suggest the kind of cultural disdain and rejection of the vulgarity of American society that it still implies. An editorial in the New York *Sun* of February 2, 1838 complained about Americans who went on holiday to Europe and adopted the attitudes of the upper classes there: "Now our young men are returned rogues and fops, with extravagant anti-American notions, and a disposition to hug and imitate all the follies of European travelers in this country."[45] In 1850, after Thomas Carlyle had his fictional character Smelfungus sneer that America was populated by "Eighteen Millions of the greatest *bores* ever seen in this world before," Ralph Waldo Emerson noted with regret that Carlyle's "violent anti-Americanism" detracted from his literary merits.[46] To respond defensively to European cultural snobbery with the charge of "anti-Americanism" is a long-standing practice, and many scholars today apply the formula *anti-American = anti-democratic*, with the corollary that any criticism of the United States is suspect as culturally elitist and politically illiberal. This myth of anti-Americanism, for all its textual roots, is worth examining more closely.

Well-to-do European travelers by the thousands visited the United States in the first half of the nineteenth century, and dozens of them wrote condescending accounts of American mores. The cultural poverty of the United States had long been an article of faith among some European elites, whether they had experienced it personally or not. The court of Louis XVI was astonished by Quaker habits of dress, and French arrivals in Philadelphia exclaimed that Americans had no fashion sense.[47] The lack of aristocratic style in American life shocked those accustomed to more rarified surroundings. "If I must stay here a year, I shall die," Talleyrand wrote in despair from his American exile. "No opera," a French count pronounces, dismissing the new country in Stendhal's *The Charterhouse of Parma*.[48] A French author in the 1850s shared a knowing wink with his readers when he published an essay entitled "Les Beaux-Arts en Amérique" ("The Fine Arts in America"), followed by three blank pages.[49]

An early inventory of American cultural deficiencies can be found in Sydney Smith's rhetorical query in the "notoriously anti-American *Edinburgh Review*."[50]

> In the four quarters of the globe, who reads an American book? Or goes to an American play? Or looks at an American picture or statue? What does the world yet owe to American physicians or surgeons? What new substances have their chemists discovered? Or what old ones have they analyzed? What new constellations have been discovered by the telescopes of Americans?[51]

This passage is a favorite in books that expose anti-Americanism among foreign elites.[52] Yet Smith was self-consciously indulging in extravagant exaggeration. He not only knew, for example, of Benjamin Franklin's discoveries, but was enthralled by them; he recommended the latest Franklin volume be published in England and added, "I will disinherit you if you do not admire everything written by Franklin" – thereby both repeating his penchant for hyperbole and undermining his claim that Americans produced nothing worthwhile.[53] Smith certainly did not believe this; as a regular book reviewer in the *Edinburgh Review*, he often criticized British travel literature for its unbalanced treatment of the United States.[54] In a letter to the *Morning Chronicle* in 1843, after Smith and other English bondholders lost money when Pennsylvania repudiated a public debt, he wrote, "I am no enemy to America . . . I meddle now in these matters because I hate fraud – because I pity the misery it has occasioned – because I mourn over the hatred it has excited against free institutions."[55] When an American correspondent insisted, asking him "Whence this morbid hatred of America?" Smith replied,

> Hate America!!! I have loved and honoured America all my life; and in the "Edinburgh Review," and at all opportunities which my trumpery sphere of action has afforded, I have never ceased to praise and defend the United States; and to every American to whom I have had the good fortune to be introduced, I have proffered all the hospitality in my power. But I cannot shut my eyes to enormous dishonesty.[56]

Thus did Smith vigorously defend himself from charges of anti-Americanism he considered to be selective and misdirected. A careful reading of the original article that landed it among the canon of anti-Americanism, moreover, shows that even the text in question was more balanced than its truncated form would suggest. C. Vann Woodward cites "Who reads an American book" as an example of European disdain for American cultural backwardness, ending the quotation as above.[57] He does not permit Smith to finish his litany of queries, which, in the original, continues: "Finally, under which of the old tyrannical governments of Europe is every sixth man a slave, whom his fellow creatures may buy and sell and torture?" This was a far more serious critique, one that had nothing to do with cultural elitism, and it connects to Smith's overall argument in the article: he brings up slavery because his polemic is directed not at American cultural inferiority per se, but at the way he feared Americans were becoming a "self-adulating race," who threatened to grow "vain and ambitious," whose newspaper editors assured them they were "the greatest, most refined, the most enlightened, and the most moral people upon earth." Even or perhaps especially the "friends and admirers of Jonathan" (an early nickname later supplanted by Uncle Sam) must puncture the inflated claims of American moral superiority, lest the country lose sight of its true ideals – ideals he shared.[58]

If there could be something other than anti-Americanism at work behind even such texts that seemed to present the United States as a cultural desert, we may need to take a second look at the conventional claim that anti-democratic snobbery explains attacks on the cultural level of the United States. To be sure, some who had the means to enjoy European palaces made possible by the centuries-old tradition of diverting resources from peasants and laborers to a glutted aristocracy sniffed at the pedestrian quality of American cities. Since even the social hierarchies of the Gilded Age would not produce such lasting architectural monuments to inequality, elites would continue to regret their absence from the American built environment. This was true even of some who, like the art critic and social reformer John Ruskin, were horrified by poverty. "Though I have kind invitations enough to visit America," wrote

Ruskin, "I could not, even for a couple of months, live in a country so miserable as to possess no castles."[59] Henry James, whose disdain for American provincialism fueled some of his best novels and contributed to his decision to expatriate himself to England, thought there was no end to what America lacked:

> No sovereign, no court, no personal loyalty, no aristocracy, no church, no army, no diplomatic service, no country gentlemen, no palaces, no castles, nor manors, nor old country houses, nor parsonages, nor thatched cottages, nor ivied ruins; no cathedrals, nor abbeys, nor little Norman churches; no great universities nor public schools – no Oxford, nor Eton, nor Harrow; no literature, no novels, no museums, no pictures, no political society, no sporting class – no Epsom or Ascot![60]

How could culture or respectable society flourish in such a place? Looking down their noses at the failure of the United States to have cultivated a culture of European-style exclusivity for the well-to-do, pampered observers could scorn American ways with enough frequency for scholars to assert that "Anti-Americanism has been endemic among the ruling classes" in Europe since 1776, linking anti-democratic politics to cultural contempt.[61] In the oft-cited formulation by Stephen Haseler, the two basic roots of anti-Americanism, apart from "envy" at American wealth, are

> the belief that American democracy destroys culture [and] the belief that American democracy is based upon excessive individualism in which "rights" have been elevated over "responsibilities." Both of these criticisms are, in essence, criticisms of democracy itself; they should be seen, and exposed, as such.[62]

Anti-Democratic Elitism or Democratic Critique?

This familiar tale of elite anti-Americanism should be modified for three reasons. First, European and Latin American elites were not the monolithic bloc that they are made to appear in the scholarly literature: elite disdain was offset by elite sympathy. Second, the specific criticisms, even those in tendentious writings, were often made by convinced democrats and shared by Americans who hoped to improve their society's deficiencies, which raises the question whether accolades or criticism are normatively more legitimate when a society has glaring flaws. Finally, the endlessly reiterated corollary to the claim of elite anti-Americanism, that the European masses were enthralled by America and proved it by moving there, on closer examination begins to erode.

If anti-Americanism appeared among literate Europeans, there was no shortage of enthusiasm as well. As the first modern republic, the United States inspired foreigners who hoped to emulate its successful creation of a constitutional democracy. "They are the hope of the human race," wrote Louis XVI's finance minister Anne-Robert-Jacques Turgot, a passionate reformer. "They may well become its model."[63] The naturalized Franco-American author

J. Hector St. John de Crèvecoeur thought his adopted country "the most perfect society now existing in the world."[64] Benjamin Franklin was so popular as ambassador to the French Court at Versailles that when he died in 1790, the National Assembly decreed three days of national mourning.[65] Despite the received wisdom that the French have always been anti-American, the United States had its impassioned defenders there. When the Marquis François-Jean de Chastellux published a diary in 1786 containing harsh impressions of his travels in America, he was immediately attacked in print by Jean-Pierre Brissot de Warville for tarnishing the image of a country that inspired progressive Europeans. "Cruel man!" wrote Brissot. "If it had been a delusion, ought you to destroy it?"[66] Talleyrand, Stendhal, or Chastellux might sniff, but Édouard-René Lefèbvre de Laboulaye, a lawyer and historian at the Collège de France, dedicated his career to the quixotic project of getting France to adopt an American-style constitution, calling Americans the "great organizers of modern democracy."[67] The historian of religion, Ernest Renan, argued that as the world "moves towards a sort of Americanism," that may "wound our refined ideas" but will contribute to "the emancipation and the progress of the human mind." As for the cultural level of the United States, Renan enjoined the complainers to consider their societies' more grievous faults: "American vulgarity would not have burned Giordano Bruno, would not have persecuted Galileo," he wrote.[68] The cadre of America's defenders among the French elite might have been outnumbered by its critics, but there were enough partisans in France heaping praise on the American political system that by 1866 the word *Américanisme* entered the Larousse dictionary to describe the "pronounced and exclusive admiration for the government, laws, and usages of the Americans, principally the inhabitants of the United States."[69]

Across the Rhine, German monarchists were predictably hostile, speaking not of the American Revolution or War for Independence but of the American "riot" or "cheekiness" (*Frechheit*) against the Crown.[70] Nonetheless, the American Revolution had its advocates in the German dispute between liberalism and reaction. The *Berlinische Monatsschrift* celebrated the American victory over Great Britain: "You are free!... Free, free now, America!... Europe's rejoicing greets the holiest of all victories!"[71] The translator of Shakespeare, Heinrich Christoph Albert, in 1793 praised the U.S. Constitution and the American people, "the only great people of the history of the world that is truly free and rules itself."[72] Romantic nationalist Johann Gottfried Herder lavished praise upon Benjamin Franklin for his "sense of humanity... clear expression... pleasing sense of humor... [and] healthy reasoning" and hoped that Europeans would read and be guided by Franklin's wisdom.[73]

Travel literature produced by German writers contained a good deal of cultural snobbery, but this too was far from a universal attitude. The German author Friedrich Gerstäcker, who traveled in the United States in his mid-twenties, wrote novels praising the freedom of America's frontier that were designed to encourage emigration there (he was posthumously made an honorary citizen of Arkansas). Gottfried Duden, who farmed in what is now

Missouri, published a best-selling book describing America as a paradise so free of imperfections that he drew angry letters from disappointed emigrants, forcing him to issue a revised edition that warned of the practical difficulties of life in the United States.[74] Even the nationalist historian Heinrich von Treitschke, who never traveled to the United States, thought Americans (and British) mediocre, but he praised the Constitution that Americans had made, and called their political system a "miracle of democracy on Earth."[75]

The great German poet Heinrich Heine is often hastily cited in scholarly accounts as an exemplar of nineteenth-century elitism and anti-Americanism for his scornful attack on "that monstrous freedom-prison, where the invisible chains would crush me even more than the visible ones at home, and where the most abominable of all tyrants, the mob, exerts its raw domination!" Harsh words indeed, as was Heine's claim that "money is their God, their only, all-powerful God."[76]

Heine's sarcasm hardly reflected a consensus. Johann Wolfgang von Goethe's ode "To the United States" turned the charge of an absence of tradition on its head, suggesting that it might be an advantage to a country to be free of old ruins and ancient hatreds. "America, you have it better" than the old continent, he wrote, for having "no dilapidated castles/And no shards" (i.e., of ancient pottery).[77] This "pro-American" voice that is held up in the studies as a counterpoint to Heine came from a man whose relationship to America was more clouded, however. Goethe's enthusiasm for American freedom evidently developed over time. Although in his memoirs he claims to have supported the American War of Independence, as head of Weimar's War Commission he actually participated in the sale of indigent prisoners to the British to deploy as footsoldiers against the American rebels.[78] When it comes to Germany's greatest writer, a simple pro- or anti-schema does not do justice to his mixed record on the United States.

Nor did Heine's disparaging view predominate among his comrades and competitors in the progressive "Young Germany" literary movement that challenged the ethnic nationalism of the Romantic period. Karl Gutzkow called America "the home of freedom."[79] Georg Büchner thought that revolution had failed in France but succeeded in the United States, because its "institutions are democratic, not only in their principle but in all their consequences."[80] Ludwig Börne, a trenchant critic of German reaction, praised the United States as a "republic without guillotines" and urged his compatriots to "make America at home": for plenty of literati, America was literally synonymous with freedom.[81]

Missing from the usual treatment of Heine himself, moreover, is the fact that his criticism was directed not against America's democratic ideals, but its insufficient fulfillment of those ideals. How could a nation claiming to champion freedom keep millions of slaves in chains? Heine's own democratic credentials were impeccable: driven into exile because of his biting satire aimed at German reactionaries, his life was devoted to the struggle to bring more political freedom to his own country. Far from being fixated on America, about which he wrote little, Heine seems to have been an equal-opportunity skeptic of powerful nations, as in the poem he wrote from his Parisian exile, "Jetzt Wohin?" ("Where to Now?"). Anti-anti-Americans like to quote its lines calling America a *Freiheitstall* (freedom barn) filled with *Gleichheitsflegeln* (equality louts) who chew tobacco and spit, but they ignore the other stanzas, in which Germany is described as the land of executions, Russia as the land of floggings, and the mere smell of Englishmen makes him want to vomit. If anti-Americanism is "the *obsessive* stereotypization, denigration and demonization of the country and the culture as a whole," Heine cannot qualify: he did not pay much attention to America and did not castigate it more strongly than he did those nations that more frequently drew his fire.[82]

Two English authors who published books about their experiences appear at the top of the typical list of elitist European anti-Americans. Charles Dickens in *American Notes* and *Martin Chuzzlewit* and Frances Trollope in *Domestic Manners of the Americans* wrote cuttingly about U.S. society. Trollope saw her name turned into a verb, *to trollopize*, meaning to criticize harshly. After *Domestic Manners* appeared in the United States, Trollope was pilloried in print, caricatured in cartoons, and even mimicked as a wax figure in the shape of a goblin. Robert Walsh, having himself weathered ad hominem attacks for his criticism of U.S. foreign policy, published a savage assault on Trollope, calling her "a vulgar and mercenary woman [with] a perverted moral sense, and a sickly appetite for slander."[83] Scholars who include Trollope and Dickens among the leading exponents of anti-Americanism have emphasized the two writers' failure to balance their criticism with praise and their condescending, apparently anti-democratic complaints about the behavior of ordinary people, "British hauteur in the face of American life."[84] A CIA report in 1963 cited *Martin Chuzzlewit* as the antecedent of modern anti-Americanism.[85] So did the philosopher Bertrand Russell, who in 1957 was commissioned to write about anti-Americanism by the *New York Times* – an interesting choice, since Russell would soon find himself on the *Times's* own list of exponents of anti-Americanism.[86] In his notes for the article on "British Anti-Americanism," Russell began with the entries "Yankee Doodle, Mrs. Trollope, *Martin Chuzzlewit*" and went on to condemn British cultural elitism.[87]

The condescension and sarcasm in these works of Trollope and Dickens can hardly fail to strike the reader. Far from a ringing call to defend elite values, however, their most impassioned passages were of a piece with the authors' lifelong commitment to producing literature in the cause of social reform in England. Dickens made a career of exposing the shocking conditions of life in urban slums, crusading against the unchecked power of the Courts of Chancery, and attacking corrupt speculators. Trollope called attention to child labor, the plight of single mothers, and abuses in the church. When they turned to the United States, they placed its society under the same bright light they used to illuminate England's failings. Here, Trollope rails against two aspects of life in the United States that certainly struck many of her American contemporaries, too, as incompatible with freedom and democracy:

You will see them with one hand hoisting the cap of liberty, and with the other flogging their slaves. You will see them one hour lecturing their mob on the indefeasible rights of man, and the next driving from their homes the children of the soil, whom they have bound themselves to protect by the most solemn treaties.[88]

It was for such critiques of slavery and the abuse of Native Americans that Mark Twain praised Trollope for "telling the truth," and credited her for learning her subject better than most foreign tourists – in return for which, he observed, she "was so handsomely cursed and reviled by this nation."[89] Dickens, who considered Trollope a rival,[90] apparently planned to refute *Domestic Manners* with a book extolling the virtues of America when he set out for its shores in 1842, only to have his expectations dashed by what he encountered there. "I *am* disappointed," he wrote. "This is not the Republic I came to see. This is not the Republic of my imagination."[91] He was outraged that unscrupulous American publishers were pirating his works and pocketing the profits from hundreds of thousands of sales, while he labored to pay his own debts. During his visit he lectured fruitlessly in support of an international copyright law and was much maligned by American journalists for sullying his hero's welcome with pecuniary issues. But it was what he discovered about American social conditions that affected him most. His visit to Five Points, the notorious Manhattan slum district, ruined his hopes of finding in America a society superior to England's. In this Dickens followed other progressive British travelers who took American rhetoric seriously and were disappointed to discover the distance between ideal and reality.

As a social reformer, Dickens, too, in *Martin Chuzzlewit* and *American Notes*, attacked slavery and took an interest in the institutions that he regularly targeted in England, including prisons, orphanages, and asylums. He deplored the "noisome vapours" of New York City's Tombs prison and was horrified by the universal practice of "hopeless solitary confinement" at Eastern State Penitentiary in Philadelphia, where every inmate was isolated for the entirety of his sentence so that the prisoners would not morally contaminate one another. But Dickens praised the way such institutions were run in Massachusetts as far superior to British ones, and he argued that Britain should take Boston's as a model.[92] His admiration was not limited to genteel Boston, as some scholars have claimed; he was awed by Niagara Falls, found the West Point Military Academy beautifully laid out and democratically run, and lauded homely Cincinnati for its free public schools. In contrast, he disliked the "wild and rabid Toryism" he encountered across the border in Toronto – a criticism one cannot attribute to loathing for the United States.[93] Some American readers responded positively to his devastating portrayal of their society's deficiencies. A critic writing in the *North American Review* lauded Dickens for suffusing his writing with "practical moral aims" and for possessing "an inexhaustible vein of the pleasantest exaggeration which keeps his readers roaring with laughter."[94] (That favorable review was promptly attacked in the

Spirit of the Times as an "anti-American article," doubtless "the production of some blind and misguided abolitionist" or possibly a "cloistered son of Harvard.")[95]

Interestingly, some scholars of anti-Americanism go further in their caricature of Dickens than he did in his portrait of the United States: he "provides an exclusively negative portrayal of America," we are told; "Dickens is outraged at every aspect of America... he flatly and uncompromisingly rejects the United States."[96] This is a curious characterization, because when one opens *American Notes*, one is immediately struck by such remarks at these:

> I sincerely believe that the public institutions and charities of this capital of Massachusetts are as nearly perfect, as the most considerate wisdom, benevolence, and humanity, can make them.
>
> [Americans] are, by nature, frank, brave, cordial, hospitable, and affectionate. Cultivation and refinement seem but to enhance their warmth of heart and ardent enthusiasm... never can [I] make again, in half-a-year, so many friends for whom I seem to entertain the regard of half a life.[97]

His fiercest criticism was reserved not for American styles but for an institution that had gone out of existence in his own country. Noting that slave owners often challenged the veracity of abolitionist writings or declared "how perfectly contented the slaves are, and how very seldom they run away," Dickens quoted from descriptions of slaves written "by their own truthful masters" in newspaper advertisements such as these:

> Ran away, a negro woman and two children. A few days before she went off, I burnt her with a hot iron, on the left side of her face. I tried to make the letter M.
>
> Ran away, a negro girl called Mary. Has a small scar over her eye, a good many teeth missing, the letter A is branded on her cheek and forehead. etc.[98]

In his gloomiest assessment in a private letter, he wrote, "I believe the heaviest blow ever dealt at Liberty's Head, will be dealt by this nation in the ultimate failure of its example to the Earth."[99] It was, indeed, not the Republic of his imagination, and what he saw would temper his attacks on English traditions, even as he continued tirelessly to agitate against abuses at home; he took a break from writing *American Notes* to pillory English mine owners who were obstructing a reform bill that would prohibit children younger than ten from working below ground.[100]

If Dickens and other critics had kept silent about the darker aspects of American society, would that have been better for the country or its people, more "pro-American"? Trollope and Dickens may have been prone to exaggeration, but they lacked the obsessive and particular hatred of the United States that scholars argue qualifies one as an anti-American, since they pursued the same social reforms in the far more numerous works they produced about their own home country. To ascribe their feelings about the United States to cultural aloofness or a fundamental hostility toward democracy and freedom overlooks their lifelong support of progressive social causes. If anything, they were consistent champions of the poor and the powerless, seeking to enlarge the notions of democracy and freedom to include those who did not yet enjoy them in Great Britain and the United States. Placing them in a tradition of anti-Americanism and suggesting that they contributed to a dangerous, irrational, and anti-democratic discourse is to hold a static view of democracy that excludes energetic critics seeking to remedy its deficiencies.

Slavery and Its Discontents

It should not be surprising that foreigners encountering slavery in the land of the free should have written critically of this central paradox of the young republic. George Washington's comrade-in-arms, the Marquis de Lafayette, once remarked that he "would never have drawn my sword in the cause of America, if I could have conceived that thereby I was helping to found a nation of slaves."[101] Isaac Candler, arriving from England full of admiration for the American ideal of equality, was shocked to find racism in northern and southern states so pervasive it was like "gangrene corrupting the whole."[102] Gustave de Beaumont, Tocqueville's traveling companion, focused his account of American society on what he saw as the country's core moral problem, tension between the races.[103] Another of Tocqueville's friends and later colleague in the diplomatic corps, Francisque De Corcelle, wrote a strong condemnation of humans owning other humans, while acknowledging that slavery still existed in French colonies and that France had nothing approaching the scale of the American abolitionist movement.[104] Tocqueville himself, who criticized slavery in America, on returning to Paris took a leading role in the Chamber of Deputies to try to accelerate France's emancipation of the quarter million slaves in its own colonies.[105]

Did this antislavery commentary constitute or stem from anti-Americanism? Surely not on the part of those, such as Tocqueville and De Corcelle, who struggled to end slavery in their own countries. That the same appeal could come from Americans themselves further complicates the question of whether criticism of slavery should be considered anti-American or whether the institution itself was the greater violation of Americanism. The African-American and abolitionist press featured early attempts to reappropriate a word that even in the antebellum period had already acquired significant symbolic power. In 1827, *Freedom's Journal*, the first African-American newspaper published in the United States, castigated proslavery forces thus: "With a savage and Anti-American barbarity they contemplate the perpetuation of slavery till the remotest generation."[106] In 1844, *The Cincinnati Weekly Herald and Philanthropist* denounced as "anti-American" the principle of the Missouri Compromise, which brought in a slave state for every new free state.[107] *The National Era* deployed the phrase in defense of abolitionists, arguing after the "Christiania Riot" of 1851 that a judge's decision to charge thirty-seven people with treason for aiding fleeing slaves was "anti-Democratic, anti-American, Anti-Christian."[108]

In the same year, Frederick Douglass published in his newspaper a letter from Bob Markle calling the state of Indiana's decision to ban the entry of free blacks "anti-American."[109] The word itself had acquired enough heft as a rhetorical weapon that opponents of slavery and slavery's apologists alike vied to control its deployment in mid-century conflicts. Of course, the fiercest proponents of slavery engaged quite literally in anti-Americanism when the Confederate States of America seceded from the Union in 1861 and made war on the United States. It might seem most logical to call "anti-American" those who tried to destroy the country by force of arms to prevent freedom from being extended to all of its inhabitants. But abolitionists and slaves, although they won the Civil War, lost that rhetorical tug-of-war over "anti-Americanism," because the expression lends itself to a vision of America that is exclusive, not inclusive. National chauvinists ever since have enthusiastically applied the term to progressives, dissenters, and ethnic minorities.

The Pleasures of the Sin of Hyperbole

Foreign writers who fail to praise American achievements or use hyperbolic language in their accounts find themselves in the sights of the anti-anti-Americans, who rightly discern a tendency toward exaggeration in much commentary about the United States, in Dickens's time and in our own. Exaggeration is mentioned explicitly in some proposed definitions of the term: "Anti-Americanism is indicated precisely when reasoned argument gives way to sweeping generalizations and hostile innuendo."[110] An anti-American view is one that "exaggerates America's shortcomings" or portrays American society or politics as "ridiculous."[111] Anti-Americanism entails the "exaggeration of the flaws and failings of American institutions."[112] To avoid anti-Americanism, the argument goes, commentators must exhibit precision and fairness in their treatment of American society and foreign policy.

Any academic committed to objectivity would urge students to follow the same general principles in their formal writing. But a dispassionate, scholarly tone is not the only style of expression that we can or should demand of all writers everywhere, certainly not in literary writing, in which irony and humorous exaggeration can be a source of pleasure and insight, or in some kinds of political writing, in which the heat that accompanies light is intended to express the force of one's convictions. Hyperbole is a useful literary device because its extravagance is effective in conveying an idea powerfully and memorably.

That is what makes so unforgettable such observations as, "It is by the goodness of God that in our country we have those three unspeakably precious things: freedom of speech, freedom of conscience, and the prudence never to practice either of them." Its author was a master of the ironic style, and it would be absurd to place him into the anti-American camp, because he is the national treasure Mark Twain. He was a penetrating critic of American society and foreign policy, a major figure in the anti-imperialist movement during the U.S. occupation of the Philippines, and a wordsmith with a celebrated gift for piercing exaggeration, whose own writings give the lie to his characteristically overstated assertion that freedom of speech is "never" practiced.[113] It is hard to imagine a writer more quintessentially American than Mark Twain, and Americans have rightly placed him in their pantheon of cultural heroes – while cherishing his gift for ironic overstatement. So venerated was this serial exaggerator that the *New York Times* once charged a foreign critic who had the temerity to doubt Twain's brilliance with "ignorance and anti-Americanism."[114]

Indeed, hyperbole is so effective that it has proved irresistible to some of the anti-anti-Americans themselves. Jean-François Revel admonishes critics of the United States for their lack of precision and judiciousness but then makes the obviously unsupportable assertion that "if you remove anti-Americanism, nothing remains of French political thought today, either on the Left or on the Right."[115] Paul Hollander attacks Bertrand Russell for comparing University of California at Los Angeles faculty meetings under a stern president to meetings of the Reichstag under Hitler – a fair reproach, had Hollander himself on another page not compared a professor of literature to Goebbels.[116] Andrei Markovits claims that Western European public opinion is so uniformly anti-American that "I would go so far as to characterize the public voice and mood in these countries as *gleichgeschaltet*" – a term that historians use to describe how the Nazis brought almost all aspects of society into ideological conformity.[117] A glance at the European press, however, will show that the range of opinion among political leaders and editorialists makes an analogy to the uniformity produced by Nazi terror far-fetched.[118] Perhaps authors who claim scholarly authority ought to be free of such exaggeration, but the fact that this rhetorical style appeals even to anti-anti-American writers should help us retain some perspective when we come across exaggeration in the writings of those who are critical of the United States. Yielding to the human affinity for hyperbole is not persuasive evidence that one is afflicted by anti-Americanism; it is simply how we write when we are impassioned.

This brings us back to European travel writers and their tendency to stereotype. It would be difficult to conceive of travel writing that did not generalize from accumulated observations to make sweeping statements about national character. That category may be slippery and unscientific, but Americans welcome such generalizations when they accentuate the positive; if a foreigner asserts that Americans are brave, or friendly, or energetic, or honest, that never draws fire from those patrolling the limits of acceptable commentary, even though such statements are patently stereotypical and incomplete. When America is celebrated as the greatest country in the world, conservatives do not protest about selectivity. It is not the imprecision that offends, but the criticism. As Tocqueville observed,

> America is a land of liberty where, in order not to offend anyone, a foreigner must not speak freely about individuals or the state, the people or the government, public or private enterprises, indeed about anything he finds there,

except perhaps the climate and the soil. In fact, one encounters Americans prepared to defend even the latter two things as though they had had a hand in making them.[119]

Tocqueville holds the distinction of being Americans' favorite foreign observer of U.S. society, and yet he, too, could readily generalize and exaggerate: "They pester you constantly for your praise, and if you hold out against their importuning, they will laud themselves. Doubtful perhaps of their own merit, they wish to have its portrait constantly before their eyes."[120] Trollope, a less sympathetic observer, found much the same thing: "Other nations have been called thin-skinned, but the citizens of the Union have, apparently, no skins at all; they wince if a breeze blows over them, unless it be tempered with adulation."[121]

Whether there was a national penchant for self-congratulation is unprovable, but it was widely remarked upon by foreigners and natives alike. Ralph Waldo Emerson dryly observed that "Our American people cannot be taxed with slowness in performance, or in praising their performance."[122] Basil Hall found most striking among Americans "their eternal bepraising of their country and its institutions."[123] Chicago humorist Finley Peter Dunne's satiric saloonkeeper, Mr. Dooley, was in agreement: "We're a great people. We are that. And the best of it is, we know we are."[124]

Self-congratulation often took the form of pride in size and scale, observed the German social historian Karl Lamprecht. "The largest in the world, the greatest in the world: how often must one hear and read that," he wrote. "In the dining car of some train I even drank the purest water in the world."[125] Canadian author Stephen Leacock, who could be equally biting about his home country, called exaggeration an American national characteristic and credited an American newspaper from 1850 with words he may well have composed himself:

> Our railway cars are bigger and run faster and pitch off the track oftener, and kill more people than all other railway cars in any other country. Our steamboats carry bigger loads, are longer and broader, burst their boilers oftener and send up their passengers higher and the captains swear harder than the captains in any other country. Our men are bigger and longer and thicker; can fight harder and faster, drink more mean whisky, chew more bad tobacco, than in every other country.[126]

Thus was exaggeration used to point to a proclivity for exaggeration. Do critical observations of this nature tell us more about Americans' habits or the prejudices of the authors? One might conclude from the frequency of repetition either that a stereotype was widely held, or that the behavior was widely practiced – or both.

Comments on American foodways displayed plenty of exaggeration, such as Talleyrand's complaint that the country had "thirty-two religions and only one dish."[127] Such remarks played into the stereotype about American cultural underdevelopment, as did observations about the pace with which meals were dispatched in the United States in contrast to the leisurely rituals afforded by European elites. Rudyard Kipling wrote that the American "has no meals. He stuffs for ten minutes thrice a day."[128] German travelers attributed Americans' haste at table to their determination not to waste time that could be devoted to the essential business of earning money. "Mute as machines, they gulp and choke down fist-sized bites of food," wrote Graf Adelbert von Baudissin. "And when they feel that the vacuum has been filled, they push back their chairs and step out of the door picking their teeth. Not a word is exchanged during the meal, no warm toasts are drunk at midday, no glass of wine drained – the 'work' of eating is mute, serious, calm, boring, and without pleasure."[129]

Von Baudissin may well have witnessed this scene during his travels, although it is unlikely to be an accurate depiction of every meal consumed in his presence. His description was not supposed to be taken as an anthropologist's field report but as a freely overstated presentation of the difference between the custom-bound aristocratic culture familiar to him and a surprisingly informal society where he mixed with people who worked for a living. A similar hyperbole characterizes the innumerable depictions of the results produced when many Americans eschewed gentlemanly snuff in favor of masticating wads of tobacco.

Spitting Distance

Frequent references to Americans' proclivity for spitting in public appear in Trollope and Dickens, and are often held up as evidence of anti-American stereotyping. This practice was noted so often that it seems to demand an explanation, and anti-Americanism might not be the best one. To be sure, those writers who relished the colorful expression indulged in it on this subject too. "America is one long expectoration," Oscar Wilde remarked after a lecture tour in the United States.[130] "To attempt to describe any phase of American manners without frequent reference to the spittoon is impossible," concurred G. A. Sala; "It would be like the play of Hamlet with the part of Hamlet omitted."[131] Rupert Brooke credited an Oxford wag with summing up the young country's manners and its material promise in a single name: "El Cuspidorado."[132] But there was some sober reporting as well, which suggests that the practice may, in fact, have simply been observably widespread. Before Trollope and Dickens, other British travelers had already noted the habit. Basil Hall complained in his 1828 traveler's report that Americans spat onto carpets, into fires, and in church. Isaac Candler in 1824 walked through a lecture hall on floors whose slickness was "occasioned entirely by the spitting of the men."[133] The London surgeon Henry Bradshaw Fearon, taken aback in 1817 at seeing spitting-boxes at the feet of every member of the House of Representatives, then entered a crowded drawing room at the home of President James Monroe and found that the evening's entertainment consisted of "Conversation, tea, ice, music, chewing tobacco, and excessive spitting."[134] Not only foreigners complained. Catharine Maria Sedgwick's popular instructional *Morals of Manners* bemoaned the ubiquity of tobacco juice. "A lady cannot walk out, without running the risk of steeping the bottom of her dress in this vile excretion," Sedgwick wrote.[135] The *New York Times* printed more than 140 news articles, editorials, and reader's letters about the public nuisance of "expectoration" between 1852 and 1914.[136] Even the outraged author of an attack on Dickens's *American Notes* in *The Spirit of the Times* concluded with the hope that the book might at least help rid the Americans of their "disgusting habit" in which they are "preeminent among the nations of the Earth."[137] Historians of medicine confirm that spitting was an "almost universal practice" in the nineteenth-century United States; by 1910, "nearly every sizable town and city across the country" had passed an anti-spitting ordinance to inhibit the spread of tuberculosis.[138]

Having established that many Americans evidently did, in fact, spit in public, it no longer makes much sense to ascribe the attention British writers paid to this practice to their inveterate "anti-Americanism." Moreover, spitting seems to have drawn the attention of British travelers in other countries, as in Candler's argument that one should not overly criticize "Americans for spitting on floors and carpets, as the French . . . do the same thing," or Dr. Johnson's remark that "the French are an indelicate people; they will spit upon any place," or George Cockburn's claim that Sicilians spit "any where, and every where," or Robert Everest's assertion that "The detestable practice of spitting is carried to a much worse extent in Sweden than in Norway."[139] Insidious anti-Swedism? Naturally there is a better explanation. As Norbert Elias noted in his landmark history of manners, the restraint of such bodily functions has long been a marker of belonging to a higher social class.[140] And as Mary Louise Pratt has documented, one purpose served by travel literature has been to reassure the readership back home of its own virtue.[141] Rather than anti-Americanism, a particular hatred of the United States and its democratic ways, we are seeing here an aspect of the construction of a sense of English identity based on Victorian self-restraint, one variant of the kind of self-justifying nationalism engaged in by all countries. The genre of travel writing often displays a highly patronizing tone toward the objects of study – as amply demonstrated in accounts by Europeans and North Americans of their visits to Latin America.[142] One could wish that every writer who undertook the task of interpreting an unfamiliar people to his or her own would have the insight and sensitivity of a Tocqueville or an Alexander von Humboldt, but to attribute to travel literature of a more mundane variety a particular kind of ideology that is hostile to freedom and democracy misleads as to both the travelers and the country they described.

Illusion and Disillusion in Latin America

If Dickens and others had hoped to find a country equal to their imaginings, a similar kind of disillusion rooted in the gap between the ideal and the reality of the United States can be found in shifting Latin American views in the nineteenth century. Comparable to the franco-French debate of left versus right or the arguments between ethno-nationalist and democratic Germans, the dispute between Conservatives and Liberals in the Latin American political class could involve symbolic meanings attributed to the United States. Bearing only slight resemblance to their homonyms in contemporary U.S. politics, Conservatives were generally the landed elites, the Catholic Church hierarchy, and ranking military officers, whereas Liberals came from the class of merchants and urban professionals. Conservatives tended to look backward nostalgically to the era of Spanish colonialism, sought a strong central government, and believed in the superiority of Catholic and Spanish culture. Liberals tended to favor free trade, individual rights, federal forms of government, secular education, and the reduction of special privileges for the clergy.

The central feature of Latin American views of the United States was the phenomenal increase in power of the "Colossus of the North" and its growing political, military, and economic presence in the region. While European observers before the twentieth century debated the nature of U.S. society and its implications as an alternative to their own, Latin Americans concerned themselves additionally with the external behavior of this most powerful of neighboring states that often affected them in profound ways.

Any discussion of anti-Americanism in Latin America should begin by acknowledging that many Latin Americans would contest the term itself as barely concealing a stark presumption of superiority: they, too, are Americans, and have long resented the arrogation of the name by one group of residents of the Americas. The fact that anyone other than a U.S. citizen might have a legitimate claim to be called an American brings a moment of cognitive dissonance in some quarters. The whole idea was ridiculed by the nationalist diplomatic historian Samuel Flagg Bemis: "some of our independent neighbors to the South would like to amuse themselves, perhaps maliciously, with the word – *horribile dictu* – Estadounidenses."[143] (Roughly translated, "I report with horror – Unitedstatesians.") Bemis evidently felt no compunction about injecting a little Latin into his talk of Latin America but had no patience for Spanish-language solutions to the linguistic dilemma – an unapologetically elitist stance reflecting a political objection veiled as an aesthetic one. Bemis may have thought *estadounidense* unpronounceable, but in the softened consonants of Latin American Spanish, it is an easily spoken word.[144] As is often the case, foreigners' claims are dismissed as irrational or malicious in the self-confident assertion of an elite American who turns out to have been misinformed.[145]

It follows that in a Latin American context, "anti-Americanism" had various meanings. Monarchists who found Latin American countries unprepared for self-rule were called *antiamericano*.[146] When the Spanish nationalist Salvador de Madariaga published a critical biography of Latin American independence leader Simón Bolívar, depicting him as a half-breed who ruined the glorious Spanish empire, he was attacked in the Latin American press, and especially in Venezuela, whose Bolivarian Society passed a resolution condemning the book as *antiamericano* – that is, anti-Latin American.[147]

More frequently, "anti-Americanism" has been a label pinned by North Americans on uncooperative or skeptical Latin Americans. Rubin and Rubin write that anti-Americanism in Latin America stems from "hurt pride" and "ultrasensitivity to imagined slights," among other factors.[148] Michael Radu calls Mexican anti-Americanism "Pavlovian," invoking an animal's salivating instinct.[149]

Such analyses follow a venerable scholarly tradition of looking down upon Latin Americans as inherently inferior, emotionally unstable, and irrational. One finds innumerable references in U.S. publications since the nineteenth century to the "Latin-American 'republics,' hot-blooded and impulsive,"[150] populated by "the hot-blooded man of Latin race,"[151] governed by "ambitious, hot-headed, and excitable leaders"[152] whose prospects are limited by "the natural incapacity of the hot-headed Latin for self-government,"[153] who has regrettably failed to overcome "tropical . . . hot blooded . . . human nature with its untamed passion,"[154] etc. The hallmark of what we might be tempted to call anti-Latin Americanism is attributing political expression to Latin American emotionality, whereas North Americans believe they reach their own views through sober reasoning.

This is a flawed analysis. Criticism of the United States from Latin Americans usually stems from geopolitical conflict and the idealist's disappointment rather than cultural hostility or psychological pathology. Anxiety over U.S. power did not derive from incomprehension, and certainly not from animosity toward freedom (or "hot blood"), but from an assessment of U.S. capabilities and actions dating to the emergence of the nation-states of the western hemisphere. Independence leaders and liberal reformers in countries that broke away from the Spanish Empire initially invested great hopes in the United States as a model republic and a potential ally, but they soon grew disillusioned by the lack of tangible support for their cause. Simón Bolívar, known as "The Liberator" in Latin America (and "the George Washington of South America" in U.S. history textbooks), in some regards had a keener sense of liberty than did Washington and Jefferson, for he manumitted his own slaves as part of his crusade for freedom, rather than benefiting from their forced labor until his death, as they did. Bolívar's warm feelings for the United States, developed during a visit there in 1807, by 1815 had turned to disappointment: "our brothers to the north have been apathetic bystanders in this struggle," he despaired.[155] For U.S. policy makers, solidarity among republics mattered less than calculation of self-interest and belief in racial hierarchy. The Madison and Monroe administrations did not wish to jeopardize relations with Spain while negotiating the cession of Florida and hoped to take advantage of the Latin American independence wars to pursue their own interests in Texas and Cuba. Many U.S. officials were skeptical that people of Catholic and mixed racial background could ever become their equals. Whereas the United States hesitated to support the anticolonial struggle, Great Britain provided loans, and even Haiti, the tiny republic of former slaves, provided armed vessels, money, rifles, and refuge to Bolívar's forces.[156] These facts, rather than passion or prejudice, led Bolívar to conclude that the United States seemed "destined by Providence to plague America with miseries in the name of Liberty."[157]

The Latin American states won their independence without the United States ever playing the role they hoped for, of aiding them against Spain in the way that France had decisively assisted Great Britain's rebellious colonies. In 1823, with the wave of Latin American independence wars largely over, President James Monroe issued the doctrine bearing his name (although written by Secretary of State John Quincy Adams) warning against future European colonization in the Americas. The Monroe Doctrine is remembered in the United States as an act of protective benevolence, but it said nothing against future U.S. territorial acquisitions in the region, an omission that made Latin Americans wary. Diego Portales, soon to become Chile's strongman, warned against "escaping one domination at the price of falling under another. We must distrust those men who take advantage of the work of our champions of freedom, without having helped us in any way."[158]

The pattern would be repeated, as positive feelings could not survive the clashes between the United States and its neighbors to the south. Conservative Latin Americans nostalgic for the imagined stability of a society based on Catholic values and Spanish culture, and Liberals, anticipating an outpouring of fraternal support from their fellow republicans to the north, both went through this cycle of disillusionment. As Mexico's foreign minister in 1823, Conservative Lucas Alamán admired the United States and hoped that the Monroe Doctrine would lead to a defensive alliance against encroachments by European monarchies.[159] But he soon tangled with the U.S. minister to Mexico, Joel Roberts Poinsett. Poinsett admired Mexican flora – he brought back from Taxco the flowering plant Mexicans called *nochebuena* and renamed it after himself, the *poinsettia* – but he did not care much for Mexicans, whom he called "a more ignorant and debauched people than their ancestors had been."[160] Whether or not Poinsett's failures should be ascribed to what one might arguably call his anti-Mexicanism, his meddling in rival factions vying for power led to a request for his recall, and Alamán judged that Poinsett's tenure in Mexico City had been "more disastrous for us than the invasion of an army."[161] He would soon have reason to alter that judgment. After watching American colonists in Texas stage a rebellion supported by the United States, followed by a war that ended in the seizure of half of Mexico's territory, Alamán's hostility grew all-encompassing toward this "people of merchants and adventurers" whose religious spirit was commercial, whose literature was derivative, and who lacked a glorious past.[162] By that point, Alamán had adopted the sweeping rejection of all things American that some define as anti-Americanism. It is clear, however, that his evolution toward that stance was driven by events rather than arising from a preexisting prejudice.

Liberals were also disappointed by the behavior of the growing United States, but scholars make a mistake when they include criticism by Liberals in the catalog of anti-Americanism, implying that it sprang from irrationality, envy, or culturally rooted hostility toward American principles. The standard anthology of "Anti-Yankee Feelings in Latin America" cites *La América en peligro (America in Danger)* by Chilean Liberal Francisco Bilbao (1823–1865) as a "pivotal" case of anti-Americanism.[163] But far from being hostile to democracy, Bilbao spent his life crusading on its behalf and suffering prison and exile as a result. In his writings he vigorously defended the right to freedom of thought and expression, and the importance of free elections and constitutional govern-ment. Rather than being obsessed with the United States, he spoke out against dictatorships in Argentina, Bolivia, Chile, Ecuador, Paraguay, Peru, Peru, and Venezuela. He called Austria, Prussia, and Russia decrepit tyrannies. Mean-while, he praised the people of England, Holland, Switzerland, and the United States, "all the greatest and freest peoples of the Earth," for their commitment to individual rights.[164] The most "anti-Yankee" remark in the book comes in a passing reference to the year "1856, when Mexico and Central America were menaced by the filibusterism of the slavocrats [*esclavocratas*] of the United States" – an attribution of expansionism to one highly anti-democratic faction within the United States, not to the country or the people itself.[165]

Rather than a career record of anti-Americanism, Bilbao seems to have had a brief period of intense disillusionment, especially in that year of 1856. It was then that he turned his pen against U.S. imperialism, and his criti-cisms were closely connected to events, as the filibusterer William Walker seized Nicaragua, proclaimed himself president, and reestablished slavery there. Bilbao now joined other Latin American Liberals who worried that future con-quests were in store. In his *Iniciativa de la América*, the author let fly his emblematic rhetorical outrage against the "fragments of América falling into the Saxon jaws of the hypnotizing boa constrictor that unrolls its tortuous coils. Yesterday Texas, then the north of Mexico, and then the Pacific greet their new master."[166] His answer was to call for a Latin American Federation to defend against an aggressive North, an idea that resonated strongly with Chilean Liberals and Conservatives alike.

Thus did Bilbao plant an "anti-American" tree among the forest of his writings. Scholars of anti-Americanism routinely cite it as evidence of "Latin American anti-Americanism."[167] But the sapling did not flourish. In the second edition of *La América en peligro*, he opened with a *cri de coeur* against "La Invasión" of Mexico, but it is a jeremiad against *France*, at the time of Napoleon III's attempted takeover of that country, not a criticism of the war of 1846–48. Soon Bilbao was again directing his fire elsewhere, and before he died in 1865, he had resumed his lavish praise of North American freedom, admiring its "most beautiful of Constitutions, which guides the destinies of the greatest, richest, wisest and freest of peoples.... Its literature is the purest and most original of modern literatures... they create what is necessary for the moral and material perfection of the human species."[168] Bilbao always expressed his views vigorously, as ready to exaggerate the positive aspects of the United States as its deficiencies. To call him an obsessive hater of the United States – an "anti-American" – shows how unhelpful is this term that is supposed to contain explanatory value.

If Liberal Latin Americans regretted U.S. actions that were not commen-surate with the values they admired, Conservative Hispanist cultural critique could also thrive even in the absence of the kind of raw confrontation that the United States had with Mexico and Nicaragua. The most enduring essay criti-cal of the United States to emerge from the Latin American republic of letters in this period was *Ariel*, published in 1900 by the Uruguayan philosopher José Enrique Rodó.[169] Writing after the United States had defeated Spain and taken control of Puerto Rico and Cuba in the War of 1898, Rodó warned that the Americas were witnessing what later scholars would call a clash of civilizations. He drew on characters from Shakespeare's *The Tempest* to contrast the North American Caliban, a vulgar, soulless materialist, to the spiritual Ariel of the South, inheritor and defender of Mediterranean culture.[170] Dubbed "one of the most important . . . anti-American works in Latin America,"[171] a book that "has perhaps done more to give dignity and a philosophical justification to the anti-American sentiment in Hispanic America than all the rest of their literature combined,"[172] this best-seller and one of the most widely read books in Latin America actually falls into the category of works that appear to be about the United States but merely use the United States to symbolize unwelcome aspects of industrial society. Rodó was not opposed to modernity; he argued that civilization rested upon "the two props" of "democracy and science,"[173] and he was a key figure in the *modernista* literary movement of his time. His negative depiction of utilitarianism was part of a broader appeal to Latin Americans to defend humanist values of idealism, selflessness, and an aesthetic sensibility – and to "challenge a hierarchy of race in which the peoples of Spanish America were not highly placed"[174] – but it was far from an utter rejection of the United States. Critical scholars, however, seem to have missed the passages in which he hopes that the values of North and South, both founded upon democracy, would result in "a reciprocity of influences and a skilful harmonizing of those attributes which make the peculiar glory of either race."[175] This is why Rodó, José Martí, and others who wrote with admiration and wariness about the United States and called for Latin American solidarity were understood by their readers to be not anti-Americans but *americanistas*.[176]

North Americans were quick to apply the pejorative label even to Martí, the Cuban revolutionary hero killed in an uprising against Spain in 1895. A prolific and widely published poet and journalist, he was one of the leading sources of information about the United States to the rest of the Americas. He had lived in New York and repeatedly praised the country's democratic system, its tolerance, and its economic achievements, while warning against its growing corruption, racism, and increasingly domineering posture toward Latin America.[177] He was well placed to observe the extent of U.S. interest in controlling Cuban affairs and predicted that Washington would seek to replace Madrid as the master of the island. As prescient as this proved, and as committed as Martí was to democracy and egalitarianism, he could not escape the usual charge. Students are taught that Martí "produced Cuba's most memorable anti-American rhetoric."[178] "Before his death," concurs a recent reference text, Martí "had become vehemently anti-American."[179]

Bilbao, Rodó, and Martí exemplify what often happens to Latin Americans when they dare to speak a discouraging word about the United States. Rather than placing their remarks in the dual context of historical events and their lifelong oeuvre, North American scholars and politicians are quick to dismiss these critics by using the anti-American label to smother a dissenting Latin American voice – often a voice that championed "American" values. Anti-Americanism, then, is not an explanatory category. It obfuscates more than it illuminates, locating the source of opposition in emotion rather than reason, neatly disparaging the critic while avoiding the substance of the critique.

The Enigma of the Masses

As we have seen, the notion of nineteenth-century elite anti-Americanism in Europe and Latin America is based on an often-cursory reading of the work of published authors, shorn of wider context. Similarly, the corollary claim that the masses "voted with their feet" by emigrating to the United States to enjoy its freedom is often repeated in studies of anti-Americanism, perhaps because, for an era before public opinion polling, they tend to employ a top-down, intellectual history approach. As C. Vann Woodward put it, "we are dependent on those opinions that found written form and were preserved. Those not written or preserved, and therefore the opinions of the great majority, are beyond our reach."[180] For the apparently silent masses, the bare fact of large-scale movement is coupled with a storybook version of the immigration experience to produce the apparently irresistible figure of speech. Andrei Markovits, Victor Davis Hanson, and Paul Hollander all have written that whereas elite Europeans disdained the United States, ordinary Europeans "voted with their feet" in favor of America.[181] Daniel Pipes concurs: "Tens of millions of immigrants have voted with their feet to slough off prior allegiances and join the boisterous experiment that makes 'life, liberty, and the pursuit of happiness' its official goal."[182]

This account of the universal "pro-Americanism" of the masses turns out to be as oversimplified and under-examined as the universal "anti-Americanism" of the elites. There is no question that the United States attracted some thirty million European immigrants before World War I and continues to draw people from around the world. But the idea that this immigration constitutes a kind of global plebiscite in which the United States is the victor represents a fundamental misunderstanding of the processes of human migration, and it contributes to the myth of anti-Americanism by confusing us about the views ordinary people held of America.

Migration scholars for decades have demonstrated that the vast majority of immigrants came seeking work, not liberty.[183] As Crèvecoeur put it, "*ubi panis ibi patria* is the motto of all emigrants" – where there is bread, there is my country.[184] Some version of the motto is indeed proverbial across Europe: *Wo ich satt werde, dort ist mein Vaterland; là où l'on est bien, là est la patrie; esa es mi patria donde todo me sobra; onde bem me vai, ai tenho mãe e pai.*[185] Material concerns were foremost. Voting for freedom might accurately describe the small fraction of immigrants who were escaping political persecution or pogroms, but they are not representative. By sheer numbers, if migration is read as a national popularity contest, an overwhelming majority vote for the home team: emigrants to the Americas in peak migration years were a tiny percentage of the whole population in every European country, from a high of 6.6 out of 1,000 annually from Norway to as low as 0.2 out of 1,000 from France.[186] Nor were the millions of Chinese who chose Australia and Southeast Asia, or Indians who chose Africa or the Middle East, taking part in a plebiscite. The United States was not unique in its appeal to many European emigrants at a time when other destinations such as Canada, Argentina, Brazil, and Australia received large numbers – in some years, larger numbers than the United States. Before 1890, more Italian emigrants left for Buenos Aires than for New York, and net immigration of Italians was greater to Argentina than to the United States in the years 1895, 1896, 1904, 1908, and 1912, but one never sees the claim that they were voting for Argentina.[187]

Those who did book passage westward passed ships filled with return migrants streaming home to Europe. When the U.S. government began keeping records in 1908, return migration rates were close to 70 percent for immigrants from the Balkans, 63 percent for Greeks, 58 percent for Italians, 34 percent for Austro-Hungarians.[188] Were they voting against America "with their feet" after they had experienced it? For the most part, return migrants had simply earned enough money to meet their goals of buying a piece of land or starting a small business in their home country. Once in the United States, moreover, many immigrants, following patterns of chain migration and cluster settlement, sought above all to replicate their familiar culture and community structures in their new homes, rather than fully embrace the new.[189] Nostalgic fables to the contrary notwithstanding, the movement of immigrants predominantly represented not a "vote" for freedom but the extension across the Atlantic of networks of labor migration.[190]

To be sure, the traditional image of the freedom-seeking immigrant has been shaped not only by official mythologizing about Pilgrim forefathers as part of the project of constructing an exceptionalist ideology but also by the carefully preserved memories of members of ethnic groups who faced persecution abroad or were engaged in struggles for liberation.[191] Partisans of Irish, Hungarian, or other independence movements found the United States a haven for their organizing efforts. Jewish immigration most closely resembled the popular narrative: a persecuted minority facing a hostile majority at home found in the United States not only a brighter economic future but religious tolerance, republican institutions, and the separation of church and state, all of which seemed essential to survival and could not readily be found elsewhere – which is why 80 percent of Jewish emigrants from Czarist Russia chose the United States and 93 percent of them stayed on after arrival.[192] Jewish immigration would appear to be a model case in support of American exceptionalism, but for the fact that it was, well, exceptional – "the clearest exception" to the larger pattern, in the words of a standard work on European migration.[193] Overall, the phrase "voting with their feet" obscures the reality of the immigration experience, which was not a perambulatory election that the United States won because of its appealing political ideals. It was instead an international quest for employment by a small fraction of the population of other countries, people whose life stories are extraordinary and meaningful – just not with the meaning usually assigned to them. The masses therefore were not "pro-American" in the sense that the anti-anti-Americans claim.

While statistical evidence weakens the myth of immigration as a popular embrace of American ideals, we need not stop there in trying to ascertain non-elite opinion in an era before public opinion surveys. The migrants' own written testimony in the form of millions of personal letters sent home show that America was a land that demanded grueling work and challenging cultural adaptation, whose rewards appeared to the immigrants above all as higher income and more plentiful food. In the industrial age of peak immigration, awareness of the growing chasm between the very rich and the very poor eroded an earlier sense of social equality, while workers' experiences, especially of mechanization and the violent repression of organized labor, diminished the symbolic power of the United States as a land of freedom.[194]

If the notion of a contrast between the largely negative views of the elite and the positive embrace of the popular classes is well entrenched, that is in large part because, as Woodward says, the sources available for the study of elite opinions are readily available, whereas the opinions of peasant and working-class populations are much more difficult to establish. Difficult, but not impossible. For while intellectual historians have uncovered a great deal of interesting commentary about the United States produced by "literate and articulate" Europeans, these writings are not the only form in which thoughts and experiences can be conveyed and preserved. Symbolic meanings of America entered idiomatic expressions, slang, proverbs, and folk songs. Such repositories of popular understanding contain surprises for those who assume that the United States stood as a beacon of liberty to downtrodden Europeans, and as a largely unworked seam of knowledge about non-elites, they are of great value. I have elsewhere explored these sources and their significance in some detail.[195] Rather than suggesting that ordinary people viewed America as an idealized land of freedom, the images of America that made their way into popular culture are far more complex; they reflected the diversity of the emigrant experience and the way the distant country affected local life.

Perhaps the most immediate sense in which America made itself felt to those in the migrant sending communities was, simply, as a place of great remoteness. In Hesse, the *Amerika-feld* was the field furthest from the farmhouse.[196] The town of Fritzhausen in the Bohemian Forest was nicknamed *Amerika* because flooding often left it cut off – literally across the water – from nearby towns.[197] A Mecklenburg farmer plowing an especially deep furrow might draw the remark "*wist wol nah Amerika*" ("you must be trying to get to America"), the way an American child playing in a sandlot might try to dig a hole "all the way to China" – to the furthest place, on the other side of the world.[198] In parts of Italy, *andare in America* meant to undertake a long journey to a distant town. *Venire d'America*, on the other hand, meant to fail to understand a simple fact or routine situation – to be as confused as a foreigner who came from a distant land.[199]

The association of America with remoteness and inaccessibility lent itself readily to imaginative metaphor. *"Dee is all in Kamerika"* ("he is in America"), Mecklenburgers might say of someone who is sleeping, or use the expression *"he is nah Amerika"* for a person sent to jail – quite the contrary of any connotation of freedom. In Rostock, *"dee hett eenen nah Amerika schickt"* ("he was sent to America") meant he had gone mad.[200] These sayings are not celebratory of the United States; their significance seems to come rather from America's inaccessibility than from any consensus on its value. *"Geh af Amerika!"* ("Go to America!") an angry West Bohemian might shout, the way an English speaker might tell someone to "go to hell" or "get out of my sight." A parent in Klentnitz lifting a naughty child might threaten *"willst Du Amerika sehen?"* ("do you want to see America?") while pouting children in Luxemburg might whine *ech gin an Amerika*, I'm going to America, as they stomped out of the room.[201]

For adults and children, then, "America" loomed large enough in their thinking to serve as a metaphor for remoteness, but not necessarily a place to which one yearned to go: it could signify a dreamland, a refuge, but also a netherworld, a site of imprisonment, a place of punishment. When positively connoted, moreover, "America" appears in these popular idioms not as a land of liberty but overwhelmingly as a land of plenty: abundance was a common meaning of *mèrica* in western Lombardy and Trentino, *mérikä* in Voghera, *america* in Rome. "To find one's America" was to strike it rich: *trovare l'America* throughout much of Italy, *catar la Merica* in Trentino, *truvà ra mérica* in Voghera. In Latin Anaunico, a dialect of Lombardy, *giatar la Merica*, to throw or cast America (like throwing a lucky seven with dice) meant to "make a fortune without having to emigrate."[202] Similar expressions could be found across Europe, referring chiefly to wealth (as in the many variations on *Dollarika*). The image of America as a land of plenty seems to be a transnational phenomenon: Chinese immigrants called the United States *"gam sann* (in Cantonese) or *jinshan* (in pinyin) which means 'gold mountain' in English." Japanese migrants spoke of *beikoku*, or rice country.[203]

Along with the favorable connotation in such locutions, there could be an element of defiance, of pride in choosing not to emigrate, running through expressions such as that from southern Hesse, *"Er hodd hie Amerika funn,"* meaning "he found America," or grew wealthy, right here.[204] When drinkers in a Wismar tavern called out the toast *"Hunn'schit Amerika, Koembuttel is min Brut"* ("dogshit for America, a bottle of caraway brandy [a local specialty] is my bride"), they were declaring their firm intention not to follow the minority of their neighbors who decided to leave.[205] In Gascony, the proverb *"las Ameriques que soun pertout"* ("one can make a fortune anywhere"), simultaneously acknowledged America's plentitude while insisting on the worthiness of a decision not to emigrate.[206]

In the emigrant sending communities, one finds a keen awareness of the daily struggle required to survive in American society. Throughout German-speaking Europe one could hear variations of the popular ditty composed in 1845 by Samuel Friedrich Sauter, *Jetzt ist die Zeit und Stunde da, wir fahren nach America* (Now the time and hour have come, we're traveling to America). In some areas with high rates of emigration, locals who had access to emigrant correspondence and the testimony of returnees changed the lyrics. Alluding to the travails their compatriots faced in the new country, residents of the Pfalz region of the Rhineland sang *"wir fahren nach Maleerika,"* a play on *das Malheur*, or misfortune.[207] In the western Swiss Alps, Romansch speakers used *America* as a nickname for fields that were worn out or unfertile, influenced by the reports in emigrants' letters of finding barren conditions on their own newly purchased lands.[208]

German folk songs sometimes celebrated America, but others struck a note of melancholy, evoking flowers with no scent and birds that cannot sing, as well as more mundane hardships such as the grueling sea voyage, the stinking holds crammed with seasick passengers, and the danger of theft in American ports. Many songs conjured up the homesickness of the emigrants, as in the line "I'd give a finger from my hand/to be back again in my fatherland."[209] Whether such sentiments echoed emigrant testimony or served to justify a decision to stay at home is impossible to know. Whereas some of the pro-America songs were written by steamship companies and emigration agencies and distributed on broadsheets in the hope of drumming up business, more skeptical texts seem intended to puncture the inflated claims of what awaited gullible emigrants in the new world, as in these lines from the derisive song "Amerika" attributed to a Thuringian barber, Johannes Hauck:

Ümharig fliehn gabratna Taubn	Roasted pigeons fly around
Kerschbrau un schönt gefüllt!	Cherry-brown, and ready-stuffed!
Ihr Flahsch is euch so weech wie Flaum	Their flesh is soft as down
Un wie Pisquit so mild.	And tender as a biscuit.
Sparrt nar die Mäuler auf, za senn	Open your mouth, they fly right in,
Sa dinn, bracht net dernach za genn.	You need not run after them.
Die Karpfn schwimma dart in Teich	Carp in ponds there swim around
Schön brau gabacken rümm,	Already baked to golden brown
Un Brad, i nu, dös hengt ja gleich	And bread, it's true, it just hangs down
Dart u den Baamern rüm...	Beneath the trees there...[210]

Other German-speaking regions produced lyrics with similarly fantastic descriptions, such as those picturing an America where "wine flows right into the windows/and the clover grows three cubits high."[211] These images can be traced back to popular sixteenth-century satires of utopia known as

Schlaraffenland, a word carrying associations both of laziness and of opu-
lence ("Land of the Feasting Monkeys").[212] Rather than a political utopia,
Schlaraffenland, like its counterparts *cocagne* in French, *cockaigne* in English,
or *cuccagna* in Italian, derived from the Latin *coquina*, kitchen, is above all
a land of plenty, where all of one's physical needs are met, and hunger – the
overriding daily concern in most peasant communities – is easily satisfied.[213]
At least since the 1830s, *Schlaraffenland* appeared in discussions of America,
in which the word satirized the naive belief that a wonderland of idleness and
easy bounty waited across the sea.[214] Of course the farmers who sang these
words knew how fish and fowl are roasted and how bread and wine are made:
with their labor. Such alluring images of abundance, although seeming on first
glance to confirm the conflation of *cockaigne* with America, can be read not
as evidence of ordinary Europeans' credulousness but of their skepticism and
sense of humor. When the barber Hauck wrote, "*Sie machen ja ahn Larm
dervuh/As wenn dart füng der Himmel uh*" ("They make such a fuss about
it/As if heaven itself begins there"),[215] he was mocking America fever, not
encouraging it.

For some Hungarian emigrants in the United States, disillusionment was a
principal theme, as in these lines from a singer planning a return to Hungary:
"America is not my native country, I never had a jolly hour there. I have
wandered a great lot, but my heart became all the more bitter."[216] Other songs
turned "America" into "Misery-ca," a land of bad luck.[217] Some Hungarian
folk songs clearly reflected not solely the imaginings of those who stayed at
home but the attestations of disappointed return migrants, since the songs
were flecked with anglicized words from their experience in the United States,
such as complaints against the *pitbósz* (pit boss), or longing for the *ókantri*
(old country). Knowing that America was commonly represented as a paradise
but vividly aware of the hardships of emigrant life, one singer resolved the
contradiction diplomatically: "Tuesday morning I went on board a ship,/ I
return to beautiful Hungary;/ God save America forever,/ But just let me get
out of there!"[218]

Europeans departing for the United States might be expected to return only
after many years or not at all, and so for their relatives bidding farewell to the
emigrants, America could be seen as the land that robbed them of their loved
ones, as in the Irish custom of calling a departure ceremony an "American
wake" (or the Japanese nickname for emigrants, *kimin*, meaning people who
had been discarded).[219] America's meaning was also influenced by the gender
of the beholder. Women who emigrated responded to some of the same array of
material considerations as male emigrants.[220] For those left behind, however,
it was a different matter. Sicilian "America widows" who wandered through
town crying out the names of their husbands or sons in the United States
would hardly have been thinking of that country as a paradise, or somehow
"voting" for it.[221] Nor did Hungarian women who lay on the tracks in front
of locomotives to try to prevent a relative from emigrating. Other Hungarian
women perhaps took bitter consolation in these lines from a folk song that

cast the country as a romantic rival: "Oh you undulating soil of America,/ How many girls have called down curses upon you!/ America, be cursed... Forever!"[222]

Such sources reveal that ordinary Europeans held a variety of often critical views of "America," ideas formed by their own experience or informed by the testimony of their compatriots, many more of whom returned from the United States than the American exceptionalist myth has ever acknowledged. Certainly the expressions collected here do not present an objective description of social conditions in the United States, much less amount to an argument for an anti-exceptionalist, dystopian understanding of "America." Nor do they diminish the significance of the political and religious freedom available in the United States to those people for whom it was above all a land where they could escape poverty and persecution. But the traces of meaning recorded in popular discourse at a minimum serve as a corrective to exceptionalism's stale platitudes, demonstrating that the myth of an unmitigated popular embrace of American freedom by the masses rests on an evidentiary foundation as shaky as that of the myth of the universal hostility of elites. The world does not simply line up as pro- or anti-American, as if cheering for a football team. Those who dwell abroad hold multifaceted views of the United States grounded in their own encounters with the country or information they may glean about it from a variety of sources.

If the evidence does not support the entrenched belief that the nineteenth century was marked by a widely shared elite hostility to American democracy that we can usefully call anti-Americanism, nor that the masses were overwhelmingly pro-American, that does not mean that the century failed to leave an important legacy with regard to anti-Americanism. It did, and that legacy was a rhetorical one of great consequence: enshrining the term *anti-American* as an enduring – and misleading – analytical category, whose dual effect of stifling dissent at home and distorting Americans' perception of foreign behavior would develop in scope and power over the course of the twentieth century.

Americanism and Anti-Americanism

The 100% American is 99% idiot.
                    – Routinely misinterpreted remark by George Bernard Shaw[1]

By the close of the nineteenth century, the concept of anti-Americanism was firmly established in American political discourse, and the struggle over its meaning was subsiding. Although "anti-Americanism" sometimes referred to diplomatic or popular resistance to U.S. expansion, especially after the War of 1898, its deeper, dual significance would expand during the twentieth century, as a rightist charge of disloyalty directed against domestic critics on the one hand, and as an ascription of irrationality to uncooperative foreigners on the other. Wars, hot and cold, shrank the political space for dissent and sharpened the sting of the anti-American label, even as "anti-Americanism" flourished as a category of analysis consecrated by journalism, academia, and government. By the second half of the century, anti-Americanism had become a fixed idea that would permanently distort Americans' perceptions of national politics and international relations.

Overseas, the frequency with which writers invoked America as a point of reference grew in proportion to the country's growing economic and military power. Negative and positive depictions of the United States became a regular feature of social and political debates in many countries, raising the question of whether foreign criticism of U.S. society revealed an ideological anti-Americanism cloaking opposition to modernity and democracy, as many of today's scholars believe, or reflected indigenous disputes at a time of social change in which America functioned as a vivid symbol. The accusation of "anti-Americanism" in domestic politics, meanwhile, became above all the rhetorical weapon of choice for national chauvinists, and others who used it unreflectively became unwitting contributors to the reinforcement of an exceptionalist stance.

100% Americanism and Anti-Americanism

In the early part of the twentieth century, numerous voices expressed anxiety that the arrival of great masses of immigrants – precisely those celebrated today for having "voted with their feet" for America – threatened the country's very existence because of their religious, racial, and political incompatibility. Supporters of non–Anglo-Saxon immigration, who believed all men were created equal, were accused of "anti-Americanism" for undermining racial uniformity.[2] Charges of "Catholic anti-Americanism" accompanied tales of Vatican conspiracies to subjugate America.[3] Brooklyn-based Congregationalist minister Newell Dwight Hillis debased Lincoln's famous aphorism to fulminate against the new immigrants. "This Republic cannot exist half American and half alien," Hillis wrote. "Either Americanism must expel anti-Americanism, or the anti-American sentiment will Bolshevise our people and destroy our Republic."[4] Chauvinists claiming the mantle of true "Americanism" had been active at least since the Know-Nothing Party was established, and hostility toward foreigners arose with each wave of new arrivals. As immigration rates peaked before World War I, this undercurrent of xenophobia broke to the surface and flooded the American political system.

No less prominent a figure than former President Theodore Roosevelt led the charge, inveighing against so-called "hyphenated Americans" – German-Americans, especially, once Britain and Germany were at war – by linking their ethnic identity to inherent disloyalty. During the 1916 election campaign in which he supported Charles Evans Hughes against President Woodrow Wilson, Roosevelt attacked "the element typified by the German-American alliances and the similar bodies, which have, in the pre-nomination campaign, played not merely an un-American but a thoroughly anti-American part." German-Americans' anti-Americanism, Roosevelt claimed, had infected even Wilson, who sought their votes and therefore refused to go to war against Germany. In a fiery speech in September, Roosevelt excoriated him with words suggesting that the president himself was undermining the country: "There has been a revival of anti-Americanism," he declared, "and President Wilson has been responsible for it." True Americanism, Roosevelt concluded, meant supporting rearmament for war.[5]

Once Wilson reversed himself and led the United States into World War I, hostility toward Germans reached new levels. Immigrants were harassed. School boards banned German language classes. Sauerkraut was renamed "liberty cabbage" (anticipating the 2003 "freedom fries" episode). German churches were set ablaze. This period of Germanophobia needs no explanation, and we have not sought one in ideology or psychology: it did not erupt because of underlying hostility toward German romantic philosophy or Germany's advanced industrial capacity, but because many Americans were at that moment angry at Germany's behavior.

The charge of anti-Americanism was leveled not only at those thought to be overly sympathetic to the Entente powers but also those judged insufficiently committed to the fight. A Chicago rally where speakers denounced the interests of munitions manufacturers and the steel and beef trusts in providing war supplies was "a field day of anti-Americanism," according to the *Tribune*.[6] The dean of the Divinity School at the University of Chicago, Shailer Mathews, asserted that "organized socialism in America has turned itself into anti-Americanism" by "pleading for peace."[7] Samuel Gompers, the head of the American Federation of Labor, formed the American Alliance of Labor and Democracy to "stamp out sedition and to confuse and confound the traitors who talk peace and anti-Americanism." The Alliance was underwritten by payments from George Creel's Committee on Public Information, the federal propaganda office, which made the fight against anti-Americanism an official cause.[8]

Wartime urgency turned the inherent charge of disloyalty that was always latent in the term "anti-Americanism" into a formal category of treasonous behavior. While all countries are less tolerant of dissent in wartime, the linguistic peculiarity that allowed loyal critics to be grouped in the same category with enemies of the state made the term "anti-Americanism" especially potent – and especially pernicious. Educational institutions came under special scrutiny. University of Illinois trustees fired four faculty members for "anti-Americanism" while the Justice Department sent agents to uncover "anti-Americans" in other universities.[9] The press called for more. "Those of proved anti-Americanism should be condemned and banished forthwith," editorialized the *Washington Post*.[10]

This era of intolerance only flourished with the end of the war. In the aftermath of the Bolshevik Revolution of 1917 and anarchist agitation at home, the first Red Scare engulfed the United States, bringing campaigns against both radicals and foreigners, and a popular conflation of the two. Alice Wood, a schoolteacher in Washington, D.C., was investigated and suspended for "anti-Americanism" after she discussed Bolshevism and the League of Nations in her classroom.[11] The dean of the School of Education at the University of Chicago recommended courses in civic morality to rid immigrant communities of their "strongly organized anti-Americanism."[12] Italian-American journalist Gino Speranza wrote an impassioned anti-immigration book he titled *Race or Nation*, attacking recent arrivals as "anti-American in spirit, ideals and aspirations" for speaking their own languages at home.[13] In this intolerant climate, African Americans who agitated for their constitutionally guaranteed civil rights were accused of being "out-and-out anti-American" for forming alliances with leftist political groups.[14]

As that example showed, in the 1920s, the charge of anti-Americanism was becoming a reliable indicator that a minority group was asserting its rights. American Zionists grew weary of having to defend themselves against accusations of "anti-Americanism" for supporting a Jewish state in Palestine, or just for being Jewish.[15] "Let us blind our eyes and stop our ears against the whirling mass of Hebraism, bolshevism, and anti-Americanism that is fomenting trouble for our country (having no country of their own)," exhorted the *American*

Organist.[16] The notorious anti-Semitic pamphleteer Robert Edward Edmondson urged his readers to *Save America! The Patriotic Crusade against Jewish Anti-Americanism*,[17] while radio demagogue Father Charles Coughlin attacked a conspiracy that, "masquerading under the name of the Jews, is officered by exponents of anti-godism, anti-Americanism and anti-Christianity."[18] The term "anti-Americanism" could be wielded by both sides in this war of words, as anti-Semites were rebuked by liberals such as Brooklyn College philosophy professor and best-selling author Harry Allen Overstreet, who urged Americans to recognize that "anti-Semitism is anti-Americanism" because it violates democratic ideals of inclusion and smacks of pro-fascist tendencies.[19] The argument that anti-Semitism is itself "a manifestation of anti-Americanism" was taken up by the Council for Democracy in a pamphlet circulated to local women's clubs.[20] By 1944, even the Communist Party USA adopted a resolution that "Anti-Semitism is anti-Americanism."[21] But the far right retained its predominance over the use of the term since more than 100 anti-Semitic organizations were active in the decade before the war, led by Coughlin and his Social Justice movement.[22] The isolationist congressman Jacob Thorkelson, Republican of Montana, claimed that "the communistic Jew and his sponsors are anti-Americans" for attacking Hitler, who, it should be remembered, "has eliminated the Communists."[23] Clare Eugene Hoffman, Republican Congressman of Michigan, demanded that "all those who are anti-American should be investigated," beginning with critics who had called him an isolationist for speaking at America First rallies.[24]

And so the promoters of an ethnically homogeneous, conservative America sought to define its narrow limits in the interwar period. Theodore Roosevelt's term "100% Americanism" became the watchword of the anti-immigrant groups that preached a blend of scientific racism, cultural conformity, and strict obedience to authority. They ranged from the American Legion, whose national convention voted in 1919 to make its basic ideal the promotion of "100 percent Americanism" and to combat "all anti-American tendencies," to the revived Ku Klux Klan, whose Imperial Wizard promised to fight "anti-Americanism of all kinds."[25] As Congress enacted the most sweeping restrictions on immigration in American history, the word "Americanism" was appropriated by the nativist right as its sole patrimony, and "anti-Americanism" linked unpopular ethnicity and progressive politics to disloyalty to the nation itself.

In this context, George Bernard Shaw's derisive aphorism from that era, "the 100% American is 99% idiot," appears in a new light. Scholars frequently cite it as a classic example of the anti-Americanism of the British cultural elite.[26] (PBS even took the line as the epigraph introducing its documentary on "The Anti-Americans.")[27] A closer look, however, shows that Shaw's remark entered the catalog of "anti-Americanism" only as a result of an ahistorical reading that does not recognize the meaning of the phrase "100% American." Shaw was directing his bon mot not at Americans in general, but at the outspoken xenophobes and nativists among them. He confirmed his intention in response to an inquiry from a correspondent in 1937: "I cannot remember the exact wording

of the statement to which you allude; but what I meant was that in my experience a man *who calls himself a 100% American* and is proud of it, is generally
150% an idiot politically." He went on to refer to the American Legion.[28]
Shaw elsewhere explained that he had "made fun of the Hundredpercent
American" to "please my American audience," but "the truth is that the Hpc
[Hundred percent] American is a harmless and well-meaning child compared to
the Hpc Englishman, Frenchman, German Nazi, or Japanese," and he further
denounced the "British conceit of moral superiority" over Americans.[29] In his
many plays, too, he directed his most insightful satire at British society, or at the
absurdities of the human condition, not at America. The standard misreading
of Shaw that places him among "the anti-Americans" not only characterizes
him unfairly as hostile, but completely misses his point, obscuring a useful
observation about a dangerous anti-democratic tendency in U.S. society that
Shaw thought was not good for America. Such has been the fate of many apt
critiques from abroad, dismissed with the usual epithet.

From Domestic Intolerance to Foreign Resistance

A hundred years of usage implying disloyalty or irrationality made those connotations permeate the term when it was deployed in the context of foreign affairs
at the beginning of the twentieth century. When some Americans objected to the
extension of U.S. power beyond its continental expanse, the "anti-American"
charge cast them not as proponents of a different kind of American republic
but as its enemies. When foreigners did not recognize and welcome the benevolence of U.S. power, Americans, surprised, found fault with the reasoning of
the foreigner.

The War of 1898 brought important new overseas island territories – Cuba,
Puerto Rico, and the Philippines – under the control of the United States,
along with Hawaii, annexed in the aftermath of the war. When inhabitants
of those islands displayed signs of resistance to their new rulers, they were
seen not merely as political opponents. The *Chicago Daily Tribune* denounced
the "ill-tempered, discontented, and carping band whose anti-Americanism"
led them to oppose the annexation of Hawaii, in what a leading American
political scientist called "a significant manifestation of anti-Americanism."[30]
The *Hartford Courant* labeled Hawaii's elected delegate to the U.S. Congress,
Robert W. Wilcox (who was on good terms with the last Hawaiian monarch,
Queen Liliuokalani), "the half-breed Liliuokalanist malcontent and agitator –
anti-American to his fingertips." The paper noted that his native supporters had
recently won a majority in the Hawaiian House and half the seats in the Senate.
The lesson of this exercise in democracy? "A great many Kanakas [Hawaiian
natives] who can read and write are utterly unfit to be trusted with the ballot,"
the paper concluded.[31] By this logic, pursuing Hawaiian interests in Hawaii was
anti-Americanism, proof that the non-white races were insufficiently mature
for self-government and inclined toward an irrational rejection of the United
States.

José Martí had warned that Cubans risked trading one master for another, and the Treaty of Paris ending the U.S. war with Spain seemed to bear him out. While Cuba was granted nominal independence, Cubans – excluded from the Paris negotiations – were subjected to military occupation and forced to include a clause in their constitution known as the Platt Amendment, giving the United States the right to intervene in Cuban affairs. As Cuban legislators debated this demand – set as a condition for the withdrawal of U.S. troops – there were protests across the island, from torchlight marches and demonstrations to petition drives by civic groups.[32] Nationalist candidates swept municipal elections and were promptly labeled "anti-Americans" in the U.S. press.[33] From a Cuban perspective, the issue was not love or hatred of the United States but a consistent commitment to independence. "We have accomplished too much to accept anything short of absolute freedom," said rebel leader Gen. Máximo Gómez, who believed his forces had weakened the Spanish through a long war of attrition – which explained why U.S. forces landing near Santiago suffered not a single casualty, the rebels having cleared the area of Spanish troops – only to see the United States arrive at the last moment and snatch away the Cuban victory.[34] Rather than sympathizing with a former colony seeking its complete independence, however, Americans took Cubans' stubborn insistence on their right to liberty as a reproach, and an irrational one. "Like all other people of Spanish origin they are hot blooded, high strung, nervous, excitable and pessimistic," complained Governor-General Charles Magoon.[35] Predictably, the *New York Times* saw nationalist complaints as evidence of "anti-Americanism" in Cuba, and dubbed the president of the Cuban House of Representatives "anti-American" for opposing the Platt Amendment.[36] The *Hartford Courant* labeled rebel veterans, who only recently were shedding blood alongside their U.S. allies, "anti-American" for opposing U.S. control.[37] Given the evolution of the term and the widespread U.S. view of Cubans as emotional or childlike, the adjective did not merely denote objection to a U.S. policy. It suggested that the inferior mental condition of foreigners was responsible for their failure to recognize that the United States knew better than they did what was in their best interests.

Although Puerto Rico remained more tranquil than Cuba, when they withheld cooperation from the U.S. project of governing the island and transforming its society, Puerto Rican politicians were labeled "anti-American."[38] The first jury trial held in U.S.-governed Puerto Rico sentenced to prison Evaristo Izcoa Díaz, editor of the newspaper *El Combate*, who had followed his criticism of Spanish excesses before 1898 with criticism of vandalism committed by some U.S. troops. The *New York Times* explained that "*El Combate* has been strongly anti-American"; Izcoa Díaz died in prison.[39] U.S. Methodist missionaries in Puerto Rico listed among "the forces opposing our work" the population's "deep-rooted immorality, Fickleness, [and] anti-Americanism," rather than a desire among Catholics to continue to pray as they pleased.[40] When 40,000 sugar workers went on strike against U.S.-owned mills to demand an increase in pay from fifty cents a day, a reporter wrote that the "feeling of

anti-Americanism all over the island" was due to Puerto Rican backwardness –
not to their poverty wages.[41] Accusations of "anti-Americanism" occurred frequently enough that some Puerto Rican politicians disputed the charge. "Don't
believe on the basis of what I say that I am or wish to be *antiamericano*. I
am not *antiamericano*, just as I am not *antiespañol*, nor *antialemán*, nor even
antiruso," wrote Epifanio Fernández Vanga, a partisan of independence. "To
be anti-anything is to be a negative quantity, and I am and wish to be something
affirmative. That is why I am simply Puerto Rican."[42]

America as World Power

If the War of 1898 was a watershed moment engendering suspicions that the
United States intended to dominate Latin America, Europeans also took notice
of the arrival of the United States as a world power after the defeat of Spain. The
massive expansion of U.S. economic and military capacity that accompanied
its rise to world leader in industrial productivity naturally drew the attention,
sometimes admiration, and occasional wariness of foreigners. The German
right, eager to increase Germany's naval presence overseas, now viewed the
United States as a direct competitor.[43] French imperialists were shocked at the
defeat of a sister European empire in what they viewed as an unprovoked act
of American aggression.[44] A French correspondent wondered whether the outcome of the war meant that the United States was about to "substitute for the
old doctrine 'America for the Americans' the new formula 'the world for the
Americans.'"[45] Six months before the war, Austrian Foreign Minister Agenor
Goluchowski rose in Parliament to warn of the "American danger" in the international commercial arena, calling for a kind of customs union for Europe to
match America's large protected market. After 1898, Goluchowski's formulation was often repeated: many took up the theme of the American menace –
le péril américain, die amerikanische Gefahr, el peligro norteamericano – and
this has entered the catalog of evidence to show how the world was growing
more and more hostile to the leading democracy.

When we examine these works, however, we see that the country was
presented as an intimidating economic competitor; the fear of an "American
danger" had nothing to do with the spread of democracy. Max Prager's
Die amerikanische Gefahr and Thomas Lenschau's *Die amerikanische Gefahr*
focused on foreign trade. Paul Sée's *Le péril américain* depicted a manufacturing goliath, not an armed empire; the country's naval strength, he noted, was
one-twentieth of Great Britain's, but its productive capacity was unmatched.
His analysis was echoed in the popular and business press.[46]

In response, the *New York Times* wondered "Why They Dislike Us" and
came to a rather calmer conclusion than some Americans would a century
later. The paper found European criticism "stimulated by the selfish nature of
our own commercial system. While we seek, and at present very successfully,
the extension of our trade in the markets of the world, we maintain intact
the barriers that bar others from our own markets. . . . Distinctly that is not a

policy to win friends."[47] In a rare instance of open-mindedness, the editorial board of a leading American newspaper examined foreign fears of American power and found them to be grounded in tangible grievances, not hostility to democracy or social equality.

Such hostility, it is true, could be found on the right wing of European politics. Along with wariness toward the new commercial rival, European conservatives expressed criticism of the United States that reflected their own commitment to exclusivist ethnic nationalism: America in their eyes was a land of racial mixing, where the melting pot of immigrants from Europe, Latin America, and Asia combined with Africans to produce, in Émile Boutmy's ugly phrase, a "mud of all the races."[48] Perhaps this was anti-Americanism, although such ideas were internationally fashionable in anthropology and biology at the time: European racists and eugenicists did not recognize the irony that their criticisms of the United States perfectly mirrored the position of the 100-percenters, who believed immigration represented "anti-Americanism" and should be restricted to keep America pure.

The Americanization of the World

Debates abroad over the transformation of society under the impact of industrialization often featured concerns about "Americanization," in which the American danger appeared in destabilizing changes wrought by the industrial age. Cities grew larger and more difficult to manage. People who might cling to a pastoral ideal found themselves surrounded by machines and their products, while the increasingly mobile workforce who operated the machines experienced closer surveillance and a loss of autonomy. Mass entertainment displaced community, religious, and family activities during leisure time. Sectors of the population traditionally excluded from the political process demanded a share of political power.

To be sure, the United States was hardly unique in going through these changes: as Daniel Rodgers puts it in his masterwork *Atlantic Crossings*, "engines of convergence" were at work in Essen, Lille, Manchester, and Pittsburgh, part of an emerging global industrial economy that was causing similar transformations.[49] On the other hand, the United States was widely associated with such changes because, with the help of massive state intervention in the economy (rarely acknowledged by celebrants of "free enterprise") in the form of land grants, subsidies, protective tariffs, and governmental strikebreaking, it was becoming the world's leading industrial producer, and its many international links of trade, migration, and media ensured the worldwide flow of information about the country's development. Moreover, the United States successfully exported many of its new ways because its vast home market and ethnically diverse population gave its exporters a dual advantage over foreign manufacturers. Economies of scale at home generated vast amounts of capital to subsidize exports, while the degree of universal appeal required to sell to people of varied cultures and tastes within the United States meant that products could more easily make inroads into diverse societies abroad.

And so began *The Americanization of the World*, as the progressive English journalist William T. Stead entitled his widely noted book published in 1901. Some scholars have listed it among the earliest anti-American tracts of the twentieth century, claiming that it "evoked nightmares" and "visions of horror," or that it "ominously...captured a set of apprehensions" about the destruction of national identities under the crushing weight of Americanization.[50] This is curious, because placing Stead among the anti-Americans reverses the argument he made: his book was actually a celebration of American power. He urged his fellow Britons to "rejoice in contemplating the achievements of the mighty nation that has sprung from our loins...cheerfully acquiesce in the decree of Destiny, and stand in betimes with the conquering American."[51] Americans had produced "a host of ingenious inventions and admirably perfected machines," Stead wrote: "We want these things. We want them now."[52] Stead not only hailed the virtues of the United States rhetorically, he actually put his and other people's money where his mouth was, raising $200,000 for civic relief work in Chicago and persuading the diamond magnate Cecil Rhodes to extend his famed scholarship program to Americans.[53] How Stead wound up on lists of anti-American writers is explainable only by some having judged a book by its cover.

Within the broad European left, views of the United States were mixed: reformers and social democrats admired its social progress, while revolutionaries noted accusingly its repression of labor. Earlier, after the victory of the Union over the Confederacy, Karl Marx had written approvingly in the preface to *Das Kapital*, "Just as in the eighteenth century the American War of Independence sounded the tocsin for the European middle class, so in the nineteenth century the American Civil War did the same for the European working class."[54] In other words, America had launched a revolution in 1776 that heralded the era of bourgeois political rule, and with the end of unfree labor in 1865, the United States would now usher in the age of working-class supremacy. This was high praise from the prophet of the proletariat. Nonetheless, America remained on the periphery of Marx's thinking: "The country that is more developed industrially only shows, to the less developed, the image of its own future," he wrote – but he was talking about England.[55]

Leftist views of the United States changed as industrialization changed America. The violence at Chicago's Haymarket Square in 1886, and the subsequent roundup of hundreds of labor leaders and execution of anarchists accused of killing policemen, drew international attention. So did the use of government troops and private militia (the Pinkertons) to crush labor unions at Carnegie's Homestead steel plant in 1892 and during the nationwide Pullman railway strike of 1894. With no laws before 1916 protecting workers' right to organize, and with federal and state governments placing the courts, the police, and the military at the service of industry to discipline the workforce, the American system could seem to the left to represent not the triumph of social equality but the domination of capital over labor. Marx's collaborator and patron Friedrich Engels traveled to the United States and was disappointed to find mere bread-and-butter unionism instead of a socialist workers' movement there.[56]

As is also the case before and after this period, however, observations abroad about the United States were often self-referential elements of a debate over the future of one's own society. Wilhelm Liebknecht, a founder of the Social Democratic Party in Germany, admired the U.S. Constitution and nick-named his vision of a classless utopia "America," the way the poets of "Young Germany" had used the name to refer to liberal democracy fifty years before. He was not claiming that the country across the Atlantic had reached this ideal; he was using the name symbolically to call for the development of a free society in Europe.[57] Karl Kautsky, a leading socialist theorist, proclaimed that "America is the freest country in the capitalist world, freer than England, even than Switzerland."[58] Socialists in France were less fascinated by a country where the strongest faction in a weak socialist movement seemed to be made up of German immigrants, and the apparent tendency of American workers to become satisfied and depoliticized by their improving standard of living dismayed European socialists ever since Werner Sombart offered that answer to his own 1906 inquiry *Why Is there No Socialism in the United States?*[59]

The explanation that took hold, at least until the crash of 1929, was that the booming American economy promised to satisfy workers' needs so well as to make socialism superfluous. With the appearance of the Soviet alternative in 1917 leading to the increasingly polarized dispute between capitalism and communism, "America" would gradually become the anti-model for the far left, and "anti-Americanism" a term that mistook an ideological standoff for hatred of a single country, blending all forms of foreign discontent into an incomprehensible, threatening mass. Before the Bolsheviks took power, however, Americans would grow concerned about an earlier social revolution much closer to home – one in which they would come to believe that "anti-Americanism" played a central role in a major foreign conflict for the first time.

Mexico: The Eruption of "Irrationality"

The Mexican Revolution of 1910–17 generated frequent references to anti-Americanism, not least because the upheavals featured recurrent denunciations of the United States, as well as attacks on American citizens and property. During the conflict and in later appraisals of it, many Americans alternately blamed the Mexican people for a kind of groundless, animalistic fury toward the North, or blamed the Mexicans' leaders for manipulating them with cynical appeals to the senseless anti-Americanism that for some puzzling reason afflicted the masses. The U.S. consul at Guadalajara, Samuel E. Magill, thought that "the anti-American sentiment is almost universal among rich and poor alike," while his counterpart at Durango, Charles M. Freeman, claimed that "this district is 95% anti-American, and that is a most conservative estimate, for I have yet to meet a Mexican who has any love for the people of the United States as a whole."[60] Lothrop Stoddard, a leading political scientist (and eugenicist), called Mexico "the center of anti-Americanism in Latin America."[61]

When they tried to account for the source of Mexican hostility, many Americans turned to classic stereotypes of Mexican emotionalism: "Jealousy of American success," believed the vice-consul at Mexico City; "a deep-seated jealousy or hatred of all things and persons American," agreed Consul Magill.[62] "Hatred" of Americans as a reason for anti-Americanism was tautological, of course. "Jealousy" at least resembles an explanatory factor, because it presumably rests upon disparities in wealth and power, but it could not explain why other poor people outside Mexico were not equally hostile. Both words implied the exercise of passion rather than reason, which fitted the stereotype when Americans looked south. A popular contemporary history of Mexico depicted it as "an unruly nation of hot-blooded half-breeds."[63] The martial poet Henry Clinton Parkhurst wrote of

> "The Mexican Peon"
> Hot blooded, deadly in his ire
> Hate sets his very veins on fire.[64]

Vanderbilt University's George Beverly Winton similarly explained in *Mexico Today* that "a spasm of anti-Americanism not unfrequently passes over the country. We are not, as we ought to be, the most popular people with them."[65] A spasm, an involuntary physical movement, is not the product of deductive reasoning or the moral pursuit of principle that Americans believed underlay their own actions.

The root of the problem, of course, was not Mexican irrationality, but widespread opposition to the conduct of the U.S. government and U.S. companies in Mexico. Memories of the U.S. seizure of half of Mexico's territory in 1848 were refreshed by more recent events. In 1914, convinced that Mexico had besmirched the honor of American sailors and that the country was tilting dangerously toward Germany, President Wilson ordered the shelling and occupation of Veracruz. He had explained his Mexico policy to a British diplomat with the words, "I am going to teach the South American republics to elect good men."[66] U.S. newspapers seemed to find no causal connection between the occupation of Veracruz and "anti-Americanism, which is reaching a dangerous pitch," although if a foreign power had bombed and occupied a U.S. city, the resulting anger would have surprised no one.[67] The State Department would later compile a list of attacks on its consular facilities in Mexico during the revolution, and found them to have been "a result of the April 21 occupation of Veracruz and the killing of several hundred Mexican citizens, mostly non-combatants, by American forces."[68]

After the offenses of 1848 and 1914 came 1916, when General John J. "Black Jack" Pershing led an army of 10,000 men into Mexico on a campaign that lasted for a year, in an effort to stop border incursions and capture rebel leader Pancho Villa. The revolutionary calculated that he could provoke U.S.

intervention and draw a larger following with appeals to defensive Mexican nationalism. His illegal raid at Columbus, New Mexico, which caused the death of 17 Americans, provoked retaliatory attacks on Mexican-Americans in the United States, resulting in some 100 deaths, including the highly publicized lynching of Antonio Rodríguez, burned alive in the presence of a large crowd in Rock Springs, Texas.[69] This brutal conflict is not explained by congenital anti-American sentiment – there was a revolution going on, and border communities were caught up in the violence – but such events did, naturally, contribute to mutual hostility in that period. As usual, an underlying geopolitical conflict produced animosities, rather than the animosities producing the conflict.

Yet U.S. newspapers in this era regularly interpreted Mexican policies as "anti-American."[70] President Venustiano Carranza's principal offense that made him "notoriously anti-American"[71] was raising taxes on foreign mining and petroleum companies. Carranza's "anti-Americanism" was evidenced by "the confiscatory policy of his Administration in dealing with foreign oil and mineral properties," wrote a couple of Democratic Party stalwarts in their laudatory account of Wilson's administration ("Eight Years of the World's Greatest History").[72] But Carranza's measures were directed at foreign companies in general, not U.S. companies only. Strikes against U.S.-owned companies were part of a broader labor movement: "Firms of all nationality were struck in the course of 1911–1913: American mines . . . British smelters . . . French factories . . . as well as numerous Mexican and Spanish-owned and/or managed enterprises," according to a leading historian of Mexico.[73]

American reports of rampant anti-Americanism in Mexico at the time struck a few observers as unreliable. Nelson O'Shaughnessy, U.S. chargé d'affaires in Mexico City, wrote in 1913 that "[I] believe active anti-Americanism much exaggerated. I am received with much cordiality everywhere."[74] H. B. Phipps, an officer of the National Automobile Chamber of Commerce, returned from a trade mission to tell a national trade convention that "this idea of Anti-Americanism is almost entirely a matter of imagination. It is a bogey."[75] Mexico's president from 1920 to 1924, Álvaro Obregón, faced charges of "anti-Americanism" from U.S. oil companies, whose executives were furious when he raised taxes on their Mexican operations, and they demanded the right to determine the level of tax they should pay. Obregón tried to explain Mexico's position: "Refusal to do certain things which have been asked of us has been mistakenly attributed to anti-American feeling," he wrote in the *New York World*. "Nothing is further from the truth." Obregón noted that the leading oil syndicate, the Doheny Group, had repatriated $28,000,000 in profits in 1920 alone and was promising its stockholders another 225 percent increase in profits for 1921; surely some portion of that wealth derived from Mexican oil could remain in Mexico without Mexicans being accused of hating Americans for wanting to fund public services. Obregón concluded by urging Americans to help "a sister Republic attain peace and prosperity" by choosing not to side with the rapacious few, but to strengthen "our confidence in the high and proved idealism of the United States."[76]

Nonetheless, the Mexican Revolution brought the beginning of what would become a scholarly industry of explaining opposition to the United States abroad as arising from foreigners' feeblemindedness.[77] Rutherford H. Platt, Jr., argued that Carranza's "policy of anti-Americanism" was the only way he could gain a following among a population of sixteen million, of whom "11,750,996 are absolutely ignorant.... As a class these 'Mexican people' know nothing, think nothing, and care nothing."[78] Edward Perry blamed anti-Americanism on ignorance and poor judgment.[79] W. E. Dunn attributed Latin American "anti-American propaganda" to ignorance and "the psychology of the southern peoples."[80] This interpretation remained popular among North American political analysts for decades. State Department economic expert Merwin L. Bohan, attending the 1945 Inter-American Conference at Chapultepec, thought he understood "the main cause of anti-Americanism – envy of our economic position."[81] A leading history textbook still teaches American students that Mexicans suffer from "virulent, almost pathological Yankeephobia."[82] Rubin and Rubin, in their study of anti-Americanism, blame it on "envious" Latin Americans who not only resented U.S. interventions but found their own weakness "frustrating and hard to explain."[83] Envy and frustration are emotional categories, not rational ones; Latin Americans apparently must laud the United States to demonstrate their rationality.

The Rubins refer as one piece of evidence to the "crown jewel of Mexican anti-Americanism," the National Museum of Interventions in Mexico City.[84] In so doing, they join other scholars who describe the museum as a monument to anti-Americanism without, to judge from their writings, ever having visited it.[85] Instead, in an example of the repetitiveness common to many studies of anti-Americanism, they rely on a single *Washington Post* article, or on another's summary of the article, that called the museum "a blend of anti-imperialism and bruised dignity."[86] Alvin Rubinstein and Donald Smith altered that quotation to "a blend of anti-Americanism and bruised dignity," as did George Grayson in several works, and the error has been repeated.[87] The original report at least acknowledged what any visitor would see, that the museum deals with Spanish, British, and French actions in addition to the many U.S. interventions in Mexico.

A visit to the object of derision would reveal that rather than a temple of anti-Americanism, the museum promotes a nationalistic, self-legitimizing narrative. (This is not uncommon in national museums; the Smithsonian's National Museum of American History does so with a grandiose exhibit on the American flag and an account of all major U.S. military conflicts entitled "The Price of Freedom," as though this were the only cause.) The Mexican museum contains an exhibit devoted to the Spanish attack against the young independent country in 1829. The so-called *Guerra de los Pasteles* or Pastry War of 1838 follows, when the French Navy bombed and blockaded Mexican ports. A prominent display is devoted to Napoleon III's ill-fated scheme to impose the Austrian Archduke Maximilian as Emperor of Mexico in the 1860s. There are, of course, extensive treatments of the war with the United States in

1846–48; had one of the European empires seized and retained half of Mexico's territory, presumably more of the exhibition space would be devoted to it. A room devoted to the 1914 U.S. occupation of Veracruz displays photographs of civilians in jackets and ties taking rifle practice to defend their city. The exhibit on Pershing's intervention makes clear that it was sparked by Villa's attack on Columbus. A concluding inscription praises Mexico for defending the principles of national sovereignty and nonintervention in international affairs, in what Octavio Paz referred to as the Mexican inclination "to accept defeat with dignity, a conception that is certainly not ignoble."[88]

U.S. journalists have regularly rediscovered the museum in the past few decades and made fun of it. "Forget the Alamo! Look at the Sins of the Yankees" was the headline of one of several condescending *New York Times* reports. The *Los Angeles Times* used scare quotes to convey its diagnosis of Mexican paranoia: "Mexico's Obsession with 'Foreign Intervention' Enshrined in Museum."[89] It is eye opening to note how U.S. journalists and scholars so readily criticize and ridicule Mexicans, attributing psychological infirmity to an entire country, whereas often these same writers strenuously object to treatments of the United States by foreigners that make sweeping disrespectful claims about its national character. Perhaps the lesson is that writers of all nations can easily be tempted to overgeneralize about other countries, a common rhetorical practice rather than an "ism" signifying opposition to first principles.

An Epidemic of Anti-Mexicanism?

Should we collect patronizing reports about the Museum of Interventions as evidence of ill-informed U.S. anti-Mexicanism? Certainly there would be no shortage of material available to show how much hostility Americans have directed at Mexico and Mexicans for nearly two centuries. Racial slurs directed against Mexicans have a long pedigree. At the time of the Mexican War, President John Tyler's envoy, Congressman Waddy Thompson, characterized Mexicans as "lazy, ignorant, and, of course, vicious and dishonest."[90] Texan leader Stephen Austin asserted that Mexicans "want nothing but tails to be more brutes than the Apes."[91] A traveler's guide to California in 1845 found Mexicans "scarcely a visible grade, in the scale of intelligence, above the barbarous tribes by whom they are surrounded."[92] And this hatred spawned violence: an estimated 597 Mexicans were lynched in the United States between 1848 and 1928.[93] In 1910, Mexican diplomats filed the first of a series of reports about the abuse of Mexicans by U.S. citizens and officials in Kansas City, South Bend, Corpus Christi, New Orleans, Philadelphia, and elsewhere.[94] By the 1920s, signs reading "No Mexicans Hired," "No Mexicans, For White Only," "No Chili, Mexicans Keep Out" appeared throughout the Southwest, as theaters, public pools, and other institutions enforced segregationist "Juan Crow" rules. More than half a million Mexicans were deported during the Great Depression, some of them U.S. citizens.[95] One could continue by citing the mass beatings of Mexican Americans during the Zoot Suit Riots in 1943, the exploitation of Mexican labor by U.S. agriculture, the stereotypical greasy bandit characters favored by Hollywood, and so on. For five years until late 2009, America's leading cable news channel turned over an hour of prime time every weeknight to a program whose chief concern seemed to be to argue that Mexicans pose a mortal threat to the United States, spreading disease, committing crimes, and draining the national treasury.[96] In July 2008, three white teenagers in Pennsylvania attacked Luis Ramirez, a 25-year-old Mexican immigrant, and beat him to death, yelling that Mexicans should get out of their town.[97]

On empirical grounds, therefore, a case for the virulence of anti-Mexicanism in the United States might be easier to construct than that of the danger posed by anti-Americanism in Mexico. In the century after the Mexican Revolution, one searches in vain for any American who could seriously be considered a victim of Mexican anti-Americanism, that is, to have been singled out for violence because of resentment of American national identity.[98]

The point is that anti-Americanism as a concept contributes nothing to understanding the relations between Mexico and the United States. On the contrary, it takes a universal phenomenon – hostility generated by friction between neighboring countries – and turns it into a particular phenomenon, a peculiarly Latin kind of irrationality given to outbursts that, it is implied, should be treated like children's tantrums. This ascribes a monopoly on reason to Americans, who claim the right to judge Mexican behavior as illegitimate, especially when that behavior involves Mexican objections to American actions.

The Nicaraguan Paradox

Since the discourse of anti-Americanism in foreign affairs intensified during the Mexican Revolution, it took little to extend the analysis to conflict arising in Central America. Baptist missionaries there complained of encountering "strong anti-Americanism" but did not wonder whether that might have had something to do with the fact that their activities were designed to uproot local traditions,[99] or with recent U.S. efforts to destabilize the government of Manuel Enrique Araujo in El Salvador, or its overthrow of José Santos Zelaya in Nicaragua.[100] As U.S. Marines remained in Nicaragua almost uninterruptedly from 1912 to 1933, directing the selection of presidents and fighting against the nationalist rebel Augusto Sandino, critics warned that military intervention had provoked "anti-Americanism" in that country.[101] The top U.S. diplomat in Managua characterized calls for a return to constitutional rule there as "a strong anti-American wave" in the National Assembly.[102]

The Nicaraguan case demonstrates how inapt are psychological or ideological explanations for anti-American sentiment, indeed, how unhelpful are the term's oversimplifying tendencies and dichotomous structure. One might call it the Nicaraguan Paradox: why was the most Americanized country in Central America, whose inhabitants went so far as to prefer baseball to soccer, also home to two of Latin America's most successful revolutionary movements of the twentieth century – bringing down the wrath of the United States upon Sandino in the 1930s and the Sandinistas in the 1980s? To find the answer, one must disaggregate political resistance to distinct policies from the assumption that behind such resistance lay psychological or cultural motives.

Nicaragua has experienced more than its share of U.S. intervention. From 1855 to 1857, it was taken over by the American filibusterer William Walker, who proclaimed himself president, made English the national language, and reinstated slavery, then was recognized by Washington. After a coalition of Central American nations defeated Walker militarily, Nicaraguan elites coupled their denunciations of U.S. military intervention with the energetic pursuit of a cosmopolitan nation-building project patterned on the United States.[103] Liberal Party stalwarts self-consciously adopted practices they understood as Americanization, while the patriarch of the Conservatives, Pedro Joaquín Chamorro, called the United States his "model Republic."[104]

Nicaraguan sentiment toward the United States did not remain in a steady state of hostility emanating from an inferiority complex or envy, but rose and fell in direct response to U.S. actions. When U.S. occupation of Cuba and its annexation of Puerto Rico followed the War of 1898, and as U.S. officials helped orchestrate the secession of Panama from Colombia, one of the most resonant voices raised against U.S. policy in the Caribbean belonged to the Nicaraguan poet Rubén Darío. This central figure in literary *modernismo* wrote an ode to Theodore Roosevelt in 1905 addressing him as "Hunter" and invoking respected elements of U.S. history and culture – George Washington's statesmanship, Walt Whitman's humanism – to condemn the trend toward the country's more recent "joining the cult of Hercules to the cult of Mammon." Defiantly, Darío addressed Roosevelt directly:

> You believe that life is a fire
> that progress is eruption;
> that wherever you place your bullet
> you place the future.
> No.[105]

That "No" was not an objection to modernity or democratic government – not from an admirer of Whitman, the bard of democracy – but to the increasingly unbridled use of U.S. power in Latin America. Yet we still encounter claims that an irrational, culturally based anti-Americanism was behind Darío's rebuke to the American president, even though the poem was clearly aimed at a particular policy. This was Roosevelt's declaration in 1904 that as the "international police power," the United States had the right to intervene in the region at will, in what came to be known as the Roosevelt Corollary to the Monroe Doctrine. This makes Darío's line "you are the future invader of indigenous America" less a sign of Latin paranoia than of taking Roosevelt at his word. The following year the poet's suspicions were confirmed when Roosevelt dispatched the Marines to Cuba for a three-year occupation after Cuban

nationalists protested a rigged election. In quick succession came U.S. occupa-
tions of Haiti, the Dominican Republic, and Nicaragua; there were more than
a dozen Marine interventions in the Caribbean basin in the two decades after
Darío's prediction.[106]

Marine occupation of Nicaragua under Roosevelt's successor, William
Howard Taft, put U.S. officials in charge of an economic arrangement ("Dollar
Diplomacy") that ensured that much of the profit from the country's resources
and productivity would be drained off to U.S. investors. In 1912, when the
U.S. official in charge of Nicaraguan customs houses blocked emergency food
imports during a drought, there were anti-U.S. demonstrations and food riots.
When U.S. bankers running Nicaragua's *Banco Nacional* cut back on agricul-
tural loans, planters driven to bankruptcy joined denunciations of Wall Street
control. Liberals "came to identify 'Wall Street' with a backward, 'feudal'
economic regime," extracting profits at the expense of Nicaraguan national
development.[107] In contrast to the discourse then circulating among European
rightists who linked Wall Street to Jewish conspiracies, the objections here
were not to the United States as a symbol of modernity, but as an obstacle to
Nicaraguan modernization.

To note the correlation between the exponential growth of the U.S. economy
and its increasingly assertive behavior overseas was not a fringe theory of
resentful Latins or wild-eyed socialists. It was Woodrow Wilson who made
this connection explicit. "Our industries have expanded to such a point that
they will burst their jackets if they cannot find a free outlet to the markets of
the world," he said. "Diplomacy, and if need be power, must make an open
way."[108] When Latin American intellectuals noticed the link between American
industry and American foreign policy, they were expressing a wary reaction to
the rise of American power that was more rational from their point of view
than the uncritical embrace for some reason expected by American nationalists
always on the lookout for any signs of anti-Americanism abroad.

Europe: The Shock of Ingratitude

In 1898, Americans had been surprised that many Cubans and Filipinos greeted
them with suspicion rather than gratitude for helping to defeat the Spanish,
especially once the United States asserted a right to control their affairs. After
the First World War, many Americans were similarly astonished that their
contribution to defeating the Germans did not bring the lasting appreciation
they expected, as Wilson's aims and achievements in peace-making diverged
from his promises, and the growing U.S. presence in the European economy
and popular culture generated resentment. When Wilson first arrived in Europe
he walked through cheering throngs of well-wishers while girls in white dresses
tossed flower petals in his path. In France he was greeted by vast crowds of
people spilling onto the sidewalks and streets, clinging to lampposts festooned
with American flags, literally shouting from the rooftops, "*Vive l'Amérique!*
Vive Wilson!" It was "the most remarkable demonstration of enthusiasm and

affection on the part of the Parisians that I have ever heard of, let alone seen," according to an American resident.[109] The ardor quickly cooled. In part this was because Wilson failed to fulfill many of the hopes he had raised so high, and partly a response to his personality, to his too-evident conviction of his own rightness. "America had the infinite privilege of fulfilling her destiny and saving the world," Wilson immodestly claimed.[110]

The first to be disappointed were the many representatives of movements for independence in the developing world who had welcomed Wilson's repeated calls for the universal right to self-determination and believed he was speaking to them. Indians under British rule, Koreans colonized by Japan, and Algerians ruled by the French marched under banners emblazoned with Wilson's slogans.[111] Ho Chi Minh, then a student in Paris, rode out to Versailles to ask for a meeting with Wilson, hoping to persuade him to support self-determination for Indochina, but his request was denied.[112] Saad Zaghlul and a delegation of Egyptian nationalists tried to make their case, but the British arrested and interned them on Malta, allowing them to proceed to Paris only after the Conference had agreed to the maintenance of a British protectorate over Egypt. Emir Faisal came seeking independence for Syria and Mesopotamia (later Iraq and Palestine), expecting to collect on a promise made by a British agent, Col. T. E. Lawrence "of Arabia," in exchange for Arab assistance fighting the Turks during the war. Faisal too would be disappointed.[113] Each of these leaders made an appeal to Wilson – Faisal noted that Arab independence "was in accord with the principles laid down by President Wilsons," and Zaghlul wrote that Egyptians desired self-determination and had "absolute faith in the fourteen points" – but Wilson championed none of their causes, because in promoting the ideal of self-determination he had never had such people in mind.[114] In this he was in agreement with his Secretary of State, Robert Lansing, who recorded privately that he was "convinced of the danger of putting such ideas into the minds of certain races...The phrase is simply loaded with dynamite."[115]

The United States was not responsible for European colonialism, but the discrepancy between Wilson's proclamations and his practice created a dissonance that undermined the likelihood of a pro-American stance among anticolonial movements. Ho Chi Minh moved on to Moscow and shifted his hopes to Soviet leader Vladimir Lenin, whose anticolonial discourse was more consistent (the Soviet Union having no overseas colonies of its own). Uprisings broke out against the British in Iraq and the French in Syria and were crushed with the use of air power.[116] The rude awakening from the Wilsonian dream would have profound and lasting effects on foreign views of the United States, in an enduring pattern repeated throughout the twentieth century: American rhetoric of selflessness and idealism is taken seriously by foreigners drawn to widely shared "American values," who then become aggrieved when the United States trades its high-flown discourse for the realpolitik practiced by all great powers. The transnational tendency to see America as a symbol of universal principles, abetted by U.S. leaders proudly speaking the language of exceptionalism, produces disillusion and resentment when the United States does not live up to that high standard. And where that disillusionment is expressed in cynical or critical remarks about the United States by foreigners, many Americans, whose faith in their exceptionalism remains unshaken, attribute those responses to an irrational anti-Americanism. It is the vicious cycle of the anti-American myth.

Contributing to this dynamic were divergent perceptions of the motives behind American behavior. In World War I, Americans thought of themselves as magnanimously entering a war not only to protect their own interests – to prevent a catastrophic default on loans made to France and Britain, and to defend free passage for neutral shipping, a long-standing principle in the diplomacy of a country that had always depended on international trade – but also to offer European allies a helping hand in the fight and guide them toward the right kind of peace when it was over: "saving the world," in Wilson's phrase. To this end, the United States had spent huge sums of money and sacrificed the lives of tens of thousands of its soldiers. Europeans saw things differently. They noted that the Americans stayed out of the fight for the first three years, and as they watched American policy and American products become more influential in their countries during and after World War I, they worried about how to preserve their own industries and interests.

These divergent perspectives colored the way each side viewed all aspects of the American war and postwar effort. When Herbert Hoover organized a massive relief effort in areas suffering shortages, Americans congratulated themselves on their altruism. Europeans welcomed the food but resented Hoover's simultaneous promotion of U.S. economic interests by such means as dumping American surplus commodities that undercut European producers.[117] Even the military effort that tipped the balance against Germany in 1918 received a lukewarm reception in some quarters. French Premier Georges Clemenceau compared the number of killed in battle: 1,364,000 French and 56,000 Americans, and concluded that American troops had remained "inactive, safely out of range."[118] André Tardieu, the French High Commissioner to the United States in charge of obtaining aid and arms, argued that Americans had mostly sat out the war: it lasted fifty-two months, of which the United States spent thirty-two in a state of neutrality and twelve in a state of "military abstention," participating only in the final eight months of fighting. Tardieu attributed the delay not to American cowardice (as Americans are wont to speak of the French military record) but to a classic realist view of international relations: cooperation between the United States and France, when it occurred, was the product not of friendship but of the alignment of interests.[119] It certainly sounded ungrateful, given that it was not an American war, and Americans might have chosen to sit out the entire conflict instead of intervening to help France win. The competing narratives on either side of the Atlantic revealed not so much the effect of prejudice as the influence of perspective upon thinking: where one stood depended on where one sat.

Disputes soon arose over American insistence that the French repay the loans they had undertaken to fund their war effort, countered by French assertions that surely they had paid part of the debt with the lives of their dead soldiers. In February 1920, someone went along the *Avenue President Wilson* at night pasting over the street signs so that they now read, resentfully, *Avenue des Américains*, as if Americans had bought and claimed a Parisian boulevard. It was a careful job, done on blue paper with white lettering, so Parisians en route to work the next morning thought their city had rebaptized the Avenue Trocadero a second time.[120] Throughout the Franco-American debt negotiations of the 1920s, attacks on "American imperialism" were frequent in the French Parliament and among the thousands of demonstrators on Paris streets. Uncle Sam was renamed "Uncle Shylock" for purportedly seeking to enslave France through indebtedness – a popular anti-Semitic image that tapped into the imaginary association of American financial power with Jewish financial power. President Calvin Coolidge blamed irresponsible American tourists and irresponsible foreigners alike for a rise in "anti-Americanism." But while some of the French turned their ire against American visitors or American society, others differentiated their continuing appreciation of American assistance in the war from their objection to seeing the U.S. government now behave more generously toward the defeated enemy (with a loan forgiveness package for Germany) than toward a former ally that had shed so much blood in the common cause.[121] As so often, Americans looked abroad expecting enduring gratitude. When they found foreigners immersed in their new concerns of the day, the dissonance could have only one explanation: anti-Americanism exercising its deplorable effects.

Ambivalent Icon: Henry Ford and the Germans

Across the Rhine, many Germans were unhappy with the outcome of a war they had expected to win and a peace they found punitive. Because German troops were still on foreign soil when the ceasefire was signed in 1918, the legend spread that they had not been beaten militarily but were "stabbed in the back" by a conspiracy of defeatist socialists and traitorous Jews. Their anger at the traditional enemy, France, increased with French exaction of reparations from the Rhineland and the Ruhr Valley. The United States had not loomed large in the German demonization of enemies during the war, except on the far right: Houston Stewart Chamberlain, the adoptive German nationalist, had written to Kaiser Wilhelm II in 1915 that the war was the product of a plot between the Jews and the Americans to take over the world.[122] But the United States gradually became a secondary target as the hopes inspired by Wilson's promises of a fair settlement yielded to resentment at the growing American role in managing Germany's affairs. In 1921, an obscure Austrian ex-corporal made clear what bothered him most about Wilson: "he came to Paris with a staff of 117 Jewish bankers and financiers," and Germany "threw itself economically and culturally into his arms," Adolf Hitler complained.[123]

Hitler's paranoia and vitriol were not directed solely or even especially at Americans, however; he had many hateful obsessions, but anti-Americanism was not among them. In his notorious treatise *Mein Kampf*, his few references to the United States ranged from praise for its excellent universities and Teutonic population to the claim that Jews dominated its financial system.[124] He lauded the benefits of Prohibition and suggested that it be replicated in Germany.[125] His second book spoke admiringly of U.S. technological innovation and high living standards and suggested the United States could serve as a model of racial hygiene, thanks to its segregation laws and immigration restriction policies, while also warning that the country could eventually become Germany's rival because it enjoyed the advantages of bountiful raw materials, a large internal market, and an energetic population drawn from Germanic stock.[126]

Far from being obsessively or consistently anti-American, Hitler, who loved to watch Walt Disney films and to read Karl May's books about the American West, sometimes looked to the United States for inspiration.[127] One of his personal role models was the American icon Henry Ford. Ford's formula combining mass production with wages high enough for workers to consume their own products came to represent the American system during the Weimar era, appearing to offer a solution to the social question that had bedeviled political theorists for decades: some even dubbed it "white socialism."[128] Ford acquired heroic status in Germany. His autobiography was a best-seller, going through thirty-two printings in German before 1939.[129] It was, said social democratic trade unionist Fritz Tarnow, "the most revolutionary work in the entire field of economics."[130] Karl Kraus, punning on the inventor's name, turned the German word for progress, *Fortschritt*, into the neologism *Fordschritt*, honoring the man who had invented the future.[131]

Ford had no greater admirer than Adolf Hitler. He hung a life-size oil portrait of Ford in his Nazi Party office in Munich, and after he became Chancellor, bestowed a medal upon the automobile magnate, impressed not only by Ford's industrial accomplishments that appealed to the enthusiast of the Autobahn and the "people's car" (*Volkswagen*) but also by Ford's active role in spreading anti-Semitism in the United States through his publication of *The International Jew*.[132] "We look to Heinrich Ford as the leader of the growing Fascist movement in America," Hitler told a *Chicago Tribune* reporter.[133] The America-fever that characterized Weimar-era discussions of political economy abated after the stock market crash of 1929, and the left recovered its bearings, challenging the "American myth" that capitalism and technology together eliminated the need for a workers' movement.[134] The Nazis' continued enthusiasm for advanced production techniques, mass media, and engineering, what Jeffrey Herf has called "reactionary modernism," made clear that embracing technology and the tools of mass communication – "Americanizing," in the language of the day – was obviously not a useful indicator for gauging commitment to democratic values.[135] Reading pro- or anti-Americanism, and thus a stance on fundamental principles of freedom or modernity, into positive or negative reactions to developments labeled "Americanization" would be as misleading as taking the Nazis' technomania and Ford-worship for approval of the democratic society in which Ford made his career.

As with any schema imposed on human behavior, the dichotomy of pro- or anti-American or pro- or anti-modern vastly oversimplifies. It forces into the same mold an array of thinkers who took note of dramatic changes associated with U.S. society and raised concerns about them, without those concerns necessarily revealing an underlying objection to the most treasured of "American values." Those commentators included, at one extreme, right-wing polemicists such as Adolf Halfeld, whose *Amerika und der Amerikanismus* contrasted the soullessness and overwork that U.S. society demanded of its members to the satisfactions to be derived from an organic German ethnic culture whose veneration led him to join the Nazi Party in 1933.[136] Charles Maurras, a French radical nationalist, monarchist, and ideological anti-Semite, thought he saw a conspiracy of German Jews from the United States seeking to take over France through their financial power.[137] In the political center was the influential French social scientist André Siegfried. Described as "the main foundation of the French intellectual anti-American tradition," Siegfried's *Les États-Unis d'aujourd'hui (The United States Today)* was a scholarly study of the impact of mass production and mass culture on U.S. society.[138] This was no right-wing rant – Siegfried was known for his opposition to reactionary demagogues in France – and he was impressed by American productivity and social cohesion even as he exhibited the same prejudicial thinking of the era's "100% Americans" by predicting that immigration would weaken the American national character.[139]

Others skeptical of American ways were anything but anti-democratic. The liberal humanist Stefan Zweig, for example, who with the rise of the Nazis would flee his native Austria for England (and eventually commit suicide in Brazil), was an idealist who hoped for a time that a cosmopolitan literary community could overcome nationalist political conflicts. He put his energy into this project, joining gatherings of the PEN Club, working closely with the pacifist and Nobel laureate Romain Rolland, helping to plan a "Moral Parliament" of leading lights from all the nations, which would have its headquarters in Geneva.[140] His love of European literature, philosophy, and psychology made him regret the cultural "monotonization" of European consciousness he associated with American cultural influence:

> [T[he conquest of Europe by America has begun . . . we are becoming a colony of their life, their life style, servants of an idea thoroughly alien to Europeans, that of the machine . . . In the cinema, in radio, in dance, in all these new means of the mechanization of humankind there lies an enormous power which cannot be overcome. Because they all fulfill the highest ambition of the mediocre: to offer pleasure without requiring exertion.[141]

This passage, which anticipated later critiques by the Frankfurt School theorists Theodor Adorno and Max Horkheimer, earned Zweig a place in accounts of interwar anti-Americanism.[142] The disdain for mass culture is read as a disdain for the masses, as if criticism of machine production were the same as criticism of those who worked on the machines. But the inclusion of Zweig among the "anti-Americans" requires the category to be extraordinarily capacious, somehow applying to a Jewish humanist fervently devoted to democracy and human rights. In a less often cited passage from his memoirs, Zweig praised Wilson's "magnificent program, which was quite our own."[143] His evocation of New York City did not include the customary depreciation of its bustle and noise or boxy forms but a reverence for its "enchanting night beauty" and "the rushing cascades of light . . . the city's dreamlike heaven which, with its billions of artificial stars, glitters at the real ones in the sky."[144] Since Zweig's hopes for a reorientation of society away from both reactionary and revolutionary violence depended on a utopian project of literary internationalism, his opposition to the commodification of culture was not a question of elitist taste but a matter, as he saw it, of preserving the possibility of a humane political future. It was not a rejection of the United States, where, he said, he had gained an insight into "the divine freedom of the country," and certainly not of democracy itself.[145]

Indeed, by the 1920s, European debates over "Americanization" were no longer about democracy or freedom in any significant respect; after decades of rapid industrial growth, the country had come to symbolize not so much a set of principles in debates over liberty or political representation as a set of material developments in debates over advanced technology, industrial capitalism, and mass consumerism. "Americanism is the new European buzzword," Rudolf Kayser wrote in 1925. "We now find ourselves in the curious situation that we have no other expression to describe the truly radical changes in our external and internal forms of life."[146] Arguments about America, in other words, were not really about America. The most extensive study of the first three decades of twentieth-century European writing about America found that hateful anti-Americanism was "an exception and an extreme position," promoted by a mere handful of proto-fascist authors, whereas most books about America were neutral in tone and aimed at a balanced portrayal, the goal of which was to explore the preeminent industrial mass society for insights into Europe's own future, not to pillory democracy or liberal values.[147]

Zweig was among the more thoughtful critics to refer to an American "colonization" of Europe in this period, but although his use of the term was metaphorical, other, less mindful writers seemed to mean it literally. Germany found itself unable to pay the steep reparations demanded by the victorious Allies in World War I, and so under a circular arrangement developed by Chicago banker Charles G. Dawes, reparations levels were reduced, and the United States lent Germany large sums to repay Britain and France, who sent much of the money back to the United States as payments on their war debts. The Dawes Plan also installed an American as overseer of reparations, placed non-Germans in charge of Germany's railways and central bank, and allowed for massive U.S. investment in Germany by General Motors, Ford, Du Pont, General Electric, and Dow Chemical. This was followed by the Young Plan of 1929–1930, which lowered reparations levels further. The plans allowed the German economy to recover but were unsatisfactory both to German nationalists, who resented the degree of foreign control, and to those in the Allied countries who had wanted reparations to come out of Germany's productive capacity (to diminish its ability to wage war), rather than being provided by New York banks in exchange for leverage over European decisions and resources.[148]

Some Europeans who disliked this postwar dependence on American capital began to compare their weakened countries to American colonies in the Caribbean. Where President Taft had thought – erroneously, as it turned out – that "Dollar Diplomacy" would serve as a progressive alternative to military intervention and colonialism, now terms like *dollardiplomatie* and *Dollarimperialismus* began to appear in ideologically distorted analyses of U.S. foreign policy in Europe. "We Germans are today the objects of Dollar Diplomacy; see the Dawes Plan," wrote Alexander Graf von Brockdorff, a leading member of the pro-imperialist *Alldeutscher Verband*.[149] "We will be handled exactly like Nicaragua, San Domingo, Haiti, Cuba etc.," with gunboats called in to collect debts, agreed Carl von Einem in 1929.[150]

Ironically, while the denunciation of real Dollar Diplomacy in Latin America came from the left, the appropriation of the term to describe U.S. financial power in Germany and France came from the far right – including from ultranationalists who heartily approved of their own countries' imperial projects. After a member of the Communist Party USA, Joseph Freeman, and his ideological colleague Scott Nearing wrote *Dollar Diplomacy* (1925), attacking U.S. imperialism in Latin America, it was translated and published in German to great acclaim in the pro-imperialist press, including the *Alldeutsche Blätter*. The Communist critique now appeared with a preface by Karl Haushofer, a retired general who taught a race-based version of geostrategy at the University of Munich, in which he blamed American capital for oppressing Germany.[151] Journalist Louis Guilaine, an apologist for French colonial control of North Africa, blamed American imperialism for seeking hegemonic control in both Latin America and Europe.[152] Roger Lambelin, a friend of Charles Maurras and cofounder with him of the proto-fascist *Action Française*, issued a warning in *Le péril juif (The Jewish Danger)*: "With Dollar Diplomacy one can find our weak spot," Lambelin opined, blaming France's postwar economic problems on the insidious power of American and "Jewish capital."[153] Nineteenth-century Social Democratic leader August Bebel had referred to anti-Semitism as "the socialism of fools" because only "dumb guys" would hold Jews responsible for capitalism. In the 1920s, the adoption of anti-imperialist rhetoric by anti-Semitic European imperialists in a perverse kind of role reversal showed that anti-Americanism, when it did appear, was often the anti-imperialism of fools.[154]

Sacco, Vanzetti, and Dreyfus: The Globalization of Protest

In the annals of anti-Americanism, as the story is usually told, the defining event of the interwar period was the international uproar over an American murder trial. In 1921, the Italian-born anarchists Nicola Sacco, a fish peddler, and

Bartolomeo Vanzetti, a shoemaker, were sentenced to death for a payroll robbery and double homicide in Braintree, Massachusetts. They were electrocuted on August 23, 1927. In the intervening years Sacco and Vanzetti became the subjects of an unprecedented wave of "anti-American" demonstrations around the world. The case was and remains controversial because of prosecutorial misconduct – witness tampering, withholding of evidence – and because it began during the First Red Scare, when fear of foreign radicalism combined with ethnic prejudice. Their humble trades, Italian origin, and leftist politics, and the bigoted utterances of various officials involved in the trial, persuaded many observers that they were the victims of a legalized lynching. Anarchist and communist groups launched protests worldwide and helped turn Sacco and Vanzetti into a cause célèbre (and a recruiting pitch). Humanitarian organizations and intellectuals saw the case as ethnic persecution and judicial abuse, an American Dreyfus affair.[155]

It would not be too much to speak of the globalization of a protest movement. During the years between the trial and the executions, protests, ranging from petition drives and large demonstrations to general strikes and even several bombings of U.S. installations took place in Algiers, Amsterdam, Asunción, Berlin, Brussels, Bucharest, Buenos Aires, Cape Town, Casablanca, Geneva, Genoa, Guadalajara, Havana, Juarez, Lisbon, London, Madrid, Marseilles, Mexico City, Montevideo, Munich, Ottawa, Paris, Quito, Rome, Stockholm, Sydney, Tokyo, and Vienna.[156] Surveying the global response, the editor of the *Nation* magazine exclaimed, "Talk about the solidarity of the human race!"[157] From the U.S. establishment point of view, these events were "anti-American demonstrations," a "mad reaction," carried out by "hot-headed youths."[158] U.S. officials generally saw only one appropriate response: steadfastness. Senator William H. Borah, chairman of the Committee on Foreign Relations, spoke for many when he argued vociferously against heeding foreign opinion: "It would be a national humiliation, a shameless, cowardly compromise of national courage, to pay the slightest attention to foreign protest," he insisted.[159]

Scholars have included these international protests among the major manifestations of twentieth-century anti-American activity, arguing that voiced concerns over injustice or attention to the details of the case were merely a "pretext for anti-Americanism."[160] Some have argued that this outpouring of global protest was an irrational negative reaction to American society itself, stemming from the accumulated frustration of intellectuals and foreign elites in their encounter with social change. Rather than sparking a backlash against modernity, however, the trial crystallized concern among liberals and the left that the United States itself in the 1920s was exhibiting worrisome antimodern tendencies, evident in the enactment of Prohibition, the exclusion of immigrants, the antiscientific trends highlighted by the Scopes Monkey Trial, and the growth of the Ku Klux Klan. Because more was expected of America, judicial abuses there were especially frightening. "One is not so surprised at occurrences of this sort in Hungary or Lithuania," wrote the British philosopher Bertrand Russell. "But in America they must be matters of grave concern to all."[161] Liberal pro-American voices were prominent in the condemnation of the trial, because America was supposed to uphold a higher standard.

Radical protest over the trials, on the other hand, sometimes specifically targeted the United States, but to describe it as "anti-Americanism" understood as a cultural reaction against modernity or derived from an abhorrence of democracy is to misread the nature of twentieth-century far left movements. Communists informed by Marx and Lenin vied with anarchists inspired by Pierre-Joseph Proudhon and Mikhail Bakunin, each offering different paths to achieve a more egalitarian society. To some workers and intellectuals, the extraordinary imbalance of power between the rich and the poor under late-nineteenth- and early-twentieth-century capitalism led them to believe that only the overthrow of such a system would resolve problems of poverty and political power. The United States loomed large in the worldview of radicals of the left, because the United States was the world's largest industrial producer, and when World War I and its aftermath displaced the globe's financial center from London to New York, America became the target of anarchists and communists who saw capitalism as the major obstacle to their vision of an ideal society. This ideological conflict would only deepen over the course of the twentieth century.

Despite recurring internecine conflict among rival factions, many communists became capital-C Communists by joining disciplined political parties increasingly subject to direction from Moscow, which could offer ideological leadership and modest material support. Dissatisfied intellectuals, workers, and unemployed were drawn to communism not as an antimodern system but as a modernizing system that promised the material sufficiency and social equality still lacking in the West. From 1917 on, Communists would look to the Soviet Union as a model (with China and Cuba later offering alternative sources of inspiration and doctrinal guidance, alongside countless variations and deviations). When Communists attacked various aspects of the United States, this was a programmatic policy resulting from an ideological party line, not a stance that emerged from a preexisting blanket prejudice against the United States. It was not anti-Americanism, in other words, that made people become Communists, but a commitment to Communism that led them to oppose the United States in an encompassing, undifferentiated, and often transparently cynical way. If they were anti-American in the sense of automatically denouncing the United States regardless of the events of the day, that was not because of culture but dogma – which made Communist "anti-Americanism" during the twentieth century predictable, self-explanatory, and from a scholarly point of view, not particularly interesting.

Anarchists had no such state sponsor and no desire for one. Instead they found congenial homes in labor organizations such as the International Workers of the World (IWW), the French *Conféderation Générale du Travail* (CGT), and the *Federación Obrera Regional Argentina* (FORA). Some embraced the tactics of *Aktionismus*, action for its own sake, and a few who clustered around the "revolutionary zealot" Luigi Galleani turned to terrorism, romanticizing violence almost as if it were a political program in its own right or could somehow cause the sudden collapse of the state.[162] This produced a series of bombings against U.S. institutions and the homes of U.S. officials starting in 1919 that brought massive retaliation in the form of the Palmer Raids, a series of arrests and deportations of foreign radicals whether they were bomb-throwers or merely readers of leftist newspapers, initiated by Attorney General A. Mitchell Palmer, himself the target of a bomb that damaged his home.

It was in this context that Sacco and Vanzetti, followers of Galleani, were arrested and tried for the murder of a clerk and a guard during a payroll robbery. Their anarchism and closeness to armed groups made them guilty by association in the eyes of their opponents, whereas their supporters depicted them as ordinary workers targeted for their unpopular ideas or their ethnicity. At first a symbol to the diaspora of Italian laborers, Sacco and Vanzetti soon became pawns in a competition among anarchist and communist groups to turn their compelling story into a marketing effort to win adherents. The Executive Committee of the Communist International in Moscow called for a world-wide campaign on their behalf. In November 1921, a coordinated bombing campaign targeted U.S. diplomatic installations abroad. Someone sent a letter bomb to the U.S. Ambassador in Paris, Myron Herrick, injuring his valet. U.S. diplomatic missions in Lisbon, Marseilles, Rio de Janeiro, and Zurich were damaged by bombs.[163]

This most radical form of protest reflected an extreme left position that considered itself to be practically in a state of war against the United States. It is worth noting that other groups with disparate goals also used bomb attacks to try to assassinate diplomats from other countries such as Argentina, Czechoslovakia, France, Great Britain, Italy, Japan, Lithuania, Poland, the Soviet Union, and Spain in the same period. That this era featured terrorism in pursuit of various other causes does not make the bombers of U.S. installations less criminal, but it does suggest that locating this violence on a spectrum of culturally based anti-Americanism is less analytically useful than placing it among various ideologically based attacks directed against a number of states by diverse radical groups of the left and the right during this era.[164]

That the bombing campaign against U.S. targets was coordinated also suggests that the terrorist cells behind it were not reflective of a widespread, culturally based anti-Americanism but represented the extreme margin of a radical ideology. They were a tiny minority compared with the scale of the demonstrations; although the violent were not representative, they naturally drew disproportionate attention.[165] This would become a recurring feature of twentieth-century protest movements directed against U.S. policies: they were often accompanied by a fringe element determined to use violence, whose discourse and practice might present the most convincing case for speaking of "anti-Americanism," even while these same characteristics make the term appropriate for only a handful of people. The same story could be told about the 1920s as it was about the 1960s, 1980s, and 2000s.[166]

Mainstream protestors, in contrast, did not display an anti-American agenda. They included renowned intellectuals and artists, some, but not all, on the left, such as Marie Curie, John Dos Passos, Albert Einstein, Anatole France, Thomas Mann, Diego Rivera, Ben Shahn, George Bernard Shaw, Upton Sinclair, and H. G. Wells.[167] Romain Rolland observed that protests against the death sentences for Sacco and Vanzetti came from "the liberals, the Christians – all the saner and better balanced elements of Europe." He went on to assert: "I am not an American, but I love America. And I accuse of high treason against America the men who have soiled her with this judicial crime before the eyes of the world."[168]

Some contemporaries dissented from the view that anti-Americanism was spreading. The president of the National Red Cross told President Coolidge in 1927 that he encountered no anti-Americanism during a trip around the world, and the U.S. ambassador in Paris played down reports of anti-American feeling there.[169] The "woman of 50 years, gray-haired, soberly and decently dressed" was not attacking the Americanization of her society when she placed a placard before the equestrian statue of George Washington in Paris reading "In the name of Christ, thou shalt not kill. We implore pardon for Sacco and Vanzetti."[170] The "thousands of men in reputable positions" who signed a French appeal to "right-thinking Americans" politely urging their intervention to stave off the execution of men whose guilt was in doubt were not objecting to modernity's impact on their culture.[171] Nor were the 140,000 members of the League of the Rights of Man who asked the Massachusetts governor "in the name of human conscience" to grant clemency.[172] They were echoing the many Americans opposed to the executions, such as the thousands of protestors who thronged Manhattan's Union Square to applaud speakers on podiums draped with American flags, or the 20,000 who marched in Philadelphia, or the editorialists of the *New York World*, the *Brooklyn Eagle*, the *St. Louis Post-Dispatch*, the *Duluth Herald*, and the *Baltimore Sun*, all of which criticized the trial. Future Supreme Court Justice Felix Frankfurter's devastating critique of the errors in the case, his own *"J'accuse,"* drew praise from future Supreme Court Justice Benjamin Cardozo (and got his phone tapped by the police).[173] Kansas newspaper editor William Allen White, the voice of middle America, wrote the Massachusetts governor, "I had no idea that one could let their passions so completely sweep their judgment into fears and hatreds, so deeply confuse their sanity. I now know why the witches were persecuted and hanged by upright and godly people."[174]

The fact that foreign protests and criticism were matched by domestic protests and criticism from the unlikeliest candidates for the anti-American label suggests that one's feelings about America were not necessary factors in a decision to speak up against what appeared to many to be unjust convictions. Comparing the uproar over Sacco and Vanzetti to a similar case from a few decades before may be even more instructive. Attributing the protests over the Sacco and Vanzetti trial to anti-Americanism would be the equivalent of

saying that anti-French sentiment was behind the international response to the
Dreyfus affair.

The Dreyfus Affair as Mirror Image

In 1894, Captain Alfred Dreyfus, the only Jewish member of the French General
Staff, was convicted of selling military secrets to Germany and sent to prison
on an island off French Guiana. For the rest of the decade, the conviction of
Dreyfus became an international cause célèbre. Thirty thousand demonstrators in London denounced his conviction, and protestors in Chicago burned
the French flag. Foreign organizations as diverse as the American Bar Association and the Swedish Association of the Blind joined the protests. The French
language acquired a new word, *boycottage*, as calls for a boycott of French
products and visits to France came from "thousands of private citizens and
scores of organizations, from San Francisco to Berlin."[175]

No one in recent times has attributed this international reaction to latent
anti-French sentiment for which the trial of Dreyfus was merely a "pretext,"
although there was no shortage of anti-French remarks during the affair.
William James criticized "the behavior of the French" (rather than that of
the military court, or the plotters, or the *anti-dreyfusards*). "You are, sir, the
leader of a filthy people," read a telegram to the French president from a British
protest committee.[176] The *Atlanta Constitution* editorialized that "France" was
"guilty" of anti-Semitism.[177] To claim that all of France was guilty is to indulge
in the kind of overgeneralizing that, when directed against the United States,
is usually called anti-Americanism. It overlooks those French who agreed with
Emile Zola, whose famous intervention *"J'accuse"* eventually led to the vin-
dication of Dreyfus, and it ignores the crowds of anarchists who broke up
anti-Semitic rallies shouting *"Vive Dreyfus!"* and *"Vive Zola!"*[178] Mark Twain
indulged in his trademark hyperbole when he fired off lines such as "Oh, the
French! The unspeakables! . . . I don't think they have improved a jot since they
were turned out of hell."[179] Despite the encompassing slur, Twain was not
driven here by anti-Gallicism, but by the same instinct for justice that led him
to criticize the corruption of Boss Tweed and the occupation of the Philippines,
and led other Americans to rally to Dreyfus's side – like the one hundred
Massachusetts lawyers who signed a protest against his treatment by the
military court, echoed thirty years later by one hundred Paris lawyers who
petitioned against the Sacco and Vanzetti sentence.[180]

Generalized negativity toward the French at the time of the Dreyfus affair
therefore should be understood not as the source of the outrage but as its product, generated by the human tendency to express indignation through hyperbole
and to speak of nations as units. Rather than blame "anti-Gallicism" or "anti-
Americanism" for the global waves of protest that arose during the Dreyfus and
Sacco and Vanzetti affairs, one may look instead to two historical factors. The
first was what today we call the globalization of media. Both trials occurred,
as Britain's Lord Chief Justice reported to Queen Victoria about the Dreyfus

case, in an era when "the telegraph and the telephone have almost brought the ends of the earth together ... it is quite impossible to treat, as a purely domestic concern, any question which, like this one, appears to touch the very foundations of justice."[181] Lisa McGirr's superb research on the global response to the Sacco and Vanzetti trial likewise shows that the "democratization of access to knowledge" fueled mobilizations thanks to high literacy rates achieved by public education and the working-class reading culture of the 1920s.[182]

The second factor was the violation of what were becoming transnational expectations of juridical fairness, invoked by the Lord Chief Justice's report and later echoed by Hannah Arendt, who explained the "vehement and united reaction" from "the rest of the world" to the Dreyfus affair this way: "The doctrine of equality before the law was still so firmly implanted in the conscience of the civilized world that a single miscarriage of justice could provoke public indignation from Moscow to New York."[183] When crowds gathered and individuals organized to protest both of these two famous trials; when the aging Dreyfus himself warned that the execution of Sacco and Vanzetti "would be the greatest moral disaster of many years, fraught with terrible consequences to American justice" – to explain all this as the product of ill-informed national prejudice does a disservice not only to the people who put their energies behind a campaign for principles but also to any effort to understand important developments in the transnational history of human rights.[184]

In the case of the Sacco and Vanzetti protests, one indicator of whether they were merely an outlet for endemic French anti-Americanism was an event that took place less than a month after the executions. On September 19, 1927, more than 20,000 members of the American Legion – a rightist organization full of WWI veterans – paraded along three miles of Parisian boulevards past two million spectators. "Not a single incident or hostile demonstration marred the pageant," according to a *Chicago Tribune* reporter. "The proletariat of Paris in all walks of life, including the strongest supporters of the Communist Party, Socialists and radicals, turned out to witness the parade, enjoy the holiday and cheer their visiting former allies of a great war." The celebrations continued into the evening, when Americans riding in open taxicabs were cheered as they toured the city, and then were treated to the largest dinner party in the city's history, prepared at Les Invalides by 500 chefs and featuring 10,000 bottles of excellent wine.[185] The *Tribune* reporter missed a few small-scale protests, mostly out of town, but at a minimum, one can safely conclude that during the era described as "the unsurpassed crest of French anti-Americanism," that flawed concept cannot account for the variety of French behavior.[186] After all, this was the same France that in the same year of 1927 gave Charles Lindbergh a delirious reception after his historic transatlantic flight.[187] Nonetheless, interpreting the global response to the Sacco and Vanzetti trial as anti-Americanism contributed to the American tendency to see the United States as better informed and morally superior to other nations and thus entitled to proceed in the face of foreign criticism, clouding America's image as admired symbol of justice and human rights.

Scenes of Life in the Future

Such disputes brought the usual surprise and self-pity. "Does England Dislike America?" asked *The Forum*. "Nobody Loves Us," sighed the *Ladies' Home Journal*. Other magazines asked "Why They Hate Us" and how the United States could have become "the best hated nation in Europe." The customary diagnosis prevailed: "jealousy" and "contempt."[188] There was, of course, plenty of published critique of the United States in this period that went beyond political or juridical issues, sometimes expressing apprehension about U.S. power or the likelihood that the world would come to resemble America's least appealing aspects. Anti-anti-American scholars have held that such anxiety is tantamount to a rejection of American principles of democratic governance and political freedom. In fact, negative portrayals of diverse facets of American society could accompany a variety of political positions, and often America's role was as a symbolic referent in arguments that were not really about the United States.

Concerns expressed about America in the interwar years were often tied to the notion that unwelcome aspects of American life presented to a foreign society "the image of its own future," in Marx's words (though he was writing about England, not America). The novelist Georges Duhamel, who had served on the battlefield in World War I, was among those Europeans whom the horrors of industrialized warfare had left with a wariness toward technology. His *Scènes de la vie future* (*Scenes of Life in the Future*) is an apocalyptic depiction of a thoroughly mechanized U.S. society in which standardization and conformity have brought an end to free will and free thought. He claimed that he was not trying to rally opposition to the United States politically or militarily, however; he was trying to stimulate discussion over changes taking place in France. "America? I am not talking of America," Duhamel claimed. "By means of this America I am questioning the future; I am trying to determine the path that, willy-nilly, we must follow."[189] (It did not help his case that his U.S. publisher changed the title of the translation to *America the Menace*, thereby contradicting his stated intent.)[190]

Rightists in the United States and abroad alike linked cultural innovations to social decline, making mass culture a political conflict zone. The booming film industry was a key example. Hollywood's successful formula appealing to diverse audiences, along with government protections such as the Webb-Pomerene Act of 1918 that exempted export associations from antitrust laws so they could form cartels and fix prices abroad, produced an extraordinary mismatch: "For every dollar of film Europe exported to the United States, the United States exported 1,500 to Europe."[191] Given the widely held belief that movie images shape moviegoers' thinking, filmmakers were not the only Europeans to wish that more "scenes" of life in the future could be generated by their own industries. Ironically, European conservatives who decried Hollywood's influence and on that basis have been labeled "anti-American," were leveling the very same charges that American conservatives made in their own campaigns against the alleged "anti-Americanism" of Hollywood itself. Columbia University psychologist Albert T. Poffenberger worried in 1921 that the motion picture was "a training school for anti-Americanism," corrupting the morals of American youth.[192] That Hollywood fueled anti-Americanism by circulating unflattering images of American society worldwide became a mantra of conservatives in the United States, who overlooked the fact that movies have also been probably the single most effective medium for spreading attractive images of American society worldwide. In film critic David Thomson's more considered judgment, "the impact of Hollywood and the movies has been to exaggerate nearly everything about America," for good or ill; their mixed reception abroad reflects the transmission of a mixed message about the United States.[193]

Chief among the concerns when Europeans looked apprehensively across the Atlantic was the apparent American obsession with material gain. This preoccupation ranged across the political spectrum. "To be successful for the average American means above all to become rich," Werner Sombart told his readers.[194] The democratic foreign minister of the Weimar Republic, Walther Rathenau, later assassinated in a plot by a far-right clique, wrote during a visit to the United States that "everything important is impossible: American culture is impossible... American philosophy, scholarship, art, or religion, even an American history. Possible is merely enterprise, technology and politics."[195] On the right, German philosopher Oswald Spengler, cultural pessimist and author of *The Decline of the West*, called Americans "a population of trappers moving from city to city on a hunt for dollars."[196] Nazi ideologue Alfred Rosenberg claimed of the average American that "the uninterrupted hunt for the dollar determines almost exclusively his entire being."[197] Even Franz Kafka, who had so memorably skewered Central European bureaucratic authoritarianism in *The Trial*, left an unfinished novel set in the United States when he died in 1924. Published posthumously as *Amerika*, it depicted a Darwinian society where "only the lucky could enjoy their good fortune" and most people survived by working twelve hours a day.[198]

Such sentiment brings charges of anti-Americanism, but the notion that the pursuit of material success occupied a central place in American life was not, of course, an invention of foreigners hostile to a democratic land. It had concerned thoughtful American critics at least since Thoreau, and by the 1920s was the stuff of mainstream commentary. In their respected investigation of "Middletown, U.S.A.," sociologists Robert and Helen Merrell Lynd found a business-dominated culture "in which everything hinges on money."[199] Sinclair Lewis, whose protagonist Babbitt became the icon of middle-class mediocrity, wrote in *Main Street* of Americans "viewing themselves as men of the world but keeping themselves men of the cash-register" (although he added, upon receiving the Nobel Prize for Literature, that Americans were also characterized by "an idealism which the outlanders who call Americans 'dollar-chasers' do not understand").[200] President Coolidge summed up the national mood with his 1925 adage, "The chief business of the American people is business." All of these commentators might have been wrong – William Allen White rebuked Coolidge that "Lincoln's whole life was devoted to showing that the business of America is freedom" – but they show that very American scholars, a very American writer, and a conservative American president all placed money-making at the center of American life.[201] Indeed, that many Americans (like many other people around the world) devote considerable energy to trying to earn money cannot be in dispute. The question is whether associating America with materialism must be evidence of anti-Americanism, of a deep, ideological hostility to democracy, or rather may reflect the same critique of actually existing aspects of U.S. society made frequently by American reformers.

Other cultural complaints or negative views of U.S. society have mistakenly been presented as evidence of an anti-democratic, illiberal mood abroad, when more differentiation is called for. Criticism or praise of the United States is not in fact a reliable guide to the pro- or anti-democratic orientation of the speaker. Attention to race relations, for example, whether critiques from the right of racial mixing or from the left of racial discrimination, was hardly the sole province of foreign complainers. Rightists who decried "miscegenation" could be found inside and outside the United States in an era of transnational interest in eugenics and biological racism, which meant that racist ideas could inform allegedly "pro-American" expressions. The British surgeon and eugenicist Robert Reid Rentoul promoted marriage restrictions and sterilization programs modeled on those of Kansas and Indiana. German eugenicist Gustav Boeters returned from five years of medical practice in the United States to spend three decades crusading for compulsory sterilization laws in Germany, citing the precedents he had witnessed "in a cultured nation of the first order – the United States of America."[202]

Just as such "pro-American" praise of U.S. racial segregation and eugenics was not a reliable indicator of modern or democratic thinking, criticism of the same practices was often the product of a commitment to democracy and social progress. Progressives who protested the mistreatment of nonwhites could be found abroad and at home. Mark Twain, forever enshrined as an American national treasure, wrote a scathing indictment of "The United States of Lyncherdom" at the end of a decade in which 1,217 African Americans were lynched.[203] After a wave of race riots in more than two dozen cities in the summer of 1919, activists called for anti-lynching laws and were promptly characterized as anti-American – even though they were seeking more democracy, not less. When a writer in the *New York Times* asserted that "Merely to mention the [obstacles to the] negro franchise is anti-American propaganda," that was less a defense of democracy and freedom than a refusal to recognize Jim Crow laws as an impediment to democracy.[204] *Time* reported on a "storm of anti-American protest" in Paris in 1923; the source of this protest was not that the United States was excessively modern or democratic, but that racist American tourists had tried to import their customs to France by throwing a "French Negro, a War veteran," off a bus when he sought to tour the battlefields, and other American visitors mistreated dark-skinned inhabitants of

Montmartre, causing a brief scandal in Parliament. *Time*'s formulation suggested that anti-Americanism, rather than anger at imported American racism, was the source of this particular problem.[205] W.E.B. Du Bois, who began his career of activism on behalf of racial justice after seeing the knuckles of lynching victim Sam Hose displayed in a shop window, also won the epithet "anti-American" for trying to improve American democracy.[206] His crime was to make alliances with Communists – one indicator of how much of the U.S. political spectrum had abdicated the struggle for racial justice to the far left: in the interwar period, Communists were among the only white Americans willing to undertake the dangerous task of civil rights organizing in the deep South.[207] They and an array of left-wing groups that protested racism in this era were said to be engaged in "anti-American activities," as though it were somehow inherently anti-American to risk beatings or jail on behalf of other Americans deprived of their rights.[208] In the era of Jim Crow and the revival of the Klan, it was, apparently, "pro-American" to praise U.S. racial discrimination, but "anti-American" to seek greater democracy.

Political debates abroad that invoked the United States could also revolve around the role of women, but these discussions often revealed more about gender anxiety than about U.S. society. Although it would have come as a surprise to American feminists who fought hard to win even the basic right to vote, some European travelers reported that the United States was ruled by women. Visiting Frenchmen reacted with incomprehension to the gender relations they encountered there. Jules Huret complained that he had been unable to seduce the prudish American woman, that "indifferent Bastille." Georges Duhamel pictured the assertive American woman literally in the driver's seat with a silent, unhappy husband in the back of the car, "smoking a cigarette like one condemned to death." Charles Crosnier de Varigny in *La Femme aux États-Unis* despaired that "the *dame*, not content with having conquered the New World, is well on her way to Americanizing the old."[209] German rightists also worried that American gender relations would spill over to their own society.[210] The United States had become a "society dominated by women," wrote Alfred Rosenberg. "The outcome of this domination of America by women is the strikingly low cultural level of the nation."[211] It was an "Amazon state," Adolf Halfeld agreed, whose *Kulturfeminismus*, as Halfeld called it (he meant the feminization of culture), went against nature, and it was insidiously spreading through the *"Girlisierung"* (girlification) of European taste under the influence of American cinema.[212]

These claims had little to do with the United States itself, any more than did progressives' praise for some aspects of American gender relations. When Alice Salomon, the "German Jane Addams," admired the political achievements of American women, she was not primarily interested in exploring American conditions so much as using an idealized American model to call for reform in German society. Such arguments may have involved America, but the stakes were self-referential, as Salomon's own experience affirmed. In the 1920s, she claimed that she wished to be reborn in America in her next life. When she actually moved there as a refugee from Nazism in the 1930s, she was "bitterly disappointed" at the lack of opportunity she encountered.[213]

By the time Salomon fled Germany, that country was adopting an official policy of anti-Americanism in state propaganda. The positive observations about America in Hitler's writings – his admiration for Ford, for America's productive "Teutonic" population, for its racial segregation and anti-immigrant policies – reflected his thinking during the 1920s. Once he seized power, as Nazi policies of internal persecution and external aggression brought Germany into growing conflict with the United States, Hitler's denunciations of America grew strident and his praise died away: "A decayed country" with nothing but "millionaires, beauty queens, stupid records, and Hollywood. . . . My feelings against America are those of hatred and repugnance; half Judaized, half negrified, with everything built on the dollar."[214] He was drawing on the classic stereotypes by now, as Nazi Germany churned out an increasing volume of hostile and vicious propaganda. Yet even in this most extreme case of a foreigner hostile to the United States, one who destroyed democracy in his own nation and declared war on America, one would be mistaken to see Hitler's rise and his launching of a world war as the inevitable culmination of a culturally based, ideological anti-Americanism turning into a dangerous geopolitical conflict. The process at work was the reverse. Hitler's ambivalent and sometimes admiring, if distorted, view of the United States evolved into enmity and scorn as the result of the geopolitical conflict he launched because of his true obsessions and most vicious prejudices – against Jews and Slavs, not Americans. As in the many cases of lesser consequence, "anti-Americanism" seems not to be a useful analytical category for understanding foreign behavior – nor, given Hitler's earlier enthusiasms for American ways, is praise or criticism a reliable guide to identifying the worst threats to democracy, peace, or American national interests.

3

The Specter Haunting Europe

Anti-Americanism and the Cold War

> I am not anti-American. I don't even know what the word means.
>
> – Jean-Paul Sartre[1]

World War II and its aftermath laid bare the stark difference between correlation and causality with regard to anti-Americanism and world affairs. The ugliest caricatures, the most vicious kinds of propaganda expressed during this most destructive of wars turned out to be transient epiphenomena of an international clash. Hostile expression directed toward the United States, unsurprisingly, intensified in enemy countries and cooled among America's allies, because geopolitical conflicts drove anti-American sentiment, not vice versa. When the war was over, the images of brutish and corrupt Americans that had abounded in the propaganda of the Axis countries rapidly faded, giving way within a few years to strong pro-American sentiment among the conquered populations of Germany and Japan who now depended on U.S. power for their protection. "Anti-Americanism" in these countries turned out to have been a superficial, temporary occurrence: an effect, not a cause, of international conflict.

The sweeping transformation of the international system and American politics by the Second World War brought lasting changes to the function of "anti-Americanism" in that system and in those politics. During the war, the United States out of necessity had allied itself with the world's leading Communist power, while the war marked the high-water point of right-wing anti-American ideology overseas. After the war was over, global political and economic competition would no longer align the United States against far-right powers but rather against those on the far left. That transition completed the decisive shift in hostile sentiment, broadly speaking, from rightist movements to leftist movements by mid-century. The Cold War that followed WWII split Europe and divided the world, according to the rhetoric of the superpowers, into two camps, globalizing the ideological arena in which many Americans would come to see criticism of the United States as a sign of alignment with its rival. As the nuclear stalemate froze armed conflict in Europe, the United States sought to thwart real or imagined Soviet meddling through a comprehensive strategy of formal alliances, foreign aid, propaganda, covert operations, and military intervention. President Harry Truman, in what would come to be known as the Truman Doctrine, promised to fight Communism anywhere in the world – a vast expansion of the sphere of American interests. Foreign policy officials in Washington now asked two questions in assessing movements and leaders around the globe: were they pro- or anti-Communist? And: were they pro- or anti-American? These twin binary oppositions melded, and they so dominated thought and discussion that many Americans came to assume all foreigners were either pro-American and anti-Communist or anti-American and pro-Communist. Such a schema allowed little room either for the varied spectrum of politics in Europe, or for the indigenous origins of nationalist movements in the developing world, especially in countries emerging from colonial rule. Nonetheless, this Manichean divide would cause Americans to see what they called "anti-Americanism," now understood as an existential threat, growing to alarming proportions around the globe.

At home, the Cold War made "anti-Americanism" and its analogue, "un-Americanism" (applied only in a domestic context), a national security issue in peacetime. General Dwight D. Eisenhower urged soldiers returning to civilian life to "attack everything anti-American now with as much vigor as you attacked the Germans and the Japs during the war." It was up to them, the future president said, "to forestall any recurrence of any type of foreignism."[2] While the House Un-American Activities Committee (HUAC) and an array of federal "loyalty-security programs" began to identify individual Americans as dangerously un-American on the basis of their political associations, thereby restricting the space for dissent and diminishing the prospects of progressive legislation, other institutions inside and outside of government began to approach the problem of foreign anti-Americanism more systematically. The U.S. government developed a lasting interest in scientific polling of foreign opinion and created permanent agencies to try to influence opinion abroad. Academics collected and analyzed data to theorize about the nature and causes of anti-Americanism. And the U.S. foreign policy bureaucracy began to treat anti-Americanism as an important factor in its deliberations. Anti-Americanism, in other words, became reified as a category of analysis during the Cold War. It was tracked, measured, and interpreted. The policies that emerged from this process were often as ill-suited to a complex world as was the simplifying rubric that shaped official thinking.

A Manichean World

As the exigencies of wartime receded, national unity gave way to intense partisan feuding almost overnight. Republicans charged Roosevelt and Truman with having sold out Eastern Europe to Communism at Yalta, and some argued that Communist agents had secretly taken over the foreign policy process. Senator Alexander Wiley (R-WI), soon to become chair of the Senate Foreign Relations Committee, declared that Russian communism had "infiltrated into high positions in American labor, in American education and in American government." He called for a "counter-offensive" that would "ferret out and expose the anti-American subversive."³ House Minority Leader Joseph W. Martin, Jr. (R-MA) asserted that only the Republican Party could defeat the "sinister...anti-American forces" trying to "dominate the Government."⁴ Conservatives now claimed that Social Security and public housing were "anti-American" elements of Soviet-style central planning.⁵ The term "anti-American" was regularly used as a synonym for Communist, and "anti-Americanism" for subversion in the service of the Soviet Union, so that the categories blended. "Anti-American," when used in diverse contexts, now carried the implication of a specific kind of disloyalty and betrayal that threatened to deliver the country to the plotters in the Kremlin.

In the era named for Senator Joseph McCarthy (R-WI) but that began well before he attracted the national spotlight, the constriction of acceptable political expression extended to the cultural realm. Rep. Karl Mundt (R-SD) urged boycotts of Hollywood films that contain "scenes which are anti-American."⁶ Robert McCormick, publisher of the conservative *Chicago Tribune*, claimed that "the New York stage is predominantly anti-American."⁷ His paper castigated New York itself as an illegitimate blight on the American landscape, criticizing "the world's largest Jewish city" where "polyglot mobs" rule the streets and "the anti-American east coast internationalists" are "critical of native American customs and traditions."⁸ Always useful to the far right as a slogan in the struggle to define the limits of American politics and culture, "anti-Americanism" became a blanket charge branding progressives of all kinds as illegitimate, thus helping to produce the suffocating atmosphere that stifled creativity in cultural production and doused the hopes of political reform movements in the 1950s.

Significantly, the Manichean view that turned anti-Communism into a national creed in the United States never captivated Western European countries to the same degree. There was apprehension about the Soviet Union and Communism among America's allies, especially in West Germany. These countries had suffered a far harsher experience of war, were physically much closer to Soviet power, more likely to be its first victims in an armed conflict, and in some cases had large domestic communist parties that were mountains to the American Communist Party's molehill. But they never developed anything resembling what we came to call McCarthyism. The United States was far stronger, at a safe distance from Soviet power at least until the deployment of intercontinental ballistic missiles in 1959, and harbored a miniscule Communist Party – some 15,000 to 20,000 members before 1956, or about 0.01% of the population – whereas the Italian Communist Party (Partito Comunista Italiano or PCI) had two million members, and the French Communist Party

(Parti Communiste Français or PCF) was France's largest political party, regularly winning more than 25% of the vote in national elections.[9] Great Britain had spy scandals, but they did not lead to the persecution of leftists or the blacklisting of writers. Why was there no McCarthyism in Europe, even though there was more Communism in Europe than in the United States? The reason seems to be that Europeans had experience with Communism as a political party among others, whose members acted within the electoral system, rather than appearing as a gang of subversives or a demonic force. Many Europeans took a realistic view of Soviet intentions and capabilities, accustomed to thinking in terms of negotiating among rival states, rather than casting international relations in theological terms of good and evil. Americans' propensity to use "crusading language," and the "verbal exaggeration customary with American politicians and Congress" were unfortunate, in the words of the Atlanticist French writer Raymond Aron, for they had a deleterious effect on policy by exacerbating tensions and constricting the room for maneuver.[10]

Under the Cold War ideology that dominated the American political culture of the 1950s, "Americanism" represented good and its opponent evil; hence to oppose American policy, to engage in "anti-Americanism," was to stand on the dark side. This transformed the valence of the "anti-Americanism" concept: as an explanation of unwelcome forces in the world, it now rested on a normative assumption of American exceptionalism made even more compelling by the transcendent conflict with the Soviet Union.

In this context, it was not at all mysterious that Communists would be anti-American. The mystery, from the point of view of U.S. officials, was why non-Communists could oppose Communism's opposite, that is, how to account for "anti-Americanism" when it seemed to come from non-Communists. They deemed this a vital matter of national security, for "the closely related attitudes of political neutralism and anti-Americanism have increased in strength," the Mutual Security Agency reported in 1952.[11] Yet even as they mobilized to try to counter anti-Americanism, U.S. officials still lacked a coherent understanding of what the term meant. State Department officials reported that the Japanese engaged in "anti-Americanism" when they protested the contamination of fishermen by fallout from a U.S. hydrogen bomb test in the Pacific.[12] The Dutch, officials claimed, displayed their "anti-Americanism" when they bristled at American support for decolonization in Indonesia, just as the postcolonial Indonesian government was engaging in "anti-Americanism" when it pursued a neutralist foreign policy.[13] The French were allegedly swept by "anti-Americanism" in response to U.S. support for decolonization in North Africa.[14] Complex events in the Middle East had been read through the same prism since before World War II, when journalists and State Department officials alike characterized Arab complaints over U.S. support for Jewish immigration as "anti-Americanism."[15] When Truman recognized the new state of Israel in 1948, there were "nasty signs of anti-Americanism growing in the Middle East."[16] These signs came from disappointed Arabs, but British criticism of the speedy recognition was also laid to British "anti-Americanism," and former

Undersecretary of State Sumner Welles feared that U.S. support for partition of Palestine would feed "anti-Americanism" among Jews in Israel too.[17]

"Anti-Americanism" therefore came to explain almost any political position not in accord with the American policy of the day, regardless of the issues at stake. That these were political disputes, not a clash of civilizations or expressions of neurosis, should have been obvious, just as it should have been clear to the British why their country grew unpopular among nationalists seeking independence from British rule. Imperial thinking, however, has its own logic. At the same time that English analysts diagnosed "indiscriminate Anglophobia" among Iraqis, Eisenhower administration officials worried about "new currents of neutralism, anti-Westernism and particularly anti-Americanism throughout the Middle East."[18]

When the United States took other actions, however, none of the alleged underlying prejudice or Arab irrationality prevented opinion from turning favorable. In September 1952, a miniature crisis brewed in Beirut, where thousands of Muslim pilgrims from all over the Middle East, clutching airplane tickets for the *hajj* or holy journey to Mecca, overwhelmed the carrying capacity of the local airlines and thronged the airport, desperate to complete the trip. Harold Minor, the alert U.S. Minister to Lebanon, suggested to Washington that this was an opportunity for the United States to show itself to be a friend to the Muslims. "Something of a miracle then happened," reported *Time* magazine: "The State Department got the point." Orders went out to U.S. military bases in Germany, France, and Libya, and soon thirteen massive C-54 Skymaster aircraft – the same plane that had supplied Berlin with food and coal through a winter's siege in 1948, winning the loyalty of a generation there – were airlifting nearly four thousand *hajjis* to Saudi Arabia. Gratitude streamed in. "Iran's bitterly anti-American religious leader" Mullah Sayyed Abolqasem Kashani thanked the U.S. pilots with kisses on both cheeks. Lebanon's Mufti Muhammad Alaya, "speaking for myself and 40 million Arab Moslems," told Minor, "this is the turning point of American relations with the Moslem world."[19]

The Psychological Strategy Board was impressed with the impact of the airlift, "a notable contribution to the national psychological effort in the area" and the only bright spot in an otherwise dismal picture of U.S. relations with Muslim countries that year.[20] Instead of prescribing more such overt aid efforts, however, the Board then recommended covert propaganda to try to manipulate Muslim opinion. Eisenhower chose to back conservative autocrats against Arab nationalists in the region, thereby making the United States the target of resentment in the same way that U.S. support for dictators in Asia and Latin America drew the ire of those who resented the repressive force of governments kept in power with U.S. aid.[21]

The assumption that foreigners should credit America's benevolence regardless of whether current policy served their interests made unreasonable "anti-Americanism" a more compelling explanation than the reasoning offered by foreigners. For a report on "Anti-Americanism in Asia," Deputy Assistant Secretary of State for South Asian Affairs Armin H. Meyer asked Prime Minister

Mohammad Daud of Afghanistan to explain why there was so much hostility toward the United States in the region "despite the fact that American policies are so well intentioned and the only American motivation is the maintenance of the freedom and independence of free countries everywhere." Daud replied that Asians became bitter when Americans attributed their aspirations for independence to Communism, and were alienated by U.S. support for European colonial powers and unpopular authoritarian regimes. He recommended that the United States should strive for good relations with nonaligned countries instead of thinking of them as enemies.[22]

Rather than take such advice, experts in and out of government solved the riddle of why noncommunists would be anti-American by turning to the customary explanation of unwelcome foreign behavior: it was irrational, linked to the negative emotions of envy, jealousy, greed, and frustration that all humans experience but which Americans often ascribe to foreigners in a realm of behavior – international politics – where they assume their own conduct is determined by reason and virtue. American scholars and analysts reinforced the official view. Reinhold Niebuhr saw "well-nigh universal anti-American sentiment throughout Europe and Asia" in 1954, blaming it principally on "the inevitable envy of our wealth and resentment of our power."[23] Henry Kissinger in 1956 agreed that "Anti-Americanism is fashionable today in many parts of the globe." He attributed the phenomenon to "frustrations" and "spiritual" weakness.[24] Whichever arguments foreigners might bring to bear, American analysts knew better: beneath any stated grievance or divergent view lay the seething emotionalism that could be overcome only by cooperating with the United States on every issue.

The Emergency of Postwar Opinion

The disjuncture between American and foreign perspectives on international affairs could be traced, like much in the Cold War, in part to the diverging experiences of World War II. When the war ended, Americans celebrated with joy, while Europeans began to take the grim measure of what had happened to their continent. Twenty-seven million Soviet civilians and soldiers were dead. Nazis had murdered six million Jews and perhaps five million other deliberately selected victims. The great cities were landscapes of destruction. Central Rotterdam was flattened by German aerial attacks. Warsaw, crossed twice by German and Soviet armies, was devastated, nearly one in five Poles killed in the war. Londoners in their threadbare clothes shuffled past the bombed-out wreck of the House of Commons and a soot-blackened Buckingham Palace that had been hit fourteen times by the bombardments that had also shattered more than three million houses. French towns and cities fought over by Allied troops and retreating Germans were so battered that 20% of the country's housing was uninhabitable. In Germany's fifty major cities, 40% of the housing was damaged or destroyed, and thirteen million homeless refugees wandered among craters, caves, mountains of rubble, debris-covered fields, ruins that hardly allowed one to imagine that they had once been houses, cables and water pipes projecting from the ground like the mangled bowels of antediluvian monsters, no fuel, no light, every little garden a graveyard and, above all this, like an immovable cloud, the stink of putrefaction. In this no-man's land lived human beings. Their life was a daily struggle for a handful of potatoes, a loaf of bread, a few lumps of coal, some cigarettes.[25]

For American postwar planners, the economic and physical devastation of Europe posed a looming threat. "Hungry people are not reasonable people," warned a State Department official.[26] They worried that impoverishment would again push Europeans toward radical political movements, and that flourishing communist parties that promised to deliver employment and meet basic needs would link up with the Soviet Union's massive army to exploit the power vacuum left by Germany's utter prostration. The Truman administration decided that the United States would try to fill that vacuum and address those needs, persuading Europeans to place their faith in American leadership rather than turn to communism for relief from their crushing postwar burdens.

Thus from a policy perspective, the concern over European and especially German opinion of the United States was not a popularity contest but an urgent question of national security. As two million U.S. troops arrived on German soil at the end of the war, one might have expected them to be greeted with hostile suspicion. "Anti-Americanism" logically should have erupted after twelve years of Nazi propaganda building on what historian Dan Diner has described as a fundamental anti-American and antimodern orientation in German culture going back to the Romantic period and continuing up to the present day. Diner argues that anti-Americanism is stronger in Germany than in France and reached "epidemic" proportions after Germany lost two world wars to the United States.[27]

This is not what came to pass. Instead, West Germans in the first two postwar decades remained staunchly anti-Soviet, not only because of years of exposure to anti-Bolshevik propaganda, but because they feared they would reap what the Nazis had sown with their scorched earth policy in the East. The Soviet military occupation of Germany exacted a harsh vengeance, beginning with the mass rape of German women and continuing with the seizure of hundreds of thousands of German workers and prisoners of war for forced labor, some of whom would never return.[28] Some Germans feared that U.S. policy would be equally severe, following the deindustrialization policy advocated by Treasury Secretary Henry Morgenthau, whom they nicknamed the "*jüdischer Racheengel*" (Jewish avenging angel), and would be carried out by the "Morgenthau-Boys" or "*Rachebengel*" (avenging rascals).[29] Instead, stern Soviet justice for ex-Nazis and the Stalinization of the political system in their zone of occupation contrasted with the relatively lenient attitude taken by the Americans and their Western allies, whose prosecutions targeted the highest-ranking officials, while other former Nazis were quickly rehabilitated and invited to resume administrative functions in postwar society.

Experience overcame apprehension as Germans realized with surprise that the American occupation would be mild, extraordinarily so compared to Nazi occupation policies or to what their compatriots further east were going through. The contrast spoke for itself, and whatever the war experience may have made them think about Americans, Germans responded to magnanimous U.S. policy with appreciation, not congenital anti-Americanism.

This appreciation, however, was gendered. A mixed reception awaited the healthy young American soldiers who appeared in the ruins, merrily dispensing chocolate bars and nylons from their satchels and displaying attributes of masculine power – weapons, authority, and relative wealth – in a society where traditional masculinity had collapsed, with millions of German men dead or disabled or in Soviet POW camps, and millions more disarmed, politically powerless, and unable to provide for their families.[30] Since German women between 20 and 40 years old outnumbered German men their age 160 to 100, many of them pursued survival strategies based on literally embracing the American presence.[31] U.S. military authorities initially tried to enforce a non-fraternization program, complete with radio spots warning that behind every apparently friendly "Fraternazi" lurked a hate-filled enemy in disguise, but the soldiers laughed off the "non-fertilization" campaign, as they dubbed it.[32] Their economic power astonished them and brought opportunities undreamed of at home: a carton of cigarettes bought for fifty cents at a military PX depot could be sold for the equivalent of $180 on the black market. Farmboys and mechanics with the right connections could buy automobiles or hire a German orchestra for the evening to impress a date.[33]

Under these circumstances, male resentment soon entered the postwar German lexicon. The *A'mizone* (American zone, pronounced with an emphasis on the first syllable) was said to be the domain of the *Amizo'ne* (accent on the third syllable), making it a play on the "American's Amazon," the German girlfriend of an American soldier. Other words to describe her status ranged from endearments to coarse insults, and their sheer variety showed just how much of a preoccupation these relationships became in the postwar argot: *Amiliebchen* (American's dearie), *Amimädchen* (American's girl), *Amidämchen* (American's little lady), and *Amine* and *Amisette*, were neologisms based on feminine diminutives, but there were also the vulgar *Amiflittchen* (American's little slut), *Amihure* (American's whore), and worse.[34] Some women suffered reprisals for dating Americans, including social ostracism, forced head shaving, and other forms of violence.[35] *Schokoladen-Weiber*, chocolate-dames, were named after the meager payment they allegedly sought for spending a night with a GI – as well as the act of racial transgression when the soldier was a black American. In the eyes of some of her compatriots this turned the woman into a *Schokoladensau* (chocolate sow), *Schokoladenhure* (chocolate whore), or a *Negerliebchen*.[36]

The proliferation of such terms reveals the extent of social tension over relations with the occupying force, but they are not signs of a particularistic anti-Americanism. The resentment directed against German women by German men for entering relationships with American soldiers had very little to do with the fact that the soldiers were Americans – any foreign force would have raised hackles, and the Russians were far more hated. Instead, it had everything to do with the acute destabilization of gender roles in the aftermath of the war's devastation. Some of the terms would survive into the 1950s and beyond, especially those that were racially charged, because prejudice against dark-skinned foreigners and their children remained more deeply entrenched than brief phases of anti-American resentments. Although anti-anti-American scholars have claimed that anti-Americanism is "similar to racism," the fact that racism outlasted anti-American sentiment is one more indication of the difference between a true prejudice and one contingent on shifting circumstances.[37]

The Emergence of Public Opinion

As the central front in the early Cold War, Germany would become the site of the first large-scale U.S. government effort to quantify foreign opinion of the United States. Scientific polling had developed in the second half of the 1930s with the work of the firms of Hadley Cantril, George H. Gallup, and Elmo Roper in the United States, Henry Durant's British Institute of Public Opinion (BIPO), and Jean Stoetzel's Institut Français d'Opinion Publique (IFOP). Gallup made his name by correctly predicting U.S. election results, and his company soon expanded its activities to international opinion research.[38] Cantril set up the Institute for International Social Research and served as a government consultant. One of his key inventions was the "self-anchoring striving scale," essentially a sketch of a ladder used "to ask respondents where they thought they were at present between a best possible life (top of the ladder) and the worst possible state of affairs (bottom of the ladder)." Soon pollsters were showing flashcards with pictures of ladders to people in Europe and the developing world.[39] This visual opinion scale was thought to provide a reliable cross-cultural measurement, because everyone knew what a ladder was. Cantril did not consider, however, that some people might see the top rung of the ladder as a precarious perch; others might be accustomed to using a ladder together with a helper; and some might expect a visual image of success to include communal rather than solitary achievement. The image provided an early example of how easily misunderstandings could arise when American experts universalized their own assumptions in trying to measure foreign cultures.

Criticism of allegedly scientific polling by Walter Lippmann and others centered on the contradiction inherent in the survey organizations' dual mission, in which the techniques for "selling toothpaste" were turned to the "plumbing of the public mind." Within the United States, as survey organizations sought to sell their research results to corporations, their work was inevitably influenced by the business world's mindset, which "worked to narrow the field of social inquiry, skew . . . samples, and affect the interpretation of poll results."[40] In the international field, with greater cultural divides to cross, marketing America overlapped with measuring its reputation, and the unexamined prejudices of the pollsters colored their findings. One of the basic flaws was that American experts assumed that praise for the United States was normal and criticism abnormal.

Beginning in October 1945, the Information Control Division of the Office of the Military Government, United States (OMGUS) conducted regular surveys of public opinion. Its successor after the formal end of occupation in 1949, the Office of Public Affairs of the U.S. High Commission for Germany (HICOG), continued the practice, employing the Deutsches Institut für Volksumfragen (DIVO, the German Institute for Population Surveys). There was an obvious problem inherent in using American service personnel or locally hired Germans who identified themselves as working for OMGUS or HICOG: respondents would realize that they were speaking to a representative of the American authorities and could be expected to try to curry favor or avoid offense. This particular concern was less present for the polling organizations set up after the war by Germans, such as the EMNID-Institut established in 1945 in Bielefeld, and the Institut für Demoskopie (IfD) founded in Allensbach in 1946.[41] To run its own growing polling program, the U.S. government turned to Dr. Leo P. Crespi, a social psychologist at Princeton and President of the World Association for Public Opinion Research. He served as senior research adviser to HICOG and the U.S. Information Agency (USIA) for 32 years.[42] Crespi tried to control for sampling problems, but he placed great faith in the explanatory value of his questionnaires and was as entrapped as his colleagues by the assumption that a positive view of the United States should be normative.[43]

Throughout the 1950s, the government sponsored regular polling of Western Europeans by such organizations to try to measure America's standing in the Cold War. The information accumulated by the pollsters is of value in two ways. The raw data explode some of the enduring myths of anti-Americanism, including the ones propagated by the pollsters themselves, because the surveys show that hostility toward the United States was not widespread among Europeans even during this period, when concern over anti-Americanism was at a peak. The pollsters' assumptions, the development of their models, and their analysis of the results also help to show why U.S. officials were led astray by the flawed concept underlying the studies. As Peter Katzenstein and Robert Keohane caution, "polls risk imposing a conceptual unity on extremely diverse sets of political processes that mean different things in different contexts."[44] Crespi's work exemplifies this problem. He reported as "Anti-Americanism" a wide range of opinions critical of the conduct of individual U.S. soldiers, the presence of U.S. military bases, U.S.-sponsored denazification efforts (regardless of whether the dissatisfaction was that they interfered in Germany's internal affairs or that they were not far-reaching enough), that the United States was "too easy with Russia" or "too tough with Russia," that the United States engaged in "economic domination," that it did not support Italy over a border dispute in Trieste, or that it interfered with European colonies.[45]

Under Crespi's formula of anti-Americanism equaling disagreement with any current U.S. foreign policy, the respondent who wanted a harder line toward the Soviet Union and the respondent who wanted a tougher denazification program both fell into the category of Europeans afflicted by "anti-Americanism." Yet these positions were entirely compatible with a fundamentally pro-democratic orientation and with support for the American side in the Cold War. Crespi and fellow HICOG analyst Hugh J. Parry claimed that a third of continental Europeans surveyed "can find nothing at all good to say about American actions since the war." As evidence, they pointed to results showing that "the bulk of such respondents simply express their ignorance or lack of favor by saying nothing."[46] That was a very free interpretation of the "no opinion, no answer" category that composed most of the allegedly hostile one-third. It required that Europeans had not only to refrain from criticizing the United States about any policy in order not to be described as anti-American but also to express positive admiration of the United States in their reply – even about subjects on which a diversity of opinion could be in harmony with broader U.S. goals, or when U.S. policies were in conflict with their own country's interests.

Crespi also placed in the category of "anti-Americans" respondents who said their overall impression of American policies was "unfavorable," but he acknowledged that a quarter of this group had favorable views of Marshall Plan aid, whereas the "pro-American" group included a quarter who disliked American criticism of French or Dutch colonial rule.[47] Either "anti-Americanism" allowed for support for U.S. policy and "pro-Americanism" allowed for opposing U.S. policy – rendering the labels meaningless – or else the binary categories had no place in "scientific" research. Moreover, Crespi subscribed to the widespread view among Americans that held criticism of the United States to be based on passion, not reason: statements by Europeans to the effect that America had too much influence in their countries "indicate an emotional reaction," he asserted.[48]

Crespi therefore generated alarmist generalizations about the high rate of "anti-Americanism" in Europe, but in neglected findings that would remain fairly constant in most countries for the next half-century, Crespi's own hard numbers showed that only 9% to 16% of Western Europeans held an "unfavorable" view of American actions. Even among Communists and their avowed sympathizers, majorities were not hostile to the United States.[49] Despite the scare headlines of the period and the ominous messages experts transmitted to government officials, in these years it was hard to find much actual anti-Americanism in Western Europe at all.[50]

Endemic Anti-Russianism

Intense animus toward the Soviet Union (generally called "Russia" in these polls) was another matter: it was evident in every country surveyed. Crespi did not use the term "anti-Russianism" to describe his finding of massive hostility toward the Soviet Union, although from 50% to 85% of respondents said

Russia had done "nothing at all" since WWII that made a favorable impression. Combining the "nothing at all" responses with the "no opinion, no answer" responses, as Crespi did to arrive at his estimate of one-third anti-Americans, would show huge majorities of from 82% to 94% hostile to Russia in every country. Even a third of European Communists viewed Soviet actions unfavorably. "Russian post-war behavior has alienated almost every group in Europe," Crespi noted correctly, but he did not ascribe Europeans' views of the Soviet Union to their emotionality or anti-Russian prejudices. Instead, he assumed it came from their rational evaluation of what they knew of Soviet actions.[51]

From the defeat of Germany in 1945 through the 1950s and thereafter, West Germans consistently viewed Americans with far more sympathy than they did the Soviets, and as the United States increased the amount and visibility of its material assistance for German reconstruction, many Germans responded with gratitude. Curiously, a belief began to develop among politicians and journalists in this period (repeated by later scholars of anti-Americanism) that it was foreign aid that caused anti-American sentiments, that "our generosity has contributed in a large measure to the current wave of anti-American feeling that now sweeps the world."[52] Foreign aid produces "an anti-American attitude,"[53] the "natural jealousy and dislike for the 'rich uncle' who provides money or gifts."[54] Yet one clearly measurable effect of aid was to increase positive views of the United States. By March 1950, although only 9% to 11% of Germans in the American Zone had received a CARE package (a food parcel from the Cooperative for American Remittances to Europe), 80% of them (and 98% of West Berliners) had heard of CARE packages.[55] Large majorities believed that "America's motives in giving the aid were good."[56] Such assistance programs contributed to the fact that by April 1951, 36% of Germans found the American occupying power sympathetic, versus only 5% for the British occupiers, 1% for the French, and 1% for the Soviets.[57] German views of American soldiers also changed with changing circumstances, from 66% who described the conduct of the occupation troops as good or very good six months after the Berlin Airlift, falling to 34% in a January 1953 poll taken after several American soldiers in different parts of Germany were court-martialed for raping civilians (there were 74 convictions for that crime by American soldiers stationed in Europe in 1952).[58] The chief military analyst of the *New York Times* provided the usual gloss: "Personal misconduct by some [American] men in uniform... played up by the sensational European press has helped to create anti-Americanism."[59] But Germans were not becoming more inherently anti-American, nor developing a sudden aversion to democracy or modernity. Rapid changes in opinion of the United States indicate an event-driven analytical process in which sentiment reflects changes in policy or actions.

The irrelevance of "anti-Americanism" to European positions on international affairs is further demonstrated by polling data on national characteristics. In this period of frantic concern over epidemic anti-Americanism, Germans were less negative toward Americans than they were toward any other nationality – including Germans. Of those interviewed in 1952, 80% ascribed negative characteristics to the Russians, 52% were negative toward the French, 40% negative toward Germans, and only 33% negative toward Americans. The most common attributes associated with Americans by the 53% of Germans who offered positive descriptions spoke to personal behavior such as "helpfulness," "good-naturedness," "fairness," "agreeability," "informality," and "fondness for children," as well as "good business sense." (The minority who used negative terms referred to "moneybags," "snobs," and "capitalists.") Russians were generally viewed as "brutal," "coarse," and "cruel" – with German women even more hostile than German men, reflecting the collective memory of sexual violence suffered at the hands of Soviet troops. Germans considered themselves to be "hardworking," "quarrelsome," and "fractious." Opinions were divided on the French, as indicated by terms ranging from "good manners" and "charming" to "nationalistic," "hate-filled," "vengeful," and "unforgiving."[60]

Drilling down further into the survey data also calls into question the conventional wisdom that Europeans who consider themselves culturally superior to Americans are anti-American, or that their feelings of cultural superiority have any bearing whatsoever on American interests. When Germans were asked between 1950 and 1956 what they could learn from Americans, most mentioned industrial methods, technology, and journalism. Only 17% to 19% thought they had something to learn from Americans about "cultural affairs/fine arts," and 50% to 60% thought they had "nothing" to learn from Americans in that category.[61] That is a pretty strong indication of a widespread belief in American cultural inferiority. HICOG analysts duly blamed "Communists" for "their reiterated propaganda to the effect that American cultural life is low and degenerate,"[62] but the most negative opinions of American culture were found among the highest socio-economic sectors, whose members were generally not receptive to Communist propaganda. Moreover, in the same period, 78% to 83% of Germans said their country should cooperate with the United States, whereas only 3% opposed such cooperation. It would be a strange sort of anti-Americanism indeed that created strong supporters of cooperation with the United States and very few opponents. Rather than being pro- or anti-American, Germans seem simply to have been able to make up their minds about different aspects of a complex country by drawing on their own impressions.

Throughout the 1950s, positive views of the United States vastly outstripped negative views: majorities of 57% to 69% expressed an overall positive opinion of the country, while those with overall negative views – the anti-Americans, as Crespi might say – ranged from 2% to 4%. Germans were always far more negatively inclined toward France (18% to 46% negative) and Russia (62% to 80% negative, with a spike following the 1956 attack on Hungary). Although anti-anti-Americans in the United States and Germany have focused on allegedly deeply rooted hostility toward America in German culture, and U.S. officials and journalists worried about surging anti-Americanism in Germany in the 1950s, were one to generalize, it would be more accurate to

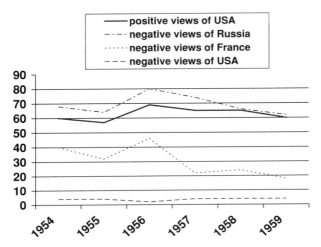

FIGURE 2. West German opinion. By the numbers, anti-Americans are a tiny minority, anti-Russians a huge majority, and the growing concern over "anti-Americanism" in this period was misplaced. According to polling data, it would have made more sense to study anti-Russianism and anti-Gallicism. *Source:* DIVO-Institut, *Umfragen 1957*, 42–44; DIVO-Institut, *Umfragen: Ereignisse und Probleme der Zeit*, 3: 39–43.

speak of an epidemic of philo-Americanism in postwar Germany, coupled with widespread anti-Gallicism and rampant anti-Russianism.[63]

If one can detect a unifying theme in the polling data, it is not anti-Americanism, but self-interest. Most West Germans in the 1950s were in agreement on the basic outlines of their country's international situation: they wanted to avoid both war and Soviet domination, and saw U.S. military protection as necessary to achieve both goals. They might not always have found American soldiers in Germany well behaved, but throughout the 1950s, majorities of 52% to 71% wanted them to stay.[64] Majorities of two to one preferred a formal alliance with the West to neutrality in the Cold War, and almost nobody was in favor of alliance with the Soviets.[65] Large majorities of nearly four to one favored mutual withdrawal of the superpowers' forces from Europe, and by four to one they replied that if the USSR should attack the United States without attacking Europe, Germany should not get involved militarily.[66] In other words, ordinary Germans hoped for a protective alliance that would not lead them back into the kind of war whose devastating effects were still fresh in their memories.

Such sentiment was widespread in Europe. Those who hoped to stay out of a war between the United States and USSR in 1957 ranged from 66% to 94% of the population in France, Italy, Belgium, Norway, Austria, and Sweden.[67] Majorities of 57% to 78% in France, Britain, the Netherlands, Germany, and Scandinavia supported the idea of a mutual withdrawal or "disengagement" of superpower forces from continental Europe. This idea, broadly unpopular in the United States, had some high-profile supporters such as George Kennan and Hugh Gaitskell, leader of the British Labor Party; in late 1957 the Soviet leadership endorsed it as well. Among European elected representatives, opinion was divided, but still far more favorable toward disengagement than among their American counterparts: of members of Parliament, 47% of British officials, 45% of Germans, and 43% of Italians supported such a proposal, but only 19% of U.S. members of Congress.[68] This discrepancy was not evidence of anti-Americanism but of the difference between U.S. and European perspectives. Eisenhower administration officials did not believe the Soviets would truly withdraw their forces behind their own borders, or worried that it would be much easier for them in a crisis to rush back along roads and railways than it would be for the United States to bring back its own forces.

Yet "disengagement has steadily assumed almost magical powers in the minds of many Europeans," in the condescending formulation by Drew Middleton of the *New York Times*, who blamed it on "marked anti-American sentiment."[69] After public relations expert Edward Bernays visited Britain on holiday, he wrote a long report called *What the British Think of Us* that warned of rising anti-Americanism and blamed it on "socio-psychological" causes.[70] The USIA's director, George V. Allen, forwarded it to the White House as an argument for increased USIA activity in friendly countries. His thinking revealed the same misjudgment as Crespi's survey reports. Anti-American views were quite rare in this period. It was rather that Europeans who favored disengagement – like those who did not – were making an independent assessment of how to pursue their own interests. Those who supported the proposal hoped that it would lead to a reduction in tensions, diminish the chance of war, and encourage the Soviets to loosen their grip on Eastern Europe once they no longer faced what they saw as an existential threat from the West. Where European supporters of disengagement differed from Americans was not in their degree of support or hostility toward the existence of the United States or its social or political makeup, but in their divergent experiences. Europeans had lived through the destructiveness of two world wars and were more leery of seeing another war break out than were Americans, who remembered the two wars largely as national triumphs that ravaged faraway places. Although a diminution of U.S. influence on the European continent was not necessarily in the long-term strategic or economic interest of the United States, that consideration was less compelling to some Germans, who would likely profit from increased influence, and many French, who hoped that their country's importance in Europe would rise as U.S. power receded.

French Anti-Americanism: The Synecdochic Fallacy

In France, where American soldiers initially received a warm welcome from the populace, tension inevitably arose between large numbers of foreign troops and the proud inhabitants of a war-damaged, impoverished country. As the euphoria of liberation turned to the daily grind of coping with shortages, bridging cultural divides, and negotiating power relations, some French citizens resentful of the continuing presence of American soldiers in their midst began to refer to Americans with the pejorative *amerlo*, formed from the same trisyllabic truncation ending in "o" beloved in French slang, as in *aristocrate – aristo, intellectuel – intello, socialiste – socialo*. For their part, American troops, mustered from all levels of society and usually innocent of any foreign travel, accumulated minor grievances as they interacted with a population that spoke little English, had its own distinctive customs, and pursued its own interests. When the U.S. Army compiled a list of popular G.I. "gripes" against foreigners, there were 35 against the Japanese but 112 against the French, including these:

> They're ungrateful.
> The French are too damned independent.
> They have to put their two cents in. But the Germans – they do just what you
>   tell them to.
> French women are immoral.
> French women are too damned expensive.
> The French are unsanitary.
> They kiss right in the open – in the streets.
> French cities are filthy.
> Why isn't there decent plumbing in French houses? The toilet facilities are
>   disgraceful.
> What did these frogs ever contribute to the world, anyway?
> The French do things differently from the way we do. That's what I don't like.[71]

It would be silly to read the soldiers' statements as evidence of entrenched anti-Gallicism linked to resentment of, say, core French values of liberty, equality, and fraternity. The "gripes" emerged from the first-time encounter with a foreign culture and a lower standard of living, unease over the wartime sexual economy, and the difficulty of negotiating the civilian–military relationship without the clear hierarchy between victors and vanquished that prevailed, for example, in Germany and Japan.

In the first years after the war, Americans were surprised at the extent to which the Communist Party enjoyed legitimacy in France. Because Americans often interpret international developments through a self-referential lens, many assumed that this was evidence of anti-Americanism, but the sources of Communist strength in France were French. The right had been thoroughly discredited by its collaboration with the Nazis under Vichy, while the Communist Party emerged with new prestige, having formed the core of the French Resistance after Hitler ordered the invasion of the Soviet Union in summer 1941. Their role in opposing Nazism won them respected members, such as the Nobel Prize-winning physicist Frédéric Joliot-Curie, the poet Paul Éluard, and the painter Pablo Picasso, all of whom joined the Party during the war. After liberation, the PCF, nicknaming itself the *Parti des fusillés* ("party of the executed," for the thousands of its members shot by the Germans), inflated the genuine heroism of many of its followers into the claim that they had lost "75,000 martyrs."[72] Exaggeration aside, the Party had a powerful nationalist argument to couple with its traditional focus on the needs of workers and the unemployed, which together reliably brought it approximately a quarter of the vote in French elections for the next decade.

Philippe Roger departs from his insightful analysis of literary sources to identify evidence of "anti-Americanism" in the results of a 1944 survey by IFOP, which posed the question, "Which country has contributed the most to the German defeat?" Sixty-one percent said it was the Soviet Union, and only 29% named the United States.[73] Perhaps some French did determine their responses on the basis of disdain for the United States or sympathy for the Soviet Union. Whatever their motives, however, the majority who credited the Soviet Union with the lion's share of responsibility for the defeat of Germany were in accord with Western military historians, who have calculated that from June 1941 to June 1944, the Red Army was fighting 80% to 90% of all German land forces, and that 75% to 80% of German losses in men and materiel took place on the Eastern Front. While doing most of the fighting, the Soviets naturally bore most of the casualties, which is why the United States and Great Britain together suffered some 600,000 combat deaths in both the Atlantic and Pacific theaters, whereas the Soviets incurred about thirteen million killed in combat and twenty-seven million total deaths.[74] The massive Western air campaign destroyed German cities and disrupted industrial production, but not nearly to the extent that its planners had expected.[75] One need not favor the Soviet system to recognize the sheer scale and significance of the Eastern Front in the war for Europe. The 29% of the French who credited the United States with doing more than the Soviet Union to defeat Germany were, if anything, less objective than the majority, who nonetheless are labeled anti-American because their answer was historically correct but politically incorrect.

As the Cold War polarized the politics of many countries into a tug-of-war between a pro-Soviet left and a pro-U.S. center-right, Communist beliefs would generally become a solid indicator of anti-American sentiment. This was true of generally party-line writers such as Pierre Courtade, André Stil, and Roger Vailland, who compared the Soviet Union favorably to the United States.[76] Despite the myth that "the French" are anti-American, however, most French workers surveyed ranked France and the United States as the best and second-best countries for workers to live in. The one-quarter who ranked the Soviet Union as the best country for workers tracked closely to the constituency of the Communist Party, demonstrating loyalty to an ideology that prescribed a hostile stance toward the United States.[77] To be sure, the link between Communism and doctrinaire anti-Americanism was not entirely reliable. Pierre de Massot, a French surrealist poet and a convinced Communist, was nonetheless "passionately pro-American on all international questions and for his breakfast each morning drank a bottle of Coca-Cola instead of a cup of *café au lait*, which he despised as being old-fashioned and chauvinist."[78] The Communist Party youth organizations quickly learned not to propagandize against American popular music when they found they could draw larger crowds of young people by organizing dances featuring *le swing* and *le bebop*.[79] Communist music critics then politicized jazz as a form of black resistance to American imperialism.

Going further than the Communists, who sought to appropriate American music in the service of recruitment, some scholars have claimed that anti-Americanism lay behind Parisians' mid-century embrace of jazz, the most American of art forms. A paradox at first glance, they argue, the anti-Americanism of French jazz enthusiasts lay in their belief that they were engaging in "counter-Americanization" by supporting "subversive" music that was marginalized in its own home country. Jazz was the music of the oppressed, and to enjoy jazz was to side with America's victims: "The taste for the American counterculture is anti-Americanism carried on by other means."[80] But to read the French taste for African American music as the product of anti-Americanism is a curious claim by the anti-anti-Americans. It assumes that true American culture is produced by a dominant white majority, while African Americans somehow are not part of America or its culture. Young French jazz fans did join protests against American racism and followed the budding civil rights movement in the magazine *Jazz hot*, but to call this anti-Americanism both denies the Americanness of black Americans and denies that the fans may have been genuinely upset over "the injustice endured by the artists they admired." Anti-racist views, indeed, became "one of the founding elements of a generational cultural identity emerging in the 1950s" that would spread to form a key element of transnational youth culture by the 1960s.[81] If the popularity of jazz and the accompanying antipathy toward American racism were but signs of a growing anti-Americanism, it would be difficult to know what a supporter of American values is supposed to have expressed – praise for segregation and disdain for the most American of musical forms?

Anti-Ugly Americanism

Postwar popular culture was but one realm in which the issue of "anti-Americanism" was now viewed as a problem affecting a broader public. The advent of mass air travel enabled many middle-class Americans to visit Europe as tourists, and U.S. officials worried that their sheer numbers – millions by the early 1950s – were becoming a source of anti-Americanism in France. As a matter of policy, the Eisenhower administration sought to make use of "the great size and psychological impact of the annual influx of American tourists in Europe" to improve America's image.[82] The challenge was that the French might not be favorably impressed by their daily encounters with Americans who do, as observed and even quantified by behavioral anthropologists, speak more loudly, dress less formally, and break eye contact sooner than most Europeans.[83] The U.S. government therefore issued a booklet in 1952 entitled "What Should I Know When I Travel Abroad?" advising against the use of terms such as "Frenchies" and "natives" to refer to the French. Passports came with a warning by President Eisenhower against obnoxious behavior.

In a *Parade* magazine article entitled "Don't Be an 'Ugly American,'" Frances Knight, head of the Passport Office, noted that anti-Americanism was fueled by tourists wearing shorts into cathedrals, exhibiting bad manners in public, and loudly proclaiming, "I only speak American."[84] In 1956, when Eisenhower launched the People-to-People Foundation to encourage exchanges between American citizens and foreigners, William Faulkner joked that if Ike really wanted to win the Cold War, he should suspend all American passports for a year.[85]

For all the evidence that tourists from the United States, like members of the tourist species from many other nations, often displayed a grating lack of cultural sensitivity abroad, this does not seem to have translated into much "anti-Americanism" on the part of the French, if we are to understand that concept as anything beyond the garden-variety stereotyping that affects all nationalities. If anti-Americanism is a deep-seated ideological opposition to the United States, leading to a desire to harm America or its interests, it was not encountered much by the tourists themselves. In 1959, four-fifths of foreign visitors to France found the French "friendly and helpful," whereas only 5% reported negative experiences. Among American tourists, eight in ten declared themselves "very satisfied" with their visit to France, and only 4% expressed a negative opinion.[86] Recurrent sensationalized stories in the U.S. media and anecdotal griping up to the present "masked the reality of largely satisfied Americans coming to France in ever-increasing numbers."[87]

That the French are congenitally anti-American has become such an article of faith that mere empirical evidence to the contrary is not likely to dislodge hardened stereotypes. The evidence shows that Americans might be less popular in France than elsewhere in Europe, but that does not mean that they have been widely hated. In 1953, asked if they liked Americans, 61% of French surveyed said yes, 8% expressed antipathy, and 15% expressed irritation. Among the working class, where the Communist Party had its base, 46% said they liked Americans, 16% felt antipathy, 9% disliked them, only 3% said they hated them, and the rest had no opinion.[88] Three-quarters expressed positive attitudes toward Americans, especially sympathy, gratitude, and admiration, and more than one-half of the respondents said they would be willing to receive American soldiers in their homes. Only 13% approved of "U.S. Go Home" graffiti, and only 4% saw the United States as a cultural threat.[89] These statistics did not prevent sociologist Arnold M. Rose from claiming that "a very large proportion of Frenchmen, of all economic classes and of all educational levels, are anti-American today."[90] John T. Marcus placed psychologically driven anti-Americanism at the heart of French politics in the Fourth Republic.[91] Philippe Roger, with his fine taste for ironic overstatement and his impatience with the more idiotic remarks of some of his compatriots over the years, describes the French in this period as divided into "solely anti-Americans of the Right, anti-Americans of the Left, and non-conformist anti-Americans."[92] A witty remark made no less witty by the fact that it is contradicted by the survey data.

Leading opinion makers in the late fifties joined the chorus of Cassandras seeing anti-Americans everywhere. Joseph Alsop wrote of "the prevalence of a vague but captious anti-Americanism." Reinhold Niebuhr claimed anti-Americanism had reached "endemic proportions." Raymond Cartier reported "Why the Americans Are Detested Today in the Whole World."[93] Headlines about rampant pro-Americanism would perhaps not sell many newspapers, but the data sustain the position of two social scientists who reported in the 1990s that while "American fears of anti-Americanism have been with us for almost four decades . . . anti-Americanism has been the view of only a limited minority in most Western European countries throughout the postwar period."[94] This view holds true not only for surveys of the public at large but for studies of elite opinion as well.[95]

Within this overall pattern of consistent pro-American sentiment in postwar Europe, there were fluctuations that were closely tied to tensions in international relations. Anti-Americanism did not cause these tensions, but anti-American sentiment could be increased by them. In October 1954, a dispute over American support for rearming Germany and apparent U.S. sympathy for Algerian independence led to increasing negatives in French opinions of America. In late 1956 and early 1957, British and French opinions of the United States declined after Eisenhower threatened to use fuel embargoes and to undercut the British pound to halt the Anglo-French attack on Egypt following President Gamal Abdel Nasser's nationalization of the Suez Canal. This provoked an "acute rise of anti-Americanism" in Britain and France, putting those countries into "a highly psychopathic state," according to CIA Director Allen Dulles.[96] French filling stations refused to sell gas to American tourists, and taxi drivers in Paris refused to drive American passengers.[97] This was clear anti-American sentiment, but if it were anti-Americanism in the sense that word has come to acquire – an expression of enduring, irrational hostility rooted in cultural rejection of modernity and democracy – one would somehow have to account for the fact that before and after the crisis, taxi drivers and filling station attendants welcomed American customers. The anger was real, but it was directly linked to a conflict in international affairs, similar to later disputes over wars in Vietnam and Iraq that would lead Americans to pour French wine down the drain. The lower ratings continued into 1957 and extended across Europe during the widely reported Little Rock desegregation crisis, then recovered in the early 1960s during Kennedy's first visit to Europe and after his famous 1963 speech in Berlin.

The concept of anti-Americanism as applied to Europe in the 1950s, then, suffered from two serious deficiencies: it was wrongly attributed to entire populations that were in fact strongly pro-American, and it ascribed foreign opinions on international affairs to an underlying psychological or cultural predisposition, even though polling data clearly showed so much fluctuation that whatever underlying condition might have afflicted foreigners, they remained quite capable of forming independent judgments about the events of the day.

The Cold War and the Race Race

The Cold War played out in multiple arenas, including an arms race, a space race, a consumer-goods race, and the race to capture world public opinion, especially in the new countries emerging from European colonialism. Because their populations identified with people of color in the developed world, that contest made domestic race relations an international issue, spurring what one might call a race race. Top Eisenhower officials recognized the damaging effect on world opinion caused by racial segregation in the United States. The Little Rock crisis was a case in point. In September 1957, the first nine African American students permitted to enroll in Central High School were blocked by a white mob backed by troops from the Arkansas National Guard. Governor Orville Faubus defied a federal court order to desegregate the schools, and white Arkansans cried that "Race Mixing is Communism."[98]

The crisis attracted the attention of the international media, which broadcast around the world images of neatly dressed black schoolchildren pursued by crowds of screaming white segregationists. Secretary of State John Foster Dulles was livid. The crisis was "ruining our foreign policy," he complained. It made him "sick at heart" to think that Little Rock was doing to the U.S. reputation abroad what the invasion of Hungary had done to the Soviets.[99] The State Department's Research and Intelligence division reported that the intense, worldwide coverage of the crisis tended to "rub the U.S. nose in its own moral principles." The good will built up by U.S. public diplomacy among Asians and Africans was "dissipated in a matter of minutes."[100] On a trip to South Africa, Dr. Chester Clark, executive secretary of the AME Missionary Department, was peppered with questions about the incident; on his return he warned that "the Little Rock crisis was a blow to America's prestige that might well rank with Pearl Harbor."[101] (While U.S. officials worried that the crisis was causing a surge in "anti-Americanism," the *Philadelphia Tribune*, an African American newspaper, refused to accept the conventional use of that term, echoing its predecessors of 100 years earlier in arguing that the crisis was a *product* of the anti-Americanism inherent in racial discrimination, namely, a test of "whether segregation and anti-Americanism, or Americanism and right, would prevail.")[102]

Seizing the initiative from the governor, Eisenhower ordered federal troops to Little Rock to escort the children to school safely, to assert federal supremacy and the rule of law, but also, he said in a televised address, because of "the harm that is being done to the prestige and influence, and indeed to the safety, of our nation in the world."[103] Polls taken in the aftermath of Little Rock showed that majorities of Western Europeans held highly negative views of U.S. race relations.[104] A survey conducted for the USIA by Gallup, DIVO, IFOP, and the Istituto Italiano dell'Opinione Pubblica in 1958 found "a basic atmosphere of esteem for the United States and for the American people" throughout Western Europe, except for two recurring complaints: "They interfere in the internal affairs of other countries," and "overwhelmingly unfavorable reaction" to the "treatment of the Negro in America."[105]

The issue would continue to aggravate the subsequent administration's efforts to improve relations with developing countries. Kennedy's halting steps toward support for civil rights legislation were driven primarily by domestic considerations, but he also responded to the imperatives of international politics.[106] The problem was vividly illustrated by the experience of African diplomats who ventured outside of Washington, where they were sometimes thrown out of restaurants, harassed by police, even beaten by white supremacists. When William H. Fitzjohn, chargé d'affaires of Sierra Leone, was denied service at a Howard Johnson restaurant in Hagerstown, Maryland, the *Lagos Daily Times* wrote, "by this disgraceful act of racial discrimination, the United States forfeits its claim to world leadership."[107] After a waitress at the Bonnie Blue Diner refused to serve Ambassador Malick Sow of Chad, she offered this excuse: "He looked like just an ordinary run-of-the-mill nigger to me. I couldn't tell he was an ambassador."[108] The State Department then assigned an officer to try to ease the foreign diplomats through a thicket of Jim Crow regulations that made it difficult for them to attend meetings in clubs or rent apartments in the District of Columbia. State Department officials started lobbying the White House to take action, and federal officials urged state legislators and restaurant owners alike to change their rules. Clarence Rosier, owner of the Cottage Inn Restaurant, rejected the pressure. "I am a patriotic American," he declared. "But when people come around here from the State Department telling me what I can do in my place, then I say this country is going Communist. I'll sell and move to Russia. There's more freedom there."[109]

Rosier might have donned the mantle of patriotism as he refused service to blacks, but his actions were almost literally anti-American, both in principle, when he enforced discrimination, and in effect, as he persisted with behavior that directly hurt American interests abroad. Kennedy's secretary of state, Dean Rusk, thought that the effects could be felt for decades. In 1980, he recalled that it had been only ten or fifteen years since an African diplomat could not get a decent meal or lodging in the segregated South, including Washington. "An African ambassador once sat in my office and asked me, 'Where can I get a haircut, Mr. Secretary?' . . . Some of these former diplomats are now prime ministers and presidents of their countries," Rusk added, "and people wonder why they hate us."[110]

Nevertheless, it was not bigots like Rosier but civil rights activists who had to defend themselves from the charge of "anti-Americanism." As their movement gathered momentum, some unsympathetic observers – including former president Harry Truman – claimed that sit-ins might be the work of Communists. The FBI reported that African American demands for equality were "inspired by anti-American sentiments."[111] Chicago NAACP leader Rev. Carl J. Fuqua tried to counter the familiar charge, arguing that "peaceful demonstrations are not synonymous with anti-Americanism, but rather give living expression to the American tradition of freedom to protest wrong."[112] Yet the charge of anti-Americanism continued to be directed at activists seeking to improve American democracy, not at white supremacists who sullied it.

During the famous March on Washington in August 1963, when Martin Luther King, Jr., spoke from the steps of the Lincoln Memorial, representatives of national liberation movements from Kenya, Mozambique, Rhodesia, South Africa, Southwest Africa, Swaziland, and Zanzibar delivered to the U.S. Embassy in Cairo a message of support for the march that also denounced discrimination in the United States.[113] Demonstrations supporting the march took place in West Berlin, The Hague, London, Madrid, Munich, Oslo, Tel Aviv, and Toronto.[114] Ten thousand Jamaicans marched through Kingston to express their sympathy with the demonstrators in Washington.[115] That same year, King wrote of the contrast between the progress in the decolonization movement and the stubborn resistance to ending official racism in the United States: "the nations of Asia and Africa are moving with jetlike speed toward the goal of political independence, and we still creep at a horse-and-buggy pace toward the gaining of a cup of coffee at a lunch counter."[116]

A Cold Warrior to the core, Kennedy decided the cost was becoming too high. Speaking to business leaders at the White House, the president acknowledged the damage done internationally by police violence against civil rights demonstrators in Alabama: "All of the money we spent for USIA might well have been saved after the picture of the Negro and the dog at Birmingham."[117] Kennedy sent Secretary Rusk to testify before the Senate in support of what would become the Civil Rights Act of 1964 on the grounds that racial discrimination in the United States damaged America's standing in the international struggle with the Soviet Union.

In the end, the alleged "anti-Americanism" represented by the intense focus abroad on racial discrimination in the United States served directly to advance the cause of civil rights – showing just how positive an effect criticism of America's failings could have in redressing a major deficit in American democracy and its standing in the world. During both the Eisenhower and Kennedy administrations, "anti-American" reactions from abroad and "anti-American" activists at home helped prod a recalcitrant U.S. government toward action on civil rights, thereby bringing American reality more in line with American ideals. In other words, so-called "anti-Americans" served a deeply pro-American purpose.

Sartre: The Poster Child of Anti-Americanism

While polling data show that the traditional concept of anti-Americanism does not apply to broad swaths of foreign opinion and it has been misdirected at American activists seeking to correct America's flaws, it also has been attributed more selectively over time to prominent individuals. A key figure in the annals of anti-Americanism is the existentialist philosopher Jean-Paul Sartre.[118] A towering presence among French intellectuals, his novels, short stories, plays, essays, and political tracts placed him at the center of debates in French society for decades. His left-wing commitments made him a hero to some but drew the ire of conservatives and scorn from those who saw him as a prominent example of the communist fellow traveler, a role he played for part of his long life as an *intellectuel engagé*, an activist intellectual. As an internationalist with a Marxist bent who believed that "the writer reveals the world from the perspective of the oppressed," Sartre's "taste for the subversive" and "absolute refusal to be resigned in the face of injustice" led him to champion dubious causes as well as take principled stands.[119] Some U.S. officials were not sure what to make of him. When J. Edgar Hoover read in 1964 that Sartre had signed an anti-American manifesto, he reportedly fired off an order: "Find out who this Sartre is."[120] That was the same year Sartre won, and declined, the Nobel Prize for Literature.

For many of today's scholars, Jean-Paul Sartre embodied postwar anti-Americanism. He was "the most prominent anti-American" in France.[121] The "Sartrean brand of anti-Americanism" dominated the 1960s.[122] His "explosive anti-Americanism set the tone of elite opinion in Europe."[123] This received wisdom needs revisiting, because Sartre lacked the disdain of American culture typically associated with anti-Americanism. His critical views of the United States were specific, politically based, and on some topics, especially race relations, perfectly in line with what has by now become an accepted part of the American national narrative that acknowledges past injustice and celebrates those who struggled against it. There is no question that Sartre sometimes wrote intemperately of Americans, and that he was a frequent critic of American foreign policy, especially during his four-year flirtation with the French Communist Party from 1952 to 1956, and again during the Vietnam War. That record, along with Sartre's writings on the defects of American cities and race relations, led John Chiddick to call him "perhaps the paradigmatic anti-American of the Cold War years."[124]

Anti-Americanism, we are told, is in evidence among those who are more hostile toward the United States than toward other countries, and who express their hatred toward all aspects of American society. It is "a systematic opposition to America as a whole," carried out by intellectuals who "organize their political thinking on the basis of anti-Americanism."[125] By these definitions, Sartre comes up short. Rather than obsess over the United States, Sartre focused his political concern and his intellectual energy on his own society and on universal dilemmas. He attacked French colonialism in Indochina and North Africa long before it became fashionable to do so and turned his magazine, *Les Temps modernes* (*Modern Times*, named for Charlie Chaplin's Hollywood film), into an anti-colonialist forum.[126] Fighting racism in France, he became an early patron of the *negritude* movement, serving on the editorial board of *Présence Africaine*, its major journal.[127] He was probably the leading French opponent of his country's brutal counterinsurgency warfare in Algeria, writing dozens of essays calling for that country's independence and denouncing the use of torture by the French military. For that he was rewarded with death threats, from thousands of war veterans who assembled on the Champs-Élysées to chant "Kill Sartre!" and from the outlawed Organisation de l'Armée Secrète (OAS), which bombed his apartment.[128] He did not choose positions merely to be trendy, or consistently oppose the U.S. position, but followed his own idiosyncratic moral compass. He admired revolutionary Cuba on a visit in 1960 but broke with Castro in 1971 over the persecution of Cuban poet Heberto Padilla. At a time when many European leftists were taking up the Palestinian cause, Sartre defended Israel, angering Arab intellectuals who had hoped that he would view the Israeli-Palestinian conflict as a parallel to the Algerian struggle.[129] He opposed the U.S. war in Vietnam, and when it ended, he called for the Vietnamese "boat people" – anti-communist refugees – to be given asylum in France.[130]

Thus his engagements were manifold, and his positions often critical of the United States during the Cold War, but this does not seem to have stemmed from an entrenched or obsessive anti-Americanism. Sartre admired New York's skyscrapers, for example: "They were the architecture of the future, just as the cinema was the art of the future, and jazz the music of the future."[131] He asserted that the "greatest literary development in France between 1929 and 1939 was the discovery of Faulkner, Dos Passos, Hemingway, Caldwell, Steinbeck."[132] Because he could not read English, he asked his partner Simone de Beauvoir, author of *The Second Sex*, to translate whole chapters of the latest American novels, which he read eagerly.[133] He explicitly called for more, not less, American influence on French literary culture, because the Americans offered "lessons in a renewal of the art of writing."[134]

Sartre first had to defend himself against the charge of anti-Americanism in 1946 after he wrote a play critical of racism in the United States. *The Respectful Prostitute* depicted the ethical conflict that a white prostitute faced when influential white citizens of a small Southern town pressured her to falsely accuse a black man, whom she had met on a train, of rape. This was hardly the invention of a fertile anti-American imagination; Sartre was inspired to write the play by the infamous Scottsboro trial of 1931, in which two white prostitutes in Alabama were pressured into falsely accusing nine young black men of raping them on a train.[135] Some French critics nonetheless accused him of anti-Americanism when the play was performed in Paris. When it opened in New York in February 1948 (beginning a run of more than 350 performances), the play again met with charges of anti-Americanism.[136] In a preface to the English translation, Sartre defended himself. "I am not anti-American. I don't even know what the word means. I am anti-racist because I do know what racism means. . . . It has been said that I saw the mote in my neighbor's eye and not the beam in my own. It is true that we French have colonies and we don't always behave well in them. But when it comes to oppression there is neither mote nor beam; one must denounce it wherever it exists."[137]

At the time, Sartre was living by that credo – he had already attacked anti-Semitism in "Childhood of a Leader" and *Anti-Semite and Jew*[138] – and he had come under fire from Communist officials for criticizing Stalinism's stultifying effect on literature. "It would be peculiar if there were people in New York to accuse me of anti-Americanism," Sartre wrote drily, "at the moment when *Pravda* in Moscow is energetically accusing me of being an agent for American propaganda."[139] His motives, Sartre argued, lay elsewhere: he had visited the United States in 1945, and he was appalled at what he learned of its race relations. "In this country, so justly proud of its democratic institutions, one man in ten is deprived of his political rights," he wrote in *Le Figaro*. He reported meeting white soldiers who told him that they would shoot their sisters if they slept with black men, and a white doctor who wanted the Red Cross to block African Americans from donating blood because "it is not good for black blood to run in our veins."[140]

The argument that this was a sign of Sartre's anti-Americanism might be more compelling if his commentary had not reflected the actual state of affairs in the United States at that time. In 1945, a majority of U.S. states still banned interracial marriages. Swedish sociologist Gunnar Myrdal found fear of interracial sex to be at the heart of white thinking on race relations while conducting interviews in the South for *An American Dilemma*.[141] During World War II, donated blood was, in fact, segregated by race, and some centers turned away African American donors.[142]

So the issue is not whether Sartre's depiction of American racism rang true – it clearly adhered closely to facts – but whether it was ill intentioned. Some Americans, such as the anticommunist cofounder of the Congress for Cultural Freedom Sidney Hook, thought that Sartre's interest in racism in the United States was merely instrumental. Hook claimed that Richard Wright was "flattered by the use which Sartre makes of him as a kind of club against American culture analogous to the use the Communists make of Robeson."[143] In this single sentence, Hook managed to depict two leading African American cultural figures as mere dupes; to deny both Richard Wright and Paul Robeson were a part of "American culture," which in Hook's formulation was exclusively white and under threat from black artists, who are somehow non-American; and to disparage Sartre's interest in fighting racism as a mere cover for an anti-American agenda. Hook was not the first to do so. When Wright attended a reception at the U.S. Embassy in Paris, he was told, "For God's sake, don't let these foreigners turn you into a brick to hurl through our windows!"[144]

Unlike Hook, Sartre took Wright seriously as a writer and as an important contributor to American culture. For him, it was not anti-American to appreciate African American cultural contributions. He not only admired them from afar but also entered into a "dialogical relationship" with black writers in transatlantic circuits of ideas on race and colonialism, as he learned from, publicized, and sometimes argued with Wright, Frantz Fanon, Leopold Senghor, and Aimé Césaire. This intellectual network helped focus Sartre's anticolonial thinking on questions of race and racism, as he was influenced by the postcolonial internationalism furthered by the Paris-based Société Africaine de Culture (the group of black Francophone intellectuals behind *Présence Africaine*) and the Congrès des Ecrivains et Artistes Noirs (International Conference of

Negro Writers and Artists).[145] Attacking racism was not an opportunistic way to slander the United States, but an absolutely central concern in Sartre's internationalism.

Nor did Sartre claim that the United States was worse than other societies, including his own. "Yes, the Negroes of Chicago are housed in hovels," he wrote. "That is neither just nor democratic. But many of our white workmen live in hovels that are even more miserable."[146] Rather than using American conditions as a foil to assert French national superiority, Sartre drew universal lessons. "No matter what evils your writers denounced, we have the same faults in our own country," he wrote. "These injustices have never seemed to us a defect of American society but rather a sign of the imperfections of our time."[147]

The anti-American label stuck, however, and it adhered to Sartre's constant companion as well. Simone de Beauvoir's name, too, appeared in scholarly treatments of anti-Americanism and in government intelligence reports. (The CIA referred more than once to "Simon" de Beauvoir; that a woman could be an influential thinker apparently produced cognitive dissonance in some Agency staff.)[148] In a 1963 report on "Intellectual Anti-Americanism," a CIA analyst who was able to spell her name correctly still got her motives wrong. "Anti-American intellectuals" including Beauvoir, the CIA report asserted, "regard Americans as barbarians who spread a low-grade mass culture of Coca Cola, Hollywood movies, fin-tailed automobiles, and hand-painted girlie neckties."[149] We do not know how Beauvoir felt about neckties, but she was a fan and frequent patron of American movies, and she referred to the large American automobile that whisked her through Chicago as "beautiful."[150] In *La Force des choses (Force of Circumstance)*, she wrote that the young American soldiers arriving in France in 1944 "incarnated liberty itself: ours, and the liberty – we had no doubt – that they were going to spread across the world." Disillusion set in after she arrived in the country that "had helped save Europe from fascism" but was now in an increasingly rightist political climate. The American intellectuals she met, even those who called themselves leftists, displayed "an Americanism that was worthy of the chauvinism of my father.... Their anti-communism verged on neurosis; they looked down upon Europe, upon France, with an arrogant condescension."[151] Her own condescension toward Americans was highlighted in a devastating review that Mary McCarthy wrote in 1952 of the translation of Beauvoir's travel narrative, *L'Amérique au jour le jour (America Day by Day)*, showing that Beauvoir's eagerness to spot capitalist oppression led her to make sloppy claims – that Fifth Avenue shops were reserved for the rich, that few professors are writers, that "the individual is nothing." More important, her determination to find evidence of growing inequality and exploitation made Beauvoir miss the fact that it was America's spreading material well-being, not poverty, that caused the social conformity of which both women disapproved.[152]

In defending America against Beauvoir's misjudgments, McCarthy made one of her own, when she ridiculed the French writer's line about "the rise, more ominous every day, of racism and reactionary attitudes" in the United States.[153]

The growing political intolerance and persecution of dissenters at that time, and the spectacle of white mobs burning their black neighbors out of their homes in Chicago's Cicero and Trumbull Park districts, suggest that Beauvoir was onto something.[154] McCarthy's objection echoed those of other white Americans who grew defensive when foreigners called attention to racism or the murder of voting rights activists such as the Rev. Walter G. Lee and Lamar Smith.[155] When foreigners condemned lynching in the American South, they were merely revealing "anti-American bias," according to the House Un-American Activities Committee.[156] HUAC member and defiant segregationist John Rankin (D-MS) argued against having the Committee investigate the activities of the Ku Klux Klan, because, unlike the "anti-American" civil rights movement, he claimed, "the Ku Klux Klan is an American institution."[157]

Such trends did not lead, as Beauvoir feared, to "fascism."[158] That over-wrought prophecy proved wrong, but it is worth noting that leading American syndicated columnist Drew Pearson shared her concern, declaring that he heard the "drums of fascism beating louder" as Joe McCarthy grew more ambitious (thereby landing himself in the senator's crosshairs).[159] Hannah Arendt shared it too, hearing in the America of the 1950s echoes of Germany in the 1930s.[160] What Pearson and Arendt feared did not come to pass, but they were not condemned as anti-American for their apprehensions.

To acquire the anti-American label, it helped to be French, of course, and to have a longer record of criticism, but when we assume that Sartre and Beauvoir were driven by an irrational and a priori hatred of the United States, we are looking for causality in all the wrong places. Both writers were regularly critical of the United States, because their philosophical convictions told them to take up the cause of the downtrodden, and their political analysis depended on Marxist principles that held capitalism responsible for the problems of the masses. Ideological consistency is not a formula for objectivity, and so their accounts of the United States were as selective as the celebratory narratives of America's Cold Warriors who could see no cracks in the edifice of American freedom. Most of the time, one could count on the French philosophers to be equally tough on other countries, especially their own. But the temporary blind spot that shielded the Soviet Union from their scrutiny until disillusion set in, and the similar investment of hope in Cuba until they could no longer counte-nance its repressive measures, revealed the degradation of critical thinking that accompanies the partisan adoption of a state ideology.

Historians have differed over how to characterize Sartre's pro-Soviet period, whether it is best understood as a clear sign of his moral weakness and failed responsibility or as a short-lived enthusiasm for fellow traveling, preceded by regular conflicts with the PCF and followed by the denunciation of Soviet bru-tality in Eastern Europe.[161] His Marxist use of class analysis to understand society was of long standing, but it was usually coupled with a commitment to individual freedom that led him to clash frequently with Communist ortho-doxy. "Stalinist policy is incompatible with an honest approach to the literary

profession," he wrote in 1947.[162] He joined a new French party, the Rassemblement Démocratique Révolutionnaire (RDR), as a third way between the United
States and the Soviet Union – leading the PCF to warn Moscow that Sartre
was building a "Third Force" and promoting a "philosophy of decadence."[163]
When his play *Dirty Hands* opened in April 1948, portraying brutally cynical Communists repressing a dissenter within their ranks, Communist attacks
on Sartre grew fierce. "Existentialist putrescence," spat Maurice Thorez, head
of the PCF.[164] Other leading Communists denounced Sartre for "foul justification of the capitalist system," "wanton contra humanism," "intellectual
fornications," and selling his honor "for 30 pieces of silver and a mess of
American pottage."[165] Jean-Paul Sartre, the pro-American stooge.

In January 1950, Sartre was still readily criticizing the Soviet Union's abuses
from a position on the independent left. *Les Temps modernes* ran an editorial
arguing that Soviet progress in raising living standards had to be measured
against the "ten million in concentration camps."[166] His magazine also published the gulag survivor Victor Serge's description of the victims of Stalin's
labor camps as "pariah-slaves" whose condition was worse than serfdom.[167]
His bristly political relations with Stalinists derived not only from his awareness
of the abuses in the Soviet Union but also stemmed from the central critique
of conventional Marxism at the heart of his existential philosophy: rather than
material forces determining individual fates, Sartre argued that the individual
shaped the world within its constraints – indeed, had a moral responsibility to
do so.[168]

Sartre's move toward reconciliation with the Communists and with Moscow
came in late 1951 and 1952, after the collapse of the RDR and in the context
of French intellectuals' disputes over whether violence was justified in anticolonial conflicts leading to a bitter falling out between Sartre and his friend Albert
Camus, who opposed Algerian independence.[169] This was also the period when
the French colonial war in Indochina was raging, and Sartre joined the PCF's
protests against it. From 1952 to 1956, Sartre set aside his misgivings and
engaged in a "four-year romance with the PCF."[170] He undertook the sup-
pression of his own work, permitting *Dirty Hands* to be performed abroad
only where the local Communist Party approved. He endorsed an article in *Les
Temps modernes* critical of the show trial of Rudolf Slansky and thirteen alleged
co-conspirators against the Communist regime of Czechoslovakia (eleven of
them Jewish). He wrote nothing of his own, however, and after eleven of the
defendants were executed, he responded not with a Zola-like eruption but by
traveling to Vienna to attend the Communist-sponsored "World Congress of
Peace."[171] The Cold War had, to his way of thinking, forced a choice between
a system designed, theoretically at least, to produce social justice, and one that
seemed incapable of meeting the demands for liberation by colonial peoples. It
was in this period that his harshest attack on the United States appeared – an
attack that was the product of his long-standing convictions and his new phase
of special pleading for the Soviet side in the Cold War.

This most-discussed "anti-American" moment of Sartre's career came in Venice in June 1953, when he learned that Julius and Ethel Rosenberg had been executed for atomic espionage. Historians have confirmed that the trial proceedings were tainted, but that the tainted proceedings led to a correct judgment of guilt for Julius. Whether the sentence fit the crime continues to be debated, especially in Ethel's case; it was the first death sentence imposed for espionage in peacetime.[172] Sartre was outraged at what he saw simply as the state-sponsored murder of two innocent Jews for their left-wing politics. Grabbing a telephone to dictate an article for *Libération*, Sartre in his anger did not hesitate to condemn the United States for failing to stop the executions, diagnosing the problem as incipient fascism. The case was evidence of "McCarthy's justice," "a legal lynching which covers a whole people with blood." The country was obviously "sick with fear," and Europe should break its ties lest it be infected. Less often quoted are his reminders that, "after all, the Rosenbergs are Americans," and that "hundreds of thousands" of "men of courage" in the United States had opposed the executions.[173]

Sartre was voicing some of the same concerns – more sharply, to be sure – that the Coordinator for Psychological Intelligence at the USIA observed in the socialist and independent press in France, Belgium, Italy, and West Germany during the trial: doubts about the Rosenbergs' guilt, coupled with the belief that "clemency will play less into the hands of Communist propagandists than will execution."[174] Many of Sartre's compatriots were convinced that the Rosenbergs were scapegoats, and Jewish scapegoats at that. As Reinhold Niebuhr put it, "The French intellectuals seemed to believe that the Rosenbergs were innocent, not only because communist propaganda insisted on their innocence but because Dreyfus was innocent."[175] There had been a massive campaign for clemency, ranging from the Catholic Church to Communist-organized demonstrations in Paris.[176] To the chairman of HUAC, Francis E. Walter (D-PA), the protestors were merely "flogging themselves into a fury of anti-Americanism."[177] Once the Rosenbergs were executed, U.S. Ambassador Douglas Dillon warned that a "flash-fire of anti-Americanism" was sweeping through France – but of course this was not a sudden upsurge in underlying prejudice; it was a reaction to a well-publicized and troubling event.[178]

Sartre's stance had more to do with French political culture than any ingrained or irrational hostility toward America. The tradition of the *intellectuel engagé* in France went back to Voltaire and Zola, and here Sartre was playing Zola to the hilt. He resisted any temptation to entitle his impassioned article "*J'accuse.*" Its actual title, "*Les Animaux malades de la rage*" ("Animals Sick with Rabies") is rarely analyzed by those who present it as evidence of his anti-Americanism. There was more to it than implying that some Americans were mad dogs. The title is an allusion to La Fontaine's seventeenth-century poem "*Les Animaux malades de la peste*" ("Animals Sick with Plague") known to every French schoolchild in Sartre's day. La Fontaine's fable, in which a harmless donkey is executed for the crime of nibbling on someone else's lawn, while ferocious, meat-eating animals judge their own bloody conduct to be above reproach, was a critique of the arbitrary exercise of judicial power.[179] Thus Sartre was positioning himself in an even longer French tradition of intellectual protest against the state's abuse of the individual.

Bernard-Henri Lévy and Raymond Aron wondered where Sartre's outraged sense of justice had been during the postwar purges of collaborators in France, conducted without due process, or the show trials in the Soviet bloc.[180] On show trials, as noted earlier, his record was mixed, but on French reprisals, the complaint is not fair. It overlooks Sartre's expression of "disgust" at the "medieval sadism" directed against female collaborators, which he published in *Combat* shortly after the liberation of Paris.[181] In 1946, he commented that Fritz Lang's *Fury*, which portrays a Chicago lynching, had been showing in Paris in late 1944, while "Frenchmen in the Midi were hanging and shooting, without much discrimination, such members of the 'militia' and collaborators as they were able to capture. They were shaving the heads of women in our provinces." An anti-American might have used a film about lynching to denigrate America, but Sartre used it to upbraid his compatriots: "we did not think about your lynchings, but of ours – we took the lesson to ourselves."[182]

His silence on Soviet crimes at this point was deliberate: Sartre was in the midst of his most pro-Moscow period when the Rosenbergs were executed. This positioning pushed him toward sloppier claims about the United States, as is typical whenever writers become propagandists for America's rivals, and it helps explain the unconcealed rage behind his *malades de la rage* piece. Just how far he had sacrificed his judgment to ideology was clear when he returned from a trip to Moscow in July 1954 and told an interviewer for *Libération*, absurdly, that Soviet citizens have "complete freedom to criticize" their government.[183] This marked the peak of his uncharacteristically fawning relationship to a state, and the nadir of his political and intellectual independence. It was a phase that would not last.

In 1956, Sartre broke with the PCF over the invasion of Hungary, which he denounced in a full-throated public protest "against the use of cannon and tanks to break the revolt of the Hungarian people and its desire for independence."[184] *Les Temps modernes* published a 487-page triple issue on the Hungarian uprising. He went further, deriding all Soviet policy since World War II as "twelve years of terror and stupidity" and the leadership of the PCF as the "product of thirty years of lies and sclerosis."[185] He was done with apologias for Moscow, although not with attacks on war-making by the great powers. In the late 1960s, he would help direct an unofficial tribunal that found the United States guilty of genocide in Vietnam, and he responded to the Soviet invasion of Czechoslovakia in 1968 by calling it "pure aggression," a "war crime" – although he added that it paled in comparison to the Vietnam War (as it did, of course, at least in scale, with 72 Czechs killed compared to 3.4 million Indochinese deaths, in Robert McNamara's estimate).[186]

One can certainly evaluate the work that Sartre and Beauvoir produced about the United States and find some of it wanting, imbalanced, or misinformed. If writing were an act of judicious evenhandedness, their books and articles should have acknowledged – and tried to account for – outcomes on the positive side of the ledger regarding the issues that most interested them, such as Truman's order desegregating the armed forces, or the dethroning of McCarthy during the Army-McCarthy hearings, or Eisenhower's dispatch of federal troops to Little Rock. It would probably be difficult to find any work of social criticism or travel impressions that did not present a selective view of a vast country and a complex society. But to dismiss Sartre and Beauvoir as anti-Americans, as if they had a singularly obsessive and malevolent view of the United States, driven by envy or irrationality, and hostile to democracy and freedom, is to misconstrue the record and misunderstand their thinking. It fails to take account of their enthusiastic embrace of American popular culture, their criticism of anti-democratic tendencies like McCarthyism and racial discrimination, and their shifting relations with Communism. In reality, it was their enduring political commitments, buffeted by the vagaries of their illusion and disillusion with the Soviet Union, which influenced their views of the United States. Sartre's lifelong search for a Marxism that sided with the downtrodden and respected the integrity of the individual, without lending support to a campaign against the harsh state that claimed to turn Marxism from theory into practice, consumed far more of his prodigious energy and prolific output, and ultimately proved a dilemma he could not resolve. America was not central to his thinking; it was an afterthought in that tortuous process.

Institutionalizing Anti-Anti-Americanism

Swayed by a fundamental misreading of the polls, and to counteract the influence of "anti-American" European leftists like Sartre as well as the larger Soviet propaganda machine, the U.S. government built up a permanent array of programs and agencies designed to influence foreign opinion through public diplomacy. The Voice of America broadcast into 100 countries in 46 languages, and a network of United States Information Centers popped up in more than 190 cities worldwide. The work became imperative not only to counter Soviet propaganda but also as a substitute for material aid when one of the most effective policy means for boosting U.S. popularity abroad, the Marshall Plan, was winding down. The agency in charge of foreign assistance programs worried about the repercussions of "the shift in the main purpose of United States aid from economic recovery and development to military defense," and wondered whether foreign gratitude would survive the shift.[187]

The development of a permanent infrastructure aimed at combating anti-Americanism was accompanied by a flurry of scholarly works devoted to parsing foreign views of the United States. The first of these was Henry Steele Commager's *America in Perspective: The United States through Foreign Eyes*, excerpting some of the classic travel accounts.[188] In 1952–53 the Social

Science Research Council, with funding from the Carnegie Corporation and the Rockefeller and Ford Foundations, sponsored a series of studies of foreign opinion. The findings were published in the *Annals of the American Academy of Political and Social Sciences* in a special issue entitled "America through Foreign Eyes," beginning with the essay "How Others See Us" by political psychologist William Buchanan, who had coauthored a study for the United Nations with Hadley Cantril, inventor of the ladder scale.[189] Four years later Franz M. Joseph commissioned essays by intellectuals from twenty countries for a volume he entitled *As Others See Us: The United States through Foreign Eyes* (rather ungenerously making no reference to Commager, Buchanan, or the *Annals* collection, despite having borrowed their titles). He began, as Buchanan had, by arguing that foreign criticism could be salutary, choosing as an epigraph lines from Robert Burns's poem "To a Louse" that express the wish that we might "see oursels as ithers see us!/It wad frae monie a blunder free us, An foolish notion."[190]

Despite the ritual acknowledgment that the United States should welcome foreign criticism as helpful for making improvements to its society or foreign policy, these studies contributed mostly to a sense within the budding foreign public opinion bureaucracy that the problem was one of inadequate communication of U.S. views abroad. Their more specific findings, for example, that foreigners seemed no longer to associate America with democracy so much as with global power, wealth, and technology, did little to affect the myth of anti-Americanism that held that opposition to U.S. policy stemmed from a rejection of democratic society.[191] When foreigners expressed negative opinions, these were not to be evaluated on the merits but remedied through better propaganda. When the Psychological Strategy Board (PSB), a coordinating body for the State Department, Defense Department, and CIA, identified an "intensification of anti-American feeling among significant elements of European opinion," the Eisenhower administration responded with increased public diplomacy efforts.[192]

President Eisenhower was an enthusiastic supporter of both overt and covert information operations who argued that "public opinion wins most of the wars and always wins the peace."[193] He tapped C.D. Jackson, *Fortune* magazine's publisher and Eisenhower's former Deputy Chief of Psychological Warfare during World War II, to develop a reorganization plan and to be the State Department's representative to the PSB. To represent the Mutual Security Agency, which coordinated foreign aid programs, he named Sigurd Larmon, an advertising executive from Young & Rubicam. William H. Jackson, a former military intelligence officer who spent a year as deputy director of the CIA, became the PSB's chair.[194] This new leadership, Eisenhower hoped, might be able to do a better job of improving America's reputation abroad.

To bring together foreign information programs with the government's growing covert operations capability, Eisenhower replaced the PSB with an Operations Coordinating Board (OCB). In June 1953, he brought all foreign propaganda efforts under the United States Information Agency, whose mission was "to persuade foreign peoples that it lies in their own interest to take actions which are also consistent with the national objectives of the United States."[195]

That assertion was breathtaking in its oversimplification of a complex world, and its limitations soon became apparent to the people charged with carrying it out. At the end of 1954, the USIA undertook a massive, six-volume self-study that produced unvarnished criticism from 142 of its officials in Washington and overseas.[196] The job of conducting the study was contracted out to survey experts at McCann-Erickson, an advertising and marketing agency with offices in Europe and Latin America, whose founding slogan was "Truth Well Told." Their findings were devastating: the Agency did not know whether its news coverage was impartial or biased, whether its anti-Communist messages were subtle or blatant, whether its impact was "important" or "infinitesimal." Staff morale was low, as indicated by such darkly humorous observations as "the only reason VOA has not done more damage to United States foreign policy is the bad quality of our engineers."[197]

When McCann-Erickson told these truths to USIA top brass, they promptly deemed the study "out of bounds" and ordered it classified. It is of interest here because the uncensored views of professionals employed by the U.S. government to combat anti-Americanism show that even they did not believe foreign criticism of the United States to be grounded in opposition to democratic principles or modernity, but that policies and actions were far more important. A single U.S. vote in the United Nations against Moroccan independence nullified any number of claims that the U.S. government supported the end of colonialism, whereas an airlift of emergency aid to pilgrims in Mecca "is worth any number of speeches or public statements." Likewise, the provision of military aircraft to the French for their fight in Indochina may be popular in the United States as an anti-Communist effort, "yet to the Indians all it means is that we are helping to bomb Asians." One USIA supervisor warned his broadcasters that it was awkward to speak of self-determination in the Arab world, where U.S. policy opposed popular movements, and offered this advice: "try to weasel your way out of the problem."[198] The bottom line, one respondent argued, is that "If the policy is either lousy or non-existent or pat, no amount of sugar-coating, no amount of propaganda will make it palatable."[199]

Thus did the leading practitioners of public diplomacy in the United States assess the value of their own work. "We cannot possibly change the mind of a man who is anti-American," argued one official. But that was the wrong aim in any case. "I don't think it makes a hell of a lot of difference in Europe whether people like us or not," argued another. "People can still act with and for the United States and U.S. objectives without liking us particularly," added a third. "Americans like to be liked, but in cold-blooded terms what we are really seeking is that [our foreign audience member] do things that are in our interest and that he thinks are also in his own interest."[200]

Instead of complaining about endemic anti-Americanism abroad as a danger to the United States, information specialists pointed to problems at home. They despaired at the contrast between the message they sought to convey about

America's open society and foreigners' knowledge of McCarthyist crackdowns on freedom of expression. They were tasked with promoting American cultural life overseas, and that presented a political dilemma when the most interesting contemporary painter to the rest of the world was Jackson Pollock, yet "the average Congressman is convinced that non-representational art is Communistic."[201] Typical of this view was Rep. George A. Dondero (R-MO): "Modern art is Communistic because it is distorted and ugly.... Art which does not glorify our beautiful country in plain, simple terms that everyone can understand breeds dissatisfaction. It's therefore opposed to our government, and those who create and promote it are our enemies."[202] Conveying the image of a flourishing American cultural life abroad was challenging when U.S. politicians spoke in such terms – and voted accordingly on appropriations for public diplomacy.

McCarthyism threatened to trump cultural appeals in other ways. American libraries overseas were popular; in Germany, 61% of Germans who lived near an America House had visited it during the preceding year, and of those, 78% urged their friends to see it.[203] In April 1953, however, Joseph McCarthy claimed there were 30,000 "Communist" books on the shelves of U.S. Embassy and USIS libraries in Europe. He sent his aides Roy Cohn and David Schine to Paris, Bonn, Frankfurt, Munich, Vienna, Belgrade, Athens, Rome, and London, where they found eighteen books by alleged Communists and seventy-eight by authors who had not cooperated with HUAC. U.S. officials felt the pressure. The State Department issued regulations prohibiting its missions abroad from stocking books by "controversial persons, Communists, fellow travelers" and anyone else considered too critical of the United States. The banned authors included Sherwood Anderson, John Dewey, Theodore Dreiser, W.E.B. Du Bois, George Gershwin, Dashiell Hammett, Ernest Hemingway, Norman Mailer, Arthur Miller, Reinhold Niebuhr, and Frank Lloyd Wright. More than three hundred titles were removed from overseas libraries, and a few overzealous embassy officials actually burned some of the books – to the astonishment of the German press, which noted that this was the first time since Hitler that books had been burned in their country. Hemingway had the distinction of having his books burned twice within two decades, first by the Nazis in 1933, and now by the U.S. government.[204]

This was no way to win converts to the American style of democracy. At the USIA, officials thought that "the fracas over the book selection did more harm to the Program than anything else that has happened to it."[205] McCarthy, in his relentless hunt for anti-Americans at home and abroad, went on to attack George Catlett Marshall – America's Chief of Staff during WWII, Secretary of State of Marshall Plan fame, and Secretary of Defense in the Korean War – whom Truman praised as "the greatest living American." When McCarthy claimed that Marshall was "implementing the will of Stalin," he drew criticism from some quarters, but he never drew the charge of "anti-Americanism."[206] McCarthy probably did more to harm America's standing in the world than any other person during his career, and he attacked the American government more ferociously than did Sartre or the authors of the books he wanted banned, but to accuse McCarthy of anti-Americanism would have been pointless. By the 1950s, the term had become a blunt instrument with which the right could beat the left at home, and a blurred lens through which Americans tried (and failed) to perceive the source of unhappiness or opposition abroad. Its meaning was fixed, and its effect on policy of far-reaching consequence.

4

Bad Neighborhood

Anti-Americanism and Latin America

> The fascist and the Communist elements agree on at least one proposition. That is
> hatred of the Yankee . . . the time to deal with this rising menace in South America
> is now.
>
>   – Secretary of State John Foster Dulles[1]

As the Cold War intensified, Americans grew accustomed to reading events in
the developing world through the lens of East-West conflict, colored by enduring assumptions of Third World inferiority. Foreign leaders and movements
were regarded as either supporters of the Free World or agents of international
communism, "pro-American" or "anti-American." From a Latin American
perspective, this schema made little sense. U.S. Marines had been landing on
Caribbean beaches since long before the Bolshevik Revolution of 1917. Successive administrations in Washington intervened to make and unmake governments in Latin America under a variety of rationales: to promote stability,
to thwart German influence, to teach democracy, to chase down bandits. By
the time the Cold War became the central concern of U.S. foreign policy,
there were already plenty of Latin American anti-communists in their own
right – especially among business leaders, military officers, large landowners,
and the Church – but although divisions between left and right were apparent in the internal political landscape, the notion of a Soviet threat to Latin
America seemed hardly credible. For most Latin Americans, political conflict
was about land tenure, access to political power, workers' rights, and disputes
with neighboring countries. When Latin Americans worried about subversion
or interference by a foreign power, they did not look with apprehension to
Moscow in the distant East, but to the nearby North. That is one reason the
Cold War seemed so different from a Latin American perspective, and one more
reason why the "anti-American" or "pro-American" labels were so ill-suited
to the Americas.

The young Mexican economist José Iturriaga tried to convey this sense in a satirical article in *El Popular* entitled "Why I Am Anti-Soviet and Anti-Russian":

> Mexico City, 27 April 1951. For more than one hundred years we have been the victims of that country.... How can a good Mexican forget that in 1846 the Czar of all the Russias, James Polkov, sent Winfield Scottisky to make war on us in order to annex the province of Texas to its immense Ukrainian steppes, in which conflict we lost not only Texas but more than half our territory.... A Mexican patriot cannot forget, either, that when we were in the midst of a civil war to oust Victoriano Huerta, the troops of the Russian fleet under Admiral Fletcherev trampled on our Mexican shores and occupied Veracruz from April to November, 1914.... We cannot ignore the humiliations suffered by our wandering farmers, who, because they want to earn a few rubles on the other side of the Volga, are discriminated against and ill-treated because they are guilty of not being Slavs.... [2]

Thus did a talented young Mexican try to call attention to the manifest source of north-south incomprehension in U.S.-Latin American relations. While Washington policy makers and the U.S. public increasingly saw Latin American events through a Cold War prism in which anti-communism was the most urgent concern, many Latin Americans began from an entirely different point of view. To them, the superpower threatening to transform their societies, dominate their economies, and undermine their political independence was not the remote Soviet Union with its miniscule presence in the region, but the colossally powerful and historically activist United States.[3]

It was hard to get the message to penetrate. The U.S. Embassy considered Iturriaga "one of the brightest of the young stars in the Mexican intellectual firmament," but when he published his satire, a U.S. diplomat bemoaned his "anti-Americanism" – thereby exquisitely missing the point.[4] The State Department, the National Security Council (NSC), academics, and journalists would spend the next decade looking for signs of Soviet and Communist manipulation of ignorant, irrational Latins whose "anti-Americanism" was assumed to be both the cause of their receptivity to radical ideas and proof of the radicals' success.

Iturriaga did not accept this notion. He sought to explain that Mexico's wariness toward its powerful northern neighbor did not spring from passion or prejudice but from historical roots. Mexican nationalists had gone from *yancofilia*, their early admiration for the U.S. political system and its Constitution, to resentment under the impact of events. In 1833, Lorenzo de Zavala had judged that the glittering wealth and republican virtues of the United States represented "the final grade of human perfection." Fray Servando Teresa de Mier assured his compatriots that the United States would lead Mexicans "to the gates of happiness.... Lifting the banner of liberty, they planted it in our hearts."[5] What soured Mexican opinion was the series of subsequent interventions at their expense. Had Russia committed those acts, Iturriaga implied, Russians would be the object of Mexican anger, and Russian analysts would be busily writing reports about the perplexing problem of Mexican anti-Russianism.

As the Cold War came to the Western Hemisphere, the predominant U.S. view, as expressed inside government, in the media, and still maintained by nonspecialists in academia, held that it would be most reasonable for Latin Americans to see their own interests as closely aligned with those of the United States, and that in their natural role as followers they should invariably support U.S. policy. Any deviation was regarded as pathological, and criticism or opposition that emerged from Latin America was taken as a sign of irrational or unjustified hostility. Rubin and Rubin, for example, listed prominent Uruguayan writer Eduardo Galeano among the anti-Americans because he echoed dependency theorists when he wrote in *Open Veins of Latin America* that "The North American economy needs Latin American minerals like the lungs need air."[6] Presumably Galeano's crime was to suggest that rather than principled values, it was a desire for Latin American resources that drove U.S. policy in the region. If so, Galeano's portrait in the rogues' gallery of "anti-American" writers should hang next to pictures of the staff analysts of the National Security Council, since their formal policy paper NSC 144 described as a key objective of U.S. policy "Adequate production in Latin America of, and access by the United States to, raw materials essential to U.S. security."[7]

The plain-spoken record of confidential NSC documents shows that within the government there was an awareness of facts that contained the potential for alternative conclusions. The NSC produced a study on "United States Objectives and Courses of Action with Respect to Latin America" that acknowledged numerous ways in which U.S. policies contributed to substantive grievances. First on the list was "resentment carried over from the days of the forced cession by Mexico of half her territory to the United States, of the secession of Panama from Colombia, and the U.S. military occupation of several other American states." Second was the disparity in wealth between the United States and its elite partners in Latin America on the one hand and the broader populations on the other, exacerbated by the fact that "returns on capital investments are high and wages low." That was a core problem in a region with the highest income inequality in the world, where foreign investors could earn higher profits than at home thanks to tax and land costs kept low through bribery and labor costs kept low through repression. The study acknowledged that Washington had not provided economic aid "on a scale remotely comparable to that of other areas" (i.e., Europe and Asia). It described the impact of quotas, tariffs, and other measures that blocked Latin American exports, helping to keep the region poor while it absorbed vast quantities of U.S. exports – one-half of U.S. automobiles, one-quarter of U.S. textiles, one-third of its iron and steel, 42% of its chemicals. In other words, Latin America helped to create U.S. wealth through its own underdevelopment.[8] This analysis placed the NSC authors quite close to Galeano in their findings about U.S. interests in Latin America.

After acknowledging these problems as sources of Latin American unhappiness with the United States, rather than make recommendations aimed at remedying the causes, the NSC study returned to the old thinking. Nationalist movements were led by "immature and impractical idealists"; the sources of "anti-Americanism" included "jealousy and feelings of inferiority." The fundamental problem was communist exploitation of social conditions, not the conditions themselves. "Because of the existence of these factors," the study concluded, "communism should be considered not only as a separate movement but also as a force which exploits and makes articulate so-called 'nationalistic aspirations' and which supplies organizational and policy guidance to *all* anti-U.S. elements."[9] The circle was complete: anti-Americanism made Latin Americans susceptible to communism, and communists controlled "all" anti-American movements.

Journalists also were prone to stating and then discarding relevant facts in favor of interpretations based on the familiar myth. In a major article in 1952 on anti-Americanism in Mexico, Flora Lewis of the *New York Times* noted that Mexicans said their wariness toward the United States was rooted in historical memory, but she thought she knew better, blaming their "pride," "envy," and "fear." Mexican intellectuals, Lewis explained, belonged to one of two groups, the "pro-Russians" or the "anti-Americans" (apparently there were no "pro-Mexicans" in Mexico).[10] This facile psychological reading of Mexican emotions was certainly less time-consuming than, for example, actually reading Mexican books. Iturriaga's 1951 study of Mexican society, which Lewis does not seem to have consulted, reached much more differentiated conclusions. He enumerated some striking recent changes in Mexican customs that Mexican nationalists had denounced as "Americanization": Cinema now drew larger audiences than theater. Traditional courtesy had yielded to informality. The midday meal and siesta at home had been superseded by an eight-hour workday interrupted by *el quick lunch*. Dress had become less austere and discreet. Women were less closely supervised by their families. Some of the new customs, Iturriaga acknowledged, were unmistakable imports, such as beauty contests, birthday cakes with candles, and Christmas trees instead of nativity scenes. Rather than blame the United States for imposing its ways upon Mexico, Iturriaga explained, one should recognize that most of these changes indicated not only Mexican receptivity to U.S. influence but transnational secular trends that reflected societies adapting to structural changes wrought by industrialization, urbanization, and the education of girls and women.[11] Indeed, comparable transformations were under way at the same time in France, Italy, and elsewhere as more women joined the paid labor force and children left it, making urban societies begin to resemble one another more than they differed. Although some of these changes were catalyzed by migrants and tourists crossing the border in both directions, to call such social transformations "Americanization" was to use a spatial term for a temporal development.[12]

A Mexican social scientist capable of such sophisticated analysis long before it became a topic in U.S. scholarship, who turned his pen against Mexican hypernationalists, Iturriaga was nonetheless dismissed as "anti-American," as were his arguments, and, for good measure, his country. It was far easier to reach for the usual epithet than to take Mexican concerns seriously and weigh their merits. This pattern of thinking was closely linked to a traditional con-descension toward Mexicans that distorted the policy-making process, as one could observe in the most varied of deliberations inside the U.S. government, from public health to immigration to border security. During an outbreak of hoof and mouth disease in Mexican cattle, the Mexican government wanted to address the epidemic through vaccination, as it had done successfully dur-ing an earlier outbreak, whereas the U.S. pressed for the immediate slaughter of a million head of cattle.[13] Although an Agriculture Department official affirmed that the Mexicans were cooperating "100 percent" on disease erad-ication efforts, the president's close advisor, Undersecretary of State Walter Bedell Smith, blamed the problem on Mexicans' closeness to their animals. "The Peon loves his cow," Smith told the Cabinet. "If it were small enough it would sleep under the bed."[14] We do not read of Smith's "anti-Mexicanism" for espousing such an over-generalized and absurd view of why Mexican ranch-ers might not want to destroy their herds – besides the obvious reasons, some believed that the U.S. cattle industry was scheming to eliminate a competitor – yet we have grown accustomed to the claim that Mexican policies emerge from "anti-Americanism."

The treatment of migrant laborers was another major point of friction between the United States and Mexico, and the notion of "anti-Americanism" served, as usual, to muddy the issue and to de-legitimize the Mexican point of view. The migration of "wetbacks," the slur for Mexican workers who crossed the Rio Grande illegally, was the subject of negotiations between the Eisen-hower administration and the government of Adolfo Ruiz Cortines. William S. Stokes, a political scientist at the University of Wisconsin whose research in Central America had been sponsored by the State Department, attributed "an exaggerated interest in Latin America in such things as racial tension in the United States, our treatment of wetbacks from Mexico," and the like to "cul-tural anti-Americanism."[15] The Mexican government requested – as it would continue to do for the rest of the twentieth century – that the United States con-front the problem by cracking down on employers who hired illegal workers. While the two governments wrestled in negotiations, an agreement on *braceros*, temporary farmhands admitted legally to fill a labor shortage during World War II, lapsed. Mexican newspapers ran unironic progovernment headlines such as "Entire Nation Supports Mexican Government," while the *New York Times* characterized both the Mexican official position and Mexican press cov-erage as evidence of "anti-Yankeeism" in Mexico. Further evidence, the paper claimed, was the denial of visas to some U.S. citizens. In vain, Mexican officials tried to persuade the *Times* that Mexican nationalism "does not necessarily mean anti-Americanism."[16] Indeed, polls taken in 1956 showed that 65% of Mexicans described their feelings toward the United States as "good" or "very good," whereas only 3% called their feelings "bad" or "very bad."[17] For all the heated reportage about "anti-gringo prejudice" and "hypersensitive pride" from the "violently anti-Yankee" Mexicans, there was little true hostility that could be measured.[18]

Meanwhile, the American practice of denying visas to many Mexican citizens soon led Eisenhower to decide on expulsion of those who arrived without papers. "Operation Wetback" began in June 1954, as the Border Patrol apprehended and deported more than a million Mexicans, some of them living in the United States legally. As Border Patrol officers used dogs to round up undocumented workers and documented residents alike, Mexican officials made comparisons to the tactics of Soviet bloc police. More than a quarter of the deportees were repatriated by cargo vessels that a Congressional investigation likened to an "eighteenth century slave ship." At least eighty-six Mexican workers died of sunstroke after thousands were unceremoniously "dumped" over the border in the desert by U.S. authorities.[19] "Anti-Americanism" in Mexico did not lead Mexicans to dump Americans in the desert; the allegedly urgent problem of "anti-Yankeeism" seems not to have produced any victims or costs of any kind. There was no great concern over "anti-Mexicanism" in this period, even though its victims were numerous: American mistreatment of Mexicans, which is partly based on prejudice, is not deemed worthy of the name, whereas Mexican objections to U.S. policies apparently merit denunciation as a malignant "ism."

By the end of the decade, Mexico's President Adolfo López Mateos would neatly sum up his country's perspective during a press conference in Washington before U.S. and Mexican journalists:

Q: "What is the principal problem Mexico faces?"
A: "The principal problem Mexico faces is the United States." (*Laughter and applause.*)[20]

Democratic Anti-Americanism, Pro-American Anti-Democrats

To describe protests against or resistance to U.S. policies as "anti-American" implicitly or explicitly suggests that the opponents are retrograde, antimodern, and hostile to the idea of a free society, but attention to inter-American relations demonstrates how unhelpful this interpretation is when applied to real policies and real events. During much of the twentieth century, U.S. policy actually favored the anti-democratic forces in Latin America, supporting "pro-American" dictators such as Anastasio Somoza of Nicaragua, Rafael Trujillo of the Dominican Republic, and Fulgencio Batista of Cuba, while often opposing democratic and modernizing forces, labeling them "pro-Communist" or "anti-American." The pro- and anti-formula was not only overly simplistic and analytically flawed; it reinforced the very habits of mind that deepened the chasm between North and South.

In 1952, the Psychological Strategy Board (PSB), a unit of the National Security Council reporting to the president and headed by the CIA director with representatives from the Departments of State and Defense, undertook what it called a "national psychological effort" to combat "anti-American attitudes" worldwide. Its plan contained a basic error in logic. The PSB first sensibly acknowledged that "anti-American sentiments and resentments" throughout the "Free World" came from "specific grievances and generalized discontents." Instead of addressing those grievances, however, the Board then recommended greater investment in covert ("non-attributable") propaganda and a larger military profile. To reduce "neutralism and anti-Americanism" in Latin America, the Board recommended "the training and equipping of national military forces" in order to contribute to "the stability of existing governments."[21]

The problem was that the major "resentments" in Latin America were directly related to U.S. support for military dictatorships, the stability of which the Board presented as the remedy for the very ailment it caused. The fall of dictators such as Honduran General Tiburcio Carías, a "consistent supporter of U.S. foreign policy," and their succession by more open governments that brought "newly-enjoyed freedoms of speech, of assembly and of the press" led, according to the State Department, to an increase in "anti-Americanism."[22] A report by the Internal Communications Branch of the CIA two years later held that strengthening Latin American security forces was more important than supporting democracies, because "If the U.S. were to create a climate of total political and economic democracy in Latin America, the Communists would certainly benefit from it and slide easily into power positions."[23]

This basic paradox – supporting dictatorships to defend democracy, while resisting democracy to ensure U.S. predominance – created a cognitive dilemma resolved through a combination of belief in the racial hierarchy of peoples, according to which strongmen were the appropriate governors for immature Latins, and an interpretive framework that viewed even democratically oriented opposition to U.S.-backed dictatorships as anti-American. As Raymond Aron noted after the Cuban Revolution, when reformers "reproach Washington for leniency toward despotism and thus appear to be anti-American, they are treated as enemies by American diplomats."[24] This valence of the term "anti-Americanism" would come to play an essential role in one of the most important events of the Cold War in Latin America: the June 1954 overthrow of Guatemala's democratically elected president, Jacobo Arbenz Guzmán, which the Mexican writer Carlos Fuentes memorably dubbed "a glorious victory against democracy in the name of democracy."[25]

Guatemala's reforms began under Arbenz's predecessor, Juan José Arévalo, who banned forced labor and racial discrimination, instituted a 40-hour work week and called for equal pay for men and women. When Arévalo's six-year term ended in 1950, he was succeeded by Arbenz, who won in a landslide, taking 65 percent of the freest vote in Guatemala's history. In his inaugural address, he promised "to convert Guatemala from a backward country with a predominantly feudal economy into a modern capitalist state."[26] At his urging, the Guatemalan Congress approved an Agrarian Reform Law that distributed small parcels, along with seeds and credits, to 100,000 poor families. Arbenz also invested in health care and education, and maintained freedom of the press. A CIA analysis of the "Personal Political Orientation of President Arbenz" reported that, while the president had some communist advisers, "Arbenz's personal idol is FDR and his reforms are patterned after New Deal reforms."[27] Meanwhile, Guatemala was ignored by Soviet leaders, who had no interest in the distant, impoverished Central American country, sending neither diplomats nor propaganda nor aid. Nonetheless, Eisenhower officials, convinced that Arbenz was a puppet of the Kremlin, armed a proxy rebel force and launched a coup that toppled the government.

This CIA operation was of extraordinary and long-lasting significance for several reasons. It marked the definitive end of the Good Neighbor policy and restored the practice of intervening to oust governments not to Washington's liking, which was the principal cause of Latin American hostility toward the United States. The CIA initially considered the coup a great success – only after it was followed by four decades of repressive military regimes and civil war that killed 200,000 people did U.S. officials come to change their minds – and U.S. presidents used it as a model for subsequent efforts in Cuba at the Bay of Pigs, in British Guiana, in Chile, in Nicaragua, and elsewhere. This made the Guatemalan intervention "the most important event in the history of U.S. relations with Latin America," according to historian Stephen Rabe.[28] Many reformers, who had hoped to address crushing levels of poverty and inequality through the electoral process, concluded that moderate governments could never bring substantial social change because the United States would overthrow them. This contributed to the radicalization of revolutionary movements throughout the region for the remainder of the Cold War. Che Guevara, who had been living in Guatemala in 1954 and whose first political article was entitled "I Saw the Fall of Jacobo Arbenz," drew the lesson that an army must be purified of counterrevolutionary elements, the peasantry armed, opposition suppressed, and other radical measures undertaken to prevent defeat by CIA-backed subversion. His experience helped persuade Fidel Castro to take a hard line after they seized power in Havana.[29]

The Myth of Guatemalan Anti-Americanism

Historians have debated whether the United States intervened to protect the United Fruit Company (UFCO), the country's largest landowner, when it protested the expropriation (with financial compensation) of its uncultivated land, or because the Eisenhower administration was convinced that Arbenz was an agent of international communism. Missing from scholarly accounts has been another factor that led Americans to think that Guatemalan reformers must be acting at the behest of Moscow. As U.S. officials and the press often repeated, Arévalo and Arbenz were "anti-Americans," whose principal objectives were to hurt the United States and its interests. Arévalo's "Red connections and rampant anti-Americanism have caused widespread concern," reported the *Washington Post*; he tilted toward the Communists "because he is anti-American."[30] A CIA report on communist influence in Guatemala claimed, "All of the anti-American and anti-imperialist propaganda was reportedly fomented by Arevalo."[31] Such rhetoric intensified after Arbenz took office. Truman's outgoing secretary of state, Dean Acheson, told the Senate Foreign Relations Committee in January 1952 that "Vociferous anti-American people [are] in the saddle" in Guatemala.[32] The *New York Times* found Guatemala "a thriving source of Soviet anti-Americanism . . . in the very heart of the Americas."[33] Serafino Romualdi, American Federation of Labor representative in Latin America, warned an AFL convention that the "anti-American Communist-Nationalist combine which controls Guatemala" had to be stopped.[34]

This was a crucial error of interpretation. Viewing the country through the Manichean lenses of pro- or anti-Americanism, Americans saw what they expected to see. They did not believe that Arévalo and Arbenz could combine an admiration for Roosevelt's New Deal with good relations with Guatemala's independent communist party to produce sensible and needed reforms. They did not realize that justifiable resentment toward United Fruit, nicknamed "the Octopus" by Guatemalans who saw its tentacles wrapped around their roads, railways, ports, and electrical system, was not the same as blanket hatred for the United States. Nor did they stop to consider that Guatemala continued to vote with the United States on Cold War resolutions at the United Nations under both presidents, as part of "the only bloc of votes we could always count on," according to a State Department official.[35] This placed "anti-American" Guatemala in the position of fulfilling a major U.S. strategic objective in Latin America as established by the National Security Council and approved by Eisenhower: "a. Hemisphere solidarity in support of our world policies, particularly at the U.N. and other international organizations."[36] Yet the overlapping frames of the assumption of Latin American inferiority and the myth of anti-Americanism contributed to the conviction that Guatemala's reform efforts were driven by hostility toward the United States and taken at the behest of a rival power. The pro- or anti-American label was of no value in analyzing Guatemalan developments, but it did explain why the United States saw the events so differently from the rest of the world.

The View from Abroad

With the lens of U.S. assumptions removed, Guatemala looked very different. For the United States was not the only North Atlantic power following events in Guatemala with interest. West Germany had not yet restored diplomatic relations with Guatemala because of a World War II-era dispute over coffee plantations seized from German citizens and nationalized in the 1940s, but this tangible economic grievance, parallel to United Fruit's complaint over the expropriation of some of its lands, did not lead German diplomats to the same conclusions reached by Washington. Ambassador Eugen Klee acknowledged his government's opposition to the Agrarian Reform law that broke up the formerly German-owned holdings, but he argued that "a renunciation of the Good Neighbor and a return to the Big Stick policy [by the United States] should be out of the question, because under current conditions this would have very unpleasant effects in Latin America."[37] Intervening against Guatemala, he added, would bring legitimate charges of "Yankee imperialism."[38]

British officials shared Klee's view. They were pleased to find that Arbenz did not press them on border disputes with British Honduras (later Belize), and observed in 1954 that the broadly popular Arbenz government "adhered to the Constitution and the Opposition were not unduly fettered up to the beginning of the recent crisis."[39] The British minister in Guatemala, Willfred Gallienne, who found U.S. policy "misguided," noted that British-owned farms were "models of compliance" with the agrarian reform program.[40]

The U.S. government and news media turned a Guatemalan purchase of military equipment from Czechoslovakia into evidence of Soviet plans to take over Central America and tried to rally other countries to intercept the shipment. Arbenz had decided to buy the arms after learning that the United States was planning his overthrow and building a mercenary army in neighboring Honduras, and the United States had imposed an arms embargo on Guatemala, even proposing that the U.S. Navy stop and search cargo ships from any nation headed for Guatemala's ports. This would, however, be a violation of international law – a fact recognized by the Justice Department and by Eisenhower's press secretary, James C. Hagerty, who recalled, "we were at war with the British in 1812 over the same principle."[41]

European countries resisted U.S. calls for a blockade. The British delegation in Guatemala City observed that the Czech equipment, mostly small arms and ammunition, was necessary because the army's "present equipment is on its last legs."[42] R.M.B. Chevallier, a British Foreign Office official closely involved in Central American issues, considered U.S. concern to be "hysteria which the circumstances really do not seem to justify," pointed out Guatemala's legitimate right to buy arms for defense, and wondered, "why the *fearful* fuss & bother?"[43] Foreign Secretary Anthony Eden wrote, "I am not convinced that these Guatemalan purchases are so dangerous as the U.S. government profess to believe."[44]

Latin American opinion was even more skeptical. Mexican ambassador to Washington Manuel Tello reported that all the Latin American diplomats he had spoken with were unanimous that Guatemala had the right to buy arms from any country that it wished.[45] The Mexican ambassador to the Organization of American States (OAS), Luis Quintanilla, scoffed at the "communist threat," expressing disbelief at U.S. claims that a Soviet submarine had delivered arms to Guatemalan subversives.[46] The experienced French ambassador in Mexico, Gabriel Bonneau, noted "unanimous sentiment" in sympathy with the Guatemalan position there, where the agrarian reform program was seen as modeled on the Mexican experience, and Mexicans remembered that their country's 1910–1917 revolution had been denounced as Marxist too.[47] Even Cuba's anti-communist dictator Fulgencio Batista refused to support sanctions against Guatemala, and Cuban editorials took the same line.[48]

One of the best-informed diplomats inside Guatemala was the Chilean ambassador, Federico Klein Reidel, a lawyer who knew the country's history well. In a lengthy dispatch, Klein refuted the notion that Guatemala had a socialist or communist government. He ticked off the government's free market economic policies: no currency controls, no import quotas, no restrictions on the export of capital, no government-owned business or industry except for lands taken from the Catholic Church in the nineteenth century and plantations seized from German nationals during the Second World War. Even those, he added, were divided up and privatized through grants to small farmers, not collectivized or turned into state enterprises: "There is nothing that resembles socialized property nor state socialism." As for Guatemala posing a threat to the United States, Klein called this "a material and moral impossibility" because "microscopic Guatemala" could not possibly endanger any other country: the Guatemalan military was weaker than those of its Central American neighbors, which were provided with modern weapons by the United States and could count on resupply in the event of a crisis. There was simply no basis in reality for considering Guatemala a Soviet beachhead.[49]

Thus a perceptual chasm separated American views of Guatemala from those of Cold War allies who could observe the situation free of assumptions about American exceptionalism. American officials' confidence in their own centrality and superior knowledge trapped them in a reductive interpretation that read developments abroad as either pro- or anti-American, rather than as generated by political processes that did not have the United States at their center. A dispatch from the British Legation in Guatemala bemoaned "the complex which tends to beset Americans here – in spite of all their friendliness – namely that they are the only people who really count in this part of the world."[50] The problem was exacerbated by the fact that, although a few among the seventy American diplomats in Guatemala were skilled and knowledgeable, most high-ranking U.S. officials knew little about Latin America. U.S. Ambassador John Peurifoy spoke no Spanish but painted with broad strokes. Guatemalans "are very placid, except when they get under the influence of whiskey," he said. "They are not jolly. They don't smile much. It is such a contrast to Greece," he added wistfully, referring to his previous post, where he had helped a military government crush a left-wing revolt.[51]

Many Americans indulged in the usual view of Latin Americans as immature and easily manipulated by outside powers. This appeared in the standard press treatments: Guatemala was "the problem child of the American continent," a "rebellious child," "the incorrigible bad boy."[52] Secretary Dulles spoke of Latin Americans as if they were children, saying, "You have to pat them on the head and make them think that you are fond of them."[53] A State Department report claimed that trying to reason with Latin Americans was "rather like consulting with babies as to whether or not we should take candy away from them."[54] This condescension was not merely offensive; it contributed to the analytical failure by making Guatemalans seem incapable of controlling their own actions in their own interests.

That could account for the pronounced difference between U.S. and non-U.S. perceptions. Increasing signs of preparations for a coup reached foreign governments, causing alarm among those puzzled by the American obsession with the Central American country. A British diplomat driving around rural Guatemala was startled to come across Americans who sought "evidence of a police state, and gazed apprehensively at the *sub-jefe* of the Guardia Civil, a pathetic old man (and a good friend of ours) who has not been paid for four months."[55] A British manager at Shell Oil reported the rather "odd" behavior of alleged U.S. "tourists" who "kept dropping into his office and saying 'have you got plenty of fuel, aviation spirit and so on and where is it kept.'"[56] (The oil storage tanks would be a prime target of rebel bombing once the coup began.)[57] The French mission in the Honduran capital monitored air shipments of cases of U.S. arms and munitions to the rebel staging areas near the Guatemalan border.[58] The Mexican ambassador in Tegucigalpa likewise reported that six U.S. cargo planes loaded with arms arrived in Honduras from the Canal Zone.[59] Ecuador and Bolivia approached Mexico through diplomatic channels to try to develop a common strategy to oppose U.S. pressure on Guatemala.[60]

American officials denied any intention of intervening. Senator Alexander Wiley (R-WI), Chairman of the Senate Foreign Relations Committee, took umbrage at the very suggestion: "This is a lie which is even lower than the usual level of Red falsehood," Wiley thundered. "The United States does not seek to exercise dominion over any people. The United States believes in a policy of non-intervention and noninterference."[61] State Department officials offered similar assurances, telling the Chilean ambassador, Aníbal Jara, that Guatemalan charges of a U.S. covert campaign were "false and ridiculous."[62] When 194 Mexican intellectuals, lawyers, journalists, artists, and doctors signed a petition published in the conservative papers *Excelsior* and *El Universal* stating that Guatemala was threatened by foreign invasion, Franklin G. Gowen, counselor of the U.S. Embassy in Mexico, dismissed it as "anti-American propaganda" produced by "ultra-nationalists and gringo-haters."[63]

All of these denials were made while the CIA was already at an advanced stage of coup preparations. Operation PBSUCCESS to bring regime change to Guatemala had been proposed and planned in the summer and fall of 1953 and formally approved on December 9. It was authorized in line with an amendment to the National Security Council directive 144/1. That document originally called for continuing the Good Neighbor policy by "Refraining from overt unilateral intervention in the internal political affairs of the other American states, in accordance with existing treaty obligations." On March 18, 1953, the NSC amended that paragraph to add

> In the event the inter-American system should fail to protect vital United States national interests in this hemisphere, it is recognized that unilateral action by the United States may be necessary.[64]

With this directive, President Eisenhower formally abrogated two decades of Good Neighbor promises and returned to the interventionist policies of the Bad Neighbor that had so embittered Latin American opinion toward the United States. The administration then moved unilaterally by building an invasion force in Honduras, convinced that Americans understood better than anyone else what was truly at stake in Guatemala – and that divergent opinions were illegitimate.

1954: The Fracas in Caracas

Before launching the coup against Arbenz, the Eisenhower administration sought support in Latin America by calling together an inter-American diplomatic conference at Caracas, Venezuela. What followed provides a nearly perfect illustration of the North-South perceptual divide. On one side, as reported by American officials and journalists, there was a glittering success of American diplomacy, a "personal triumph" for Secretary Dulles, who rallied U.S. allies and routed the "bush league Reds."[65] The conference, and the coup that followed, were "a clear-cut victory for the United States and for hemispheric solidarity," claimed the leading diplomatic historian Thomas A. Bailey.[66] But when he stepped through the looking glass at Caracas, Dulles encountered an array of determined Latin American diplomats who fiercely opposed a return to interventionism and wrested the agenda from his hands, completely transforming the meaning of the event. This contrast between U.S. and Latin American perceptions explains why an American "triumph" was actually a fiasco that greatly increased the scale of outrage when the CIA moved against Guatemala – outrage that would, once again, be misinterpreted as "anti-Americanism."[67]

On March 13, 1954, the 10th Inter-American Conference voted in favor of a resolution against Communist inroads in the Americas. The vote was reported as 17 to 1 in favor, with only Guatemala voting against. U.S. officials and the press held up this result as a sign of hemispheric unity behind American leadership. "At Caracas a Vote of Confidence for the U.S." headlined the *Baltimore Sun*.[68] In his memoirs, Eisenhower praised "the strength of the inter-American resolve" embodied in the resolution. To have failed to arm the anti-Arbenz forces afterwards, Eisenhower claimed, would have been "contrary to the letter and spirit of the Caracas resolution," as if the diplomacy at Caracas had forced his hand: "The American republics wanted no Communist regime within their midst," he wrote. The coup against Guatemala, in other words, was the result of a pan-American consensus that Arbenz must be overthrown.[69]

Digging into the record of Caracas, however, yields a remarkably different picture of what happened at the meeting. Instead of a hemisphere united against Communist aggression, what emerges is a sordid tale of a desperate U.S. effort to create the illusion of Latin American support for action against Guatemala by engaging in bullying, vote buying, and concessions that did not merely water down the American draft resolution but reversed it from a license to intervene into a prohibition against intervention. Caracas signified the opposite of what Eisenhower claimed.

The lopsided voting tally and talk of Dulles's "triumph" obscured some basic facts. The total was actually 17–1–2, with two of the most powerful Latin American countries, Mexico and Argentina, abstaining. Of the sixteen that voted with the United States, half were dictatorships dependent on aid from Washington for their survival. Dulles acknowledged as much in an executive session of the House Committee on Foreign Affairs. "It was more or less assumed that we would have the support of the so-called dictator countries," he admitted, "and their support was sometimes a bit embarrassing."[70]

Even dictators, however, needed some persuasion, because the U.S. position that Guatemala was a danger was so out of step with the prevailing view in the region. To reach the final vote, the U.S. government began with lavish vote buying, ran into stern and principled opposition, and then ultimately abandoned the core elements of its diplomatic agenda. The strategy was straightforward: the usually fiscally conservative Republican administration made multimillion dollar deals benefiting each country that it was courting at the expense of U.S. producers, taxpayers, or consumers. Uruguay received an exemption from a planned 18% tariff on its principal export. With Cabinet approval, once in Caracas, Dulles told the head of the Uruguayan delegation, José A. Mora, that Eisenhower would veto wool tariffs if the Uruguayans voted with the United States on the anti-communist resolution.[71] Dulles then announced that the Export-Import Bank, which had frozen loans to Latin America, would resume lending, beginning with $12 million for the Cuban Electric Company.[72] Venezuela, host of the conference, received a three-year exemption from oil import quotas (enraging U.S. oilmen), a benefit worth about $100 million per year.[73] The administration also expedited more than $10 million in military sales to Venezuela, waiving restrictions on advanced equipment.[74] Eisenhower topped off the package in November by decorating Venezuela's dictator Marcos Pérez Jiménez with the Legion of Merit.[75] For Chile, the United States reversed its position and purchased 100,000 tons of copper above the market price, a $60 million deal that settled Chilean government balance sheets for the year.[76] Price-fixing investigations by the Federal Trade Commission and the Senate Banking Committee threatened to result in caps and lower income to coffee exporters, but Dulles persuaded the Cabinet to ignore public sentiment and promise that there would be no ceiling set on coffee prices, just in time for him to announce the news at Caracas that a billion-dollar export market for Latin American producers had been preserved.[77]

Other emoluments were simpler. Costa Rica received accelerated delivery of arms shipments.[78] Peru obtained a $30 million loan a week before the opening gavel, "permitting this government to participate in the Caracas Conference in relatively satisfactory conditions."[79] Bolivia received $4 million in "special economic aid" and another $3 million in food assistance.[80] Colombia, the only Latin American country to have sent troops to fight alongside Americans in the Korean War, had accrued a $10 million debt for using American equipment and logistical support there.[81] As Dulles ran into stiff resistance in Caracas, the Cabinet met again, and Eisenhower authorized forgiveness of the Colombian debt, added $7 million for construction on the Pan-American Highway, and approved another $10.5 million in various aid programs.[82] Reporting the latest round of Cabinet decisions to Dulles by cable, Undersecretary Smith told him that they "can be communicated quietly to any delegation you think it may influence." Dulles promptly paid a visit to the Colombian foreign minister to inform him confidentially that the debt would be forgiven.[83]

Tallying these measures makes clear that hundreds of millions of dollars were at stake in the various deals, either in the form of direct payments or loans from the U.S. government and related institutions, or in access to the U.S. market on preferential terms in competition with American producers or financed by American consumers. Spending vast sums to obtain a diplomatic objective, of course, is a hallowed practice in international relations. But in this case, the objective itself was not achieved.

The original U.S. resolution called for "appropriate action in accordance with existing treaties" to combat "the domination of any American State by the international communist movement" or "an extracontinental power."[84] Dulles later explained to the NSC that his main goal at Caracas was to obtain agreement that "Communist subversion" was "tantamount to external aggression," so that the resolution would enable the United States to "avoid the charge of interference in the affairs of any other sovereign state" when it proceeded with action against Guatemala.[85]

Latin American delegates understood this intention perfectly, and most did not agree with it. Latin American diplomacy since the late nineteenth century has developed a tradition known as *principismo*, marked by legalism, the defense of national sovereignty, and an effort to rein in powerful states. This approach emerged from each end of Latin America, developed especially by Argentina and Mexico, regional powers whose particular relationship to the United States was shaped by their geographical location: one so far away that it developed a self-conscious identity as an opposing pole for orientation in the inter-American system, one so close that its entire foreign policy was developed in the shadow of its powerful neighbor. Mexico's commitment to the principles of nonintervention and juridical equality of states could be expected of a country that had lost half its territory in war. Obsessed with intervention because it has been the object of the obsessive attentions of intervening powers, Mexico made nonintervention the foundation of its foreign policy. For years, Argentina, too, had been raising objections to the U.S. deployment of overwhelming force in the Americas. At a 1928 inter-American conference held in Havana, the Argentine delegation led broad Latin American demand for an agreement against intervention in light of three decades of U.S. Marine landings in Central America and the Caribbean. The accord would come during the era of the Franklin Roosevelt administration's Good Neighbor policy, codified at inter-American conferences in 1933 and 1936, the first affirming that "no state has the right to intervene in the internal or external affairs of another" and the second prohibiting intervention "directly or indirectly, and for whatever reason, in the internal or external affairs of the parties."[86]

It was with these traditions of *principismo* firmly established – not because of cultural or emotional resentment of the United States – that Mexico and Argentina staked out their opposition to the U.S. resolution on Guatemala at

Caracas. The Argentine delegate, Foreign Minister Jerónimo Remorino, carried instructions to ensure the inclusion of a clause that "preserves the sovereign right of American peoples to decide their own destiny and give themselves their own political institutions."[87] In his opening remarks, Remorino invoked "the principle of non-intervention in internal and external affairs, and the juridical equality of states." Any weakening of the nonintervention principle, he warned, would "deal a death blow to the free self-determination of the peoples of America."[88]

Dulles listened to the words but did not realize they were embedded in a tradition of diplomatic principle widely shared in the whole region. He heard only, as he complained to an aide, that Argentina "seemed inclined to 'play footsie' with the Guatemalans."[89] Although Dulles would have liked to ignore the Argentines, other delegations took up the cause. The Bolivian delegate stated that the resolution could not be used in reference to the internal politics of any country. The Chilean delegate said the principle of nonintervention was at the heart of the inter-American system, and his country could not accept any action that would undermine this principle.[90] At key moments during the negotiations, the United States found itself almost alone, with supporters of its position reduced to Brazil, Panama, and Nicaragua, and then to only Brazil (which in 1953 had received more than $50 million in military aid from Washington).[91] Even the Brazilian delegate, the closest ally of the United States at the conference, whose instructions were "to vote in agreement with the United States delegation," noted that the best protection against "infectious germs of subversive ideologies" was not "intervention in the internal affairs" of any country but "raising the standard of living."[92]

The sharpest riposte came from the Uruguayan delegate, Foreign Minister Justino Jiménez de Aréchaga, who represented the strongest democracy in Latin America and who most directly confronted the U.S. arguments. "We are not afraid of the international character of political movements in general. We not afraid of the internationalization of ideas," he said.[93] "Uruguay, following its constitutional precepts that enshrine freedom of expression and freedom of thought, cannot accept norms or recommendations that tend to limit the diffusion of these or other ideas."[94] Latin American opposition to U.S. policy on Guatemala might appear as so much "anti-Americanism" to observers in the United States,[95] but these arguments were made in favor of democratic principles, not against them.

Caving In

Faced with this united front of opposition, Dulles surrendered. In the event of foreign ideological intervention in the Americas, instead of Washington's "call for appropriate action," the resolution as amended at the insistence of Latin American delegates read "call for a meeting of consultation to consider the adoption of appropriate action" – a watery phrase that ensured Latin American governments would have another opportunity to restrain the United

States at a future meeting. Dulles did get the language that he wanted, saying that "the domination or control of the political institutions of any American State by the international communist movement...would constitute a threat to the sovereignty and political independence of the American States." But the final paragraph gutted any possible interventionist reading of the summit's outcome:

> This declaration...is designed to protect and not to impair the inalienable right of each American State freely to choose its own form of government and economic system and to live its own social and cultural life.[96]

This second change, proposed by Mexico and seconded by Uruguay, turned a resolution for action against Guatemala into a resolution prohibiting action against Guatemala. Some of those who voted yes nonetheless did so apprehensively. One delegate told a reporter that distasteful as it was to vote for a resolution that the United States had intended as a means to pressure Guatemala, it was best to try to exercise a moderating influence. "If we did not agree, the U.S. might resort to unilateral action," he said. "That would be far worse."[97] Argentina abstained, standing by its traditional opposition to diplomatic moves that might infringe on the national sovereignty of any state. The Mexican delegate said that his country could not vote for the resolution because it might be used in the future to return to interventionism. "We have seen it in the past," he said. "Mexico has suffered interventions in its territory...We know what we are talking about."[98] Mexico's stance at Caracas, predictably, became the first item of evidence in a *New York Times* story claiming that "anti-Yankeeism is on the rise in Mexico to an alarming degree."[99]

The Italian Foreign Ministry noted that the emphasis on nonintervention in the resolution had ruined the main U.S. objective.[100] The Italian view was neatly summarized in the newspaper *Il Tempo*, which understood the draft resolution had been transformed from its original intention of giving a "free hand" to the United States and was now an anti-interventionist accord: "Now it is certain that the United States cannot intervene in any way whatsoever in that small Central American republic if they do not want to run the risk of alienating nearly all the countries of Latin America."[101]

1954: The Coup

That, of course, is precisely what happened next. Invigorated by its incongruously triumphant reading of Caracas, the Eisenhower administration proceeded to launch its coup against the Guatemalan government, instantly alienating nearly all the countries of Latin America. That surprised the administration – why would a hemisphere united in its anti-communism react negatively when the United States acted against communism? The cognitive dissonance was assuaged with the usual reminder about Latin American behavior: emotional and irrational anti-Americanism, rather than diplomatic consistency and principled outrage, caused the protests against the American-backed coup.

Although the Eisenhower administration initially denied all involvement, the world was not convinced. The CIA spent at least $7 million to build a force of several hundred mercenaries in Honduras, trained by Americans and backed by three Thunderbolt fighter-bomber planes flown by American pilots. The Agency selected Carlos Castillo Armas, a "bold but incompetent" Guatemalan colonel, in his handler's words, to lead the force.[102] On June 18, the rebels crossed the border and immediately bogged down, outfought in skirmishes with Guatemalan troops and police. Castillo Armas pleaded for air support, supported by Peurifoy. "Bomb repeat Bomb," the ambassador cabled Allen Dulles.[103] Eisenhower approved the dispatch of three more Thunderbolts, which bombed towns and strafed roads in Guatemala, machine-gunned a girls' school, blew up the radio station of a Protestant missionary from New Jersey, and sank a British cargo ship. CIA propagandists circulated stories of large rebel columns converging on Guatemala City. Arbenz, believing his capital to be under attack by the world's most powerful country, ceded power to Guatemalan officers who promised to continue his reforms. Peurifoy swept them aside to make way for Castillo Armas to take over.

Eisenhower was overjoyed. "Thanks, Allen, and thanks to all of you," he told a group of CIA officers assembled at the White House. "You've averted a Soviet beachhead in our hemisphere."[104] Secretary Dulles was "elated" over the "happier situation" in Guatemala: It was, he said, a "great triumph" for American diplomacy, "the biggest success in the last five years against Communism."[105] The House Select Committee on Communist Aggression called it "one of the few clear-cut victories for the West in the cold war." The only problem was a rise in "anti-Yanquism," which the Committee blamed on a failure "to counter Communist propaganda." In other words, Latin Americans needed only to be better informed, and then they would be pleased with the coup.[106]

The view from abroad was quite different. Once the invasion began, the United Nations immediately became the scene of an international effort to stop the coup. "My people . . . are being machine-gunned," cried Guatemala's U.N. ambassador, Eduardo Castillo Arriola, in an appeal to the Security Council.[107] French and British diplomats went into action. The French ambassador to the United Nations, Henri Hoppenot, had spent time in Guatemala that winter, and he backed a Guatemalan request for Security Council intercession.[108] British officials joined in to support a resolution calling for "the immediate termination of any action likely to cause bloodshed," the end of "assistance to any such action," and the dispatch of a U.N. commission to Guatemala.[109] This led to days and nights of intense diplomatic wrangling with their U.S. counterparts, and not a few shouting matches. Ambassador Henry Cabot Lodge responded with "bad humor and clenched teeth" and tried to sidetrack Guatemala's complaint to the Organization of American States.[110] Hoppenot quoted Lodge's own remark only a day before the Guatemala meeting, when in connection with a request from Thailand regarding violence in Southeast Asia, Lodge had declared, "I hope that I will never live to see the day when a small country comes to the United Nations and asks for protection against war and is simply greeted with the question: what is the hurry?"[111] Robert Speaight in the British Foreign Office noted that although the U.N. Charter allows members to use regional arrangements before turning to the Security Council, the U.S. argument that Guatemala therefore had no right to appeal to the United Nations before going through the OAS overlooked Article 52, section IV, which says that the existence of regional organizations "in no way impairs" the right of any member state to go to the Security Council.[112] On June 24, a clearly irritated Dulles called in the French ambassador in Washington, Henri Bonnet, to demand that Hoppenot follow Lodge's lead.[113] He pursued Bonnet at a dinner that night, vehemently denouncing the lack of solidarity on the part of the French and the British.[114]

If anything, Dulles was angrier at the British. In a tirade "full of exaggerations and inaccuracies," he told British Ambassador Sir Roger Makins that London's support on Guatemala "might well be the touchstone of the Anglo-American alliance."[115] Finally matters were settled at the very top. Eisenhower ordered Dulles to "show the British that they have no right to stick their nose into matters which concern this hemisphere entirely.... Let's give them a lesson."[116] Dulles met Eden and Prime Minister Winston Churchill at the Washington airport and threatened to withdraw U.S. support for the British in the Middle East and for the French in North Africa if they did not fall into line.[117] Eden and Churchill caved in, and the French followed. The European career diplomats involved were appalled at this instance of crass *realpolitik*, calling the decision to yield to U.S. bullying "fantastic," "indefensible," an act that "will surely wreck the moral authority of the United Nations."[118] But Churchill overruled his Foreign Service. He did not think the issue was important enough to risk alienating the United States and losing its support for British global interests. "I'd never heard of this bloody place Guatemala until I was in my seventy-ninth year," he fumed, and insisted on accepting the U.S. line in public.[119] That shut down the U.N. effort to stop the coup.

A Global Backlash from Pro-Americans

In his memoirs, Eisenhower justified his support for Castillo Armas's forces by invoking the Caracas resolution and claimed, "The rest of Latin America was not in the least displeased."[120] Reading the international press and diplomatic reports from the far-flung embassies of several countries shows the contrary: that the coup elicited overwhelmingly negative response from around the globe and that criticism did not fall along Cold War lines but crossed the political spectrum. Much of what Americans dismissed as "anti-American" criticism derived instead from different perspectives, allowing foreigners who worked outside the frame of pro- or anti-Americanism to develop much better information, reaching positions that were not incompatible with "American ideals," and would have served as a guide to better policy had the United States been more open to foreign opinion.

The French press was highly critical, regardless of party affiliation. The anti-Stalinist paper linked to Albert Camus, *Combat*, called the coup a "Pyrrhic victory" that damaged U.S. and U.N. prestige, handed the Communists a powerful argument, and represented "one of the terrible examples of injustice in History."[121] *Le Monde* found it "strange that the great republic that...considers itself the model of democracies openly favors dictatorships installed by force."[122] Anthropologist Jacques Soustelle, one of France's leading Latin Americanists, member of Parliament, and an adviser to the rightist *Rassemblement du Peuple Français*, wrote an impassioned attack on the intervention. "The first victim of this senseless war was not little Leticia Torres, murdered by unmarked planes that bombed the flowering city of Guatemala; it is the confidence that the Latin Americans can place in their neighbors to the north." Echoing the Mexican economist Iturriaga, he argued, "Go tell a Mayan peasant from Atitlán that his Enemy No. 1 is Russia...he will reply that it was not Russian planes that bombed Guatemala!"[123]

The most staunchly anti-communist of the major European allies, West Germany, was also the scene of outrage at the coup. Its leading conservative newspaper, the *Frankfurter Allgemeine Zeitung*, editorialized on its front page that "whoever wishes to fight the tyranny of Bolshevism must have clean hands," but the coup had vitiated America's moral standing in the Cold War: "The image of the United States as the leader of the West is endangered," the paper concluded.[124] British officials in West Germany expressed surprise at the extent to which traditionally Atlanticist voices there were critical of the United States role in the coup. The *Bonner Rundschau*, a paper close to the anti-communist Christian Democratic government, defended Arbenz's reforms as "socially and economically justified" and suspected the influence of the banana companies behind U.S. support for the rebels. The liberal *Frankfurter Rundschau* wrote that it was not possible to take Guatemala seriously as a danger to the United States or to the Panama Canal, and that if the Eisenhower administration had truly felt threatened, it should have taken up the issue at the U.N. Security Council.[125]

The British press, too, was broadly critical. The *Economist* wrote that in this "War Through the Looking Glass" the United States had lost more than it had gained and would see mistrust increase among the smaller nations of the world.[126] For a Latin American politics expert writing in the *Observer*, the coup brought back "memories of United States intervention in Mexico, Haiti, Nicaragua and the Dominican Republic....The U.S. will be more feared, less loved."[127] The British Foreign Office found that public opinion in Britain was solidly critical of the U.S. overthrow of the Arbenz government.[128] Diplomats fielding appeals by trade unions and Labor Party organizations struggled to find reasonable formulas for defending Churchill's defense of the coup. "I wish we *had* more irrefutable facts," grumbled one official.[129]

Criticism flowed in from all of America's friends. Canada's *Ottawa Citizen* editorialized that the United States had damaged the cause of all Western countries, which cannot "afford to have a U.S.-hating peasantry in

Latin-America, with only the Communists to turn to for support in their desire for a better life."[130] A Danish paper wrote that the coup had "weakened the confidence of the Danish people in the United States," reflecting a widely held sentiment, according to the French Embassy in Copenhagen.[131] Swedish newspapers wrote that the coup showed imperialism and McCarthyism were alive and well.[132] The conservative *Svenska Dagbladet* stated flatly that Guatemala had never posed a threat and that the rebels were getting aid from the United States.[133] "The same story all over Europe," observed a British official reading the reports.[134]

Shock and anger were expressed around the world. In Arab countries, "rightist and government-controlled papers as well as the leftist press widely interpreted the Guatemalan affair as an example of U.S. colonialism." Mainstream Israeli papers published equally critical editorials. Condemnation of the intervention against a legally elected government came from Ceylon, Burma, Japan, Vietnam, and Indonesia. Even in India's conservative *Statesman*, one could read that "if there was nothing wrong in US encouragement to right-wing insurgents in Central America, there was nothing wrong with Chinese support of left-wing insurgents in Southeast Asia." The only support seems to have come from a few right-wing papers in Greece, Turkey, Taiwan, and South Korea, all countries heavily dependent on U.S. aid – and even some of them acknowledged the legitimacy of Guatemala's land reform.[135]

The most sustained and strongest criticism came, of course, from Latin Americans, who seemed to fear a return of U.S. intervention and the end of the Good Neighbor policy. Assistant Secretary of State for inter-American affairs Henry Holland saw "serious anti-American consequences in a number of Latin American states."[136] In Venezuela, host of the recent conference aimed at preventing precisely what had taken place, public opinion and the press now sympathized with Guatemala, and "sharp criticism in diplomatic circles" was expressed against the United States as "resentment felt by many Latin Americans" over the Caracas fiasco was "rekindled."[137] Costa Rica's democratic president, José Figueres, angrily denounced the United States for returning to the era of the Big Stick and for "seeing communists everywhere."[138]

In Uruguay, dubbed a model democracy by Eisenhower, the Chamber of Deputies passed a resolution condemning the attack on Guatemala, backed by every political party from left to right.[139] Italian diplomats there observed "a true moral uprising against Washington's policy, and against the methods of that government, not only specifically against Guatemala but in dealing with all the Latin American countries. This uprising is expressed in every forum and in every circle."[140] Chile's Ambassador Klein in Guatemala told his ministry that many Latin American diplomats there believed the United States was committing "a grave error . . . it will produce a profound resentment in *nuestra América*," he wrote, using José Martí's term.[141]

While Mexican artist Diego Rivera painted a mural showing the Dulles brothers passing money to Castillo Armas over the bodies of dead Guatemalan children, across Latin America anger over the coup erupted in the streets.[142] In

Buenos Aires, Mexico City, Havana, Rio de Janeiro, and Santiago, large crowds of protestors burned the American flag and effigies of Dulles and Eisenhower. "No one could recall so intense and universal a wave of anti-U.S. sentiment in the entire history of Latin America," wrote Daniel James, hired by the State Department to prepare a lengthy report on Guatemala.[143] Secretary Dulles told his brother that officials at the State Department were so "frightened by reactions all over" that they complained that "we can't carry on very well at the diplomatic level the way things are.... Demonstrations are bad."[144] The Secretary was unrepentant, however, dismissing all the "anti-Americanism" across Latin America as Communist-inspired and of no consequence. "The Reds...throughout the Americas are presently staging anti-America demonstrations in every capital," he summarized, "but cannot do anything but make a lot of noise."[145] CIA reports acknowledged that "a great segment of public opinion in Latin America" opposed the attack on Guatemala but claimed that the demonstrations "revealed a surprising and embarrassing influence of Communists on public opinion."[146]

One might try to imagine a response in which the U.S. government, taking seriously the evidence of this overwhelming international rejection of its conduct, might have reassessed the decision to launch the coup and reevaluated the policy-making process that led to such a globally unpopular action. Instead, Secretary Dulles yearned for more unilateralism, remarking that "the happiest day of his life will be when we don't have to modify our policies etc. to keep up a façade of unity."[147] Faced with the anger of a disapproving world, the Eisenhower administration responded the way the U.S. government often responded to opposition abroad during the Cold War and beyond: dismissively toward the content of the complaints, and by launching a public relations and propaganda campaign. Declassified CIA documents show that the Agency's Psychological and Paramilitary Operations Staff coordinated an international effort to "counteract unfavorable world reaction to the recent events in Guatemala." Field agents tried to plant positive stories in news outlets in Albania, Denmark, the Federal Republic of Germany, Greece, Italy, Japan, Malaya, the Netherlands, Norway, the Philippines, Sweden, Thailand, and the Vatican.[148] It had no more success in Britain, where the Foreign Office rejected as "ridiculous" the CIA's suggestion that the press be told that the United States had not been involved in the coup.[149] When on July 1 Dulles gave a speech reiterating that Guatemala had been an outpost of international Communist conspiracy, Speaight found it "distressing.... In places it might almost be Molotov speaking about e.g. Czechoslovakia – or Hitler about Austria!"[150] Chevallier wrote a point-by-point rebuttal of Dulles's "dubious claims," showing that Moscow had never taken an interest in Guatemala, that the Caracas conference demonstrated the power of U.S. pressure rather than hemispheric unity, that ordinary Guatemalans had not joined any uprisings against Arbenz, and that British opinion was "now undoubtedly on the side of the ousted regime."[151] As a self-study by the United States Information Agency at the end of the year put it, "American actions have an effect on foreign public opinion which far outshadows anything done by the Information Program.... Propaganda can never be better than policy."[152]

Too many U.S. observers isolated themselves from world opinion either by not taking any notice of it or by explaining it away in the same manner as Dulles. The National Security Council quickly resumed blaming "anti-Americanism" on the fact that "many Latin Americans are jealous and resentful of the size and wealth of the United States."[153] Guatemala faded from the headlines in the aftermath of the coup, as Castillo Armas evicted the 100,000 families who had received land under the agrarian reform, abolished all political parties, stripped the vote from the majority of uneducated peasants, and banned labor unions. He then had his reign ratified by a phony plebiscite in which he received 99.99% of the vote.[154] As his security forces began arresting and executing hundreds of his opponents, unleashing four decades of bloodletting by successive military regimes pitted against a determined peasant uprising, the Mexican Embassy located across from the presidential palace in Guatemala City took in asylum seekers fleeing for their lives. The State Department reacted swiftly to Castillo Armas's hunt for Arbenz loyalists: it sent emissaries to press the Mexicans to hand the refugees over to the Guatemalan regime to meet their fates.[155] Only later, much later, would an element of regret filter into U.S. memory of the coup. In 1980, a U.S. official, trying to cajole Guatemala's brutal ultrarightist regime to institute some of the same reforms for which the CIA had overthrown Arbenz, surveyed the bloody Guatemalan landscape and confessed to a reporter: "What we'd give to have an Arbenz now."[156]

1958: Another Fracas in Caracas

In the spring of 1958, Eisenhower's Vice President, Richard Nixon, embarked on a goodwill tour of South America, where, the NSC reported, he came face to face with "anti-Americanism." Demonstrators in Peru "shouted anti-American slogans" and threw rocks and eggs at his motorcade. Others yelled all night in front of Nixon's hotel in Colombia. In Caracas, a hostile crowd at the airport spat so vigorously on Nixon's entourage that he thought he was being pelted with water balloons. A mob stormed his limousine on the open highway, beating the car with metal pipes and nearly overturning it before his driver was able to speed away and deliver Nixon to the safety of the U.S. Embassy.[157] An enraged President Eisenhower put a thousand Marines on alert and considered extracting Nixon by helicopter, while reports came in of other anti-American demonstrations in Burma, Lebanon, and France.[158] There was a shocked sense in the White House that a quiescent world had suddenly and inexplicably turned hostile. "Another of the worst days of our lives," wrote Eisenhower's private secretary Ann Whitman in her diary. The president fumed. "I am about ready to go put my uniform on," he snapped.[159]

The uproar in Latin America – Walter Lippmann dubbed it "a diplomatic Pearl Harbor" – caught U.S. officials completely off guard.[160] Only two months before, Roy Rubottom, the State Department's top official for Latin American affairs, had appeared at a Senate hearing, where Senator J. William Fulbright (D-AR) asked him: "Do you believe, Mr. Rubottom, that there is widespread discontent in Latin America with United States policies?" Rubottom blithely replied, "No, sir; I do not."[161]

The source of discontent in Caracas should not have been mysterious. Not only had Eisenhower recently granted asylum to deposed Venezuelan strong-man Marcos Pérez Jiménez and his despised secret police chief, the torturer Pedro Estrada, but his administration had then imposed oil quotas on the country for the first time – an act generally interpreted by Venezuelans as "punishment" for their having ousted a "pro-American" dictator, one upon whom Eisenhower had bestowed a medal.[162]

Reactions to the Caracas incident revealed a good deal about the perceptual gap between North and South. Venezuela's reformist politician and future pres-ident, Rómulo Betancourt, who would become a key ally of John F. Kennedy, blamed anger over U.S. support for coups and dictatorships.[163] Costa Rica's President Figueres observed, "People cannot spit on a foreign policy, which is what they meant to do."[164] The NSC, on the other hand, thought the fault lay elsewhere: the Soviet Union had "used its propaganda and diplomatic apparatus to foster anti-American sentiments" in areas afflicted by "misunder-standings . . . about the United States." Communist disinformation was evident, according to a lengthy State Department report, in the words appearing on ban-ners carried by student protestors such as "Little Rock," "Guatemala," and "McCarthyism" – textual clues to the true sources of anger; instead they were read by U.S. officials as a sign of ignorance. Interestingly, Radio Moscow and other Soviet propaganda outlets reaching Latin America had not stepped up their criticism of the United States before or during Nixon's trip – a point stressed by the State Department to excuse its officers for failing to anticipate the protests, but one that rather undermined the claim that Moscow was behind the upheaval.[165]

Nixon drew a different kind of lesson. A "democratic form of government," he asserted, "may not always be in each country the best of all possible courses, particularly in those Latin American countries which are completely lacking in political maturity."[166] *Time* magazine reported on the basis of an interview with Nixon that the riots were produced by "hate-building emotion" derived from "envy" and "Latin American embarrassment over the political imma-turity shown in the frequency of revolutions." Attacks on the United States, *Time* assured its readers, "are simply irrational."[167] Thomas L. Hughes, direc-tor of the State Department's Research and Intelligence Division, was soon blaming the students' "immaturity, spotty academic training, parochialism, and general frustration."[168] A Senate study on "Communist Anti-American Riots" blamed the "anti-American emotional climate" among "uninformed and excitable teenagers, students, and illiterates." What perplexed the senators was why on earth anyone should object to U.S. policies, since "the traditions of American diplomacy are predicated upon peaceful negotiation with duly authorized representatives of other nations on the basis of solemn agreements and treaties, in accord with international law and usage."[169] That assertion was made only six years after the Guatemalan coup and in the midst of planning for the Bay of Pigs invasion, and it was matched by Nixon's assertion that "our policies and actions were generally correct." The need therefore was not for a rethinking of policy, but for renewed efforts "to get our story across" to ordinary people, to "join the battle in Latin America on the field of propaganda."[170]

Nor did allegedly scientific surveying of public opinion come to different conclusions, because it operated within the same limiting framework. In a five-country survey about the anti-Nixon demonstrations, International Research Associates asked Latin Americans to say who had organized the protests, and provided its pollsters with a list of anticipated responses. These ranged from the sinister ("Communists," "Professional Agitators," "Fascists") to the vague ("Leftists," "Nationalists"), and from the generic ("Students," "Workers") to the illogical ("Almost Everybody"). There was no category on the list for Venezuelans who were angry that the United States had conferred a medal and a visa upon the dictator they had recently overthrown, nor for Latin Americans embittered over the fate of Guatemala's democracy.[171] That the demonstrators' cries of "Little Rock! Little Rock!" might have arisen from a concern about racial injustice among a nonwhite population keenly aware of the civil rights struggles in the United States was acknowledged in the United States only in the black press.[172]

Failing to understand the phenomenon made it no less worrisome. By mid-1958, the NSC listed "yankeephobia" as a leading threat to U.S. interests in Latin America.[173]

1959–1961: A Revolution in Anti-Americanism

After the attack on Nixon, senior research staff at the CIA called for a "serious and objective study of anti-Americanism" worldwide. Then came the Cuban revolution of 1959, lending urgency to the question of anti-Americanism in Latin America even as officials maintained their belief in Latin American psychological pathology.[174] White House and State Department officials reported that the "unreasoning" Fidel Castro "had a broad streak of irrationality on the Hitler pattern" and that he had "gone haywire." Eisenhower called him a "madman."[175] Castro's "psychotic anti-American campaign" was falling on fertile ground, thanks to Latin Americans' predilection for impassioned, unthinking behavior.[176] Such views were bipartisan. Senator Thomas Dodd (D-CT) denounced "the berserk anti-American propaganda conducted by Castro." Senator Barry Goldwater (R-AZ) thought Castro's triumph was "a shot of adrenalin to latent anti-Americanism, and today that ugly phenomenon is shaking its fist throughout every nation of Central and South America."[177]

The Cuban revolution set off a new surge of official interest in anti-Americanism. Members of Congress were soon taking to the floor to speak about anti-Americanism or anti-Americans an average of 350 times per year.[178]

They detected this menace at home and abroad, in Europe, in East Asia, and above all in Latin America. Over the dozen years following 1959, the number of internal U.S. foreign policy documents addressing "anti-Americanism" would double compared with the preceding 12 years, nearly half dealing with Cuba.[179]

In identifying "anti-Americanism" as the source of Castro's recent actions, however, officials overlooked several facts. At the age of twelve, Castro had mustered his schoolboy English to write a letter telling "My good friend" Franklin Roosevelt how happy he was to learn of his reelection (and asking FDR for a ten-dollar bill).[180] During the 1950s, Castro's 26th of July Movement did not denounce the United States, and his speeches invoked the American Declaration of Independence. When conflict with the Eisenhower and Kennedy administrations over his expropriation of U.S. businesses led him to attack "Yanqui imperialism," he was careful to distinguish between what he viewed as the ill effects of U.S. military and economic power in Cuba from the welcome presence on the island of American tourists, Ernest Hemingway, and his favorite sport, baseball, which he continued to play avidly. His speeches acquired a relentless focus on U.S. aggression as the conflict with the United States increased, but the hostility was a product of that conflict, not its source. Warning of plots by the powerful enemy to the north served as a convenient excuse to repress critics all the more effectively because some of the warnings were accurate. While Castro's policies were undoubtedly driven by his efforts to seize and hold power, transform Cuban society to serve the interests of the poor, and crush any opposition, U.S. officials persisted in applying the conventional interpretation of irrationality.

This logic led to such tortured formulations as the CIA's assertion that Castro was "incit[ing] anti-Americanism by [making] accusations that the US is aiding forces working to defeat his revolution."[181] The accusations were true, as the Agency very well knew, because it was already planning what would become the failed invasion at the Bay of Pigs, even though State Department officials recognized that "the majority of Cubans support Castro."[182] Castro was not the only leader to learn of this planning and object to it. In July 1960, British Prime Minister Harold Macmillan warned Eisenhower directly by personal letter not to invade the island, not to support exiled counterrevolutionaries, and to avoid escalating the war of words and sanctions that was, he believed, driving the Cubans into the arms of the Soviets. In a private exchange of letters, Eisenhower replied that the United States was determined to continue to do everything short of outright invasion; after all, he reasoned, Castro could not long retain the support of the Cuban population, since the average Cuban just "wants to receive his earnings in cash and go to the store, buy a white guayabera, white shoes, a bottle of rum and go to a dance."[183]

British officials continued their warnings right up until the Bay of Pigs operation, which they knew about in advance, although they had never been consulted. The Foreign Office was receiving a "continual flow of reports" about the "disquieting" preparations for an invasion. "For a long time past we have been impressing on the Americans how damaging it would be to their position in most countries in Latin America if they were to intervene in Cuba," wrote a diplomat, adding that the British had "done all we can to prevent any rash act which could have the most unfortunate consequences."[184] The French and the Germans knew of the preparations as well, because their informants had observed anti-Castro exiles training in Central American camps.[185] So, of course, did Cuban counterintelligence; even the Norwegian government learned in January 1961 of plans for a U.S.-backed exile operation and tried to persuade the Americans not to carry it out because it would not succeed and would only increase East-West tensions.[186]

Given such advance warnings, Undersecretary of State Chester Bowles noted that U.S. officials were anticipating "a new wave of anti-Americanism" as a result of the operation.[187] Arthur Schlesinger, Jr., Special Assistant to the President for Latin American Affairs, also expected it to "add fuel to the fires of anti-Americanism throughout Europe."[188] When the invasion began, worldwide reaction was swift in coming. Betancourt, Kennedy's friend (and no friend to Castro), was appalled by the armed attack upon a neighboring country, calling it "stupid and criminal."[189] Fifty thousand people protested in Mexico City, carrying placards reading "Yesterday Veracruz – today Cuba."[190] Eighty thousand rallied in Cairo. There were demonstrations in Caracas, La Paz, Morelia, Montevideo, and every major city in Colombia.[191]

The world's press was unusually unified. *Pravda*, of course, had a field day. The Arab nationalist press condemned the invasion, but so did the independent newspapers. *Nahar*, an independent Beirut daily, regretted the fact that the progressive American president's first step onto the world stage took the form of attacking another country. Moroccan papers that had welcomed Kennedy's election were more critical of the United States than they had ever been before.[192] The Pakistani press condemned the return to "gunboat diplomacy" that handed an effortless victory to the Soviet Union; the *Times of India* said the Bay of Pigs was "Kennedy's Folly" and called U.S. denials of involvement "grotesque."[193] Afghanistan, which had welcomed American development projects and usually followed a policy of strict neutrality, made its strongest attack on the United States in memory, deploring the unwelcome spectacle of a great power invading a small neighboring country, an event that hit close to home.[194]

In Canada, the *Globe and Mail* tallied up the effects: the Cuban government strengthened and handed an excuse for repression; Castro pushed further into the Soviet camp; U.S. prestige damaged by its "resorting to undercover methods of warfare normally associated with the Communist bloc."[195] France's *Combat* ridiculed American claims of noninvolvement, and pointed out that bringing democracy to Cuba had not seemed so urgent while Batista was making its beaches and brothels available to American tourists.[196] British newspapers unanimously deplored the invasion; the *Daily Mail* compared it to the self-inflicted disaster when Britain and France attacked Egypt after Gamal Abdel Nasser's nationalization of the Suez Canal. Like Nasser after the Suez fiasco, the paper said, Castro would now achieve the status of a "demi-god."[197] *Der Spiegel* was astonished that Kennedy's advisers seemed not to realize that an attempt to create a revolution requires a revolutionary situation first, and presciently warned that Soviet Premier Nikita Khrushchev was likely to use any means necessary to defend Cuba in the future.[198]

The diplomatic response, whether public or private, was similarly uniform. Anti-Soviet Argentine diplomats gave speeches reasserting the sacred principle of nonintervention.[199] Brazil's foreign minister condemned all intervention in Cuba and argued that democracy cannot be created through force.[200] The Italian foreign ministry worried that this would be the first of more unilateral actions to come, which would break the unity of NATO.[201] The British Foreign Office, "without rubbing it in," made a point of reminding its contacts in Washington that for months it had been warning that an invasion would be unlikely to spark an uprising.[202] Arthur Schlesinger went on a listening tour of Western Europe, where he got an earful. Most of the politicians, intellectuals, and journalists he spoke with were "baffled and incredulous," he told Kennedy. "They could not believe that the U.S. Government had been quite so incompetent, irresponsible and stupid." The invasion had caused "acute shock and disillusion." He heard this from the broad spectrum of European politics, from Christian Democrats and Social Democrats, Atlanticists and Gaullists, Tories and Labor. They were angry at the invasion, not at its failure.[203]

This worldwide condemnation might appear to have been the anticipated "new wave of anti-Americanism," except that it was not the expression of deep-seated hatred or resentment of the United States. The same people complaining to Schlesinger were those who only weeks before "had been making heavy emotional and political investments in the new American administration," he reported. Kennedy's youth, intelligence, dynamism, and promises of a new era in world affairs "had excited tremendous anticipation and elation. The new American President in three months had reestablished confidence in the maturity of American judgment and the clarity of American purposes." The invasion of Cuba, however, made the new administration seem "as self-righteous, trigger-happy and incompetent as it had ever been in the heyday of John Foster Dulles," Schlesinger wrote. "Now, in a single stroke, all this seemed wiped away."[204]

These critics were voicing unhappiness not with America and Americans, but at the violation of the professed ideals of the United States, of international law, of the advice of allies, and of the principle that large countries cannot simply invade small ones at will if the world is to avoid endless war. Anti-Americanism, an ideological predisposition to hate the United States for reasons based in cultural conflict or a dislike of democracy, had nothing to do with it, but Americans in government and the press decided that it did, and with those blinders on, they were unable to learn the obvious lessons of the experience. Instead of taking seriously the reaction from abroad, they ascribed it to anti-Americanism, and the Kennedy administration proceeded to ratchet up its confrontation with Cuba: with the sabotage campaign of Operation Mongoose, with repeated assassination attempts, and with large-scale military exercises in which U.S. troops carried out the mock invasion of an island off Puerto Rico to overthrow a mythical ruler named "Ortsac" – Castro spelled backwards.[205] That policy spurred Khrushchev to station nuclear missiles in Cuba as a deterrent to invasion, provoking a crisis that nearly resulted in global nuclear war. The myth of anti-Americanism once more had fostered perceptions and policies that damaged America's own interests.

1963: Another Coup against Anti-Americanism

While the Kennedy administration watched "anti-Americanism" spread in the aftermath of the failed invasion of Cuba, U.S. officials were busily building intelligence files on the "anti-American" ex-leader of Guatemala whom Castillo Armas had expelled after the 1954 coup: former president Juan José Arévalo. Regularly reported by U.S. sources to be not a Communist but an "anti-American" during his time in office, as an exile dedicated to protesting the Guatemalan dictatorship after the coup, he entered the select ranks of those individuals formally classified as "anti-Americans" by the U.S. government. His impending return to Guatemala to run for the presidency now provoked a crisis that in 1963 would bring another coup d'état supported by the United States.

U.S. officials and journalists had characterized Arévalo as anti-American when his crime in office had been to pursue a reformist program even more modest than Arbenz's. Thereafter the former university professor drew official American ire for two books he wrote after the 1954 coup: *Anti-Kommunism in Latin America* and *The Shark and the Sardines*. The shark was a powerful United States interfering in the small countries of Latin America, the vulnerable sardines. When it appeared in English translation in the United States, it caused a minor tempest.[206] "I am not anti-American," Arévalo protested. "I am a Christian and an idealistic anti-Marxist."[207] He embraced John F. Kennedy's proposals for an ambitious development program known as the Alliance for Progress. Arévalo explained that he had written the book as a reaction to the overthrow of his country's elected government, not because of animus toward the United States.[208]

"Anti-Kommunism" was the sarcastic moniker – inspired by a Madison Avenue fad for the letter "k" – he gave to the campaigns by anti-Communists against Communists who existed only in their imaginations. In Latin America, where real Communists were a negligible minority without power and pro-Soviet organizations were usually docile, law-abiding parties, right-wing dictators could collect lucrative support from the United States by labeling all manner of reformers and social movements "Communists" and promising to fight them. Arévalo counted himself among the imaginary Communists – the "Kommunists" – who were the victims of "anti-Kommunism."[209]

Presidential elections were scheduled for 1963 in Guatemala, and Arévalo made plans to return from exile to run again. The State Department's Bureau of Intelligence and Research (INR), after careful investigation, judged him "not under the control of international communism" and his political program "consistent with specific reform goals of the Alliance for Progress." Because of his "record of substantial accomplishments in the fields of social security, education, and labor legislation between 1945 and 1951," it concluded, he "would win a free election in 1963."[210] A resumption of his moderate reform program would seem to have been exactly what the Alliance for Progress called for, but Arévalo bore the scarlet letter. The INR study aside, U.S. officials engaged in the traditional analysis that equated criticism with hostility based in irrationality. Arévalo was "hopelessly obsessed with a psychopathic hatred of the United States," according to State Department guidelines on Guatemala.[211] Officials reported that Arévalo's "deep prejudice against the United States" had become a "psychopathic obsession," one "fed by a consuming hatred and contempt of the United States."[212] The CIA called him the "rabidly anti-U.S. former president of Guatemala" and a "rabid critic of the United States," who regrettably enjoyed "wide popularity."[213] U.S. Ambassador to Guatemala John O. Bell thought Arévalo "passionately and pathologically antagonistic to the United States and all its works."[214]

This was as misguided in 1963 as it had been nearly two decades earlier. In 1947, Arévalo had approved the so-called *Pacto del Caribe*, a network of exiles from Caribbean dictatorships who pledged that if they came to power they would "ally themselves in perpetuity with the United States and Mexico for the common defense."[215] Marxism-Leninism, he wrote, was a failed system, "the philosophy of the firing squad."[216] Despite his unhappiness over the 1954 coup, Arévalo drew a sharp distinction between U.S. actions in the era of Dulles and Eisenhower, "the old imperial policy of the Republican Party," versus the spirit of the Kennedy administration, "men of the university, educated in Harvard, sympathizing with the working class, like us."[217] It took a powerful faith in U.S. infallibility and Latin American irrationality to move from Arévalo's words and actions to the conviction that he was a menace to the United States and had to be stopped, even if that meant overruling the will of the majority of the Guatemalan people.

That is precisely what happened next. In September 1962, Ambassador Bell reported from Guatemala City that Arévalo was likely to win an election, but that the defense minister, Enrique Peralta Azurdia, had suggested that the Army would block Arévalo from returning if the United States blessed a coup to overthrow the sitting president, Miguel Ydígoras Fuentes, and cancel the election. "It is quite conceivable," wrote Bell, "that in the final analysis the decision of these people as to whether or not to attempt a coup will depend on U.S. attitudes."[218] In October, the State Department's Latin America Policy Committee (LAPC) decided to try to block Arévalo's election. The U.S. country team for Guatemala, headed by the ambassador and comprising the senior members of each U.S. military and civilian agency there, understood its mission to be "preventing Arevalo's succession to power." The team report noted that respecting constitutional processes might "produce disastrous consequences" because Arévalo, with his "pathological hatred of the United States," was likely to win a free election.[219]

In January 1963, Kennedy himself began to focus on the problem. He requested and received State Department reports indicating that Arévalo held "deep prejudice" against the United States and that the Department was seeking "acceptable civilians and military men who could govern if Ydígoras is displaced by a coup."[220] At a White House meeting on Guatemala, Kennedy quizzed experts from the State Department and CIA, including CIA Director Richard Helms. A tape recording of the meeting, heavily excised, opens with a statement from Edwin Martin, Assistant Secretary of State for Inter-American Affairs. Martin, who spoke no Spanish and had little experience in what he called the "immature and inexperienced societies" of Latin America, summed up the policy that held that Guatemalans should not be permitted to freely elect their own leader.[221]

> MARTIN: "There's unanimous agreement that Arévalo would be a very bad president from our standpoint, and that, uh, we ought to seek to do what we can to prevent him from becoming president.... "
> *Excision: 1 minute, 16 seconds*
> KENNEDY: "What was it in the past, in his past record, that convinced us that he was a communist or a fellow traveler?"
> PARTICIPANT: "During the Arbenz regime, he was perhaps his most outspoken defender. At that time, he was a roving ambassador based in Santiago, Chile. And he made the most vicious speeches attacking the United States . . . "
> *crosstalk*
> KENNEDY: " – a crypto – "
> PARTICIPANT: "Not a communist. Not a card-carrying, not a communist, but a very [unintelligible]-minded man who is very tolerant of communism–"
> PARTICIPANT: "He's also the most popular man in Guatemala.... "
> PARTICIPANT: "He's the fellow that wrote *The Shark and the Sardines*."
> PARTICIPANT: "That's right."
> MARTIN: "It's rather a slicing attack on –"
> PARTICIPANT: "Violently anti-American. Very violent."

Martin went on to allude to ongoing Guatemalan plots aimed at "throwing Ydígoras out . . . to forestall Arévalo." Kennedy gave his order: "make our plans to prevent" the election of Arévalo.[222]

Kennedy also expressed a desire to learn the views of Venezuela's democratic president, Rómulo Betancourt. Betancourt was "all that we admire in a political leader," said Kennedy, who had a direct telephone line installed between the White House and Miraflores, Betancourt's presidential palace.[223] In February the two presidents spoke about Guatemala, and Betancourt clearly did not share the view that Arévalo was an anti-American. He told Kennedy that although Arévalo had been associated with Communists after leaving office, "Communists had burned Arévalo's books in Venezuela and recently the Cuban radio had attacked him." He pointed out that Arévalo's closest advisers included Dr. Manuel Noriega Morales, one of the "nine wise men," a panel of U.S.-approved experts helping to administer Alliance for Progress operations – tangible evidence of his professed sympathy for the Kennedy program. Betancourt added that he did not trust Arévalo entirely, and he was not the Venezuelan leader's first choice for a Guatemalan president, but he was clearly the Guatemalans' first choice, and that fact seemed to be important to Betancourt.[224] The British Embassy in Guatemala also reported that Arévalo was "anxious to cooperate with the U.S."[225]

Neither Betancourt's cautions, the views of allies, nor Arévalo's own words would change U.S. assessments. When Guatemalan Foreign Minister Jesús Unda Murillo visited Washington, he came away with the impression that the United States wanted to "'help' in defeating Arévalo... without 'intervention' on an open basis."[226] Ydígoras's disloyal Defense Minister, Peralta, told the U.S. Embassy that the army was reluctant to take action because of "uncertainty as to United States reaction to a coup," especially the possibility of economic aid being reduced or cut off, as Washington had done after a coup in Peru the previous year. "I gathered he felt the Army group, before acting, would want some kind of assurance from the United States that we would not look askance at the action," wrote Embassy counselor Robert F. Corrigan.[227] Ambassador Bell pushed hard from Guatemala City, arguing in March that "the fact is that a coup becomes harder to get as Arévalo's campaign gains momentum." He characterized Arévalo as "the anti-American, super egotistical 'spiritualist'" and concluded: "It is the opinion of nearly all Americans in Guatemala, official and unofficial, that it is of great importance to prevent Arévalo from success."[228]

As the date of Arévalo's return to Guatemala approached, Kennedy started dealing with the issue personally on a weekly basis, attending White House meetings on Guatemala with State Department and CIA officials on March 5 and March 14, then flying to an inter-American summit meeting in Costa Rica on March 20 where, having arranged for a private encounter with President Ydígoras with no aides and only one interpreter present, he asked Ydígoras not to permit Arévalo to return. "He would be dangerous if he won the elections," Kennedy told Ydígoras.[229] He followed up two days later with another White House meeting on Guatemala with Martin and CIA Director Richard Helms.[230]

On March 27, Arévalo, wearing a wig and disguised in a laborer's clothes, flew secretly from Mexico to an airstrip in Guatemala and called a press conference to which journalists were driven in blindfolds. Asked if he was a *communista* he replied that as long as Kennedy was president of the United States he would be a *kennedista*, but if a new John Foster Dulles were to appear, he would have to write a sequel to *The Shark and the Sardines*.[231] While Arévalo stayed underground, moving from safe house to safe house, Bell expressed the hope that "at long last [Peralta] might yield to pressures to attempt coup."[232] He would not have long to wait. On March 30, the Army moved against the sitting president, who had failed to prevent Arévalo's return. Peralta led the two principal army garrisons in Guatemala City to the Presidential Palace and took Ydígoras into custody. Arévalo's leading supporters were arrested.

The army then suspended the Constitution, dissolved Congress, and placed all executive and legislative power in the hands of Peralta. Arévalo fled back to Mexico. When Peralta heard that the leaders of the Guatemalan Congress wanted to call a special session, his response was "What Congress?"[233] Peralta also announced that when elections were held later that year, Arévalo would not be permitted to run. A British diplomat at the Foreign Office's American Desk observed dryly, "One wonders what sort of 'elections' there will be, if the candidate who is unarguably the most popular is not allowed to stand."[234]

U.S. officials initially greeted the coup as a success. "This is a gain," stated a State Department summary.[235] Bell wrote that the coup had "achieved, in at least a provisional sense, our objective of seeing the corrupt, inefficient Ydígoras Government replaced by a friendly government which blocked the presidential road for Juan José Arevalo, the pathologically anti-American ex-President." However, the regrets had begun to set in. Bell added that the Peralta regime was now "a particularly difficult one to work with and influence" because of its "sensitivity and overdeveloped sense of dignity with respect to 'sovereignty.'"[236] Assistant Secretary Martin believed that by "driving all political activity underground," Peralta's government "promoted rather than inhibited extremist subversion through violence."[237] Within three years of Peralta's takeover, the CIA would admit that while the Guatemalan elite considered "any reformist" to be a Communist, "actually, there have never been many Communists in Guatemala." It was political repression, intelligence analyst Sherman Kent reported, that was "likely to drive the moderate left further toward extremism."[238] He was right. As the military government embarked on "perhaps the cruelest campaign of state repression in twentieth-century Latin America," leftists favoring dialogue or negotiation were tortured and executed by a regime that ultimately murdered 200,000 of its own citizens, and the only remaining challenge to dictatorship in Guatemala was a tenacious, peasant-based insurgency that would fight on until the 1990s.[239]

Nonetheless, very little was learned from this tragic outcome because U.S. officials were so unwilling to see Latin Americans as independent actors, to view any criticism of the United States as rational or grounded in experience, or to take Latin American opinion seriously. This dynamic was most evident in the response to Betancourt's furious reaction. He wrote to Kennedy directly, outside normal channels, to denounce the coup in Guatemala. Military coups, he wrote, brought inept government, increased political persecution, and swelled the ranks of the Communist movements, as well as causing "a visible deterioration in relations between the United States and the people of Latin America."[240] By the time Kennedy hand-signed a personal reply a month later, he was ready to claim with a straight face:

> I view military coups d'état against freely elected, constitutional governments as deplorable events which impair the cause of representative democracy. . . . I would like to emphasize again that it is the unalterable position of the Government of the United States to support representative, constitutional processes.[241]

At a press conference six weeks before his death, Kennedy followed up with the statement that "we are opposed to an interruption of the constitutional system by military coups," because "dictatorships are the seedbeds from which Communism ultimately springs up."[242]

These words were intended for public consumption and to soothe the anger of his closest Latin American ally. But even if Kennedy believed them to be true, the argument that undermining democracy fuels dictatorship and communist revolution was overwhelmed by the exigencies of the Cold War and the power of the myth of anti-Americanism. This myth held that opposition to the United States was a sign of relentless hostility to democracy. In Guatemala for a second time in the space of a decade, American belief in the myth of anti-Americanism had contributed to the destruction of democracy abroad.

It was at this time that Mexico's leading writer, Carlos Fuentes, a longtime admirer and critic of the United States, spoke out to object to the U.S. claim to represent the "free world" when it backed so many dictatorships. Preparing an appeal to the American people, he wrote, "Ask them [the Latin Americans], whether we believe in the free world of Franco, Salazar, Chiang Kai-Shek and Ngo Dinh Diem. Ask them, and they will explain to you, why they spat on Nixon." As the Kennedy administration turned to counterinsurgency and increased military aid in response to a rise in revolutionary movements in the Third World, Fuentes urged Americans to "try to see further than the intellectual provincialism of the Cold War permits. Try to understand what we, the people of the underdeveloped, hungry, revolutionary world want. We do not want the destruction of the American people, whom we love for what its greatest individuals have brought to expression, its great politicians – Lincoln, Franklin Roosevelt – and its great artists – Poe, Melville, Faulkner, Marian Anderson, O'Neill, Miller." He ended with this plea: "Don't be provincial. Try to understand the diversity of the world."[243]

This is what Fuentes planned to say in a debate scheduled on NBC television with the Assistant Secretary for Inter-American Affairs, but the State Department denied him a visa because, explained Undersecretary George Ball, "he is an anti-American."[244] The debate never took place, and Americans never heard the plea.

5

Myth and Consequences

De Gaulle, Anti-Americanism, and Vietnam

A 'mortal enemy,' a 'renegade friend,' a 'cynic,' a 'demagogue,' a 'homicidal lunatic' inspired by 'implacable hostility toward the United States' and 'the most ungrateful man since Judas Iscariot...'
> – Members of Congress on Charles de Gaulle[1]

We have fought together, suffered together, triumphed together. It is hand in hand that our two countries must walk towards the future.
> Long live the American Army! Long live the United States of America!
> – Charles de Gaulle to General Dwight D. Eisenhower, 1945[2]

The Vietnam War brought a twin culmination to the history of anti-Americanism: a cresting of worldwide protest against the United States, and such widespread employment of the term *anti-Americanism* to explain foreign behavior as to harden it into an accepted truth. By 1968, foreign opinion of the United States had sunk to the lowest level ever measured, and charges of anti-Americanism were hurled in all directions. What has not been shown until now is that the very war that wrought this state of affairs was itself partly the product of the confused notion of anti-Americanism. Vietnam was a devastating illustration of what could happen when the U.S. political class and the public in general so fully absorbed the myth of anti-Americanism into their thinking that they became incapable of considering advice and criticism that might have spared their country from marching off that particular cliff. In a self-fulfilling prophesy, or a feedback loop, the conviction that anti-Americanism explained opposition to the United States abroad prevented Americans from taking seriously proposals and warnings that might have saved them from policies that increased foreign opposition abroad, which they read as more anti-Americanism. Prisoners of a discursive system that reduced complexities and choices to the misleading rubrics of pro- and anti-Americanism, they failed to see that there were paths available that would not lead into deadly quagmire.

This chapter examines the U.S. intervention in Vietnam and its resonance around the world from a new angle: the role of the anti-American myth. First, it demonstrates that the best-informed government on Indochina in the West – that of French President Charles de Gaulle – tried to warn the Kennedy administration against intervening in Vietnam but was pilloried as anti-American and its potentially life-saving advice ignored. The misleading but hardened image of de Gaulle as an anti-American leader is shown to have been born largely of ignorance of the French side of the Franco-American relationship. The archives of other key allies are examined, revealing that British and West German officials who were knowledgeable about Southeast Asia shared the French view but placed a priority on not offending Americans and did not express those dissenting views forcefully, as the French did. As a result, the "pro-American" allies concealed what they knew to be true in order to ingratiate themselves with a U.S. government that tolerated little opposition. These governments turned out to have had the same conviction as the French, that the American escalation in Vietnam was ill-advised. While the "pro-American" and "anti-American" distinction did not provide a good guide to foreign assessments and actions, it did lead several governments either to suppress their best estimates or to watch, perplexed, as their motives were misrepresented as hostile. Thus did a concept that distorted U.S. perceptions of foreign behavior contribute to a series of disastrous foreign policy decisions.

The Defamation of Charles de Gaulle

Two weeks after the last surviving U.S.-trained counterrevolutionaries were hauled out of the swamp at the Bay of Pigs, on May 31, 1961, John and Jacqueline Kennedy flew to France on an official state visit. French President Charles de Gaulle broke with tradition to drive to the airport to meet Air Force One and try out a greeting in English: "Have you had a good aerial voyage?" As the limousines rolled into the city past a million cheering Parisians lining the route, de Gaulle remarked, "Look how happy Paris is to see you!"[3] Part of the enthusiasm was for Jackie, whose beauty, glamour, and effortless French so charmed her hosts that JFK introduced himself at a news conference as "the man who accompanied Jacqueline Kennedy to Paris."[4] But the French crowds were also celebrating the visit of an American leader, just as they had cheered Eisenhower the previous year. Entrenched American beliefs to the contrary notwithstanding, French hostility toward the United States, rather than toward some of its aspects or policies, has always been a minority position.

The good feelings did not last. In the months that followed, de Gaulle launched an array of initiatives at variance with what U.S. officials desired, for which they blamed his anti-Americanism, stemming from Gallic irrationality, French cultural prejudice, and de Gaulle's own personal grievances. Well before Kennedy was elected president, top American officials routinely diagnosed French intransigence in the face of American demands as a neurotic condition. President Franklin D. Roosevelt described de Gaulle as "a nut" and nicknamed him "Joan of Arc," adding insult to the injury of preferring to deal with Vichy French officials instead of the head of the French resistance.[5] Secretary of State Dean Acheson found the French people as a whole to be "mentally ill."[6] "I don't like the son of a bitch," remarked President Harry S. Truman, exclaiming that the "French ought to be taken out and castrated."[7] The *New York Times* explained in 1953 that French "anti-Americanism" stemmed from "an inferiority complex" and a "hidden sense of shame."[8] The top U.S. general in Europe called the French "psychopathic" when the Assemblée Nationale voted against the proposed European Defense Community in 1954.[9] According to the interagency Psychological Strategy Board, "manifestations of anti-Americanism" came from French unhappiness with modern life. "The French mind rebels at pragmatism," the Board explained. "The Frenchman disassociates his thoughts from the facts."[10]

By the time Kennedy took office, the habit of explaining French behavior on the basis of irrational anti-American hostility was well established. Undersecretary of State George Ball found the French "psychotic"[11] and argued that "de Gaulle's policy ... is largely animated by anti-American prejudice."[12] Kennedy's ambassador to France, Charles Bohlen, agreed. "We must definitely recognize," wrote Bohlen, "that one of the motivating forces of de Gaulle's conduct of foreign policy is his anti-American obsession."[13] The State Department's Bureau of Intelligence and Research concurred that de Gaulle's policy was driven by his anti-Americanism, which Johnson's National Security Advisor Walt Rostow attributed to de Gaulle's "somewhat disturbed frame of mind."[14] In a tape-recorded meeting with his National Security Council, President Kennedy summarized the contemporary American view this way: "They put out some pretty vicious stuff out of Paris every day. ... I mean these bastards just live off the fat of the land and spit on us every chance they get."[15]

Ascribing de Gaulle's actions to irrational anti-Americanism placed more weight on his imperious manner and his unhappiness over the snubbing that he got from Roosevelt than an analysis of his broader foreign policy agenda. De Gaulle's overarching goal was the restoration of France as a great power active on the world stage, and his strategy had four parts. First, he sought for France the means to defend itself independently, without relying on the United States, chiefly through the nuclear deterrent of a *force de frappe* (nuclear strike force). Second, he hoped to foster European unity through Franco-German rapprochement, ending the enmity that had erupted in three traumatic wars in less than a century. Third, he actively pursued détente with the Communist powers by recognizing China and improving relations with the Soviet Union in a post-Stalin era. On this, de Gaulle was an early leader; he spoke the word "détente" ten times in speeches between 1960 and 1962.[16] He was not willing to see a weakening of Western defenses or to cede control of West Berlin to the Soviets – "if the Russians occupy Germany, we are lost ... if they arrive at the Rhine by force or by politics, we are finished" – but neither did he see any reason for needless provocation.[17] His amorphous formula of a Europe united "from the Atlantic to the Urals" was, he explained, not a pro-Moscow shift away from the Atlantic alliance, but historical anticipation, a way to show the Russians that a European Union would not be directed against them, while offering some hope to eastern Europeans.[18] His understanding of international affairs emphasized nations, not ideologies; he did not believe in a monolithic Communist threat, as many Americans did, but sought to exploit the Sino-Soviet split, and thought that a thousand years of Vietnamese hostility to the Chinese meant a Vietnam under Communist rule would remain independent, like Josip Tito's Yugoslavia.[19]

Finally – and this fourth element was neglected by Americans – de Gaulle's strategy included an opening to the developing world: completing the withdrawal from Algeria to end France's status as a colonial power, then offering developing countries French leadership and support as an alternative to Cold War polarization between the Soviet Union and the United States.[20] This strategy would not only improve France's prestige on the world stage, de Gaulle hoped, but also could mean that the forces of nationalism in decolonizing states in Africa and Asia, encountering skepticism in Washington, might not rush headlong into the open arms of the Communist bloc and would turn to France instead. In contrast to the United States, stubborn opposition to nationalism from Vietnam to Cuba to the Congo, France would offer an alternative: a non-Communist great power ready to provide understanding and material aid to postcolonial nations, helping to keep them tied to the West rather than the East.[21]

Seen in this light, de Gaulle's divergence from U.S. policy in the developing world is more intelligible, emerging not from pique or anger at Americans, but as part of a different strategic vision, and naturally enough, an emphasis on French rather than American interests. The aim of offering developing countries French leadership was, of course, condescending, beginning with the presumption that developing countries are childlike, in need of direction from a more mature power that could provide them "wisdom," as de Gaulle remarked to Averell Harriman.[22] The idea of French leadership of a decolonized world did find some resonance, however, especially when it was backed by concrete policies, such as the most generous foreign aid program of any major power. (In 1963 French aid to developing countries represented 2.5% of national income, compared with 1% for Great Britain and the United States.)[23] American officials grew troubled by their sense that "de Gaulle is worshipped in African capitals, adulated in Phnom Penh and greeted with delirium in Latin America."[24] A survey by *Jeune Afrique* in 1965 found that de Gaulle was the most popular man in Africa.[25] Prince Norodom Sihanouk of Cambodia observed that, given positions taken on the Vietnam War, "Without France, we would have despaired entirely of the West."[26] In 1965, planners of an Afro-Asian conference discussed inviting only three non-Afro-Asian guests of honor: Fidel Castro, Josip Tito, and Charles de Gaulle.[27]

The ambitious vision de Gaulle laid out for French leadership of the developing world never materialized for the simple reason that the leaders and populations of newly independent former colonies were not interested in being any country's followers. But this vision explains his motives better than the American remarks about neuroses and anti-American obsession. De Gaulle's leading biographer noted that, on many occasions, public and private, de Gaulle expressed sympathy and appreciation for Americans, whom he viewed as friends, allies, and liberators – but not as superiors.[28] He was not obsessed with America; he wrote hundreds or thousands of words every day, in private correspondence and in notebooks to clarify his thinking, or for publication in one of his nine books – and almost none of them concerned the United States.

It was a different nation that obsessed Charles de Gaulle. "All my life," he wrote, "I have had a certain idea of France. . . . France is not truly herself unless she is in the front rank. . . . France cannot be France without greatness."[29] With a sense of national mission that Americans find suspicious when it refers to any country but their own, de Gaulle would try to play a weak hand with enough verve to allow France to "aim high and stand up straight."[30] To Col. Vernon Walters, a top aide to Eisenhower and later U.S. military attaché in Paris, de Gaulle explained, "I have a nation which was once great but which fell into the gutter. I know I cannot raise it back to where it once was, but if it is to carry its weight in the defense of freedom, I must lift it part of the way. If therefore, I sometimes say things that seem harsh or unreasonable, please remember the context in which I say them."[31] Despite all of the psychologizing and national character analysis popular in Washington, French opposition to U.S. foreign policy, like critiques coming from other countries, was rooted not in irrationality or an obsession with the United States but in independent agendas and assessments of world affairs.

Put simply, American and French officials had different assumptions of how French foreign policy should be made. The French believed they should pursue French interests based on French analyses. Top American officials thought that the French should understand that American and French interests were congruent, and they should therefore accept decisions made by the more powerful partner. National Security Adviser McGeorge Bundy remarked, "decent Frenchmen [support us] and the General is an indecent Frenchman."[32] Secretary of State Dean Rusk thought the United States should "insist that they join with us in all matters involving the alliance."[33] George Ball agreed, in a message to Kennedy: "We should never forget that the United States is the leader of the Atlantic world and that the great mass of Europeans look to America – and . . . to you, as President – for guidance and direction," he wrote. "This is for them a conditioned reflex."[34] When that "reflex" did not function as expected, it was time for diagnosis.

Scholars have debated whether to oppose U.S. policy in this way was to be anti-American. Richard Kuisel writes that "De Gaulle was anti-American in trying to subvert [an] international order that the United States believed served its best interests."[35] Philippe Roger disagrees, because he defines anti-Americanism as a consistent discourse of malignant representations, a practice in which de Gaulle did not engage.[36] The French Communist Party did not see him as an anti-American; in fact, when it issued a pamphlet unmasking a "fifth column" of twenty-three American agents active in French politics, they included the name of Charles de Gaulle.[37] If anti-Americanism were so profoundly entrenched in French culture as to bear the explanatory weight assigned it by U.S. officials and some scholars as the source of French resistance to U.S. policies, it is strange that one finds very little trace of classic anti-American ideas and images in the writings of French officials. In their internal memoranda, classified correspondence, diaries, memoirs, and speeches, de Gaulle and his principal subordinates display almost none of this supposedly endemic and consequential cultural prejudice. The presence of anti-American tropes in French literary works does not seem to have bled over into policy writings.

Stephen Haseler's general argument would seem to apply well to de Gaulle: "Just as calculations about national advantage should be distinguished from anti-Americanism, so too should the enduring desire for independence and self-determination."[38] If anti-Americanism is understood as a true "ism," that is, an ideology, or enduring and causal prejudice, it cannot be merely a synonym for opposing U.S. policies – especially when those policies also are opposed by many Americans. Influential U.S. observers who are never accused of anti-Americanism, from Walter Lippmann to Henry Kissinger, were sympathetic to de Gaulle's approach to international relations.[39] A careful look at the documentary record reveals a very different de Gaulle, one who was not particularly interested in the United States as a country or a culture, who was devoted to restoring French power, and who was increasingly uneasy about French strategic dependence on the Americans – not because they were Americans, but because he wanted an independent France, and several key incidents vividly demonstrated that dependence might drag France into an unnecessary war.

"Annihilation Without Consultation"

From 1958 onward, de Gaulle stressed his desire that the United States consult with its NATO allies, not just make policy and then expect adherence. During extensive talks with Dulles in July over a regional political crisis in the Middle East that threatened the government of Lebanon, where France had historic interests, the two countries agreed on mutual consultation and cooperation before taking any action. Ten days later, without warning, Eisenhower ordered 14,000 U.S. troops to land at Beirut to back up the government of President Camille Chamoun, coordinating with a simultaneous dispatch of British troops to Jordan – but leaving the French in the dark. De Gaulle was incensed. "There was no consultation among the three powers," he wrote to British Prime Minister Harold Macmillan, even though the British and Americans could have counted on France's support. Privately, he wondered whether the two leaders had been planning behind his back even while Dulles was giving him assurances.[40]

Only a month later, tensions between the People's Republic of China (PRC) and the Nationalists in Formosa flared up, as China resumed shelling the disputed coastal islands of Quemoy and Matsu. Jiang Jieshi's Nationalist forces in 1954 had occupied these islands lying 15 miles from the mainland and 150 miles from Formosa in the Taiwan Straits. This presented a dilemma to Eisenhower and Dulles. They did not want them to be taken over by the PRC, because that could lead in their overwrought estimation to another "Munich," which would "destroy the whole position of the free world from Japan to New Zealand."[41] But America's allies did not think the coastal islands were worth a war.[42] Discussing the islands with congressional leaders in 1955, Eisenhower exclaimed, "How nice it would be if they'd sink!"[43]

In August 1958, Dulles announced that the United States would respond to a Chinese invasion with force and it would not remain "a limited operation."[44] Since the Soviets had promised to back the Chinese, this threat held the possibility that the conflict could escalate into a world war. American officials confirmed privately to the French that if the PRC invaded Quemoy and Matsu, the United States would strike mainland China – without previous consultation, and even at the risk of Soviet retaliation against Europe.[45] The British and the French were both taken aback at the saber-rattling that might lead to the destruction of their own countries.[46] Australia's Prime Minister Robert Menzies worried that "if the Americans fight for Quemoy," the consequences "may well concern us all."[47] Richard Casey, Australia's longest-serving foreign minister, sought a joint approach with the British to try to tone down the American hard line.[48] Macmillan and his Foreign Secretary Selwyn Lloyd urged Dulles to negotiate a withdrawal of Nationalist forces from the islands: "The matter must not be settled by force," Lloyd insisted.[49] Dulles nonetheless claimed that American allies "have been in entire accord with the position which we have taken."[50]

That allied apprehensions were not misplaced is confirmed by the declassification of a top secret report of a meeting on Quemoy and Matsu between Dulles and the Joint Chiefs of Staff, at which they called for the use of atomic weapons in the event of a PRC attack on the islands, even if such a move were unpopular and likely to provoke Soviet intervention:

> Are we to risk loss of U.S. prestige and influence in the world, through loss of the Offshore Islands occasioned by failure to exert a maximum defense; or are we to risk loss of prestige and influence, through limited use of nuclear weapons to hold the Islands.
> It was the consensus that we should take the second risk.[51]

This was brinkmanship on a grand scale, and among allied leaders unnerved by the American stance, de Gaulle was the one to take action. He responded to the crises over Lebanon and Quemoy and Matsu with a memorandum addressed to Macmillan and Eisenhower calling for tripartite cooperation in security matters, to avoid the possibility of what historian Frank Costigliola dubbed "annihilation without consultation."[52] Under the current system, "risks are shared," wrote de Gaulle, but not decisions.[53] Rather than the current NATO architecture, in which Americans led and Europeans followed, or the Americans and the British acted together while marginalizing the other European powers, de Gaulle sought a strategic directorate of all three powers that would consult and act in concert not only on the defense of Western Europe but also in international matters that could affect the security of all countries concerned. This was not a peculiarly Gaullist proposal but had been a French aim in 1950, when French Premier Bidault had called for an "Atlantic High Council for Peace," and Hervé Alphand, then French representative to the North Atlantic Council, recommended a three-power "inner council."[54] By reviving the demand, de Gaulle was not attacking the United States but reasserting a long-standing French policy goal of having an equal voice with Great Britain in matters of crucial importance to France's interests. Maurice Couve de Murville, France's longest-serving Foreign Minister since the *ancien régime*, who was close to de Gaulle and shared his views, wrote that this recalibration of relations with the United States "was certainly not on the level of sentiment or of friendship, nor on the pact of alliance that linked the two states, but on the level of the habits that had developed and the systems that had become accepted." The essential issue for France, he said, was "to know whether she might be drawn into a war that she had neither wanted nor decided upon."[55]

Eisenhower rebuffed the request for a formal system of consultation, and de Gaulle would regularly raise the issue for the next three years. During Kennedy's visit to Paris in 1961, de Gaulle asked for a system of consultation before any use of nuclear weapons, especially since those weapons were likely to be used in Europe. The American government was, unsurprisingly, not willing to cede any control over its nuclear arsenal.[56] The French viewed Kennedy's policy of "flexible response" with concern. Did it mean that the United States would meet a Soviet invasion of Western Europe with tactical nuclear weapons on the battlefield, meaning widespread destruction in France and Germany, but not use strategic nuclear weapons (intercontinental ballistic missiles [ICBMs]) against Soviet territory, to spare their own from retaliation from ICBMs?[57] De Gaulle had already raised this obvious strategic dilemma to explain to Eisenhower the French need for an independent nuclear deterrent, asking, "How can we French be certain, if you are not bombed directly on United States soil, you would intervene in a way that would bring death down upon your heads?" Eisenhower acknowledged that he had a point.[58] Kennedy's assurance that he would come to the aid of France was "possible, but not certain," de Gaulle observed, and since no one could know who would govern the United States in future years, operating on trust was not an adequate way to protect his country.[59]

In a tape-recorded meeting with his National Security Council, Kennedy expressed frustration over Gaullist complaints. "They either attack us for trying to dominate Europe, or they attack us for withdrawing from Europe, or that we won't use our nuclear force, or that we'll get them into a war in which they're not consulted," Kennedy said exasperatedly.[60] He was right.

De Gaulle's worry was twofold – that the Americans would not be willing to start a nuclear war when it was necessary to defend France (or to credibly deter an attack), but might start a nuclear war elsewhere over interests that were not vital from the French point of view. Hervé Alphand, who served for ten years as France's ambassador in Washington, wrote that de Gaulle feared both "American hegemony and withdrawal, which appears contradictory but can also be concurrent."[61] There were positions between the absolutes that de Gaulle found more appropriate, and his efforts to move France and the United States closer to the middle caused consternation. Interestingly, when French officials disliked U.S. positions, such as Eisenhower's pressure to stop the invasion of Egypt during the Suez crisis in 1956, or Kennedy's speech as senator expressing sympathy with Algerian rebels in 1957, or the U.S. vote at the United Nations against French policy in Algeria in 1959, they might respond with anger or resentment, but never assumed that Americans were engaging in psychologically based anti-Gallicism.

Solidarity in Crisis

Despite these differences on policy, de Gaulle recognized the many common interests France shared with the United States, and he did not want to drive the countries apart. "Our relations with the United States must remain good," de Gaulle told Alphand in August 1962. "I have only friendly and well-disposed feelings toward Kennedy."[62] He soon had the opportunity to prove his point, when Soviet Premier Nikita Khrushchev sent nuclear-armed missiles to be stationed in Cuba.

That de Gaulle declared his unconditional support for Kennedy during the Cuban Missile Crisis is often mentioned, sometimes with surprise, in standard accounts by scholars perplexed by this gesture of solidarity from an allegedly anti-American leader. Rarely acknowledged is the more concrete assistance that France provided the United States on Cuba. De Gaulle followed up his gesture during the Missile Crisis with an immediate order to the French mission at the United Nations to back the American position in the Security Council, whatever it might be.[63] Even more far-reaching was de Gaulle's secret and lasting arrangement to provide Washington with same-day intelligence reports from the French embassy in Havana. The Foreign Ministry at the Quai d'Orsay in January 1961 instructed its Havana embassy to send duplicates of all its political dispatches directly to Washington, without clearing them through Paris first, in order to keep the Americans well-informed. Since the U.S. embassy was closed, this was one of the few remaining Western sources of information from inside Cuba – an arrangement that carried substantial risks for the French, who were under constant "hostile surveillance."[64] For this critical and dangerous service, Secretary Rusk on three separate occasions personally expressed his thanks.[65]

The information, moreover, was quite useful: Ambassador Roger Robert du Gardier reported from Havana in August 1962 that embassy officials traveling at night saw a convoy of heavy trucks bearing "missile launch ramps about a dozen meters long." At least 4,000 Slavic personnel had debarked from Soviet ships, and Cuban High Command officers were studying Russian intensively.[66] Having delivered this intelligence, French officials were startled when Kennedy denied in late August that he had any information about the presence of missiles in Cuba.[67] In the midst of the October crisis, when the Cubans cut off U.S. communications with its interests section at the Swiss Embassy in Havana, the French stepped forward with increased reporting from the interior of the island.[68]

De Gaulle's usually unacknowledged assistance is hardly compatible with his image as an embittered anti-American, nor is his reaction to the Missile Crisis. Kennedy sent former Secretary of State Dean Acheson to carry photographs of the missiles to Paris, where he was smuggled into the Élysée through the basement to avoid reporters. As Acheson recalled the encounter, the French president's first question was, "Do I understand that you have come from the President to inform me of some decision taken by your President – or have you come to consult me about a decision he should take?" Acheson replied, "I have come to inform you of a decision he has taken," and offered to show him the photographic evidence. De Gaulle waved it away, saying "a great nation like yours would not act if there was any doubt about the evidence, and, therefore, I accept what you tell me as a fact without any proof of any sort needed. . . . You may tell your President that France will support him in every way in this crisis."[69] A few days later, Bohlen reported de Gaulle's statement to him that "if developments in this affair should unfortunately lead to war, the U.S. could be sure that France with its limited means would be at our side in the war."[70]

This made de Gaulle the firmest supporter of the United States in Europe during the crisis, and it was the second time de Gaulle had given a message of unconditional solidarity with the United States during an emergency.[71] The first was when the May 1960 Paris summit between Eisenhower and Khrushchev collapsed over the discovery that American U-2 spy aircraft were flying over Soviet territory. During Khrushchev's angry outbursts, de Gaulle took Eisenhower aside and said, "I do not know what lies ahead but whatever does we are with you all the way." Acting as Eisenhower's interpreter, Vernon Walters was impressed: "I will never forget what he said and particularly the circumstances under which he said it."[72] The Deputy Chief of Mission at the U.S. Embassy in Paris, Cecil B. Lyon, one of a handful of mid-level dissenters from the American "theology" on de Gaulle, thought these two crises showed that "in the important East-West conflict it will be seen that de Gaulle thoroughly honors his commitments to the Alliance."[73]

While vowing to stand by the United States, French officials nonetheless drew their own lessons from the Missile Crisis. Alphand noted that the crisis showed how determined the Americans were to act unilaterally in an emergency, and to make decisions alone, even a decision that might start a war involving the allies.[74] By August 1963, de Gaulle was complaining to Alphand, "they never consult us."[75]

Such existential questions, rather than pique, were the true sources of Franco-American tensions. Raymond Aron wrote that although Americans found de Gaulle perplexing, his policy was "wholly in accord with traditional practices, for a state's wish to have its hands free and not to be reduced to the rank of a protected state is part and parcel of the very essence of an independent diplomacy."[76] Each decision was made, not out of prejudice against the United States or a desire to harm it, but with the question in mind that de Gaulle often interjected to settle long policy debates among his advisers: "What is the national interest?"[77]

A Global Policy

Those who placed great weight upon personal and symbolic actions in measuring anti-Americanism seemed not to know what to make of de Gaulle's response to Kennedy's death. His spontaneous eulogy for JFK upon hearing the news from Dallas might have been the highest tribute *le Général* could give: "He died as a soldier, under fire. . . . "[78] The French president then became the first foreign head of state to ask to attend the funeral, beginning an international practice that endures today. On arrival he spoke with "perceptible emotion," as an American diplomat noted, of his admiration for Kennedy, of France's affection for the United States, of the closeness of ties between the two countries. "That is the reality," he said with solemn emphasis and deliberation. "That is the only thing that counts."[79] As he marched in the cortege behind Kennedy's casket, he carried in the pocket of his tunic a flower given to him by Jacqueline Kennedy out of gratitude for his gesture. On the first anniversary of JFK's death, he would write to her, "each day we see more clearly all that the United States has lost and, at the same time, many other nations, perhaps above all its friend France, by losing this man."[80]

But the charge of anti-Americanism imputed to de Gaulle stuck, and it distorted American interpretations of a whole range of French policy decisions. When France extended diplomatic recognition to the People's Republic of China in 1964, Bohlen explained the decision as "primarily" an act demonstrating independence of American control, and the press linked it to rising "anti-Americanism."[81] (The British had recognized China 14 years earlier to protect their investments in Hong Kong, but nobody called that an anti-American act.)[82] De Gaulle offered three rationales for his action: widening the Sino-Soviet split, pursuing French economic interests, and resolving the Southeast Asian crisis. "In Asia, there can be neither war nor peace without China being involved," he said, and his government used its ability to speak to the Chinese to press for negotiations to end the Vietnam War.[83] Edgar Faure, the main French official involved in the opening to China, said afterward that recognition of the PRC was far from being an anti-American move:

"we had vaguely in mind that the Americans would be able to derive an advantage . . . from our [China] initiative, particularly as regards Vietnam."[84] Shortly before his death, Kennedy had told Bundy that he, too, planned to recognize China in his second term.[85] Johnson also "would have liked to" recognize China, but knew such a move was politically impossible.[86] De Gaulle had merely done what these two U.S. presidents wished they could have done, and what Richard Nixon, with no fear of being outflanked on the right, finally did.

De Gaulle's visit to Latin America in 1964 also produced the usual commentary. When he addressed a cheering crowd of 400,000 in Mexico City (without notes, in flawless Spanish), the *Los Angeles Times* reported that "Washington Fumes in Private."[87] William Tyler, assistant secretary for European affairs, thought the trip showed de Gaulle's belief that "the way to handle Uncle Sam is to kick him in the shins until he smiles."[88] This although his speeches were "studiously free of anti-American attacks," and the trip itself had been suggested by Kennedy the year before, when he explicitly requested that France take on a larger role in Latin America: "everything you can do to be more present there would be very helpful to us."[89] De Gaulle had explained to Chancellor Ludwig Erhard of West Germany that France's interest in Latin America was "not to oppose the United States, nor to embarrass them and much less to condemn them" but to provide a complementary source of development aid to alleviate the poverty that fueled communism.[90] When de Gaulle spoke with Chile's President Eduardo Frei, he "never uttered a word against the U.S.," Frei noted. De Gaulle "made no anti-American statements of any kind. Rather he had taken the line he did not wish to create any difficulties for the U.S." in Latin America.[91]

"Gaullefinger" the Villain

The same misunderstanding applied to de Gaulle's effort to insulate France from inflation caused by U.S. monetary policy. As the international reserve currency, the dollar was essential to world trade. The United States spent far more overseas – largely to finance its worldwide military presence – than it sold to foreign countries, causing huge balance-of-payments deficits. As a result, foreign countries built up large dollar holdings. This was a problem for both sides. If the value of the dollar declined, so did the value of foreign countries' savings.

Officially, dollars were backed by gold reserves in the United States, but while the U.S. could simply print more dollars, it could not suddenly produce more gold. This meant a steady erosion of the value of the currency as the United States lived beyond its means throughout the 1960s, especially when successive administrations decided to pay for overseas troop deployments and the Vietnam War by printing dollars rather than by raising taxes. In 1961, several European countries – but not France – nervous over the inflation-caused decline in the value in the dollar, cashed in nearly $1 billion for gold, as the rules permitted. There was no outcry that this was an anti-American move. When France followed suit, however, requesting the exchange of $112 million for gold the following year under the same rules, the move was held up as further evidence of de Gaulle's anti-Americanism. De Gaulle pointed out that by racking up debt, the United States was exporting its inflation, and then using devalued dollars to take over European companies at a discount. Because France cooperated in this scheme by holding the surplus dollars, in effect, exclaimed de Gaulle, "we are paying them to buy us!" In 1965 and 1966, France turned in nearly $1.5 billion in exchange for gold from the United States, adding dramatic flair for domestic consumption by having French Air Force planes collect the bullion and bring it to France. De Gaulle continued the policy for two more years.[92]

Press reaction was predictable. The papers spoke of a "gold war." Russell Baker nicknamed him "Gaullefinger," after the villain in the 1964 James Bond film *Goldfinger*.[93] The "Gaullist anti-American policy of turning dollars into gold," newspaper readers were told, came from de Gaulle's "paranoiac compulsion. He sees the Stars and Stripes . . . and he reacts like a Gallic bull with a phobia for red flags."[94]

De Gaulle's gold policy was executed ostentatiously, but it did not differ significantly from that of other allies who did not incur Americans' wrath. In mid-August 1971, the British government asked for a guarantee in gold for the entire $3 billion of its official dollar holdings. When Nixon then took the dollar off the gold standard, the American currency's value plummeted. This was a double-barreled assault on Europeans' economic interests: it lessened the value of their dollar holdings overnight and hurt their competitiveness with American exports, because the falling dollar meant discounted prices for American goods. National Security Adviser Henry Kissinger and Treasury Secretary John Connally thought this was tantamount to economic warfare against the other industrial democracies.[95] In the words of a leading political scientist, "the Nixon administration's international monetary policies testified belatedly to the logic of the French analysis."[96] American policy with respect to gold and the dollar varied over time; it was never made with the intention of harming other countries or out of animosity toward them, but simply to promote American economic interests. In the same way, French monetary policy had nothing to do with anti-Americanism and everything to do with a strategy to promote French economic interests.

Lost in Translation

The American assumption that the French had a malicious and irrational aim of injuring the United States lent credibility to even the unlikeliest reports. A high-level CIA assessment reported that de Gaulle had told Italian leaders privately, "France is violently opposed to the blatant American imperialism now rampant in the world" and would attack U.S. policy in Latin America, Asia, and Africa.[97] This report, influential within the U.S. government and repeated in published accounts, was an example of what today is described politely as "flawed intelligence."[98] Declassified transcripts of the conversation between de Gaulle and visiting Italian leaders show a crucial semantic and contextual difference. De Gaulle actually stated that France's "future lay with those who can resist the Soviets," first among them the United States. "We want an alliance with America, a solid one, but on a different basis than today.... I have no grievances against the Americans," he added. Nonetheless he saw in Europe, Latin America, Japan, India, and South Korea "a kind of American hegemony which is inevitable."[99]

Hegemony is not a synonym for imperialism. Imperialism implies an active conquest that crushes resistance. Hegemony, whether defined by Antonio Gramsci, Walter Russell Mead, or the dictionary, describes a state of power relations in which consent no longer need be obtained by force; it can refer simply to the "predominant influence" of one state over others.[100] Hegemony is such a useful way of describing the preponderance of American power that it was used in the same period not only by de Gaulle but also by writers such as Reinhold Niebuhr and Raymond Aron, neither of whom can reasonably be accused of anti-Americanism. Niebuhr wrote of the United States as a "hegemonous nation" exercising "hegemonous power," of uniting European democracies "under the hegemony of our nation," and claimed, "nobody doubts this hegemony."[101] Aron, whom Ball deemed "the most distinguished political writer in France," a "completely trustworthy" friend who was "pro-alliance and pro-American," reminded his readers that hegemony's original Greek meaning was leadership – a word that does not exist in French.[102] De Gaulle usually made careful distinctions when he was comparing the two superpowers. In his televised speeches in the 1960s, he only once used the word "imperialist" and once the word "imperialism," both times to refer to the Soviet Union.[103] In private discussions with his spokesman, Alain Peyrefitte, he spoke of Europe as divided between "Soviet occupation" and "American hegemony," and as "under the communist boot" but "under the American protectorate."[104] Elsewhere, too, he referred not to "imperialism" but to "American hegemony," as did his top officials in their private correspondence.[105] It was his custom to choose his words with care. An American diplomat who watched de Gaulle closely for five years remarked that "de Gaulle's command of French is about on a par with Churchill's command of English." Moreover, he was not given to outbursts, since by nature he was "calm, logical, unemotional, very reserved, solid, cool and extremely dignified."[106]

So the image of a ranting de Gaulle promising to confront "American imperialism" around the world does not ring true; in fact, it is based on either a mistranslation or bad reporting. According to the transcript of the meeting with the Italians misinterpreted by the CIA, when Foreign Minister Giuseppe Saragat objected that the Americans were not "imperialists," de Gaulle replied: "In speaking of the United States, I have never employed the word imperialism...I spoke of their hegemony." Saragat then agreed: "The word hegemony is more appropriate."[107] That is the conversation the CIA inflated into a Gaullist plan to attack American imperialism around the world. It was the Italian who used the offending word, not de Gaulle, but as so often occurs, the true meaning was lost in translation.

In and Out of NATO

Nevertheless, the predominant view among American officials still could be summed up, as McGeorge Bundy characterized it, as "My God, these French people are no damn good but even though they are no damn good you have got to talk to them and see what happens, whether they are still no damn good."[108] This applied to de Gaulle's decision to remove U.S. troops from French soil. He thought that the presence of tens of thousands of foreign troops not under French command was not in keeping with the principle of national sovereignty. In March 1966 he withdrew France from the NATO integrated command structure and asked the Americans to withdraw their troops from France, telling his ministers that the decision was the consequence of the American failure to consult: "We are not disposed to follow the Americans into all the adventures into which they deem it good to launch themselves."[109] Secretary Rusk was livid, and asked de Gaulle bitterly, "Does that include the dead Americans in military cemeteries as well?"[110]

Some U.S. officials recognized that this was not the end of the West. As Vice President Hubert Humphrey tried to explain in a television interview, "Many people think that France has really withdrawn from NATO. She hasn't withdrawn from her participation in terms of the defensive structure of NATO. She has withdrawn the control of her troops from the NATO command. But she still has her two divisions in Germany, she still is a very powerful nation, and she still has her alliance with us and with other countries, and I have a feeling that General de Gaulle will keep that commitment and that alliance."[111] De Gaulle himself wrote that his intention was not to withdraw from the "Atlantic Alliance," but "from NATO's integrated structure under American command," in order to preserve France's independence.[112]

For most Americans, however, it was merely another poke in Uncle Sam's eye from an ungrateful and exasperating Frenchman. Protest reached the popular level. In New York, women returned French handbags to department stores. Entrepreneurs produced de Gaulle dartboards and de Gaulle voodoo dolls. A Miami restaurant owner announced he would stop serving French wine as a protest against what he called de Gaulle's "anti-American statements and actions."[113] The American Legion urged a boycott on travel to France.[114] Congressman Mendel Rivers (D-SC), chair of the House Armed Services Committee, in a common refrain, invoked the memory of the more than 60,000 American soldiers buried in France "after giving their lives to save that nation from a disgraceful defeat. Perhaps we should make our removal from French soil complete by reinterring the bodies of these American men on American soil."[115] De Gaulle's reputation as an anti-American was sealed.

Vietnam

Of all the points of friction, none angered American officials and the public so much as de Gaulle's criticism of the war in Vietnam. Traditional accounts hold that de Gaulle tried to undermine the U.S. effort in Southeast Asia as an act of prideful vengeance, hoping that the United States would not succeed where France had failed. On closer examination, however, anti-Americanism as an explanation for French opposition to the Vietnam War turns out to be a red herring, and even worse: it was an obfuscating concept that clouded American vision where both France and Vietnam were concerned. The conviction that anti-Americanism lay behind de Gaulle's skepticism on the war distorted American analyses of the issues at stake and prevented U.S. officials from seriously considering well-informed words of warning against the tragic decisions they were making in Southeast Asia.

The first category of evidence refuting the charge that anti-Americanism explains de Gaulle's position on Vietnam is to be found in the neglected record of early, discreet Gaullist diplomacy intended to discourage American escalation before it began. Rather than suddenly surprising the Americans with his first public statement on Vietnam in August 1963, as has often been claimed, de Gaulle actually engaged for several years in quiet diplomacy beforehand, using multiple channels to urge the Kennedy administration not to make the mistake of sending combat troops to fight in Southeast Asia. These warnings were sober, consistent, and now look prescient. They were not accompanied by leaks to the media, nor in any other way manipulated for political effect. Whether this represented the well-intentioned advice of a concerned ally or was part of a larger effort to preserve French influence in an area formerly under its colonial control, it was good counsel privately delivered, and therefore cannot be characterized as a hostile, anti-American act.

The second category of evidence against an interpretation that emphasizes personal pique and anti-Americanism shows that de Gaulle's view of conditions in Vietnam was not idiosyncratic: it was widely shared throughout the French foreign policy bureaucracy, from respected diplomats on the Asia desk in the Quai d'Orsay to the lowliest attaché in the embassy in Saigon. French professional diplomats may have rolled their eyes at other Gaullist initiatives, sometimes even letting their American counterparts know privately that they did not agree with every démarche emerging from the presidential palace, the Elysée.[116] They were, according to Bohlen, "on the whole, favorably disposed towards the U.S."[117] But while de Gaulle's personal views on history and strategy may well account for other policies controversial in French policy-making circles, such as his withdrawal from the NATO command or his rhetorical support for an independent Quebec, on Vietnam, French diplomats were united. Their realistic assessment of conditions in Indochina was based on 80 years of French experience there, including their own military defeat at the hands of determined Vietnamese nationalists, and on their having retained the best contacts with North and South Vietnamese of any country in the West. De

Gaulle did not invent a stance against U.S. military intervention and in favor of a political settlement as a reaction to personal slights: his was the consensus view held by French experts, whether Gaullists or not.

The third category of evidence comes from archives in third countries, and it reveals that America's other major allies shared French pessimism about U.S. efforts in Vietnam from an early date. British and German diplomats, who were never accused of anti-Americanism and chose not to challenge the United States publicly, nevertheless came to the same conclusions as de Gaulle about the futility of a military approach and the necessity of a negotiated settlement. This suggests that anti-Americanism cannot usefully explain the source of the French assessment, because diplomats understood to be "pro-American" held the same views in private.

Taken together, these three kinds of evidence challenge the enduring myth that de Gaulle, driven by his own animosity toward Americans, took an emotional, not to say irrational, stance on Vietnam. He is shown instead to have been much more in the mainstream of French and Western European thinking about the situation on the ground in Indochina, and to have been more constructive and less dramatic than scholars have claimed, in his efforts to convince the Americans not to go forward with a policy that he believed would damage their own interests and the interests of the West. For U.S. leaders to have labeled his efforts anti-Americanism at the time was misguided and brought serious consequences when policymakers ignored his advice and escalated the war. To continue to call it anti-Americanism today is to fail to adjust our view even with the advantages of hindsight and archives, and contributes to an ongoing flaw in U.S. perception of the wider world that tends to identify foreign opposition as prejudice or malevolence.

Quiet Diplomacy

If U.S. officials typically rejected Gaullist opposition as irrational, serious academic studies, too, have held his personality responsible for worsening Franco-American relations and preventing France from taking more effective steps to try to influence his American ally. Marianna Sullivan's widely cited work argues that

> de Gaulle preferred drama to persuasion. It did not suit his political style to present his arguments against United States policy in Vietnam in private or in conjunction with other interested parties. Instead, he launched a unilateral public attack on American policy in Southeast Asia.... De Gaulle's preference for dramatic public statements was at odds with the quiet persuasion that might have convinced the United States of its errors in Vietnam.[118]

This analysis, although widely accepted, is refuted by the international documentary record, which has not been sufficiently analyzed by historians.[119] De Gaulle's first public statement on Vietnam, one that incensed American officials, was a rather mild and ambiguous call for Vietnamese neutralization, issued by his spokesman Alain Peyrefitte, on August 29, 1963. It was an expression of sympathy for "the Vietnamese people" and of the hope that Vietnam would enjoy "unity" and "independence from foreign influences." The Vietnamese people, "and they alone," should choose the means to reach that goal, but if they sought assistance, de Gaulle extended an offer of France's "cordial cooperation" toward these ends.[120]

Although French officials thought "foreign influences" referred to the Americans, the French, the Soviets, and the Chinese, Kennedy's reaction was as straightforward as it was dismissive: "De Gaulle made his statement to annoy the United States," an aide paraphrased the president's private remarks.[121] Administration officials expressed "surprise and resentment" at this "anti-American mischief," seeing de Gaulle's move as "another effort to undercut the United States position."[122] James Reston decried "the new diplomacy" of damaging public statements compared to "the traditional diplomacy" which was "private and discreet."[123]

Whether one understands this first public Gaullist statement on Vietnam as a mild and possibly useful diplomatic overture or an ill-spirited shot across the bow of the Americans, by the time it was made, de Gaulle had already been engaged *for more than two years* precisely in what Sullivan and Reston said he should have undertaken but did not: "quiet persuasion," "present[ing] his arguments against United States policy in Vietnam in private." De Gaulle and other French officials continued their quiet diplomacy through the early 1960s, going public with sharper criticism only when the Americans dismissed their advice and escalated the war.

The private warnings were numerous, direct, and eerily prophetic. During private talks with Kennedy in Paris in May 1961, de Gaulle warned him to resist the temptation to "rekindle a war which we had ended. I predict that you will sink step by step into a bottomless military and political quagmire, despite the lives and treasure you may squander there."[124] An escalation of the conflict would increase hostility to Western nations and provoke Soviet intervention, de Gaulle said, whereas neutralizing the region would allow the United States to retain some influence, just as the French had achieved once they accepted a settlement and no longer represented a foreign military occupation.[125] The French interpreter recalled that de Gaulle argued that only a political solution could succeed, one that would replace the unpopular South Vietnamese regime of Ngo Dinh Diem with a democratic government willing to compromise with the opposition. De Gaulle offered to use France's excellent contacts in Vietnam to try to help move the Americans toward this goal. Kennedy declined.[126]

But de Gaulle's words left an impression. Back in Washington, Kennedy resisted the idea of sending troops to neighboring Laos, recalling that "General de Gaulle, out of painful French experience, had spoken with feeling of the difficulty of fighting in this part of the world."[127] De Gaulle passed the same warning to the U.S. ambassador in Paris, General James Gavin, also in May 1961: "Our own experience taught us," de Gaulle said, "that men who hold power by virtue of foreign intervention [i.e., Diem] will fail. . . . I fear that you are getting bogged down in a vain enterprise from which it will become more and more difficult to extract yourselves."[128]

French efforts to persuade the Americans not to go to war in Vietnam continued. In November 1961, French diplomats worked behind the scenes to try to discourage the United States from increasing its military commitment, including helicopters and ground troops, as recommended by General Maxwell Taylor's fact-finding mission to Vietnam. They held discussions with British diplomats to coordinate an effort to persuade Kennedy not to send more troops.[129] The French ambassador in Saigon advised U.S. Ambassador Frederick Nolting to "weigh seriously the consequences" of sending U.S. soldiers who, whether advertised as flood relief workers or advisers, would be seen as the spearhead of U.S. military intervention by Hanoi, Peking, and Moscow.[130] Etienne Manac'h, the respected director of Asian affairs at the Quai d'Orsay, instructed Ambassador Alphand in Washington to try to get through to the Americans before they reached a decision on the Taylor recommendation, because it would be "essential" to convey French reservations before the Kennedy administration committed itself to a policy to avoid giving offense. This was to be a confidential, diplomatic approach, made while there might still be time to influence the fateful decision of an ally – a far cry from any public America-bashing.

Alphand therefore requested and was granted a meeting with Secretary Rusk to caution him against sending U.S. combat forces to Vietnam. Indochina presented an inhospitable political and physical environment for Western troops, Alphand said, and warned that "an intervention of American troops in Vietnam, rather than containing the communist menace in South-East Asia, would precipitate a crisis that would engulf the whole region." For emphasis, Alphand reiterated France's opposition to the introduction of U.S. troops four times.[131]

All these French appeals fell on deaf ears. Kennedy ordered the helicopters and several thousand "advisers" to Vietnam, bringing total U.S. military forces to more than 3,000 by the end of the year. They would reach 11,000 by the end of 1962, and 17,000 by the time of his death in November 1963. As the French objected to each increase, President Kennedy continued to believe that "de Gaulle's fundamental attitude was based on his experience with Americans in World War II." He said so in May 1962 to de Gaulle's visiting Minister of Culture, André Malraux, and added that he found it very hard to understand "this latent, almost female, hostility."[132] Malraux disagreed, adding that he "did not think any French member of government had this kind of hostility toward the United States," and that de Gaulle's policies were aimed at "rebuilding the French nation politically."[133]

In May 1963, Couve de Murville once again tried to explain the French point of view to Kennedy. The French thought that there could be no military solution in Vietnam, and the path to peace would require the neutralization of Southeast Asia. Kennedy asked twice: why do you always give your policies "an anti-American aspect?" Couve replied that what Kennedy saw as anti-Americanism was either a divergence of interests or different views.[134]

All of these diplomatic exchanges took place privately, before de Gaulle ever made a public statement on Vietnam. But none of it made any difference to U.S. officials, who repeatedly ascribed French policy to de Gaulle's personality flaws and the weakness of French character generally. A Department of State official explained to a German colleague that French actions in Southeast Asia were "strongly influenced by their emotions."[135] Secretary Rusk praised a dispatch explaining that French officials are "undoubtedly marked by the emotional experience of French defeat and withdrawal from the area."[136] The Joint Chiefs of Staff observed derisively, "The French also tried to build the Panama Canal" – in other words, the United States would succeed where the French had failed.[137] Faith in the dichotomy of French irrationality and American objectivity persisted, at a time when de Gaulle was predicting that American escalation would bring ten years of war – an almost perfectly accurate forecast[138] – while Americans, presuming themselves to be free of emotional influences on their own assessments, kept seeing light at the end of the tunnel.

When de Gaulle finally issued his August 1963 statement supporting neutralization, Bundy, feeling "personal irritation" over de Gaulle's statement, urged the president simply to "ignore Nosey Charlie" on Vietnam.[139] U.S. officials did indeed ignore French counsel, to the point where the French Foreign Ministry's Asia desk noted a year-long hiatus in American consultation or requests for information during the crucial period of Diem's final, crisis-ridden months in office, and, following his overthrow and assassination, the subsequent turbulent succession of unstable governments.[140]

The dismissive and hostile American response was an unfortunate product of the assumption that de Gaulle's stance emerged from an inflexible anti-Americanism. Other observers free of that particular assumption read the August 1963 statement quite differently. Walter Lippmann was a rare American voice of support, writing with foresight, "If there is no settlement such as Gen. de Gaulle proposes, then a protracted and indecisive war of attrition is all that is left."[141] Jean-Marie Garraud, in a commentary for *Le Figaro*, a paper friendly to the United States, noted that de Gaulle's statement was not a one-sided attack but meant several things: a call for an end to all foreign interference, including that of the United States in the South and the Soviets and Chinese in the North; a criticism of authoritarian regimes, both the Ngo family's in the South and Ho Chi Minh's in the North; and an appeal to Vietnamese nationalists to unite for a peaceful settlement.[142] At the British embassy in Paris, an analyst thought the statement was a sensible response to recent French discoveries of emerging interest among the North Vietnamese leadership in an end to the fighting that would enable them to escape the growing influence of the Chinese and the Soviets.[143] T.J. Everard of the British Foreign Office thought the de Gaulle approach "might prove the only way out," even if neutralization led to a unified Vietnam under independent Communist leadership, because "the prize of a Tito-istic Vietnam would be a great let-out for the West," an escape from looming disaster.[144] Couve de Murville observed that in urging the United States to accept the inevitable, to come to terms and leave Vietnam, de Gaulle was recommending the same path that the French took in Algeria, where despite superior military power they arrived at a settlement, withdrew their troops, and "were not diminished in the eyes of the world."[145]

Bernard Fall, the widely admired Franco-American journalist, former resistance fighter, and Howard University scholar who was considered the West's best-informed student of contemporary Vietnam until he was killed there while accompanying U.S. troops, thought that it was wrong for Americans to dismiss French skepticism "simply as another case of French paranoid anti-Americanism."[146] In his books and articles, he tried to explain the French perspective to an American audience. De Gaulle, he wrote, simply "wants Vietnam to be reunified in independence. That is a wish that every western statesman trots out whenever he visits a divided country like Germany, Korea, and Vietnam, or a city like Berlin." Fall concluded that "French preoccupations with Vietnam stem from reasons that are more realistic than the desire to nettle the young men in Washington."[147] He characterized the notion that the French wanted to "get even" with the United States as "thoroughly simple-minded." Had de Gaulle truly been interested in damaging American prestige, Fall said, he would have wanted the Vietnam War to continue, because it was so unpopular and such a drain on American resources.[148]

As a point of comparison, de Gaulle's statement was far milder than the speech made by President Eisenhower condemning a French military intervention seven years before. When France, Great Britain, and Israel jointly attacked Egypt after Nasser nationalized the Suez Canal in 1956, Eisenhower was furious that "the United States was not consulted in any way" before its allies escalated a conflict that he thought would exacerbate the hostility of postcolonial nationalists toward the West. He declared that it is "our right – if our judgment so dictates – to dissent." Eisenhower proceeded to do so strongly. "We believe these actions to have been taken in error. For we do not accept the use of force as a wise or proper instrument for the settlement of international disputes." To say this, he added, "is in no way to minimize our friendship with these nations, nor our determination to maintain those friendships."[149] Eisenhower then backed his words with sanctions, withholding oil from Europe and preventing the International Monetary Fund from coming to the aid of the plummeting British pound.[150] France and Britain yielded to the intense pressure and withdrew their forces. Despite the hardball, nobody accused Eisenhower of anti-Europeanism. Eisenhower's insight that friendship might require dissent when one's ally seems bent on ill-advised action resonated in de Gaulle's stance on Vietnam.

The French Diplomatic Consensus

But if Americans admired Eisenhower's tough peacemaking, they thought that de Gaulle acted out of wounded pride. Two months after the August statement, Kennedy told Alphand at a dinner in Palm Beach that he thought all of

de Gaulle's actions could be explained by the general's determination to maintain "relations of acrimony and bitterness."[151] Yet unhappy personal experience could not account for the fact that de Gaulle's position represented the
consensus view across the spectrum of experienced French diplomats. Before
the August statement, while de Gaulle maintained his discreet public silence
and private frankness to the Americans about Vietnam, the East Asia experts
in the French foreign ministry independently developed their own analysis of
American policy that mirrored his conclusions: the United States was bent on
military victory in Vietnam, but since the bulk of the population supported
Ho Chi Minh, the only likely outcomes were either a Korea-style ground war
leading to stalemate or a negotiated solution under "mediocre" conditions.[152]
At the time of the Taylor report urging an increase in combat troops, the
Quai's Asia desk accurately predicted that such action would lead to the intensification of ground combat in South Vietnam, spark intervention by external
Communist powers, and draw Laos and Cambodia's Prince Sihanouk into
the conflict, ultimately pushing Cambodia into the Communist camp.[153] This
assessment was not driven by disdain for the United States but was a judgment
widely shared by French officials at all levels. Asia desk chief Manac'h had
determined as early as 1960 that American backing for the unpopular Diem
government was an illustration of the fundamental error of "supporting an
artificial regime" (i.e., one without domestic support), which would only fuel
resistance.[154]

American diplomats in Paris were impressed by Manac'h, both by his
formidable intellect and his determination to maintain good relations with
them. "Manac'h genuinely wishes to be helpful," wrote a State Department
official. "He is certainly an intelligent and knowledgeable student of the
Vietnamese scene. . . . he does as much for us as his instructions can be stretched
to permit and perhaps even a bit more."[155] A U.S. embassy officer who saw
Manac'h once a week in Paris during the 1960s remembered him as "far
from being anti-American. He told me one day, with some sentimentality,
how well he remembered when President Woodrow Wilson arrived in France
in 1918 and how he, as a young boy, stood there waving a flag welcoming
the American 'liberator.' . . . Manac'h considered himself all his life a friend
of America."[156] Manac'h later was instrumental in preparing the way for the
Paris peace talks of 1968, physically carrying messages back and forth between
U.S. and North Vietnamese diplomats who were not yet willing to be together
in one room. Yet this "friend of America" was the source of many of the analytical reports that led the French government to determine that the Americans could not win militarily in Vietnam and must seek a negotiated solution. Again, anti-Americanism as an explanation for de Gaulle's stance on
Vietnam does not convince, when we realize that French "pro-Americans"
shared his view.[157]

French diplomats were unified not because of any emotional stance toward
the United States but because France, logically enough after 80 years of colonial
rule, had the best contacts in Indochina of any Western power. Seventeen

thousand French citizens lived in South Vietnam, where they formed but one source available to the well-informed French ambassador, Roger Lalouette, and other knowledgeable French diplomats such as Jacques Boizet and Georges Perruche ("extremely talented and able," observed a U.S. diplomat).[158] Boizet called U.S. hopes that their aid would encourage Diem toward democratic reforms a "vain illusion," and the Quai's Asia desk predicted, accurately, that the Americans would ultimately decide to overthrow him in a coup.[159]

The French retained access to other sources of high-quality information that contributed to their assessment of conditions in Vietnam. Vietnamese exiles in Paris were in close touch with Foreign Ministry officials.[160] The best French journalists in Southeast Asia (all eventually expelled by Diem) thought that South Vietnam could not be defended militarily.[161] Officials in the Elysée benefited from Bernard Fall's private counsel, at a time when Washington disdained him for following the "crypto-Communist line" and the FBI placed him under surveillance.[162] The *Washington Post's* chief diplomatic correspondent charged Fall with "anti-American bias."[163] An American diplomat warned simply, "You've got to watch Bernard Fall. Remember, he's French."[164]

Fall was unable to persuade decision makers in his adopted hometown of Washington before he stepped on a mine and was killed while accompanying U.S. troops on reconnaissance in the Vietnamese jungle in 1967. American military leaders would come to have a different view of Fall after his death. He became something of a cult figure among American officers, who read him at West Point; from John McCain to David Petraeus, they respected his books, especially *Street without Joy*.[165] Colin Powell wrote in his autobiography that "if President Kennedy or President Johnson had spent a quiet weekend at Camp David reading that perceptive book, they would have returned to the White House Monday morning and immediately started to figure out a way to extricate us from the quicksand of Vietnam."[166] They did not listen to Fall at the time, but French officials did.[167]

Sources in North Vietnam were sparser, but a French consul in Hanoi maintained direct and cordial contact with the leadership. Some of these officials, including President Ho Chi Minh himself, were French-educated intellectuals who could acknowledge some affective ties to France now that the era of French colonialism was definitively over. French diplomats arranged discreet meetings with National Liberation Front (NLF) representatives in Algiers, Phnom Penh, Cairo, and Djakarta.[168] Since at least 1957, they provided crucial information about conditions in North Vietnam while, as Secretary Rusk acknowledged, the Americans lacked any direct access to that country.[169] Their contacts told them that the North Vietnamese were open to a settlement in part because they knew that as the war intensified, so would unwelcome Chinese influence in Hanoi.[170]

This broad, diverse network of contacts produced information that, whatever the tensions between the Elysée and the Quai d'Orsay, did rise to the top.[171] French officials kept in close contact with a committee of Vietnamese exiles opposed to Diem. By the time de Gaulle issued his August 29 statement, the Quai d'Orsay had concluded that interest in neutralism in both North and South Vietnam had grown to the point where it was a realistic prospect: the North realized that escalation was increasing its dependence on Chinese aid while provoking greater American involvement, and Diem's government was growing increasingly nationalistic and resentful of the foreign presence in the country.[172] This was the basis of de Gaulle's call for a neutral solution, but Americans saw only another piqued Frenchman putting a spoke in their wheel.

False Friends

Having dismissed French positions on Vietnam as irrational anti-Americanism, most Americans looked no further for the source of French analyses. Yet British and West German officials dealing with Southeast Asia came to conclusions similar to those of their French counterparts. Unlike the French, their governments did not openly challenge U.S. policy. But the fact that private assessments from European diplomats who were never tarred with the anti-American brush often reflected a similar reading of the situation in Vietnam again suggests that dismissing French assessments as anti-Americanism made little sense.

British officials first learned of American plans to increase ground forces in Vietnam in 1961 when a Canadian diplomat reported in early June that two Americans, "perhaps a little flushed with wine," told him that the United States would soon send not an expected one hundred but one thousand military instructors.[173] This plan carried "grave implications," the British embassy in Saigon believed, because it was not likely to lead to success and would be a violation of the 1954 Geneva accords prohibiting outside intervention in Vietnam.[174]

The British ambassador in Saigon, Gordon Etherington-Smith, argued that the injection of a large number of U.S. ground troops "seems most unwise.... The *'présence américaine'* has already reached serious proportions and constitutes a distinct political liability."[175] At the Foreign Office, J.I. McGhie of the South-East Asia Department wrote, "I entirely agree with Mr. Etherington-Smith's views. Direct training of the Viet-Namese Army will be of doubtful value and the attachment of military officers to combat teams will lead to endless dangers and complications."[176] In November, while awaiting a decision about the Taylor report, Britain's Foreign Secretary Lord Home sent a message to the French government stating that he hoped there would be no "direct American intervention in South Vietnam before a Laos settlement [i.e., political neutralization] is reached" because war in either place would be "very difficult and dangerous."[177]

In the spring and summer of 1963, before de Gaulle made his public statement on neutralization, the British consul general in Hanoi was arguing that neutralization was the only possible solution in Vietnam. He thought that American support for the Diem regime was pointless, because Vietnamese from all walks of life in both North and South hated Diem and admired Ho

Chi Minh. The French position should be encouraged, because "the French can talk to the Vietnamese in a way that no other nation (least of all the Russians) can do."[178]

In 1964, as the Johnson administration was preparing to bomb North Vietnam and to increase the number of American combat troops, British officials concluded that taking the war to the North would be "disastrous."[179] They took pains to emphasize to the Americans multiple times that their public stance on Vietnam was "support *for your present defensive policy* in South Viet Nam," not for escalation.[180] When McGeorge Bundy visited London, he was told bluntly that the British thought the only solution in Vietnam was to hold an international conference leading to neutralization, not to escalate the war.[181] Even British counterinsurgency expert Robert Thompson, who had hoped to be able to replicate in Vietnam a version of the British success in thwarting a revolutionary movement in Malaya, by August 1964 concluded the war would be lost and therefore wrote to "strongly advocate that the earliest possible opportunity should be taken to open negotiations while a measure of control remains in South Vietnam."[182] In November, a Foreign Office paper laying out British policy for Prime Minister Harold Wilson's cabinet explained that British rhetorical support for the Americans was aimed at retaining the "influence which this will give us towards restraining them from the graver risks of escalation."[183]

In Washington, British ambassador Harold Caccia put his government's dilemma this way: "We do not want the Americans to follow what seems to us a dangerous and mistaken course, but still less do we want to incur the odium of persuading them to cut their losses."[184] The danger, another British official agreed, was that "even to express our fears might be resented and bring down on our heads a charge of defeatism. We do not want to run any avoidable risk of finding ourselves accused of having caused what we had actually done no more than predict."[185]

At the end of 1964, Wilson directed his Foreign Office to try to develop a "British initiative aimed at enabling the U.S. Government to extricate themselves from the worsening situation in Viet-Nam."[186] That included his secret diplomacy with the Soviets to try to drum up support for an international conference.[187] Johnson's rage at Wilson confirmed British apprehension about American sensitivities. "I won't tell you how to run Malaysia and you don't tell us how to run Vietnam," Johnson snapped. "If you want to help us some in Vietnam, send us some men."[188] The British eschewed the French route of going public with criticism of U.S. policy on Vietnam, but that was out of a desire to avoid American wrath. In private, their views were in harmony with French analyses. Anti-Americanism explained neither country's stance, but American faith in the anti-American myth – and the accompanying intolerance of disagreement – accounted for both British silence and American anger at French outspokenness.

German diplomats faced a dilemma similar to that of the British. Contrary to conventional accounts that depict West Germany as backing the United

States unconditionally in Vietnam, German officials privately tried to steer the Americans toward ending the war because they did not think that it could be won. The West German embassy in Saigon reported in March 1963 that war-weariness was widespread, and that despite the high body counts touted by the Americans, rebel attacks had made large areas of the countryside only a few kilometers from the capital unsafe for travel.[189] Ambassador Yorck Alexander Freiherr von Wendland estimated that 80 percent of the population supported neutralization as the only path to peace.[190] De Gaulle's neutralization proposal was, he thought, "the secret desire of all of the small countries of Southeast Asia."[191]

Unlike the French but like the British, the Germans did not come out publicly for neutralization. Chancellor Ludwig Erhard, on the contrary, had assured Johnson of his "unrestricted" support, even while severely restricting it to modest financial assistance and sending a single hospital ship, the *Helgoland*, in response to Johnson's request for "more flags" to be shown by America's allies in Vietnam.[192] Foreign Minister Gerhard Schröder was still arguing with Couve de Murville in June 1964 that the most important issue was the solidarity of the West when the United States asked for it. Couve replied that he thought "the best expression of solidarity was that one should say what one thinks."[193]

Yet "the French have correctly judged the situation," wrote State Secretary Karl Carstens in July 1964.[194] Now, agreed Foreign Ministry Director Josef Jansen, it was time to change the public posture of uncritical solidarity. The Americans' "very optimistic" belief in victory had been proved "erroneous," because after vast amounts of U.S. military assistance, it had not been possible to free a single province from the communists, who had reached the Saigon city limits. He argued that the United States should be told that Germany thought that the time for a political solution in Vietnam had arrived.[195]

In August 1964, the Germans quietly pressed the United States to hold an international conference to resolve the conflict. When Johnson sent U.S. Ambassador to Vietnam Henry Cabot Lodge to urge German officials in Bonn to increase support for the U.S. war effort, Lodge began by declaring that the United States planned to win in Vietnam and was opposed to an international conference. State Secretary Ludger Westrick, trying to put a positive spin on Lodge's words, diplomatically replied that he welcomed what he characterized as Lodge's remark that the United States would be prepared to seek a political solution through an international conference "when the time is right" (a significant reconfiguration of Lodge's refusal). He then questioned the American view that an international conference would be a political defeat, because, he argued, world opinion would welcome it as a sign of détente and evidence that the United States was working for peace. Lodge stuck to his guns, and the assembled German diplomats were shocked to hear him restate his confidence in military victory.[196]

From February 1 to 4, 1965, German diplomats from all over Asia gathered in Bonn to confer with their Foreign Ministry colleagues, and found that they were almost unanimous in thinking that there could be no military solution in Vietnam. They noted that after every engagement, one heard of fifty or more *écartés* (deserters) from South Vietnamese units, but almost none from the Viet Cong. They reported that support for de Gaulle's neutralization proposal was widespread in Asia; even rivals Pakistan and India were in rare agreement on this point. Wendland's successor as ambassador in Saigon, Guenther Schlegelberger, noted with regret that Johnson and Taylor spoke often about maintaining U.S. "credibility" in Vietnam, even though America's allies did not think that it strengthened U.S. credibility to pursue a futile, costly, and dangerous policy.[197]

The German leadership suppressed its doubts over Vietnam for the same reason as the British: to bow to American sensitivities. This was the case while the Christian Democrats were in office, and it continued initially under the Social Democratic Party (SPD). Fritz Erler, head of the SPD's parliamentary faction, told the editor of the *Bild-Zeitung* that given Berlin's dependence on the Americans for protection, it was unwise to "kick them in the balls." Willy Brandt, foreign minister from 1966 to 1969 and then Chancellor, repeatedly warned his colleagues that Germans of all people had no right to engage in moral finger-pointing about the conduct of war, and that solidarity with the United States was more important to Germany's national interest than was a faraway conflict about which he admitted he knew little. In 1967 he changed his mind and later concluded his position had been a mistake based on what he called an *inneres Denkverbot*, an internal ban on thinking freely when it came to criticizing the United States. The refrain used by German politicians, *Berlin wird am Mekong verteidigt* (Berlin is defended on the Mekong), implied that America's credibility as a military power – a vital part of West Berlin's deterrence-based defense – was at stake in Vietnam, but it had always rung hollow because Germany refused to send troops there. By 1968 the SPD was opposing the war openly, as Brandt concluded that Vietnam was damaging rather than preserving U.S. credibility, and that the formula about the Mekong had it backward: the Vietnam debacle was putting Berlin's future in jeopardy by undermining détente and weakening the United States.[198]

The British and German positions of calculated insincerity – public statements of support despite a private assessment that the war could not be won and a marked preference for a negotiated settlement along the lines of de Gaulle's proposal – were based almost entirely on a recognition that the Americans were intolerant of criticism and that professions of support were the price of good relations. That the French were willing to take their dissent public beginning in August 1963 does highlight a difference in the value that each European government placed on the public appearance of harmony with the United States, as well as the priority each placed on the crisis in Southeast Asia, where French interests were greater than British or German ones. The fact that all three major European powers reached similar conclusions about Vietnam, however, refutes the interpretation that the French assessment must have been caused by the distortions of anti-American prejudice. Indeed, one might well

ask how "pro-American" it was to offer insincere support for an ally's futile
and self-destructive policy in full knowledge that it was doomed to failure.

Escalation

Johnson continued Kennedy's policy of ignoring de Gaulle. As the war intensified in 1964 and 1965, the French promoted their vision of a neutral settlement and tried through diplomacy to improve its prospects for success.[199]
They explained to U.S. officials that they thought that Vietnam could become
a neutral state like Finland, Austria, or India; that its neutrality should be
established through a multipower conference modeled on the 1954 Geneva
accords, including the United States, France, Great Britain, China, and the
Soviet Union, followed by an agreement by the United States and China to
refrain from military intervention in Vietnam; that no one could guarantee
that a neutral country would not slide toward communism, but that continuing a war against the wishes of the population was likely to ensure just such an
outcome.[200]

A few high officials in the United States concurred, such as Senate Majority
Leader Mike Mansfield (D-MT), a former professor of Asian history. "The de
Gaulle approach to Southeast Asia offers a faint glimmer of hope," Mansfield
argued. "If there is any hope of a satisfactory solution in Viet Nam and, indeed,
throughout Indochina it rests very heavily on France. . . . We should be prepared
to listen most intently and with an open ear and mind to whatever the French
may have to say on Vietnam."[201] Instead of listening, Johnson told the French
to keep their opinions to themselves. In April 1964, he sent Bohlen to ask de
Gaulle whether he could at least support the U.S. war rhetorically in public. De
Gaulle replied that he could not, because a military solution was impossible.[202]
Instead, the French continued to work behind the scenes toward a peaceful
settlement in Vietnam. During the summer, de Gaulle collaborated with U.N.
Secretary General U Thant and with Prince Sihanouk of Cambodia, who had
been pushing for the neutralization of Southeast Asia since 1960, to try to build
support for an international conference.[203]

Having established diplomatic relations with China (over U.S. objections),
de Gaulle and Couve de Murville then pressed the Chinese to agree to a confer-
ence and to drop their precondition that the United States must first abandon
Taiwan, and tried to persuade the Americans to talk with the Chinese.[204] The
American refusal was summed up by Lodge, who told de Gaulle's cabinet
minister Louis Joxe, who had led the negotiations leading to withdrawal from
Algeria in 1962, that the Americans were merely following the example of
French counterinsurgency in Algeria. Joxe disagreed:

> JOXE: You have spoken of Algeria. . . . We realized that by taking things in
> hand and crushing terrorism, we were not able to kill the spirit that had led
> to terrorism. This is just as true for Vietnam, and that is why we believe
> that there is no other solution but negotiation.

LODGE: But such an accord would not be respected. The Chinese would vio-
late it immediately, just like Hitler did.... I can't imagine talking with an
aggressor.[205]

In this exchange, it is clear that rather than being prompted by national or
personal animosities, the divide arose from clashing interpretations of historical
events.

Indeed, when they interacted with de Gaulle, U.S. officials were sometimes
surprised that he did not live up to the caricature that they had helped to
draw of him. In 1964 George Ball, by then a skeptic of escalation, told British
officials that after meeting de Gaulle, he found him "far from unfriendly. His
attitude did not appear to have been governed by pique nor did he appear to
be crowing over difficulties in South East Asia. He seemed genuinely anxious
that the advance of communism should be arrested in the area and Mr. Ball
had not derived the impression that his motive was to create difficulties for the
United States."[206]

Ball appears in historical accounts as the highest-ranking internal critic of
the war. Few have noted his own explanation for how he came to take that
unusual stance: it was his intimate knowledge of the French experience. At his
high-powered law firm of Cleary Gottlieb, Ball won the French government
as a client after WWII, spending part of every month in Paris throughout the
1950s personally advising French officials and industrial leaders. He worked
closely with and admired French Premier Pierre Mendès-France for "the skill
and incisiveness with which he had extracted his country from its 'dirty war'
in Indochina," and later wished that America had its own Mendès-France to
help end "its own 'dirty war'... when America compulsively repeated all of
France's mistakes on the same hostile terrain and against essentially the same
enemy."[207]

Walter Lippmann, too, continued to argue that de Gaulle should be taken
seriously. "We are missing the main point and we are stultifying our influence
when we dismiss the French policies as not really serious, as expressions of
personal pique or personal vanity on the part of General de Gaulle, as inspired
by 'anti-Americanism' and a wish to embarrass us," he wrote. Lippmann argued
with President Johnson in person at the White House, fruitlessly.[208] De Gaulle
might be irritating, Lippmann held, but he deserved a hearing, because so often
he had been right in the past that he seemed to be "endowed with second sight
about the future... a prophetic man."[209]

Ignoring the prophecy, in an anguished process marked by his own private
pessimism, Johnson steadily escalated the war. In August 1964 he obtained
from Congress a resolution authorizing "all necessary measures" in Vietnam
after inflating reports of an attack on an American warship in the Gulf of
Tonkin. He began a bombing campaign against North Vietnam, Operation
Rolling Thunder, in February 1965. He ratcheted up troop levels to 180,000
by late 1965, 300,000 by mid-1966, and a half million by 1968. De Gaulle
opposed each stage of the escalation, continuing to call for, and push his

diplomats to promote, an international conference to settle the war. In an interview in December 1965, when asked whether he was anti-American, de Gaulle scoffed, "I have always heard myself called anti-something-or-other." He pointed out that the Americans had not come to the aid of France in 1914 but in 1917, not in 1940 but in 1944. "I don't call them anti-French because they did not always accompany us," he continued. "Well then! I am not anti-American just because at the moment I do not always accompany them, in particular, for example, in the policy they are carrying out in Asia."[210]

In September 1966, de Gaulle flew to Cambodia and was given a hero's welcome. A quarter million Cambodians – half the population of Phnom Penh – crowded into a stadium to hear him denounce the war. "There is no chance that the peoples of Asia will subject themselves to the law of the foreigner who comes from the other shore of the Pacific, whatever his intentions, however powerful his weapons." He invoked two centuries of Franco-American friendship and called on Americans to realize that a distant military expedition without benefit or justification could be replaced by an international arrangement to oversee a peaceful settlement. This "would involve nothing, absolutely nothing, that could injure its pride, contradict its ideals, or damage its interests. On the contrary, by taking such a path in harmony with the genius of the West, what an audience would the United States recover from one end of the world to the other, and what an opportunity would peace find on the scene and, especially, beyond!"[211]

The British chargé d'affaires was impressed. "There is no question that the great mass of the Cambodian people welcomed Charles de Gaulle with joy," he wrote. The "brilliantly successful state visit" struck "a shrewd indirect blow at Communist influence over Cambodia" by showing that France had displaced China as "Cambodia's Friend Number One.... Western values generally began to look more respectable than they have for years hereabouts." De Gaulle's policy had been "to the general advantage of the West."[212]

But Americans were furious. The *New York Times* slammed "the anti-American tone of General de Gaulle's remarks."[213] The *Philadelphia Inquirer* called him "the implacable enemy of this country."[214] Political columnist William S. White, writing in the *Washington Post*, attacked "the now open determination of Charles de Gaulle to degrade or destroy the United States, the savior of France from Hitler two decades ago, for reasons more suitable to a psychoanalyst's couch than to the area of public affairs."[215] From Saigon, Lodge accused de Gaulle of undermining American efforts, "due to anti-Americanism or to a desire to have us fail where they failed."[216]

Americans who were enraged had, naturally enough, focused on the criticism and overlooked de Gaulle's mention of friendship and alliance with the United States, his remark that American military power could not be defeated, and his belief that a settlement would restore and not damage U.S. prestige. Bernard Fall regretted the "hectoring tone" of the speech but thought it important that de Gaulle had warned the North Vietnamese three times that the United States could not be defeated, given that their public objective was military victory. He also made the argument that U.S. credibility was being injured, not defended, by the war: "The sight of heavily armed Americans being stymied in South Viet-Nam by lightly armed peasants and by the infantry of a fifth-rate power does perhaps more harm to American prestige than it would if the Americans were not there and the setbacks were not primarily 'American' setbacks."[217]

The Path to Peace Runs through Paris

These divergent views were too far apart to be bridged, but French officials continued to reach out privately with constructive efforts. After the Phnom Penh speech, de Gaulle authorized Jean Sainteny to undertake a mission to Hanoi as intermediary. Sainteny, a hero of the Resistance who had negotiated with Ho Chi Minh in the 1940s and 1950s, was respected by Vietnamese and Americans alike. He was "the best informed Frenchman on North Vietnam and the closest to the principal personalities in Hanoi," according to Bohlen and Harriman.[218] De Gaulle now sent him to meet with Ho and Prime Minister Pham Van Dong, both of whom he knew personally, to determine their interest in a settlement. When Sainteny returned, he told Bohlen that the North Vietnamese were willing to cease sending infiltrators to the South if the United States stopped aerial bombardment.[219] He then met with Henry Kissinger, who was visiting Paris at the State Department's request. Kissinger's notes show that Sainteny conveyed a stark picture of North Vietnamese tenacity but also indicated there was some potential for progress. He had arrived in Hanoi two days after the city had been bombed. "The North Vietnamese leaders seemed furious and determined. A number of ministers had told Saintenny [sic] that they would not be treated like little boys getting a spanking. They were prepared to fight in the jungles and to see their cities razed. They had made preparations accordingly. Sainteny believed them." Sainteny came away convinced that "all Vietnamese – including the leaders of Hanoi – profoundly distrust China." Pham had told him that if the Americans ended the bombing, they would respond with concessions; Hanoi seemed "in no hurry to unify the country," and when Sainteny said he thought there might have to be a five-year interim settlement before national elections and unification could take place, both Ho and Pham said "that they were patient and could wait – provided American troops were withdrawn before the end of that period." Although de Gaulle could be "exasperating," Sainteny added, the point of his Cambodia speech had been to address Hanoi's phobia about American occupation turning into colonial rule, and to outline an agreement that could lead to U.S. withdrawal, rather than require American withdrawal as a precondition to an agreement. Kissinger concluded by saying that he had known Sainteny for ten years and considered him "honorable and decent [and] anguished by the situation in Viet-Nam."[220]

De Gaulle continued to make his case every time he saw an American official. When Senator Robert Kennedy visited him in Paris in 1967, de Gaulle told him that the United States had enjoyed a morally and therefore politically strong position in the world, "due not only to its resources but to its humanity, a special spirit, and in particular its respect for the right of peoples to self-determination. What is happening in Vietnam contradicts this image, and we think it would be better for the United States to retain it." Although the United States thought it was fighting communism in Vietnam, de Gaulle said, "it could, on the contrary, be serving communism there."[221] He told Averell Harriman that the French wanted U.S. withdrawal "because we believe that this would be better for the United States itself.... [I]f the United States can bring an end to it, neither their prestige nor their power will be diminished."[222]

The French effort to maintain open lines of communication to all parties involved in the conflict in Southeast Asia would be vindicated when the warring sides finally agreed to pursue peace talks and chose Paris as the only acceptable site. Participants from all factions praised the French for managing those difficult talks successfully.[223] Once Johnson changed his policy and sought negotiations in 1968, everything changed in Franco-American relations as well. De Gaulle called Johnson's new policy "an act of reason and political courage."[224] The French provided security, arranged secret contacts, and helped to initiate meetings to keep the talks going. Manac'h, Sainteny, and Raymond Aubrac were among those with good contacts in North Vietnam whom de Gaulle authorized to aid the Americans in conducting the negotiations. The French were highly professional about this: although the secret meetings they enabled between U.S. and North Vietnamese officials lasted for years, ultimately resulting in the settlement that ended the war, there were no leaks.[225] "As it turned out," reflected Dean Rusk, "Paris proved to be very satisfactory as a site because President de Gaulle acted very correctly, and the French did everything they could to facilitate the talks."[226] This was only one reason Kissinger, who admired de Gaulle's farsighted and early pursuit of détente, wrote, "I believed then, as I believe now, that de Gaulle was extremely helpful to the Western world."[227]

While some have wondered, "Was de Gaulle anti-American?"[228] this chapter has posed a different question: "Did the assumption that French policy stemmed from anti-Americanism hinder U.S. officials from considering France's advice on Vietnam?" The answer should come from a figure at the center of the events:

> I believe we should have explored the idea of a neutral solution [in Vietnam] with the French. It is true that de Gaulle was difficult to deal with. But in matters of war and peace, these things just have to be put aside.

These are the words of former Secretary of Defense Robert McNamara, at one station of his confessional peregrination in the last years of his life. "My point in referring to the repudiation of various neutral solutions is not that my colleagues and I were wrong, though I believe we *were* wrong," he continued. "My point is that we didn't properly analyze the *idea* of a neutral solution. It wasn't taken seriously. It was simply rejected. And that, I believe, was a basic mistake – a failure of imagination."[229]

The imagination of top American officials failed in part because they could not conceive then of the possibility that Vietnamese Communists hoped to avoid war and dependence on the Chinese, and might have traded peace for neutrality in the Cold War, or at least for a Yugoslav-style independence. The failure of imagination McNamara bemoaned was also due to the fact that it seemed impossible for some Americans to conceive of the utility or good faith of foreign criticism, especially when it came from the French. U.S. officials, peering through the fog of their own assumptions, believed they saw "anti-Americans," French leaders inveterately prejudiced against them, rather than people acting in their own interests whose painful historical experience might have given them something useful to say. The erroneous conviction that anti-Americanism was the engine of French policy prevented Americans from listening to the best-informed officials in the West on an issue of vital national interest. This error would be compounded as Americans escalated the war, then read the worldwide protests it sparked through the same fogged lens.

6

Anti-Americanism in the Age of Protest

> How can such nice people make such terrible foreign policy?
> – German Green Party foreign affairs expert Ludger Volmer, 1984[1]

While diplomats in foreign ministries worried about Vietnam and whether to convey their doubts to their American allies, the more visible opposition to the war was happening on the streets. Small, isolated demonstrations in the early 1960s gathered momentum as the war grew in scope, the marches and chants fueled by a bourgeoning antiauthoritarian youth culture until they erupted in a worldwide wave of protest. This transnational movement was frequently characterized as an unprecedented level of "anti-Americanism" sweeping the globe, as if in order to prove their commitment to democracy, freedom, and justice, young foreigners should have set aside their concerns and supported the war in Vietnam merely because it was an American war. Some demonstrations were launched by a kaleidoscope of leftist groups whose professional ideologues argued over whether objective truth emanated from Moscow, Havana, or Beijing. The hundreds of thousands of young protestors who made up the crowds, however, were members of a thoroughly "Americanized" generation, both in their commitment to democratizing their own societies and in their taste for American popular culture in music, film, slang, and style of dress. The '68ers – *soixante-huitards, Achtundsechziger, sessantottini, sesenta y ocheros* – would make their societies culturally and politically more like America, nowhere more so than in West Germany, the main focus of this chapter, even as it is placed in a broader European context. As the protests of the 1960s flowed into a variety of social movements for peace, environmental protection, and women's rights in the next two decades, and as the thawing of the Cold War in the era of détente made Manichean visions of international affairs even less persuasive abroad, the myth of anti-Americanism would continue to come between Americans and perceptions of the changing world around them.

Vietnam crystallized the paradigm into permanence. By 1967, sentiment against the war was so strong abroad that when Vice President Hubert

Humphrey began a tour of European capitals in the spring, he was "dogged by anti-American demonstrations in Rome, Florence, Bonn, Paris, Berlin, and Brussels."[2] He opened his tour by declaring, "We have nothing to apologize for," then spent the rest of the trip ducking for cover.[3] In Florence, a protestor threw an egg into his car and another struck him in the face with a lemon. Demonstrators in Milan, ranging from communists to *capelloni* (longhairs), fought the police and thirty people were arrested. In Rome, Humphrey dodged a pouch of yellow paint as his motorcade was rerouted around the demonstrations. Safely inside a government building, Humphrey listened to his Italian counterpart and fellow social democrat Pietro Nenni compare the Vietnamese guerrillas to the Italian partisans fighting against fascism in World War II. Whatever one might think of the noisy crowds outside, Nenni said, "broad swaths of European public opinion and Italian opinion that are not identified with the communists" favored an end to U.S. bombing and a negotiated settlement. Humphrey asked for more solidarity from America's European friends. "Europe does not understand America any longer," Nenni said. "America does not understand Europe. The root of the discord is the Vietnam War." The inconclusive meeting over, Humphrey slipped out a hidden exit to avoid the throngs.[4]

From the Italian frying pan Humphrey went into the Parisian fire. Demonstrators dogged him from the airport into the city, splattering his motorcade with white paint, then defacing the American Cultural Center and smashing windows at the American Express building. Meeting the French president, Humphrey noted that the United States had pulled its troops out of the Dominican Republic, as de Gaulle had urged when they met two years before. "You did well to withdraw your troops," de Gaulle snapped. "You would do even better to withdraw them from Vietnam."[5] Humphrey then braved the crowds to lay a wreath at the statue of George Washington at the Place d'Iéna and returned to the embassy. As two of his Marine honor guards folded up the American flag used in the ceremony, they were set upon by protestors. A U.S. official report on the incident described the Marines bravely fighting their way through the mob with their fists as "French police positioned at either end of the block made no move to disperse the crowd or come to the assistance of the Marines." The demonstrators then moved on to the Avenue George V, where they tore down and burned an American flag. "No policemen were to be seen during the ten minutes it took to burn the flag," the report said.[6] Conservative columnists Rowland Evans and Robert Novak sharpened the account of the incident and blamed it on de Gaulle. "Some 25 Communist toughs assaulted two U.S. Marines during Vice President Hubert Humphrey's visit here while French policemen watched impassively," they wrote, calling it "a surface indication of the strong anti-American offensive waged on many fronts by de Gaulle."[7] Scholars have continued to refer to the incident as a vivid example of French anti-Americanism under de Gaulle's leadership.[8]

It is understandable that after years of linking France and de Gaulle to anti-Americanism, Americans would tease this narrative out of the events, not only because of the beating of the Marines and the burning of the flag but also because assumptions often prevent the intrusion of incompatible facts. These facts included, to begin with, that de Gaulle was a target, not an instigator, of the demonstrations. Cries of *"Humphrey assassin!"* ("Humphrey is a murderer!") were followed by *"De Gaulle complice!"* ("De Gaulle is his accomplice!"). Another chant was "Charonne!" – a reference to the police killing of nine antifascist demonstrators during a protest over Algeria at the Charonne metro station in February 1962. Where Americans saw only French anti-Americanism in the streets of Paris, French protestors were focused on a number of issues of intense concern to the left, from Vietnam and the French colonial past to police repression.[9] As Humphrey himself noticed, "there was heckling by these people during the French national anthem as well as our own."[10]

The second set of inconvenient facts missing from the tale of vicious French anti-Americanism is that French police did not stand by, and Parisians did not attack the Marines that day; American expatriates did. Before the ceremony began, police intercepted a group of American antiwar protestors, confiscated their placards and banners, and directed them to a spot on the median at the edge of the Place d'Iéna, where they could demonstrate without blocking traffic. They yelled at Humphrey as he placed the wreath, and then police began arresting some of them, along with two English journalists in their midst, Harold Sieve and Jack Gee. Sieve and Gee would later send a letter to *Le Monde* confirming that the protestors were Americans.[11]

After the ensuing brawl and arrests, French detectives investigating the events were not given access to the Marines, but they did interview three members of the American Legion who had been present for the ceremony. One of the veterans, Richard M. Anderson, told police that most of the crowd was made up of Americans of student age. All three veterans confirmed that there were no police nearby when the fighting started, but twenty-five policemen stationed 200 meters away rushed to break up the fight when they were alerted by a passerby that demonstrators had attacked the American flag bearers.[12] In the flag-burning incident on the Avenue George V, police radio logs show a lag of only two minutes between the time the flames were first spotted by a patrol car and the arrival of a commander with twenty-five of his men to disperse the crowd.[13] What looked from afar like a paroxysm of de Gaulle-inspired anti-Americanism resulting in the beating of two U.S. servicemen under the unfeeling gaze of French police looked to English and American eyewitnesses like American expatriates turning a protest against the Vietnam War into a mini-riot that was quickly suppressed by French authorities.

This episode, as reported across the Atlantic, resonated strongly among Americans already accustomed to thinking of the French as driven by anti-American hatred. An Associated Press report about rioting Parisians attacking two U.S. Marines was reprinted widely, and Americans from all walks of life responded. Alan Cummings, a wealthy Consolidated Foods executive who liked to take $50,000 French vacations, resolved never to return to Paris.[14]

William Cornelius Hall, president of Chemtree Corporation, sent de Gaulle the AP photo of the flag-burning, demanded an apology, and declared that such an affront "would not here be permitted to happen to the flag of any nation with whom diplomatic relations existed, least of all to a nation with friendly ties as old as those between the U.S.A. and France."[15] He spoke too soon. Two days later, a twenty-four-year-old telephone company worker in Boston bought a French flag and assembled ten friends to burn it on the steps of the French consulate.[16] In Chicago, two men called the press and then tried to burn a French flag in front of the consulate there. Surrounded by forty reporters and four television broadcasting trucks, they managed to create a baseball-sized hole in the flag they had brought with them before they were arrested for disorderly conduct.[17]

This tit-for-tat shows how national flags can become targets for people expressing indignation over actions blamed on that nation, whether they be Americans angry at France over the Humphrey riots or French (and Americans) angry at the United States for its conduct of the war in Vietnam. It is not surprising that many Americans have come to see "anti-Americanism" behind the act of flag burning. The flag can stand symbolically as a representation of the state, or it can stand metonymically for the nation, so that to damage it is to attack the whole nation and its people. All-encompassing hatred of American values and a desire to injure Americans may motivate some flag-burners, but the semiotic power of the act ("I am burning America") is often more far-reaching in effect than the protestor who is seeking the attention of news cameras may intend to convey ("I am angry at U.S. actions").

A few American journalists tried to contextualize the Humphrey protests. The *Los Angeles Times* noted that French authorities could not have prevented the demonstrations "short of adopting police-state methods to suppress rights of assembly and free speech."[18] Bernard Redmond, in Paris for news station WINS, reported that the incidents were "sincerely deplored here," even though they represented "in exaggerated form the real feeling of the French and of most Europeans against Washington's Vietnam involvement. The French as a whole aren't anti-Humphrey or anti-American but they disapprove of the Johnson Administration's Vietnam policy, and more in sorrow than in anger."[19] CBS correspondent Peter Kalisher observed that the scale of the protests "showed that even to the friendliest of governments, Vietnam is becoming a political albatross."[20]

That became clear when Humphrey arrived in Germany. He drew applause from West Berliners pleased to hear another prominent American politician promise to stand by them, but they were less impressed by his argument on Vietnam.[21] Antiwar demonstrations accompanied each of his speaking events, screened by a massive police presence because of an elaborate plot that the rightist press depicted as a conspiracy by radical students to use "chemical high explosives" provided by the Chinese Embassy to assassinate Humphrey. Hundreds of students yelling "Vice Killer" threw eggs and bottles at the parked Cadillacs of his motorcade, but the "explosives" turned out to be bags of pudding mix, and eleven students jailed after the initial reports of plotting had to be freed.[22]

The argument over the Vietnam War was embedded in domestic disputes in which the clashing sides used America as a symbol of the true democracy that each claimed to champion. West Berlin Mayor Heinrich Albertz supported Humphrey's claim that Berlin's freedom was being defended in Vietnam. The Student Union of the Free University protested his "false historical analogy" and produced an "open letter to the Mayor of Berlin" reproaching him and Humphrey for comparing officials in Berlin's democratically elected government to those of Vietnam's military regime.[23] Reinhard Lettau, a professor of German literature who had studied in the United States and returned there in 1967 to teach at the University of California at San Diego, defended the student demonstrators against charges of anti-Americanism. He asked why club-wielding German police who concealed their badge numbers and beat up peaceful demonstrators while barking "this isn't kindergarten" were labeled pro-American heroes, while the opponents of the war were called anti-American. "Or are the 120,000 New Yorkers who demonstrated against the war yesterday also anti-American? I insist: We were the pro-American demonstrators!"[24]

Humphrey's last stop was in London, where a hard rain drove away most of the protestors, and their scarcity on the ground seemed to revive the buoyant politician. He spoke at the U.S. Embassy, remarking that he had enjoyed his tour of Europe, although some of the countries seemed to have a problem of surplus egg production.[25] On his return to Washington, he was less diplomatic. In a report to Johnson, he compared Europe to "a young man just arriving at the age of maturity," in need of guidance from the more mature United States (an inversion of the cliché that, when used by Europeans to describe the United States, draws cries of "anti-Americanism"). "No one with whom I spoke," Humphrey wrote implausibly, "indicated basic disagreement with our presence and objectives in Vietnam." Instead, Humphrey claimed that criticism of the war was a problem of "public relations" that could be remedied through cultivation of European journalists.[26] Humphrey evidently had not been listening carefully to the people inside or outside the government buildings he visited, not to Italy's Nenni, who had told him Vietnam should be left to the Vietnamese and that Europe "loathed" the war, nor to Prime Minister Harold Wilson of Britain, who had urged him to support British efforts to nurture a peace settlement with the help of the Soviets, nor to Foreign Secretary George Brown, who criticized U.S. bombing, nor to Wilson's Parliamentary Secretary Harold Davies, who said that the North Vietnamese leaders were not irrational Neanderthals but "experienced, cultured diplomats" with whom one could negotiate.[27] As they had for several years, many British and Italians continued to harbor misgivings similar to those of their French counterparts, but those who publicly called the war ill-advised were labeled anti-American, whereas those who put up a public front of support for a war that they knew to be wrong were regarded as the true friends of America.

Anti-Americanism in the Streets?

For foreigners outside government who took their views of the Vietnam War into the streets, the labeling was even more ironic. The most thoroughly Americanized generation of young people in history, who marched through Paris, Frankfurt, and Rome wearing blue jeans and singing American folk songs, were dubbed "anti-American" as they adopted American protest methods to oppose a war that was damaging the United States.

To challenge U.S. policy openly marked a sea change in European opinion, especially among the young. "America" had been positively connoted in the fifties among German fans who went wild for Elvis or rocked around the clock with Bill Haley and the Comets. French fans of Jacques Brel may have preferred his *chansons* to imported rock, but they knew what he meant when he sang "Madeleine is my hope, she is my very own America."[28] When Italians danced to Renato Carosone and Nicola Salerno's *"Tu vuo' fa' l'americano"* ("You wanna do the American"), they smiled at its gentle teasing about the whiskey and Camel cigarettes that they consumed with relish – just as Carosone and Salerno *facevano l'americano* by playing a frantic kind of swing.[29] Cultural enthusiasts of America, this is the generation that, along with millions of young Americans, came out against the American war a decade later. It was fanciful to attribute this opposition to an irrational hatred of the United States as if European (and American) youth secretly disliked democracy or no longer wanted to be modern. Instead, one must consider the content and context of their protests.

The antiwar movement in Europe was slow to develop and partly inspired by its American counterpart. Like the American Students for a Democratic Society (SDS), German student activists began with a cultural critique of their own society. They were reacting against the stultifying political climate under Chancellor Konrad Adenauer in the 1950s, when "the Old Man" campaigned on the slogan "No Experiments." The German SDS, the *Sozialistischer Deutscher Studentenbund*, founded in 1946 as a youth organization of the Social Democratic Party (*Sozialdemokratische Partei Deutschlands*, SPD), diverged from the larger party initially out of concern that the SPD was insufficiently resolute against German militarism and the far right: in 1959 and 1960 the SDS publicized the presence of former Nazis in the justice system, and in 1960 broke with the party in protest against the possibility that Germany might acquire nuclear arms.[30] (To many Germans scarred by the war's destructiveness and their responsibility for it, the prospect of a German atomic bomb was anathema, and they were disturbed by Adenauer's blithe description of atomic weapons as merely "the further development of artillery.")[31] The SDS was firmly grounded in democratic and pacifist aims when it held a teach-in at the Free University in West Berlin in December 1965 to protest the Vietnam War. Participants included noted intellectuals and writers such as Ernst Bloch, Heinrich Böll, Hans Magnus Enzensberger, Helmut Gollwitzer, Jürgen Habermas, Erich Kästner, and Martin Niemöller, all of them committed antifascists who spent their lives grappling with and trying to atone for Germany's Nazi past.

Some scholars have characterized opposition to the Vietnam War in Germany as an expression of endemic German anti-Americanism, but the texture of German political culture was too complex to be reduced to any single-minded antagonism toward the United States. One could detect an element of displacement, or the working through of feelings of guilt, in the occasional use of Nazi imagery on the German left and right in condemnations of America's leadership and actions. Antiwar protests featured posters of Lyndon Johnson's face juxtaposed to Adolf Hitler's, while crowds of demonstrators chanted "USA-SA-SS." Letters to the editor in conservative newspapers decried the American "final solution" and "war of extermination" in Vietnam, deliberately using Nazi terminology familiar from World War II. Signs reading "Dresden, Würzburg, Vietnam – terror bombers on the attack" equated German and Vietnamese victimhood.[32]

There is enough evidence of this aspect of the German reaction to Vietnam that some scholars have presented it as the primary cause of opposition to the war. "West German students were protesting not so much against the current American actions in Southeast Asia," writes Wilfried Mausbach, "as against past German atrocities in Europe. For them, Vietnam represented an opportunity to break away from their parents' generation of perpetrators and assuage their inherited national guilt."[33] Dan Diner agreed that American crimes in Vietnam were conflated with "the crimes of the fathers," as young Germans found relief in shifting their unbearable burden of guilt onto the shoulders of the Americans.[34] Perhaps some of the protestors were pleased to be able to point elsewhere when there was talk of atrocities, but if a discussion of the Vietnam-era protests in Germany might start with Freudian speculation, it should not end there.

To begin with, comparison is a useful tool: displaced guilt over the crimes of one's parents' generation cannot explain the motives of young antiwar demonstrators who filled the streets in Paris, Copenhagen, and Mexico City, or, for that matter, Berkeley, Chicago, and New York. Moreover, the pop-psychological explanation ignores the many overlapping currents of German politics and historical memory intersecting with official and unofficial relations between Germans and Americans at the time. People often look to their own national histories to make comparisons in explaining foreign events, as when Americans dub sympathetic revolutionary leaders "the George Washington of [insert name of country]." Günther Anders, a harsh critic of the war, wondered why it was forbidden to compare Vietnam to World War II if Secretary of State Dean Rusk felt free to compare critics of the war to Neville Chamberlain, or the *Wall Street Journal* could compare Ho Chi Minh to Hitler.[35] Everyone, it seemed, was drawn to inexact analogies. The most traumatic event of the twentieth century remained a touchstone in discussions of national and international affairs, and if it usually brought more heat than light, it was certainly common.

If comparing any leader to Hitler is a fool's game, in this case the comparison was unusually inapt. Johnson had no ambition for foreign conquest, and he pursued a progressive domestic agenda with nothing remotely approaching the Nazi repressive apparatus. When this generation of Germans invoked the Nazis, however, there was something other at work than the transference of guilt. Many of the young people in the streets were the same ones who had deliberately dragged the dark deeds of the past into the daylight of the present, confronting their parents' generation over their complicity with fascism. Angry over the "second silence" of respectable postwar German society, which had not objected to Auschwitz and now was silent over Vietnam, they demanded more accountability, democracy, and freedom in their own society, not less.[36] Their professors and mentors were the same ones who vigilantly patrolled the boundaries of German politics for any hint of the reemergence of prefascist tendencies, hoping to inculcate a democratic political culture that would preclude a return to the dark years through active civic engagement, public commemoration of German crimes, and the de-legitimization of military force. Jürgen Habermas, young philosophical sage of the democratic left, gained fame for promoting what would come to be known as *Verfassungspatriotismus*, or constitutional patriotism, a rather American notion of allegiance to the constitution rather than to an ethnicity, a ruler, or a mythical common origin. Drawing on their own past as the most essential of cautionary tales, they worried that another powerful country might now be going down a dangerous road. They watched with growing horror as the American leaders who had inspired them, Martin Luther King and the Kennedy brothers, were gunned down and feared a repetition across the Atlantic of the kind of endemic political violence that had afflicted the fragile Weimar regime and led to the collapse of German democracy in the 1930s. As tough responses from the police and the political right contributed to an escalation of rhetoric and actions, the radical vanguard of the student movement moved further to the left, some of them arguing that the violence of war in the Third World justified engaging in violent protest at home.

It took some time for a mass movement of Germans to coalesce around the opposition to an American policy, partly because of the positive feelings that so many held toward Americans. Karl-Heinz Bohrer remembered nostalgically how "we young people saw the American gods stride out of the ocean in 1945, chewing their gum and being friendly to us and playing this wonderful new music, which the Nazis in the stupidest satire had ridiculed as 'nigger jazz.'"[37] That admiration sparked emulation from the very beginning, as when children who saw American convoys roll through Göttingen in 1945 ran into the fields to strip wheat kernels from the stalks and chew them for hours into a sticky paste they called *Kaugummi* (chewing gum).[38] American-inspired trends in dress, food, and entertainment soon followed. Arnulf Baring wrote that in those years the United States became a kind of "ersatz Fatherland" for grateful West Germans who had no other anchor, their old Germany discredited by Nazism, their new one shrunken and stripped of its nationalist mythology by the criminal aims that German pride had so recently served.[39]

Which politician in the world do you trust the most
in the current crisis to preserve world peace?

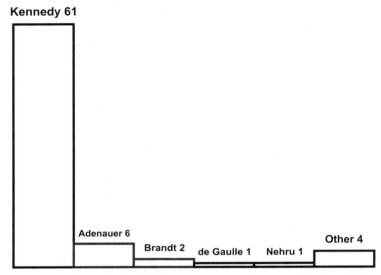

FIGURE 3. Percentage of West Germans surveyed in 1963 who chose Kennedy over other world figures as the most trusted leader. *Source: Emnid-Informationen* 34 (1963): 3.

These were the Germans who in the second half of the 1960s would allegedly unleash an underlying anti-American hatred produced by a transference of unprocessed guilt. If this were true, it would have required an extraordinary mental shift within the space of a few years, given the warm embrace these same Germans gave Kennedy in 1963 (Figure 3).

Could enthusiasts of Kennedy turn so quickly into hate-filled anti-Americans? To assert that a large population in the middle years of the 1960s suddenly decided to displace their sense of guilt and turned from warm, supportive pro-Americans into embittered anti-Americans rests on the confusion of psychology with politics. Whatever underlying psychological dilemmas this generation might have borne, they would not have been radically altered between 1963 and 1967. There was, however, an external factor that Germans who turned from praising to criticizing the United States said was the cause of that change, and that was what they learned about U.S. conduct of the war in Vietnam.

For many young Germans, their first knowledge of the Vietnam War came from an unusual source: a book of poetry. When Erich Fried published his collection *und Vietnam und* in 1966, there had been so little attention to that country in Germany that his publisher included a map and a chronology of events to help orient the reader. The book was ignored by most of the mainstream press, but it began to circulate in schools and churches and strongly influenced many of its mostly young readers. Inspired by Brechtian pedagogical verse, Fried encapsulated the dilemma of the "second silence" in his poetry. "The Americans freed us from Hitler," he wrote,

> But how long
> Can I still say "Friends"
> "Friends you have made a mistake
> in Vietnam and Santo Domingo"
>
> I have spoken out
> against Russian tanks in Hungary
> Should I be silent today?[40]

In his poem "Amerika," Fried praised American student protestors, "beaten down with clubs made of hickory," and called on Germans to show solidarity with America by demonstrating in solidarity with American demonstrators. In "Einleuchtend" ("Enlightening"), he took on the voice of an uncritical German to address the dangerous implications for German democracy of unquestioning support for the American war:

> It cannot be
> that the Americans
> unnecessarily
> burn Vietnamese children
>
> It cannot be
> that the Americans
> support Marshal Ky
> if he truly is a scoundrel
>
> They truly support him
> so he cannot be so bad
> and what he says
> cannot be so incorrect
>
> He truly does say
> his model is Adolf Hitler
> so it cannot be so bad
> for one to take Hitler as a model
>
> Hitler also burned children
> and not in Vietnam but nearby
> So why does one get upset
> when the Americans do it[41]

The invocation of Hitler in the context of an American war is grating, but the comparison originated with the American ally, South Vietnamese Prime Minister Nguyen Cao Ky. He had told a reporter, "People ask me who my heroes are. I have only one – Hitler. I admire Hitler because he pulled his country together when it was in terrible shape in the early thirties. But the situation here is so desperate now that one man would not be enough. We need four or five Hitlers in Viet Nam."[42]

As to Fried's use of the comparison, in the interest of accuracy and moral reasoning one might point out that the Nazis deliberately rounded up children for murder, whereas the Americans did not. In fact, the power of the juxtaposition of Hitler's war and the Vietnam War lies partly in one's awareness of the obvious differences, within which any similarities become shocking. Of course, Fried was not writing history or political science; he was trying to provoke indignation. The method worked. His lines soon began appearing in political pamphlets, letters of protest, and school newspapers. By connecting to young Germans' deep unhappiness over the crimes of their parents, he helped lead them to protest the worst crimes they saw happening in their own time.

Whether one believes that Nazism and the Holocaust constitute a sacrosanct topic that should never be raised in a context beyond itself, or, on the contrary, one is unsurprised that Germans think of the Nazis when speaking of war, it would be inaccurate to call Fried's impassioned criticisms of the Vietnam War psychological displacement or anti-democratic symptoms. Fried's antifascist credentials were obvious: he was a Viennese Jew who fled to London after his father was beaten to death by Nazis during the *Anschluß* in 1938. He had no reason to feel any guilt over Germany's past nor to look for ways to rid himself of a burden that he did not carry. Although Fried's stance against the Vietnam War became well known, he was also, like so many others who shared his views, not obsessed with America but deeply engaged in many struggles, especially those in Germany – both Germanys. East German functionaries resented his BBC broadcasts indicting their state for censorship and false propaganda.[43] The German right disliked him because he insisted on pointing out the lingering presence of Nazis in the government of the Federal Republic of Germany (FRG). When he wrote a poem questioning why left-wing terrorists in the 1970s received harsher sentences for murder than did Nazis who had murdered thousands of Jews, a Christian Democratic politician exclaimed that Fried's writing should be "burned."[44] This was one of many episodes in the political controversy that swirled around one of the best-loved poets writing in the German language, but Fried's work and commitments had nothing to do with any ingrained dislike of the United States or its most cherished principles.

"Pro-Americans" Against Americanization

If psychoanalyzing anti-fascist and democratic-minded Germans who opposed the Vietnam war as "anti-Americans" is misleading, those who at the time were considered "pro-Americans" should also be reexamined to see whether their values were more in line with American ideals. When President Kennedy worried in 1963 about anti-Americanism in Europe, he acknowledged that the most reliably "pro-American" voices came from the very sectors that used to be blamed for aristocratic snobbery toward the United States. "We may be able to appeal to conservative elements over there, and to the rich," he told his advisers.[45] Indeed, the staunchest defender of the American war effort was the Christian Democratic establishment. These conservative German politicians had by the early 1960s become convinced Atlanticists: they supported NATO and the presence of U.S. troops as their best hope for defense against the Communist threat from the East, and they supported the Vietnam War because they believed in the slogan from those days, "Berlin is defended on the Mekong." Christian Democrats were the first to call anti-war demonstrators in Germany "anti-Americans," just as they had spread the word that their Social Democratic rivals were "anti-American."[46] Because of West Germany's particular history after 1945, one of the peculiar characteristics of the anti-Americanism debate in that country was that the term itself came to be used as a political weapon by the right against the left, acquiring a similar function to the one it served in the United States: to discredit critics by implying that their criticism was based in the irrational rejection of the leading democratic power. Every invocation of the American role in helping to free the country from Nazi tyranny reinforced the notion that to be anti-American was to regret the outcome of World War II.

Yet German right-wing politicians were also those who had spent more than a decade inveighing against the creeping "Americanization" of German society. Like many parents and clergy, they looked with horror upon the transformation of Germany's youth, the questioning of authority in universities and the family, the premarital sex, the so-called "jungle rhythms" of rock music: it was older rightists who first denounced "the Coca-Colonization of Germany" under the growing American influence.[47] Whereas the political left, the Social Democrats and trade unions, "had a broadly pro-American tradition at least since 1949, if not going back to the Weimar Republic," sweeping rhetorical rejection of America and Americanization came from the political right.[48] Those most reliably "pro-American" in supporting the Vietnam War were also the most complacent about the presence of former Nazis in the West German bureaucracy and least tolerant of American cultural influence – neither pro-democratic nor pro-American beyond the exigencies of *realpolitik*.

This paradox should have called into question the whole notion of using the term anti-Americanism as if it were comprehensive and ideologically coherent. Instead, it came to designate opposition to a single, controversial U.S. policy – thereby emptying the concept of all deeper meaning. But just as criticism of the United States should be analyzed in context, supportive comments should also be placed under the microscope. Hilmar Bassler, a German diplomat and former Nazi Party member, supported the deployment of more American troops to clear South Vietnam of rebels. By using the verb *reinigen* (to cleanse or purify), he placed himself in a discourse familiar from the Eastern Front that treated partisans as vermin.[49] For ex-Nazis, the war in Vietnam was a continuation of the struggle against Bolshevism and the "barbaric Asiatic hordes" that Germany had fought in two world wars.[50] Jürgen Habermas thinks that German rightists found a pro-American stance to be a useful "instrument of forgetting," as they were able to couch their brand of anti-Communism – anti-Slavic, anti-Semitic, and anti-Asian, as one of the unbroken continuities from the Nazi era, it should have been suspect – in terms of a Western, democratic alliance. "Anti-Communism in the Federal Republic was so widespread," Habermas said, "it required an anti-anti-Communist movement to create space for real democracy in this country."[51]

The intertwining of debate over the U.S. role in Vietnam with German concerns about their own postfascist society was evident at every turn. In 1968, playwright Peter Weiss staged a piece of agitprop called "Vietnam Diskurs" in Frankfurt. Weiss, strongly influenced by the political theater of Bertolt Brecht and Erwin Piscator, had most recently provoked the establishment with "The Investigation," which turned the uncomfortable audience into participants in the Auschwitz trial that was then confronting West Germany with its first national conversation about its murderous past. (In "The Song of the Lusitanian Bogey," he attacked Portuguese colonialism.) In "Vietnam Diskurs," Weiss turned his attention to the American war, criticizing the comfortable lifestyle of middle-class spectators who experienced the war only through their television sets. On opening night, far-right groups had called in bomb threats, and so uniformed policemen were stationed inside the theater. A heckler started yelling that they should be thrown out, and the mood began to turn ugly. At this moment Habermas, who was in the audience, calmed the crowd by saying that they should stay, because when would these gentlemen ever get another chance to see such a play?[52]

It is notable that many critics on the left measured the United States strictly against its own self-proclaimed values, rather than rejecting those values; indeed, leftist Germans rejected many of the traditional *German* values that the old right had celebrated (nationalism, racial supremacy, respect for authority, faith in the superiority of German *Kultur*, etc.).[53] This observation could lead one to question who was more "anti-American": the students seeking to democratize their society, who loved American culture and hated the war, or their parents and grandparents who supported the war on anti-Communist grounds and hated the way American culture was "corrupting" Germany's youth. Moreover, since the war was terribly damaging to the United States, those "pro-Americans" who supported its escalation might be said to resemble an alcoholic's enabling buddies rather than the true friend who urges him to sober up.[54]

As the Free University theologian Helmut Gollwitzer put it, "it is not anti-American, but pro-American, to raise my voice against this mistake of American policy whose consequences affect us all." Precisely because he was not anti-American, Gollwitzer argued, did he care enough to want Americans not to follow misguided and brutal policies: "I find the carpet bombing of a dirt-poor, courageous people by the combined military power of the world's largest industrialized country simply abhorrent.... In Rome a Vietnamese bishop told me that in his diocese a thousand people are killed by American bombs every week. If that leaves us cold, we should at least stop calling ourselves Christians and celebrating Christmas."[55] In his phrasing, Gollwitzer was not far from a disillusioned Secretary of Defense Robert McNamara, who wrote to President Johnson that "the picture of the world's greatest superpower killing or seriously injuring 1,000 noncombatants a week, while trying to pound a tiny backward nation into submission on an issue whose merits are hotly disputed, is not a pretty one."[56] Raymond Aron, whom Undersecretary Ball considered a "completely trustworthy" friend who was "pro-alliance and pro-American," went even further: America's "monstrous" and "inordinate violence" in Vietnam "pounded a people and polluted an environment.... Seldom did the image of a David and Goliath seem so symbolic as during this long-drawn-out trial of strength between huge machines and little men.... Was dumping millions of tons of bombs on Vietnam the way to defend the free world?"[57] That three men with such different perspectives could reach the same conclusion suggests that it was the object of their commentary (the war) and not the subjectivity of the commentator (some inherent pro- or anti-American orientation) that caused them to oppose this particular U.S. policy.

Horkheimer vs. Marcuse; Horkheimer vs. Horkheimer

The inadequacy of the pro- and anti-American schema is laid bare when we try to impose it on individuals at the center of the controversy. Max Horkheimer and Herbert Marcuse, two German Jewish refugees from Nazism who had fled to the United States, played key roles in the public debate over Vietnam. Horkheimer returned to Germany after World War II to help refound the Frankfurt School for Social Research with Theodor W. Adorno, while Marcuse taught at several American universities, finishing his career at the University of California at San Diego. Their writings were instrumental in helping to move the New Left away from the traditional Marxist notion that workers would revolt against exploitation and scarcity, and toward an analysis of wealthier societies that emphasized alienation in the midst of affluence, putting the focus on students and academics as potential bearers of social change. The leading anti-anti-American scholar Paul Hollander condemns "the whole Frankfurt School" for its claim that industrial mass culture limited the capacity for independent thought, what Hollander considers an attack on "virtually all the institutions of American society."[58] Placing them in the anti-American category does not explain their thinking, however, nor is it a good indicator of the positions they took on the war. Horkheimer was a staunch supporter of U.S. policy. At the height of the protests, he gave speeches defending the United States and the war, admonishing the student activists, "Don't forget that we would not be here together and able to speak freely, if America had not intervened and saved Germany and Europe from the worst totalitarian terror."[59] Marcuse, meanwhile, opposed the war and became a kind of guru to the student movements in both the United States and Germany.

From this information, it might seem evident who would be "anti" and who would be "pro," but the facts are more complex. Marcuse liked America so much that he made it his home, while Horkheimer never felt comfortable

there. Marcuse's warning that modern workers were becoming extensions of
the commodities they produced – "they find their soul in their automobile,
hi-fi set, split-level home, and kitchen equipment" – resonated strongly with
young people in both the United States and West Germany who had not found
personal satisfaction in being the first generation able to take material abundance for granted.[60] In May 1966, Marcuse gave the keynote address at the
national congress of the German SDS, calling on German students to emulate
the antiwar activism of American students. The congress's final communiqué
expressed solidarity with the American antiwar and civil rights movements,
opposing a U.S. war by allying with Americans who opposed it.

In part, the differences between Marcuse and Horkheimer reflected the
different lessons they took from the Second World War. Horkheimer's message was that one must remain grateful to America no matter what it does.
Marcuse's lesson was that one must not remain silent about any crimes even
if committed by the former savior. Habermas remembers marching next to
Marcuse in an antiwar demonstration in Frankfurt in 1967, when Marcuse
said to him gravely, "You have no idea how sad it makes me to have to be
here, because America saved me."[61]

It is even harder to pin on Horkheimer a simple pro- or anti-American label.
While he lauded the "inner freedom" that Americans exhibited because they
expected their government to serve them and not vice versa, he also attacked
McCarthyism in unusually strong language, condemning "the irresistible historical tendency making America resemble terroristic Russia."[62] This comparison was as inaccurate as any Sartrian or Marcusian claim that America was
coming to resemble a fascist country, yet it came from the country's public
champion. Moreover, in his journal, Horkheimer acknowledged Vietnam to
be a "dirty war" and wrote that America's "foreign policy is grounded in
lies."[63] His private notes include bitter remarks about America's "alliances
with the most reactionary governments in the world...Mass murderers are
caressed and embraced." Having fought against Nazism, the United States
now supported Nazism's "ilk throughout the whole world."[64]

Further complicating an assessment of whether Horkheimer should be classified as pro- or anti-American is the fact that at times he expressed sentiments about America's and Americans' cultural poverty that were squarely in
line with aristocratic traditions of America-bashing that he, like later scholars, considered illegitimate. Conversations with Americans were shallow and
dull. "American civilization cannot bring forth anything new. It has no depth.
Thought is powerless," he wrote. "Why is thought powerless? Because it does
not serve specific interests. In the United States only that may prosper which is
directly aimed at furthering interests."[65]

Under the terms of the scholarly consensus, these ideas qualify Horkheimer
as a double anti-American, first of the left for maligning U.S. foreign policy,
then of the right for disdaining American culture and society in such generalized
terms. His comparison of America to "terroristic Russia," however, was not
meant to suggest an equivalence of the two societies or a whitewash of the
gulag but rather reflected his view that political systems in the modern era are

characterized – and cursed – by an instrumental rationality that places ends above means, inevitably producing victims and suffering in what he and Adorno called the "dialectic of Enlightenment."[66] His feelings of social alienation while in exile in America did not lead him to become obsessed with hurting the United States or its interests. His claim that U.S. "foreign policy is grounded in lies" was made when it became known that the Gulf of Tonkin incident Johnson presented as America's *casus belli* never took place. His criticisms were deep and genuine, yet to a reporter, he described his feeling for America as one of "love."[67] All-or-nothing categories like "anti-American" do not leave much room for a sensitive observer of a country to which he was grateful and whose faults he noted with sorrow.

Americanized "Anti-Americans"

The antiwar student movement in Germany also expressed admiration for aspects of America – just not for its martial aspects. It is commonplace to note as a paradox that the young people marching through Frankfurt and Berlin carrying signs against the Vietnam War were dressed in blue jeans and singing songs by Bob Dylan. They invited others to join *ein Teach-In* or *ein Sit-In* where they linked arms and intoned "Ve shall overcome." Dismissing their own country's high culture as hopelessly tainted by Nazism, they adopted American popular culture "to the point of slavish imitation," recalled the poet and editor Hans Magnus Enzensberger. "It is bizarre – one went to the anti-American demonstration, then one went afterwards to the cinema to watch the latest American western."[68]

This appears contradictory only if one assumes a monolithic Americanism encompassing everything that the U.S. government does and everything American culture produces, which then must be embraced or rejected in toto. In the real world, where America, in Walt Whitman's words, is "vast" and "contains multitudes," it was no contradiction that the most Americanized generation of Germans in history protested an American war. Some of them attributed their stance partly to the success of the American effort to reeducate Germans politically after 1945, which inculcated a spirit of pacifism and independent thought to replace traditional German militarism and obedience.[69] For Enzensberger, who at age fifteen was drafted into the *Volkssturm* (people's militia) in the last days of World War II, Americans had rescued Germans by ending the war and treating them generously: "I am grateful to the Americans for saving my life. Without them, I would have been dead. Period." But then "the Vietnam War came as such a shock because I had idealized America."[70] He expressed his disapproval by abruptly resigning a fellowship at Wesleyan in 1968, telling the university president that he could not stay in a country reminiscent of Germany in the 1930s, where "a racial minority was repressed and persecuted, the arms budget grew alarmingly, and the government increasingly intervened in a counterrevolutionary war." He went to revolutionary Cuba instead but soon abandoned his romantic image of that society as he learned more about its failures.[71] Enzensberger might have been politically radical, but anti-Americanism does not convey the eclecticism of his concerns. His journal *Kursbuch* occasionally discussed American topics but never displayed an obsessive anti-Americanism; like much of what had become a German New Left, it reflected wide-ranging interests in political movements in Europe and the global South, carrying an article urging Germans to follow the Auschwitz trial of 1965 and others on German police surveillance and the defense industry, on South African apartheid, Iranian torture, the Cuban Communist Party, and war in the Congo, and further exploring linguistics, mathematics, the treatment of the insane, and futurology and science fiction.

The *Kursbuch* article that is most frequently cited as evidence of the journal's anti-Americanism was Reinhard Lettau's lengthy 1970 piece on "Daily Fascism" in the United States. Lettau's article consisted of just a brief introduction in his own words, followed by a collection of newspaper clippings from the *Los Angeles Times* and other papers reporting a rise in police violence, the White House's secret dispatching of construction workers to beat up antiwar demonstrators, and the efforts of Nixon's hagiographers to present him as an infallible leader. The title, quoted without context in scholarly treatments of German anti-Americanism, implies that the author was drawing not only a comparison but an equivalence between Nazi Germany and the United States in 1970. The article itself, however, clearly states otherwise. Before presenting his compendium of what Lettau thought might be harbingers of the germination of a fascist system in the United States, he made clear in his introduction that he intended no comparison to the Nazis but wished to warn about trends he found worrisome.[72] In this concern he was in the company of such respected Americans as Martin Luther King, Jr., who worried that in his "society gone mad on war," the extreme right might take power and bring about "fascism's triumph."[73]

Above all, for German left-liberal criticism of the war, there was the imperative to avoid at all costs the tendency toward complaisance and complicity that they saw in their past, without resorting to national hatreds. "The Americans are our closest allies, our closest political friends," wrote the novelist Martin Walser. But he felt that he had to speak up. Because Americans described the war as defense of the "Free World . . . they are conducting this war in our name too," he noted. "To be silent when one is a witness is intolerable." He argued that "one could practice German-American friendship" by supporting "the internal American opposition against the Vietnam War."[74] Walser's ambivalence toward the United States was capacious, multifaceted, and well informed enough to lead him to denounce U.S. policy in Vietnam and satirize what he saw as the excesses of West Germans' philo-Americanism in *Tintenfisch* (1969), and then a few years later to write a Whitmanesque tribute containing these lines:

> Think of it, one can *become* an American. Europe, I believe, is a funereal culture that overestimates itself.
> Could my homesickness for America be homesickness for the future?[75]

For many anti-war Germans like Walser, there was a deliberate and conscious emulation of aspects of American culture, politics, and public figures they admired. One can see this reflected in collections of "grey literature," the pamphlets and other ephemera produced by the student movement. A leaflet distributed at the Free University of Berlin invoked American opponents of the war such as "Senator Robert F. Kennedy, holder of an honorary doctorate from the Free University" and "the Nobel Peace laureate Martin Luther King, holder of an honorary doctorate from the Berlin Theological Seminary, who has called resistance to the U.S. Vietnam policy the moral duty of every American."[76] In March 1967, the Social Democratic University Club's national organization voted a resolution of sympathy with other prominent Americans who had called for an end to the war, including Senators J. William Fulbright and Wayne Morse, and the influential diplomat George Kennan.[77] When the Free University's Vietnam Committee called for demonstrations, including *Sit-ins*, in May, they quoted Henry David Thoreau in English: "When the law is of such injustice that it compells [sic] you to do injustice to another person, then I say: break the law."[78] Other students modeled their protests in style and tactics on those of their American counterparts in the Student Non-Violent Coordinating Committee and the Free Speech Movement.[79] "For me as a German at the time," recalled Andreas Huyssen, "in a country that had an authoritarian mentality, to understand civil disobedience as part of the practice of democracy was enormously important."[80] Thus were some German opponents of the American war becoming Americanized not only culturally but also, to an extent, philosophically as well.

The student leader Rudi Dutschke, who would later be shot in the head by a self-declared anti-Communist from the German far right who claimed to be inspired by Martin Luther King's assassin, edited a report on American atrocities in Vietnam (drawing on stories from Reuters and the *New York Times*) that offered an analysis that was far from "anti-American." (He certainly liked some Americans; his wife Gretchen was from Chicago.) "One knows the American soldier from the Second World War as a fair opponent who sought to avoid unnecessary victims on both sides," began his pamphlet *Why Is the American Soldier Brutalized by a War to Free the Vietnamese People from Communism?* Dutschke's text offered not a condemnation of American racism, or references to Indian-fighting, or similar attributions of violence to the American character, but explained that in the context of a war in which it was hard to distinguish the enemy from civilians and progress was measured by body counts, soldiers would inevitably grow desensitized to their civilian victims.[81] Dutschke, a gifted student and a committed leftist, was relentless in opposing the war and came to sympathize with the Viet Cong, but his stance did not stem from particularized hatred of America or some misplaced sense of guilt for his country's past: it was the latest incarnation of the Marxist tradition of anti-imperialism that went back to Rosa Luxemburg.

Daniel Cohn-Bendit, a leader of student protests in Paris, Frankfurt, and Berlin, whose parents were Jews who had fled Hitler's Germany for France,

explains the link between an acute awareness of the Nazi past and the determination to protest the Vietnam War. "We all talked about the Holocaust
and the Nazi seizure of power in 1933, and vowed that it would never happen again," he said. "Then we looked at our own time and developed the
theory of anti-imperialism. We sympathized with the struggles of the Vietnamese and the Algerians against French rule. In the sixties, we saw the United
States as carrying out an imperialist policy in Vietnam. Did that make us
anti-American?" He answered the question in the most personal terms. "I am
genetically pro-American. I was conceived at the first possible opportunity after
the Normandy landings, when my parents celebrated their new freedom. That
is why I am fundamentally grateful to the Americans: without them, I would
not exist."[82] His admittedly singular perspective is borne out by an exhaustive
recent study of student publications that found them to contain much criticism
of U.S. intervention in Vietnam and American backing of right-wing dictators,
but a "general lack of genuine anti-Americanism" in the pamphlet literature,
which more frequently featured "praise [for] American democratic values and
achievements."[83]

The Violent Fringe

Perhaps the contrast between the image of wild-eyed America-hating '68ers
and the articulated views of many of those involved in the anti-war movement
is explained by the selective focus of the media and some historians on a
radical fringe of the demonstrators. In early 1967, Professor Richard Lowenthal
estimated that of the 15,000 students at the Free University, several thousand
were interested in politics – mostly on the left – but of these only 50 were
radicals. Unfortunately, he remarked, the press, eager for the dramatic story,
had made the radical into a caricature of the student.[84] As the most committed
among the protestors, the radicals were willing to take personal risks and to
neglect their studies and families, and as the most doctrinaire, they were often
able to shout down rivals, dominate meetings, and stage highly visible actions.
Some of them sought to create instant utopian communities by squatting in
rundown buildings where they indulged in free expression and free love (and,
given their financial straits, a more mundane diet of dry bread and spaghetti
with ketchup), while they dreamed of liberating a repressed and materialistic
society from all forms of authority.[85]

The numbers of the angry, small at first, grew after police beatings of demonstrators. In June 1967, the shooting of a nonviolent student named Benno
Ohnesorg during a protest against the visit to Berlin of the Shah of Iran persuaded many that they faced the ominous return of the heavy hand of the
state in alliance with dictatorships.[86] Riots in Berlin now were deemed "anti-
American" because they included protest of the Vietnam War as well as the
Shah's rule. Only five years before, 10,000 rioters in West Berlin, angered by
the killing of a young refugee by East German border guards, were deemed to
be engaging in "anti-Americanism" because they decried the passivity of U.S.

soldiers who were not permitted to cross the Wall to help the victim as he bled to death in no-man's-land. Whatever the stated goal of a protest, it seemed to the American press, "anti-Americanism" lay behind it.[87] Young Berliners could shout against the Iranian dictatorship, the war in Vietnam, or political repression in East Germany, but Americans invariably assumed themselves to be at the center of their mental world.

The growing fear of authoritarianism was exacerbated by the shooting of Dutschke and by Parliament's 1968 passage of the Emergency Laws allowing constitutional rights to be suspended. Opposing the Emergency Laws on democratic grounds became a major issue for the student movement, as the SDS warned that "the post-fascist system in the Federal Republic of Germany has become a pre-fascist system."[88] The students now focused on intra-German politics and turned their attention to university reform (along with internecine factionalism) as America began to fade from their literature after 1968.[89]

A hard core became enamored of violence and celebrated spectacular acts. When an underground Belgian group set fire to a crowded Brussels department store showcasing American goods, some 300 shoppers were killed in the conflagration. Radicals in the Berlin group *Kommune I* – so far out of the mainstream protest movement they were excluded from the SDS – made light of the dead and linked them to American military casualties in a pamphlet entitled "New! Unconventional! Why Are You Burning, Consumer?" Gleefully mocking the Belgian victims as well as the GIs "shedding their Coca-Cola blood in the Vietnamese jungle," the *Kommune* polemicists expressed the hope that Berlin's department stores would be the next to go up in flames, so that the complacent could feel what it was like to be Vietnamese.[90] It was as if shopping – or being drafted – had become a capital crime. To gloat over the deaths of hundreds of Belgians whose only offense had been to take their wages and go shop for clothes was so far beyond the pale that it does not seem to make sense to say that "anti-Americanism" was at work – nor anti-Belgianism, for that matter. Members of the *Kommune I* and its less well-known counterpart *Kommune II* were drawn in various directions: some reveled in their ability to shock German society and staged illegal but nonviolent protests, hoping that countercultural "happenings" could awaken passersby from their materialistic somnolence. A few went underground and turned their more violent fantasies into reality by joining terrorist groups.

The most notorious of these in Germany was the Red Army Faction (RAF) headed by Ulrike Meinhof and Andreas Baader. These self-proclaimed urban revolutionaries bought guns from drug dealers, torched department stores, and set off bombs in the right-wing Springer publishing house, blaming its hostile tabloid coverage of Dutschke for inciting his attacker. Their support among the left declined as they moved from targeting empty buildings to people. They smuggled bombs into American military bases in 1972, killing four servicemen in "retaliation" for B-52 bombings of Haiphong Harbor. Protestors in Berlin had gone as far as holding up signs praising Ho Chi Minh, but the RAF members believed they could literally become part of the war and bring the battlefield to Germany. Nurturing their desire to feel kinship with genuine Third World revolutionaries, some RAF members went to train in Palestinian guerrilla camps in the Middle East. But they soon clashed with the Palestinians over doctrine and goals and returned to Germany, where the RAF accepted payments from East German intelligence and developed the notion that capitalism was directly responsible for poverty and starvation in the global South, which in their eyes justified killing bankers. They launched the so-called "German autumn" of 1977 with the kidnapping and murder of the head of the national German business association, Hanns-Martin Schleyer, and hijacked a planeload of German tourists. The RAF was responsible for more than thirty deaths.[91]

The terrorists' crimes were shocking, and some of them were directed against American targets. It is misleading, however, to explain their violence as the product of a continuum of "anti-Americanism" that begins with German disdain for American culture, flourishes in opposition to an American war, and culminates in the shooting of U.S. soldiers and German business leaders, as if the culture and the protestors were responsible for the path taken by a few people scattered in the midst of the crowds. The terrorists' ideology, for what it is worth, worked differently, combining a yearning for the putative moral clarity and daring of romanticized revolutionary struggles in the Third World with a free interpretation of the classical dilemma of *Tyrannenmord*. Since the time of the ancient Greeks, philosophers have asked whether it was permissible to commit the injustice of murder to relieve a people of an unjust tyrant. Schiller took up this question in his plays, and members of the anti-Nazi resistance debated it in Hitler's time. RAF members now not only answered in the affirmative but also convinced themselves that bankers and bureaucrats were the tyrants of their day. This placed them at the margins of political thought and required a denial of their victims' humanity, but it was their thinking about Germany and global politics that made them turn to violence, not an obsession with the United States. Although they may have evoked some muddled sympathy or given a *frisson* of rebellious excitement to some outsiders (while drawing sharp condemnation from Böll, Dutschke, Gollwitzer, Habermas, and others), it would require a very narrow aperture to peer at the broader German New Left and see its chief characteristic as the potential for terrorist violence rather than a generational conflict over how to put democratic principle into practice. When critics claim that "1968" was the culmination of a dangerous anti-American current in German political culture, they really mean "1977," and they are speaking of a minority of a minority, because most students never joined the terrorist fringe.[92]

Taking delight in violence was a rare enough quality that the terrorists contributed to the degeneration of the broad, mass-based movement into splinter groups, while many of the students who had been involved in it moved on into the middle-class professions, became academics and civil servants and social workers, or turned their attention to environmentalism and local politics. They helped to push through reforms that democratized and modernized the universities, ending the era when professors bestrode the campus like royalty, their briefcases carried by trailing research assistants. These and other reforms – in the family, where stern paternalism weakened, and in the workplace, where some hierarchies were leveled – contributed to the further "Americanization" of German society: 1968's legacy helped further the country's democratic reeducation that had been the goal of American occupation authorities since 1945.[93]

Transnational Protest

The broader European movements of the sixties displayed transnational similarities and connections that were rooted in generational and national experiences.[94] When President Johnson asked the CIA for a report on youth and student movements worldwide, the Agency investigated nearly 25 countries. Its report dismissed Communist infiltration as insignificant and emphasized national issues, university politics, and the Vietnam War as central to student concerns; but then the Agency blamed the "emotional crises" of adolescence for the outbreaks of unrest, undermining any notion that the students should be taken seriously.[95] Elsewhere, American observers, in typical fashion, depicted European peace activists as motivated by "emotional, wildly oversimplified" views and "irrational anti-Americanism."[96] William S. Schlamm, a former advisor to Henry Luce who cofounded the conservative *National Review*, argued that anti-Americanism by "neurotically disturbed" Europeans was driven by their scorn for American impotence evidenced by failure in Vietnam.[97] The *Chicago Tribune*, explaining once more "Why They Hate Us," argued that the failure to defeat Vietnamese guerrillas unleashed "the wild waves of Europe's anti-American subconscious," leading Europeans to act with "a woman's passionate contempt for a lover who proves not only inadequate but cowardly to boot."[98] Psychologically based anti-Americanism, apparently, was endemic among Europeans, who were gendered feminine, which reinforced their characterization as "passionate" and irrational. The prescribed cure was more virile American military force.

Such explanations might seem preposterous were they not part of a long-standing tradition that preceded the sixties and endures even today. Providing flip commentary about the collective mental state of foreigners instead of careful investigation of political conditions abroad, they misdiagnosed what was actually going on across Western Europe. As in Paris during Humphrey's visit, the angriest and most violent anti-war demonstrators in London were American students, according to U.S. Ambassador David Bruce, who watched them from behind embassy windows and read police surveillance reports.[99] In one scholar's assessment, "in general, criticism of American foreign and defense policy was far more important for the general shape of British protest discourses than anti-Americanism."[100] British protestors were also encouraged by prominent Americans, such as James Baldwin, Marlon Brando, Allen Ginsberg, Arthur Miller, Philip Roth, and others who signed an open letter in the London *Times* in 1967: "We assure you that any expression of your horror of this shameful war – a war which is destroying those very values it claims to uphold – ought not to be regarded as anti-American but, rather, as support for that America we love and of which we are proud."[101]

In 1967, British and French opponents of the war held a mock trial intended to publicize American war crimes, whose panel of judges was headed by famed philosophers Bertrand Russell and Jean-Paul Sartre. When convened, the tribunal compiled testimony and evidence – most of it already reported in the press – about aerial attacks on civilian hospitals, mistreatment of prisoners, and the like, in a one-sided examination that largely ignored crimes such as summary executions and torture committed by North Vietnam and the National Liberation Front, and concluded with Sartre's judgment that the United States was engaged in "genocide" in Vietnam. This was taken as yet more evidence of French national anti-Americanism at work.[102]

That overlooked a few key facts. As soon as French authorities got wind of the project in August 1966, they started finding ways to prevent the tribunal from convening in France, ranging from discreet personal approaches to Russell and Sartre to imposing visa controls and invoking legal prohibitions on impersonating a judge. The planned tribunal posed "a political problem, not a juridical one," wrote the Foreign Ministry's Director of Asian Affairs Etienne Manac'h, arguing that the overriding French interest was to maintain "a position of perfect objectivity" on Vietnam so that France could serve more effectively in pursuing peace among the parties.[103] De Gaulle himself bluntly told Sartre that he could not hold the tribunal in France because, despite differences with the United States, "a state . . . which remains her traditional friend, shall not be, on her territory, the object of a procedure that violates international law and practice."[104] When the tribunal finally opened in Sweden in May 1967, Sartre in his position as judge tried to play a moderating role, cutting off personal attacks on Lyndon Johnson and speaking in "measured tones" compared with Russell, in the view of a British diplomatic observer.[105] He also called for the establishment of a permanent war crimes tribunal that would be empowered to take up future conflicts of all kinds, not only those involving the United States. "When will the tribunal start investigating Communist aggression?" asked placards held up by about twenty protestors standing in the snow outside the meeting. Russell's response to that question came a little more than a year later, when the Bertrand Russell Peace Foundation organized a conference in Stockholm condemning the Soviet invasion of Czechoslovakia. It was not a full-fledged tribunal, and the 96-year-old philosopher did not attend in person, but he sent a message denouncing the Soviets.[106]

Sweden was now in line for the anti-Americanism charge, given its willingness to host the tribunal, its admission of American draft resisters, and its Prime Minister from 1969 to 1976, Olof Palme, who openly expressed his criticism of the war. Gunnar Myrdal pleaded with Americans to understand that nonetheless "there is hardly a trace of basic anti-Americanism in Sweden," with its long-standing ties to the United States developed through large-scale immigration. Sweden's fundamental "pro-Americanism" was no contradiction, he said, to the fact that "practically the whole Swedish people, with the exception of a few mavericks, condemns the Johnson government's war policy in Vietnam." Myrdal, whose *An American Dilemma* helped move the United States toward desegregation, now wrote, he said, as a "tried and tested friend" of America, "not in anger" but "in sorrow and the deepest anxiety."[107]

It took retirement for some U.S. officials to be able to view such global protests with equanimity. The former research director of the United States Information Agency looked back on the long 1960s and observed that "researchers have been hard-pressed to find much anti-Americanism" anywhere in the world. He cited surveys in eighty-two countries and major cities from 1963 to 1972 that showed only one place on earth – Karachi, Pakistan – where unfavorable opinions of the United States exceeded favorable opinions. Everywhere else, majorities were "very strongly positive." The same surveys showed consistent, strongly negative views of U.S. policy in Vietnam. This was not a contradiction: anti-Americans would have hated both the policy and the country that made it, but most people disliked only the policy that the country had made.[108]

Maturing Protest Movements

The thaw in the Cold War made possible a different relationship to the United States. Willy Brandt, the social democratic West German chancellor whose *Ostpolitik* did more to nurture détente than any previous Cold War policy (and got him accused of "fostering anti-Americanism" by the German right), wanted to maintain but recalibrate the partnership with the United States.[109] As foreign minister from 1966 to 1969, he wrote that he never could forget Americans' role in saving Germany after the war with the Marshall Plan, saving Berlin from Soviet pressure with the 1948 airlift, and while he was mayor of West Berlin, standing against Communist efforts to absorb the city into East Germany. He came to oppose the Vietnam War, however, because it damaged the chances of easing Cold War tensions and hurt America's own interests – as many Americans also understood, he wrote. "We Germans are not in a position to lecture about world affairs," he told American socialist leader Norman Thomas. "But we should certainly not be mere followers either, not a satellite that finds everything good and nice that the leading western power thinks correct. I argue especially against simplified, factually unsound comparisons between Vietnam and Berlin." Brandt called for a negotiated settlement, even as he tried to tamp down hostility toward the United States in his party's youth wing and committed West Germany to an enduring alliance with the United States.[110]

If Adenauer had pursued *Westbindung*, the integration of West Germany into Western European economic, political, and military structures, Brandt's *Ostpolitik* did not call any of that into question, it merely sought to complement it with an opening to the East that could permit Germany to regain the trust of countries that it had devastated in World War II. The ultimate aim was the end of the Cold War and reunification of divided Germany and divided

Europe. Beginning in the early 1970s, *Ostpolitik* began to bear fruit in the form of increased travel, cultural exchanges, and reduced tensions with the Eastern bloc, and some West Germans began to wonder whether the 300,000 U.S. troops stationed in their country were necessary. As fear of the Soviets lessened, local concerns came to the fore. When the U.S. army announced plans to turn a forest into a base for tank maneuvers, 80,000 Germans signed petitions arguing that although the soldiers were there "to defend our freedom," the base was unnecessary and posed a risk that children could be injured by stray ammunition. Other communities became the scene of protests against the noise from military helicopters and abuses committed by GIs. The *New York Times* reported all of these events under the heading of "anti-American incidents," even though some U.S. Army officials suggested that they were evidence not of hostility but of a maturing democratic spirit in West Germany that led citizens to take action on issues that concerned them.[111]

Increasing civic engagement by the generation of '68 helped fuel a diverse array of social movements in the 1970s and 1980s focused on promoting women's rights, alleviating poverty in the Third World, and protecting the environment. At the end of the 1970s, NATO plans to deploy medium-range Pershing II and cruise missiles in Europe in response to Soviet installation of SS-20 missiles helped to spark a massive peace movement and were accompanied by more open criticism of U.S. foreign policy in the media and in opinion polls. The antimissile movement was strongest in Germany, and reaction to it followed the familiar pattern. "Anti-America Feelings Sweep West Germany," headlined the *Chicago Tribune*.[112] *Time* magazine claimed that a "disproportionately influential faction of West German journalism is assertively anti-American."[113] The philosopher André Glucksmann called West Germany "the most anti-American country in Western Europe today."[114]

Despite such claims, there is little evidence to suggest that the antinuclear protestors – any more than the antiwar protestors of a decade earlier – were driven by an encompassing rejection of American values and of all things American. The demonstrators, as in all peace movements, were multigenerational but disproportionately young. They indulged in plenty of cheap ridicule of American leaders and playful alteration of recognizable American iconography, such as replacing the stars on the American flag, or the teeth in President Jimmy Carter's smile, with bombs. At the same time, they continued to take their cues from American protest traditions and to express themselves in the idioms of American popular culture even while following in the footsteps of the Christian antinuclear Easter March movement of the 1950s and 1960s. Social Democratic peace activists further worried that the deployments posed a threat to détente, their party's overarching foreign policy goal since 1970. (Initially supported by party leader and Chancellor Helmut Schmidt, the missiles were opposed by a majority of party members.)

Critics of the new missile deployments offered reasoned arguments rather than mere disparagement of America: the weapons' short flight time and the cruise missile's radar-evading ability made them appear to the Soviets as destabilizing, first-strike weapons that increased the risk of war rather than reducing it through deterrence. That argument might not have been compelling to all strategists, but it convinced enough people to build a movement. The Green Party, a coalition of grassroots activists interested in environmental issues, women's rights, and peace, took up the cause and received enough votes to enter parliament in 1983. Some of these activists were critical of the United States, but not its democratic nature; surveys of peace activists found that they were better educated than the average person and strongly supported democracy and constitutional government.[115]

Anti-anti-Americans like Paul Hollander have seen in the environmental and antinuclear movements an extension of "anti-industrialism," "aversion to modern technology," and "a generalized questioning of the moral foundation of the Western world" that have allegedly informed German criticism of America going back to the Romantic era.[116] This notion of a technophobic, anti-American German *Sonderweg* (special path), however, would not explain why German demonstrations were matched by massive antinuclear protests in Great Britain and the United States. For that matter, President Ronald Reagan himself experienced "genuine anxiety" after witnessing the superpowers come close to accidental nuclear war during NATO's 1983 "Able Archer" exercises, and his fears led him to change course and begin disarmament talks with the Soviets in earnest in his second term. No one ever accused Reagan of an aversion to modern technology (or of anti-Americanism) even when he became a latter-day nuclear abolitionist.[117]

Against "Euroshima"

To explain why millions of Germans and other Europeans suddenly joined protests against the planned missile deployments and the nuclear arms race after 1980, it makes less sense to plumb the psychological depths of their alleged anti-Americanism (which would presumably be a constant and not a new factor) than to consider a more obvious independent variable that arose at this time: a marked change in U.S. policy. Notorious statements by Reagan aides seemed to imply that they believed the United States could fight and win a nuclear war. Secretary of State Alexander M. Haig spoke of responding to a conventional Soviet invasion with "a nuclear warning shot."[118] Undersecretary of Defense Frank C. Carlucci said that the United States needed a "nuclear war-fighting capability." T.K. Jones, the Pentagon official in charge of civil defense, told a reporter that an atomic attack would be survivable if Americans had "enough shovels" to run out and dig backyard shelters.[119] With such rhetoric accompanying a massive military buildup, the prevailing view in most of Western Europe was that "U.S. policies have increased the risks of war."[120]

It was not as an amorphous movement railing against the United States, then, but as a direct response to the perceived increased danger to their survival that some three to five million Europeans marched in a single week of protest in the fall of 1983 in Bonn, Brussels, Dublin, Helsinki, London, Madrid, Paris, Rome,

Stockholm, and Vienna, turning out for demonstrations, candlelight vigils, and 60-mile-long human chains connecting American military bases.[121] That same year the international hit was German New Wave singer Nena's "99 Luftballons," the most popular song across Europe and the second most popular in the United States (unprecedented for a recording with German lyrics). Nena's success reflected the transnational youth culture's interest in the antinuclear movement: the lyrics described the release of toy balloons that inadvertently trigger global nuclear war when the militaries of several countries overreact. The tune was catchy, but there were plenty of catchy tunes pressed into vinyl that year; "99 Luftballons" resonated strongly with a generation who had lost confidence in their leaders' judgment and feared that militarism might destroy the world. Another 1983 hit by a New Wave band, Geier Sturzflug ("Vulture Nosedive"), depicted the atomic destruction of London, Paris, and Cologne, and urged listeners to "visit Europe – while it's still standing." Blockbuster sales in the United States suggest that those haunted by the messages of these apocalyptic pop songs were not anti-American but afraid of dying in a mushroom cloud, just like their European peers.

Among the broad European public, there was a strong aversion to war when it seemed clear that it would involve nuclear explosions on their soil, perhaps in their cities, leading to nightmare visions of "Euroshima." In 1983, majorities of 78% in Germany, 82% in France, and 85% in Italy thought that preserving peace was more important than going to war to defend the standard of living, liberty, or human rights.[122] The sense that continental Europeans have a stronger abhorrence of war than do Americans stems not from Europeans' supposed hedonism or effeminized weakness, as Robert Kagan has argued, but from their different collective memories of the largest wars of the twentieth century, which were fought in their homelands at a great distance from American soil.[123] The divergence is reflected in linguistic usage: American politicians regularly call for wars on drugs, on poverty, and on crime, but European politicians would not win points by calling for *Krieg* or *guerre* as a policy metaphor.[124]

Vietnam aside, if Americans still generally took pride in the wars that their country had fought and assumed they were defensive and justified, decades of democratic education had persuaded most Germans that the wars of their own past had been illegitimate acts of aggression, and that war brought only incalculable suffering and loss. A medical student in Ulm protesting the Pershing deployments wrote on his placard, "My Grandfather Died on the Western Front. My Father Died on the Eastern Front. Where Will I Die?"[125] To people horrified by war, Reagan's depiction of the Soviet Union as an "evil empire" in the "age of Armageddon" sounded like dangerous theology. Reagan's little joke – "My fellow Americans, I am pleased to tell you I just signed legislation which outlaws Russia forever. The bombing begins in five minutes" – was known to 77% of West Germans, of whom 86% thought it was out of line; 45% believed it was not merely a joke but expressed a secret desire.[126] Each year, West Germans were asked which superpower seeks peace in the world.

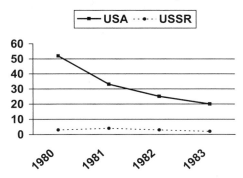

Which seeks world peace?

FIGURE 4. The impact of Reagan's military buildup and rhetorical belligerence. When U.S. policy changed, opinions changed. *Source*: Mueller and Risse-Kappen, "Origins of Estrangement," 58.

Very few named the Soviet Union. The figures for the United States declined precipitously once Reagan took office (Figure 4).

Similar results were produced by the question "Do you agree or disagree with the American President" on foreign and defense policy: In 1980, despite Carter's many problems, 42% of Germans said they agreed with his policies. Under Reagan, that figure fell to 19% by 1983.[127] At the same time, more than half of the Germans surveyed continued to say they "like the Americans," 78% thought that U.S. troops stationed in Germany helped to maintain peace, and 80% called for continued close cooperation with the United States. Any psychologically based or long-term culturally rooted explanation for opposition to the United States would presumably have shown a high degree of continuity, but this precipitous fall-off in support for U.S. foreign policy shows rapid change, because the declining approval was directed at the administration and its policies and not at the country as a whole.

Reagan's conduct of foreign affairs undermined the validity of the formula that held that to support U.S. policy was evidence of a democratic orientation and to oppose it was anti-democratic. Such categories were scrambled when Reagan praised Filipino strongman Ferdinand Marcos, for example, as "a respected voice for reason" and sent Vice President George Bush to attend Marcos's third inauguration, where he listened to a 1,000-voice choir serenade their leader with Handel's Hallelujah Chorus ("And he shall reign for ever and ever") before toasting the dictator with the words, "We love your adherence to democratic principles and to the democratic process, and we will not leave you in isolation."[128] The democratic image was also undercut when Reagan emphasized friendship with the apartheid regime in South Africa, "a country that has stood beside us in every war we have fought," whose minerals were "essential to the free world" (he did not explain how black South Africans should enjoy the benefits of that freedom).[129] U.S. journalists worried over what they called increasing "anti-Americanism" as Reagan's sympathy for the white regime angered many black South Africans.[130] When the U.S. Congress imposed sanctions on South Africa over Reagan's objections, that move sparked "anti-Americanism" among white South African nationalists upset at the interference in their affairs.[131] Anti-Americanism seemed to come in many colors. In fact, there was little anti-Americanism in any meaningful sense in that conflict; instead, there were people angry at the United States over U.S. policy, and the groups who were angry changed as the policy did.

Reagan's major undertaking in Central America, trying to topple Nicaragua's leftist Sandinista government, was also a major source of foreign disapproval. Before he took office, 38% of West Germans surveyed opined that the United States intervenes in the affairs of smaller states. By 1983, that figure had risen to 61%.[132] Domestically, critics of Reagan's Central America policies drew the usual label. Assistant Secretary of State Elliott Abrams charged journalist Anthony Lewis with "anti-Americanism" for criticizing the Iran-Contra affair, in which Abrams, Oliver North, and other U.S. officials illegally sold arms to Iran at a profit and raised other money abroad in order to transfer the funds secretly, in violation of express Congressional law, to the U.S.-backed counterrevolutionaries, the contras.[133] Thus did Abrams arrogate to himself the right to judge as anti-American an American critic who was defending the democratic process against Abrams's violation of the Constitutional separation of powers.

The Sandinistas themselves were, unsurprisingly, also labeled "anti-Americans"; for them, according to David Brooks, "anti-U.S. feeling was visceral." As evidence he pointed to their "new national anthem that included the proposition, 'The Yankee is the enemy of humanity.'"[134] That phrase sounds categorical, although the composer of the "Hymn of Sandinista Unity," Carlos Mejía Godoy, explained his intention in an interview: "When we speak of the Yankees, we are not speaking of a baseball team, nor are we speaking of those who are in musical groups nor of organizations that work for peace. We are speaking of the Yankees in power."[135] As indiscriminate as his original line may have sounded, it was obviously conceived during an era of geopolitical confrontation, when the Sandinistas were fighting a desperate struggle first against the U.S.-backed dictator Anastasio Somoza, whose dynasty enjoyed U.S. support for half a century, and then against the contras, who deliberately used terrorist attacks against civilian targets as part of a calculated strategy developed under CIA guidance. Nicaraguan resentment of that record was not exactly irrational.[136]

Of Continuity and Change

Across decades of surveys, a clear pattern emerges in public opinion about the United States, showing that foreigners react to changing events in international affairs rather than to an inner prejudice. Taking West Germany as an example, we see that the favorable rating peaks in the early 1960s, when President

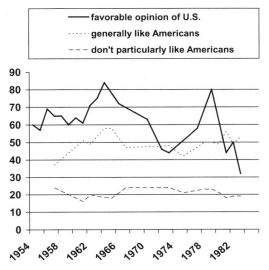

FIGURE 5. *Source: Allensbacher Jahrbuch der Demoskopie 1993–1997* (Munich: K.G. Saur, 1997), X: 1106.

Kennedy announced his solidarity with West Germany and delivered his famous speech in Berlin. Beginning only two years later there is a decline that accelerates after 1968, as the legitimacy of the U.S. war effort in Vietnam came increasingly into question. A low point comes in the early 1970s, the era of Watergate and revelations about CIA covert actions, including assassination attempts, in the Third World. The election of Carter, who promised to restore morality and respect for human rights to the U.S. government, coincides with a revival of favorable opinion toward the United States, but then Reagan's interventionism, his confrontational stance toward the Soviet Union, and his advisers' loose talk about limited nuclear war precipitate another rapid decline.[137]

The solid line that fluctuates greatly is the opinion of "the United States" (Figure 5). The steadier, dotted lines answer a different question, about whether Germans like "Americans" or not. The difference between the former and the latter two reflects the distinction that many foreigners make between the actions of the U.S. government, which they might approve of or disapprove of depending on the nature of each action, and the American people, who remain fairly popular in most periods. Even the minority of negative responses, moreover, is probably somewhat inflated here by the wording of the question. *"Mögen Sie eigentlich die Amerikaner oder mögen Sie sie nicht besonders?"* does not reveal the number of people who "don't like Americans," but who "don't particularly like the Americans" – thus measuring a lack of especially positive feeling rather than the presence of a negative feeling, thereby establishing a lower threshold for a negative response that is not congruent with hatred or enmity.

It is difficult to make the case that German anti-Americanism is evident in these data. The number of Germans stating that they like Americans hovered within a few points of 50% year in and year out, while the number holding a favorable opinion of the United States in the same years varied widely, from 30% to more than 80%, closely correlating to developments in international affairs. These spikes and troughs were not somehow the sign of a sudden and temporary change in the underlying culture of a foreign country. They did not respond to a surge in prejudice or the sudden outbreak of hostility toward first principles. Transitory periods of increased negative views of the United States reflected differences over policy, rather than causing those differences. If foreign views of the United States were rooted in envy of American wealth and power, or reflected an aversion to democracy or modernity, or emerged from a collective cultural memory of negative images and metaphors, the favorable and unfavorable ratings would not be expected to change so much from year to year, since American wealth and power and democratic organization have remained strong over time. It makes little sense to see a change and ascribe it to a continuity.

In other words, the United States was not "damned if you do, damned if you don't," as the anti-anti-Americans claim; it was damned when it did something unwelcome.[138] When its policies and actions were seen as consistent with professed American values or with the national interests of foreign countries, their populations generally expressed sympathy or support for the United States. When U.S. policies or actions seemed to diverge from its principles or the national interests of foreign countries, their populations expressed opposition. Changing policies provoked changing responses.

Lone voices took public exception to the view that behind these disagreements lay an ominous rise in anti-Americanism. U.S. Ambassador Richard Burt, seeking to mend fences, remarked that after a year and a half in Germany, he had yet to encounter any anti-Americanism worthy of the name. "Criticism of the government is a daily occurrence at home," he observed. "That doesn't scare me."[139] Ambassador Burt's distinction between anti-Americanism and criticism of the U.S. government, one rarely made by U.S. official or media sources, was reinforced by two leading German political scientists who closely studied polling data and documents from German political parties and concluded, "This general hostility is *not* focused on the whole United States nor on the concept of a German alliance with it. Rather, it is more narrowly focused on the policies of the Reagan Administration."[140] A careful study for the German Bundestag of 2,500 articles taken from West German newspapers between 1968 and 1984 found very little in the way of underlying anti-American prejudice but indicated that the press, liberal and conservative alike, tended to endorse measures that advanced international cooperation while generally condemning military intervention and state repression, regardless of whether these acts were taken by the United States or the Soviet Union. Editorials condemned the 1979 Soviet invasion of Afghanistan and the imposition of martial law in Poland two years later. The press was wary of Reagan's armament program, military intervention in Central America, and 1983 invasion of Grenada, but supported his willingness to enter negotiations with the Soviet Union. None of this showed a basic anti-American orientation among the German press but rather reflected independent assessments of changing policies.[141]

The notion that anti-Americanism was the best explanation for opposition to the Reagan nuclear buildup is further called into question by the simultaneous rise of an American movement favoring a freeze on nuclear weapons production and deployment, one that received over 70% public support in recurrent polls, was endorsed by 370 city councils and the House of Representatives, and led to a 1982 demonstration in New York City by nearly a million Americans that was the largest political rally in U.S. history up to that time.[142] The movements on both sides of the Atlantic peaked in 1983 after losing the battle over the missile deployments, but demonstrations of half a million or more continued over the next few years. Despite the myth that anti-Americanism motivated the European peace movement (and despite the effort of the KGB to capitalize on its small-scale infiltration of some peace groups), the protestors played a constructive role in bringing about a tectonic shift in the international system that was to the benefit of the United States.[143] Pressure from below in Western Europe and the United States helped drive the Reagan administration toward arms control negotiations and a resumption of détente beginning in 1985. That gave Soviet premier Mikhail Gorbachev political space to pursue the reforms that opened the way for Eastern European protest movements to flourish, and in 1989, bring down Communist rule. Détente had always been in the long-term interest of the United States and of the eventual restoration of a Europe "whole and free."[144] The allegedly "anti-American" Europeans who were early and consistent supporters of winding down the Cold War helped to end it on terms that enhanced America's security and standing.

The Cold War Ends; "Anti-Americanism" Lives On

If disagreement over policy during the Cold War was often taken as a sign of anti-Americanism, so too were disagreements over responsibility for its end. "The outpouring of warmth toward Gorbachev on his visit to West Germany in 1989 and survey results showing that he was far more favorably regarded than President Reagan," writes Hollander, "are further indications of anti-American sentiment."[145] In the same period, however, survey results showed that the most common adjective that Germans applied to Americans was "friendly" (picked by 82.5% of respondents).[146] And what are we to make of the finding that Americans, too, admired Gorbachev more than they admired George H. W. Bush, whom they had just elected president?[147] Either Bush was about to lead a nation of anti-Americans, or else many Americans, like many Europeans, were able to form independent judgments about Gorbachev's central role in setting Eastern European free and ending the most dangerous international conflict in world history.

With its end, the collapse of Communism changed the character of discourse about the United States. The Soviet alternative, whether inspiration or menace, was gone. Shorn of its Cold War context, "America" could resume its preeminent role as a convenient allusion in debates about the organization of society, one that was at once symbolic and concrete, because of Washington's tangible steps to promote internationally its neoliberal model. When foreigners argued over how far the state should intervene in the market to protect workers, families, and the environment, or regulate media monopolies, provide subsidized health care, or discourage fossil fuel consumption, they often used the United States as recognizable shorthand for a pro-business, laissez-faire approach.

Another way that the end of the Cold War affected "anti-Americanism" was in a new wave of publications by scholars interested in understanding and defining the phenomenon. Hollander published his major work in this period, casting so wide a net as to catch almost anyone who had a discouraging word for the United States.[148] In a more sober approach, Konrad Jarausch suggested that opposition to U.S. foreign policy be renamed *Amerikakritik* (America-critique) rather than anti-Americanism, because "it is often tied to attempts to improve the USA" and to urge a return to its original values, rather than to do it harm.[149] Peter Krause tried to develop a clear formula for distinguishing legitimate criticism from anti-Americanism: anti-Americans, he wrote, judge and reject America "as a totality," interpreting individual disliked aspects as "immutable characteristics of the United States."[150] Dan Diner was moved to write a book about German anti-Americanism after he thought that he saw it reaching "epidemic" proportions in "the reactions of the German public to American involvement in the Gulf War of 1991."[151]

In fact, the comparisons of American bombers over Dresden and over Basra, or the depictions of an aggressive and brutal American military machine that Diner dwells on, were marginal positions. During the fighting in Iraq, 76% of Germans expressed support for American policy, and peace groups were unable to muster anything like the same crowds that had come together against the Pershing missiles only a few years before.[152] That the opponent, Saddam Hussein, was an aggressive dictator who brutalized his people made for uneasiness among leftists who were now torn between their twin slogans of "never again war" and "never again fascism." Nor was it easy, as Saddam rattled his saber and fired his SCUD missiles against Israel, to evade the knowledge that German firms had helped to produce the Iraqi rockets and poison gas that now might again be used for the mass murder of Jews. Hans Magnus Enzensberger and Wolf Biermann, leading figures respectively in the movements against the Vietnam War and the Pershing deployments, decided that Saddam's similarity to Hitler was so strong that it compelled support for American military action. Green Party member and later Foreign Minister Joschka Fischer urged solidarity with Israel and deplored slogans against the United States. Jürgen Habermas defended the armed response to Iraq's invasion as legally sanctioned by the U.N. Security Council and morally necessary to protect Israel.[153]

Inevitably, protestors against the Gulf War were labeled "anti-American," not only by Americans but also by conservative Germans seeking to disparage the leftist opposition, as "the silly club that nobody is afraid of was hauled out once more," in the words of a skeptical journalist. If the charge of anti-Americanism had been inaccurate during protests over Vietnam and the Pershings, "this time it was even dumber, because some leaders among the intellectual left, gritting their teeth, endorsed the war.... But merely the fact that [some] demonstrated against the war sufficed to make them anti-Americans – which apparently to some simple persons in Bonn is something horrible."[154]

Gesine Schwan, leading political scientist and later candidate for the German presidency, tried to bring some sense to the discussion with a thoughtful and narrow definition of anti-Americanism. Conscious that the term had served chiefly as a political weapon of the right to discredit the left, she recommended that a distinction be made between legitimate critique, on the one hand, and "a basic, normative rejection of what the person in question understands as the core of Americanism," on the other.[155] To name America's failings was not a sign of anti-Americanism, Schwan wrote. To engage in anti-Americanism was "to totalize [those failings] as the necessary essence of American democracy, and therefore to implicitly or explicitly reject liberal democracy" that is the hallmark of the anti-American, anti-Western tradition.[156]

Schwan's view might seem to resemble that of the anti-anti-American scholars, except for a key difference: she understood such a basic rejectionist stance to be exceedingly rare and thus assigned the term only where it seemed to fit a small handful of ideologues. In this way, her interpretation might bring some needed perspective to the concept of anti-Americanism after two centuries of partisan instrumentalization, just at the moment when the rise of a new ideology in a new century makes disaggregating the sources of hostility toward the United States a matter of vital importance to America's national well-being.

Epilogue

The Anti-American Century?

"Why do they hate us?" It was September 2001. Nearly 3000 people had been killed in a terrorist attack that destroyed New York's tallest buildings, smashed a gaping hole in the Pentagon, and brought down four airliners crowded with travelers. In our shock and pain, Americans, led by the president, asked the question with more urgency than ever before.[1] Here, it seemed, was the tragic fulfillment of the danger posed by anti-Americanism: prejudice and irrational hostility had finally produced a catastrophe whose consequences were incalculable. Soon, commentators and scholars were depicting a continuum of anti-Americanism, beginning with the disdainful accounts of nineteenth-century travel writers, running through twentieth-century political rhetoric, and ending with fiery crashes into the premier symbols of American power.

The question "why do they hate us?" could have led to new insights and more effective ways to confront terrorism, had the word "they" been understood to refer to a small, focused group of terrorists and their active supporters and not to a hostile, anti-American world. Indeed, the initial response of the wider world was a tremendous outpouring of sympathy. As images of the smoking ruin of the World Trade Center were relayed around the globe, American diplomats in Beijing, Berlin, Helsinki, Moscow, Paris, and many other cities could look out their embassy windows and see crowds of ordinary people massing outside not to shout slogans but to place endless bouquets of flowers or hold candlelight vigils deep into the night. A sympathetic French government decreed three minutes of silence in every school and public office in the country. Drivers in Denmark and Germany stopped their cars and stood in respectful silence at noon. Hungarian fire trucks flew black flags of mourning for their fellow firefighters killed in New York. Across Europe, thousands queued up for hours at consulates and hospitals to sign condolence books or donate blood. Even in Tehran, a stadium grew hushed as soccer fans observed a moment of silence despite the official hostility of their regime. To be sure, there were pockets of celebration in Arab communities that held America responsible for their own suffering, including in Iraq and the

West Bank – although hundreds of Palestinians also gathered to pray for American victims. It was a moment of global goodwill that brought tangible assistance: for the first time in NATO's history, its members formally invoked Article 5 of the common defense treaty, declaring the attack on America an attack upon them all.[2]

The leading French newspaper *Le Monde*, so often charged with anti-Americanism in the past, caught the mood in an editorial: "We are all Americans! We are all New Yorkers, as surely as John Kennedy declared himself, in 1963 in Berlin, to be a Berliner. How could one not feel, as in the most serious moments of our history, profound solidarity with this people and this country, the United States, to which we are so close, and to whom we owe liberty, and thus our solidarity." The editorial, a complete and utter rejection of terrorism penned by the paper's editor, Jean-Marie Colombani, warned that to blame poverty as a justification of the attack would be to insult the poor. The attackers "do not want a better, more just world. They simply want to erase ours from the map." Colombani also reminded his readers that Osama bin Laden had cooperated with the CIA when he fought the Soviets in Afghanistan, perhaps an unwelcome observation to Americans still reeling from the assault, but a fact of no small importance for anyone interested in thinking through how to reduce the dangers of blowback in the future. Colombani expressed the hope that the inevitable retaliation would focus on those responsible for the attack and would not play into their hands with a disproportionate response that might lead Muslims to think that they had to choose sides between the extremists and a United States hostile to Islam.[3]

The editorial was remarkable both for its unconditional sympathy and for its prescient – and unheeded – warning. The George W. Bush administration quickly moved from a retaliatory attack on al-Qaeda and the Taliban regime in Afghanistan to preparing an unrelated and unprovoked invasion of Iraq that rapidly dissipated international goodwill. Resistance to the Iraq war was perplexing to much of the American public, a majority of whom mistakenly believed that Saddam Hussein was both actively supporting al-Qaeda and deploying weapons of mass destruction.[4] Many could not account for the active opposition of the French and German governments to the U.S. position on Iraq, and on February 15, 2003 they were bewildered by the more than one million people who marched past Rome's Coliseum to protest the looming invasion, the half million marching past the Brandenburg Gate in Germany's largest demonstration since World War II, more than a million each in Madrid and Barcelona and London, all part of a coordinated protest that began in Australia and New Zealand that day and then circled the globe to encompass the largest coordinated political demonstration in the history of humankind. There were rallies on literally every continent, including forty-six residents of McMurdo Sound Station on Ross Island in Antarctica who joined the protest against the coming war, and half a million New Yorkers whose feelings about 9/11 were still raw but who were not willing to see their anger diverted to a target that had nothing to do with the attack.[5]

The Iraq war and its global unpopularity sent the discussion of anti-Americanism off the rails. The "they" in "why do they hate us" came to refer to a hostile world in general, or all Arabs or Muslims, or western Europeans, or foreign opponents of U.S. foreign policy, as analytical inquiry about the causes of international disputes was subsumed into the familiar, scattershot charges of "anti-Americanism" that blurred distinct movements, actors, and conflicts into a single, frightening image of global hatred. "The fact is the world hates us for our wealth, our success, our power," seethed Charles Krauthammer. "They hate us into incoherence.... The search for logic in anti-Americanism is fruitless."[6] The February demonstration was "the most well-orchestrated and choreographed exhibition of anti-Americanism ever," wrote Robert Patterson.[7] There were "millions of Europeans demonstrating against America," according to the *Washington Times*.[8] As had happened in every military conflict since the War of 1812, belligerent voices in the United States were quick to lump domestic opponents with foreign enemies. "When your country is under attack, as ours is, you can't have a peace movement. You can only have an appeasement movement, and a movement to betray your own country," argued David Horowitz.[9] The *Chicago Tribune* denounced "the anti-American peace movement."[10] Dinesh D'Souza declared "the cultural left" – including Hillary Clinton, Maureen Dowd, Spike Lee, and Kurt Vonnegut – to be "secretly allied" with al-Qaeda and "the primary reason for Islamic anti-Americanism."[11] Consistent with historical practice, the epithet did not adhere to right-wingers no matter how outlandish their claims, such as evangelists Pat Robertson and Jerry Falwell, who declared on national television that the attacks of 9/11 were the expression of God's wrath against America for its sins, and were "probably what we deserve," in Falwell's formulation.[12]

A few observers expressed skepticism about whether we were witnessing a worldwide wave of hatred. Reporter Eric Alterman went searching for the new European anti-Americanism and found himself at a Bruce Springsteen concert in a sold-out arena in Paris, surrounded by 15,000 French fans screaming "I was born in the USA!"[13] Ann Richter wrote to the *Washington Post* from Munich to ask, "If Europe is seething with anti-Americanism, why is Bill Clinton so popular all over Europe?"[14] Some demonstrators tried to make the same point. German student Henrik Buchhorn rode seven hours on a bus to reach the Berlin protest, where he insisted, "I'm not anti-American. I'm against the way the Bush administration has handled Iraq."[15] Sixty-five-year-old Janet Rutherford stood in frigid London weather that did not deter her or her fellow Britons from mounting the largest demonstration in the city's history. She said she had come because of her concern that an invasion of Iraq would "only escalate terrorist attacks here. It can only end badly."[16] (It would not take long before her fears were confirmed, when explosions tore through the public transportation systems of London and Madrid.)

Nonetheless, in the United States it became axiomatic that growing French, European, and worldwide anti-Americanism was the source of opposition to U.S. policy on Iraq. The National Press Club sponsored a forum on "Why They

Hate Us: The Rise of Anti-Americanism around the World."[17] Scholars asked whether the "American Century," begun in 1945, was being succeeded by the Anti-American Century.[18] Book publishers favored a sky-is-falling tone for a growing list of alarmist titles: *America against the World; America on Notice; Hating America: A History; Hating America: The New World Sport.*[19] Paul Hollander was invited to speak at the State Department on anti-Americanism, and his explanation that anti-Americanism was caused by foreigners' irrationality was cited in Congressional hearings.[20] The influential historian Niall Ferguson urged Americans to quit whining and act like a real imperial power, now that "Hatred of America Unites the World."[21]

Anti-Americanism, it seemed, was now an existential threat. The U.S. Government Accountability Office reported that "anti-Americanism is spreading and deepening around the world," threatening increased terrorism, military conflict, and damage to trade.[22] The Council on Foreign Relations warned that anti-Americanism was "endangering our national security."[23] Senator Christopher S. Bond (R-MO) asked: "We all know that anti-Americanism is growing throughout the world. So how do we respond to this ideology, and to the terrorism that results?" (He recommended "sending troops to defend America.")[24] The most influential interpretations were those that reaffirmed the assumptions of American exceptionalism. Robert Kagan explained Europeans' unhappiness over the Iraq war by arguing that "Americans are from Mars and Europeans are from Venus": if Europeans had invested in large, manly militaries rather than effeminizing social programs, he argued, they would not have left "the burden of maintaining order in far-flung regions of the world" to the Americans.[25] (Kagan's analysis managed to overlook both European assistance in Afghanistan and the fact that intervening in Iraq did not maintain order but destabilized it, with grave consequences that were foreseen by Europeans.) Russell Berman went further, explaining that failure to back the United States on Iraq stemmed from a "desire to avoid the moral order":

> For Western Europeans, and perhaps for many others, it has always been more comfortable to ignore the violence of totalitarian states. Because the United States sets a higher moral standard in a way that causes discomfort to the appeasers, it becomes the target of resentment: another source of anti-Americanism.[26]

The "moral order" established by the Bush administration, of course, drew fire not because of foreign indifference to injustice, but because that order included needless war, indefinite detention without trial, the physical abuse of suspects, and the weakening of international institutions. Nor had the United States itself been innocent of ignoring the violence of totalitarian states in the past, from the period of U.S. neutrality in the face of totalitarian violence in Europe and Asia before December 1941, to its modi vivendi with the Soviet Union and China during periods of the Cold War, not to mention the aid provided to Saddam Hussein himself in the 1980s and to a roster of other tyrants whenever grand strategy seemed to call for it. Morality is rarely a useful category of analysis for explaining the behavior of states.

Saddam Hussein had few enthusiasts among those opposed to the Bush administration policy, nor were its opponents expressing an endemic anti-Americanism. Instead, they were making differentiated judgments. In 2002, majorities of those surveyed in France, Germany, Italy, and the UK supported two major U.S. policies and opposed two others. They approved of the initial military campaign in Afghanistan and of President Bush's promise to increase foreign aid to developing countries. They disapproved of Bush's lumping Iraq, Iran, and North Korea into an "Axis of Evil," and they insisted that the United States should invade Iraq only with the United Nations' approval. This was a discriminating response to different U.S. policies based on an assessment of their merits, not the expression of instinctive, blanket hostility. It reflected a preference for multilateralism and support for international institutions – a preference shared by a majority of Americans.[27]

When U.S. unilateralism was combined with diplomatic slights – Secretary of Defense Donald Rumsfeld dismissed Germany and France as irrelevant members of "old Europe" and refused even to speak to his German counterpart – the unhappiness was palpable.[28] In March 2003, Fareed Zakaria, after talking with officials in dozens of countries, reported, "with the exception of Britain and Israel, every country the administration has dealt with feels humiliated by it." As Jorge Castañeda, former foreign minister of Mexico, told Zakaria, he and his colleagues "are not anti-American types. We have studied in the United States or worked there. We like and understand America. But we find it extremely irritating to be treated with utter contempt."[29]

The French Paradox

Such nuances were beyond the capacity of a concept, anti-Americanism, that claimed that "they" hate America, and that "Anti-Americanism . . . is illogical, irrational, contradictory, and mysteriously primitive."[30] The worst tension arose with France, French gestures of sympathy notwithstanding. Back in 1963, Charles de Gaulle had been the first world leader to ask to attend President Kennedy's funeral to demonstrate his solidarity with the United States in a time of national crisis. Now Jacques Chirac was the first foreign head of state to arrive in New York after September 11 and to stand at the side of "my friend George" at the White House.[31] His pledge of solidarity included a willingness to fight America's attackers in Afghanistan. It did not extend to the planned invasion of Iraq, however. "Be careful," Chirac urged Americans in an interview on CNN. "Think twice before you do something which is not necessary and may be very dangerous."[32] Like de Gaulle's initial warnings against escalation in Vietnam, Chirac's had begun with an earnest, private message based on French assessments and experience: Iraq did not support al-Qaeda and was too weak to present an imminent danger; the occupation of Iraq would generate bloody resistance; and the Muslim world would view the intervention as illegitimate, thereby increasing rather than diminishing the ranks of terrorists endangering U.S. and European security. In a private conversation with Bush in Prague in November 2002, Chirac recalled his own service as a conscript in France's unsuccessful campaign to suppress Algerian rebels. He warned of the force of Arab nationalism and the endemic violence that would accompany an occupation. The best way to protect U.S. and European cities, in the French view, was relentlessly to pursue al-Qaeda and related terrorist networks using investigative and judicial methods – the same targeted techniques that had enabled Americans to arrest and convict the 1993 bombers of the World Trade Center and enabled French intelligence to identify and track the "millennium bomber" Ahmed Ressam until he was arrested at the U.S.–Canadian border en route to set off a car bomb in Los Angeles, after the French tipped off the Canadians and the FBI.[33]

As the Bush administration ignored these warnings and France's disapproval moved into the public sphere, to be joined by official German opposition to the invasion, Chirac's arguments were drowned out by choruses charging him with "anti-Americanism," and French-bashing came back into vogue. The *New York Post* branded France and Germany "the axis of weasel," superimposing rodent heads onto photos of the French and German ambassadors to the United Nations.[34] But American fury was directed for the most part against France, not Germany. In part, that reflected the fact that France had threatened to use its U.N. veto to thwart a resolution endorsing war, whereas Germany had no such veto. It also reflected long-standing national stereotypes: an editorial cartoonist could hardly depict a jackbooted German in a spiked helmet saying "no war." Inveighing against the French, however, resonated strongly with existing prejudices about weakness and effeminization. Editorialists gleefully skewered the "cheese-eating surrender monkeys."[35] The *Wall Street Journal* depicted Chirac as a "transvestite" and a "pygmy Joan of Arc." Dinesh D'Souza urged Americans to ignore advice "from men who carry handbags."[36] Bumper stickers exhorted "Iraq first, then France." The editor of the conservative *Weekly Standard*, Fred Barnes, argued that the French deserved what they were getting because French opposition to the war showed they were "breathtakingly, unprecedentedly, and perhaps even unforgivably, ungrateful."[37]

Anger over the perceived ingratitude and anti-Americanism of the French was widespread, and it was expressed in forms identical to those made during the dispute with de Gaulle over Vietnam. House Speaker Dennis Hastert (R-IL) called for sanctions on French goods. A Palm Beach bar owner dumped his entire stock of French wine and champagne into the street. A Las Vegas radio station hired an armored vehicle to drive over photographs of Chirac, pictures of the French flag, bottles of French wine and a loaf of French bread.[38] Congress came up with one innovation, the official renaming of French fries as "Freedom fries," French dressing as "Freedom dressing," and French toast as "Freedom toast" on its cafeteria menu. "I took the Grey Poupon out of my cupboard," boasted Rep. Duke Cunningham (R-CA), unwittingly naming an American product manufactured by Kraft Foods. For the most part, we

had seen this play before: Florida Republican Rep. Ginny Brown-Waite even
echoed Congressman Mendel Rivers's 1966 call to disinter and repatriate the
bodies of American soldiers buried in French soil.[39]

Jokes that alluded to French cowardice abounded. House Majority Whip
Roy Blunt (R-MO) chuckled: "Somebody was telling me about the French
Army rifle that was being advertised on eBay the other day – the description
was 'Never shot. Dropped once.'"[40] This theme was as enduring as its selectivity
was curious, because the French air force had joined the United States in flying
missions against the Taliban in Afghanistan, and French soldiers were at that
very moment risking and losing their lives side by side with American troops.
An American officer in Kabul praised the courage of the French forces he
worked with in the field, and added, "Out here, we've still got French fries."[41]
But for armchair commentators, the cracks about French cowardice persisted
without regard to French actions. Speaking before an audience of hundreds of
fellow Republicans, Blunt told another one:

> Q: Do you know how many Frenchmen it takes to defend Paris?
> A: Nobody knows. It's never been tried.[42]

Syndicated columnist George Will repeated the same joke, adding that it was
quite popular in Washington circles.[43] Americans could chortle over the fee-
ble French because the historical narrative in their minds about World War II
combines French fecklessness in 1940 with American heroics in 1944. Blunt
and Will seem unmoved by the roughly 1,300,000 French soldiers who died
defending Paris in the First World War, or another 100,000 who died trying
to defend Paris against the Nazi blitzkrieg in 1940 while Americans remained
neutral behind a protective ocean. The contrast between the collaborationist
Vichy regime and the dogged courage of Churchill's British contributes to the
notion of French cravenness, even though British pluck was backed by something that the French lacked – the 20-mile-wide tank trap known as the English
Channel. But it is a long way to go from condemning Vichy to producing spu-
rious insults about national cowardice that have Americans guffawing over the
endless graves of the French dead.

National stereotyping is not a pretty thing, whether it is done by foreigners about Americans or by Americans about foreigners, but it seems to be a
common human response to cultural difference, especially in times of international conflict, rather than a peculiarly foreign pathology requiring elevation
to the level of an "ism" only when the United States is on the receiving end.
Disagreements between France and the United States over trade, debt, and
war have produced intermittent anger on both sides, but that hostility ebbed
and flowed depending on the contingencies of the moment. Surveys showed
that Americans' favorable impression of France slipped from 79% in February
2002, before the argument over Iraq, to 29% in May 2003.[44] This was not
an eruption of psychological anti-Gallicism any more than French opposition
to American policies constituted enracinated anti-Americanism. The disputes
that arise between nations are best understood by evaluating their competing

claims and interests, rather than seeking answers in irrationality or national character.

Chirac himself tried earnestly to explain his view of America, invoking his student days. "I've known the U.S. for a long time," he told *Time* magazine,

> I've studied there, worked as a forklift operator for Anheuser-Busch in St. Louis and as a soda jerk at Howard Johnson's. I've hitchhiked across the whole United States . . . I know the U.S. perhaps better than most French people, and I really like the United States . . . I've made many excellent friends there, I feel good there . . . When I hear people say that I'm anti-American, I'm sad – not angry, but really sad.

The source of the dispute with U.S. officials, Chirac concluded, was that "I simply don't analyze the situation as they do. . . . A war of this kind cannot help giving a big lift to terrorism. It would create a large number of little bin Ladens."[45] Because this was a foreign truth that could not reach most Americans' ears, we would learn it through experience.

The Continuum of Anti-Americanism

Philippe Roger, who chides his compatriots eloquently for their rhetorical excesses, offered a reproach influenced by the attack he had witnessed while writing at a desk in lower Manhattan one clear September morning. "French anti-Americanism has of course no direct connection with the aggression committed that day," he says, but French critics of the United States should ask themselves "to what extent systematic anti-Americanism, French and otherwise, has had a hand in the global process of demonization that facilitates slippage from a war of words to a war of the worlds."[46] As Roger implies, the concept of anti-Americanism ultimately assumes a direct line from Trollope and Dickens by way of Sartre and de Gaulle to Osama bin Laden and the catastrophe he visited upon the United States.

It is a charge of great consequence when leveled at critics who, for the most part, engaged in criticism of the United States and their own societies in order to try to make them more just. If the logical corollary of the concept of anti-Americanism were true, who could dare speak a discouraging word, knowing it might contribute to a slippage that led to the deaths of thousands?

That argument, however, has been made by many of the anti-anti-Americans. When developed in more detail, the notion that 9/11 was the logical outcome of anti-Americanism invokes the intellectual founding father of radical Islam, Sayyid Qutb, leading member of the Egyptian Muslim Brotherhood. Qutb spent two years on a scholarship in the United States in the late 1940s and apparently turned from a cultural anti-American into a radical Islamist warrior, a path that presumably others risk following if they take the first step of criticizing American culture. It is true that Qutb came away from his student days in the United States with a strong animus against the country for what he viewed as its sexual licentiousness, its "animalistic" jazz, and its violent contact sports. He experienced American racism – denied admission to a movie theater because of his dark skin – even as he himself disparaged the "primitive instincts" of American "Negroes."[47] He was angered, too, by American support for Israel, a position that he viewed as a betrayal of the Arabs. Radicalized not by his sojourn in a foreign culture but after being tortured in Egyptian prisons, Qutb's hostility toward the United States blended into an anticolonial, anti-Western, and antimodern stance, as he condemned secularism, the mingling of the sexes, the privileging of science over faith, and the Western "master who tramples our honor and enslaves us."[48] When the inheritors of that tradition in al-Qaeda a generation later mouthed some of the same words and called for the installation of theocratic Islamic rule in a new caliphate, it seemed to support the interpretation of terrorism as a civilizational clash that began in the irrational rejection of U.S. culture.

Those most knowledgeable about al-Qaeda and bin Laden argue otherwise. They see political resentments, rather than an anti-Americanism rooted in objections to American modernity or democracy, as central to bin Laden's violent worldview. Peter Bergen writes that bin Laden's arguments against the West and the United States in particular were "quite consistent over time," depicting an America committing violence against Muslims in the Middle East and beyond. "What bin Laden has done is unforgivable," writes Bergen. "But bin Laden is a man and we need to understand him neither through a fog of our own propaganda – he has never, for instance, expressed an interest in attacking the West because of our 'freedoms' – nor through the mythomania of his supporters, who style him as a defender of Islam, despite the fact that the Koran is full of injunctions against the killing of civilians."[49] Michael Scheuer, former head of the CIA's bin Laden unit, says that radical Islamist resentment toward the United States is a reaction to its perceived foreign policy, not its perceived values.[50] Thomas Hegghammer cautions that "Islamism and anti-American militancy are not the same thing. There are millions of Islamists out there, but only some engage in violence and only a tiny fraction fight America." Religious fundamentalists of all faiths reject consumerism and sexual promiscuity, he notes, but for Islamists who oppose Westernization and turn to militancy, their violence "is nearly always directed at other Muslims, typically against regimes in Arab countries." (Qutb himself, for example, devoted his life to fighting the secular Egyptian government, not the United States.) The small groups of radicals who do attack American targets, including the al-Qaeda recruits that Hegghammer studied, say they are motivated most strongly not by the cultural issues asserted by the "clash of civilizations" theory, but by the desire to fight "non-Muslims who kill Muslims and occupy Muslim territory," as they see it.[51]

Those who interviewed bin Laden's associates report that whatever disdain for American culture bin Laden might have held, it did not prevent him from showing Hollywood movies to trainees in his camps and permitting his sons to play video games. More to the point, it did not prevent him from allying himself with the U.S.-funded insurgency against the Soviet occupation of Afghanistan in the 1980s.[52] "Thank you for bringing the Americans to help us get rid of the secularist, atheist Soviets," he told Saudi Prince Bandar at the time.[53] Something then changed to make bin Laden turn his wrath from one superpower to the next, but the character of American society and the existence of critical texts and stereotypes about America were consistent variables both during his alliance with and subsequent war on the United States. One factor that had changed between the 1980s and the 1990s, on the other hand, constituted his main concern, as expressed in his 1996 "Declaration of War against the Americans Occupying the Land of the Two Holy Places," which denounced the arrival of Christian troops in his home country of Saudi Arabia.[54] His recruits generally cited perceived oppression of Muslims in Palestine or Chechnya, or the presence of "Crusaders on the Arabian Peninsula," as their reasons for militancy.[55] Other analysts who emphasize the global ambitions and messianic self-image of Islamist terrorists emphasize that this fringe position is not representative of larger Muslim populations, nor even of the guerrilla forces, such as the Taliban, that U.S. troops find themselves fighting. Counterinsurgency expert David Kilcullen, adviser to American generals, argues that "while neo-Salafi 'jihadists' – a small, elusive minority in any society – are often implacable fanatics, the local guerrillas they exploit . . . fight Westerners primarily because we are intruding into their space."[56]

Misunderstanding what draws adherents to al-Qaeda and its ilk will not further the effort to combat them, nor will confusing bin Laden's brand of zealotry with the broad range of political discourse, social criticism, and disputes arising from an infinite number of local and national contexts that have for so long been forced to fit into the simplifying catch-all concept of "anti-Americanism." Distinguishing threats from non-threats is critical to America's future security. It may be discomforting to see that the United States is unpopular in some Muslim countries, and that conspiracy theories about September 11 combining anti-Semitic and anti-American calumnies circulate on the Internet and at newspaper kiosks in many Arab cities. It is lamentable, as Edward Said wrote, that he found it hard to persuade even some well-educated Arabs that "United States foreign policy is not in fact run by the CIA, or a conspiracy" responsible for "virtually every event of significance in the Middle East."[57] But to turn that into evidence of a "clash of civilizations" pitting Western democracy against a premodern culture does not accord with survey research showing that even people who strongly disfavor the United States are objecting not to American society or values but to its actions as perceived abroad.[58] The World Values Survey of nine Muslim nations showed that 87% of their populations approved of democratic ideals, and 68% approved of the way in which democracy actually functions.[59] Political movements and leaders in the Middle East and elsewhere (such as Hugo Chávez of Venezuela, Vladimir Putin of Russia, and Mahmoud Ahmadinejad of Iran) can try to instrumentalize anti-U.S. rhetoric and symbols, inflating and repeating any real or imagined grievances against the United States in order to mobilize nationalist sentiment, but their power to distract or mislead is limited, far outweighed in the eyes of their constituents by their ability to deliver the material conditions their people want. This was borne out during the 2011 "Arab Spring," when massive pro-democracy demonstrations in Egypt, Tunisia, and other countries throughout the region unfolded without attacks on American institutions or the burning of American flags, giving the lie to the notion that the Arab masses are easily duped into redirecting their grievances against America.[60]

More broadly, most nationalities around the world "give America high marks for its respect for the personal freedoms of its people," reports the Pew Global Attitudes Project, refuting President Bush's claim that America is hated for its freedom. "Admiration for U.S. science and technology remains nearly universal" – as opposed to the image of a hostile world united by opposition to modernity – "and despite resistance to the spread of U.S. ideas and customs in many parts of the world, the appetite for American movies, music and television shows remained strong."[61] Respondents in nearly every country agreed that democracy, despite its problems, was the best form of government; majorities also supported free enterprise and the free market.[62]

Sometimes, hostility toward the United States arises in defense of democracy, not in antagonism to it. We have seen this in Latin America during the Cold War, when successive U.S. administrations aligned themselves with anti-democratic forces, helping authoritarian regimes to repress social movements and even toppling elected governments when grand strategy trumped principle. Former U.S. Ambassador Wendy Chamberlin has dated the growth of anti-U.S. sentiment in Pakistan to 1979, when Washington supported General Zia ul-Haq after he overthrew and executed the popular elected president, Zulfikar Ali Bhutto. Another wave of anger arose in response to U.S. support for General Pervez Musharraf, who trampled on democratic processes. The Pakistani media's dissemination of conspiracy theories about U.S. plotting in the country contributes to the hostility, but so do U.S. actions taken in the real world. "The same media that in 2005 showed U.S. helicopters distributing aid to earthquake victims in remote areas of Pakistan," reported the Voice of America in 2010, "are now showing drone attacks on al-Qaida and Taliban militants every day – alongside civilian casualties."[63] Not only have critics such as the University of Michigan's Juan Cole concluded, "It's the foreign policy, stupid."[64] After studying U.S. relations with Muslim countries, a Defense Department task force commissioned by Secretary Rumsfeld reached the following conclusion: "Muslims do not 'hate our freedoms,' but rather, they hate our policies." The Defense Science Board Task Force on Strategic Communication report continues: "American direct intervention in the Muslim World has paradoxically elevated the stature of and support for radical Islamists, while diminishing support for the United States to single-digits in some Arab societies." Deviating from the position taken since Dean Acheson was Secretary of State that Arab anti-Americanism should be redressed through public information campaigns, the task force recommended strengthening not U.S. official propaganda but "the U.S. Government's ability to understand global public opinion."[65] Unfortunately, while talented Foreign Service Officers seek to pursue dialogue abroad, "strategic communication" as understood in the U.S. government usually means selling the official line, not hearing what others have to say.

Given the widespread support around the world for democracy and freedom and many aspects of American culture, and the fact that conflict over land, power, sovereignty, or resources is at the root of most international disputes, there is not much practical utility in the interpretive conceit of "anti-Americanism." It conflates large majorities with small minorities, non-threats with real threats, and critics with enemies and traitors. Carefully discriminating among these will be more helpful than blending them together.

The Bush Effect

Attempts to measure "anti-Americanism" in the early twenty-first century have been hobbled by a conceptual failure. A favorite shorthand for journalists, academics, and intelligence analysts, the formula "anti-Americanism is on the rise" usually refers to negative responses in polls. When favorable opinions of the U.S. fell by half in many countries between 2000 and 2004, such headlines followed.[66] We were told that "European anti-Americanism . . . goes far beyond specific policies and entails a much larger and generalized disdain for America and Americans."[67] Yet the same populations who could no longer say they looked favorably on the United States during the Bush administration's first term still liked Americans: in 2004, 32% of the French held a favorable opinion of the United States, but 53% were favorable toward Americans. Among the British, it was 58% for the United States, 72% for Americans; in Germany, 38% for the United States, and 68% for Americans.[68] This apparent contradiction is mysterious only if one clings to the interpretive fiction of "anti-Americanism," which holds that hatred of a country and its people are the same as disapproval of its policies.

Concern over anti-Americanism rises to a fever pitch precisely when there is widespread opposition abroad to U.S. foreign policy – such as during the Vietnam War, the early Reagan era, and the George W. Bush administration. The term is used to refer to and explain the motivation of uncooperative foreign leaders, the falling poll numbers in international surveys, and the protestors in the streets. "Anti-Americanism is on the rise": if anti-Americanism is simply to be a synonym for opposition to U.S. policy, then the journalistic formulation would be unobjectionable, but "anti-Americanism" has come to be understood as "a well-established 'ism' – thus bespeaking its entrenched institutionalization and common usage as a modern ideology."[69] Anti-Americanism is not *synonymous* with opposition to U.S. policies; it is the *cause* of opposition to U.S. policies, according to those who are most exercised about it.

On the contrary, recent research shows that anti-American sentiments have neither a necessary nor a sufficient connection to stances against any given U.S. policy. Rather than anti-Americanism causing negative responses to U.S. actions, we see some U.S. actions generating increased negative views of the

United States. In 2002, 64% of people surveyed in 44 countries held a favorable view of the United States. Over the next three years, in tandem with the Iraq war, favorable ratings declined. In Indonesia, favorable views plummeted from a high of 75% in the last year of the Clinton administration to a low of 15% during the Iraq war, recovering to 38% after the United States deployed its military resources for emergency rescue and relief efforts in response to the devastating tsunami of 2004, then climbing back up to 63% after the election of an American president who had spent part of his childhood in Jakarta. Favorable ratings among Pakistanis saw some improvement after the United States provided emergency earthquake assistance in 2005 but declined again with an increase in the number of terrorist bombings and civilian casualties that many blamed on the escalation of the "American war" in Afghanistan, whose goal seemed to be to stabilize a pro-Indian government.[70] These results demonstrate the surpassing importance of political conflict rather than culture or psychology in foreign views of the United States. Rather than mistaking change for continuity, we should recognize that deep-seated prejudices and irrational thinking do not rise and fall from month to month and year to year.[71]

The Obama Effect

In the summer of 2008, the leading candidate for the American presidency, who took pride in proclaiming that "only in America is my story possible," strode onto a stage within sight of the Brandenburg Gate and addressed a cheering crowd of 200,000 Europeans, many waving American flags. Having queued up all afternoon with the rest of them to file past security checkpoints, I looked around for some sign of the "generalized disdain for America and Americans" supposedly endemic among these people, but it was nowhere in evidence.[72] There was no counterdemonstration, no angry crowds of tens of thousands of protestors penned in by police cordons, such as those that mobilized when Ronald Reagan and George W. Bush had visited Berlin in previous years. A sole protestor held up a cardboard sign and shouted that the death penalty was immoral, while other audience members shushed him so that they could better understand the words of the American they had stood in the sun for hours to hear.

Barack Obama's extraordinary popularity in Europe and throughout much of the world required some intellectual adjustments on the part of those who had been decrying the pandemic of anti-Americanism sweeping the globe. If the problem were not contingent on U.S. policy but an enduring, irrational hatred of all things American rooted in cultural fears and anti-democratic tendencies, the pattern of foreign opinion after the end of Bush's term in office should have remained consistent. But the change was spectacular. In September 2009, the Transatlantic Trends survey showed that Obama's approval rating in Germany was 92%, compared with the 12% for Bush when he left office. Support for the American president jumped 77 points in France, 70 in Portugal, and 64 in

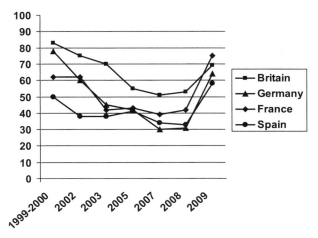

The Bush Effect:
Favorable Opinion of the United States
in Western Europe, 1999-2009

Britain
Germany
France
Spain

FIGURE 6. Western European opinion of the United States was highly variable in the first decade of the twenty-first century, from majority positive in the Clinton years, plummeting during the Bush presidency, then recovering sharply in the first year of Obama's term. This is evidence not of ingrained anti-Americanism but support for the multilateralist policies of two charismatic presidents and opposition to the unilateralist policies of a less gifted one. *Source*: Pew Global Attitudes Project, "Confidence in Obama Lifts U.S. Image around the World," July 23, 2009.

Italy.[73] These Europeans were still discussing the president of the same country, but it was a different president with different policies and a very different style. A small segment of the U.S. far right might not have considered Obama an American, but Europeans certainly did, so this astonishing transformation in opinion polls can only mean that the massive disapproval directed across the Atlantic during the Bush administration was largely anti-Bush sentiment rather than anti-Americanism. (See Figure 6.)

That logic did not persuade those who preferred to continue wielding the term as a club, however awkwardly. When the Nobel Committee awarded the new president the 2009 Peace Prize, surprising everyone including Obama, some on the right quickly joined the Taliban in condemning the decision. Literally. "We all agree with the Taliban and Iran," averred talk show host Rush Limbaugh. "He doesn't deserve the award."[74] Some of Limbaugh's ideological comrades tied themselves in knots in their eagerness to apply the dubious formula, explaining that the "anti-American" Nobel Committee had engaged in "a purely anti-American gesture" by awarding the Nobel Peace Prize to the American president.[75]

The hard right, having spent eight years deriding as dangerous anti-Americans anyone who dared criticize the U.S. president, now began ferociously to criticize the U.S. president. Representative Joe Wilson (R-SC), who had once attacked a fellow congressman as "viscerally anti-American" for having the temerity to recall that the United States had supplied Saddam Hussein with materials used in chemical weapons, now forgot his 28 years of military discipline and shouted "you lie!" at his commander-in-chief as the president addressed a joint session of Congress.[76] Conservatives developed a new charge against Obama: that he failed to claim that the United States is morally superior to all other societies.[77] "This is a guy," groused former Vice President Dick Cheney, "who doesn't fully understand or share that view of American exceptionalism that I think most of us believe in."[78] Republican presidential candidate Mitt Romney wrote that Obama's "reorientation away from a celebration of American exceptionalism is misguided." Former Arkansas governor Mike Huckabee complained that "to deny American exceptionalism is in essence to deny the heart and soul of this nation."[79]

This brand of American exceptionalism, Thomas Bender observed, produces "an odd combination of parochialism and arrogance."[80] Obama's version was different. He tried to be as clear as possible: "I believe in American exceptionalism," he declared. "We have a core set of values that are enshrined in our Constitution, in our body of law, in our democratic practices, in our belief in free speech and equality, that, though imperfect, are exceptional." He continued, however, in terms that would not please those who think that American exceptionalism means American infallibility: "Now, the fact that I am very proud of my country and I think that we've got a whole lot to offer the world does not lessen my interest in recognizing the value and wonderful qualities of other countries, or recognizing that we're not always going to be right, or that other people may have good ideas, or that in order for us to work collectively, all parties have to compromise and that includes us."[81] Obama here articulated a possible solution to exceptionalism's paradox that holds the United States to be simultaneously unique and a model for other societies to replicate. Where national chauvinists resolved the paradox of an inimitability that requires imitation by scorning uncooperative foreigners for their benightedness, Obama suggested that Americans could both feel pride and join with other countries to address common problems without demanding that foreigners behave merely as followers.

Finding solutions to common problems will remain difficult as long as a substantial portion of the American public continues to view critical discussion of basic issues in policy and social organization as anti-American. This attitude has greatly constrained the possible scope of needed reforms in the United States. For Russell Berman, criticism of the United States in any systematic manner, such as "conjuring up nonspecific American conditions," is a sign of anti-Americanism.[82] But there must be a way of discussing what is a pronounced difference between European social democracy, however attenuated in recent decades, or Latin American and Asian state-managed development, however imperfect, and an American political economy of deregulated market capitalism that has seen inequality increase dramatically since the late 1970s, the result of a broad shift of tax and social policies that turned the United States into the world's leader among wealthy countries in income disparity, hours worked, cost of education, crime rates, percentage of population in prison, health care costs, and bad health outcomes.[83] "American conditions" have undoubtedly been positive for those able to better their circumstances, such as immigrants who overcome obstacles to find social integration generally easier than it is in Europe, or those consumers who still have disposable income to spend on inexpensive goods. But those who have benefited the most have been the wealthiest 0.01% of Americans, whose annual income increased 384% from 1979 to 2005 (compared with a median 14% for the population) while their federal tax rates declined – a trend that has helped the top 1% of Americans earn a higher share of the nation's income today than that at any time since the 1920s.[84] The richest 10% of American families now own 70% of their nation's wealth, compared with Germany, 44%; Italy, 48%; Japan, 39%; and the United Kingdom, 56%.[85] Cherished assumptions must be rethought. Social mobility – measured by the disparity between fathers' and sons' incomes in adulthood – is now higher in six European countries and Canada than in the United States: the American Dream has been outstripped by the Danish Dream and the German Dream.[86] Yet suggestions that the market and tax structure that has ushered the United States into a new Gilded Age should be amended often raise cries of an "anti-American" turn toward "a European-style socialist utopia" or worse.[87] Discussion of the conditions that drive these basic differences – whose impact on society is far-reaching – is not only legitimate, but it will be essential to the future well-being of the United States and other societies seeking a workable social model for the twenty-first century.[88] The same is true for a self-interested and effective foreign policy.

Bearing the Burden

"The majority lives in perpetual adoration of itself; certain truths can reach the ears of Americans only from foreigners or from experience."[89] Alexis de Tocqueville made this observation more than a century before Americans decided to shut their ears to foreigners' warnings and intervene in Guatemala, Cuba, Vietnam, and Iraq. Whether we learned certain truths from the experience remains to be seen.

That foreigners might have valuable perspectives to offer remains as true for the United States as it does for any other country. None has a monopoly on virtue or wisdom. Just as taking the opinion of their American ally more seriously might have helped Britain and France avoid their debacle at Suez in 1956, more American respect for foreign views might have helped this country avoid its most damaging adventures. Increasing the number of players involved in a decision decreases the chances of action, to be sure, even while it increases the chances that action taken will have legitimacy. When it comes to wars of choice, both are salutary effects.

This book has argued that the misuse of the concept of anti-Americanism has constricted policy choices and diminished opportunities for pursuing U.S. interests in cooperation with foreign countries. When foreigners oppose U.S. policy, their advice too often is dismissed as anti-American, ill-intentioned, and therefore illegitimate, preventing U.S. officials and the U.S. public from gaining access to other assessments and from considering alternative policies that might be more successful. A predisposition to find anti-Americanism in the motives of so many foreigners is the opposite of a cosmopolitan, multilateralist outlook that would serve this country well.

It is widely recognized that the Manichean division of the world into two camps during the Cold War, one called the "free world" despite its authoritarian members, and the other labeled "global communism" despite its diverse national movements, brought an array of negative consequences for the United States. These ranged, from overlooking the potential advantages of the Sino-Soviet split to mistaking Vietnamese nationalism for international communism, to backing brutal regimes that waved an anti-communist flag, all while narrowing the scope of acceptable debate over social reform at home to the exclusion of sensible policies (such as universal health insurance) proven effective elsewhere. Imagining the world as divided into binary opposites was an exercise in self-deception that was neither analytically sound nor in the interests of the United States. Today, however, the predilection of many Americans for praising our society as normatively superior to all others has led us again to divide the world in two: there is pro-Americanism, and there is anti-Americanism. If anything, this distinction makes even less sense than the Cold War formula, because at least international communism existed as a fractured movement with identifiable actors. Yet while there is prejudice and hostility today toward the United States, whose popularity abroad will continue to rise and fall with changing leadership and changing events, there is no global anti-American conspiracy uniting the Left Bank with the West Bank and Baghdad with Berlin. To behave as if there were can only increase the estrangement between America and the world and fuel an unhealthy unilateralism that will damage this country's long-term interests.

Half a century ago, Reinhold Niebuhr surveyed growing anti-American sentiment that he diagnosed as partly a side effect of great power status, but partly the product of foreigners' understandable alienation from the excesses of McCarthyism and the atomic saber-rattling of "massive retaliation" that seemed to threaten global nuclear war. Where he saw anger at the United States abroad, Niebuhr urged Americans "to learn to live with the burden of this animus," not only because his Christian realist faith taught him that even moral nations are constrained by limits to their power but also because he saw a good deal of value in much foreign opinion. He advised Americans faced with hostile rhetoric "to bear the unjustified attacks against us with sufficient patience so that we may learn from the justified criticisms."[90] If rethinking anti-Americanism enables us to do as Niebuhr counseled, we may yet turn the burden into a gift.

Notes

Introduction

1. "Why Do They Dislike Us?" *New York Times*, Sep 10, 1913, 8; "Why Do Canadians Dislike Us? Here Are Some of Their Reasons," *New York Times*, Oct 5, 1913, SM4.
2. Sons of the American Revolution pamphlet entitled *A Welcome to Immigrants and Some Good Advice* (1901), cited in Gino C. Speranza, "How It Feels to Be a Problem: A Consideration of Certain Causes which Prevent or Retard Assimilation," *Charities* 12:18 (1904): 458.
3. "Why They Hate Us," *New York Times*, Nov 5, 1899, 22.
4. Peter Ford, "Why Do They Hate Us?" *Christian Science Monitor*, Sep 27, 2001.
5. As per a Lexis-Nexis search of English-language newspapers performed on Sep 1, 2011.
6. "Why the World Loves to Hate America," *Financial Times*, Dec 7, 2001, 23; Roger Cohen, "Anti-Americanism is One 'Ism' that Thrives," *International Herald Tribune*, Nov 26, 2005, 2; Jay Nordlinger, "An Irrational Hatred," *New York Sun*, Jul 19, 2004, 1; Paul Johnson, "Hating America, Hating Humanity," *National Review*, Sep 12, 2005.
7. Paul Hollander, *Anti-Americanism: Critiques at Home and Abroad, 1965–1990* (NY: Oxford University Press, 1992), 410.
8. Fouad Ajami, "The Falseness of Anti-Americanism," *Foreign Policy* (September/October 2003): 52–61.
9. J. William Fulbright, *The Arrogance of Power* (NY: Random House, 1967), 3.
10. This term came into vogue to describe European defenders of America's reputation after September 11, 2001. It has appeared in print, however, at least since 1926. "Foreign News: A bas les Américains!" *Time*, Aug 2, 1926.
11. Hollander, *Anti-Americanism*, and idem, ed., *Understanding Anti-Americanism: Its Origins and Impact at Home and Abroad* (Chicago: Ivan R. Dee, 2004).
12. Victor Davis Hanson, "Fear and Loathing," *National Review*, Oct 25, 2004, 54.
13. Russell A. Berman, *Anti-Americanism in Europe: A Cultural Problem* (Stanford, CA: Hoover Institution Press, 2004), 113–14.
14. For example, Hollander, *Anti-Americanism*; Barry Rubin and Judith Colp Rubin, *Hating America: A History* (NY: Oxford University Press, 2004); Dan Diner,

America In the Eyes of the Germans: An Essay on Anti-Americanism, English language ed. (Princeton, NJ: Markus Wiener Publishers, 1996); Andrei S. Markovits, *Uncouth Nation: Why Europe Dislikes America* (Princeton, NJ: Princeton University Press, 2007); Philippe Roger, *L'ennemi américain: Généalogie de l'antiaméricanisme français* (Paris: Seuil, 2002). More examples are cited in the bibliography.

15. Claude Lévi-Strauss, *Structural Anthropology* (NY: Basic Books, 1963).

16. Roland Barthes, *Mythologies* (Paris: Seuil, 1957); Roger, *L'ennemi américain*, 11.

17. See the Epilogue for details on France and the Iraq war.

18. See Chapter 5.

19. Robert S. McNamara, James Blight, Robert Brigham, Thomas Biersteker, and Herbert Schandler, eds., *Argument without End: In Search of Answers to the Vietnam Tragedy* (NY: Public Affairs, 1999), 102, 150.

20. For an excellent overview, see Brendon O'Connor, ed., *Anti-Americanism: History, Causes, and Themes, vol. 1: Causes and Sources* (Oxford: Greenwood Press, 2007), especially O'Connor's own "Causes and Sources of Anti-Americanism," xiii–xix, and "What Is Anti-Americanism?" 1–22.

21. Hollander, *Understanding Anti-Americanism*, 8; Josef Joffe, *Überpower: The Imperial Temptation of America* (NY: W.W. Norton, 2006), 77.

22. Ivan Krastev, "The Anti-American Century?" *Journal of Democracy* 15:2 (April 2004): 5–16, quoted at 7.

23. Brendon O'Connor and Katherine Delaney, "The ABC and Anti-Americanism," *Australian Journal of Political Science* 44:3 (2009): 389–404, quoted at 390; Brendon O'Connor and Martin Griffiths, "Making Sense of Anti-Americanism," in Brendon O'Connor and Martin Griffiths, eds., *The Rise of Anti-Americanism* (NY: Routledge, 2006), 1.

24. Diner, *America in the Eyes of the Germans*, viii; Peter Krause, "Amerikakritik und Antiamerikanismus in der deutschen Presse am Beispiel der Berichterstattung zur Grenada-Intervention und zum Golfkrieg," in *Antikommunismus und Antiamerikanismus in Deutschland: Kontinuität und Wandel nach 1945*, ed. Gesine Schwan (Baden Baden: Nomos Verlag, 1999), 248–73; Markovits, *Uncouth Nation*, 17.

25. Rubin and Rubin, *Hating America*, ix. The authors state that this is one of four characteristics anti-Americans may have. Another is portraying American society, policies, or goals as "ridiculous," which would place just about every editorial cartoonist out of bounds, not to mention quite a few U.S. politicians who have used humor to skewer policies that they opposed.

26. See Chapter 3.

27. See Chapter 4.

28. See Chapter 6.

29. Alan McPherson, *Yankee No! Anti-Americanism in U.S.-Latin American Relations* (Cambridge, MA: Harvard University Press, 2003), 6. See also idem, ed., *Anti-Americanism in Latin America and the Caribbean* (NY: Berghahn Books, 2006), and Ivan Krastev and Alan McPherson, eds., *The Anti-American Century* (Budapest: Central European Press, 2007).

30. Richard F. Kuisel, *Seducing the French: The Dilemma of Americanization* (Berkeley and Los Angeles: University of California Press, 1993), 236.

31. J.G.A. Pocock, "Verbalizing a Political Act: Toward a Politics of Speech," in Michael Shapiro, ed., *Language and Politics* (NY: New York University Press,

1984), 38–39; Quentin Skinner, "Rhetoric and Conceptual Change," *Finnish Yearbook of Political Thought* 3 (1999): 60–73; Otto Brunner, Werner Conze, and Reinhardt Koselleck, eds., *Geschichtliche Grundbegriffe: Historisches Lexikon zur politisch-sozialer Sprache in Deutschland*, 8 vols. (Stuttgart: Ernst Klett Verlag, 1972–1997). See also W.B. Gallie, "Essentially Contested Concepts," in Max Black, ed., *The Importance of Language* (Edgewood Cliffs, NJ: Prentice-Hall, 1962), 121–46.

32. The standard account is Seymour Martin Lipset, *American Exceptionalism: A Double-Edged Sword* (NY: Norton & Co., 1996). Lipset's cautions against American crusades are taken up by Godfrey Hodgson in *The Myth of American Exceptionalism* (New Haven, CT: Yale University Press, 2009).

33. Nils Gilman, *Mandarins of the Future: Modernization Theory in Cold War America* (Baltimore: Johns Hopkins University Press, 2007), 187.

34. Hollander, *Anti-Americanism*, 29–36, 151.

35. See Chapter 6.

36. Senator Jesse Helms (R-NC) claimed that King held an "anti-American ideological view of U.S. foreign policy," *Congressional Quarterly* 129:130 (Oct 3, 1983): S13452–13461. Rep. John Ashbrook (R-OH) said he "preached an anti-American theme," *Cong. Rec.* (Sep 26, 1977), 30941.

37. Jean-François Revel, *L'obsession anti-américaine* (Paris: Plon, 2002), 16.

38. Stephen Haseler, *The Varieties of Anti-Americanism: Reflex and Response* (Washington, DC: Ethics and Public Policy Center, 1985), 44.

39. Diner, *America in the Eyes of the Germans*, 108.

40. See Chapter 4.

41. See the Epilogue.

42. C. Vann Woodward, *The Old World's New World* (NY: Oxford University Press, 1991), 4–12.

43. Diner, *America in the Eyes of the Germans*; Ulrich Ott, *Amerika ist anders. Studien zum Amerika-Bild in deutschen Reiseberichten des 20. Jahrhunderts* (Frankfurt am Main: Peter Lang, 1991); Roger, *L'ennemi américain*; Schwan, *Antikommunismus und Antiamerikanismus*; Egbert Klautke, *Unbegrenzte Möglichkeiten: "Amerikanisierung" in Deutschland und Frankreich (1900–1933)* (Stuttgart: Franz Steiner, 2003).

44. See Chapter 1.

45. Among the growing corpus of useful works on the subject are Dan Diner, *Verkehrte Welten: Antiamerikanismus in Deutschland: ein historischer Essay* (Frankfurt am Main: Eichborn, 1993); Denis Lacorne, Jacques Rupnik, and Marie-France Toinet, eds., *L'Amérique dans nos têtes: un siècle de fascinations et d'aversions* (Paris: Hachette, 1986); Rob Kroes, Maarten van Rossem, and Marcus Cunliffe, *Anti-Americanism in Europe* (Amsterdam: Free University Press, 1986); Jacques Portes, *Fascination and Misgivings: The United States in French Opinion, 1870–1914*, trans. Elborg Forster (NY: Cambridge University Press, 2000); Alexander Stephan, *The Americanization of Europe: Culture, Diplomacy, and Anti-Americanism after 1945* (NY: Berghahn Books, 2006).

46. Hollander, *Anti-Americanism*, 393.

47. Pew Global Attitudes Project, "Among Wealthy Nations, U.S. Stands Alone in its Embrace of Religion," Dec 19, 2002.

48. "Global Public Opinion in the Bush Years," Pew Research Center Global Attitudes Project, Dec 18, 2008.

49. Paul Hollander, "The Politics of Envy," *The New Criterion* 21 (November 2002): 14.
50. Max Horkheimer, *Gesammelte Schriften* (Frankfurt am Main: S. Fischer, 1988), 14: 408.
51. Alvin H. Rosenfeld, "Anti-Americanism and Anti-Semitism: A New Frontier of Bigotry," American Jewish Committee, August 2003; Diner, *America in the Eyes of the Germans*, 20.
52. See Berel Lang, "On the 'the' in 'the Jews': from Grammar to Anti-Semitism," *Midstream* 14 (May/June 2003): 9–11.

Chapter 1. History of a Concept

1. Dickens to William Charles Macready, Mar 22, 1842, in Mamie Dickens and Georgina Hogarth, eds., *The Letters of Charles Dickens* (London: Chapman and Hall, 1882), I: 65.
2. Andrew Kohut and Bruce Stokes, *America against the World: How We Are Different and Why We Are Disliked* (NY: Henry Holt and Co., 2006), 22.
3. Andrei Markovits, *Uncouth Nation: Why Europe Dislikes America* (Princeton, NJ: Princeton University Press, 2007), 3.
4. Michael Radu, "A Matter of Identity: The Anti-Americanism of Latin American Intellectuals," in Paul Hollander, ed., *Understanding Anti-Americanism: Its Origins and Impact at Home and Abroad* (Chicago: Ivan R. Dee, 2004), 144–64, quoted at 144.
5. See below for a discussion of this common figure of speech.
6. Stephen Haseler, *The Varieties of Anti-Americanism: Reflex and Response* (Washington, DC: Ethics and Public Policy Center, 1985), 30.
7. Gerbi, a gifted and prolific amateur historian and economist, and a Jew by birth, fled to South America after Italy allied itself with Nazi Germany. See Antonello Gerbi, *La disputa del Nuovo Mondo: storia di una polemica, 1750–1900* (Milan: Ricciardi, 1955), first published in Spanish as *Viejas polémicas sobre el Nuevo Mundo: En el umbral de una conciencia americana* in 1946 by the Banco del Crédito del Peru, where he served as chief economist while in exile. His longer version was published in Jeremy Moyle's translation as *The Dispute of the New World: The History of a Polemic, 1750–1900* (Pittsburgh: University of Pittsburgh Press, 1973).
8. The phrase is E.P. Thompson's in *The Making of the English Working Class* (London: Victor Gollancz, 1963), 12.
9. "[T]he word 'Anti-Americanism' itself might not have been explicitly used until the beginning of the twentieth century," according to Markovits, *Uncouth Nation*, 19; he refers to a 1901 article, "Europe and America," *The Atlantic Monthly* 88 (November 1901): 577–88.
10. "From the Monthly Review for January 1767," *Boston Evening-Post*, May 25, 1767, 2.
11. St. Vincent Troubridge, "Notes on DAE: I. Words of the Colonial and Revolutionary Periods," *American Speech* 20, no. 4 (December 1945): 265–76, quoted at 269.
12. "Philadelphia, April 19," *New-York Journal*, Apr 27, 1775, 1.
13. Camden to Lord Chatham, February 1775, in Thomas Erskine May, *The Constitutional History of England since the Accession of George Third, 1760–1860* (Boston: Crosby and Nichols, 1863), 2: 30, n. 1.

14. *Courier de l'Europe*, Dec 13, 1776, quoted in Paul Imbs, ed., *Trésor de la langue française* (Paris: Éditions du Centre National de la Recherche Scientifique, 1973), 745.

15. John Fothergill to Franklin, Mar 19, 1775; Benjamin Snowden to Franklin, Aug 25, 1777; Stephen Sayre to Franklin, Mar 21, 1779; in *The Papers of Benjamin Franklin*, now online at www.yale.edu/franklinpapers.

16. Adams, Franklin, and Jay to the President of Congress, Sep 10, 1783, *Revolutionary Diplomatic Correspondence*, 6: 690; Morris to Washington, Sep 18, 1790, *The Papers of George Washington: Presidential Series*, Dorothy Twohig, ed. (Charlottesville, VA: University of Virginia Press, 1996), 6: 470–77, quoted at 477.

17. Jefferson to Edward Rutledge, Jun 24, 1797, and Jefferson to James Brown, Oct 27, 1808, in Paul Leicester Ford, ed., *The Works of Thomas Jefferson in Twelve Volumes*, online at memory.loc.gov.

18. *Windham Herald*, Jul 26, 1798, 3.

19. *The Centinel*, May 22, 1798, 1; May 15, 1798, *Journal of the House of Representatives: John Adams Administration 1797–1801*, vol. 2, 5th Cong., 2nd Sess. (Wilmington, DE: Michael Glazler, Inc., 1977), 475–76; "Chronicle," *Niles' Weekly Register*, Nov 13, 1819, 175.

20. New Jersey's *Sentinel of Freedom* 17:4 (Oct 13, 1812): 3, and in Maine's *American Advocate* 5:42 (Nov 5, 1813): 3.

21. "Prospect of Peace," *New-Jersey Journal*, Apr 6, 1813, 2; Peleg Sprague, *An Oration Pronounced at Worcester July 4, 1815* (Worcester, ME: Henry Rogers, 1815), 11; "From the *Boston Patriot*: Unthinking Bostonians," *Daily National Intelligencer*, May 17, 1818, 2.

22. Thomas Cooper, "Political Economy," *The Banner of the Constitution*, Jan 13, 1830, 57.

23. Carlos Vicuña, *La Tiranía en Chile* (Santiago: LOM Editorial, 2002 [1928]), 536–8.

24. Denis Peschanski, *Vichy 1940–44: contrôle et exclusion* (Paris: Éditions Complexe, 1997), 60; James Shields, *The Extreme Right in France: From Pétain to Le Pen* (NY: Routledge, 2007), 222. "Jean Maxe," a pseudonym, published pamphlets entitled *Les Cahiers de l'anti-France* in the 1920s, purporting to unmask members of the conspiracy.

25. Lillian Guerra, "Beyond Paradox: Counterrevolution and the Origins of Political Culture in the Cuban Revolution, 1959–2009," in Greg Grandin and Gilbert M. Joseph, eds., *A Century of Revolution* (Durham: Duke University Press, 2010), 199–230.

26. Robert Horvath, *The Legacy of Soviet Dissent: Dissidents, Democratisation and Radical Nationalism in Russia* (NY: Routledge, 2005), 151.

27. "Objections," *New York Sentinel and Working Man's Advocate*, Jun 9, 1830, 1; "A Letter to the Candidates for the Offices of President and Vice-President of the United States," *Workingman's Advocate*, Aug 24, 1844, 4; "Nativism vs. Republicanism," *Workingman's Advocate*, Feb 1, 1845, 3; "Who Are Foreigners?" *The Catholic Telegraph*, Aug 21, 1845, 260.

28. "Parting Address," *The Free Enquirer*, Aug 21, 1830, 337.

29. Review of James Fenimore Cooper, *The American Democrat*, in *Boston Quarterly Review* 1: 3 (July 1838): 360; Cooper to Mrs. Cooper, Jun 3, 1850, in James Fenimore Cooper, ed., *Correspondence of James Fenimore Cooper* (New Haven, CT: Yale University Press, 1922), II: 680; Kermit Vanderbilt, *American Literature*

and the Academy: The Roots, Growth, and Maturity of a Profession (Philadelphia: University of Pennsylvania Press, 1986), 64.

30. An American Pat-riot, "Foreigners Especially the Irish – Riots in Boston," *Cincinnati Daily Gazette*, reproduced in *The Catholic Telegraph*, Aug 3, 1837, 278.

31. Ronald Lora and William Henry Longton, eds., *The Conservative Press in Eighteenth- and Nineteenth-Century America* (Westport, CT: Greenwood Publishing, 1999), 51–4.

32. "The American Review of History and Politicks, and General Repository of Literature and State Papers," *The Select Reviews of Literature, and Spirit of Foreign Magazines* V (1811): 217–24.

33. "The American Review," 221.

34. "The American Review," 221–22. Emphasis in original.

35. Ronald Lora and William Henry Longton, eds., *The Conservative Press in Eighteenth- and Nineteenth-Century America* (Westport, CT: Greenwood Publishing, 1999), 51–4.

36. Joseph Eaton, "From Anglophile to Nationalist: Robert Walsh's *An Appeal from the Judgments of Great Britain*," *Pennsylvania Magazine of History and Biography* 132:2 (April 2008): 141–72, quoted at 141.

37. "The U. States, Mexico, and Texas," *National Intelligencer*, reproduced in *Niles' National Register* Jul 6, 1844, 294.

38. "The Mexican Question," *The United States Magazine and Democratic Review* 14, no. 83 (1845): 419.

39. "Anti-Americanism," *Pittsfield Sun*, Jul 16, 1846, 2.

40. "Anti-American: The Speech of Mr. Clay," *National Era* 1:48 (Dec 2, 1847): 2; see also Carl Schurz, *Life of Henry Clay*, vol. 2 (NY: Houghton, Mifflin, 1894), 290.

41. "Letter from Mexico," *Morris's National Press*, May 2, 1846, 3; "The Mexican War," *The Commercial Review of the South and West*, 2:1 (July 1846): 21; "Northern Mexico," *Arizonian*, May 5, 1859, reprinted in the *New York Times*, May 26, 1859, 2.

42. William Gannaway Brownlow, *Americanism Contrasted with Foreignism, Romanism, and Bogus Democracy* (Nashville, n.p.: 1856), 179–81.

43. Cong. Marshall of Kentucky, May 25, 1858, *Congressional Globe*, 35th Cong. 1st. sess., 2357.

44. "Influence of the Press on Education," *American Annals of Education and Instruction* 5:10 (October 1835): 434.

45. James S. Buckingham, *America[:] Historical, Statistical, and Descriptive*, 3 vols (London: Fisher, Son, & Co., 1841), 1:173.

46. Carlyle, *Latter-Day Pamphlets* (London: Chapman and Hall, 1850), 25; Emerson journal entry from December 1865 in Linda Allardt et al., eds., *The Journals and Miscellaneous Notebooks of Ralph Waldo Emerson* (Cambridge, MA: Belknap, 1982), 15: 82.

47. Philippe Roger, *L'ennemi américain: généalogie de l'antiaméricanisme français* (Paris: Seuil, 2002), 80.

48. Roger, *L'ennemi américain*, 63.

49. A. D'Alembert, *Flânerie parisienne aux Etats Unis* (Paris 1856), 145–47, quoted in C. Vann Woodward, *The Old World's New World* (NY: Oxford University Press, 1991), 48.

50. Kermit Vanderbilt, *American Literature and the Academy* (Philadelphia: University of Pennsylvania Press, 1989), 34.

51. Sydney Smith, "Review of Seybert's Annals of the United States," *The Edinburgh Review*, January 1820.

52. Gerald Emanuel Stearn, *Broken Image: Foreign Critiques of America* (NY: Random House, 1972), 23; Toby Miller, "Anti-Americanism and Popular Culture," in Richard A. Higgott and Ivona Malbasic, *The Political Consequences of Anti-Americanism* (NY: Taylor & Francis, 2008), 62; Woodward, *Old World*, 47.

53. Smith to Bennet, November 1816, in *Letters of Sydney Smith*, ed. Nowell C. Smith (London: Oxford University Press, 1953), 217.

54. Sheldon Halpern, *Sydney Smith* (NY: Twayne Publishers, 1966), 118.

55. *The Works of the Rev. Sydney Smith* (London: Longmans, Green, Reader, and Dyer, 1869), III: 799.

56. *The Works of the Rev. Sydney Smith*, III: 802.

57. Woodward, *Old World*, 47.

58. Sydney Smith, "Review of Seybert's Annals of the United States," *The Edinburgh Review*, January 1820.

59. John Ruskin, *Praeterita*, 1885–1889, quoted in Peter Yapp, ed., *The Travellers' Dictionary of Quotation* (London: Routledge & Kegan Paul, 1983).

60. Quoted in Graham Clarke, ed., *Henry James: Critical Assessments* (London: Routledge, 1991), I: 211.

61. Herbert J. Spiro, "Anti-Americanism in Western Europe," *Annals of the American Academy of Political Science* (May 1988): 124.

62. Haseler, *Varieties of Anti-Americanism*, 44.

63. Woodward, *Old World*, 16. Those sentiments did not prevent Turgot from opposing French aid to the American revolutionaries because he feared it would burst the king's budget. "Pro-American" utterances are no better indicator of tangible support than are "anti-American" utterances a reliable sign of hostile action to come.

64. Woodward, *Old World*, 17.

65. Gordon S. Wood, *The Americanization of Benjamin Franklin* (NY: Penguin, 2004), 231.

66. J.P. Brissot de Warville, *Examen Critique des Voyages dans l'Amérique Septentrionale de M. le Marquis de Chatellux; ou Lettre à M. le Marquis de Chatellux, dans laquelle on refute principalement ses opinions sur les Quakers, sur les Nègres, sur le Peuple, et sur l'Homme* (London, 1786), published in English by Joseph James, Philadelphia, 1788. Thomas Jefferson kept a copy in his library at Monticello.

67. Laboulaye, *La république constitutionelle* (Paris: Charpentier, 1871), 16, quoted in Roger, *L'ennemi américain*, 142.

68. Ernest Renan, *Souvenirs d'enfance et de jeunesse* (Paris : Calmann-Lévy, 1883), 13, 18.

69. Larousse 19th ed. (1866), cited in Imbs, *Trésor de la langue française*, 745.

70. Otto Brunner, Werner Conze and Reinhardt Koselleck, eds., *Geschichtliche Grundbegriffe: Historisches Lexikon zur politisch-sozialer Sprache in Deutschland* (Stuttgart: Ernst Klett Verlag, 1972), V: 618.

71. "Die Freiheit Amerikas," *Berlinische Monatsschrift* (April 1783), quoted in Brunner et al., *Geschichtliche Grundbegriffe*, V: 724.

72. Brunner et al., *Geschichtliche Grundbegriffe*, V: 618.

73. Ernst Fraenkel, ed., *America im Spiegel des deutschen politischen Denkens. Äusserungen deutscher Staatsmänner und Staatsdenker über Staat und Gesellschaft in den Vereinigten Staaten von Amerika* (Cologne: Westdeutscher Verlag, 1959), 74–7.

74. Alexander Schmidt, *Reisen in die Moderne: Der Amerika-diskurs des deutschen Bürgertums vor dem Ersten Weltkrieg im europäischen Vergleich* (Berlin: Akademie Verlag, 1997), 88–9.

75. Fraenkel, *Amerika im Spiegel*, 118–23.

76. Fraenkel, *Amerika im Spiegel*, 106–7. Josef Joffe, for example, writes that "the long-running story of European anti-Americanism... was as old as Heinrich Heine's denunciation of the United States in the early 19th century." Josef Joffe, "Dissecting Anti-Isms," *The American Interest* 1:4 (Summer 2006).

77. In Fraenkel, *America im Spiegel*, 108.

78. Lesley Sharpe, *The Cambridge Companion to Goethe* (NY: Cambridge University Press, 2002), 212.

79. Karl Gutzkow, *Öffentliche Charaktere* (Hamburg: Hoffmann und Campe, 1835), 209.

80. Maurice B. Benn, *The Drama of Revolt: A Critical Study of Georg Büchner* (NY: Cambridge University Press, 1976), 19, 25.

81. Ludwig Börne, *Gesammelte Schriften* (Milwaukee: E. Luft, P. Bickler, & Co., 1858), 91, 164, 264.

82. Joffe, "Dissecting Anti-Isms," emphasis added.

83. "British Opinions of America," *American Quarterly Review* 20:40 (December 1836): 405.

84. Robert Lawson-Peebles, "Dickens Goes West," in Mick Gidley and Robert Lawson-Peebles, eds., *Views of American Landscapes* (Cambridge: Cambridge University Press, 1989), 111–28, quoted at 113.

85. CIA, "Bi-Weekly Propaganda Guidance: Intellectual Anti-Americanism," May 20, 1963, CIA-RDP78–03061A00020001009–1, CREST.

86. Drew Middleton, "The Deeper Meaning of British Neutralism," *New York Times*, Dec 11, 1960, SM12.

87. "Anti-American Feeling in Britain [1957]," in Andrew Bone, ed., *The Collected Papers of Bertrand Russell, vol. 29: Détente or Destruction* (NY: Routledge, 2005), 187. The resulting essay appeared as "Three Reasons Why They Dislike Us" in the *New York Times Magazine*, Sep 8, 1957, 20.

88. Frances Trollope, *Domestic Manners of the Americans* (NY: Penguin, 1997 [1832]), 168.

89. Twain's marginal notes from his own copy of *Domestic Manners* quoted in Richard Mullen, "Introduction" to Frances Trollope, *Domestic Manners of the Americans* (New York: Oxford University Press, 1985 [1832]), xxxvi.

90. He accused her, too expansively, of stealing ideas from his *Nicholas Nickleby* to write her indictment of child labor, *Michael Armstrong the Factory Boy* – a book Dickens thought she might as well have named "Ticholas Tickleby." Susan S. Kissel, *In Common Cause: The "Conservative" Frances Trollope and the "Radical" Frances Wright* (Bowling Green University Popular Press, 1993), 116.

91. Dickens letter to William Charles Macready quoted in Mullen, "Introduction," xxxii.

92. Dickens, *American Notes for General Circulation* (London: Chapman and Hall, 1842), chs. III, VI, VII, XVII. Dickens thought the main difference attributable to the state subsidy provided to poorhouses and orphanages in Massachusetts.

93. Michael Slater, *Charles Dickens* (New Haven, CT: Yale University Press, 2009), 186–89; Dickens, *American Notes*, 80–1.

94. *The North American Review* 56:118 (January 1843): 217.

95. "Charles Dickens and his 'Notes,'" *Spirit of the Times*, Feb 18, 1843, 603.

96. Markovits, *Uncouth Nation*, 72–3.

97. Dickens, *American Notes*, 17, 19, 170.

98. Dickens, *American Notes*, 162–63. Dickens drew here upon a compilation of newspaper advertisements quoted in the American Anti-Slavery Society's *Anti-Slavery Examiner* in 1839.

99. Slater, *Charles Dickens*, 192.

100. Slater, *Charles Dickens*, 199.

101. James M. McPherson, *Battle Cry of Freedom: The Civil War Era* (NY: Oxford University Press, 1988), 210.

102. [Isaac Candler], *A Summary View of America* (London: T. Cadell, 1824), 280.

103. Gustave de Beaumont, *Marie ou L'esclavage aux États-Unis: Tableau de moeurs américaines* (Paris: L. Hauman et Cie., 1835).

104. Francisque de Corcelle, "De L'escalavage aux Etats-Unis," *Revue des deux mondes* 4:6 (1836): 227–46.

105. Louis Kern, "'Slavery Recedes but the Prejudice to which it Has Given Birth Is Immovable': Beaumont and Tocqueville Confront Racism and Slavery in Ante-Bellum America and Orléanist France," in William L. Chew, ed., *National Stereotypes in Perspective: Americans in France, Frenchmen in America* (Amsterdam: Rodopi, 2001), 143–86.

106. "American Colonization Society: Objections Answered," *Freedom's Journal*, Oct 26, 1827.

107. "Anti-American Doctrine," *The Cincinnati Weekly Herald and Philanthropist*, May 1, 1844, 3.

108. "In Treason there Are No Accessories," *The National Era*, Oct 16, 1851.

109. Bob Markle to Frederick Douglass, Aug 30, 1851, in "Communications: The Constitution – Colonization," *Frederick Douglass Paper*, Sep 4, 1851.

110. Russell A. Berman, *Anti-Americanism in Europe: A Cultural Problem* (Stanford, CA: Hoover Institution Press, 2004), 34.

111. Rubin and Rubin, *Hating America*, ix.

112. Paul Hollander, *Anti-Americanism: Irrational and Rational* (New Brunswick, NJ: Transaction Publishers, 1995), xiv.

113. Mark Twain, *More Tramps Abroad* (London: Chatto & Windus, 1897), 127.

114. "French Sneer at Mark Twain," *New York Times*, Apr 24, 1910.

115. Revel, *La grande parade* (Paris: Plon, 2000), 308, quoted in James Ceaser, "The Philosophical Origins of Anti-Americanism in Europe," in *Understanding Anti-Americanism*, 45.

116. Hollander, *Anti-Americanism*, 373 and 157, where he writes "not unlike Goebbels" of Prof. Louis Kampf's observation that "the very concept of culture is rooted in elitism... [it can be] difficult not to gag on the word." Presumably, Hollander here is making the common mistake of misattributing to Goebbels the line "When I hear the world culture, I release the safety-catch on my revolver [*Wenn ich Kultur höre, entsichere ich meinen Browning*]." It actually comes from the play *Schlageter* by Hanns Johst that premiered on Hitler's birthday, April 20, 1933. John London, *Theatre under the Nazis* (Manchester: Manchester University Press, 2000), 7.

117. Markovits, *Uncouth Nation*, 3.

118. Even Markovits acknowledges that the leading German newspapers *Die Zeit* and *Die Welt*, along with the British *Daily Telegraph* and *The Times*, cannot be characterized as anti-American publications. Needless to say, the Nazis never permitted such variety. The point is not that Markovits is wrong to detect widespread negativity toward the United States in the European press, but by exaggerating his findings for rhetorical effect, he unwittingly reveals the stylistic impetus behind some of the texts he dislikes.

119. Alexis de Tocqueville, *Democracy in America* (NY: Library of America, 2004 [1835]), 271–72.

120. Tocqueville, *Democracy in America*, 719.

121. Trollope, *Domestic Manners*, 2: 276.

122. Ralph Waldo Emerson, "Success," *Society and Solitude 1870*, in Yapp, *The Travellers' Dictionary*.

123. "Capt. Basil Hall's, *Travels in North America*," *The Westminster Review* 11:22 (October 1829): 428.

124. Finley Peter Dunne, *Mr. Dooley Remembers*, Philip Dunne ed., in Yapp, *The Travellers' Dictionary*.

125. Karl Lamprecht, *Americana. Reiseeindrücke, Betrachtungen, Geschichtliche Gesamtansicht* (Freiburg: Hermann Heyfelder, 1906), 67–72, reprinted in Fraenkel, *Amerika im Spiegel*, 202–4.

126. Leacock quotes from "An old American newspaper of the year 1850" in his essay, "American Humour," in *Essays and Literary Studies* (NY: John Lane Co, 1916).

127. David Lawday, *Napoleon's Master: A Life of Prince Talleyrand* (NY: Macmillan, 2007), 79.

128. Rudyard Kipling, *From Sea to Sea*, in Kipling, *Works*, vol. 8 (NY: Doubleday, 1914 [1899]), 454.

129. Graf Adelbert von Baudissin, *Peter Tütt. Zustände in Amerika* (Altona: Mentzel, 1862), 70–1, in Heike Paul, "Tasting America: Food, Race, and the Anti-American Sentiments in Nineteenth-Century German-American Writing," in Tobias Doring et al., *Eating Culture: The Poetics and Politics of Food* (Heidelberg: Winter Verlag, 2003).

130. Oscar Wilde, 1882, quoted in Yapp, *The Travellers' Dictionary*.

131. G.A. Sala, *My Diary in America in the Midst of War*, 1865, quoted in Yapp, *The Travellers' Dictionary*.

132. Rupert Brooke, *Letters from America* (Whitefish, MT: Kessinger Publishing, 2004 [1916]), 20.

133. Candler, *A Summary View*, 59.

134. Fearon similarly disapproved of New York shopkeepers "smoking segars and spitting in every direction, to a degree offensive to any man of decent feelings." Fearon, *Sketches of America: A Narrative of a Journey of Five Thousand Miles through the Eastern and Western States of America* (London: Longman, 1818), 291, 12.

135. Catharine Maria Sedgwick, *Morals of Manners, Or Hints for Our Young People* (NY: G.P. Putnam & Co, 1854 [1846]), 26–8.

136. Search of *Times* archives database.

137. "Charles Dickens and his 'Notes,'" *Spirit of the Times*, Feb 18, 1843, 603.

138. Suellen Hoy, *Chasing Dirt: The American Pursuit of Cleanliness* (NY: Oxford University Press, 1995), 9; Marilyn T. Williams, *Washing "the Great Unwashed": Public Baths in Urban America, 1840–1920* (Columbus: Ohio State University

Press, 1991), 83–4; Katherine Ott, *Fevered Lives: Tuberculosis in American Culture Since 1870* (Cambridge, MA: Harvard University Press, 1996), 119.

139. Boswell, *Boswell's Life of Johnson*, I: 403; George Cockburn, *A Voyage to Cadiz and Gibraltar, Up the Mediterranean to Sicily and Malta in 1810 & 11* (London: J. Harding, 1815), 1: 436; "A Journey through Norway, Lapland, and part of Sweden, &c., by the Rev. Robert Everest," *The London Literary Gazette* 655 (Aug 8, 1829): 517.

140. Norbert Elias, *The Civilizing Process: Sociogenetic and Psychogenetic Investigations*, revised ed. (Hoboken, NJ: Wiley-Blackwell, 2000 [1939]), 130–35.

141. Mary Louise Pratt, *Imperial Eyes: Travel Writing and Transculturation* (London: Routledge, 1992).

142. For a sample, see Frank MacShane, *Impressions of Latin America: Five Centuries of Travel and Adventure by English and North American Writers* (NY: Morrow, 1963).

143. Samuel Flagg Bemis, "'America' and 'Americans'," *Yale Review* 57 (1968): 326.

144. In English, the letter D is a "hard" alveolar made by pressing the tip of the tongue against the gum ridge, but in Spanish it is a "soft" laminal denti-alveolar, that is, formed by the flat forward top of the tongue caressing the upper front teeth to produce a sound closer to the English "TH." The letters N, S, and T are also laminal, allowing a Spanish speaker to keep the tongue in roughly the same position throughout the act of pronouncing the word. In other words, although Bemis may have had trouble with it, in Latin America, *estadounidense* literally rolls off the tongue.

145. *Estadounidense's* imperfection lies in its assignment to the people of the *Estados Unidos de América*, and not to their neighbors in the *Estados Unidos Mexicanos*. The common use of *norteamericano* to mean "of the United States" is a geographical imprecision that does the customary injustice to Canadians and again, strictly speaking, to Mexicans. "Latin American" ignores the non-"Latin" influence of pre-Columbian, African, Dutch, and Anglo cultures in the region. In other venues I have avoided the use of *America* and *Americans* to refer to the United States, in deference to the sensibilities and sensible arguments of Latin Americans. For the present work, I was unable to avoid using *America* and *American* in a book about the history of the concept of anti-Americanism – which points to yet another flaw in the term.

146. *Boletín bibliográfico* (Peru) 3–4 (1927–1929): 256.

147. The resolution is reported in the Venezuelan *Boletín de la Academia Nacional de la historia* (1952): 363.

148. Rubin and Rubin, *Hating America*, 121.

149. Michael Radu, "A Matter of Identity: The Anti-Americanism of Latin American Intellectuals," in *Understanding Anti-Americanism*, 144–64, quoted at 146.

150. Charles Fletcher Lummis, "In the Lion's Den," *Land of Sunshine* 4 (May 1896): 236.

151. Grover Flint, *Marching with Gomez* (Boston: Lamson, Wolffe and Company, 1898), 195.

152. "Mexico in Disorder," *The Outlook*, Apr 13, 1912, 796.

153. Archibald Ross Colquhoun, *Greater America* (NY: Harper, 1904), 201.

154. Robert E. Speer, *Missions in South America* (NY: Board of Foreign Missions of the Presbyterian Church, 1909), 157.

155. Bert Ruiz, *The Colombian Civil War* (Jefferson, NC: McFarland, 2001), 189.

156. Piero Gleijeses, "The Limits of Sympathy: The United States and the Independence of Spanish America," *Journal of Latin American Studies* 24:3 (October 1992): 481–505.

157. John Lynch, *Simón Bolívar: A Life* (New Haven, CT: Yale University Press, 2006), 264.

158. Fredrick B. Pike, *Chile and the United States, 1880–1962* (Notre Dame, IN: University of Notre Dame Press, 1963), 25.

159. Salvador Méndez Reyes, *El hispanoamericanismo de Lucas Alamán, 1823–1853* (Mexico City: Universidad Autónoma, 1996), 141–43.

160. Lars Schoultz, *Beneath the United States: A History of U.S. Policy toward Latin America* (Cambridge, MA: Harvard University Press, 1998), 19.

161. Méndez Reyes, *El hispanoamericanismo*, 212.

162. Charles A. Hale, *El liberalismo mexicano en la época de Mora* (Mexico City: Siglo Veintiuno, 1972), 219.

163. F. Toscano and James Hiester, *Anti-Yankee Feelings in Latin America* (Washington, DC: University Press of America, 1982), ix, 8.

164. Francisco Bilbao, *La América en peligro*, 2nd ed. (Buenos Aires: Bernheim y Boneo, 1862), 9–13, 16–17, 53–4.

165. Bilbao, *La América*, 98.

166. Printed in Francisco Bilbao, *Obras completas* (Buenos Aires: Imprenta de Buenos Aires, 1866), 289–92.

167. For example, Rubin and Rubin, *Hating America*, 104; Alan McPherson, ed., *Anti-Americanism in Latin America and the Caribbean* (NY: Berghahn Books, 2006), 12.

168. *El evangelio americano* (1864), quoted in Solomon Lipp, *Three Chilean Thinkers: Bilbao, Letelier, Molina* (Waterloo, Ontario: Wilfrid Laurier University Press, 1975), 42.

169. José Enrique Rodó, *Ariel* (Montevideo: Dornaleche y Reyes, 1900).

170. Roberto Fernández Retamar would later reappropriate the figure of Caliban as the marginalized embodiment of Latin America's postcolonial revolutionary potential in *Caliban and other Essays* (Minneapolis: University of Minnesota Press, 1989 [1973]).

171. Rubin and Rubin, *Hating America*, 108.

172. W.E. Dunn, "The Post-War Attitude of Hispanic America toward the United States," *Hispanic American Historical Review* 3:2 (1920): 177–83, quoted at 179.

173. José Enrique Rodó, *Ariel*, tr. Frederic Jesup Stimson (NY: Houghton Mifflin, 1922), 78.

174. Nicola Miller, *In the Shadow of the State: Intellectuals and the Quest for National Identity in Twentieth-Century Spanish America* (London: Verso, 1999), 176.

175. Rodó, *Ariel* (1922), 95. See also Leslie Bethell, *Ideas and Ideologies in Twentieth Century Latin America* (Cambridge: Cambridge University Press, 1996), 180.

176. For example, F. García Godoy, *Americanismo literario* (Madrid: Editorial-América, 1910).

177. See John M. Kirk, "José Martí and the United States: A Further Interpretation," *Journal of Latin American Studies* 9:2 (November 1977): 275–90; Philip S. Foner, ed., *José Martí, Inside the Monster: Writings on the United States and American Imperialism* (NY: Monthly Review Press, 1975).

178. Thomas E. Skidmore and Peter H. Smith, *Modern Latin America*, 2nd ed. (NY: Oxford University Press, 1989), 249.

179. Heather L. McCrea, "Iberia and the Caribbean," in John Michael Francis, ed., *Iberia and the Americas: Culture, Politics, and History* (Santa Barbara, CA: ABC-CLIO, 2006), 19–26, quoted at 25.

180. Woodward, *Old World*, xv.

181. Victor Davis Hanson, "Goodbye to Europe?" *Commentary* 114:3 (October 2002); Andrei S. Markovits, *European Anti-Americanism (and Anti-Semitism): Ever Present Though Always Denied* (Cambridge, MA: Harvard University Gunzburg Center for European Studies Working Paper Series, 2003), 10; Hollander, ed., *Understanding Anti-Americanism*, jacket copy.

182. Daniel Pipes, "Hating America's Success," *New York Sun*, Oct 12, 2004.

183. Roger Daniels, *Coming to America: A History of Immigration and Ethnicity in American Life*, 2nd ed. (NY: Perennial, 2002), 17–18, 43–44; George E. Pozzetta, ed., *Emigration & Immigration: The Old World Confronts the New*, vol. 2 (NY: Garland, 1991), viii; Wolfgang J. Helbich, *"Alle Menschen sind dort gleich . . ." Die deutsche Amerika-Auswanderung im 19. und 20. Jahrhundert* (Düsseldorf: Schwann, 1988), 38; Walter Nugent, *Crossings: The Great Transatlantic Migrations, 1870–1914* (Bloomington: Indiana University Press, 1992); Rudolph J. Vecoli and Suzanne M. Sinke, eds., *A Century of European Migrations, 1830–1930* (Champaign: University of Illinois Press, 1991).

184. Hector St. John de Crèvecoeur, *Letters from an American Farmer* (NY: Oxford University Press, 1998), 43.

185. Emanuel Strauss, *Dictionary of European Proverbs* (NY: Routledge, 1994), 356.

186. Annual averages cited in Leslie Page Moch, *Moving Europeans: Migration in Western Europe since 1650* (Bloomington: Indiana University Press, 1992), 149.

187. Samuel L. Baily, *Immigrants in the Lands of Promise: Italians in Buenos Aires and New York City, 1870–1914* (Ithaca, N.Y.: Cornell University Press, 1999), 56. Moreover, during all phases of the period 1876–1976, more Italians moved to other parts of Europe than to North America. Ibid., 24.

188. J.D. Gould, "European and Inter-Continental Emigration. The Road Back Home: Return Migration from the United States," *Journal of European Economic History* 9 (Spring 1980): 41–112, 57. See also Mark Wyman, *Round-Trip to America: The Immigrants Return to Europe, 1880–1930* (Ithaca, NY: Cornell University Press, 1993).

189. John Bodnar, *The Transplanted: A History of Immigrants in Urban America* (Bloomington: Indiana University Press, 1985); Jon Gjerde, *The Minds of the West: Ethnocultural Evolution in the Rural Middle West, 1830–1917* (Chapel Hill: University of North Carolina Press, 1997).

190. Patrizia Audenino, "The Paths of the Trade: Italian Stonemasons in the United States," in *Emigration & Immigration: The Old World Confronts the New*, ed. George E. Pozzetta (NY: Garland, 1991), 31–47.

191. John Bodnar, *Remaking America: Public Memory, Commemoration, and Patriotism in the Twentieth Century* (Princeton: Princeton University Press, 1992).

192. Simon Kuznets, "Immigration of Russian Jews to the United States," *Perspectives in American History* 9 (1975): 336–37.

193. Moch, *Moving Europeans*, 150. Nonetheless, Jews chose to return to Europe in surprising numbers during the peak years of Jewish migration. Jonathan D. Sarna debunks what he rightly calls "The Myth of No Return: Jewish Return Migration to Eastern Europe, 1881–1914," in Colin Holmes, ed., *Migration in European History* (Cheltenham: Edward Elgar, 1996), 2: 454–66.

194. Marianne Debouzy, ed., *In the Shadow of the Statue of Liberty: Immigrants, Workers, and Citizens in the American Republic, 1880–1920* (Urbana: University of Illinois Press, 1992).

195. See my "Beyond 'Voting with their Feet': Toward a Conceptual History of 'America' in European Migrant Sending Communities, 1860s to 1914," *Journal of Social History* 40:3 (Spring 2007): 557–75, or the synopsis in "Survey of notable articles," *The Wilson Quarterly* (Summer 2007): 79.

196. Friedrich Maurer and Rudolf Mulch, *Südhessisches Wörterbuch* (Marburg: Elwert Verlag, 1965).

197. Heinz Engels, *Sudetendeutsches Wörterbuch* (Munich: Oldenbourg Verlag, 1988).

198. Richard Wossidlo and Hermann Teuchert, *Mecklenburgisches Wörterbuch*, vol. 1 (Neumünster: Karl Wachholtz Verlag, 1942).

199. Max Pfister, *LEI. Lessico etimologico italiano* (Wiesbaden: Ludwig Reichert Verlag, 1987).

200. Wossidlo and Teuchert, *Mecklenburgisches Wörterbuch*.

201. Engels, *Sudetendeutsches Wörterbuch; Luxemburger Wörterbuch* (Luxemburg: P. Linden, 1950), 23.

202. Pfister, *LEI*. See also Salvatore Battaglia, *Grande dizionario della lingua italiana* (Torino: Editrice Torinese, 1961), 389.

203. Jon Gjerde, "Response," *Journal of American Ethnic History* 18:4 (Summer 1999): 152–56.

204. Maurer and Mulch, *Südhessisches Wörterbuch*.

205. Wossidlo and Teuchert, *Mecklenburgisches Wörterbuch*.

206. Simin Palay, *Dictionnaire du béarnais et du gascon modernes* (Paris: Éditions du Centre National de la Recherche Scientifique, 1961), 34.

207. Ernst Christmann and Julius Krämer, *Pfälzisches Wörterbuch* (Wiesbaden: Franz Steiner Verlag, 1965), 200.

208. Chasperr Pult et al., eds., *Dicziunari rumantsch grischun* (Cuoira: Bischofberger, 1939–1946), 236.

209. Lutz Röhrich, "Auswandererschicksal im Lied," in *Der große Aufbruch. Studien zur Amerikaauswanderung*, ed. Peter Assion (Marburg: Jonas Verlag, 1985), 71–108, 91.

210. Lyrics written by Johannes Hauck (1806–1880), a shoemaker's son who worked as the town barber in Gompertshausen, in Heinz Sperschneider, ed., *Wälder, Felder, Bergeshöhn. Eine Anthologie Thüringer Mundartdichtung* (Leipzig: Friedrich Hofmeister, 1968), 91–3. Translation mine.

211. Röhrich, "Auswandererschicksal im Lied," 87.

212. Hermann Pleij, *Der Traum vom Schlaraffenland. Mittelalterliche Fantasien vom vollkommenen Leben* (Frankfurt am Main: S. Fischer Verlag, 2000).

213. Pleij, *Der Traum vom Schlaraffenland*, 40–52.

214. Peter Assion, "Schlaraffenland schriftlich und mundlich," in Lutz Röhrich and Erika Lindig, eds., *Volksdichtung zwischen Mündlichkeit und Schriftlichkeit* (Tübingen: Gunter Narr, 1989), 109–23.

215. Sperschneider, *Wälder, Felder, Bergeshöhn*, 91.

216. Béla Gunda, "America in Hungarian Folk Tradition," *The Journal of American Folklore* 83:330 (1970): 406–416. Gunda provides translations but not the original Hungarian texts.

217. Puskás, *Ties that Bind*, 84.

218. Gunda, "America in Hungarian Folk Tradition."

219. Bernard Share, *Slanguage: A Dictionary of Slang and Colloquial English in Ireland* (Dublin: Gill & Macmillan, 1997), 4; Gjerde, "Response," 155.

220. Donna Gabaccia, ed., *Seeking Common Ground: Multidisciplinary Studies of Immigrant Women in the United States* (Westport: Praeger, 1992).

221. Linda Reeder, *Widows in White: Migration and the Transformation of Rural Italian Women, Sicily, 1880–1920* (Toronto: University of Toronto Press, 2003), 65–6. See also Vito Teti, "Noti sui comportamenti delle donne sole degli 'americani' durante la prima emigrazione in Calabria," *Studi emigrazione* 24:87 (1987): 13–46.

222. Gunda, "America in Hungarian Folk Tradition."

Chapter 2. Americanism and Anti-Americanism

1. See analysis below.

2. John H. Denison, "The Survival of the American Type," *The Atlantic Monthly* 75 (January 1895): 16–29.

3. Jeremiah J. Crowley, *The Parochial School: A Curse to the Church, a Menace to the Nation* (n.p., 1905), 22, 349.

4. Newell Dwight Hillis, *The Great Refusal and Other Evangelistic Sermons* (NY: Revell Company, 1923), 140.

5. "Colonel Assails Wilson in Maine; Charges that Anti-Americanism is Due to Lack of Courage on Mr. Wilson's Part," *New York Times*, Sep 1, 1916, 6; "America Indicted By Theodore Roosevelt," *The Argus*, Sep 2, 1916, 19. In the event, the German-American vote split nearly evenly for Wilson and Hughes. "Both Candidates Got Hyphen Vote," *New York Times*, Nov 9, 1916, 6.

6. "Pacifists Hold Anti-American Talk Carnival," *Chicago Daily Tribune*, Aug 20, 1917, 1.

7. Shailer Mathews, "The Moral Value of Patriotism," *The Biblical World* 52:1 (July 1918): 26.

8. "Labor Loyalty: Workers Urged to Observe Lincoln's Birthday Week in Combating Anti-Americanism," *Chicago Daily Tribune*, Jan 7, 1918, 8; Ernest Freeberg, *Democracy's Prisoner: Eugene V. Debs, the Great War, and the Right to Dissent* (Cambridge, MA: Harvard University Press, 2008), 57.

9. "U. of I. Teachers Called Disloyal," *Chicago Daily Tribune*, Nov 2, 1917, 1; "Illinois University Men Are Accused: Instructors Charged with Anti-Americanism," *Los Angeles Times*, Nov 3, 1917, I3.

10. "A Persistent Menace," *Washington Post*, Nov 3, 1917, 6.

11. Bessie Louise Pierce, *Public Opinion and the Teaching of History in the United States* (NY: Knopf, 1926), 128.

12. Samuel Chester Parker, "Civic-Moral Teaching in French Secular Schools, Part II," *The Elementary School Journal* 20:9 (May 1920): 660–69, quoted at 669.

13. Gino Speranza, *Race or Nation: A Conflict of Divided Loyalties* (Indianapolis: Bobbs-Merrill, 1923), 199–200.

14. "Negroes of World Prey of Agitators," *New York Times*, Aug 24, 1919, 1; *Pittsburgh Courier*, Aug 29, 1925, 14.

15. *Report of the Proceedings of the 24th Annual Convention of the Zionist Organization of America* (ZOA, 1921), 78.

16. *American Organist* 2 (1919): 397.

17. NY: Edmondson Economic Service, 1936.

18. *An Answer to Father Coughlin's Critics* (Royal Oak, MI: Radio League of the Little Flower, 1940), 17.

19. Harry Allen Overstreet, *Our Free Minds* (NY: W.W. Norton & Co., 1941), 38.

20. *Defense on Main Street: A Guide-Book for Local Activities for Defense and Democracy* (NY: Council for Democracy, 1941), 15.

21. *The Communist* 23:9 (September 1944): 860.

22. David S. Wyman, *The Abandonment of the Jews: America and the Holocaust, 1941–1945* (NY: Pantheon Books, 1984), 9.

23. Representative Thorkelson (MT), "That Our Nation May Survive," 76th Cong., 3d sess., *Cong. Rec.* (Jan 16, 1940), 86, pt. 13: 224–27.

24. 79th Cong., 1st sess., *Cong. Rec.* (Jan 22, 1945), 91, pt. 1: 420; Ellen H. Posner, "Anti-Jewish Manifestations," *American Jewish Year Book* 46 (1945): 137.

25. Jacob Armstrong Swisher, *The American Legion in Iowa, 1919–1929* (Iowa City: State Historical Society of Iowa, 1929), 17; House Committee on Rules, *Hearings on the Ku Klux Klan* (Washington, DC: Government Printing Office, 1921), 89; "Denizens of the Rural Slums," *Chicago Tribune*, Sep 19, 1926, 10; Frederick Lewis Allen, *Only Yesterday: An Informal History of the 1920s* (NY: Wiley, 1997 [1931]), 47; Higham, *Strangers*, 204–5, and *passim*. See also Thomas R. Pegram, *One Hundred Percent American: The Rebirth and Decline of the Ku Klux Klan in the 1920s* (Chicago: Ivan R. Dee, 2011).

26. Dan Diner, *America in the Eyes of the Germans: An Essay on Anti-Americanism* (Princeton, NJ: Markus Wiener Publishers, 1996), 23; Walter Laqueur, *Fin de Siècle and Other Essays on America and Europe* (New Brunswick, NJ: Transaction Publishers, 1997), 58; Wolfgang Wagner, "Das Amerikabild der Europäer," in *Amerika und Westeuropa. Gegenwarts- und Zukunftsprobleme*, ed. Karl Kaiser and Hans-Peter Schwarz (Stuttgart: Belser, 1977), 20.

27. www.pbs.org/weta/crossroads/about/show_anti-americans.html, accessed Jun 6, 2008.

28. George Seldes, *Never Tire of Protesting* (NY: Lyle Stuart, 1968), 18. Emphasis added.

29. George Bernard Shaw, *The Political Madhouse in America and Nearer Home* (London: Constable, 1933), 5.

30. "Selfish, Disloyal Sugar-Beeters," *Chicago Daily Tribune*, Jun 4, 1898, 12; James Wilford Garner, "Record of Political Events," *Political Science Quarterly* 18:4 (December 1903): 723–51, quoted at 725.

31. Reprinted in the *Washington Post*, Nov 23, 1900, 9.

32. Louis A. Pérez, Jr., *Cuba between Empires 1878–1902* (Pittsburgh: University of Pittsburgh Press, 1998), 324.

33. "The Election in Cuba: Majority of Delegates Anti-American," *Hartford Courant*, Sep 21, 1900, 1.

34. Pérez, *Cuba between Empires*, 139. Born in the Dominican Republic, Gómez fought the Spanish in Cuba for years and was probably the most popular revolutionary leader there.

35. Quoted in Lars Schoultz, *That Infernal Little Cuban Republic: The United States and the Cuban Revolution* (Chapel Hill: University of North Carolina Press, 2009), 27.

36. "Anti-Americanism in Cuba," *New York Times*, Nov 19, 1902, 9.

37. "Opinions in Cuba," *Hartford Courant*, Jul 26, 1899, 1.

38. "Porto Rico Politics: Federals Are Bitterly Anti-American and Allow No Participation in Celebration over American Occupation of Mayaguez," *Hartford Courant*, Aug 18, 1900, 1.
39. "First Jury Trial in Puerto Rico," *New York Times*, Oct 14, 1899, 4.
40. *The Gospel in All Lands* (journal of the Methodist Episcopal Church Missionary Society) 22 (1901): 368–69.
41. "Porto Ricans Strike and Burn Cane Fields," *Atlanta Constitution*, Apr 3, 1915, 12.
42. Fernández Vanga to Muñoz Rivera, Aug 6, 1912, *Boletín Histórico de Puerto Rico* IX (1922): 292.
43. See Nancy Mitchell, *The Danger of Dreams: German and American Imperialism in Latin America* (Chapel Hill: University of North Carolina Press, 1999); Thomas Schoonover, *Germany in Central America: Competitive Imperialism, 1821–1929* (Tuscaloosa: University of Alabama Press, 1998).
44. Thomas D. Schoonover, *The French in Central America: Culture and Commerce, 1820–1930* (Lanham, MD: Rowman and Littlefield, 2000).
45. F.E. Johannet, "Le monde aux Américains," *Le Correspondant* (Aug 10, 1898): 498, cited in Jacques Portes, *Fascination and Misgivings: The United States in French Opinion, 1870–1914* (NY: Cambridge University Press, 2000), 399.
46. Paul Sée, *Le Péril américain* (Lille: L. Danel, 1903), 44; Thomas Lenschau, *Die amerikanische Gefahr* (Berlin: Franz Seimenroth, 1902); Max Prager, *Die amerikanische Gefahr* (Berlin: L. Simion, 1902). See also Octave Noël, *Le Péril américain* (Paris: De Soye et fils, 1899); "Le péril américain," *Revue économique internationale* 2 (1905): 451.
47. "Why They Dislike Us," *New York Times*, May 27, 1901, 6.
48. Émile Boutmy, *Élements d'une psychologie politique du peuple américain* (Paris: A. Colin, 1911 [1902]), 61, quoted in Philippe Roger, *L'ennemi américain: généalogie de l'antiaméricanisme français* (Paris: Seuil, 2002), 239.
49. Daniel Rodgers, *Atlantic Crossings: Social Politics in a Progressive Age* (Cambridge, MA: Harvard University Press, 2000), 44.
50. Diner, *America in the Eyes of the Germans*, 48; Richard Pells, "Double Crossings: The Reciprocal Relationship between American and European Culture in the Twentieth Century," in Alexander Stephan, ed., *Americanization and Anti-Americanism* (NY: Berghahn Books, 2005), 189.
51. W.T. Stead, *The Americanization of the World; or, the Trend of the Twentieth Century* (London: Horace Markley, 1901), 5.
52. Stead, *The Americanization of the World*, 350–52.
53. Eldon J. Eisenach, *The Social and Political Thought of American Progressivism* (Indianapolis, IN: Hackett Publishing, 2006), 290.
54. Karl Marx, *Capital: A Critique of Political Economy*, ed. Ben Fowkes et al. (NY: Penguin Classics, 1976 [1867]), 91.
55. Marx, *Capital*, 91.
56. Werner Kremp, "Von der Höhe sozialisitischer Kultur zur neuen Macht auf dem Welts-chachbrett: Sozialdemokratische Amerikabilder 1890–1914," in *Zwei Wege in die Moderne: Aspekte der deutsch-amerikanischen Beziehungen 1900–1918*, ed. Ragnhild Fiebig-von-Hase and Jürgen Heideking (Trier: Wissenschaftlicher Verlag, 1998), 119–27.
57. Lars Fischer, *The Socialist Response to Antisemitism in Imperial Germany* (NY: Cambridge University Press, 2007), 162.

58. Karl Kautsky, "Der amerikanische Arbeiter" in *Die Neue Zeit* [1906?], reproduced in Ernst Fraenkel, ed., *America im Spiegel des deutschen politischen Denkens. Äusserungen deutscher Staatsmänner und Staatsdenker über Staat und Gesellschaft in den Vereinigten Staaten von Amerika* (Cologne: Westdeutscher Verlag, 1959), 220–3. See also Kremp, "Von der Höhe."

59. Werner Sombart, *Warum gibt es in den Vereinigten Staaten keinen Sozialismus?* (Tübingen: Mohr Verlag, 1906); Philippe Roger, *The American Enemy: The History of French Anti-Americanism* (Chicago: University of Chicago Press, 2006), 227–45.

60. Frederick C. Turner, "Anti-Americanism in Mexico, 1910–1913," *Hispanic American Historical Review* 47:4 (November 1967): 502–18, quoted at 502–3.

61. Stoddard, *The Rising Tide of Color against White World-Supremacy* (NY: Scribner, 1920), 136.

62. Turner, "Anti-Americanism in Mexico," 506.

63. Ethel Alec-Tweedie, *Mexico: From Díaz to the Kaiser* (NY: George H. Doran Co., 1917), 129.

64. Clint Parkhurst, *Songs of a Man Who Failed: The Poetical Writings of Henry Clinton Parkhurst* (Lincoln, NE: The Woodruff Press, 1921), 215.

65. George Beverly Winton, *Mexico Today: Social, Political and Religious Conditions* (Missionary Education Movement of the United States and Canada, 1913), 171.

66. Leslie Bethell, *The Cambridge History of Latin America: 1870–1930* (NY: Cambridge University Press, 1986), 107.

67. "Mexicans May Open Attack on Vera Cruz," *Chicago Daily Tribune*, Nov 7, 1914, 1.

68. "Assaults on United States Installations Abroad, 1900–1965," Research Project No. 709, Sep 1965, NSF, Gordon Chase Files, Box 7, LBJL.

69. Friedrich Katz, *The Life and Times of Pancho Villa* (Stanford, CA: Stanford University Press, 1998), 566; Alan Knight, *The Mexican Revolution: Counter-Revolution and Reconstruction* (Lincoln: University of Nebraska Press, 1990), 344; Frederick C. Turner, *The Dynamic of Mexican Nationalism* (Chapel Hill: University of North Carolina Press, 1968), 87.

70. Burt Morton McConnell, *Mexico at the Bar of Public Opinion: A Survey of Editorial Opinion in Newspapers of the Western Hemisphere* (NY: Mail and Express Publishing Company, 1939), *passim*.

71. Stoddard, *Rising Tide*, 136.

72. Frank B. Lord and James William Bryan, *Woodrow Wilson's Administration and Achievements* (Washington, DC: James William Bryan Press, 1921), 30.

73. Knight, *The Mexican Revolution*, 428.

74. O'Shaughnessy to SecState, Sep 17, 1913, Doc. 497, in *FRUS 1913* (Washington, DC: USGPO, 1920), 831.

75. *Official Report of the Fourth National Foreign Trade Convention* (NY: National Foreign Trade Convention, 1917), 349.

76. *New York World*, Jun 26, 1921, reprinted in Senate Finance Committee Hearing, "Tariff Act of 1921 (H.R. 7456), Schedule 15" (Washington, DC: US GPO, 1922), 4588–89.

77. Greg Grandin also noticed this trend and cites examples in his superb essay, "Your Americanism and Mine: Americanism and Anti-Americanism in the Americas," *American Historical Review* (October 2006): 1042–66, n. 20.

78. Rutherford H. Platt, Jr., "What Kind of Intervention for Mexico?" *The World's Work: A History of Our Time* 34 (November 1919): 385–400, quoted at 392, 393, 395.

79. Perry, "Anti-American Propaganda in Hispanic America," *Hispanic American Historical Review* 3:1 (1920): 17–40.

80. W.E. Dunn, "The Post-War Attitude of Hispanic America toward the United States," *Hispanic American Historical Review* 3:2 (1920): 177–83, quoted at 177.

81. Bohan memcon, Jan 29, 1945, *FRUS 1945*, IX: 73.

82. Michael C. Meyer and William L. Sherman, *The Course of Mexican History*, 7th ed. (NY: Oxford University Press, 2003 [1979]), 335.

83. Rubin and Rubin, *Hating America*, 101.

84. Rubin and Rubin, *Hating America*, 121.

85. Alvin Z. Rubinstein and Donald Eugene Smith, *Anti-Americanism in the Third World: Implications for U.S. Foreign Policy* (NY: Praeger, 1985), 31; Paul Hollander, *Anti-Americanism: Irrational & Rational* (New Brunswick, NJ: Transaction Publishers, 1995), 359; George W. Grayson, *The United States and Mexico: Patterns of Influence* (NY: Praeger, 1984), 8.

86. Marlise Simons, "U.S. Interventions Are Star Attraction at New Museum in Mexico," *Washington Post*, Dec 28, 1981, A-21.

87. Rubinstein and Smith, *Anti-Americanism in the Third World*, 31; Grayson, ed., *Prospects for Democracy in Mexico* (New Brunswick, NJ: Transaction Publishers, 1990), 239; idem, *Oil and Mexican Foreign Policy* (Pittsburgh: University of Pittsburgh Press, 1988), 10; idem, "Mexico: A Love-Hate Relationship with North America," in Hans Binnendijk, *National Negotiating Styles* (U.S. Department of State Foreign Service Institute, 1987), 125.

88. Octavio Paz, *The Labyrinth of Solitude*, tr. Lysander Kemp (NY: Grove Press, 1985), 31.

89. Larry Rohter, "Forget the Alamo! Look at the Sins of the Yankees," *New York Times*, Jan 7, 1988, A4; Dan Williams, "Mexico's Obsession with 'Foreign Intervention' Enshrined in Museum," *Los Angeles Times*, Jun 5, 1986, 21; Tim Weiner, "Of Gringos and Old Grudges: This Land is Their Land," *New York Times*, Jan 9, 2004, A4; Dianne Klein, "Mexico's View of the Vanquished – Itself," *Chicago Tribune*, Jul 5, 1985, N3.

90. Waddy Thompson, *Recollections of Mexico* (NY: Wiley and Putnam, 1846), 23.

91. Quoted in Piero Gleijeses, "The Limits of Sympathy: The United States and the Independence of Spanish America," *Journal of Latin American Studies* 24:3 (Oct. 1992): 490.

92. Lansford W. Hastings, *The Emigrants' Guide to Oregon and California* (Cincinnati: George Conclin, 1845), 113.

93. William D. Carrigan and Clive Webb, "The Lynching of Persons of Mexican Origin or Descent in the United States, 1848 to 1928," *Journal of Social History* 37:2 (Winter 2003): 411–38.

94. León de la Barra to SRE, "Exclusión de niños mexicanos," 1910, legajo 352.9/17; Bartolomé Carabajal y Rosas, "Maltrato a mexicanos," 1911, legajo 378.4/17; ConsulMex San Antonio to SRE, "Atropellos contra ciudadanos mexicanos," 1914, legajo 447.24/32; ConsulMex Filadelfia to SRE, "Racismo contra mexicano en Filadelfia," 1914, legajo 445.8/31; ConsulMex Nueva Orleans, "Discriminación contra niños mexicanos," 1915, legajo 494.14/18; Eliseo Arredondo to SRE, "Abuso de autoridades estadounidenses contra mexicanos," 1916, legajo

493.13/19; De Negri to SRE, "Iniciativa de ley en contra de mexicanos en Arizona," 1917, legajo 523.31/41; Luis Rincón, "Discriminación a mexicanos," 1918, legajo 635(I).18/59; Bonillas to SRE, "Discriminación en contra de ciudadanos mexicanos," 1919, legajo 580.10/15; and 49 similar reports in Archivo de la Embajada de México en EEUU, Archivo Histórico Genaro Estrada, Secretaría de Relaciones Exteriores, Mexico City (hereafter AHGE).

95. Frederick B. Pike, *FDR's Good Neighbor Policy: Sixty Years of Generally Gentle Chaos* (Austin: University of Texas Press, 1995), 103; Camille Guerin-Gonzalez, *Mexican Workers and American Dreams: Immigration, Repatriation, and California Farm Labor, 1900–1939* (New Brunswick, NJ: Rutgers University Press, 1994); Francisco E. Balderrama and Raymond Rodriguez, *Decade of Betrayal: Mexican Repatriation in the 1930s* (Albuquerque: University of New Mexico Press, 1995).

96. The reference is to "Lou Dobbs Tonight" on CNN.

97. "3 Coal-region Teens Held in Hate-Crime Killing," *Philadelphia Inquirer*, Jul 26, 2008.

98. Drug violence and crime against tourists are in a different category: prejudice and ideology do not seem to motivate crimes committed for profit, whose chief victims in Mexico are Mexicans.

99. *Missions: An International Baptist Magazine* 7 (1916): 731.

100. Thomas D. Schoonover, "A United States Dilemma: Economic Opportunity and Anti-Americanism in El Salvador, 1901–1911," *Pacific Historical Review* 58 (November 1989): 403–28.

101. Anna I. Powell, "Relations between the United States and Nicaragua, 1898–1916," *Hispanic American Historical Review* 8:1 (February 1928): 43–63, quoted at 44 and 64; see also Wallace Thompson, "The Doctrine of the 'Special Interest' of the United States in the Region of the Caribbean Sea," *Annals of the American Academy of Political and Social Science* 132 (July 1927): 153–9.

102. F.M. Gunther to SecState, Jan 15, 1913, *FRUS 1912*, 995.

103. Michel Gobat, *Confronting the American Dream: Nicaragua under U.S. Imperial Rule* (Durham: Duke University Press, 2005), ch. 2.

104. Gobat, *Confronting*, 50.

105. Rubén Darío, "A Roosevelt," *Cantos de vida y esperanza* (Bogotá: Ediciones Dipón, 1994 [1905]), 37.

106. Darío, "A Roosevelt," 37.

107. Gobat, *Confronting*, 127.

108. William Appleman Williams, *The Tragedy of American Diplomacy* (NY: Dell, 1962), 66.

109. Margaret Macmillan, *Paris 1919: Six Months that Changed the World* (NY: Random House, 2003), 18.

110. Arthur S. Link, ed., *The Papers of Woodrow Wilson*, v. 63 (Princeton University Press, 1966), 469.

111. See Erez Manela, *The Wilsonian Moment: Self-Determination and the International Origins of Anticolonial Nationalism* (NY: Oxford University Press, 2007).

112. A.J. Langguth, *Our Vietnam: The War, 1954–1975* (NY: Simon & Schuster, 2000), 35.

113. Ernest Hamlin Abbott, "An Interview with Prince Faisal," *Outlook*, Apr 2, 1919, 556.

114. Douglas Little, *American Orientalism: The United States and the Middle East since 1945* (London: I.B. Tauris, 2003), 159–60.

115. Robert Lansing, *The Peace Negotiations: A Personal Narrative* (NY: Houghton Mifflin, 1921), 97.

116. Michael Provence, *The Great Syrian Revolt and the Rise of Arab Nationalism* (Austin: University of Texas Press, 2005).

117. Macmillan, *Paris 1919*, 61.

118. Clemenceau, *Grandeurs et misères d'une victoire* (Paris: Plon, 1930), 146, 46, quoted in Roger, *L'ennemi américain*, 344–5.

119. André Tardieu, *Devant l'obstacle. L'Amérique et nous* (Paris: Éd. Émile-Paul Frères, 1927), 295, 6, quoted in Roger, *L'ennemi américain*, 346.

120. Alberto J. Pani to Venustiano Carranza, Mar 1, 1920, Box L-E-1445, AHGE.

121. David Strauss, *Menace in the West: the Rise of French Anti-Americanism in Modern Times* (Westport, CT: Greenwood Press, 1978), 130; Jean Louis Chastanet, *L'Oncle Shylock, ou, L'impérialisme américain à la conquête du monde* (Paris: Flammarion, 1927); "Parisians Insult American Tourists," *New York Times*, Jul 24, 1926, 1; "Coolidge Cautions American Tourists," *New York Times*, Jul 28, 1926, 1; Egbert Klautke, *Unbegrenzte Möglichkeiten: "Amerikanisierung" in Deutschland und Frankreich, 1900–1933* (Stuttgart: Franz Steiner Verlag, 2003), 181.

122. Joachim Scholtyseck, "Anti-Amerikanismus in der deutschen Geschichte," *Historisch-politische Mitteilungen* 10 (2003): 23–42, cited at 30.

123. Eberhard Jäckel and Axel Kuhn, eds., *Hitler. Sämtliche Aufzeichnungen 1905–1924* (Stuttgart: Deutsche Verlags-Anstalt, 1980), 458.

124. Adolf Hitler, *Mein Kampf*, tr. James Murphy (London: Hurst and Blackett Ltd., 1939 [1925]), chs. XI, XIII.

125. Clemens Vollnhals, ed., *Hitler: Reden, Schriften, Anordnungen. Die Wiedergründung der NSDAP, Februar 1925-Juni 1926* (Munich: K.G. Saur, 1992), 363, 364, 388–89.

126. Gerhard L. Weinberg, ed., *Hitler's Second Book: The Unpublished Sequel to Mein Kampf* (NY: Enigma Books, 2003), viii, 118, 231; Adam Tooze, *The Wages of Destruction: The Making and Breaking of the Nazi Economy* (NY: Viking Press, 2006), 9–11; Detlef Junker, *Kampf um die Weltmacht: die USA und das Dritte Reich, 1933–1945* (Düsseldorf: Schwann-Bagel, 1988); Philipp Gassert, *Amerika im Dritten Reich: Ideologie, Propaganda und Volksmeinung, 1933–1945* (Stuttgart: Franz Steiner, 1997).

127. Klaus P. Fischer, *Hitler and America* (Philadelphia: University of Pennsylvania Press, 2011), 11–45, 170–74, and *passim*.

128. Gérard Imhoff, "Der Amerikanismus der zwanziger Jahre oder die Versuchung einer alternativen Weltbildes," *Revue d'Allemagne* 22 (1990): 427–37.

129. Thomas Raithel, "'Amerika' als Herausforderung in Deutschland und Frankreich in den 1920er Jahren," in Metzger and Kaelble, *Deutschland – Frankreich – Nordamerika*, 90.

130. Mary Nolan, *Visions of Modernity: American Business and the Modernization of Germany* (NY: Oxford University Press, 1994), 34.

131. Charlotte Lütkens, "Die Amerikalegende," *Sozialistische Monatshefte* 38/1 (1932): 45, cited in Diner, *America in the Eyes of the Germans*, 69.

132. Neil Baldwin, *Henry Ford and the Jews: The Mass Production of Hate* (NY: Public Affairs, 2001), 172–185.

133. Raymond Fendrick, "'Heinrich' Ford Idol of Bavaria Fascisti Chief. Anti-Jewish Articles Circulate by Millions," *Chicago Tribune*, Mar 8, 1923, 2.
134. Charlotte Lütkens, "Die Amerikalegende," *Sozialistische Monatshefte*, Jan 16, 1932, 45–50.
135. Jeffrey Herf, *Reactionary Modernism: Technology, Culture, and Politics in Weimar and the Third Reich* (NY: Cambridge University Press, 1985).
136. Adolf Halfeld, *Amerika und der Amerikanismus: Das Gegenstück zu Henry Ford* (Jena: Diederich, 1927).
137. Roger, *L'ennemi américain*, 402.
138. Colin Nettelbeck, "Anti-Americanism in France," in Brendon O'Connor, ed., *Anti-Americanism: History, Causes, Themes*, vol. 3 (Westport, CT: Greenwood Publishing, 2007), 135; Roger, *The American Enemy*, 205, 271–74; André Siegfried, *Les États-Unis d'aujourd'hui* (Paris: A. Colin, 1927).
139. André Siegfried, *Tableau politique de la France de l'ouest sous la troisième république* (Paris: Libraririe Armand Colin, 1913), 413.
140. Lionel B. Steiman, "The Eclipse of Humanism: Zweig between the Wars," *Modern Austrian Literature* 14:3/4 (1981): 147–93.
141. Stefan Zweig, "Die Monotonisierung der Welt," 1925, in Scholtyseck, "Anti-Amerikanismus in der deutschen Geschichte," quoted at 27–8.
142. Scholtyseck, "Anti-Amerikanismus"; Petra Goedde, *GIs and Germans: Culture, Gender, and Foreign Relations, 1945–1949* (New Haven: Yale University Press, 2003), 216.
143. Stefan Zweig, *Die Welt von Gestern: Erinnerungen eines Europäers* (Frankfurt: Fischer, 1982 [1943]), 321.
144. Stefan Zweig, *The World of Yesterday: An Autobiography* (NY: Viking Press, 1943), 148.
145. Zweig, *World of Yesterday*, 149.
146. Rudolf Kayser writing in the *Vossische Zeitung* 27 Sept 1925, cited in Anton Kaes, ed., *Weimarer Republik. Manifeste und Dokumente zur deutschen Literatur 1918–1933* (Stuttgart: Metzler, 1983), 265.
147. Klautke, *Unbegrenzte Möglichkeiten*, 335.
148. H.J. Braun, *The German Economy in the Twentieth Century* (NY: Routledge, 1990), 45–7; Ron Chernow, *The House of Morgan: An American Banking Dynasty and the Rise of Modern Finance* (NY: Grove Press, 2001), 249–54.
149. Klautke, *Unbegrenzte Möglichkeiten*, 164.
150. Carl von Einem, "Amerikas wahre Regierungsmethoden III," in *Zeitschrift für Geopolitik* 6:1 (1929), 63–9, cited in Klautke, *Unbegrenzte Möglichkeiten*, 162.
151. Karl Haushofer preface to Scott Nearing and Joseph Freeman, *Dollar-Diplomatie. Eine Studie über amerikanischen Imperialismus*. Tr. Paul Fohr (Berlin: Vowinckel, 1927), v–viii, quoted in Klautke, *Unbegrenzte Möglichkeiten*, 163.
152. Louis Guilaine, *L'Amérique latine*, cited in Klautke, *Unbegrenzte Möglichkeiten*, 176.
153. Roger Lambelin, *Le péril juif: le règne d'Israël chez les Anglo-Saxons* (Paris: Grasset, 1921), 162, quoted in Klautke, *Unbegrenzte Möglichkeiten*, 174.
154. Although usually attributed to Bebel (and sometimes to Karl Marx), the phrase *Sozialismus der dummen Kerle*, "socialism of idiots" or "socialism for dumb guys," may have first come from Austrian democrat Ferdinand Kronawetter, and was common among late-nineteenth-century German Social Democrats. Richard

J. Evans, *The Coming of the Third Reich: A History* (NY: Penguin, 2004), 496 n 31.

155. See, for example, Paul Avrich, *Sacco and Vanzetti: The Anarchist Background* (Princeton, NJ: Princeton University Press, 1996); Bruce Watson, *Sacco and Vanzetti: The Men, the Murders, and the Judgment of Mankind* (NY: Viking, 2007); Lisa McGirr, "The Passion of Sacco and Vanzetti: A Global History," *Journal of American History* 93:4 (March 2007): 1085–1115; Moshik Temkin, *The Sacco-Vanzetti Affair: America on Trial* (New Haven: Yale University Press, 2009).

156. G. Louis Joughin and Edmund M. Morgan, *The Legacy of Sacco and Vanzetti* (NY: Harcourt, Brace, 1948), 146, 274–77, 296, 313; David Felix, *Protest: Sacco-Vanzetti and the Intellectuals* (Bloomington: Indiana University Press, 1965), 97–99, 169–71, 183–84, 204.

157. Oswald Garrison Villard, "Justice Underfoot," *The Nation*, Aug 17, 1927, quoted in McGirr, "The Passion," 1086.

158. Edwin L. James, "Defiant Reds Plan March on Embassy. Anti-American Demonstration in Paris Today," *New York Times*, Oct 23, 1921, 1; "Mad Reaction to Sacco-Vanzetti Plea Stirs Paris," *Chicago Tribune*, Nov 21, 1921; "Mexican Meeting Call Denounces Americans, Boycott Talk if Sacco Dies," *Washington Post*, Jul 4, 1927, 1; "Americans Are Leaving Italy for Switzerland as Animosity Is Shown over the Sacco Case," *New York Times*, Aug 7, 1927, 1.

159. McGirr, "The Passion," 1110.

160. Pierre Rigoulot, "American Justice as a Pretext for Anti-Americanism," *Human Rights Review* 4:3 (April 2003), 55–62. See also Ian Tyrrell, "American Exceptionalism and Anti-Americanism," in Brendon O'Connor, ed., *Anti-Americanism: Historical Perspectives*, v. 2 (Westport, CT: Greenwood Publishing, 2007), 113; Stephen Duggan, *The Two Americas: An Interpretation* (NY: C. Scribner's Sons, 1934), 240; Roger, *L'ennemi américain*, 182; Strauss, *Menace in the West*, 172.

161. Temkin, *The Sacco-Vanzetti Affair*, 139.

162. Avrich, *Sacco and Vanzetti*, 48–59.

163. McGirr, "The Passion," 1091, 1093, 1095–97.

164. "Bomb Perils British," *Chicago Daily Tribune*, Mar 20, 1920, 2; "Bomb Thrown in House Wounds Lithuanian Finance Minister," *New York Times*, Nov 26, 1921, 15; "Italian Consulate Bombed in Lisbon," *New York Times*, Dec 25, 1922, 27; "Consul Fears Widespread Plot," *New York Times*, Nov 25, 1923, 6; "Six Bombs Exploded in Brazil's Capital; One Blew Up in Front of Argentine Embassy as Envoy Was about to Enter," *New York Times*, Sep 1, 1924, 14; "Throws Bomb at Japanese Consulate in Shanghai," *Chicago Daily Tribune*, Sep 15, 1926, 1; "French Consul is Killed by a Bomb at Canton," Jun 20, 1924, 1; "Bomb Kills Seven at Buenos Aires; Explodes in Italian Consulate," *New York Times*, May 24, 1928, 1; "Red Envoy Imperiled by Bomb in Warsaw; Plot against Soviet Legation Is Thwarted," *New York Times*, Apr 27, 1930.

165. "Bomb Sent Herrick; Valet of U.S. Envoy Injured in Opening 'Gift' Package," *Washington Post*, Oct 20, 1921, 1; "Radicals Condemn Blasts as 'Outrage,' Sacco Sympathizers Disavow Any Connection With Plot – Some Blame Capitalists. Others See Lunatic's Hand," *New York Times*, Aug 7, 1927, 1.

166. See Chapter 6 and the Epilogue.

167. McGirr, "The Passion," 1105–6.

168. Joughin and Morgan, *The Legacy*, 337.

169. "Payne Fails to Find Any Anti-Americanism on His World Jaunt," *Chicago Daily Tribune*, May 22, 1927, A12; "France Will Pull Through Says Herrick; Reports of Anti-Americanism Are 'Greatly Exaggerated,'" *Hartford Courant*, Aug 18, 1926, 5; "Denies Paris Crowd Insulted Our Flag. Herrick Cables Kellogg He Has Heard Nothing of Anti-Americanism Over Nungesser Flight," *New York Times*, May 12, 1927, 1.

170. "French Intellectuals Send New Sacco Plea," *New York Times*, Aug 4, 1927, 3.

171. "French Intellectuals."

172. "Sacco Processions Barred in Paris; 4,000,000 German Workers Make a Protest," *New York Times*, Aug 7, 1927, 1.

173. John L. Goldman, "Frankfurter's Phone Was Tapped in Sacco-Vanzetti Case," *Los Angeles Times*, Sep 13, 1977, A7.

174. Watson, *Sacco and Vanzetti*, 281, 295, 300; "Sacco-Vanzetti Protest," *New York Times*, Jul 4, 1927, 20; Felix Frankfurter, "The Case of Sacco and Vanzetti," *The Atlantic* (March 1927), published in book form as *The Case of Sacco and Vanzetti: A Critical Analysis for Lawyers and Laymen* (Boston: Little, Brown, 1927). On Cardozo see Watson, *Sacco and Vanzetti*, 287–88.

175. Michael Burns, *France and the Dreyfus Affair: A Documentary History* (NY: Palgrave Macmillan, 1999), 151, 159; Egal Feldman, *The Dreyfus Affairs and the American Conscience, 1895–1906* (Detroit: Wayne State University Press, 1981), passim.

176. Burns, *France and the Dreyfus Affair*, 152.

177. "A Mockery of Justice," *Atlanta Constitution*, Feb 11, 1898, 6.

178. "Riots Disturb Paris: Anarchists Break Up an Anti-Semitic Meeting," *Washington Post*, Jan 18, 1898, 1.

179. Quoted in Louis J. Budd, *Mark Twain: Social Philosopher* (Columbia: University of Missouri Press, 2001), 172.

180. Joughin and Morgan, *The Legacy*, 296.

181. Baron Russell of Killowen quoted in Burns, *France and the Dreyfus Affair*, 153.

182. McGirr, "The Passion," 1101.

183. Hannah Arendt, *The Origins of Totalitarianism* (NY: Harcourt, Brace, 1951), 91.

184. Duggan, *Two Americas*, 240; Joughin and Morgan, *The Legacy*, 296.

185. Henry Wales, "Peace Army of Yanks Thrills Paris Throngs," *Chicago Tribune*, Sep 20, 1927, 1.

186. "Paris Reds Stage Anti-Legion Riot as Parade Is Held," *Atlanta Constitution*, Sep 20, 1927, 1; Roger, *The American Enemy*, 273.

187. "Lindbergh Lands at Paris Ending Epic Dash; Wildly Acclaimed in France and America," *Hartford Courant*, May 22, 1927, 1.

188. Adelheid von Saldern, "Emotions of Comparisons: Perceptions of European Anti-Americanism in U.S. Magazines of the 1920s," in Jessica C.E. Gienow-Hecht, ed., *Emotions in American History: An International Assessment* (NY: Berghahn Books, 2010), 139–57, cites these: C.E.M. Joad, "Does England Dislike America?" *The Forum* (November 1928): 692–98; Barton W. Currie, "Nobody Loves Us," *Ladies' Home Journal* condensation in *Reader's Digest* (September 1922): 425; Frederick Palmer, "Why They Hate Us," *Collier's* condensation in *Reader's Digest* (September 1925): 439–40; George E.G. Catlin, "America Under Fire: A European Defense of Our Civilization," *Harper's Magazine* (1927): 222–27. Quotations from Catlin.

189. Georges Duhamel, *Scènes de la vie future* (Paris: Mercure de France, 1930), quoted in C. Vann Woodward, *The Old World's New World* (NY: Oxford University Press, 1991), 82.

190. Georges Duhamel, *America the Menace*, tr. Charles Miner Thompson (NY: Houghton Mifflin, 1931).

191. Victoria de Grazia, *Irresistible Empire: America's Advance through Twentieth-Century Europe* (Cambridge, MA: Belknap Press, 2005), 285, 288, 299.

192. A. T. Poffenberger, "Motion Pictures and Crime," *Scientific Monthly* 12:4 (April 1921): 336–39, quoted at 337.

193. David Thomson, "Hollywood Confidential," *The Guardian*, Feb 23, 2007.

194. Sombart, *Warum*, 22.

195. Walter Rathenau, *Gesammelte Schriften* (Berlin: Fischer Verlag, 1918), 4: 131–37, quoted in Fraenkel, *Amerika im Spiegel*, 257–60.

196. Oswald Spengler, *Jahre der Entscheidung* (Munich: Beckscher Verlag, 1933), 48. See also idem, *The Decline of the West* (NY: Knopf, 1926).

197. Alfred Rosenberg, from *Der Mythos des 20. Jahrhunderts*, 5th ed. (Munich: Hoheneichen Verlag, 1933), 501–2, cited in Fraenkel, *America im Spiegel*, 314.

198. Franz Kafka, *Amerika* (Frankfurt am Main: Fischer Taschenbuch Verlag, 1994 [1927]), quoted at 37.

199. Robert Staughton Lynd and Hellen Merrell Lynd, *Middletown: A Study in Contemporary American Culture* (NY: Harcourt, Brace and Co., 1929), 206.

200. Sinclair Lewis, *Main Street* (NY: New American Library, 1920), 260; idem, "Autobiography," in *Nobel Lectures, Literature 1901–1967*, ed. Horst Frenz (Amsterdam: Elsevier Publishing Company, 1969).

201. William Allen White, *Calvin Coolidge: The Man Who Is President* (NY: The Macmillan Company, 1925), 218. Coolidge's original remark is often paraphrased as "The business of America is business."

202. Edwin Black, *War against the Weak: Eugenics and America's Campaign to Create a Master Race* (NY: Thunder's Mouth Press, 2003), 208–9, 261.

203. Mark Twain, "The United States of Lyncherdom" (1901) in Charles Neider, ed., *The Complete Essays of Mark Twain* (Cambridge, MA: Da Capo Press, 2000), 673–79; Patrick Scott Washburn, *The African American Newspaper: Voice of Freedom* (Evanston, IL: Northwestern University Press, 2006), 63.

204. P.W. Wilson, "An Anonymous Canadian Fears for American Freedom," *New York Times*, May 22, 1927, BR12.

205. "Jacques Corbeau," *Time*, Aug 13, 1923. That's roughly French for "Jim Crow."

206. David Levering Lewis, *W.E.B. Du Bois: Biography of a Race, 1868–1919* (NY: Henry Holt, 1993), 226; Du Bois to President Wilson, Aug 3, 1915, in Herbert Aptheker, ed., *The Correspondence of W.E.B. Du Bois: Selections, 1877–1934* (Amherst: University of Massachusetts Press, 1997), 213; Paul Gordon Lauren, *The Evolution of International Human Rights* (Philadelphia: University of Pennsylvania Press, 2003), 76.

207. Robin D. G. Kelley, *Hammer and Hoe: Alabama Communists during the Great Depression* (Chapel Hill: University of North Carolina Press, 1990); Philip S. Foner and Herbert Shapiro, eds., *American Communism and Black Americans: A Documentary History, 1930–1934* (Philadelphia: Temple University Press, 1991).

208. "Gompers Charges Garland's $800,000 Helps Revolution," *New York Times*, Apr 13, 1923, 1.

209. All three quoted in Roger, *L'ennemi américain*, 247–50.

210. Klautke, *Unbegrenzte Möglichkeiten*, 28, finds authors in France and Germany unanimous in agreeing that American women had more independence than European women.
211. Quoted in Ernst Fraenkel, *America im Spiegel*, 314.
212. Halfeld, *Amerika und der Amerikanismus*, x, 209, 214.
213. Kathryn Kish Sklar, Anja Schüler, and Susan Strasser, eds., *Social Justice Feminists in the United States and Germany* (Ithaca, NY: Cornell University Press, 1998), 159–67; Leila J. Rupp, *Worlds of Women: The Making of an International Women's Movement* (Princeton, NJ: Princeton University Press, 1997), 100; Nolan, *Visions of Modernity*, 122.
214. James V. Compton, *The Swastika and the Eagle: Hitler, The United States, and the Origins of World War II* (NY: Houghton Mifflin, 1967), 17. See also Fischer, *Hitler and America*; Jeffrey Herf, *The Jewish Enemy: Nazi Propaganda during World War II and the Holocaust* (Cambridge, MA: Belknap Press, 2006), 47–8.

Chapter 3. The Specter Haunting Europe

1. Jean-Paul Sartre, "Objections Noted; French Writer Answers His Varied Critics," *New York Times*, Mar 21, 1948, X3.
2. "Eisenhower Gets B.U. Honor Degree," *New York Times*, Feb 1, 1946.
3. Alexander Wiley statement of Aug 20, 1945, quoted in 92 Cong. Rec. A4122 (1946).
4. Rep. John Jennings, "Extension of Remarks," 92 Cong. Rec. A3258 (1946).
5. Charles B. Brownson (R-IN), quoting George O. Browne, "Americanism or Marxism," House of Representatives, Aug 6, 1951, 97 Cong. Rec. A4999.
6. Rep. Karl Mundt (R-SD), Apr 9, 1947, "Extensions of Remarks," 93 Cong. Rec. A1581.
7. Robert R. McCormick, Sep 17, 1947, quoted in 93 Cong. Rec. A4474.
8. Eugene Griffin, "New York City Like an Alien Island in U.S.," *Chicago Tribune*, Apr 12, 1947, 1.
9. Frederic Spotts and Theodor Wieser, *Italy, a Difficult Democracy* (NY: Cambridge University Press, 1980), 60; Ronald Tiersky, *French Communism, 1920–1972* (NY: Columbia University Press, 1974), 183–84.
10. Raymond Aron, *The Imperial Republic: The United States and the World 1945–1973*, trans. Frank Jellinek (Englewood Cliffs, NJ: Prentice-Hall, Inc., 1974), 52, 58.
11. "Summary of a Report by Field Staff Representatives of the Mutual Security Agency," Aug 1, 1952, CIA-RDP80–01065A000500070006–0, CIA Records Search Tool (hereafter CREST).
12. NSC 5509, "Status of United States Programs for National Security as of December 31, 1954," Mar 2, 1955, *FRUS 1955–57*, IX: 517.
13. Chapin [The Hague] to SecState, Nov 1, 1949, *FRUS 1949*, VII: 559; Cumming [Djakarta] to SecState, Feb 2, 1954, *FRUS 1952–1954*, XII: 409.
14. Dillon to DoS, Mar 2, 1956, and Murphy to Hoover, Mar 3, 1956, *FRUS 1955–57*, XVIII: 115, 117.
15. "Anti-Americanism Sweeps Holy Land Arabs; Plan Boycott," *New York Times*, Oct 29, 1938, 5; Berle to FDR, May 25, 1939, *FRUS 1939*, IV: 768.
16. C.L. Sulzberger, "Exit of Americans in Mid-East Shaped," *New York Times*, Jul 11, 1948, 10.

17. Herbert L. Matthews, "Britain Fears U.S. Will Arm Israel," *New York Times*, May 22, 1948, 2; Sumner Welles, "What of the Fate of Israel?" *St. Petersburg Times*, Oct 12, 1948, 6.
18. Stephen Hemsley Longrigg, *Iraq, 1900–1950: A Political, Social, and Economic History* (Oxford: Oxford University Press, 1953), 189, 250; Dana Adams Schmidt, "Washington Eyes Uneasy Mid-East," *New York Times*, Oct 10, 1955, 2.
19. "Middle East: Airlift for Allah," *Time*, Sep 8, 1952.
20. Psychological Strategy Board, "Progress Report on the National Psychological Effort for the Period July 1, 1952 through September 30, 1952," Oct 30, 1952, CIA-RDP80–01065A000500090001–3, CREST.
21. Ussama Makdisi, "'Anti-Americanism' in the Arab World: An Interpretation of a Brief History," *Journal of American History* 89:2 (September 2002): 538–56.
22. Meyer, "Anti-Americanism in Asia," Jul 6, 1958, *FRUS 1958–60*, XV: 235.
23. Reinhold Niebuhr, "Why They Dislike Us," *The New Leader*, 37:15 (1954), 3.
24. Henry A. Kissinger, "Reflections on American Diplomacy," *Foreign Affairs* 35: 1 (October 1956): 37–56, quoted at 52.
25. Peter Duignan and Lewis H. Gann, *The Rebirth of the West: the Americanization of the Democratic World, 1945–1958* (Lanham, MD: Rowman & Littlefield, 1996), 23–4, quoting Gordon Craig, *The Germans* (NY: New American Library, 1982), 35, who cites Willy Brandt's memoirs. Figures for war damage in *United States Strategic Bombing Survey: Summary Report (European War)* ([Washington, DC: U.S. Government Printing Office], 1945), 15; Maureen Waller, *London 1945: Life in the Debris of War* (London: Macmillan, 2005), 4–9.
26. Thomas G. Paterson, *On Every Front: The Making and Unmaking of the Cold War*, 2nd ed. (NY: Norton, 1992), 98.
27. Dan Diner, *America in the Eyes of the Germans: An Essay on Anti-Americanism* (Princeton: Markus Wiener Publishers, 1996), 148, vii, 24.
28. Norman Naimark, *The Russians in Germany: A History of the Soviet Zone of Occupation, 1945–1949* (Cambridge: Belknap Press of Harvard University Press, 1995).
29. Claus-Dieter Krohn, "Remigranten und Rekonstruktion," in *Die USA und Deutschland im Zeitalter des Kalten Krieges 1945–1968*, ed. Detlef Junker (Stuttgart: DVA, 2001), 803–13, quoted at 809.
30. Petra Goedde, *GIs and Germans: Culture, Gender, and Foreign Relations, 1945–1949* (New Haven, CT: Yale University Press, 2003); Maria H. Höhn, *GIs and Fräuleins: The German-American Encounter in 1950s West Germany* (Chapel Hill: University of North Carolina Press, 2002); Frank Biess, "Survivors of Totalitarianism: Returning POWs and the Reconstruction of Masculine Citizenship in West Germany, 1945–1950," in Hanna Schissler, *The Miracle Years: A Cultural History of West Germany, 1949–1968* (Princeton, NJ: Princeton University Press, 2001), 57–82.
31. Petra Goedde, "Macht im Spiegel der Geschlechter- und Rassenbeziehungen: US-Soldaten und die deutsche Bevölkerung," in *Die USA und Deutschland im Zeitalter des Kalten Krieges 1945–1968*, ed. Detlef Junker (Stuttgart: DVA, 2001), 785–94.
32. Klaus-Dietmar Henke, *Die amerikanische Besetzung Deutschlands* (Munich: Oldenbourg Verlag, 1995), 188–193.
33. Frances Stonor Saunders, *The Cultural Cold War: The CIA and the World of Arts and Letters* (NY: New Press, 1999), 8–9.

34. Heinz Küpper, *Illustriertes Lexikon der deutschen Umgangssprache*, vol. 1 (Stuttgart: Klett, 1982), 112–13.
35. Henke, *Die amerikanische Besetzung*, 199–200; Heide Fehrenbach, *Race after Hitler: Black Occupation Children in Postwar Germany and America* (Princeton, NJ: Princeton University Press, 2005), 63.
36. Henke, *Die amerikanische Besetzung*, 199; Höhn, *GIs and Fräuleins*, 289 n. 6; Fehrenbach, *Race after Hitler*, 63.
37. "Similar to racism": Paul Hollander, "Introduction: The New Virulence and Popularity," in *Understanding Anti-Americanism: Its Origins and Impact at Home and Abroad*, ed. Paul Hollander (Chicago: Ivan R. Dee, 2004), 9.
38. John Gray Geer, *Public Opinion and Polling around the World: A Historical Encyclopedia* (Santa Barbara, CA: ABC-CLIO, 2004), 389–407; Jean Converse, *Survey Research in the United States: Roots and Emergence 1890–1960* (New Brunswick, NJ: Transaction Publishers, 2009).
39. For example, IISR, "Dominican Republic – General Public," Nov 1960, Dominican Republic – IISR November 1960 Hopes & Fears, Dominican Republic, Roper Center, Storrs, CT.
40. Daniel J. Robinson, *The Measure of Democracy: Polling, Market Research, and Public Life, 1930–1945* (Toronto: University of Toronto Press, 1999), 62–3.
41. Richard L. Merritt, *Democracy Imposed: U.S. Occupation Policy and the German Public, 1945–1949* (New Haven, CT: Yale University Press, 1995), 82–3.
42. Adam Bernstein, "Leo Crespi, 91, Directed Opinion Polls for U.S.," *Washington Post*, Jul 17, 2008.
43. J.A.W. Gunn, "'Public Opinion' in Modern Political Science," in James Farr et al., *Political Science in History* (NY: Cambridge University Press, 1995), 99–122, qtd. at 105.
44. Peter J. Katzenstein and Robert O. Keohane, "Varieties of Anti-Americanism: A Framework for Analysis," in Katzenstein and Keohane, eds., *Anti-Americanisms in World Politics* (Ithaca, NY: Cornell University Press, 2007), 19.
45. Hugh J. Parry and Leo P. Crespi, "A Survey of Public Opinion in Western Europe," HICOG Report 169-S, January 1953, 26.
46. HICOG Report 169-S, 24.
47. HICOG Report 169-S, 25.
48. HICOG Report 169-S, 35.
49. HICOG Report 169-S, 27.
50. A careful review of the data by Norbert Muhlen concluded, "'anti-Americanism' of the violent, obsessively prejudiced type [was] very rare in Germany, and usually to be found among the 'lunatic fringe' of unreconstructed Nazis and Communists, comprising together less than 3 per cent of the total population." Norbert Muhlen, "America and American Occupation in German Eyes," *Annals of the American Academy of Political and Social Science* 295 (September 1954): 52–61, quoted at 61.
51. HICOG Report 169-S, 37–42.
52. Rep. Hugh Quincy Alexander (D-NC), Aug 15, 1957, 103 Cong. Rec.14930 (1957).
53. Rep. Lawrence Henry Smith (R-WI), Jul 15, 1957, 103 Cong. Rec.11747 (1957).
54. Hanson W. Baldwin, "Rising Neutralism a Hurdle for NATO: Anti-Americanism Grows," *New York Times*, Jan 13, 1953, 8.

55. Anna J. Merritt and Richard L. Merritt, *Public Opinion in Semisovereign Germany: The HICOG Surveys, 1949–1955* (Urbana: University of Illinois Press, 1980), 58.
56. Merritt and Merritt, *Public Opinion*, 237.
57. *Emnid-Informationen* 41 (1951): 1.
58. Merritt and Merritt, *Public Opinion*, 58; *Emnid-Informationen* 1 (1953): 11; "Georgia Soldier Sentenced on Assault Charges," *Rome News-Tribune*, Dec 12, 1952, 7; "Court Told GI Bragged of His Attack on Girl," *Chicago Daily Tribune*, Dec 19, 1952, A10; "Six Month Crime Record of GIs in Europe 1,399," *Chicago Daily Tribune*, Dec 9, 1952.
59. Baldwin, "Rising Neutralism," 8.
60. *Emnid-Informationen* 27 (1952): 5–7.
61. HICOG surveys reprinted in Fischer, "Das Amerikabild," 60. I have dropped the figures for the July 1950 survey because, unlike in other years, it excluded Germans under 25 years of age. Leaving out young people artificially lowered the already low totals of fans of American culture.
62. Fischer, "Das Amerikabild," 63.
63. DIVO-Institut, *Umfragen 1957: Ereignisse und Probleme des Jahres im Urteil der Bevölkerung* (Hamburg: Europäische Verlagsanstalt, 1958), 42–44; DIVO-Institut, *Umfragen: Ereignisse und Probleme der Zeit im Urteil der Bevölkerung, Band 3/4* (Hamburg: Europäische Verlagsanstalt, 1960), 39–43.
64. DIVO-Institut, *Umfragen 1957*, 30.
65. DIVO-Institut, *Umfragen 1957*, 23.
66. DIVO-Institut, *Umfragen: Ereignisse und Probleme der Zeit im Urteil der Bevölkerung, Band 2* (Hamburg: Europäische Verlagsanstalt, 1959), 21, 23.
67. DIVO-Institut, *Umfragen 1957*, 27.
68. DIVO-Institut, *Umfragen: Ereignisse, Band 2*, 22. See also the cautiously optimistic analysis of the proposal by Chester Bowles after his conversation with Khrushchev, "Our Objective in Europe – and Russia's," *New York Times*, May 12, 1957, SM5. On Kennan see the excellent discussion in Anders Stephanson, *Kennan and the Art of Foreign Policy* (Cambridge, MA: Harvard University Press, 1989), 152–6.
69. Drew Middleton, "East, West Weigh a Neutral Zone: Disengagement in Central Europe Is Viewed by Many as Key to Other Issues," *New York Times*, Jan 26, 1958, 3; Drew Middleton, "A British 'Great Debate,'" *New York Times*, Feb 18, 1958, 17.
70. Edward L. Bernays, *What the British Think of Us: A Study of British Hostility to America and Americans and Its Motivation* (NY: English Speaking Union, 1958), 22; Nicholas Cull, *The Cold War and the United States Information Agency: American Propaganda and Public Diplomacy, 1945–1989* (NY: Cambridge University Press, 2008), 159.
71. Quoted in Laurence Wylie, "Teaching French Culture," in *Contemporary French Culture and Society/Société et culture de la France contemporaine*, ed. Georges Santoni (Albany: State University of New York Press, 1981), 19–20.
72. Maxwell Adereth, *The French Communist Party: A Critical History* (Manchester: Manchester University Press, 1984), 112–17.
73. *Bulletin d'Informations de l'IFOP* 1, Oct 1, 1944, cited in Roger, *L'ennemi américain*, 430.
74. Norman Davies, *No Simple Victory: Europe at War, 1939–1945* (London: Macmillan, 2006), 244; Isaac Deutscher, *Stalin: A Political Biography*, rev. ed. (NY: Penguin Books, 1966), 485–86; Clive Ponting, *Armageddon* (NY: Random

House, 1995), 96–7, 128, 203, all cited in Robert Bideleux and Ian Jeffries, *A History of Eastern Europe: Crisis and Change*, 2nd ed. (NY: Taylor & Francis, 2007), 419.

75. See the *United States Strategic Bombing Survey: Summary Report (European War)* ([Washington, DC: U.S. Government Printing Office], 1945).

76. John Flower, "The American Dream – or Nightmare: Views from the French Left, 1945–1965," *French Cultural Studies* 20:1 (February 2009): 47–64.

77. De Grazia, *Irresistible Empire*, 354–55.

78. Janet Flanner, *Paris Was Yesterday* (NY: Viking Press, 1972), xiv.

79. Anthony Beevor and Artemis Cooper, *Paris after the Liberation, 1944–1949* (NY: Doubleday, 1994), 263.

80. Roger, *The American Enemy*, 443. See also Ludovic Tournès, "La réinterpretation du jazz: un phénomène de contre-américanisation dans la France d'après-guerre (1945–1960)," in *L'antiaméricanisme. Anti-Americanism at Home and Abroad*, ed. Sylvie Mathé (Aix-en-Provence: Université de Provence, 2000), 167–83.

81. Tournès, "La réinterpretation du jazz," 181.

82. Psychological Strategy Board, "Progress Report on the National Psychological Effort for the Period July 1, 1952 through September 30, 1952," Oct 30, 1952, CIA-RDP80–01065A000 500090001–3, CREST.

83. Edward T. Hall, *The Hidden Dimension* (Garden City: Doubleday, 1966); O. Michael Watson, *Proxemic Behavior: A Cross-Cultural Study* (The Hague: Mouton, 1970).

84. Harvey A. Levenstein, *We'll Always Have Paris: American Tourists in France since 1930* (Chicago: University of Chicago Press, 2004), 139–40.

85. Christopher Endy, *Cold War Holidays: American Tourism in France* (Chapel Hill: University of North Carolina Press, 2004), 147.

86. Endy, *Cold War Holidays*, 159.

87. Endy, *Cold War Holidays*, 163.

88. Levenstein, *We'll Always Have Paris*, 146.

89. From Richard Kuisel's analysis of a poll taken by the Institut français d'opinion publique (IFOP) in early 1953, "Les Etats-Unis, les Américains, et la France, 1945–1953," *Sondages* 2 (1953): 3–78, in his thoughtful *Seducing the French: The Dilemma of Americanization* (Berkeley and Los Angeles: University of California Press, 1993): 30–33.

90. Arnold M. Rose, "Anti-Americanism in France," *Antioch Review* 12:4 (Winter 1952), 468–84.

91. John T. Marcus, *Neutralism and Nationalism in France* (NY: Bookman Associates, 1958), 18.

92. Roger, *L'ennemi américain*, 354.

93. Joseph Alsop, "Devil Take the Hindmost," *New York Tribune*, Aug 1, 1957; Reinhold Niebuhr, "The French Do Not Like Us: The Roots of the Anti-American Sentiment in France," Box 15, Speech, Article and Book File, Niebuhr Papers, LC; Cartier's article in *Match* cited in J.A. Rogers, "Are Americans Most Disliked People on Earth?" *Pittsburgh Courier*, Jun 16, 1956, 10.

94. Steven K. Smith and Douglas A. Wertman, *U.S.-West European Relations during the Reagan Years: The Perspective of West European Publics* (Basingstoke: Macmillan, 1992), 91, 101.

95. Daniel Lerner and Morton Gorden, *Euratlantica: Changing Perspectives of the European Elites* (Cambridge, MA: MIT Press, 1969).

96. Memcon of 305th Meeting of the National Security Council, Nov 30, 1956, *FRUS 1955–57*, XVI: 1218.
97. Irwin M. Wall, *France, the United States, and the Algerian War* (Berkeley and Los Angeles: University of California Press, 2001), 62.
98. See John T. Bledsoe's photograph from *U.S. News & World Report* collection donated to the Library of Congress Prints and Photographs Division, LC-U9-2908-15.
99. "Telephone Call to Attorney General Brownell," Sep 24, 1957, and "Telephone Call from Sen. Knowland from California," Sep 23, 1957, Box 7, Telephone Calls Series, Dulles Papers, Dwight D. Eisenhower Library, Abilene, Kansas (hereafter DDEL).
100. Intelligence Production Division, "The World Looks at Little Rock," Oct 2, 1957, Box 14, Special Reports, 1953–63, Office of Research and Intelligence, RG 306, National Archives, College Park, Maryland (hereafter NARA).
101. "Little Rock, Singer on Africans' Lip," *Baltimore Afro-American*, May 3, 1958, 19.
102. "Daisy Bates Home Fired On, Stoned," *Philadelphia Tribune*, Sep 30, 1958, 1.
103. "Eisenhower Address on Little Rock Crisis," *New York Times*, Sep 25, 1957, 14.
104. Hazel Erskine, "The Polls: World Opinion of U.S. Racial Problems," *Public Opinion Quarterly* 32 (1968): 299–312.
105. USIA Office of Research and Analysis, "The Image of America in Western Europe," October 1959, Box 17, Special Reports, 1953–63, RG 306, NA, quoted at ii, 22, 57.
106. Among the many excellent studies of the intersection of the Cold War and the struggle for civil rights, see Thomas Borstelmann, *The Cold War and the Color Line: American Race Relations in the Global Arena* (Cambridge, MA: Harvard University Press, 2001); Mary Dudziak, *Cold War Civil Rights: Race and the Image of American Democracy* (Princeton, NJ: Princeton University Press, 2000); Brenda Gayle Plummer, *Rising Wind: Black Americans and U.S. Foreign Affairs, 1935–1960* (Chapel Hill: University of North Carolina Press, 1996); Penny Von Eschen, *Race against Empire: Black Americans and Anticolonialism, 1937–1957* (Ithaca, NY: Cornell University Press, 1997).
107. Calvin B. Holder, "Racism toward Black African Diplomats during the Kennedy Administration," *Journal of Black Studies* 14:1 (September 1983): 31–48, quoted at 34.
108. "Big Step Ahead on a High Road," *Life*, Dec 8, 1961, 32.
109. "Big Step Ahead," 34.
110. Lawrence A. Still, "Rusk Says Past U.S. Acts Cause Anti-Americanism," *Atlanta Daily World*, Jan 1, 1980, 1.
111. Robert A. Hill, ed., *The FBI's RACON: Racial Conditions in the United States during World War II* (Boston: Northeastern University Press, 1995), 407.
112. "Local Leaders Blast Harry's Sit-In Views," *Chicago Defender*, Jun 14, 1960, A3.
113. Cairo BBC Monitoring Service, "Africans March in Support of U.S. Negroes," Aug 28, 1963, FO 371/168485, NA-K; "Cairo Rally Suppressed," *New York Times*, Aug 29, 1963, 19.
114. "March Gets Big Play in World Newspapers," *Washington Post*, Aug 30, 1963, A5.

115. Kingston to Commonwealth Relations Office, Aug 29, 1963, FO 371/168485, NA-K.
116. Martin Luther King, Jr., "Letter from a Birmingham Jail," in *Why We Can't Wait* (NY: Penguin, 2000 [1963]), 69.
117. Renee Romano, "No Diplomatic Immunity: African Diplomats, the State Department, and Civil Rights, 1961–1964," *Journal of American History* 87:2 (September 2000): 546–79, at 551.
118. For a more extensive analysis, see my "Of Sartre, Race, and Rabies: 'Anti-Americanism' and the Transatlantic Politics of Intellectual Engagement," *Atlantic Studies* 8:3 (September 2011): 361–77.
119. "The writer reveals": Jonathan Judaken, *Jean-Paul Sartre and the Jewish Question: Anti-Antisemitism and the Politics of the French Intellectual* (Lincoln: University of Nebraska Press, 2006), 161; "taste" and "absolute refusal": Michael Winock, co-author with Jacques Julliard of the *Dictionnaire des intellectuels français* (Paris: Seuil, 1996), quoted by Alan Riding, "To Honor Sartre, France Buffs a Pedestal the Writer Rejected," *New York Times*, Mar 16, 2005.
120. Gordon Wright, "Blurred and Distorted Images: France Viewed from the American Shore, 1880–1990," *French American Review* 61:2 (1990): 22. A slightly different version appears in Kuisel, *Seducing the French*, 29.
121. Seth D. Armus, *French Anti-Americanism (1930–1948): Critical Moments in a Complex History* (Lexington, MA: Lexington Books, 2007): 155–6.
122. Hilton Kramer, *The Twilight of the Intellectuals: Culture and Politics in the Era of the Cold War* (Chicago: Ivan R. Dee, 2000), 287.
123. Roger Kimball, "Anti-Americanism Then and Now," in Hollander, *Understanding Anti-Americanism*, 239–57, quoted at 240.
124. John Chiddick, "The Cold War and Anti-Americanism," in Brendon O'Connor, ed., *Anti-Americanism: History, Causes, Themes*, vol. 2 (Oxford: Greenwood, 2007), 151–77, quoted at 152.
125. Ivan Krastev, "The Anti-American Century?" *Journal of Democracy* 15:2 (April 2004): 5–16, quoted at 7; James Ceaser, "The Philosophical Origins of Anti-Americanism in Europe," in Hollander, ed., *Understanding Anti-Americanism*, 45. For more examples of such claims by scholars, see the Introduction.
126. See Jean-Paul Sartre, *Colonialism and Neocolonialism* (NY: Routledge, 2001); Jonathan Judaken, ed., *Race after Sartre: Antiracism, Africana Existentialism, Postcolonialism* (Albany: State University of New York Press, 2008).
127. Judaken, *Race after Sartre*, 4.
128. Lewis R. Gordon, "Sartre and Black Existentialism," in Judaken, ed., *Race after Sartre*, 157.
129. Bernard-Henri Lévy, *Sartre: The Philosopher of the Twentieth Century*, tr. Andrew Brown (Cambridge: Polity, 2003), 347; Amina Elbendary, "Of Words and Echoes," *Al-Ahram Weekly* 477 (Apr 13–19, 2000). On Sartre's turn to Maoism after 1968, see Richard Wolin, *Wind from the East: French Intellectuals, the Cultural Revolution, and the Legacy of the 1960s* (Princeton, NJ: Princeton University Press, 2010).
130. Riding, "To Honor Sartre."
131. Jean-Paul Sartre, "New-York – ville coloniale," in Sartre, *Situations III* (Paris: Gallimard, 1949), 122–23.
132. Jean-Paul Sartre, "American Novelists in French Eyes," *Atlantic Monthly* 178 (August 1946): 114–18, quoted at 114.

133. Anna Boschetti, "Sartre and the Age of the American Novel," in Jean-François Fourny and Charles D. Minahen, eds., *Situating Sartre in Twentieth-Century Thought and Culture* (NY: Palgrave Macmillan, 1997), 71–92; Simone de Beauvoir, *The Second Sex* (NY: Knopf, 1953 [1949]).

134. Sartre, "American Novelists," 118.

135. Michel Contat and Michel Rybalka, *The Writings of Jean-Paul Sartre* (Evanston: Northwestern University Press, 1974), 138.

136. Julien Murphy, "Sartre on American Racism," in Julie K. Ward and Tommy Lee Lott, *Philosophers on Race: Critical Essays* (Oxford: Wiley-Blackwell, 2002), 222–41; David Caute, *The Dancer Defects: The Struggle for Cultural Supremacy during the Cold War* (NY: Oxford University Press, 2005), 309–10.

137. Jean-Paul Sartre, "Objections Noted; French Writer Answers His Varied Critics," *New York Times*, Mar 21, 1948, X3.

138. "L'enfance d'un chef" in *Le Mur* (Paris: Gallimard, 1939); *Réflexions sur la question juive* (Paris: Morihien, 1946).

139. Sartre, "Objections Noted"; "Sartre Now Target of Pravda's Attacks," *New York Times*, Jan 24, 1947, 19.

140. Jean-Paul Sartre, "Ce que j'ai appris du problème noir," *Le Figaro*, Jun 16, 1945, 2.

141. Renée Christine Romano, *Race Mixing: Black-White Marriage in Postwar America* (Cambridge, MA: Harvard University Press, 2003), 30–3; Gunnar Myrdal, *An American Dilemma: The Negro Problem and Modern Democracy* (NY: Harper & Bros, 1944).

142. Thomas A. Guglielmo, "'Red Cross, Double Cross': Race and America's World War II-era Blood Donor Service," *Journal of American History* 97:1 (June 2010): 63–90.

143. Saunders, *The Cultural Cold War*, 69.

144. Beevor and Cooper, *Paris after the Liberation*, 351.

145. Gordon, "Sartre and Black Existentialism," 161; Plummer, *Rising Wind*, 254–55. See also Jean-Paul Sartre, *Orphée Noir*, published as the preface to Leopold Senghor's anthology of negritude poetry, *Anthologie de la nouvelle poésie nègre et malgache de la langue française* (Paris: Presses Universitaires de France, 1948).

146. Sartre, "American Novelists," 117.

147. Sartre, "American Novelists," 116.

148. CIA, "The Crisis of International Communism: Impact of Hungarian Events on the Movement Outside the Bloc," Feb 11, 1957, CIA-RDP78–00915R000600090009–7; CIA Office of Central Reference, Mar 1, 1958, CIA-RDP81S00991R000200150004–2, CREST.

149. CIA, "Bi-Weekly Propaganda Guidance: Intellectual Anti-Americanism," May 20, 1963, CIA-RDP78–03061A00020001009–1, CREST.

150. Simone de Beauvoir, *America Day by Day*, trs. Carol Cosman (Berkeley and Los Angeles: University of California Press, 2000 [1948]), 101.

151. Simone de Beauvoir, *La Force des choses* (Paris: Gallimard, 1963), 12, 174–75.

152. Mary McCarthy, "Mlle. Gulliver en Amérique" (1952), in *On The Contrary: Articles of Belief, 1946–1961* (NY: Farrar, Straus and Cudahy, 1961), 24–31; Simone de Beauvoir, *L'Amérique au jour le jour* (Paris: Editions Paul Morigien, 1948).

153. McCarthy, "Mlle. Gulliver en Amérique."

154. Christopher Robert Reed, *The Chicago NAACP and the Rise of Black Professional Leadership, 1910–1966* (Bloomington: Indiana University Press, 1997), 150–55.

155. Louis Berg, "What's Happened to 'Hate America,'" *Los Angeles Times*, Aug 21, 1955, H7; Bern Price, "Race Conflict Flares in Mississippi," *Washington Post*, Aug 21, 1955, E1.

156. Referring to a petition against lynching presented to Secretary of State Byrnes in Paris, in HUAC's "Report on American Youth for Democracy," in Rep. John E. Rankin (D-MS), Extension of Remarks, Apr 16, 1947, 93 Cong. Rec. A1715.

157. Wyn Craig Wade, *The Fiery Cross: The Ku Klux Klan in America* (NY: Oxford University Press, 1998), 274.

158. De Beauvoir, *America Day by Day*, 94.

159. Quoted in David M. Oshinsky, *A Conspiracy So Immense: The World of Joe McCarthy* (NY: Oxford University Press, 2005), 347.

160. Volker R. Berghahn, *America and the Intellectual Cold Wars in Europe: Shepard Stone between Philanthropy, Academy, and Diplomacy* (Princeton, NJ: Princeton University Press, 2002), 136.

161. For example, compare Tony Judt, *Past Imperfect: French Intellectuals, 1944–1956* (Berkeley and Los Angeles: University of California Press, 1994), to Irwin M. Wall, "From Anti-Americanism to Francophobia: The Saga of French and American Intellectuals," *French Historical Studies* 18:4 (Autumn 1994): 1083–1100.

162. Beevor and Cooper, *Paris after the Liberation*, 294.

163. Beevor and Cooper, *Paris after the Liberation*, 334–5.

164. Ian H. Birchall, *Sartre against Stalinism* (NY: Berghahn Books, 2004), 87.

165. Caute, *The Dancer Defects*, 310–16.

166. Birchall, *Sartre against Stalinism*, 110–12.

167. Birchall, *Sartre against Stalinism*, 113.

168. Sartre develops this theme most clearly in *La Nausée* [Nausea] (Paris: Gallimard, 1938) and *Critique de la raison dialectique* [Critique of Dialectical Reason] (Paris: Gallimard, 1960).

169. Ronald Aronson, *Camus and Sartre: The Story of a Friendship and the Quarrel that Ended It* (Chicago: University of Chicago Press, 2004).

170. Birchall, *Sartre against Stalinism*, 214.

171. Birchall, *Sartre against Stalinism*, 138, emphasizes Sartre's published statement taking "full responsibility" for the article by Marcel Péju, which showed the trial to be rigged and marked by anti-Semitism. Judt, *Past Imperfect*, 185, emphasizes Sartre's failure to write anything himself.

172. See, for example, Ronald Radosh and Joyce Milton, *The Rosenberg File*, 2nd ed. (New Haven, CT: Yale University Press, 1997).

173. Jean-Paul Sartre, "Les Animaux malades de la rage," *Libération*, Jun 22, 1953, 1.

174. MacKnight to Evans, "European Reactions to the Rosenberg Case," Jan 14, 1953, Box 2, Special Papers, Coordinator for Psychological Intelligence, 1952–54, RG 306, NARA.

175. Niebuhr, "The French Do Not Like Us."

176. Saunders, *The Cultural Cold War*, 180–82.

177. Walter report in Daniel J. Flood extension of remarks, Mar 19, 1958, 104 Cong. Rec. 4830.

178. Frank C. Costigliola, *France and the United States: The Cold Alliance since World War II* (NY: Twayne Publishers, 1992), 79.

179. Jean de la Fontaine, *One Hundred Fables* (NY: Ginn, 1906), 58–60.

180. Lévy, *Sartre*, 323–7; Raymond Aron, *The Opium of the Intellectuals* (New Brunswick, NJ: Transaction Publishers, 2001 [1955]), 225.

181. "La Délivrance est à nos portes," *Combat*, Sep 2, 1944, excerpted in Contat and Rybalka, *The Writings*, 102–3.

182. "American Novelists," 116.

183. Quoted in Lévy, *Sartre*, 328.

184. CIA, "The Crisis of International Communism: Impact of Hungarian Events on the Movement Outside the Bloc," Feb 11, 1957, CIA-RDP78–00915R000600090009–7, CREST.

185. Saunders, *The Cultural Cold War*, 305; Aronson, *Camus and Sartre*, 202.

186. "Sartre Terms Invasion by Soviet a War Crime," *New York Times*, Aug 26, 1968, 16. See also Kieran Williams, *The Prague Spring and its Aftermath: Czechoslovak Politics, 1968–1970* (NY: Cambridge University Press, 1997), 158. McNamara gives his estimate in the documentary *Fog of War*, transcript available at www.errolmorris.com/film/fow_transcript.html. On the Vietnam tribunal, see Chapter 6.

187. "Summary of a Report by Field Staff Representatives of the Mutual Security Agency," Aug 1, 1952, CIA-RDP80–01065A000500070006–0, CREST. See also Cull, *The Cold War and the USIA*; Walter L. Hixson, *Parting the Curtain: Propaganda, Culture, and the Cold War, 1945–1961* (New York: St. Martin's Press, 1997).

188. NY: Random House, 1947.

189. *Annals of the American Academy of Political and Social Sciences* 295 (September 1954): 1–12; William Buchanan and Hadley Cantril, *How Nations See Each Other* (Urbana: University of Illinois Press, 1954).

190. Franz M. Joseph, *As Others See us: The United States through Foreign Eyes* (Princeton, NJ: Princeton University Press, 1959). Ole R. Holsti took up the theme in his *To See Ourselves as Others See Us: How Publics Abroad View the United States after 9/11* (Ann Arbor: University of Michigan Press, 2008).

191. Arvid Brodersen, "Themes in the Interpretation of America by Prominent Visitors from Abroad," *Annals* 295, 32.

192. Cull, *The Cold War and the USIA*, 100.

193. Hixson, *Parting the Curtain*, 22.

194. Anthony Leviero, "U.S. To Take Offensive in Psychological War," *New York Times*, Feb 1, 1953, E6.

195. Hixson, *Parting the Curtain*, 25.

196. "A Study of USIA Operating Assumptions," December 1954, Box 7–8, Special Reports, 1953–63, RG 306, NARA. A version was subsequently published in Leo Bogart, *Premises for Propaganda: The United States Information Agency's Operating Assumptions in the Cold War* (NY: Free Press, 1976).

197. "A Study of USIA," 2, E-9.

198. "A Study of USIA," RF-14.

199. "A Study of USIA," P-6.

200. "A Study of USIA," O-21, T-25, O-22.

201. "A Study of USIA," PA-26.

202. 95th Cong., 3rd sess., *Cong. Rec.* (Aug 16, 1949), 11584–87; Saunders, *Cultural Cold War*, 256.

203. Merritt and Merritt, *Public Opinion*, 215.

204. Timothy G. Turner, "West Germans Declared Amazed by Book Furor," *Los Angeles Times*, Jul 2, 1953, A3; C.P. Trussell, "Some Books Literally Burned After Inquiry, Dulles Reports," *New York Times*, Jun 15, 1953, 1; Richard H. Pells, *Not Like Us: How Europeans Have Loved, Hated, and Transformed American Culture since World War II* (NY: Basic Books, 1998), 80–82.
205. "A Study of USIA," L-39.
206. Oshinsky, *A Conspiracy So Immense*, 197–201.

Chapter 4. Bad Neighborhood

1. "The Americas: Policy Preview," *Time*, Feb 9, 1953.
2. José Iturriaga, "Porque soy anti-soviético y anti-ruso," *El Popular*, Apr 27, 1951.
3. Popularity contests were a different issue. Most Mexicans *were* anti-Russian, insofar as only 27% told pollsters they had a good or fair opinion of Russia and 42% had a bad or very bad opinion. Iturriaga's point was that Russia was not important to most Mexicans, because it was remote, but the U.S. loomed very large in their lives. International Research Associates, SA de CV, "Barometer Study of Public Opinion – Mexico," December 1956, in folder MXUSIA56-LA**, Roper Center, Storrs, CT (hereafter RC).
4. Raine to DoS, May 4, 1951, 611.12/5–451, RG 59, National Archives, College Park, MD (hereafter NARA).
5. José E. Iturriaga, *La estructura social y cultural de México* (Mexico City: Fondo de Cultura Económica, 1951), 217–18.
6. Barry Rubin and Judith Colp Rubin, *Hating America: A History* (NY: Oxford University Press, 2004), 119. Michael Radu called *Open Veins* "primitive... the Bible of the anti-American left." Michael Radu, "A Matter of Identity: The Anti-Americanism of Latin American Intellectuals," in Paul Hollander, ed., *Understanding Anti-Americanism: Its Origins and Impact at Home and Abroad* (Chicago: Ivan R. Dee, 2004), 153–54.
7. "United States Objectives and Courses of Action with Respect to Latin America," Mar 4, 1953, Box 20, NSC 144, Formal Policy Papers, 1947–61, RG 273, NARA.
8. "United States Objectives and Courses of Action with Respect to Latin America: Staff Study," Mar 4, 1953, Box 20, NSC 144 Annex, Formal Policy Papers, 1947–61, RG 273, NARA. A redacted version was published in FRUS 1952–54 IV: 6–10.
9. "United States Objectives and Courses of Action."
10. Flora Lewis, "Why There Is Anti-Americanism in Mexico," *New York Times*, Jul 6, 1952, SM10.
11. Iturriaga, *La estructura social*, 221.
12. C. Vann Woodward, *The Old World's New World* (NY: Oxford University Press, 1991), 35; John Tomlinson, *Cultural Imperialism* (London: Continuum, 1991), 75–6.
13. Josefina Zoraida Vázquez and Lorenzo Meyer, *The United States and Mexico* (Chicago: University of Chicago Press, 1985), 166.
14. L. Arthur Minnich, Jul 3, 1953, Box 2, Cabinet Series, White House Office, Office of the Staff Secretary, Dwight D. Eisenhower Presidential Library, Abilene, Kansas (hereafter DDEL); "U.S. Shuts Border to Mexican Cattle," *New York Times*, May 24, 1953, 39.

15. William S. Stokes, "Cultural Anti-Americanism in Latin America," in *Issues and Conflicts: Studies in Twentieth Century American Diplomacy*, ed. George L. Anderson (Lawrence: University of Kansas Press, 1959), 315–38, quoted at 315.

16. "Nación entera apoya gobierno mexicáno," *El Popular*, Jan 17, 1954; "Respaldo unánime al gobierno por su actitud a fin de proteger a los braceros," *El Nacional*, Jan 18, 1954; "Aplauso unánime al patriotismo de Ruiz Cortines," *Novedades*, Jan 19, 1954; Sydney Gruson, "Anti-Yankeeism Is Seen in Mexico," *New York Times*, May 13, 1954, 8.

17. International Research Associates, SA de CV, "Barometer Study of Public Opinion – Mexico," December 1956, in folder MXUSIA56-LA**, RC.

18. Holmes Alexander, "Mexicans Welcome American Aid but Resent Patronizing Attitude," *Los Angeles Times*, Feb 24, 1959, F5.

19. Mae M. Ngai, *Impossible Subjects: Illegal Aliens and the Making of Modern America* (Princeton, NJ: Princeton University Press, 2004), 156; Lester D. Langley, *Mexico and the United States: The Fragile Relationship* (Boston: Twayne, 1991), 46.

20. "Un adiós a López Mateos," *Excelsior*, Nov 30, 1964, reporting a National Press Club event of Oct 12, 1959.

21. Psychological Strategy Board, "Progress Report on the National Psychological Effort for the Period July 1, 1952 through September 30, 1952," Oct 30, 1952, CIA-RDP80–01065A000500090001-3, CIA Records Search Tool, NARA (hereafter CREST).

22. "Policy Statement Prepared in the Department of State: Honduras," Feb 6, 1951, FRUS 1951, II: 1466.

23. "Comment on 'Lessons of Guatemala' by Daniel James," Aug 19, 1954, SS-2003–00002, CIA-FOIA.

24. Raymond Aron, "Reflections on American Diplomacy," *Daedalus* 91:4 (Fall 1962): 717–32, quoted at 725.

25. Carlos Fuentes, "Farewell, Monroe Doctrine," *Harper's* 263, no. 1575 (August 1981): 29–35, quoted at 29. On the 1954 coup and its significance, see Nick Cullather, *Secret History: The CIA's Classified Account of its Operation in Guatemala, 1952–1954* (Stanford, CA: Stanford University Press, 1999); Piero Gleijeses, *Shattered Hope: The Guatemalan Revolution and the United States, 1944–1954* (Princeton, NJ: Princeton University Press, 1992); Greg Grandin, *The Last Colonial Massacre: Latin America in the Cold War* (Chicago: University of Chicago Press, 2004); Richard H. Immerman, *The CIA in Guatemala: The Foreign Policy of Intervention* (Austin: University of Texas Press, 1983); Schlesinger and Kinzer, *Bitter Fruit*; Stephen M. Streeter, *Managing the Counterrevolution: The United States and Guatemala, 1945–1961* (Athens: Ohio University Press, 2000).

26. Quoted in Jim Handy, *Gift of the Devil: A History of Guatemala* (Toronto: Between the Lines, 1984), 115.

27. "Personal Political Orientation of President Arbenz/Possibility of a Left-Wing Coup," Central Intelligence Agency Information Report No. 00-B-57327, Oct 10, 1952, in FRUS 1952–54, *Guatemala*, 38–40.

28. Stephen Kinzer, "Iran and Guatemala, 1953–54: Revisiting Cold War Coups and Finding Them Costly," *New York Times*, Nov 30, 2003.

29. Hilda Gadea, *Ernesto: A Memoir of Che Guevara* (NY: Doubleday, 1972), 53–7.

30. Benjamin Muse, "Shrewd Temporizer Bosses Pinkish Guatemala," *Washington Post*, Nov 29, 1950, B2; Fitzhugh Turner, "Guatemala is 'Halfway to Poland,'" *Washington Post*, Feb 12, 1950, B2.

31. CIA, "Communist Influence in Guatemala and El Salvador," Feb 7, 1951, CIA-RDP82–00457R006800130001–9, CREST.
32. US Congress, SCFR, vol. 4, 1952, 28, cited in Gleijeses, *Shattered Hope*, 226.
33. Milton Bracker, "Guatemala Poses Dilemma for U.S.," *New York Times*, Mar 5, 1954, 3.
34. Sam Stavisky, "'Dazed Quarterback,' Morse Says of Taft," *Washington Post*, Sep 29, 1952, 13.
35. Assistant Secretary Miller at the House Committee on Foreign Affairs Subcommittee on the Western Hemisphere, "Briefing on Inter-American Relations," Mar 16, 1951, 387. For Guatemala backing the United States in U.N. votes, see, for example, "46 Nations Support U.N. Action on Korea," *New York Times*, Jul 9, 1950, 2; Walter Sullivan, "Asian Move Loses, U.N. Unit Declares Peiping Aggressor," *New York Times*, Jan 31, 1951, 1; "U.N. Unit Approves Korea Relief Plan; Political Committee Endorses Aid Program by 54–5 Vote – Soviet Bloc Dissents," *New York Times*, Mar 10, 1953, 5.
36. "United States Objectives and Courses of Action with Respect to Latin America," Mar 4, 1953, Box 20, NSC 144, Formal Policy Papers, 1947–61, RG 273, NARA.
37. Klee, "Die Lage in Guatemala," Jan 16, 1953, Box 104, Sig. 205–00/25, B 11 GUA, Politisches Archiv des Auswärtigen Amtes (hereafter PAAA), Berlin.
38. Klee, "Die Lage in Guatemala," Mar 2, 1953, Box 104, Sig. 205–00/25, B 11 GUA, PAAA.
39. Allen to FO, Jul 9, 1954, FO 371/108930, National Archives, Kew, Great Britain (hereafter NA-K).
40. Sharon I. Meers, "The British Connection: How the United States Covered Its Tracks in the 1954 Coup in Guatemala," *Diplomatic History* 16 (Summer 1992): 409–28, here 412.
41. "Hagerty Diary," Jun 19, 1954, Box 1, Hagerty Papers, DDEL.
42. Andrew to FO, May 19, 1954, FO 371/108962, NA-K.
43. Chevallier minute, Jun 15, 1954, FO 371/108963, NA-K; Chevallier minute, May 25, 1954, FO 371/108962, NA-K.
44. Meers, "The British Connection," 415–16.
45. Tello to SRE, May 27, 1954, Box III-2538-2-6a Parte, Archivo Histórico Genaro Estrada, Secretaría de Relaciones Exteriores, Mexico City (hereafter AHGE).
46. Quintanilla to SRE, May 17, 1954, Box III-2538-2-Ia Parte, AHGE.
47. Bonneau to Bidault, "La question guatémaltèque et l'opinion mexicaine," Jun 10, 1954, and Bonneau to Bidault, Jun 11, 1954, sous-série Guatemala 1952–1963, No. 21, série Amérique, Ministère des Affaires Etrangères, Paris (hereafter MAE).
48. Bosques to SRE, May 27, 1954, Box III-2538-2-3a Parte, AHGE.
49. Federico Klein to MRE, "Informa sobre realidad económico-social e infiltración comunista en Guatemala," Feb 13, 1954, Guatemala: Embachile Conchile Confidenciales 1954, vol. 3792, AGHMRE.
50. Allen to FO, Dec 8, 1954, FO 371/108934, NA-K.
51. "Situation in Guatemala and Costa Rica," in *Committee on Foreign Relations*, House of Representatives (1954), 474–75.
52. "Communism at Caracas," *Wall Street Journal*, Mar 2, 1954; Fitzhugh Turner, "Guatemala is 'Halfway to Poland,'" *Washington Post*, Feb 12, 1950, B2; "At Caracas a Vote of Confidence for the U.S.," *Baltimore Sun*, Mar 18, 1954.

53. David F. Schmitz, *Thank God They're on Our Side: The United States and Right-wing Dictatorships, 1921–1965* (Chapel Hill: University of North Carolina Press, 1999), 182.

54. Quoted in Michael Krenn, "Their Proper Share: The Changing Role of Racism in U.S. Foreign Policy since World War One," *Nature, Society, and Thought* 4 (1991): 57–79, cited in Schmitz, *Thank God*, 149.

55. Andrew to Man, Apr 27, 1954, FO 371/108938, NA-K.

56. Chevallier memcon, Jun 27, 1954, FO 371/108927, NA-K.

57. "Oil Tanks Fliers' Targets," *New York Times*, Jun 20, 1954, 3.

58. Colonna-Cesari to MAE, Jun 23, 1954, sous-série Guatemala 1952–1963, No. 21, série Amérique, MAE.

59. Armendariz del Castillo to SRE, May 25, 1954, Box III-2538-2-Ia Parte, AHGE.

60. Martínez de Alva to SRE, May 22, 1954, Martínez de Alva to SRE, May 31, 1954, Martínez de Alva to SRE, Jun 3, 1954, and Lagarde to SRE, Jun 10, 1954, Box III-2538-2-3a Parte, AHGE.

61. Alexander Wiley, Jan 14, 1954, 100 Cong. Rec. I: 249–50.

62. Anibal Jara, "El problema de Guatemala," Feb 11, 1954, Embachile EEUU, Oficios Confidenciales, vol. 3761, AGHMRE.

63. Gowen to DoS, Dec 16, 1953, 611.14/12–1653, RG 59, NARA.

64. "United States Objectives and Courses of Action with Respect to Latin America: Staff Study," Mar 18, 1953, Box 20, NSC 144/1, Formal Policy Papers, 1947–61, RG 273, NARA.

65. Alexander Holmes, "A Christian Gentleman Among the Heathen," *Los Angeles Times*, Mar 31, 1954, A5.

66. Thomas A. Bailey, *A Diplomatic History of the American People*, 10th ed. (Upper Saddle River, NJ: Prentice Hall, 1980), 830.

67. For a detailed account of this event, see my "Fracas in Caracas: Latin American Diplomatic Resistance to United States Intervention in Guatemala in 1954," *Diplomacy and Statecraft* 21:4 (2010): 1–21.

68. "At Caracas a Vote of Confidence for the U.S.," *Baltimore Sun*, Mar 18, 1954.

69. Dwight David Eisenhower, *The White House Years: Mandate for Change, 1953–1956* (Garden City, NJ: Doubleday, 1963), 326, 421.

70. *Selected Executive Session Hearings of the Committee on Foreign Affairs* (Washington, DC: U.S. Government Printing Office, 1954), 16:502.

71. José A. Mora to MRE, "Primer Informe," Mar 4, 1954, Box CI.X.8, X Conferencia Interamericana: Grupos de Trabajo, Organismos Internacionales, Dirección de Política Exterior, Archivo Histórico-Diplomático del Ministerio de Relaciones Exteriores, Montevideo (hereafter AHDMRE); Cabot to Smith, Feb 15, 1954, FRUS 1952–54, IV: 293.

72. "Informal Remarks of W. Randolph Burgess, Deputy to the Secretary of the Treasury," Mar 13, 1954, Box 2, Mann Papers, DDEL.

73. "Notes of a Meeting of the Guatemalan Group," Department of State, Jun 9, 1954, *FRUS 1952–1954 Volume IV: American Republics (Guatemala Compilation)* doc. 57; "Venezuela Trade Tied to Oil Sales," *New York Times*, Apr 14, 1954, 43; "Hits Proposal to Put Curb on Venezuelan Oil," *Chicago Daily Tribune*, May 7, 1954, C7; "Creole Head Takes Issue with Move to Cut Oil Imports," *Los Angeles Times*, May 14, 1954; "Oil Sales Held Base of Venezuela Trade," *New York Times*, May 19, 1954, 51; Torleif Meloe, *United States Control of Petroleum Imports: A Study*

in the Federal Government's Role in the Management of Domestic Oil Supplies (Arno Press, 1979), 54–8.

74. Nolting to Stassen, Jan 15, 1954, FRUS 1952–54, IV: 1662–3.
75. Robert J. Alexander, "Citation of Perez Jimenez," *New York Times*, Nov 8, 1954, 20.
76. Cattafari to MAE, Apr 20, 1953, Box 1606, Visita Milton S. Eisenhower in America Latina, Ufficio VI, Serie Affari Politici 1950–57, Archivio Storico Diplomatico, Ministero degli Affari Esteri, Rome (hereafter ASDMAE); Anibal Jara, "Renuncia de Cabot," Feb 19, 1954, Embachile EEUU, Oficios Confidenciales, vol. 3761, AGHMRE; Barros to MRE, Mar 12, 1954, X Conferencia Interamericana, Caracas 1954, Vol. 3964, AGHMRE; "Minutes of Cabinet Meeting," Mar 12, 1954, Box 3, Cabinet Series, Ann Whitman File, DDEL; L. Arthur Minnich, Mar 12, 1954, Box 2, Cabinet Series, White House Office, Office of the Staff Secretary, DDEL.
77. "Telephone Conversation with Dr. Hauge," Feb 25, 1954, Box 10, Telephone Calls Series, Dulles Papers, DDEL; "Minutes of Cabinet Meeting," Feb 26, 1954, Box 3, Cabinet Series, Ann Whitman File, DDEL; "On the March," *Time*, Jan 4, 1954.
78. "Notes of a Meeting of the Guatemalan Group."
79. Woodward to Hardesty, Feb 24, 1954, FRUS 1952–54, IV: 1513; ItAmbPeru to MAE, Feb 25, 1954, Box 1603, Xa Conferenza Interamericana – Caracas, Ufficio VI, Serie Affari Politici 1950–57, ASDMAE.
80. Charles R. Norberg, "Meeting of the Working Group on the Caracas Conference," Mar 16, 1954, Box 71, Latin America (2), OCB Central File Series, National Security Council Staff Papers, DDEL.
81. Joseph I. Sisco, "Colombian Reimbursement," Sep 14, 1954, FRUS 1952–54, IV: 810–11; Charles R. Norberg, "$5,000,000 Columbian [sic] Debt," Jun 17, 1954, Box 72, Latin America (7), OCB Central File Series, National Security Council Staff Papers, DDEL.
82. "Minutes of Cabinet Meeting," Mar 5, 1954, Box 3, Cabinet Series, Ann Whitman File, DDEL.
83. Smith to Dulles, Mar 9, 1954, FRUS 1952–54, IV: 293.
84. "Declaration of Solidarity for the Preservation of the Political Integrity of the American States Against International Communist Intervention," Box 72, Latin America (4), OCB Central File Series, National Security Council Staff Papers, DDEL.
85. "Discussion at the 189th Meeting of the National Security Council," Mar 19, 1954, Box 3, NSC Series, Ann Whitman File, DDEL.
86. G. Pope Atkins, *Encyclopedia of the Inter-American System* (Westport, CT: Greenwood Publishing, 1997), 102.
87. MRE, "Decima conferencia interamericana: instrucciones impartidos a la Delegación Argentina," 1954, Decima Conferencia Interamericana – Caracas 1954, Archivo del Ministerio de Relaciones Exteriores y Culto, Buenos Aires (hereafter AMREC); Delegamex to Rodriguez Cano, Mar 12, 1954, 433/259, Ruíz Cortines Papers, Archivo General de la Nación, Mexico City (hereafter AGN).
88. *Argentina en la X conferencia interamericana* (Buenos Aires: Ministerio de Relaciones Exteriores y Culto, 1954), 19, 22, 63.
89. Durward V. Sandifer, Mar 24, 1954, FRUS 1952–54, IV: 468.
90. SRE, "X Conferencia Interamericana – Boletín de Prensa No. 23," Mar 12, 1954, 433/259, Ruíz Cortines Papers, AGN.

91. ItAmbVen to MAE, "X Conferenza Panamericana," Mar 29, 1954, Box 1603, Xa Conferenza Interamericana – Caracas, Ufficio VI, Serie Affari Politici 1950–57, ASDMAE; Jan Knippers Black, *United States Penetration of Brazil* (Manchester: Manchester University Press, 1977), 164.

92. SRE, "X Conferencia Interamericana – Boletín de Prensa No. 6," Mar 4, 1954, 433/359, Ruíz Cortines Papers, AGN; Wayne A. Selcher, *The Afro-Asian Dimension of Brazilian Foreign Policy, 1956–1972* (Gainesville: University of Florida, 1974), 14.

93. "Discurso pronunciado por el Dr. Justino Jiménez de Aréchaga," Mar 10, 1954, Box CI.X.8, X Conferencia Interamericana, Organismos Internacionales, Dirección de Política Exterior, AHDMRE; "Palabras pronunciadas por el Dr. Justino Jiménez de Aréchaga en la sesión del 12 de marzo," Mar 12, 1954, Box CI.X.8, X Conferencia Interamericana, Organismos Internacionales, Dirección de Política Exterior, AHDMRE.

94. MRE, "Instrucciones para la delegación de la república que concurrira a la X Conferencia Interamericana," March 1954, Box CI.X.7, X Conferencia Interamericana, Organismos Internacionales, Dirección de Política Exterior, AHDMRE.

95. "Anti-American Sentiment Grows in Latin-America," *Associated Press*, Jun 24, 1954; "Guatemala Problem Seems to Be Solving," *Los Angeles Times*, Jun 29, 1954.

96. "Declaration of Solidarity for the Preservation of the Political Integrity of the American States Against International Communist Intervention," Box 72, Latin America (4), OCB Central File Series, National Security Council Staff Papers, DDEL.

97. "Success at Caracas," *Time*, Mar 22, 1954, 27.

98. SRE, "X Conferencia Interamericana – Boletín de Prensa No. 24," Mar 12, 1954, 433/259, Ruíz Cortines Papers, AGN.

99. Sydney Gruson, "Anti-Yankeeism Is Seen in Mexico," *New York Times*, May 13, 1954, 8.

100. MAE circular telegram, "Dichiarazione di Caracas," Apr 22, 1954, Box 1603, Xa Conferencia Interamericana – Caracas, Ufficio VI, Serie Affari Politici 1950–57, ASDMAE.

101. "L'América Latina diffida della casa bianca," *Il Tempo*, Apr 1, 1954, 6.

102. Tim Weiner, *Legacy of Ashes: The History of the CIA* (NY: Random House, 2008), 110.

103. Weiner, *Legacy*, 115.

104. David Atlee Phillips, *The Night Watch* (NY: Atheneum, 1977), 51.

105. "Telephone Call to Mr. McCardle," Jun 28, 1954, Box 8, Chronological Series, Telephone Calls, Dulles Papers, DDEL; "Minutes of Cabinet Meeting," Jul 9, 1954, Box 3, Cabinet Series, Ann Whitman File, DDEL; "Hagerty Diary," Jun 28, 1954, Box 1, Hagerty Papers, DDEL; "Telephone Call to Mr. McCardle," Jun 29, 1954, Box 2, Telephone Calls Series, Dulles Papers, DDEL.

106. House Select Committee on Communist Aggression, *Report of the Subcommittee to Investigate Communist Aggression in Latin America* (Washington, DC: U.S. Government Printing Office, 1954).

107. U.N. Security Council, "Verbatim Record of the Six Hundred and Seventy-Fifth Meeting," Jun 20, 1954, FO 371/108743, NA-K.

108. "Telephone Conversation with Ambassador Lodge (NY)," Jun 22, 1954, and "Memorandum of Telephone Conversation between the Secretary and Ambassador Lodge," Jun 25, 1954, Box 8, Chronological Series, Telephone Calls, Dulles Papers, DDEL.

109. "Resolution adoptée par le Conseil de sécurité le 20 juin 1954 à sa 675ème séance," Jun 20, 1954, sous-série Sécretariat des Conferences 1945–59, No. 242, série Nations Unies et Organisations Internationales, MAE; "Telephone Conversation from Amb. Lodge," Jun 24, 1954, Box 8, Chronological Series, Telephone Calls, Dulles Papers, DDEL.

110. ItAmbLegUN to MAE, Jun 24, 1954, Box 1612, Guatemala-U.S.A., Ufficio VI, Serie Affari Politici 1950–57, ASDMAE.

111. U.N. Security Council, "Verbatim Record of the Six Hundred and Seventy-Fifth Meeting," Jun 20, 1954, FO 371/108743, NA-K.

112. R.L. Speaight, "Guatemala," Jun 24, 1954, FO 371/108743, NA-K.

113. Bonnet to MAE, Jun 24, 1954, sous-série Guatemala 1952–1963, No. 21, série Amérique, MAE.

114. Bonnet to MAE, Jun 25, 1954, sous-série Guatemala 1952–1963, No. 21, série Amérique, MAE.

115. R.L. Speaight, "Guatemala," Jun 24, 1954, FO 371/108743, NA-K.

116. "Hagerty Diary," Jun 24, 1954, Box 1, Hagerty Papers, DDEL.

117. "Memorandum of Telephone Conversation between the Secretary and Ambassador Lodge," Jun 24, 1954, Box 8, Chronological Series, Telephone Calls, Dulles Papers, DDEL; "Hagerty Diary," Jun 26, 1954, Box 1, Hagerty Papers, DDEL.

118. "Appalling": Pridham minute, Jul 2, 1954, FO 371/108743, NA-K; "fantastic": Hoppenot to MAE, Jun 21, 1954, sous-série Guatemala 1952–1963, No. 21, série Amérique, MAE; "indefensible... wreck the moral authority": Foreign Office to New York, Jun 24, 1954, FO 371/108742, NA-K.

119. Cullather, *Secret History*, 111.

120. Eisenhower, *The White House Years*, 421–26.

121. "L'agression contre le Guatemala au Conseil de Sécurité," *Combat*, Jun 21,1954, 1; V. Pellegrino, "La Guerre paysanne en Amérique centrale," *Combat*, Jun 22, 1954, 1; "Le Président du Guatemala démissionne et se réfugie à Buenos-Aires," *Combat*, Jun 29, 1954, 1.

122. Paul Rivet, "Néocolonialisme," *Le Monde*, Jun 23, 1954, 3.

123. Jacques Soustelle, "'Libération' du Guatemala," *L'Express*, Jun 26, 1954.

124. "Ueberfall," *Frankfurter Allgemeine Zeitung*, Jun 21, 1954, 1.

125. Bonn to FO, Jun 25, 1954, FO 371/108928, NA-K.

126. "War Through the Looking Glass," *Economist*, Jun 26, 1954.

127. J. Halcro Ferguson, "Guatemala in Perspective," *Observer*, Jun 27, 1954.

128. Chevallier minute, Jul 6, 1954, FO 371/108929, NA-K.

129. See file for August 1964, FO 371/108934/G1015/210, NA-K.

130. "U.S. Policy in Guatemala," *Ottawa Citizen*, Jun 22, 1954, 30.

131. Bourdeillette to MAE, Jun 29, 1954, sous-série Guatemala 1952–1963, No. 21, série Amérique, MAE.

132. Du Chayla to MAE, Jun 21, 1954, sous-série Guatemala 1952–1963, No. 21, série Amérique, MAE.

133. Stockholm to FO, Jun 21, 1954, FO 371/108927, NA-K.

134. M.B.C. minute, Jul 8, 1954, FO 371/108930, NA-K.

135. "World Reactions to the Guatemalan Revolution," Sep 2, 1954, Box 9, Special Reports, 1953–63, Office of Research and Intelligence, RG 306, NARA.
136. Jun 23, 1954, *FRUS 1952–1954*, American Republics (Guatemala Compilation), IV: Doc. 72.
137. Smith to FO, Jun 25, 1954, FO 371/108929, NA-K.
138. Costa Rica to FO, Jun 24, 1954, FO 371/108930, NA-K.
139. Cerisola to SRE, Jul 13, 1954, Box III-2538–2-Ia Parte, AHGE.
140. ItAmbUruguay to MAE, Jun 28,1954, Box 1612, Guatemala-U.S.A., Ufficio VI, Serie Affari Politici 1950–57, ASDMAE.
141. Federico Klein to MRE, "Acontecimientos en Guatemala," Jun 17, 1954, Guatemala: Embachile Conchile Confidenciales 1954, vol. 3792, AGHMRE. See also Mark T. Hove, "The Arbenz Factor: Salvador Allende, U.S.-Chilean Relations, and the 1954 U.S. Intervention in Guatemala," *Diplomatic History* 31:4 (September 2007): 623–663.
142. Cullather, *Secret History*, 112. Rivera's painting is reproduced on the book cover.
143. Daniel James, *Red Design for the Americas: Guatemalan Prelude* (NY: John Day, 1954), 13.
144. "Telephone Conversation with Mr. Allen Dulles," Jun 24, 1954, Box 2, Telephone Calls Series, Dulles Papers, DDEL.
145. "Hagerty Diary," Jun 28, 1954, Box 1, Hagerty Papers, DDEL.
146. "Possible Action by Organization of American States Regarding Guatemalan Situation," Jun 14, 1954, SS-2003–00002, CIA-FOIA; "Comment on 'Lessons of Guatemala' by Daniel James," Aug 19, 1954, SS-2003–00002, CIA-FOIA.
147. "Memorandum of Telephone Conversation between the Secretary and Ambassador Lodge," Jun 25, 1954, Box 8, Chronological Series, Telephone Calls, Dulles Papers, DDEL.
148. Information Coordination Division, "Report on Actions Taken to Counteract Unfavorable World Reaction to Overthrow of Arbenz Regime in Guatemala," Jul 26, 1954, SS-2003–00002, CIA-FOIA.
149. Speaight minute, Jul 6, 1954, FO 371/108934, NA-K.
150. Speaight minute, Jul 7, 1954, FO 371/108929, NA-K.
151. Chevallier minute, Jul 6, 1954, FO 371/108929, NA-K.
152. "A Study of USIA Operating Assumptions," December 1954, Box 7–8, Special Reports, 1953–63, RG 306, NARA.
153. Operations Coordinating Board, "Outline Plan of Operations against Communism in Latin America," Apr 18, 1956, *FRUS 1955–1957* VI: 63. The draft for this report was begun in early 1955 and approved by Eisenhower.
154. Gleijeses, *Shattered Hope*, 383.
155. "Intervención del gobierno de los Estados Unidos de América del Norte en cuestión de los refugiados políticos," Aug 1954, Box B1–184-21, AHGE.
156. Alan Riding, "Guatemala: State of Siege," *New York Times*, Aug 24, 1980, 66. A "State Department official" repeated the same phrase to Marlise Simons, "Guatemala: The Coming Danger," *Foreign Policy* 43 (Summer 1981): 103.
157. "Vice President Nixon's Trip to South America," May 26, 1958, Box 42, NSC 5613/1, Formal Policy Papers, 1947–61, RG 273, NA; Alan L. McPherson, *Yankee No! Anti-Americanism in U.S.-Latin American Relations* (Cambridge, MA: Harvard University Press, 2003), 26–30.
158. "Telephone Call to Mr. Hagerty," May 13, 1958, Box 13, Telephone Calls Series, Dulles Papers, DDEL.

159. May 13, 1958, Box 10, May 1958 (1), Ann Whitman Diary, Ann Whitman File, DDEL.
160. Marvin R. Zahniser and W. Michael Weis, "A Diplomatic Pearl Harbor? Richard Nixon's Goodwill Mission to Latin America in 1958," *Diplomatic History* 13:2 (April 1989): 163–90.
161. Senate Committee on Foreign Relations, "Review of Foreign Policy," Mar 3–10, 1958 (Washington, DC: USGPO, 1958).
162. Robert Alexander, *Rómulo Betancourt and the Transformation of Venezuela* (New Brunswick, NJ: Transaction Books, 1982), 405.
163. Betancourt to Kennedy, Jul 22, 1963, Box 192A, Venezuela – General, Countries, PSF, John F. Kennedy Presidential Library, Boston (hereafter JFKL).
164. Quoted in McPherson, *Yankee No!*, 9.
165. Annex C, "Vice President Nixon's Trip to South America," May 26, 1958, Box 42, NSC 5613/1, Formal Policy Papers, 1947–61, RG 273, NARA. This portion of the report was prepared by the State Department.
166. "Discussion at the 366th Meeting of the National Security Council," May 22, 1958, Box 10, NSC Series, Ann Whitman File, DDEL.
167. "The Hemisphere: Why It Happened," *Time*, May 26, 1958.
168. Hughes to Secretary, "Anti-US Student Sentiment in Latin America," Oct 23, 1963, Box WH-40, White House Files, Schlesinger Papers, JFKL.
169. Senate Committee on the Judiciary, "Communist Anti-American Riots: Mob Violence as an Instrument of Red Diplomacy. Bogotá – Caracas – La Paz – Tokyo," Aug 26, 1960 (Washington, DC: USGPO, 1960).
170. "Discussion at the 366th Meeting of the National Security Council," May 22, 1958, Box 10, NSC Series, Ann Whitman File, DDEL.
171. INRA, "Latin American Reactions to Nixon's Visit," May 22, 1958, Mexico IRA #301, Mexico, RC.
172. "Nixon Jeered by Mob Crying 'Little Rock!'," *Norfolk Journal and Guide*, May 17, 1958, B24.
173. Operations Coordinating Board, "U.S. Policy toward Latin America," NSC 5613/1, 4–5, May 21, 1958, DDRS.
174. CIA Senior Research Staff on International Communism, "Autobiography of SRS," Apr 27, 1961, CIA-RDP80–01445R000100360001–8, CREST. Although dated 1961, this report deals with discussions of anti-Americanism held immediately after the attack on Nixon in 1958.
175. Alan L. McPherson, "Myths of Anti-Americanism: The Case of Latin America," *Brown Journal of World Affairs* 10:2 (Winter/Spring 2004): 141–52.
176. Lloyd Free, "The Cuban Situation," FRUS 1958–60, VI: 891.
177. 107 Cong. Rec. p. 642 (1961) Extensions of Remarks – Wednesday, Jan 11, 1961; 107 Cong. Rec. p. 583 (1961) Senate – Wednesday, Jan 11, 1961.
178. Based on a search of Hein Online's *Congressional Record* database.
179. Greg Grandin made this estimate on the basis of the Declassified Document Reference System. See his insightful article, "Your Americanism and Mine: Americanism and Anti-Americanism in the Americas," *American Historical Review* 111: 4 (November 2006), fn. 92.
180. A copy of the letter from Nov 6, 1940 is at the National Archives website, www.archives.gov/exhibits/american_originals/castro.html.
181. CIA, "Central Intelligence Bulletin," Oct 26, 1959, CIA-RDP79T00975A004-700480001–7, CREST.

182. Mallory to Rubottom, "The Decline and Fall of Castro," Apr 6, 1960, FRUS 1958–1960, VI: 885.

183. Macmillan to Eisenhower, Jul 25, 1960, PREM 11/3688, NA-K; Eisenhower to Macmillan, Aug 8, 1960, PREM 11/3688, NA-K.

184. Hankey to Busk, Apr 13, 1961, FO 371/156178, NA-K.

185. Pons to MAE, Apr 12, 1961, sous-série Généralités, No. 134b, série Amérique 1952–63, MAE; Guatemala City to AA, Apr 20, 1961, Box 195, Sig. B 33 Kuba, PAAA.

186. Binoche to MAE, Jan 13, 1961, sous-série Généralités, No. 134b, série Amérique 1952–63, MAE.

187. Bowles to Rusk, Mar 31, 1961, FRUS 1961–1963, X: 178–81.

188. Schlesinger to Kennedy, "Cuba: Political, Diplomatic and Economic Problems," Apr 10, 1961, *FRUS Cuba, 1961–1962* Doc. 86 (1961), X.

189. Caracas to AA, Apr 24, 1961, Box 195, Sig. B 33 Kuba, PAAA; Robert Alexander, *Venezuela's Voice for Democracy: Conversations and Correspondence with Rómulo Betancourt* (NY: Praeger, 1990), 77.

190. Mexico City to AA, Apr 25, 1961, Box 195, Sig. B 33 Kuba, PAAA.

191. "Contact rompu entre les anticastristes á Cuba et leur quartier général," *Combat*, Apr 20, 1961, 1; Bogotá to AA, May 4, 1961, Box 195, Sig. B 33 Kuba, PAAA.

192. Beirut to AA, Apr 25, 1961, Box 195, Sig. B 33 Kuba, PAAA; Rabat to AA, Apr 27, 1961, Box 195, Sig. B 33 Kuba, PAAA.

193. Karachi to AA, Apr 25, 1961, Box 195, Sig. B 33 Kuba, PAAA; Von Heyden to AA, Apr 21, 1961, Box 195, Sig. B 33 Kuba, PAAA.

194. Kabul to AA, Apr 25, 1961, Box 195, Sig. B 33 Kuba, PAAA.

195. "The Cuban Tragedy," *Globe and Mail*, Apr 21, 1961, 6.

196. "Les envahisseurs cubains essaient de couper l'île en deux," *Combat*, Apr 18, 1961, 1; "L'URSS tire des avantages diplomatiques de la maladresse américaine," *Combat*, Apr 21, 1961, 1.

197. Herwarth to AA, Apr 21, 1961, Box 195, Sig. B 33 Kuba, PAAA.

198. "Kuba: Guevara-Taktik," in *Der Spiegel*, Apr 26, 1961, 73–4.

199. DELARGENU to MRE, Apr 19, 1961, Cables de DELARGENU 1961, AMREC.

200. FM Arnios reported in Dittmann to AA, May 19, 1961, Box 195, Sig. B 33 Kuba, PAAA.

201. "Traccia per i colloqui con l'On. Segretario di Stato per gli Affari Esteri Lord Home," May 2–5, 1961, Gran Bretagna, Sig. Busta 13, Fasc. A46, Presidenza del Consiglio dei Ministri, Ufficio del Consigliere Diplomatico, Archivio Centrale dello Stato, Rome (hereafter ACS).

202. FO to Washington, Apr 28, 1961, FO 371/156181, NA-K.

203. Schlesinger to JFK, May 3, 1961, Doc. 196, *FRUS 1961–63*, vol. XI, Cuba.

204. Ibid.

205. See, for example, James G. Blight, Bruce J. Allyn, and David A. Welch, *Cuba on the Brink: Castro, the Missile Crisis, and the Soviet Collapse* (Lanham, MD: Rowman & Littlefield, 2002); Aleksandr Fursenko and Timothy J. Naftali, *One Hell of a Gamble: Khrushchev, Castro, and Kennedy, 1958–1964* (NY: W.W. Norton, 1997).

206. Juan José Arévalo, *The Shark and the Sardines*, tr. June Cobb and Dr. Raul Osegueda (NY: Lyle Stuart, 1961).

207. "Guatemala: Echoes from a Sardine," *Time*, Jan 5, 1962.

208. Juan José Arévalo, *Carta política al pueblo de Guatemala* (Guatemala City: Editorial San Antonio, 1963), 4.

209. Juan José Arévalo, *Antikomunismo en América Latina: radiografía del proceso hacia una nueva colonización* (Buenos Aires: Editorial Palestra, 1959). Arévalo was playing with the trend in business names such as Korner Kafe and Kwik Kar Wash. The letter "k" does not occur in Spanish, except in foreign words like *kilo* and *kiwi*.

210. Hilsman to Martin, March 1963, Box WH-36, White House Files, Schlesinger Papers, JFKL.

211. "Guatemala: Department of State Guidelines for Policy and Operations," February 1963, American Republics Microfiche Supplement, 10–12: Doc. 134.

212. "Agencia Prensa Latina (APL)," Jun 3, 1959, Box 2, Requestor Only Reports, Latin America, 1958–1960, Classified Research Reports, USIA Classified Research Reports, 1954–84, RG 306, NA; Brubeck to Bundy, Jan 21, 1963, Box 101, CF, PSF, JFKL; Fisher to Siracusa, Aug 21, 1962, in folder "Guatemala," Bureau of Inter-American Affairs, Office of Central American and Panamanian Affairs, Subject and Country Files, 1955–1963, Box 5, RG 59, NARA; Collins to Martin, Jan 21, 1963, in folder "Guatemala – 1963," Bureau of Inter-American Affairs, Office of Central American and Panamanian Affairs, Subject and Country Files, 1955–1963, Box 6, RG 59, NARA.

213. CIA, "Central Intelligence Bulletin," Nov 9, 1959, CIA-RDP79T00975A004-700480001-1, CREST.

214. Bell to DoS, Sep 11, 1962, Box WH-36, White House Files, Schlesinger Papers, JFKL.

215. Piero Gleijeses, "Juan Jose Arévalo and the Caribbean Legion," *Journal of Latin American Studies* 21:1 (February 1989): 133–45.

216. Arévalo, *Carta política*, 32.

217. Arévalo, *Carta política*, 4, 38.

218. Bell to DoS, Sep 11, 1962, Box WH-36, White House Files, Schlesinger Papers, JFKL.

219. "Status of U.S. Country Team Plans, Both Short and Long-Term Military and Political Objectives, for Guatemala," Oct 10, 1962, Declassified Documents Reference System (hereafter DDRS).

220. Brubeck to Bundy, Jan 24, 1963, Box 118, Guatemala Security 1961–1963, Country Files, POF, JFKL; Brubeck to Bundy, Jan 21, 1963, Box 101, CF, PSF, JFKL.

221. Rabe, *The Most Dangerous Area*, 16.

222. "Meeting on Haiti and Guatemala," Jan 22, 1963, Presidential Recordings, Tape 70, POF, JFKL. According to the White House Appointment Books, present at the meeting in addition to Kennedy and Martin were State Department officials John H. Crimmins, Director of the Office of Caribbean and Mexican Affairs; V. Lansing Collins, Director of the Office of Central American and Panamanian Affairs; and Ralph Dungan, Special Assistant to the President for Latin American affairs and later ambassador to Chile. White House Appointment Books, Card Files, 1963, JFKL. Collins's memo did not list Dungan but added Col. J.C. King, Chief of the Western Hemisphere Division of the CIA's Directorate of Operations, and CIA Director Richard Helms. See V. Lansing Collins, "Memcon: Meeting at the White House," Jan 22, 1963, *American Republics Microfiche Supplement*, FRUS 1961–1963, 10–12: Doc. 133; Collins, "Meeting at the White House," Jan 22, 1963, 714.00/1–2263, RG 59, NARA. The National Archives turned my FOIA request

over to the CIA as the "interested agency," and the CIA refused to declassify the omissions.

223. Rabe, *The Most Dangerous Area*, 99–101.
224. "Second and Final Conversation between President Kennedy and President Betancourt of Venezuela – Guatemala," Feb 20, 1963, Box 192A, Venezuela – General, Countries, PSF, JFKL.
225. Buxton to Parsons, Feb 25, 1963, FO 371/168074, NA-K.
226. Bell to SecState, Mar 6, 1963, Box 101, CF, PSF, JFKL.
227. Corrigan to SecState, Mar 13, 1963, Box 101, CF, PSF, JFKL; Corrigan to SecState, Mar 12, 1963, in folder "POL 6 – GUAT," Subject-Numeric Files, Box 3920, RG 59, NARA.
228. Bell to LAPC, "Guatemala," Mar 8, 1963, Box WH-40, White House Files, Schlesinger Papers, JFKL.
229. "Memcon Kennedy-Ydígoras," Mar 20, 1963, POL 15-1 US/Kennedy, RG 59, NA; Rusk to AmEmbGuatemala, Mar 27, 1963, Box 101, Guatemala – General, Countries, PSF, JFKL; Ydígoras-Bell-Corrigan Memcon, Mar 16, 1963, in folder "Guatemala – 1963," Bureau of Inter-American Affairs, Office of Central American and Panamanian Affairs, Subject and Country Files, 1955–1963, Box 6, RG 59, NARA; Bell to SecState, Mar 22, 1963, in folder "POL – GUAT," Subject-Numeric Files, Box 3919, RG 59, NARA.
230. White House Appointment Books, Card Files, 1963, JFKL.
231. Manuel Cabieses, "Con Peluca y Disfrazado de Obrero Entró Arévalo en Guatemala," *El Nacional*, Apr 17, 1963, 24; CIA, "Arevalo's Return to Guatemala," Mar 29, 1963, CIA Electronic Reading Room, foia.cia.gov.
232. Bell to SecState, Mar 30, 1963, in folder "POL 6 – GUAT," Subject-Numeric Files, Box 3920, RG 59, NARA.
233. Williams to Home, Apr 8, 1963, FO 371/168075, NA-K.
234. S.C. minute, May 28, 1963, FO 371/168076, NA-K.
235. "Nature of Threat," [April 1963], typescript in folder "Guatemala – Internal Defense Plan," Bureau of Inter-American Affairs, Office of Central American and Panamanian Affairs, Subject and Country Files, 1955–1963, Box 4, RG 59, NARA.
236. Bell to DoS, Sep 7, 1963, Box WH-36, White House Files, Schlesinger Papers, JFKL.
237. Martin to Special Group (CI), "Guatemala Internal Defense Plan," Sep 25, 1963, Box WH-36, White House Files, Schlesinger Papers, JFKL.
238. Sherman Kent, "Guatemala's Dilemma," Jan 18, 1966, EO-1998–00646, CIA-FOIA.
239. Grandin, *The Last Colonial Massacre*, 74.
240. Betancourt to Kennedy, Jul 22, 1963, Microfilm 24, The Papers of Rómulo Betancourt; see also State Department translation in Betancourt to Kennedy, Jul 22, 1963, Box 192A, Venezuela – General, Countries, PSF, JFKL.
241. Kennedy to Betancourt, Aug 16, 1963, Box 192A, Venezuela – General, Countries, PSF, JFKL.
242. USIS, "President Kennedy's Press Conference," Oct 10, 1963, FO 371/168415, NA-K.
243. Carlos Fuentes, "Rede an die Bürger der USA," *Kursbuch* 2 (1965): 56–71.
244. Ball to Johnson, "Nonimmigrant Visa Case of Carlos Fuentes Macias," May 13, 1964, DDRS.

Chapter 5. Myth and Consequences

1. Cited in John Hess, *The Case for de Gaulle* (NY: William Morrow and Co., 1968), 1.

2. AmEmbParis to General Eisenhower, Nov 9, 1945, Box 34, Charles de Gaulle, DDE Papers, Pre-Presidential, 1916–52, Principal File, DDEL.

3. Vincent Jauvert, *L'Amérique contre de Gaulle: Histoire sécrete 1961–1969* (Paris: Seuil, 2000), 19.

4. Arthur M. Schlesinger Jr., *A Thousand Days: John F. Kennedy in the White House* (NY: Houghton Mifflin, 2002), 356.

5. Wahl, Introduction to Paxton and Wahl, eds., *De Gaulle and the United States*, 4.

6. Frank C. Costigliola, *France and the United States: The Cold Alliance since World War II* (NY: Twayne Publishers, 1992), 30, 101.

7. Irwin M. Wall, "Harry S. Truman and Charles de Gaulle," in Robert O. Paxton and Nicholas Wahl, eds., *De Gaulle and the United States: A Centennial Reappraisal* (Oxford: Berg, 1994), 118.

8. Hanson W. Baldwin, "Rising Neutralism a Hurdle for NATO: Anti-Americanism Grows," *New York Times*, Jan 13, 1953, 8.

9. Gen. Alfred M. Gruenther in 1954, quoted in Costigliola, *France and the United States*, 97.

10. Psychological Strategy Board, "Evaluation of the Psychological Impact of United States Foreign Economic Policies and Programs in France," Feb 9, 1953, CIA-RDP80–01065A000 400090004–1, CREST.

11. Bromley K. Smith, Summary Record of NSC Executive Committee No. 39, Jan 1, 1963, Meetings and Memoranda, PSF, John F. Kennedy Library, Columbia Point, Massachusetts (hereafter JFKL).

12. Ball to Bohlen and Rusk, Sep 25, 1963, France Security 1963, Country Files, POF, JFKL.

13. Bohlen to SecState, Jul 1, 1967, Declassified Documents Retrieval System (hereafter DDRS). Bohlen later denied that he ever found de Gaulle anti-American: Jean Lacouture, *De Gaulle: Le souverain, 1959–1970* (Paris: Editions du Seuil, 1986), 344. In a 1967 press briefing, he said, "I don't think he's anti-American at all." Hess, *The Case for de Gaulle*, 2. Yet he used the word frequently in dispatches. See, e.g., Bohlen, "Reflections on Current French Foreign Policy and Attitudes toward the United States and Recommendations," Mar 10, 1964, Box 2168; Bohlen to SecState, Jul 24, 1964, Box 2178; and Bohlen to SecState, May 20, 1965, Box 2178, POL France 1964–66, Subject-Numeric Files 1964–66, RG 59, NARA. In his memoirs he again bemoaned "de Gaulle's anti-American tone." Charles E. Bohlen, *Witness to History, 1929–1969* (NY: Norton, 1973), 515. The contradictions of America's closest observer on this subject reflect the general imprecision that make this a term of little value, but great cost.

14. Hughes to Secretary, "De Gaulle's Stepped-Up Anti-Americanism and the Crisis of French Foreign Policy," Jul 26, 1967, DDRS, and enclosed Rostow note. See also the CIA's "Situation Appraisal in France: Indications of Anti-Americanism," Jan 31, 1964, in folder "France – Cables 11/63–3/64," NSF Country Files, France, Box 169, Lyndon B. Johnson Library, Austin (hereafter LBJL).

15. Meeting with the National Security Council on NATO, Jan 31, 1963, Presidential Recordings, Tape 70, POF, JFKL.

16. Jean-Marie Cotteret and René Moreau, *Recherches sur le vocabulaire du Général de Gaulle* (Paris: Armand Colin, 1969), 72. See also Irwin Wall, "The United

States and Two Ostpolitiks: De Gaulle and Brandt," in *The Making of Détente*, ed. Wilfried Loth and Georges-Henri Soutou (NY: Routledge, 2008), 133–150.

17. Audience accordée par le Général de Gaulle au gouverneur Rockefeller, Oct 3, 1963, *Documents Diplomatiques Français 1963* (Paris: Ministère des Affaires étrangères, 1963, hereafter *DDF*), 2: 335.

18. Hervé Alphand, *L'Étonnement d'être: Journal, 1939–1973* (Paris: Fayard, 1977), 385.

19. Laurent Césari, "Que reste-t-il de l'influence politique française en indochine (1954–1966)?," in *Du conflit d'Indochine aux conflits indochinois*, ed. Pierre Brocheux (Paris: Éditions Complexe, 2000), 21–36. On de Gaulle's strategic outlook, see especially Frédéric Bozo, *Two Strategies for Europe: De Gaulle, the United States, and the Atlantic Alliance*, trans. Susan Emanuel (Lanham, MD: Rowman and Littlefield, 2001); Charles G. Cogan, *Oldest Allies, Guarded Friends: The United States and France since 1940* (Westport, CT: Praeger, 1994); Frank C. Costigliola, "The Failed Design: Kennedy, de Gaulle, and the Struggle for Europe," *Diplomatic History* 8:3 (Summer 1984): 227–51; idem, *France and the United States: The Cold Alliance, 1940–1990* (NY: Twayne Publishers, 1992); Michael Harrison, *The Reluctant Ally: France and Atlantic Security* (Baltimore and London: Johns Hopkins University Press, 1981); Stanley Hoffmann, "The Will to Grandeur: de Gaulle as Political Artist," *Daedalus* (Summer 1968): 829–87; Lacouture, *De Gaulle: Le souverain, 1959–1970*; Paxton and Wahl, *De Gaulle and the United States*; Maurice Vaïsse, *La grandeur: Politique étrangère du général de Gaulle, 1958–1969* (Paris: Fayard, 1998); Alexander Werth, *De Gaulle: A Political Biography* (NY: Simon and Schuster, 1966). Also see Thomas L. Hughes, "De Gaulle at Bay?" INR Research Memorandum, Sep 2, 1964, in folder "France, 1964–66," NSF Komer Files, Box 20, LBJL.

20. Maurice Couve de Murville, *Une Politique Etrangère, 1958–1969* (Paris: Plon, 1971), 24. On Algeria see Matthew Connelly's excellent *A Diplomatic Revolution: Algeria's Fight for Independence and the Origins of the Post-Cold War Era* (NY: Oxford University Press, 2002).

21. Edward A. Kolodziej, *French International Policy under de Gaulle and Pompidou: The Politics of Grandeur* (Ithaca, NY: Cornell University Press, 1974), 447–52.

22. "Entretien entre le Général de Gaulle et M. Averell William Harriman à l'Elysée," Mar 4, 1961, sous-série Entretiens et Messages, No. 13, série Secrétariat Général, Ministère des Affaires Étrangères, Paris (hereafter MAE).

23. Werth, *De Gaulle*, 341.

24. Bovey to SecState, "How to Succeed in the Third World without even Trying," Oct 29, 1964, Box 2168, POL France 1964–66, Subject-Numeric Files 1964–66, RG 59, NARA.

25. Wladyslaw W. Kulski, *De Gaulle and the World: The Foreign Policy of the Fifth French Republic* (Syracuse: Syracuse University Press, 1966), 321.

26. Philippe Devillers, "Le Général de Gaulle et l'Asie," in *De Gaulle et le tiers Monde*, ed. Institut Charles de Gaulle (Paris: Pédone, 1984), 299–327, here 320.

27. Werth, *De Gaulle*, 342.

28. Jean Lacouture, *De Gaulle: Le politique, 1944–1959* (Paris: Editions du Seuil, 1985), 633; idem, *De Gaulle: Le souverain*, 349.

29. Charles de Gaulle, *Mémoires de guerre: L'Appel, 1940–42*, vol. I (Paris: Plon, 1999 [1954]), 7.

30. De Gaulle, *Mémoires de guerre*, I:7.
31. Walters to Harriman, Apr 7, 1961, Box 454, De Gaulle, Charles, Harriman Papers, LC.
32. "Bundy-Ball Telcon," Aug 15, 1963, Box 4, France, Ball Papers, JFKL.
33. Jan 15, 1963, Box 317A, Meetings & Memoranda, PSF, JFKL.
34. Ball to Kennedy, "The Mess in Europe and the Meaning of Your Trip," Jun 20, 1963, Box WH-33, White House Files, Schlesinger Papers, JFKL.
35. Richard F. Kuisel, *Seducing the French: The Dilemma of Americanization* (Berkeley and Los Angeles: University of California Press, 1993), 145. This is one of the best examinations of postwar French attitudes toward the United States.
36. Philippe Roger, *L'ennemi américain: Généalogie de l'antiaméricanisme français* (Paris: Seuil, 2002), 438.
37. *La Cinquième Colonne, la voici!* (Paris: SEDIC, n.d. [1950]), cited in Roger, *L'ennemi américain*, 354.
38. Stephen Haseler, *The Varieties of Anti-Americanism: Reflex and Response* (Washington, DC: Ethics and Public Policy Center, 1985), 4.
39. Ronald Steel, *Walter Lippmann and the American Century* (Boston: Little, Brown, 1980), 549–50; Henry Kissinger, *The Troubled Partnership: A Re-appraisal of the Atlantic Alliance* (NY: McGraw-Hill, 1965); Kissinger, "Dealing with de Gaulle," in Paxton and Wahl, *De Gaulle and the United States*, 331–42; Kissinger to Bundy, Mar 6, 1962, Box 463A, Kissinger Series, PSF, JFKL.
40. De Gaulle to Macmillan, Aug 9, 1958, PREM 11/2335, National Archives, Kew, London (hereafter NA-K); Roberts to FO, "General de Gaulle's Pique," Aug 1, 1958, PREM 11/2335, NA-K.
41. "Memcon," Sep 22, 1958, PREM 11/3738, NA-K; Peking to FO, Sep 29, 1958, PREM 11/3738, NA-K.
42. Chauvel to Couve de Murville, Aug 29, 1958, *DDF 1958*, 2: 300–1.
43. L. Arthur Minnich, Jan 18, 1955, Box 1, Minnich Series, White House Office, Office of the Staff Secretary, DDEL.
44. E.W. Kenworthy, "Eisenhower Sees Increased Need to Guard Quemoy," *New York Times*, Aug 28, 1958, 1.
45. "Consultations tripartites de Washington," Feb 5, 1959, and "Consultations tripartites de Washington sur l'Extrême-Orient," Feb 7, 1959, sous-série Entretiens et Messages, No. 6b, série Secrétariat Général, MAE.
46. Couve de Murville, *Une Politique Etrangère*, 33, 57–8; Drew Middleton, "British Are Wary of Nuclear War: Diplomats in London Weigh Possibility U.S. May Use Atom Bombs in Far East," *New York Times*, Sep 24, 1958, 3.
47. Menzies to Macmillan, Sep 26, 1958, PREM 11/3738, NA-K.
48. Caccia to FO, Oct 14, 1958, PREM 11/3738, NA-K.
49. FO to Washington, Oct 22, 1958, and Macmillan to Menzies, Oct 3, 1958, PREM 11/3738, NA-K.
50. Caccia to FO, Oct 15, 1958, PREM 11/3738, NA-K.
51. "The Case for U.S. Intervention," Sep 2, 1958, Box 3, Sep 1958 – Jan 1959 (1), Subject Series, State Dept. Subseries, White House Office, Office of the Staff Secretary, DDEL.
52. Frank Costigliola, "Kennedy, de Gaulle, and the Challenge of Consultation," in Paxton and Wahl, *De Gaulle and the United States*, 173.
53. De Gaulle to Macmillan, Sep 17, 1958, PREM 11/3002, NA-K.
54. Harrison, *The Reluctant Ally*, 17.

55. Couve de Murville, *Une Politique Etrangère*, 53, 57.
56. De Gaulle to Couve de Murville, Nov 24, 1960, No. CM 7, Couve de Murville Papers, CHEVS.
57. Couve de Murville, *Une Politique Etrangère*, 59.
58. Charles de Gaulle, *Mémoires d'Espoir: Le renouveau 1958–1962* (Paris: Plon, 1970), 226. Eisenhower's view reported by his interpreter, Vernon Walters, later military attaché in Paris and a CIA official, cited in Lacouture, *De Gaulle: Le souverain*, 352–53.
59. Alphand, *L'Étonnement d'être*, 385.
60. "Meeting with the National Security Council on NATO," Jan 31, 1963, Presidential Recordings, Tape 70, POF, JFKL.
61. Alphand, *L'Étonnement d'être*, 407.
62. Alphand, *L'Étonnement d'être*, 384.
63. Carbonnel to New York, Oct 23, 1962, sous-série Généralités, No. 135b, série Amérique 1952–63, MAE.
64. Roché to Ambafrance La Havane, Jan 31, 1961, sous-série Généralités, No. 134b, série Amérique 1952–63, MAE. See the French ambassador's request for more American discretion about the source of their information: Robert du Gardier to MAE, Nov 13, 1962, sous-série Cuba, No. 36, série Amérique 1952–63, MAE; Robert du Gardier to MAE, Dec 3, 1962, sous-série Généralités, No. 137c, série Amérique 1952–63, MAE.
65. For Rusk's thanks to de Gaulle, Alphand, and Couve de Murville, see respectively "Compte rendu, audience accordée par le Général de Gaulle à M. Dean Rusk," Apr 8, 1963, *DDF 1963*, 1: 377; Alphand to MAE, Sep 7, 1962, sous-série Généralités, No. 135a, série Amérique 1952–63, MAE; "Compte rendu de la conversation de M. Couve de Murville avec M. Rusk," Oct 7, 1962, sous-série Entretiens et Messages, No. 17, série Secrétariat Général, MAE.
66. Robert du Gardier to MAE, Aug 18, 1962, sous-série Généralités, No. 135a, série Amérique 1952–63, MAE.
67. "False," wrote a Foreign Ministry official in the margin of a report of Kennedy's claim. Lebel to MAE, Aug 30, 1962, sous-série Généralités, No. 135a, série Amérique 1952–63, MAE.
68. Alphand to MAE, Oct 26, 1962, sous-série Cuba, No. 36, série Amérique 1952–63, MAE.
69. Contrary to some accounts, after their conversation de Gaulle did then take a look at the photographs, studying them with interest and asking technical questions. Dean Acheson Oral History, interviewed by Lucius D. Battle, Apr 27, 1964, 24–8, JFKL Oral History Program.
70. Bohlen to SecState, Oct 27, 1962, Cuban Missile Crisis Collection CC01557, National Security Archive.
71. Wahl, Introduction to Paxton and Wahl, eds., *De Gaulle and the United States*, 5.
72. Walters to Harriman, Apr 7, 1961, Box 454, De Gaulle, Charles, Harriman Papers, LC.
73. Lyon to DoS, "General de Gaulle," May 17, 1963, Box 3910, POL France 1963, Subject-Numeric Files 1963, RG 59, NARA. The phrase "the theology" on de Gaulle is Bundy aide David Klein's in Klein to Bundy, Nov 27, 1962, Box 71A, CF, PSF, JFKL. Hugh G. Appling of the European desk at State also thought "the General's policies were rather pro-French than anti-American." Appling, "French

Policies," Mar 9, 1964, Box 2168, POL France 1964–66, Subject-Numeric Files 1964–66, RG 59, NARA.

74. Alphand to Couve de Murville, Oct 28, 1962, sous-série Généralités, No. 136b, série Amérique 1952–63, MAE.

75. Alphand, *L'Étonnement d'être*, 402.

76. Raymond Aron, *The Imperial Republic: The United States and the World 1945–1973*, trans. Frank Jellinek (Englewood Cliffs, NJ: Prentice-Hall, Inc., 1974), 85.

77. Couve de Murville, *Une Politique Etrangère*, 480.

78. Alphand, *L'Étonnement d'être*, 412–13.

79. Memcon, "President de Gaulle's Comments on the Death of President Kennedy," Nov 24, 1963, in folder "France – Cables 11/63–3/64," NSF Country Files, France, Box 169, LBJL.

80. De Gaulle to Jacqueline Kennedy, Nov 17, 1964, 5 AG 1/205, AN.

81. Bohlen, "Reflections on Current French Foreign Policy and Attitudes toward the United States and Recommendations," Mar 10, 1964, Box 2168, POL France 1964–66, Subject-Numeric Files 1964–66, RG 59, NARA; Drew Middleton, "Bias against U.S. Rising in France," *New York Times*, Feb 25, 1964, 9; Max Frankel, "Many French Programs Seen in Direct Conflict with U.S. Policy," *New York Times*, Mar 8, 1964, E3; Henry J. Taylor, "There's No Question of De Gaulle Alliance with Soviet, Red China," *Los Angeles Times*, Mar 20, 1964, A5.

82. R. Ovendale, "Britain, the United States, and the Recognition of Communist China," *Historical Journal* 26:1 (1983): 139–58.

83. Devillers, "Le Général de Gaulle et l'Asie," 307. A CIA study acknowledged this in Office of National Estimates, "Indications of French Policy toward the Indochina States," Feb 5, 1964, in folder "France – Cables 11/63–3/64," NSF Country Files, France, Box 169, LBJL.

84. Charles Cogan, "Lost Opportunity or Mission Impossible: De Gaulle's Initiatives in China and Vietnam, 1963–1964," *French Politics & Society* 13:1 (1995): 54–77, quoted at 58.

85. Cogan, "Lost Opportunity," 60.

86. Thomas Alan Schwartz, *Lyndon Johnson and Europe: In the Shadow of Vietnam* (Cambridge, MA: Harvard University Press, 2003), 31.

87. "De Gaulle's Hemispheric 'Invasion,'" *Los Angeles Times*, Mar 16, 1964, A4; Richard Reston, "De Gaulle Latin Trip Exacerbates Feud," *Los Angeles Times*, Mar 15, 1964, L3.

88. Tyler to Rusk, "Whether to Send a Message to de Gaulle before He Leaves for Latin America," Sep 19, 1964, Box 2178, POL France 1964–66, Subject-Numeric Files 1964–66, RG 59, NARA.

89. Boonstra to DoS, Mar 26, 1964, Box 2178, POL France 1964–66, Subject-Numeric Files 1964–66, RG 59, NARA; "studiously free" in Alexander Werth, *De Gaulle: A Political Biography* (NY: Simon and Schuster, 1966), 334; "Entretien entre le Président des États-Unis et le Ministre des Affaires étrangères à Washington," May 25, 1963, *DDF 1963*, 1: 533–43.

90. "Entretien en tête-à-tête entre le Général de Gaulle et le Chancellier Erhard," Feb 15, 1964, sous-série M. Couve de Murville (1958–1967), No. 377, série Cabinet du Ministre, MAE.

91. Paris to SecState, Jul 12, 1965, in folder "Chile Memos," NSF Country File, Box 13, LBJL; Bohlen to DoS, Jul 12, 1965, Box 544, Dominican Republic Crisis 4, Harriman Papers, LC.

92. Alphand to Couve de Murville, Jul 17, 1962, No. CM 7, Couve de Murville Papers; Francis J. Gavin, *Gold, Dollars, and Power: The Politics of International Monetary Relations, 1958–1971* (Chapel Hill: University of North Carolina Press, 2004), 76, 121.

93. Don Cook, "Is U.S. Prepared to Fight Back in Gold War?" *Los Angeles Times*, Dec 17, 1967, K1; Russell Baker, "Lorraine's Cross Gains Fort Knox," *New York Times*, Feb 7, 1965, E10.

94. Max Lerner, "Kissinger Makes Canny Decision," *Los Angeles Times*, May 16, 1969; "Headache for Free World," *Rome (GA) News-Tribune*, Mar 31, 1965, 4.

95. Costigliola, *France and the United States*, 169–70.

96. Kolodziej, *French International Policy*, 562.

97. Helms to Director, CSDB-3/659,794, Mar 10, 1964, CK3100381093, in folder "France – Cables 11/63–3/64," NSF Country Files, France, Box 169, LBJL. The report, from an Italian source, was given high priority and disseminated to more than a dozen high-ranking officials in the White House and intelligence agencies. Bundy to Johnson, Mar 11, 1964, in folder "McGeorge Bundy 11/63–2/64," NSF Memos to the President, Box 1, LBJL.

98. Cited, for example, in Costigliola, *France and the United States*, 139; Geoffrey Perret, *Commander in Chief* (NY: Macmillan, 2008), 214; Adrian W. Schertz, *Die Deutschlandpolitik Kennedys und Johnsons* (Vienna: Böhlau, 1992), 312.

99. Compte-rendu de la réunion tenue entre le Général de Gaulle et le Président Segni, Feb 20, 1964, sous-série M. Couve de Murville (1958–1967), No. 377, série Cabinet du Ministre, MAE. The word *hegemony* also appears in Lucet circular telegram, Feb 22, 1964, sous-série Italie 1944–70, No. 393, série Europe, MAE.

100. Peter Ives, *Language and Hegemony in Gramsci* (London: Pluto Press, 2004); *American Heritage Dictionary of the English Language*, 4th ed. (NY: Houghton Mifflin, 2000), 813. Mead notes that U.S. military and economic power "sustain U.S. hegemony and make something as artificial and historically arbitrary as the U.S.-led global system appear desirable, inevitable, and permanent." Walter Russell Mead, "America's Sticky Power," *Foreign Policy* 141 (March/April 2004), 48.

101. Reinhold Niebuhr, "The Two Imperial Nations in an Anti-imperialistic Age," n.d. [1961], "American Hegemony and the Prospects for Peace," n.d. [1962], Book Chapters, and "General de Gaulle and France," n.d. Box 15, Article and Book File, Niebuhr Papers, Manuscripts Division, Library of Congress, Washington, DC (hereafter LC), the last of these published as "New Voice in the West," *New Leader* 42:42 (Dec 7, 1959): 12.

102. Aron, *The Imperial Republic*, 59; Ball to Moyers, May 22, 1966, in folder "France – Memos 1/66–9/66," NSF Country Files, France, Box 172, LBJL. The Greek word *hgemon* translates as "leader," from *hgeisthai*, to lead.

103. Cotteret and Moreau, *Recherches sur le vocabulaire*, 77, 87.

104. Alain Peyrefitte, *C'était de Gaulle* (Paris: Fayard, 1997), 2: 33, 35.

105. De Gaulle to Couve de Murville, Nov 24, 1960, No. CM 7, Couve de Murville Papers. Malraux made this toast at a dinner at the White House: "There has been an Assyrian Empire, a Byzantine Empire, a Roman Empire. There is no American empire." "Discours de Monsieur Malraux," May 11, 1962, Box 71, CF, PSF, JFKL.

106. Lyon to DoS, "General de Gaulle," May 17, 1963, Box 3910, POL France 1963, Subject-Numeric Files 1963, RG 59, NARA.

107. Compte-rendu, Feb 20, 1964, op. cit.

108. "Bundy-Ball Telcon," Dec 31, 1962, Box 4, France, Ball Papers, JFKL.

109. Devillers, "Le Général de Gaulle et l'Asie," 314.

110. Costigliola, *France and the United States*, 145.

111. Transcript of NBC Today Show interview from April 12, 1967 in Béliard to Couve de Murville, Apr 12, 1967, sous-série États-Unis 1964–70, No. 582, série Amérique, MAE.

112. De Gaulle, *Mémoires d'Espoir*, 214.

113. Nicholas Wahl, "Introduction," James Chace and Elizabeth Malkin, "The American Media and De Gaulle," and Robert O. Paxton, "Comments," in Paxton and Wahl, *De Gaulle and the United States*, 2, 361, 418; "Wine and Dine American: Protest against de Gaulle," *St. Petersburg Times*, Dec 12, 1967, 18.

114. Christopher Endy, *Cold War Holidays: American Tourism in France* (Chapel Hill: University of North Carolina Press, 2004), 161, 179.

115. "Withdraw Dead from France Too?" *Associated Press*, Sep 16, 1966; see also "U.S. War Dead in France," *Chicago Tribune*, Apr 21, 1966, 24.

116. For example, Bovey to SecState, "Comments of Foreign Office Official on US Position vis-a-vis de Gaulle," Feb 19, 1963, Box 3911, POL France 1963, Subject-Numeric Files 1963, RG 59, NARA; GerEmbWashington to AA, "Personalveränderungen in der französischen Botschaft Washington," Jan 7, 1963, Box 480, Sig. B 24 FRA, Politisches Archiv des Auswärtigen Amtes, Berlin (hereafter PAAA).

117. Bohlen to SecState, Dec 13, 1963, Box 3909, POL France 1963, Subject-Numeric Files 1963, RG 59, NARA.

118. Marianna P. Sullivan, *France's Vietnam Policy: A Study in French-American Relations* (Westport, CT: Greenwood Press, 1978), xiii, 27. Lawrence S. Kaplan similarly called de Gaulle's campaign for a peaceful settlement in Indochina "retribution for America's ouster of France ten years before." See his "The Vietnam War and Europe: The View from NATO," in *La Guerre du Vietnam et l'Europe 1963–1973*, ed. Christopher Goscha and Maurice Vaïsse (Brussels: Emile Bruylant, 2003), 89–102.

119. Fredrik Logevall, *Choosing War: The Lost Chance for Peace and the Escalation of War in Vietnam* (Berkeley and Los Angeles: University of California Press, 1999), is one of the few American studies of the Vietnam War to integrate European sources. It is excellent on the year *after* de Gaulle's August 1963 neutralization proposal. Anne Sa'adah's fine analysis of de Gaulle's published statements does not delve into the archival record: "Idées Simples and Idées Fixes: De Gaulle, the United States, and Vietnam," in Paxton and Wahl, *De Gaulle and the United States*, 295–316.

120. "Declaration sur le Vietnam faite par le Général de Gaulle au Conseil des Ministres du 29 août 1963," Aug 30, 1963, sous-série Sud-Vietnam, No. 91, série Asie-Océanie, MAE.

121. Memcon, "Europe and the Problem of France," Oct 4, 1963, *Foreign Relations of the United States* (hereafter FRUS) 1961–1963 (Washington, DC: United States Government Printing Office), 13: 219–23; Alphand, *L'Étonnement d'être*, 408; Waverley Root, "Paris Denies Anti-U.S. Viet View," *Washington Post*, Sep 6, 1963, A14; "Dr. De Gaulle's Old Remedy," *Los Angeles Times*, Sep 1, 1963, G6.

122. Tad Szulc, "Paris Premature on Vietnam Unity . . . U.S.-French Rift Widens: Anti-U.S. Effort Seen," *New York Times*, Aug 31, 1963, 1; Don Shannon, "Paris Tries

to Soften Slap at U.S. Viet Policy," *Los Angeles Times*, Aug 31, 1963, 5; "No Excuses for Gen. de Gaulle," *Los Angeles Times*, Sep 3, 1963, B4.
123. James Reston, "How to Make Things Worse than They Really Are," *New York Times*, Sep 4, 1963, 38.
124. De Gaulle, *Mémoires d'Espoir*, 269.
125. "Entretien entre le Général de Gaulle et le Président Kennedy," May 31, 1961, 5 AG 1/200, Archives Nationales, Paris (hereafter AN).
126. Philippe Devillers, editor-in-chief of *France-Asie* from 1965 to 1970, reported on this interview with de Gaulle's interpreter Roger Vaurs in Devillers, "Le Général de Gaulle et l'Asie," 304.
127. *FRUS 1961–63* 14: 148, 161n.
128. "Entretien entre le Général de Gaulle et l'Ambassadeur des États-Unis d'Amérique," May 1961, 5 AG 1/201, AN.
129. Chauvel to MAE, Nov 14, 1961, sous-série Sud-Vietnam, No. 79, série Asie-Océanie, MAE.
130. Lalouette to MAE, Oct 27, 1961, sous-série Sud-Vietnam, No. 76, série Asie-Océanie, MAE.
131. Alphand to Couve de Murville, Nov 13, 1961, *DDF 1961*, 2: 584–6; L.D. Brown, Memcon, Nov 13, 1961, *FRUS 1961–1963*, I: Doc. 241.
132. Bundy, Meeting in the Cabinet Room, May 11, 1962, CF, PSF, JFKL.
133. Ibid.; Bohlen to Bundy, May 14, 1962, Box 71, CF, PSF, JFKL.
134. "Entretien entre le Président des États-Unis et le Ministre des Affaires étrangères à Washington," May 25, 1963, *DDF 1963*, 1: 533–43.
135. Knappstein to AA, Mar 6, 1964, Band 64, B 37 Süd- und Ostasien, PAAA.
136. Anschuetz to SecState, "Factors Underlying French Thinking on Viet Nam," Oct 5, 1963, Box 3910, POL France 1963, Subject-Numeric Files 1963, RG 59, NARA.
137. L.M. Mustin, "Memorandum for the Chairman," Nov 10, 1964, in Mike Gravel, ed., *The Pentagon Papers: The Defense Department History of Decision Making in Vietnam* (Boston: Beacon Hill Press, 1971), 3: 621–28.
138. On April 7, 1965, de Gaulle told Peyrefitte that if the Americans did not withdraw soon, the war would last ten years. It ended on April 30, 1975. Peyrefitte, *C'était de Gaulle*, 2: 507.
139. Bundy to JFK, Sep 1, 1963, CF, PSF, JFKL.
140. Klaiber to AA, Feb 29, 1964, Band 64, B 37 Süd- und Ostasien, PAAA.
141. Walter Lippmann, "De Gaulle May Be Right about Making Viet-Nam Neutral Nation," *Los Angeles Times*, Sep 4, 1963, B5.
142. "La France prête à organiser avec le Vietnam une cordiale coopération," *Le Figaro*, Aug 30, 1963.
143. Ramsbotham to Warner, Sep 12, 1963, FO 371/170107, NA-K.
144. Everard minute, Sep 12, 1963, FO 371/170107, NA-K.
145. Couve de Murville, *Une Politique Etrangère*, 158.
146. Bernard B. Fall, *Anatomy of a Crisis* (NY: Doubleday, 1969), 147.
147. Bernard B. Fall, "What de Gaulle Actually Said about Vietnam," *Reporter* 29 (1963): 39–41.
148. Bernard B. Fall, *The Two Viet-Nams*, 2nd revised ed. (NY: Praeger, 1967 [1963]), 400, 401.
149. "Text of Eisenhower Broadcast on the Mideast Crisis," *New York Times*, Nov 1, 1956, 14.

150. William Stivers, "Eisenhower and the Middle East," in Richard A. Melanson and David Mayers, *Reevaluating Eisenhower: American Foreign Policy in the 1950s* (Champaign: University of Illinois Press, 1987), 192–219.

151. Alphand, *L'Étonnement d'être*, 410.

152. Direction Asie-Océanie, "Politique américaine au Vietnam," Feb 10, 1962, sous-série Sud-Vietnam, No. 77, série Asie-Océanie, MAE.

153. Direction Asie-Océanie, "Aspects politiques d'une intervention armée américaine au Sud-Vietnam," Nov 6, 1961, sous-série Sud-Vietnam, No. 14, série Asie-Océanie, MAE.

154. Manac'h to Fourier-Ruelle, Apr 19, 1960, *DDF 1960*, 1: 462.

155. Flott to Harriman, "Impressions of Manac'h," Nov 25, 1966, Box 554, Manila Summit Conference 10, Harriman Papers, LC.

156. John Gunther Dean oral history, interviewed by Charles Stuart Kennedy, Sep 6, 2000, Jimmy Carter Library.

157. For example, Manac'h, "Réflexions sur le problème d'Indochine vu dans son ensemble," Sep 17, 1963, sous-série Sud-Vietnam, No. 18, série Asie-Océanie, MAE; Manac'h, "La crise au Vietnam (perspectives)," Nov 4, 1963, sous-série Sud-Vietnam, No. 17, série Asie-Océanie, MAE.

158. Anschuetz to DoS, Oct 10, 1962, Box 56, "V" 1962, Paris Embassy: Classified General Records, RG 84, NA; Lalouette to Couve de Murville, Jan 9, 1962, *DDF 1962*, 1: 8–9.

159. Boizet to Couve de Murville, Aug 18, 1961, sous-série Sud-Vietnam, No. 13, série Asie-Océanie, MAE; Direction Asie-Océanie, "Perspectives vietnamiennes," Dec 11, 1961, sous-série Sud-Vietnam, No. 12, série Asie-Océanie, MAE

160. On excellent French contacts among Vietnamese exiles see "Note pour Paul," Sep 4, 1963, Box 199, CF, PSF, JFKL; "Commentaires recueillis dans les milieux vietnamiens de la capitale," Feb 26, 1964, sous-série Sud-Vietnam, No. 79, série Asie-Océanie, MAE; Cabinet du Ministre, Aug 21, 1963, and "Position de M. Tran Van Huu, ancien Chef du Gouvernement du Vietnam," Nov 20, 1963, sous-série Sud-Vietnam, No. 18, série Asie-Océanie, MAE; G. de la Grandière, "Transcription de la conversation avec Mr. Le-Quang," Sep 1963, 5 AG 1/241, AN.

161. Fall, *The Two Vietnams*, 402, naming especially Max Clos, Georges Chaffard, and Jean Lartéguy.

162. Fall's widow obtained his FBI file two decades after his death. Dorothy Fall, *Bernard Fall: Memories of a Soldier-Scholar* (Dulles, VA: Potomac Books, 2006), 190–203.

163. Chalmers M. Roberts, "1954 Heralded Today in Vietnam," *Washington Post*, Jan 31, 1967, A16.

164. Laurence Stern, "Two Worlds and their Terrible Collision," *Washington Post*, Aug 6, 1972, BW1.

165. Christopher E. Goscha, "'Sorry about that . . .' Bernard Fall, the Vietnam War and the Impact of a French Intellectual in the U.S.," in Goscha and Vaïsse, *La Guerre*, 363–82; Steve Coll, "The General's Dilemma: David Petraeus, the Pressures of Politics, and the Road Out of Iraq," *The New Yorker*, Sep 8, 2008; Matt Bai, "The McCain Doctrines," *New York Times Magazine*, May 18, 2008, 40; Bernard B. Fall, *Street without Joy: Indochina at War, 1946–54* (Harrisburg, PA: Stackpole Books, 1961).

166. Colin Powell with Joseph E. Persico, *My American Journey* (NY: Random House, 1996), 143.
167. See Bernard Fall letter in Maillard papers, Mar 20, 1963, 5 AG 1/241, AN.
168. Chambon to Couve de Murville, Mar 29, 1961, *DDF 1961*, 1: 408; De la Bossière to Couve de Murville, Jun 3, 1961, *DDF 1961*, 1: 710–11; G. de la Grandière, "Transcription de la conversation avec Mr. Le-Quang," Sep 1963, 5 AG 1/241, AN. See also Pierre Journoud, "Le Quai d'Orsay et le processus de paix, 1963–1973," in Goscha and Vaïsse, *La Guerre*, 385–400.
169. Gassouin to MAE, Oct 16, 1957, and Millet to Gassouin, Oct 22, 1957, sous-série Etats-Unis 1952–1963, No. 416, série Amérique, MAE; "Compte rendu, entretien entre M. Rusk et M. Couve de Murville," Apr 7, 1963, *DDF 1963*, 1: 361–74.
170. Lalouette, "Le problème vietnamien – Premières perspectives d'une solution politique?," Jun 21, 1963, sous-série Sud-Vietnam, No. 16, série Asie-Océanie, MAE; G. de la Grandière, "Transcription de la conversation avec Mr. Le-Quang," Sep 1963, 5 AG 1/241, AN.
171. Some of the key documents appear in the files of Pierre Maillard, de Gaulle's diplomatic counselor, and are marked "vues par le Général." 5 AG 1/241, AN.
172. Jean Brèthes, "Perspectives actuelles de la guerre du Vietnam," Mar 26, 1963, *DDF 1963*, 1: 310–13; Lalouette, "Le problème vietnamien – Premières perspectives d'une solution politique?," Jun 21, 1963, sous-série Sud-Vietnam, No. 16, série Asie-Océanie, MAE.
173. Stewart to FO, Jun 9, 1961, FO 371/160157, NA-K.
174. Stewart to FO, Jun 9, 1961, FO 371/160157, NA-K.
175. Gordon Etherington-Smith to McGhie, Jul 3, 1961, FO 371/160157, NA-K.
176. McGhie minute, Jul 14, 1961, FO 371/160157, NA-K.
177. Chauvel to MAE, Oct 25, 1961 and Nov 14, 1961, sous-série Sud-Vietnam, No. 79, série Asie-Océanie, MAE, and Manac'h to Ambafrance Washington, Nov 12, 1961, sous-série Sud-Vietnam, No. 76, série Asie-Océanie, MAE.
178. Blackwell to Murray, May 24, 1963, FO 371/170103, NA-K.
179. Blackwell to Cable, Feb 25, 1964, FO 371/175495, NA-K.
180. FO to Washington, Feb 28, 1964, FO 371/175494, NA-K, emphasis added; FO to Washington, Feb 28, 1964, FO 371/175494, NA-K; Cable to Etherington-Smith, Mar 10, 1964, FO 371/175494, NA-K.
181. FO, "Record of Discussions with Mr. Bundy," May 29, 1964, PREM 11/4759, NA-K.
182. Thompson to Peck, Aug 13, 1964, FO 371/175501, NA-K. A Foreign Office official noted on the message that Thompson's views were "significantly in line with the last [Joint Intelligence Committee] paper."
183. Foreign Secretary, "British Policy towards South-East Asia," Nov 19, 1964, CAB 148/17/10, NA-K.
184. Peck to Stewart, Nov 27, 1964, FO 371/175503, NA-K.
185. J.E. Cable to Forster, Oct 6, 1964, FO 371/175503/DV103145/199G, NA-K.
186. J.E. Cable, "Vietnam," Dec 29, 1964, FO 371/175503, NA-K.
187. Detailed in Peck to Wright, Feb 19, 1965, and accompanying documents in PREM 13/692, NA-K.
188. "Record of a Telephone Conversation between the Prime Minister and President Johnson," Feb 11, 1965, PREM 13/692, NA-K.
189. Jansen to Staatssekretär, Mar 12, 1963, Band 60, B 37 Süd- und Ostasien, PAAA.

190. Wendland to AA, Jan 17, 1964, Band 64, B 37 Süd- und Ostasien, PAAA.

191. Wendland to AA, "Erneuter Staatsstreich in Südvietnam," Feb 17, 1964, Band 60, B 37 Süd- und Ostasien, PAAA.

192. "Bundeskanzler Erhard an Präsident Johnson," May 8, 1964, *AAPD 1964*, I: 514–18; Alexander Troche, *"Berlin wird am Mekong verteidigt": Die Ostasienpolitik der Bundesrepublik in China, Taiwan und Süd-Vietnam 1954–1966* (Düsseldorf: Droste Verlag, 2001), 291–99.

193. "Gespräch des Bundesministers Schröder mit dem französischen Außenminister Couve de Murville," Jun 8, 1964, *AAPD 1964*, I: 615–25.

194. Carstens memorandum, Jul 27, 1964, Doc. 210, *AAPD 1964* (Munich: R. Oldenbourg Verlag, 1995), II: 893. *Staatssekretär* corresponds to Undersecretary of State; there can be more than one at a time.

195. Jansen to Lahr, "Besuch des US-Sonderbotschafters H. Cabot Lodge," Aug 20, 1964, Band 65, B 37 Süd- und Ostasien, PAAA; Jansen to Lahr, "Die Haltung der Bundesregierung zur Südvietnam-Frage," Aug 24, 1964, Band 62, B 37 Süd- und Ostasien, PAAA.

196. Bassler memorandum, Aug 25, 1964, Band 225, B 32 USA, PAAA.

197. "Protokoll der Süd- und Ostasien-Konferenz," Feb 4, 1965, Band 6766, AV Neues Amt, PAAA. See also Troche, *"Berlin wird am Mekong verteidigt,"* 327–32.

198. See the minutes of the SPD's parliamentary faction on Jan 18, 1966 in Heinrich Potthoff, ed., *Die SPD-Fraktion im Deutschen Bundestag. Sitzungsprotokolle 1961–1966*, vol. 2 (Duesseldorf: Droste Verlag, 1993), 781–83; Hans-Jürgen Grabbe, *Unionsparteien, Sozialdemokratie und Vereinigte Staaten von Amerika 1945–1966* (Düsseldorf: Droste Verlag, 1983), 556–59; Troche, *"Berlin wird am Mekong verteidigt,"* 308, 350, 353–55.

199. "Chronologie des principales interventions françaises à propos du Vietnam," Apr 6, 1965, sous-série Conflit Vietnam, No. 162, série Asie-Océanie, MAE.

200. Pierre Maillard, "La position de la France au sujet de la neutralité du Viet Nam," Apr 1, 1964, 5 AG 1/201, AN.

201. Mansfield to Johnson, "The Vietnamese Situation," Feb 1, 1964, in folder "McGeorge Bundy 11/63–2/64," NSF Memos to the President, Box 1, LBJL. See also Logevall, *Choosing War*, 26–30, 83–4.

202. "Compte rendu de l'entretien entre le général de Gaulle et l'Ambassadeur des États-Unis," Apr 2, 1964, *DDF 1964*, 1: 346.

203. "Compte rendu de l'entretien du général de Gaulle et de M. Thant, secrétaire général de l'ONU," Jul 21, 1964, *DDF 1964*, 2: 80–84; "Le concept de la neutralité et les Etats de l'ancienne Indochine," Sep 17, 1963, sous-série Sud-Vietnam, No. 18, série Asie-Océanie, MAE; Devillers, "Le Général de Gaulle et l'Asie," 309; Fall, *Anatomy of a Crisis*, 210–14.

204. "Compte rendu de l'entretien de M. Couve de Murville avec l'Ambassadeur de Chine," Jul 21, 1964, *DDF 1964*, 2: 85–6.

205. "Compte rendu de l'entretien de M. Joxe avec M. Cabot Lodge," Aug 17, 1964, *DDF 1964*, 2: 164–72.

206. FO, "Record of Conversation," Jun 8, 1964, PREM 11/4759, NA-K.

207. Ball told columnist Mary McGrory that his years advising the French government affected his view of Indochina. Ball-McGrory Telcon, May 27, 1966, and Jun 3, 1966, Papers of George Ball, Box 5, folder "Misc.," LBJL. See also George W. Ball, *The Past Has Another Pattern: Memoirs* (NY: Norton, 1982), 94, 101–2,

153; James A. Bill, *George Ball: Behind the Scenes in U.S. Foreign Policy* (New Haven, CT: Yale University Press, 1997), 2, 42.

208. Ronald Steel, "Walter Lippmann and Charles de Gaulle," in Paxton and Wahl, *De Gaulle and the United States*, 387.
209. Walter Lippmann, "Today and Tomorrow," *Hartford Courant*, Jan 31, 1963, 10.
210. Cotteret and Moreau, *Recherches sur le vocabulaire*, 119.
211. "Le texte intégral du discours de Pnom Penh," *Le Figaro*, Sep 2, 1966, 5.
212. Fielding to Brown, "President de Gaulle in Phnom Penh," Sep 16, 1966, PREM 13/916, NA-K.
213. "Response to de Gaulle," *New York Times*, Sep 3, 1966, 17.
214. Quoted in "Opinion at Home and Abroad," *New York Times*, Sep 4, 1966, 145.
215. William S. White, "Low Blow: De Gaulle Aids U.S. Foes," *Washington Post*, Sep 3, 1966, A13.
216. Lodge to SecState, Sep 2, 1966, Box 2174, POL France 1964–66, Subject-Numeric Files 1964–66, RG 59, NARA. Yuko Torikata's fine "Reexamining de Gaulle's Peace Initiative on the Vietnam War," showing de Gaulle acted rationally, nonetheless calls the speech "the climax of his anti-Americanism." *Diplomatic History* 31:2 (2007): 909–38.
217. Fall, *The Two Vietnams*, 403, 411.
218. Harriman to DoS, Dec 4, 1966, Box 554, Manila Summit Conference 10, Harriman Papers, LC.
219. William Conrad Gibbons, *The U.S. Government and the Vietnam War: Executive and Legislative Roles and Relationships*, vol. 4 (Princeton, NJ: Princeton University Press, 1995), 391.
220. Kissinger memcon, Sep 9, 1966, Box 554, Manila Summit Conference 10, Harriman Papers, LC.
221. "Entretien entre le Général de Gaulle et le Senateur Robert Kennedy," Jan 31, 1967, 5 AG 1/202, AN.
222. "Entretien entre le Général de Gaulle et Monsieur Averell Harriman," May 21, 1968, 5 AG 1/202, AN.
223. John Gunther Dean oral history; Vu Son Thuy, "The French Role in Finding a Peaceful Solution to the Vietnam War," in Goscha and Vaïsse, *La Guerre*, 415–28.
224. Devillers, "Le Général de Gaulle et l'Asie," 317.
225. Sullivan, *France's Vietnam Policy*, 123; Vu, "The French Role," 418; "Witness: Jean Lacouture," in Paxton and Wahl, *De Gaulle and the United States*, 324–25.
226. Dean Rusk Oral History, interviewed by Paige E. Mulhollan, Jul 28, 1969, LBJL.
227. Kissinger, "Dealing with De Gaulle," 339.
228. Richard Kuisel, "Was de Gaulle Anti-American?" *Tocqueville Review* 13:1 (1992).
229. Robert S. McNamara, James Blight, Robert Brigham, Thomas Biersteker and Herbert Schandler, eds., *Argument without End: In Search of Answers to the Vietnam Tragedy* (NY: Public Affairs, 1999), 150, 102.

Chapter 6. Anti-Americanism in the Age of Protest

1. Michael Groth, "Die Regression des politischen Denkens und Stobbes Position," *Frankfurter Allgemeine Zeitung*, Oct 30, 1984, 5.
2. "Humphrey Escapes Hail of Eggs in Belgium; Heads Back to U.S.," *Los Angeles Times*, Apr 10, 1967, 1.

3. "Hubert Defends U.S. Viet Policy in Europe Talk," *Chicago Tribune*, Mar 28, 1967, 2.

4. "Conversazione Nenni-Humphrey," Mar 31, 1967, Visita de H. Hubert Humphrey in Italia, Sig. Busta 114, Fasc. 2384, Serie Governo, Pietro Nenni Papers, ACS; Bernard Noel, "Manifestation d'hostilité en Italie sur le passage de M. Humphrey," *Le Monde*, Apr 2, 1967; "Manifestation anti-Américaine à Rome," *AFP*, Mar 31, 1967; Nenni diary entry of Mar 31, 1967 quoted in Leopoldo Nuti, "The Center-Left Government in Italy and the Escalation of the Vietnam War," in *America, the Vietnam War, and the World: Comparative and International Perspectives*, ed. Andreas W. Daum, Lloyd C. Gardner and Wilfried Mausbach (NY: Cambridge University Press, 2003), 259–78.

5. "Entretien entre le Général de Gaulle et le Vice-Président Hubert Humphrey," Apr 7, 1967, 5 AG 1/202, AN.

6. "Summary of anti-American acts committed during Vice President Humphrey's visit," n.d. [April 1967], sous-série États-Unis 1964–70, No. 582, série Amérique, Ministère des Affaires Etrangères, Paris (hereafter MAE).

7. Rowland Evans and Robert Novak, "The Policies of De Gaulle: An Anti-American in Paris," *St. Petersburg Times*, May 1, 1967, 14A.

8. Marianna P. Sullivan, *France's Vietnam Policy: A Study in French-American Relations* (Westport, CT: Greenwood Press, 1978), 95.

9. Jurgensen to Secretaire Général, "Manifestations lors de la visite du Vice-Président Humphrey," Apr 10, 1967, sous-série États-Unis 1964–70, No. 582, série Amérique, MAE.

10. Humphrey to Johnson, Apr 8, 1967, in folder "Vice President – Visit to Europe," NSF International Meetings and Travel File, Box 26, LBJL.

11. "Circonstances de l'interpellation de deux journalistes anglais," Apr 7, 1967, sous-série États-Unis 1964–70, No. 582, série Amérique, MAE.

12. "Militaires américains et porteurs de drapeaux molestés Avenue Pierre Ier-de-Serbie," Apr 7, 1967, sous-série États-Unis 1964–70, No. 582, série Amérique, MAE.

13. "Incendie d'un drapeau américain Avenue George V," Apr 7, 1967, sous-série États-Unis 1964–70, No. 582, série Amérique, MAE.

14. Debré to Couve de Murville, Feb 15, 1968, sous-série M. Couve de Murville (1958–1967), No. 160, série Cabinet du Ministre, MAE.

15. Hall to de Gaulle, Apr 8, 1967, sous-série États-Unis 1964–70, No. 582, série Amérique, MAE; "Riot in Paris over Hubert," *Chicago Tribune*, Apr 8, 1967, 1.

16. John Sullivan, "French Flag Burner Explains Hub Action," *Boston Record American*, Apr 13, 1967, 3.

17. Mandereau to Lucet, Apr 20, 1967, sous-série États-Unis 1964–70, No. 582, série Amérique, MAE.

18. "The Flag-Burning Incident in Paris," *Los Angeles Times*, Apr 11, 1967, A4.

19. Béliard to MAE, Apr 11, 1967, sous-série États-Unis 1964–70, No. 582, série Amérique, MAE.

20. Béliard to MAE, Apr 11, 1967, sous-série États-Unis 1964–70, No. 582, série Amérique, MAE.

21. John W. Finney, "Berliners Applaud Humphrey Speech on War in Vietnam," *New York Times*, Apr 7, 1967, 1.

22. Siegward Lönnendonker and Tilman Fichter, eds., *Freie Universität Berlin 1948–1973: Hochschule im Umbruch* (Berlin: Pressestelle der FU Berlin, 1975), IV: 151–52; 429–30.
23. "Offener Brief an den Regierenden Bürgermeister von Berlin," [April 1967], Doc. 662, *Freie Universität Berlin*, IV: 407.
24. Reinhard Lettau, "Von der Servilität der Presse," *Berlin EXTRA-Dienst* 4:31 (May 31, 1967), 6, in *Freie Universität Berlin*, IV: 413–14.
25. Joseph W. Grigg, "Le séjour à Londres du Vice-Président Humphrey," *UPI*, Apr 3, 1967.
26. Humphrey to Johnson, Apr 10, 1967, in folder "Vice President – Visit to Europe," NSF International Meetings and Travel File, Box 26, LBJL.
27. White House Situation Room to Walt Rostow, Apr 1, 1967, in folder "Vice President – Visit to Europe," NSF International Meetings and Travel File, Box 26, LBJL; Humphrey to Johnson, "Meeting with Prime Minister Wilson, Chequers, Sunday, April 2, 1967," Apr 4, 1967, DDRS; memcon of Humphrey-Brown meeting, Apr 20, 1967, DDRS.
28. Brel may have been channeling John Donne's tribute "To His Mistress Going to Bed": "O, my America, my Newfoundland!" E.K. Chambers, ed., *Poems of John Donne*, vol. 1 (London: Lawrence & Bullen, 1896), 149.
29. Alessandro Portelli calls the song "a declaration of surrender" to soft rock in "The Centre Cannot Hold: Music as Political Communication in Post-War Italy," in Luciano Cheles and Lucio Sponza, eds., *The Art of Persuasion: Political Communication in Italy from 1945 to the 1990s* (Manchester: Manchester University Press, 2001), 258–77.
30. Kristina Schulz, "Studentische Bewegungen und Protestkampagnen," in Roland Roth and Dieter Riucht, eds., *Die sozialen Bewegungen in Deutschland seit 1945* (Campus Verlag, 2008), 418–46.
31. Wolfgang Kraushaar, "Die Wiederkehr der Traumata im Versuch sie zu bearbeiten," in *Exilforschung. Ein Internationales Jahrbuch. Band 9, Exil und Remigration*, ed. Claus-Dieter Krohn et al. (Munich: Text & Kritik, 1991), 46–67.
32. Bernd Greiner, "Saigon, Nuremberg, and the West: German Images of America in the Late 1960s," in *Americanization and Anti-Americanism: the German Encounter with American Culture after 1945*, ed. Alexander Stephan Frankfurt: (NY: Berghahn Books, 2005), 51–62.
33. Wilfried Mausbach, "Auschwitz and Vietnam: West German Protest Against America's War During the 1960s," in *America, the Vietnam War, and the World: Comparative and International Perspectives*, ed. Andreas W. Daum, Lloyd C. Gardner and Wilfried Mausbach (NY: Cambridge University Press, 2003), 279–98, quoted at 279.
34. Dan Diner, *America in the Eyes of the Germans: An Essay on Anti-Americanism* (Princeton, NJ: Markus Wiener Publishers, 2006 [2003]), 128–37.
35. Günther Anders, *Visit Beautiful Vietnam. ABC der Aggressionen heute* (Cologne: Pahl-Rugenstein, 1968), 27; "Atrocities and Policies: A Key Difference," *Wall Street Journal*, Dec 3, 1969.
36. Mausbach, "Auschwitz and Vietnam," 288.
37. Christian Schwaabe, *Antiamerikanismus: Wandlungen eines Feindbildes* (Munich: Wilhelm Fink Verlag, 2003), 110.

38. I thank Jochen Kreuser for this story from his boyhood, recounted to the author in Göttingen in June 2005.
39. Arnulf Baring, *Unser neuer Grössenwahn: Deutschland zwischen Ost und West* (Munich: Deutsche Verlags-Anstalt, 1988), 122.
40. Erich Fried, *und Vietnam und* (Berlin: Verlag Klaus Wagenbach, 1966), 13.
41. Fried, *und Vietnam und*, 57.
42. Drew Pearson, "Saigon Premier: He Likes Hitler, Purple, Poems," *Washington Post*, Aug 12, 1965.
43. For example Erich Fried, "Intimus," BBC radio transcript: German Soviet Zone Programme, Nov 7, 1960, in Ursula Seeber et al., eds., *"All right, what's left": Historische und aktuelle kritische Positionen im Andenken an Erich Fried* (Vienna: Zirkular, 2001), 23–5.
44. Erich Fried, *100 Gedichte ohne Vaterland* (Berlin: Wagenbachs Taschenbücherei, 1978), 123.
45. "Meeting with the National Security Council on NATO," Jan 31, 1963, Presidential Recordings, Tape 70, POF, JFKL.
46. Dietrich Orlow, "Ambivalence and Attraction: The German Social Democrats and the United States, 1945–1974," in Reiner Pommerin, ed., *The American Impact on Postwar Germany* (NY: Berghahn Books, 1997), 35–82.
47. Ute Poiger, *Jazz, Rock, and Rebels: Cold War Politics and American Culture in a Divided Germany* (Berkeley and Los Angeles: University of California Press, 2000), 31–70; Christoph Hendrik Müller, *West Germans against the West* (NY: Palgrave Macmillan, 2010), 120–78; Kaspar Maase, *BRAVO Amerika: Erkundungen zur Jugendkultur der Bundesrepublik in den fünfziger Jahren* (Hamburg: Junius, 1992), 141–50 and *passim*; Jost Hermand, "Resisting Boogie-Woogie Culture, Abstract Expressionism, and Pop Art: German Highbrow Objections to the Import of 'American' Forms of Culture, 1945–1965," in Stephan, ed., *Americanization and Anti-Americanism*, 67–77.
48. Müller, *West Germans against the West*, 181.
49. "Protokoll der Süd- und Ostasien-Konferenz," Feb 4, 1965, Band 6766, AV Neues Amt, PAAA; Auswärtiges Amt, *Biographisches Handbuch des deutschen Auswärtigen Dienstes 1871–1945* (Paderborn: Schöningh, 2000).
50. Peter Jahn, "Befreier und halbasiatische Horden," in Deutsch-Russisches Museum Berlin-Karlshorst, ed., *Unsere Russen – Unsere Deutschen. Bilder vom Anderen 1800 bis 2000* (Berlin: Links Verlag, 2007), 14–29.
51. Interview with the author, Elmau, Germany, Jun 27, 2011.
52. I thank dramaturge Marion Hirte for telling me this story in Berlin in August 2005, and Habermas for confirming that he was present and that "I might well have said something then; in any case, that would have been *ganz in meinem Sinne*" (wholly in accordance with my beliefs). Interview with the author, Elmau, Germany, Jun 28, 2011.
53. Schwaabe, *Antiamerikanismus*, 126.
54. I borrow this comparison from President Kennedy's remark that sending American troops to Vietnam was "like taking a drink. The effect wears off, and you have to take another." Arthur M. Schlesinger, *A Thousand Days: John F. Kennedy in the White House* (NY: Houghton Mifflin, 1965), 547.
55. Helmut Gollwitzer, "Warum ich protestiere," *FU-Spiegel* 54 (Dec 1966): 19, in *Freie Universität Berlin 1948–1973*, IV: 267–68, doc. 602.

56. Quoted in A.J. Langguth, *Our Vietnam: The War, 1954–1975* (NY: Simon and Schuster, 2000), 446.

57. Ball to Moyers, May 22, 1966, in folder "France – Memos 1/66–9/66," NSF Country Files, France, Box 172, LBJL; Raymond Aron, *The Imperial Republic: The United States and the World* (Englewood Cliffs, NJ: Prentice-Hall, 1974), 99–103, 117.

58. Paul Hollander, *Anti-Americanism: Critiques at Home and Abroad, 1965–1990* (NY: Oxford University Press, 1992), 217.

59. Max Horkheimer, *Gesammelte Schriften* (Frankfurt: S. Fischer, 1988), 7: 646–47.

60. Marcuse, *One-Dimensional Man: Studies in the Ideology of Advanced Industrial Society* (Boston: Beacon Press, 1964), 9; see also Jeremi Suri, "The Rise and Fall of an International Counterculture, 1960-1975," *American Historical Review* 114:1 (February 2009): 45–68.

61. Interview with the author, Elmau, Germany, Jun 27, 2011.

62. Horkheimer, *Gesammelte Schriften*, 8: 86, 14: 63.

63. Horkheimer, *Gesammelte Schriften* 14: 474, 364.

64. Horkheimer, *Gesammelte Schriften* 6: 332.

65. Horkheimer, *Gesammelte Schriften* 14: 288.

66. *Dialektik der Aufklärung* (Frankfurt am Main: S. Fischer, 1969); see Martin Jay, *The Dialectical Imagination: A History of the Frankfurt School and the Institute of Social Research, 1923–1950* (Boston: Little, Brown, 1973).

67. Horkheimer, *Gesammelte Schriften* 7: 473.

68. Hans Magnus Enzensberger, unpublished interview with Jennifer Ruth Hosek, Aug 14, 2006, Munich, courtesy of Hosek.

69. For another argument that rising American influence produced more criticism of America's flaws, see Philipp Gassert, "The Anti-American as Americanizer: Revisiting the Anti-American Century," *German Politics & Society* 27:1 (2009): 24–39.

70. Enzensberger interview.

71. Hans Magnus Enzensberger, "Warum ich Amerika verlasse," *Die Zeit*, Mar 1, 1968, 16; Klaus Peter, "Supermacht USA. Hans Magnus Enzensberger über Amerika, Politik und Verbrechen," in *Amerika in der deutschen Literatur*, ed. Sigrid Bauschinger, Horst Denkler and Wilfried Malsch (Stuttgart: Reclam, 1975), 368–81.

72. Reinhard Lettau, "Täglicher Faschismus. Eine Zeitungs-Collage," *Kursbuch* 22 (December 1970): 1–44. Lettau expanded this report into book form in *Täglicher Faschismus: Amerikanische Evidenz aus 6 Monaten* (Munich: Carl Hanser Verlag, 1971).

73. *A Testament of Hope: The Essential Writings and Speeches of Martin Luther King, Jr.*, James Melvin Washington, ed. (NY: HarperCollins, 1991), 232, 472.

74. Martin Walser, "Praktiker, Weltfremde und Vietnam," *Kursbuch* 9 (1967): 168–76.

75. Martin Walser, "Versuch, ein Gefühl zu verstehen," *Dimension* 9 (1976), quoted in Ulrich Ott, *Amerika ist anders. Studien zur Amerika-Bild in deutschen Reiseberichten des 20. Jahrhunderts* (Frankfurt: Peter Lang, 1991), 442.

76. "Offener Brief an den Regierenden Bürgermeister von Berlin," April 1967, Doc. 662, in *Freie Universität Berlin 1948–1973*, IV: 407.

77. AStA and Konvent, "Konventsdrucksache Nr. XIX/30," Doc. 712, in *Freie Universität Berlin*, IV: 444–46.

78. "Resolution des Vietnam-Komitees an der Freien Universität Berlin," May 25, 1967, Doc. 711, in *Freie Universität Berlin*, IV: 444.

79. See Martin Klimke, *The Other Alliance: Student Protest in West Germany and the United States in the Global Sixties* (Princeton: Princeton University Press, 2010).

80. Quoted in Jennifer Ruth Hosek, "Interpretations of Third World Solidarity and Contemporary German Nationalism," in Karen Dubinsky et al., eds., *New World Coming: The Sixties and the Shaping of Global Consciousness* (Toronto: Between the Lines, 2009), 68–76.

81. "Warum wird der amerikanische Soldat durch einen Krieg brutalisiert, der in Vietnam das Volk vom Kommunismus befreien soll?" in *Informationen über Vietnam und Länder der dritten Welt* 3 (Berlin: SDS, 1966), edited by Rudi Dutschke et al., Doc. 588, in *Freie Universität Berlin*, IV: 357.

82. Interview with the author, Elmau, Germany, Jun 28, 2011.

83. Müller, *West Germans against the West*, 179–82.

84. "Die Krise an der FU: ABEND-Gespräch mit Professor Richard Löwenthal," Jan 19, 1967, *Der Abend*, in *Freie Universität Berlin 1948–1973*, IV: 394, doc. 640.

85. For an evocative account, see Belinda Davis, "The City as Theater of Protest: West Berlin and West Germany, 1962–1983," in Gyan Prakash and Kevin M. Kruse, eds., *The Spaces of the Modern City: Imaginaries, Politics, and Everyday Life* (Princeton: Princeton University Press, 2008), 247–74.

86. Ohnesorg's killer, a plainclothes policeman named Karl-Heinz Kurras, was later unmasked as an informant for the East German secret police – although that capacity seems to have had no direct bearing on his actions that day. See, for example, "East German Spy Shot West Berlin Martyr," May 22, 2009, Spiegel Online International.

87. "Anti-Americanism on Rise among West Berlin Students," *Hartford Courant*, Dec 25, 1967, 36B; "Brandt Seeks Halt to Berlin Riots," *UPI*, Aug 21, 1962; 258.

88. Mausbach, "Auschwitz and Vietnam," 294.

89. Compare the SDS publications reproduced in *Freie Universität Berlin 1948–1973*, vols. V (1967–69) and VI (1969–73).

90. Kommune I, "Neu! Unkonventionell! Warum brennst Du, Konsument? Neu! Atemberaubend!" and "Wann brennen die Berliner Kaufhäuser?" May 24, 1967, in *Freie Universität Berlin 1948–1973*, IV: 442, doc. 708, 709.

91. That figure includes the collective suicide of the group's leadership in prison. See Stefan Aust, *Baader Meinhof: The Inside Story of the RAF* (NY: Oxford University Press, 2009); Wolfgang Kraushaar, ed., *Die RAF und der linke Terrorismus*, 2 vols. (Hamburg: Hamburger Edition, 2006); Dorothea Hauser, "Terrorism," in Martin Klimke and Joachim Scharloth, eds., *1968 in Europe: A History of Protest and Activism, 1956–1977* (NY: Palgrave Macmillan, 2008), 269–80; Bruce Hoffman, *Terrorism*, 2nd ed. (NY: Columbia University Press, 2006), 75–80.

92. See Diner, *America in the Eyes of the Germans*, 128–37; Donatella della Porta, Belinda Davis, Geoff Eley, and Sven Reichardt, "Forum: 1977, The German Autumn," *German History* (July 2007): 401–21; Jeremy Varon, *Bringing the War Home: The Weather Underground, the Red Army Faction, and Revolutionary Violence in the Sixties and Seventies* (Berkeley and Los Angeles: University of California Press, 2004).

93. Heinrich August Winkler, *Der lange Weg nach Westen: Deutsche Geschichte vom 'Dritten Reich' bis zur Wiedervereinigung* (Munich: C.H. Beck, 2001), 251–53. On the politics of university reform see A. Dirk Moses, *German Intellectuals and the Nazi Past* (NY: Cambridge University Press, 2007), 131–218.

94. For an overview of the explosion of recent literature on the mass movements associated with 1968 and 1989 in both East and West, see Belinda Davis, "What's Left? Popular and Democratic Political Participation in Postwar Europe," *American Historical Review* 113: 2 (April 2008): 363–90; Vladimir Tismaneanu, *Promises of 1968: Crisis, Illusion, and Utopia* (Budapest: Central European University, 2011).

95. "Restless Youth," Study no. 0613/68, September 1968, in folder "Youth and Student Movements – CIA Report," NSF, Files of Walt W. Rostow, Box 13, LBJL.

96. R.K. Webb, "Britain Faces the Sixties," *Foreign Policy Association of New York Headline Series* 156 (November-December 1962), 15, 48.

97. William S. Schlamm, "Europe United against U.S.," *National Review* 20 (May 1968): 441–2.

98. "Why They Hate Us," *Chicago Tribune*, May 12, 1968, 24.

99. David Bruce Oral History, 6, AC73–39, LBJL.

100. Holger Nehring, "Great Britain," in Klimke and Scharloth, *1968*, 125–36.

101. "An American View," *The Times*, Jun 2, 1967.

102. Jean-Paul Sartre, *On Genocide* (Boston: Beacon Press, 1968).

103. Jurgensen to Secretaire Général, Aug 4, 1966; Jurgensen to Secretaire Général, Aug 5, 1966; Manac'h to Couve de Murville, Aug 19, 1966; De Leusse to Courcel, Sep 7, 1966; all in sous-série M. Couve de Murville (1958–1967), No. 103, série Cabinet du Ministre, MAE.

104. Philippe Devillers, "Le Général de Gaulle et l'Asie," in *De Gaulle et le tiers Monde*, ed. Institut Charles de Gaulle (Paris: Pédone, 1984), 299–327, at 321.

105. P.H. Grattan, "Bertrand Russell War Crimes Tribunal," May 17, 1967, FCO 9/755, NA-K. American observers reported the "quick gavelling down" of witnesses who attacked American officials personally. AmEmbStockholm to DoS, May 5 and 7, 1967, in folder "Vietnam: The Bertrand Russell 'Trial,'" NSF, Country File Vietnam, Box 191, LBJL.

106. Dana Adams Schmidt, "Sartre Indicates 'Tribunal' Will Score Johnson," *New York Times*, May 3, 1967; "Russell Attacks Czech Occupation," *New York Times*, Feb 2, 1969, 28.

107. Gunnar Myrdal, "America and Vietnam," *Transition* 33 (October-November 1967), 15–18.

108. Richard E. Bissell, "Implications of Anti-Americanism for U.S. Foreign Policy," in Alvin Z. Rubinstein and Donald E. Smith, eds., *Anti-Americanism in the Third World: Implications for U.S. Foreign Policy* (NY: Praeger, 1985), 252–3.

109. "Brandt Parries Barzel Attack by Affirming Loyalty to NATO," *New York Times*, Apr 3, 1973, 10.

110. Willy Brandt, *Friedenspolitik Europa* (Frankfurt: Fischer Verlag, 1968), 88–98; Roon Lewald, "Anti-Americanism Charges Stir Fiery Bonn Parliament Debate," Associated Press, Apr 6, 1973.

111. "Anti-U.S. Feeling Rises in Germany," *New York Times*, Mar 25, 1973, 10.

112. Alice Siegert, "Anti-America Feelings Sweep West Germany," *Chicago Tribune*, Sep 27, 1981, 4.

113. William A. Henry III, "Making Hostility a Media Event: In West Germany, Uncle Sam is a Journalistic Whipping Boy," *Time*, Aug 29, 1983, 24–5.

114. Karl-Heinz Reuband, "Antiamerikanismus – ein deutsches Problem?" *S&F (Sicherheit und Frieden)* 3:1 (1985): 46–52.

115. Harald Mueller and Thomas Risse-Kappen, "Origins of Estrangement: The Peace Movement and the Changed Image of America in West Germany," *International*

Security 12:1 (Summer 1987): 52–88, at 64; Alice Holmes Cooper, *Paradoxes of Peace: German Peace Movements since 1945* (Ann Arbor: University of Michigan Press, 1996).

116. Hollander, *Anti-Americanism*, 47, 379. See also Diner, *America in the Eyes of the Germans*, 137.

117. Beth A. Fischer, *The Reagan Reversal: Foreign Policy and the End of the Cold War* (Columbia: University of Missouri Press, 1997), 122–38.

118. Fischer, *The Reagan Reversal*, 124.

119. Robert Scheer, "Détente Yields to Nuclear Superiority," *Los Angeles Times*, Sep 28, 1981, C1; Robert Scheer, *With Enough Shovels: Reagan, Bush, and Nuclear War* (NY: Vintage Books, 1983), 18–23; Laurence W. Beilenson, *Survival and Peace in the Nuclear Age* (Washington, DC: Regnery, 1980), 35ff.

120. 1984 USIA survey cited in Lawrence S. Wittner, *Toward Nuclear Abolition: A History of the World Nuclear Disarmament Movement, 1971-Present* (Stanford, CA: Stanford University Press, 2003), 168.

121. Frederick Painton, "Europe: The Weekend that Was: A Peace Movement Peacefully Masses against Missiles," *Time*, Oct 31, 1983; Wittner, *Toward Nuclear Abolition*, 168.

122. Andrew H. Ziegler, "The Western European Public and the Atlantic Alliance," Ph.D. diss., University of Florida, 1987, 209.

123. Robert Kagan, *Paradise and Power: America and Europe in the New World Order* (NY: Knopf, 2003).

124. As usual, Britain stands between America and Europe: in 1951, Harold Wilson coined the phrase "War on Want," which became the name of a London anti-poverty organization.

125. "Missile Protests Near Finale in West Germany," *Associated Press*, Oct 22, 1983.

126. Ziegler, "The Western European Public," 197.

127. Mueller and Risse-Kappen, "Origins of Estrangement," 60.

128. Milt Freudenheim, Henry Giniger, and Katherine J. Roberts, "Marcos Gets a Boost in Washington," *New York Times*, Sep 19, 1982; "Philippines: Together Again," *Time* Jul 13, 1981.

129. Joseph Lelyveld, "Reagan's Views on South Africa Praised by Botha," *New York Times*, Mar 5, 1981.

130. James F. Smith, "Divisions among Blacks on White Role a Generation Old," *Associated Press*, Jan 28, 1985.

131. William Claiborne, "Botha Speech Leads Backlash in S. Africa against Sanctions," *Washington Post*, Nov 22, 1986, A1.

132. Mueller and Risse-Kappen, "Origins of Estrangement," 58.

133. Lloyd Grove, "Elliott Abrams in the Hour of Combat," *Washington Post*, Jan 13, 1987, D1.

134. David Brooks, "Nicaraguan Anti-Americanism," in Paul Hollander, ed., *Understanding Anti-Americanism: Its Origins and Impact at Home and Abroad* (Chicago: Ivan R. Dee, 2004), 165–89, quoted at 178.

135. "Carlos Mejía Godoy reafirma su militancia opositora en el MRS, pero 'no soy fanático,'" *Radio la Primerísima*, Sep 23, 2007.

136. As if to confirm the temporal contingency of such rhetoric, Daniel Ortega had his party remove the line from their hymn in 1996, when he was running for election as a moderate social democrat. He then restored "enemies of humanity" to his own speeches in 2005 when he aligned himself with Fidel Castro and Hugo Chávez of Venezuela. "La derecha liberal y el sandinismo frente a frente," *Clarín*,

Oct 17, 1996; "Palabras del Comandante Daniel Ortega Saavedra," *Granma*, May 1, 2005.

137. Gebhard Schweigler, "Anti-Americanism in German Public Opinion," in Dieter Dettke, ed., *America's Image in Germany and Europe* (Washington, DC: Friedrich-Ebert-Stiftung, 1985), 11–12.

138. Andrei S. Markovits, *European Anti-Americanism (and Anti-Semitism): Ever Present Though Always Denied* (Cambridge, MA: Harvard University Gunzburg Center for European Studies Working Paper Series, 2003), 22.

139. Klaus Liedtke, "Verraten wir Amerika?," *Stern*, Jun 10, 1987, 74–92.

140. Mueller and Risse-Kappen, "Origins of Estrangement," 55.

141. Martin Kaiser, "Kontinuität und Wandel des Amerikabildes in der bundesdeutschen Presse zwischen 1968 und 1984," Sep 1984, Sig. 162757, Stiftung Wissenschaft und Politik, Berlin.

142. Wittner, *Toward Nuclear Abolition*, 176–84.

143. On the ambivalent Soviet role in the protests see Wittner, *Toward Nuclear Abolition*, 268–74.

144. George H.W. Bush, "A Europe Whole and Free: Remarks to the Citizens in Mainz," May 31, 1989, usa.usembassy.de.

145. Hollander, *Anti-Americanism*, 383.

146. Wolfgang G. Gibowski and Holli A. Semetko, *Public Opinion in the USA and the Federal Republic of Germany: A Two Nation Study* (Gummersbach: Friedrich-Naumann-Stiftung, 1990).

147. "Mr. Popularity: Gorbachev Is 2nd only to Reagan in Eyes of U.S. Public, Poll Shows," *San Jose Mercury News*, Jan 5, 1989, 1A. Gorbachev also edged out Pope John Paul II and Donald Trump.

148. Hollander, *Anti-Americanism*, passim.

149. Konrad H. Jarausch, "Mißverständnis Amerika: Antiamerikanismus als Projektion," in *Antiamerikanismus im 20. Jahrhundert: Studie zu Ost- und Mitteleuropa*, ed. Jan C. Behrends et al. (Bonn: Dietz, 2005), 34–49.

150. Peter Krause, "Amerikakritik und Antiamerikanismus," in Schwan, *Antikommunismus und Antiamerikanismus*, 248–73.

151. Diner, *America in the Eyes of the Germans*, vii, ix.

152. Cooper, *Paradoxes of Peace*, 245, 252.

153. Cooper, *Paradoxes of Peace*, 253–60; Hans Magnus Enzensberger, "Hitlers Wiedergänger," *Der Spiegel*, Feb 4, 1991, 26–8; Wolf Biermann, "Kriegshetze, Friedenshetze," *Die Zeit*, Feb 1, 1991, 51.

154. Reino Schönberger, "Kleine Geschichte des Anti-Amerikanismus," *Frankfurter Rundschau*, Apr 20, 1991, 16.

155. Schwan, *Antikommunismus und Antiamerikanismus*, 19.

156. Schwan, *Antikommunismus und Antiamerikanismus*, 43.

Epilogue

1. George W. Bush quoted in Peter Ford, "Why Do They Hate Us?" *Christian Science Monitor*, Sep 27, 2001.

2. Dan Barry, "The Vigils: Surrounded by Grief, People around the World Pause and Turn to Prayer," *New York Times*, Sep 15, 2001; Carol J. Williams, "World Reaction: World Leaders Condemn 'New Evil,'" *Los Angeles Times*, Sep 12, 2001, A13; Warren Hoge, "Outpouring of Grief and Sympathy for Americans Is Seen throughout Europe and Elsewhere," *New York Times*, Sep 14, 2001.

3. Jean-Marie Colombani, "Nous sommes tous Américains," *Le Monde*, Sep 13, 2001.

4. Sixty percent of Americans believed those statements. For viewers of the Fox news channel, the figure was 80%. Steven Kull, "Misperceptions, the Media, and the Iraq War," Program on International Policy Attitudes (PIPA), Oct 2, 2003, www.worldpublicopinion.org.

5. Sidney Tarrow and Donatella Della Porta, "'Globalization,' Complex Internationalism, and Transnational Contention," in *Transnational Protest and Global Activism* (Lanham, MD: Rowman & Littlefield, 2005), 227–46. Tarrow and Della Porta estimate 16 million total participants; Robert Patterson (cited below) claims 25 million.

6. Charles Krauthammer, "To Hell with Sympathy," *Time*, Nov 17, 2003, 156, quoted in Ole R. Holsti, *To See Ourselves as Others See Us: How Publics Abroad View the United States after 9/11* (Ann Arbor: University of Michigan Press, 2008), 182.

7. Robert Patterson, *War Crimes: The Left's Campaign to Destroy Our Military and Lose the War on Terror* (NY: Random House, 2008), 171.

8. Dennis Prager, "Nature of the Rift," *Washington Times*, Feb 22, 2003.

9. Interviewed by Wes Vernon, "'Hate-America Leftists' Lead the Appeasement Movement," *NewsMax.com*, Feb 27, 2003.

10. Robert Graham, "Goofy Protests," *Chicago Tribune*, Feb 16, 2003.

11. Dinesh D'Souza, *The Enemy at Home: The Cultural Left and Its Responsibility for 9/11* (NY: Doubleday, 2007), 2, 23, 289–92.

12. John F. Harris, "Falwell Apologizes for Remarks," *Washington Post*, Sep 18, 2001, C4.

13. Eric Alterman, "USA Oui! Bush Non!" *The Nation*, Feb 10, 2003.

14. "It's Called Democracy," *Washington Post*, Feb 18, 2003, A24.

15. "The Scene: Berlin, New German Unity at Old Dividing Line," *New York Times*, Feb 16, 2003.

16. "Wide Range of Ages, Races and Parties Unite on Iraq," *New York Times*, Feb 16, 2003.

17. *Washington Daybook*, Feb 10, 2003.

18. Ivan Krastev and Alan L. McPherson, eds., *The Anti-American Century* (Budapest: Central European University Press, 2007); Julia E. Sweig, *Friendly Fire: Losing Friends and Making Enemies in the Anti-American Century* (NY: Public Affairs, 2006). To their credit, they remained skeptical, being more interested in the content of critiques from abroad than in name-calling.

19. Andrew Kohut and Bruce Stokes, *America against the World: How We Are Different and Why We Are Disliked* (NY: Henry Holt & Co., 2006); Glenn E. Schweitzer and Carole D. Schweitzer, *America on Notice: Stemming the Tide of Anti-Americanism* (Amherst, NY: Prometheus Books, 2006); Barry Rubin and Judith Colp Rubin, *Hating America: A History* (NY: Oxford University Press, 2004); John Gibson, *Hating America: The New World Sport* (NY: Regan Books, 2004).

20. "Anti-Semitism in Europe," Senate Committee on Foreign Relations, S. Hrg. 108–370, Oct 22, 2003; Greg Grandin, "The Narcissism of Violent Differences," in Andrew Ross and Kristin Ross, eds., *Anti-Americanism* (NY: NYU Press, 2004), 17.

21. Niall Ferguson, "Hatred of America Unites the World," *Telegraph*, Feb 25, 2007.

22. "U.S. Public Diplomacy: Interagency Coordination Efforts Hampered by the Lack of a National Communication Strategy," GAO-05-323, April 2005.
23. Jane Perlez, "U.S. Asks Muslims Why It Is Unloved," *New York Times*, Sep 27, 2003, A3.
24. "State, Foreign Operations, and Related Programs Appropriations for Fiscal Year 2010," Senate Committee on Appropriations, S. Hrg. 111–199, May 20, 2009.
25. Robert Kagan, *Of Paradise and Power: America and Europe in the New World Order* (London: Atlantic Books, 2003), 1, 29, 31, 33.
26. Russell A. Berman, *Anti-Americanism in Europe: a Cultural Problem* (Stanford, CA: Hoover Institution Press, 2004), 78, xi, xii, xvi.
27. Pew Global Attitudes Project, "Americans and Europeans Differ Widely on Foreign Policy Issues," Apr 17, 2002, and Chicago Council on Foreign Relations and German Marshall Fund of the United States, "Worldviews 2002," Oct 2, 2002.
28. Steven Erlanger, "German Chancellor Trying to Mend His Rift with the U.S.," *New York Times*, Sep 24, 2002.
29. Fareed Zakaria, "The Arrogant Empire," *Newsweek*, Mar 24, 2003, 29.
30. Paul Johnson, "Hating America, Hating Humanity: Yup, That's What They Do – Especially the Intellectuals," *National Review*, Sep 12, 2005.
31. Keith Richburg, "Why Chirac Is Defying His American Friends," *Toronto Star*, Feb 16, 2003, B03.
32. Paul Starobin, "The French Were Right," *National Journal*, Nov 7, 2003.
33. Starobin, "The French Were Right," citing a French transcript of the conversation.
34. David B. Caruso, "French Roasted: France's Reluctance to Back War Sends Bashing to New Heights," *Associated Press*, Feb 21, 2003.
35. Originally a line from the television cartoon *The Simpsons*, it was popularized by columnist Jonah Goldberg in regular diatribes such as "Frogs in Our Midst," *National Review Online*, Jul 16, 2002.
36. Robert Stam and Ella Shohat, *Flagging Patriotism: Crises of Narcissism and Anti-Americanism* (NY: Routledge, 2007), 126–29.
37. Fred Barnes, "How Many Frenchmen Does It Take ... Nobody Likes an Ingrate," *The Daily Standard*, Feb 13, 2003.
38. David B. Caruso, "French Roasted: France's Reluctance to Back War Sends Bashing to New Heights," *Associated Press*, Feb 21, 2003.
39. Frank Rich, "The Ides of March 2003," *New York Times*, Mar 18, 2007; Stam and Shohat, *Flagging Patriotism*, 129.
40. Sharon Kehnemui, "French Jokes Gain Wide Audiences," *Foxnews.com*, Feb 21, 2003.
41. Andrew Higgins, "For U.S., Waging Peace Still Requires Support from Contrarian Allies," *Wall Street Journal* (Europe), Jun 17, 2003, quoted in Denis Lacorne, "Anti-Americanism and Americanophobia," in Lacorne and Tony Judt, eds., *With Us or Against Us: Studies in Global Anti-Americanism* (NY: Palgrave Macmillan, 2005), 5.
42. Jo Mannies, "Republicans Poke Fun at France, Not Democrats," *St. Louis Post-Dispatch*, Feb 16, 2003, A10.
43. George F. Will, "After Powell, Before War," *Newsweek*, Feb 17, 2003, 72.
44. "America's Image Slips," Pew Global Attitudes Project Report, Jun 13, 2006.
45. Bruce Crumley and James Graff, "France Is Not a Pacifist Country," *Time*, Feb 24, 2003.

46. Philippe Roger, *The American Enemy: The History of French Anti-Americanism*, tr. Sharon Bowman (Chicago: University of Chicago Press, 2006), xviii.

47. Adnan Musallam, *From Secularism to Jihad: Sayyid Qutb and the Foundations of Radical Islamism* (Westport, CT: Greenwood Publishing, 2005), 111–36; Lawrence Wright, *The Looming Tower: Al-Qaeda and the Road to 9/11* (NY: Knopf, 2006), 9–37.

48. Wright, *The Looming Tower*, 27.

49. Peter Bergen, *The Osama Bin Laden I Know: An Oral History of Al-Qaeda's Leader* (NY: Simon & Schuster, 2006), xxix, 165.

50. Michael Scheuer, *Through Our Enemies' Eyes: Osama bin Laden, Radical Islam, and the Future of America* (Dulles, VA: Brassey's, 2003), 244–5.

51. Thomas Hegghammer, *Jihad in Saudi Arabia: Violence and Pan-Islamism since 1979* (NY: Cambridge University Press, 2010), 64, 69, 135, 137, 147, 193; idem, "Lady Gaga vs. the Occupation," *Foreign Policy Magazine*, Mar 31, 2010. See also Samuel P. Huntington, *The Clash of Civilizations and the Remaking of World Order* (New York: Simon & Schuster, 2011 [1997]).

52. Wright, *The Looming Tower*, 288, 343; Bergen, *The Osama Bin Laden I Know*, 170.

53. Wright, *The Looming Tower*, 172.

54. Quoted in Wright, *The Looming Tower*, 265.

55. Hegghammer, *Jihad in Saudi Arabia*, 193.

56. David Kilcullen, *The Accidental Guerrilla: Fighting Small Wars in the Midst of a Big One* (NY: Oxford University Press, 2009), xiv. See also Olivier Roy, *Globalized Islam: The Search for a New Ummah* (NY: Columbia University Press, 2004).

57. Edward W. Said, *Culture and Imperialism* (NY: Knopf, 1993), 294.

58. "Global Polling Data on Opinion of American Policies, Values, and People," House Committee on Foreign Affairs, Subcommittee on International Organizations, Human Rights, and Oversight, Serial No. 110–4 (Washington, DC: USGPO, 2007), 7.

59. Juan Cole, "Anti-Americanism: It's the Policies," *American Historical Review* 111:4 (October 2006): 1120–29. See also John L. Esposito and Dalia Mogahed, *Who Speaks for Islam? What a Billion Muslims Really Think* (NY: Gallup Press, 2008).

60. A notion advanced inter alia by Barry Rubin, "The Real Roots of Arab Anti-Americanism," *Foreign Affairs* 81:6 (Nov-Dec 2002): 73–85. For a rebuttal based on empirical research, see Sigrid Faath, ed., *Anti-Americanism in the Islamic World* (Princeton, NJ: Markus Wiener, 2006). For earlier instrumentalization strategies, see Alan McPherson, *Yankee No! Anti-Americanism in U.S.-Latin American Relations* (Cambridge, MA: Harvard University Press, 2003).

61. "Global Public Opinion in the Bush Years," Pew Research Center Global Attitudes Project, Dec 18, 2008.

62. "Global Polling Data," 8.

63. Ravi Khanna, "Experts Say Anti-American Sentiment in Pakistan at All-Time High," VOA News.com, Jul 8, 2010.

64. Cole, "Anti-Americanism: It's the Policies," 1129. See also Sergio Fabbrini, "Anti-Americanism and U.S. Foreign Policy: Which Correlation?" *International Politics* 47:6 (November 2010): 557-73.

65. *Report of the Defense Science Board Task Force on Strategic Communication* (Washington, DC: Office of the Under Secretary of Defense for Acquisition,

Technology, and Logistics, 2004), 40, 6; Acheson, "Anti-Americanism in the Arab World," DoS airgram, May 1, 1950, National Security Archive online.

66. Pew Global Attitudes Project, "America's Image Slips," Jun 13, 2006, www. pewglobal.org.

67. Berman, *Anti-Americanism in Europe*, xiii.

68. Pew Global Attitudes Project, "Confidence in Obama Lifts U.S. Image around the World," Jul 23, 2009.

69. Andrei S. Markovits, *Uncouth Nation: Why Europe Dislikes America* (Princeton: Princeton University Press, 2007), 17.

70. Pew Global Attitudes Project, "Confidence in Obama Lifts U.S. Image around the World," Jul 23, 2009.

71. For a sophisticated statistical analysis of world opinion concluding that "popular anti-Americanism is mostly benign and shallow," see Giacomo Chiozza, *Anti-Americanism and the American World Order* (Baltimore: Johns Hopkins University Press, 2009), 4.

72. Berman's definition of anti-Americanism in *Anti-Americanism in Europe*, xiii.

73. "Survey: Support for U.S. Leadership Skyrockets in Europe," German Marshall Fund of the United States, Sep 9, 2009, www.gmfus.org.

74. "8 Most Outrageous Attacks on Obama's Nobel Peace Prize," *Huffington Post*, Oct 9, 2009.

75. Matt Canham, "Republicans Incredulous, Critical over Obama's Peace Prize," *Salt Lake Tribune*, Oct 9, 2009; James F. Oshust, "Disgusting Gaffe," *Salt Lake Tribune*, Oct 13, 2009. See also: Obama's Nobel "reveals the vehemently anti-American view of the Oslo committee," Larry Horist, "Nobel Panel is Anti-American," *Chicago Sun-Times*, Oct 11, 2009, A25; William Kristol: "This is an anti-American committee, they've now given the prize to President Obama." *Fox News Sunday*, Oct 11, 2009.

76. Lloyd Grove, "On C-SPAN, Talk of War Gets Awfully Belligerent," *Washington Post*, Sep 25, 2002; "Obama Heckled by GOP during Speech to Congress," *Washington Post*, Sep 9, 2009.

77. Geoffrey Hodgson, *The Myth of American Exceptionalism* (New Haven, CT: Yale University Press, 2009).

78. "Cheney Rips 'Radical' Obama," FOXNews.com, Dec 9, 2009.

79. Karen Tumulty, "Conservatives' New Focus: America, the Exceptional," *Washington Post*, Nov 29, 2010.

80. Hodsgon, *The Myth*, 128.

81. Jonathan Chait, "The Exceptionalism Myth Goes Mainstream," *The New Republic*, Aug 29, 2011.

82. Russell Berman, "Anti-Americanism and Americanization," in Alexander Stephan, ed., *Americanization and Anti-Americanism: The German Encounter with American Culture after 1945* (NY: Berghahn Books, 2007), 11–25, quoted at 14.

83. Richard Wilkinson and Kate Pickett, *The Spirit Level: Why Greater Equality Makes Societies Stronger* (NY: Bloomsbury Press, 2009).

84. David Leonhardt, "In Health Bill, Obama Attacks Wealth Inequality," *New York Times*, Mar 23, 2010; Eduardo Porter, "Study Finds Wealth Inequality Is Widening Worldwide," *New York Times*, Dec 6, 2006.

85. James B. Davies et al., "Estimating the Level and Distribution of Global Household Wealth," *World Institute for Development Economics Research Paper No. 2007/77* (Helsinki: United Nations University, 2007), 23.

86. Wilkinson and Pickett, *The Spirit Level*, 159–61.
87. Rep. Dan Burton, "The Danger of Underestimating Obama," *Washington Times*, Aug 8, 2011; Steve Benen, "DeMint Calls Administration 'Anti-American,'" *Washington Monthly* Political Animal Blog, Aug 11, 2011.
88. Wilkinson and Pickett's *The Spirit Level* demonstrates that an array of social pathologies, from poor health to illiteracy and crime, correlate not with insufficient national wealth but with excessively unequal wealth. For a discussion see Tony Judt, *Ill Fares the Land* (NY: Penguin, 2010).
89. Alexis de Tocqueville, *De la Démocratie en Amérique*, 8th ed. (Paris: Charles Gosselin, 1840), II: 145.
90. Reinhold Niebuhr, "Why They Dislike Us," *The New Leader* 37:15 (April 1954), 3–5.

Sources

Archives

Argentina

Archivo del Ministerio de Relaciones Exteriores y Culto, Buenos Aires (AMREC)

Chile

Archivo General Histórico del Ministerio de Relaciones Exteriores, Santiago (AGHMRE)
Archivo Nacional de la Administración Central del Estado, Santiago (ARNAD)

France

Archives d'Histoire Contemporaine, Centre d'Histoire de Sciences Po, Paris (CHEVS – formerly Centre d'Histoire de l'Europe du Vingtième Siècle)
Archives Nationales, Paris (AN)
Ministère des Affaires Etrangères, Paris (MAE)

Germany

Archiv der Ausserparlamentarischen Opposition und Sozialen Bewegungen, Berlin (APOSB)
Institut für Zeitgeschichte, Munich (IfZ)
Politisches Archiv des Auswärtigen Amtes, Berlin (PAAA)
Stiftung Wissenschaft und Politik, Berlin (SWP)
Zentralarchiv für Empirische Sozialforschung, Cologne (ZES)

Great Britain

National Archives, Kew (NA-K – formerly Public Record Office)

Italy

Archivio Centrale dello Stato, Rome (ACS)
Archivio Storico Diplomatico, Ministero degli Affari Esteri, Rome (ASDMAE)

Mexico

Archivo General de la Nación, Mexico City (AGN)
Archivo Histórico Genaro Estrada, Secretaría de Relaciones Exteriores, Mexico City (AHGE)

Uruguay

Archivo Histórico-Diplomático del Ministerio de Relaciones Exteriores, Montevideo (AHDMRE)

USA

Central Intelligence Agency Records Search Tool, NARA (CREST)
Dwight D. Eisenhower Presidential Library, Abilene, Kansas (DDEL)
John F. Kennedy Presidential Library, Boston, Massachusetts (JFKL)
Lyndon B. Johnson Presidential Library, Austin, Texas (LBJL)
Manuscript Division, Library of Congress, Washington, DC (LC)
National Archives and Records Administration, College Park, Maryland (NARA)
Roper Center Public Opinion Archives, Storrs, Connecticut (RC)

Published Documents

Akten zur Auswärtigen Politik der Bundesrepublik Deutschland. Munich: R. Oldenbourg Verlag, various dates.
Congressional Record, various dates.
Documents Diplomatiques Français. Paris: Ministère des Affaires Etrangères, various dates.
Foreign Relations of the United States. Washington, DC: U.S. General Printing Office, various dates.
Freie Universität Berlin 1948–1973: Hochschule im Umbruch, Siegward Lönnendonker and Tilman Fichter, eds. Berlin: Pressestelle der FU Berlin, 1975. 6 vols.
The Papers of Benjamin Franklin. www.yale.edu/franklinpapers.
The Papers of George Washington: Presidential Series. Dorothy Twohig, ed. Charlottesville: University of Virginia Press, 1996.
The Papers of Rómulo Betancourt. Scholarly Resources, Inc. 66 reels.
The Revolutionary Diplomatic Correspondence of the United States. Francis Wharton, ed. Washington, DC: Government Printing Office, 1889.
Die SPD-Fraktion im Deutschen Bundestag. Sitzungsprotokolle 1961–1966. Vol. 2. Potthoff, Heinrich, ed. Duesseldorf: Droste Verlag, 1993.
The Works of Thomas Jefferson in Twelve Volumes, Paul Leicester Ford, ed., memory.loc.gov.

Newspapers and Magazines (various dates)

The Age
Agence France Presse
Alerta
American Advocate
The Argus
Arizonian
Atlanta Constitution
Atlanta Daily World
The Atlantic Monthly
Baltimore Afro-American
Baltimore Sun
Boston Evening-Post
Boston Record American
Brooklyn Eagle
The Catholic Telegraph
The Centinel
Chicago Daily Tribune
Chicago Defender
Chicago Sun-Times
Christian Science Monitor
The Cincinnati Weekly Herald and Philanthropist
Clarín
Combat
El Comercio
The Commercial Review of the South and West
Corriere della Sera
Daily National Intelligencer
The Daily Standard
Deseret News
The Eclectic Review
Economist
The Edinburgh Review
Excelsior
L'Express
Le Figaro
Financial Times
Foreign Affairs
Foreign Policy
France-Soir

Frankfurter Allgemeine Zeitung
Frankfurter Rundschau
The Free Enquirer
Freedom's Journal
La Gente
Globe and Mail
Granma
The Guardian
Hartford Courant
Harvard Crimson
The Hindu
Houston Chronicle
The Independent
International Herald Tribune
Jet
Life
Littell's Living Age
The London Literary Gazette
Los Angeles Times
Manchester Guardian
El Mercurio
Midstream
Le Monde
Monthly Review
Morris's National Press
El Nacional
The Nation
National Era
National Intelligencer
National Journal
The National Register
National Review
Neue Zurcher Zeitung
New-England Magazine
New-Jersey Journal
New York Daily News
New York Herald Tribune
New-York Journal
The New York Review
New York Sentinel and Working Man's Advocate

New York Sun
New York Times
New York Times Magazine
New York Tribune
New York World
The New Yorker
Newsweek
Niles' National Register
Niles' Weekly Register
Norfolk Journal and Guide
The North Star
Novedades
Observer
Ottawa Citizen
The Outlook
Paris-Match
Philadelphia Bulletin
Philadelphia Tribune
Pittsburgh Courier
Pittsburgh Post-Gazette
Pittsfield Sun
El Popular
Rome News-Tribune
Salt Lake Tribune
San Jose Mercury News
Seattle Post-Intelligencer
The Select Reviews of Literature, and Spirit of Foreign Magazines
Sentinel of Freedom
Southern Literary Messenger
Der Spiegel
Spirit of the Times
St. Louis Post-Dispatch
St. Petersburg Times
Stern
Süddeutsche Zeitung
La Suisse
Il Tempo
Time
The Times
Times of India

Toronto Star
The United States Magazine and Democratic Review
U.S. News & World Report
USA Today
Wall Street Journal
Washington Post
Washington Times
The Weekly Inspector
The Westminster Review

Selected Books (The length of a comprehensive bibliography proved impractical, so a list of key texts appears here. Many others are found in the notes.)

Adereth, Maxwell. *The French Communist Party: A Critical History*. Manchester: Manchester University Press, 1984.

Adorno, Theodor W., Else Frenkel-Brunswik, Daniel Levinson, and Nevitt Sanford. *The Authoritarian Personality*. NY: Harper & Row, 1950.

Alexander, Robert. *Rómulo Betancourt and the Transformation of Venezuela*. New Brunswick, NJ: Transaction Books, 1982.

———. *Venezuela's Voice for Democracy: Conversations and Correspondence with Rómulo Betancourt*. NY: Praeger, 1990.

Allison, Graham T., and Philip Zelikow. *Essence of Decision: Explaining the Cuban Missile Crisis*. 2nd ed. NY: Longman, 1999 [1971].

Alphand, Hervé. *L'Étonnement d'être: Journal, 1939–1973*. Paris: Fayard, 1977.

Anders, Günther. *Visit Beautiful Vietnam. ABC der Aggressionen heute*. Cologne: Pahl-Rugenstein, 1968.

Aptheker, Herbert, ed. *The Correspondence of W.E.B. Du Bois: Selections, 1877–1934*. Amherst: University of Massachusetts Press, 1997.

Arendt, Hannah. *The Origins of Totalitarianism*. NY: Harcourt, Brace, 1951.

Arévalo, Juan José. *Antikomunismo en América Latina: radiografía del proceso hacia una nueva colonización*. Buenos Aires: Editorial Palestra, 1959.

———. *Carta política al pueblo de Guatemala*. Guatemala City: Editorial San Antonio, 1963.

———. *The Shark and the Sardines*. Translated by June Cobb and Dr. Raul Osegueda. NY: Lyle Stuart, 1961.

Armus, Seth D. *French Anti-Americanism (1930–1948): Critical Moments in a Complex History*. Lexington, MA: Lexington Books, 2010.

Aron, Raymond. *The Imperial Republic: The United States and the World 1945–1973*. Translated by Frank Jellinek. Englewood Cliffs, NJ: Prentice-Hall, Inc., 1974.

———. *The Opium of the Intellectuals*. New Brunswick, NJ: Transaction Publishers, 2001 [1955].

Aronson, Ronald. *Camus and Sartre: The Story of a Friendship and the Quarrel that Ended It*. Chicago: University of Chicago Press, 2004.

Baily, Samuel L. *Immigrants in the Lands of Promise: Italians in Buenos Aires and New York City, 1870–1914*. Ithaca, NY: Cornell University Press, 1999.

Balderrama, Francisco E., and Raymond Rodriguez. *Decade of Betrayal: Mexican Repatriation in the 1930s*. Albuquerque: University of New Mexico Press, 1995.

Baldwin, Neil. *Henry Ford and the Jews: The Mass Production of Hate.* NY: Public Affairs, 2001.

Ball, George. *The Past Has Another Pattern: Memoirs.* NY: Norton, 1982.

Baring, Arnulf. *Unser neuer Grössenwahn: Deutschland zwischen Ost und West.* Munich: Deutsche Verlags-Anstalt, 1988.

Barthes, Roland. *Mythologies.* Paris: Seuil, 1957.

Beals, Carleton. *Rio Grande to Cape Horn.* NY: Houghton Mifflin Co., 1943.

———. *What the South Americans Think of Us.* NY: McBride & Company, 1945.

Beevor, Anthony, and Artemis Cooper. *Paris after the Liberation, 1944–1949.* NY: Doubleday, 1994.

Beisner, Robert L. *Twelve against Empire: The Anti-Imperialists, 1989–1900.* NY: McGraw-Hill, 1968.

Bergen, Peter. *The Osama Bin Laden I Know: An Oral History of Al-Qaeda's Leader.* NY: Simon & Schuster, 2006.

Berger, Joachim. *Berlin. Freiheitlich und rebellisch.* Berlin: Goebel Verlag, 1987.

Berghahn, Volker R. *America and the Intellectual Cold Wars in Europe: Shepard Stone between Philanthropy, Academy, and Diplomacy.* Princeton, NJ: Princeton University Press, 2002.

Berman, Russell A. *Anti-Americanism in Europe: A Cultural Problem.* Stanford, CA: Hoover Institution Press, 2004.

Bernays, Edward L. *What the British Think of Us: A Study of British Hostility to America and Americans and Its Motivation.* NY: English-Speaking Union, 1958.

Bethell, Leslie. *Ideas and Ideologies in Twentieth Century Latin America.* Cambridge: Cambridge University Press, 1996.

Bilbao, Francisco. *La América en peligro.* 2nd ed. Buenos Aires: Bernheim y Boneo, 1862.

———. *Obras completas.* Buenos Aires: Imprenta de Buenos Aires, 1866.

Birchall, Ian H. *Sartre against Stalinism.* NY: Berghahn Books, 2004.

Blight, James G., Bruce J. Allyn, and David A. Welch. *Cuba on the Brink: Castro, the Missile Crisis, and the Soviet Collapse.* Lanham, MD: Rowman & Littlefield, 2002.

Bogart, Leo. *Premises for Propaganda: The United States Information Agency's Operating Assumptions in the Cold War.* NY: Free Press, 1976.

Bohlen, Charles E. *Witness to History, 1929–1969.* NY: Norton, 1973.

Bone, Andrew, ed. *The Collected Papers of Bertrand Russell, vol. 29: Détente or Destruction.* NY: Routledge, 2005.

Borstelmann, Thomas. *The Cold War and the Color Line: American Race Relations in the Global Arena.* Cambridge, MA: Harvard University Press, 2001.

Bozo, Frédéric. *Two Strategies for Europe: De Gaulle, the United States, and the Atlantic Alliance.* Translated by Susan Emanuel. Lanham, MD: Rowman and Littlefield, 2001.

Brandt, Willy. *Friedenspolitik Europa.* Frankfurt: Fischer Verlag, 1968.

Brunner, Otto, Werner Conze, and Reinhardt Koselleck, eds. *Geschichtliche Grundbegriffe: Historisches Lexikon zur politisch-sozialer Sprache in Deutschland.* Stuttgart: Ernst Klett Verlag, 1972.

Buchanan, William, and Hadley Cantril. *How Nations See Each Other.* Urbana: University of Illinois Press, 1954.

Burns, Michael. *France and the Dreyfus Affair: A Documentary History.* NY: Palgrave Macmillan, 1999.

Cau, Jean. *L'Ivresse des Intellectuels – Paris, Whisky et Marxisme.* Paris: Plon, 1992.

Caute, David. *The Dancer Defects: The Struggle for Cultural Supremacy during the Cold War.* NY: Oxford University Press, 2005.

Ceaser, James. *Reconstructing America: The Symbol of America in Modern Thought.* New Haven, CT: Yale University Press, 1997.

Chaban-Delmas, Jacques. *Mémoires pour demain.* Paris: Editions Flammarion, 1998.

Chastanet, Jean Louis. *L'Oncle Shylock, ou, L'impérialisme américain à la conquête du monde.* Paris: Flammarion, 1927.

Chiozza, Giacomo. *Anti-Americanism and the American World Order.* Baltimore: Johns Hopkins University Press, 2009.

Cogan, Charles G. *Oldest Allies, Guarded Friends: The United States and France since 1940.* Westport, CT: Praeger, 1994.

Commager, Henry Steele. *America in Perspective: The United States through Foreign Eyes.* NY: Random House, 1947.

Connelly, Matthew. *A Diplomatic Revolution: Algeria's Fight for Independence and the Origins of the Post-Cold War Era.* NY: Oxford University Press, 2002.

Contat, Michel, and Michel Rybalka. *The Writings of Jean-Paul Sartre.* Evanston: Northwestern University Press, 1974.

Converse, Jean. *Survey Research in the United States: Roots and Emergence 1890–1960.* New Brunswick, NJ: Transaction Publishers, 2009.

Cooper, Alice Holmes. *Paradoxes of Peace: German Peace Movements since 1945.* Ann Arbor: University of Michigan Press, 1996.

Costigliola, Frank C. *France and the United States: The Cold Alliance since World War II.* NY: Twayne Publishers, 1992.

Cotteret, Jean-Marie, and René Moreau. *Recherches sur le vocabulaire du Général de Gaulle.* Paris: Armand Colin, 1969.

Couve de Murville, Maurice. *Une Politique Etrangère, 1958–1969.* Paris: Plon, 1971.

Crèvecoeur, Hector St. John de. *Letters from an American Farmer.* NY: Oxford University Press, 1998 [1782].

Cull, Nicholas J. *The Cold War and the United States Information Agency: American Propaganda and Public Diplomacy, 1945–1989.* NY: Cambridge University Press, 2008.

Cullather, Nick. *Secret History: The CIA's Classified Account of its Operation in Guatemala, 1952–1954.* Stanford, CA: Stanford University Press, 1999.

Daniels, Roger. *Coming to America: A History of Immigration and Ethnicity in American Life.* 2nd ed. NY: Perennial, 2002.

Davis, Richard Harding. *Three Gringos in Venezuela and Central America.* NY: Harper & Brothers, 1896.

De Beaumont, Gustave. *Marie ou L'esclavage aux États-Unis: Tableau de moeurs américaines.* Paris: L. Hauman et Cie., 1835.

De Beauvoir, Simone. *L'Amérique au jour le jour.* Paris: Editions Paul Morigien, 1948.

———. *La Force des choses.* Paris: Gallimard, 1963.

———. *Les Mandarins.* Paris: Gallimard, 1954.

De Gaulle, Charles. *Mémoires de guerre: L'Appel, 1940–42.* Vol. I. Paris: Plon, 1999 [1954].

———. *Mémoires d'Espoir: Le renouveau 1958–1962.* Paris: Plon, 1970.

De Grazia, Victoria. *Irresistible Empire: America's Advance through Twentieth-Century Europe.* Cambridge, MA: Belknap Press, 2005.

Dickens, Charles. *American Notes for General Circulation.* London: Chapman and Hall, 1842.

———. *Martin Chuzzlewit*. London: Chapman and Hall, 1844.

Dickens, Mamie, and Georgina Hogarth, eds. *The Letters of Charles Dickens*. London: Chapman and Hall, 1882.

Diner, Dan. *America in the Eyes of the Germans: An Essay on Anti-Americanism*. English language ed. Princeton, NJ: Markus Wiener Publishers, 1996.

———. *Feindbild Amerika: über die Beständigkeit eines Ressentiments*. Munich: Propyläen, 2002.

———. *Verkehrte Welten. Antiamerikanismus in Deutschland: ein historischer Essay*. Frankfurt am Main: Eichborn, 1993.

Doeberitz, Hugo von Knebel. *Besteht für Deutschland eine amerikanische Gefahr?* Berlin: E.S. Mittler und Sohn, 1904.

D'Souza, Dinesh. *The Enemy at Home: The Cultural Left and Its Responsibility for 9/11*. NY: Doubleday, 2007.

Dubinsky, Karen et al., eds. *New World Coming: The Sixties and the Shaping of Global Consciousness*. Toronto: Between the Lines, 2009.

Dudziak, Mary. *Cold War Civil Rights: Race and the Image of American Democracy*. Princeton, NJ: Princeton University Press, 2000.

Duhamel, Georges. *America the Menace*. Translated by Charles Miner Thompson. NY: Houghton Mifflin, 1931.

Eisenhower, Dwight David. *The White House Years: Mandate for Change, 1953–1956*. Garden City, NJ: Doubleday, 1963.

Elias, Norbert. *The Civilizing Process: Sociogenetic and Psychogenetic Investigations*. Revised ed. Wiley-Blackwell, 2000 [1939].

Endy, Christopher. *Cold War Holidays: American Tourism in France*. Chapel Hill: University of North Carolina Press, 2004.

Engerman, David C. *Modernization from the Other Shore: American Intellectuals and the Romance of Russian Development*. Cambridge, MA: Harvard University Press, 2003.

Eschen, Penny von. *Satchmo Blows Up the World: Jazz Ambassadors Play the Cold War*. Cambridge, MA: Harvard University Press, 2004.

Faath, Sigrid, ed. *Anti-Americanism in the Islamic World*. Princeton, NJ: Markus Wiener, 2006.

Fabre, Michel. *From Harlem to Paris: Black American Writers in France, 1840–1980*. Champaign: University of Illinois Press, 1993.

Falcoff, Mark. *A Culture of Its Own: Taking Latin America Seriously*. New Brunswick, NJ: Transaction Publishers, 1998.

Fall, Bernard B. *Anatomy of a Crisis: The Laotian Crisis of 1960–1961*. NY: Doubleday, 1969.

———. *Street without Joy: Indochina at War, 1946–54*. Harrisburg, PA: Stackpole Books, 1961.

———. *The Two Viet-Nams*. 2nd revised ed. NY: Praeger, 1967 [1963].

Fall, Dorothy. *Bernard Fall: Memories of a Soldier-Scholar*. Dulles, VA: Potomac Books, 2006.

Fearon, Henry Bradshaw. *Sketches of America: A Narrative of a Journey of Five Thousand Miles through the Eastern and Western States of America*. London: Longman, 1818.

Feldman, Egal. *The Dreyfus Affairs and the American Conscience, 1895–1906*. Detroit: Wayne State University Press, 1981.

Ferguson, Niall. *Colossus: The Price of America's Empire*. NY: Penguin Press, 2004.

————. *Empire: The Rise and Demise of the British World Order and the Lessons for Global Power*. London: Allen Lane, 2002.

Fischer, Beth A. *The Reagan Reversal: Foreign Policy and the End of the Cold War*. Columbia: University of Missouri Press, 1997.

Flanner, Janet. *Paris Was Yesterday*. NY: Viking Press, 1972.

Fombona, Rufino Blanco. *Grandes escritores de América*. Madrid: Renacimiento, 1917.

Foner, Philip S., and Herbert Shapiro, eds. *American Communism and Black Americans: A Documentary History, 1930–1934*. Philadelphia: Temple University Press, 1991.

Foner, Philip S., ed. *José Martí, Inside the Monster: Writings on the United States and American Imperialism*. NY: Monthly Review Press, 1975.

Ford, Henry. *The International Jew: The World's Foremost Problem*. Dearborn, MI: Dearborn Publishing Co., 1922.

Fraenkel, Ernst, ed. *America im Spiegel des deutschen politischen Denkens. Äusserungen deutscher Staatsmänner und Staatsdenker über Staat und Gesellschaft in den Vereinigten Staaten von Amerika*. Cologne: Westdeutscher Verlag, 1959.

Fried, Erich. *100 Gedichte ohne Vaterland*. Berlin: Wagenbachs Taschenbücherei, 1978.

————. *und Vietnam und*. Berlin: Verlag Klaus Wagenbach, 1966.

Fursenko, Aleksandr, and Timothy J. Naftali. *One Hell of a Gamble: Khrushchev, Castro, and Kennedy, 1958–1964*. NY: W.W. Norton, 1997.

Gadea, Hilda. *Ernesto: A Memoir of Che Guevara*. NY: Doubleday, 1972.

Gassert, Philipp. *Amerika im Dritten Reich: Ideologie, Propaganda und Volksmeinung, 1933–1945*. Stuttgart: Franz Steiner, 1997.

Gellman, Irwin F. *Secret Affairs: Franklin Roosevelt, Cordell Hull, and Sumner Welles*. Baltimore: Johns Hopkins University Press, 1995.

Gerbi, Antonello. *La disputa del Nuovo Mondo: storia di una polemica, 1750–1900*. Milan: Ricciardi, 1955.

————. *The Dispute of the New World: The History of a Polemic, 1750–1900*. Pittsburgh: University of Pittsburgh Press, 1973.

Gibson, John. *Hating America: The New World Sport*. NY: Regan Books, 2004.

Gilderhus, Mark T. *Pan American Visions: Woodrow Wilson in the Western Hemisphere, 1913–1921*. Tucson: University of Arizona Press, 1986.

Gilman, Nils. *Mandarins of the Future: Modernization Theory in Cold War America*. Baltimore: Johns Hopkins University Press, 2007.

Gleijeses, Piero. *Shattered Hope: The Guatemalan Revolution and the United States, 1944–1954*. Princeton, NJ: Princeton University Press, 1992.

Gobat, Michel. *Confronting the American Dream: Nicaragua under U.S. Imperial Rule*. Durham: Duke University Press, 2005.

Godoy, F. García. *Americanismo literario*. Madrid: Editorial-América, 1910.

Goedde, Petra. *GIs and Germans: Culture, Gender, and Foreign Relations, 1945–1949*. New Haven: Yale University Press, 2003.

Grabbe, Hans-Jürgen. *Unionsparteien, Sozialdemokratie und Vereinigte Staaten von Amerika 1945–1966*. Düsseldorf: Droste Verlag, 1983.

Graebner, Norman A. *The Age of Global Power: The United States since 1939*. NY: Wiley, 1979.

Grandin, Greg. *The Last Colonial Massacre: Latin America in the Cold War*. Chicago: University of Chicago Press, 2004.

Guerin-Gonzalez, Camille. *Mexican Workers and American Dreams: Immigration, Repatriation, and California Farm Labor, 1900–1939*. New Brunswick, NJ: Rutgers University Press, 1994.

Hale, Charles A. *El liberalismo mexicano en la época de Mora*. Mexico City: Siglo Veintiuno, 1972.

Halfeld, Adolf. *Amerika und der Amerikanismus: Das Gegenstück zu Henry Ford*. Jena: Diederich, 1927.

Halpern, Sheldon. *Sydney Smith*. NY: Twayne Publishers, 1966.

Handy, Jim. *Gift of the Devil: A History of Guatemala*. Toronto: Between the Lines, 1984.

Harrison, Michael. *The Reluctant Ally: France and Atlantic Security*. Baltimore and London: Johns Hopkins University Press, 1981.

Haseler, Stephen. *The Varieties of Anti-Americanism: Reflex and Response*. Washington, DC: Ethics and Public Policy Center, 1985.

Henke, Klaus-Dietmar. *Die amerikanische Besetzung Deutschlands*. Oldenbourg: Wissenschaftsverlag, 1996.

Henningsen, Manfred. *Der Fall Amerika. Zur Sozial- und Bewusstseinsgeschichte einer Verdrängung*. Munich: List, 1974.

Herf, Jeffrey. *The Jewish Enemy: Nazi Propaganda during World War II and the Holocaust*. Cambridge, MA: Belknap Press, 2006.

———. *Reactionary Modernism: Technology, Culture, and Politics in Weimar and the Third Reich*. NY: Cambridge University Press, 1985.

Hess, John. *The Case for de Gaulle*. NY: William Morrow and Co., 1968.

Higgott, Richard, and Ivona Malbašić, eds. *The Political Consequences of Anti-Americanism*. NY: Routledge, 2008.

Higham, John. *Strangers in the Land: Patterns of American Nativism, 1860–1925*. Rutgers: Rutgers University Press, 1988 [1955].

Hill, Robert A., ed. *The FBI's RACON: Racial Conditions in the United States during World War II*. Boston: Northeastern University Press, 1995.

Hitchcock, William I. *France Restored: Cold War Diplomacy and the Quest for Leadership in Europe, 1944–1954*. Chapel Hill: University of North Carolina Press, 1998.

Hitler, Adolf. *Mein Kampf*. Translated by James Murphy. London: Hurst and Blackett Ltd., 1939 [1925].

Hixson, Walter L. *Parting the Curtain: Propaganda, Culture, and the Cold War, 1945–1961*. NY: St. Martin's Press, 1997.

Hodgson, Godfrey. *The Myth of American Exceptionalism*. New Haven, CT: Yale University Press, 2009.

Hoffman, Bruce. *Terrorism*. 2nd ed. NY: Columbia University Press, 2006.

Hofstadter, Richard. *Anti-Intellectualism in American Life*. NY: Vintage Books, 1963.

Höhn, Maria H. *GIs and Fräuleins: The German-American Encounter in 1950s West Germany*. Chapel Hill: University of North Carolina Press, 2002.

Hollander, Paul. *Anti-Americanism: Critiques at Home and Abroad, 1965–1990*. NY: Oxford University Press, 1992.

———. *Anti-Americanism: Irrational and Rational*. New Brunswick, NJ: Transaction Publishers, 1995.

———, ed. *Understanding Anti-Americanism: Its Origins and Impact at Home and Abroad*. Chicago: Ivan R. Dee, 2004.

Holsti, Ole R. *To See Ourselves as Others See Us: How Publics Abroad View the United States after 9/11*. Ann Arbor: University of Michigan Press, 2008.

Horkheimer, Max. *Gesammelte Schriften*. Frankfurt: S. Fischer, 1988.

Horne, Gerald. *Black and Red: W.E.B. Du Bois and the Afro-American Response to the Cold War, 1944–1963.* Albany: State University of New York Press, 1986.

Hosek, Jennifer Ruth. *Sun, Sex, and Socialism: Cuba in the German Imaginary.* Toronto: University of Toronto Press, forthcoming.

Houtin, Albert. *L'Americanisme.* Paris: Librairie Émile Nourry, 1904.

Immerman, Richard H. *The CIA in Guatemala: The Foreign Policy of Intervention.* Austin: University of Texas Press, 1983.

Iturriaga, José E. *La estructura social y cultural de México.* Mexico City: Fondo de Cultura Económica, 1951.

Jäckel, Eberhard, and Axel Kuhn, eds. *Hitler. Sämtliche Aufzeichnungen 1905–1924.* Stuttgart: Deutsche Verlags-Anstalt, 1980.

James, Daniel. *Red Design for the Americas: Guatemalan Prelude.* NY: John Day, 1954.

Jauvert, Vincent. *L'Amérique contre de Gaulle: Histoire sécrete 1961–1969.* Paris: Seuil, 2000.

Jay, Martin. *The Dialectical Imagination: A History of the Frankfurt School and the Institute of Social Research, 1923–1950.* Boston: Little, Brown, 1973.

Joffe, Josef. *Überpower: The Imperial Temptation of America.* NY: W.W. Norton, 2006.

Johnson, Samuel. *Taxation No Tyranny: An Answer to the Resolutions and Address of the American Congress.* London: T. Cadell, 1775.

Joseph, Franz M. *As Others See Us: The United States through Foreign Eyes.* Princeton, NJ: Princeton University Press, 1959.

Judaken, Jonathan. *Jean-Paul Sartre and the Jewish Question: Anti-Antisemitism and the Politics of the French Intellectual.* Lincoln: University of Nebraska Press, 2006.

———, ed. *Race after Sartre: Antiracism, Africana Existentialism, Postcolonialism.* Albany: State University of New York Press, 2008.

Judt, Tony. *Ill Fares the Land.* NY: Penguin, 2010.

———. *Past Imperfect: French Intellectuals, 1944–1956.* Berkeley and Los Angeles: University of California Press, 1994.

Junker, Detlef. *Kampf um die Weltmacht: die USA und das Dritte Reich, 1933–1945.* Düsseldorf: Schwann-Bagel, 1988.

Kafka, Franz. *Amerika.* Frankfurt am Main: Fischer Taschenbuch Verlag, 1994 [1927].

Kagan, Robert. *Paradise and Power: America and Europe in the New World Order.* NY: Knopf, 2003.

Katz, Friedrich. *The Life and Times of Pancho Villa.* Stanford, CA: Stanford University Press, 1998.

Katzenstein, Peter J., and Robert O. Keohane, eds. *Anti-Americanisms in World Politics.* Ithaca, NY: Cornell University Press, 2007.

Kazin, Michael, and Joseph A. McCartin, eds., *Americanism: New Perspectives on the History of an Ideal.* Chapel Hill: University of North Carolina Press, 2006.

Kepner, Charles David, Jr. and Jay Henry Soothill. *The Banana Empire: A Case Study of Economic Imperialism.* NY: The Vanguard Press, 1935.

Kinzer, Stephen. *Overthrow: America's Century of Regime Change from Hawaii to Iraq.* NY: Macmillan, 2007.

Kissel, Susan S. *In Common Cause: The "Conservative" Frances Trollope and the "Radical" Frances Wright.* Bowling Green University Popular Press, 1993.

Kissinger, Henry. *The Troubled Partnership: A Re-appraisal of the Atlantic Alliance.* NY: McGraw-Hill for the Council on Foreign Relations, 1965.

Klautke, Egbert. *Unbegrenzte Möglichkeiten: "Amerikanisierung" in Deutschland und Frankreich 1900–1933*. Stuttgart: Franz Steiner Verlag, 2003.

Kloppenberg, James T. *The Virtues of Liberalism*. NY: Oxford University Press, 1998.

Knight, Alan. *The Mexican Revolution: Counter-Revolution and Reconstruction*. Lincoln: University of Nebraska Press, 1990.

Kohut, Andrew, and Bruce Stokes. *America against the World: How We Are Different and Why We Are Disliked*. NY: Henry Holt and Co., 2006.

Kolodziej, Edward A. *French International Policy under de Gaulle and Pompidou: The Politics of Grandeur*. Ithaca, NY: Cornell University Press, 1974.

Krastev, Ivan, and Alan McPherson, eds. *The Anti-American Century*. Budapest: Central European Press, 2007.

Kroes, Rob, Maarten van Rossem, and Marcus Cunliffe. *Anti-Americanism in Europe*. Amsterdam: Free University Press, 1986.

Kuisel, Richard. *Seducing the French: The Dilemma of Americanization*. Berkeley and Los Angeles: University of California Press, 1993.

Kuklick, Bruce. *Blind Oracles: Intellectuals and War from Kennan to Kissinger*. Princeton: Princeton University Press, 2006.

Kulski, Wladyslaw W. *De Gaulle and the World: The Foreign Policy of the Fifth French Republic*. Syracuse: Syracuse University Press, 1966.

Lacorne, Denis, Jacques Rupnik, and Marie-France Toinet, eds. *L'Amérique dans nos têtes: un siècle de fascinations et d'aversions*. Paris: Hachette, 1986.

Lacorne, Denis, and Tony Judt, eds. *With Us or Against Us: Studies in Global Anti-Americanism*. NY: Palgrave Macmillan, 2005.

Lacouture, Jean. *De Gaulle: Le politique, 1944–1959*. Paris: Editions du Seuil, 1985.

———. *De Gaulle: Le souverain, 1959–1970*. Paris: Editions du Seuil, 1986.

LaFeber, Walter. *The New Empire: An Interpretation of American Expansion, 1860–1898*. 35th anniversary ed. Ithaca, NY: Cornell University Press, 1998.

Langguth, A.J. *Our Vietnam: The War, 1954–1975*. NY: Simon & Schuster, 2000.

Langley, Lester D. *The Banana Wars: An Inner History of American Empire, 1900–1934*. Lexington: University Press of Kentucky, 1983.

———. *Mexico and the United States: The Fragile Relationship*. Boston: Twayne, 1991.

Laqueur, Walter. *Fin de Siècle and Other Essays on America and Europe*. New Brunswick, NJ: Transaction Publishers, 1997.

Lenschau, Thomas. *Die amerikanische Gefahr*. Berlin: Franz Seimenroth, 1902.

Lerner, Daniel, and Morton Gorden. *Euratlantica: Changing Perspectives of the European Elites*. Cambridge, MA: MIT Press, 1969.

Lettau, Reinhard. *Täglicher Faschismus: Amerikanische Evidenz aus 6 Monaten*. Munich: Carl Hanser Verlag, 1971.

Levenstein, Harvey A. *We'll Always Have Paris: American Tourists in France since 1930*. Chicago: University of Chicago Press, 2004.

Lévi-Strauss, Claude. *Structural Anthropology*. NY: Basic Books, 1963.

Lévy, Bernard-Henri. *Sartre: The Philosopher of the Twentieth Century*. Translated by Andrew Brown. Cambridge: Polity, 2003.

Lewis, Sinclair. *Main Street*. NY: New American Library, 1920.

Lipp, Solomon. *Three Chilean Thinkers: Bilbao, Letelier, Molina*. Waterloo, Ontario: Wilfrid Laurier University Press, 1975.

Lipset, Seymour Martin. *American Exceptionalism: A Double-Edged Sword*. NY: Norton & Co., 1996.

Little, Douglas. *American Orientalism: The United States and the Middle East since 1945*. London: I.B. Tauris, 2003.

Logevall, Fredrik. *Choosing War: The Lost Chance for Peace and the Escalation of War in Vietnam*. Berkeley and Los Angeles: University of California Press, 1999.

Lynch, John. *Simón Bolívar: A Life*. New Haven, CT: Yale University Press, 2006.

Lynd, Robert Staughton, and Helen Merrell Lynd. *Middletown: A Study in Contemporary American Culture*. NY: Harcourt, Brace and Co., 1929.

Maase, Kaspar. *BRAVO Amerika: Erkundungen zur Jugendkultur der Bundesrepublik in den fünfziger Jahren*. Hamburg: Junius, 1992.

Mackenzie, Frederick Arthur. *The American Invaders*. London: Grant Richards, 1902.

Macmillan, Margaret. *Paris 1919: Six Months that Changed the World*. NY: Random House, 2003.

MacShane, Frank. *Impressions of Latin America: Five Centuries of Travel and Adventure by English and North American Writers*. NY: Morrow, 1963.

Mandelbaum, Michael. *The Case for Goliath*. NY: PublicAffairs, 2005.

Manela, Erez. *The Wilsonian Moment: Self-Determination and the International Origins of Anticolonial Nationalism*. NY: Oxford University Press, 2007.

Markovits, Andrei S. *Uncouth Nation: Why Europe Dislikes America*. Princeton, NJ: Princeton University Press, 2007.

———, and Philip S. Gorski. *The German Left: Red, Green, and Beyond*. NY: Oxford University Press, 1993.

Marx, Leo. *The Machine in the Garden: Technology and the Pastoral Ideal in America*. NY: Oxford University Press, 1964.

Mathé, Sylvie, ed. *L'antiaméricanisme*. Aix-en-Provence: Université de Provence Service des Publications, 2000.

McNamara, Robert S., James Blight, Robert Brigham, Thomas Biersteker, and Herbert Schandler, eds. *Argument without End: In Search of Answers to the Vietnam Tragedy*. NY: Public Affairs, 1999.

McPherson, Alan, ed. *Anti-Americanism in Latin America and the Caribbean*. NY: Berghahn Books, 2006.

———. *Yankee No! Anti-Americanism in U.S.-Latin American Relations*. Cambridge, MA: Havard University Press, 2003.

Merrill, John C. *Gringo: The American as Seen by Mexican Journalists*. Gainesville: University of Florida Press, 1963.

Merritt, Anna J., and Richard L. Merritt. *Public Opinion in Semisovereign Germany: The HICOG Surveys, 1949–1955*. Urbana: University of Illinois Press, 1980.

Merritt, Richard L. *Democracy Imposed: U.S. Occupation Policy and the German Public, 1945–1949*. New Haven, CT: Yale University Press, 1995.

Miller, Nicola. *In The Shadow of the State: Intellectuals and the Quest for National Identity in Twentieth-Century Spanish America*. London: Verso, 1999.

Moses, A. Dirk. *German Intellectuals and the Nazi Past*. NY: Cambridge University Press, 2007.

Müller, Christoph Hendrik. *West Germans against the West: Anti-Americanism in Media and Public Opinion in the Federal Republic of Germany, 1949–68*. Basingstoke: Palgrave Macmillan, 2010.

Müller, Jan-Werner. *Another Country: German Intellectuals, Unification and National Identity*. New Haven, CT: Yale University Press, 2000.

Munson, Henry Lee. *European Beliefs Regarding the United States*. NY: Common Council for American Unity, 1949.

Musallam, Adnan. *From Secularism to Jihad: Sayyid Qutb and the Foundations of Radical Islamism*. Westport, CT: Greenwood Publishing, 2005.

Myrdal, Gunnar. *An American Dilemma: The Negro Problem and Modern Democracy*. NY: Harper & Bros, 1944.

Naimark, Norman. *The Russians in Germany: A History of the Soviet Zone of Occupation, 1945–1949*. Cambridge: Belknap Press of Harvard University Press, 1995.

Ngai, Mae M. *Impossible Subjects: Illegal Aliens and the Making of Modern America*. Princeton, NJ: Princeton University Press, 2004.

Nieto, Clara. *Masters of War: Latin America and United States Aggression from the Cuban Revolution through the Clinton Years*. Boston: Seven Stories Press, 2003.

Noël, Octave. *Le Péril américain*. Paris: De Soye et fils, 1899.

Nolan, Mary. *Visions of Modernity: American Business and the Modernization of Germany*. NY: Oxford University Press, 1994.

O'Connor, Brendon, ed. *Anti-Americanism: History, Causes, and Themes*. 4 vols. Oxford: Greenwood Press, 2007.

———. *Beyond Anti-Americanism: The Case for Criticism not Prejudice*. NY: Routledge, 2011.

Oshinsky, David M. *A Conspiracy So Immense: The World of Joe McCarthy*. NY: Oxford University Press, 2005.

Ott, Ulrich. *Amerika ist anders. Studien zum Amerika-Bild in deutschen Reiseberichten des 20. Jahrhunderts*. Frankfurt am Main: Peter Lang, 1991.

Paterson, Thomas G. *On Every Front: The Making and Unmaking of the Cold War*. 2nd ed. NY: Norton, 1992.

Patterson, Robert. *War Crimes: The Left's Campaign to Destroy Our Military and Lose the War on Terror*. NY: Random House, 2008.

Paxton, Robert O., and Nicholas Wahl, eds. *De Gaulle and the United States: A Centennial Reappraisal*. Oxford: Berg, 1994.

Paz, Octavio. *The Labyrinth of Solitude*. Translated by Lysander Kemp. NY: Grove Press, 1985.

Pells, Richard H. *Not Like Us: How Europeans Have Loved, Hated, and Transformed American Culture since World War II*. NY: Basic Books, 1998.

Pérez, Louis A., Jr. *Cuba between Empires 1878–1902*. Pittsburgh: University of Pittsburgh Press, 1998.

Peyrefitte, Alain. *C'était de Gaulle*. Paris: Fayard, 1997.

Pike, Fredrick B. *FDR's Good Neighbor Policy: Sixty Years of Generally Gentle Chaos*. Austin: University of Texas Press, 1995.

Plummer, Brenda Gayle. *Rising Wind: Black Americans and U.S. Foreign Affairs, 1935–1960*. Chapel Hill: University of North Carolina Press, 1996.

Poiger, Ute. *Jazz, Rock, and Rebels: Cold War Politics and American Culture in a Divided Germany*. Berkeley and Los Angeles: University of California Press, 2000.

Portes, Jacques. *Fascinations and Misgivings: The United States in French Opinion, 1870–1914*. NY: Cambridge University Press, 2000.

Powell, Colin, with Joseph E. Persico. *My American Journey*. NY: Random House, 1996.

Prager, Max. *Die amerikanische Gefahr*. Berlin: L. Simion, 1902.

Pratt, Mary Louise. *Imperial Eyes: Travel Writing and Transculturation*. London: Routledge, 1992.

Provence, Michael. *The Great Syrian Revolt and the Rise of Arab Nationalism*. Austin: University of Texas Press, 2005.

Rabe, Stephen G. *Eisenhower and Latin America: The Foreign Policy of Anticommunism*. Chapel Hill: University of North Carolina Press, 1988.

———. *The Most Dangerous Area in the World: John F. Kennedy Confronts Communist Revolution in Latin America*. Chapel Hill: University of North Carolina Press, 1999.

Radosh, Ronald, and Joyce Milton. *The Rosenberg File*. 2nd ed. New Haven, CT: Yale University Press, 1997.

Renan, Ernest. *Souvenirs d'enfance et de jeunesse*. Paris: Calmann-Lévy, 1883.

Retamar, Roberto Fernández. *Caliban and other Essays*. Minneapolis: University of Minnesota Press, 1989 [1973].

Revel, Jean-François. *Anti-Americanism*. San Francisco: Encounter Books, 2003.

———. *L'obsession anti-américaine*. Paris: Plon, 2002.

Reyes, Salvador Méndez. *El hispanoamericanismo de Lucas Alamán, 1823–1853*. Universidad Autónoma del Estado de México, 1996.

Richter, Dieter. *Schlaraffenland. Geschichte einer populären Phantasie*. Cologne: Diederichs Eugen, 1984.

Richter, Melvin. *The History of Political and Social Concepts: A Critical Introduction*. NY: Oxford University Press, 1995.

Robinson, Daniel J. *The Measure of Democracy: Polling, Market Research, and Public Life, 1930–1945*. Toronto: University of Toronto Press, 1999.

Rodgers, Daniel. *Atlantic Crossings: Social Politics in a Progressive Age*. Cambridge, MA: Harvard University Press, 2000.

Rodó, José Enrique. *Ariel*. Montevideo: Dornaleche y Reyes, 1900.

Roger, Philippe. *The American Enemy: The History of French Anti-Americanism*. Translated by Sharon Bowman. Chicago: University of Chicago Press, 2006.

———. *L'ennemi américain: généalogie de l'antiaméricanisme français*. Paris: Seuil, 2002.

Ross, Andrew, and Kristin Ross, eds. *Anti-Americanism*. NY: NYU Press, 2004.

Rowley, Hazel. *Richard Wright: The Life and Times*. Chicago: University of Chicago Press, 2008.

Roy, Olivier. *Globalized Islam: The Search for a New Ummah*. NY: Columbia University Press, 2004.

Rubin, Barry, and Judith Colp Rubin. *Hating America: A History*. NY: Oxford University Press, 2004.

Rubinstein, Alvin Z., and Donald Eugene Smith. *Anti-Americanism in the Third World: Implications for U.S. Foreign Policy*. NY: Praeger, 1985.

Sartre, Jean-Paul. *Colonialism and Neocolonialism*. NY: Routledge, 2001.

———. *On Genocide*. Boston: Beacon Press, 1968.

———. *Réflexions sur la question juive*. Paris: Morihien, 1946.

Saunders, Frances Stonor. *The Cultural Cold War: The CIA and the World of Arts and Letters*. NY: New Press, 1999.

Scheer, Robert. *With Enough Shovels: Reagan, Bush, and Nuclear War*. NY: Vintage Books, 1983.

Scheuer, Michael. *Through Our Enemies' Eyes: Osama bin Laden, Radical Islam, and the Future of America*. Dulles, VA: Brassey's, 2003.

Schlesinger, Arthur M., Jr. *A Thousand Days: John F. Kennedy in the White House*. NY: Houghton Mifflin, 2002.

Schlesinger, Stephen C., and Stephen Kinzer. *Bitter Fruit: The Untold Story of the American Coup in Guatemala*. NY: Doubleday, 1982.

Schmidt, Alexander. *Reisen in die Moderne: Der Amerika-diskurs des deutschen Bürgertums vor dem Ersten Weltkrieg im europäischen Vergleich*. Berlin: Akademie Verlag, 1997.

Schmitz, David F. *Thank God They're on Our Side: The United States and Right-Wing Dictatorships, 1921–1965*. Chapel Hill: University of North Carolina Press, 1999.

Schoonover, Thomas D. *The French in Central America: Culture and Commerce, 1820–1930*. Lanham, MD: Rowman and Littlefield, 2000.

———. *Germany in Central America: Competitive Imperialism, 1821–1929*. Tuscaloosa: University of Alabama Press, 1998.

Schoultz, Lars. *Beneath the United States: A History of U.S. Policy Toward Latin America*. Cambridge, MA: Harvard University Press, 1998.

Schwaabe, Christian. *Antiamerikanismus: Wandlungen eines Feinbildes*. Munich: Wilhelm Fink Verlag, 2003.

Schwan, Gesine, ed. *Antikommunismus und Antiamerikanismus in Deutschland: Kontinuität und Wandel nach 1945*. Baden Baden: Nomos Verlag, 1999.

Schwartz, Thomas Alan. *Lyndon Johnson and Europe: In the Shadow of Vietnam*. Cambridge, MA: Harvard University Press, 2003.

Schweitzer, Glenn E., and Carole D. Schweitzer. *America on Notice: Stemming the Tide of Anti-Americanism*. Amherst, NY: Prometheus Books, 2006.

Sée, Paul. *Le Péril américain*. Lille: L. Danel, 1903.

Servan-Schreiber, Jean-Jacques. *Le défi américain*. Paris: Seuil, 1967.

Shaw, George Bernard. *The Political Madhouse in America and Nearer Home*. London: Constable, 1933.

Sheinin, David, ed. *Beyond the Ideal: Pan Americanism in Inter-American Affairs*. Westport, CT: Greenwood Publishing, 2000.

Shields, James. *The Extreme Right in France: From Pétain to Le Pen*. NY: Routledge, 2007.

Siegfried, André. *Les États-Unis d'aujourd'hui*. Paris: A. Colin, 1927.

———. *Tableau politique de la France de l'ouest sous la troisième république*. Paris: Libraririe Armand Colin, 1913.

Slater, Michael. *Charles Dickens*. New Haven, CT: Yale University Press, 2009.

Smith, Steven K., and Douglas A. Wertman. *U.S.-West European Relations during the Reagan Years: The Perspective of West European Publics*. Basingstoke: Macmillan, 1992.

Sombart, Werner. *Warum gibt es in den Vereinigten Staaten keinen Sozialismus?* Tübingen: Mohr Verlag, 1906.

Spengler, Oswald. *The Decline of the West*. NY: Knopf, 1926.

Speranza, Gino. *Race or Nation: A Conflict of Divided Loyalties*. Indianapolis: Bobbs-Merrill, 1923.

Stam, Robert, and Ella Shohat. *Flagging Patriotism: Crises of Narcissism and Anti-Americanism*. NY: Routledge, 2007.

Stead, W.T. *The Americanization of the World; or, the Trend of the Twentieth Century.* London: Horace Markley, 1901.

Stearn, Gerald Emanuel. *Broken Image: Foreign Critiques of America.* NY: Random House, 1972.

Steel, Ronald. *Walter Lippmann and the American Century.* Boston: Little, Brown, 1980.

Stephan, Alexander, ed. *Americanization and Anti-Americanism: the German Encounter with American Culture after 1945.* NY: Berghahn Books, 2005.

————. *The Americanization of Europe: Culture, Diplomacy, and Anti-Americanism after 1945.* NY: Berghahn Books, 2006.

Stephanson, Anders. *Kennan and the Art of Foreign Policy.* Cambridge, MA: Harvard University Press, 1989.

Strauss, David. *Menace in the West: the Rise of French Anti-Americanism in Modern Times.* Westport, CT: Greenwood Press, 1978.

Streeter, Stephen M. *Managing the Counterrevolution: The United States and Guatemala, 1945–1961.* Athens, OH: Ohio University Press, 2000.

Sullivan, Marianna P. *France's Vietnam Policy: A Study in French-American Relations.* Westport, CT: Greenwood Press, 1978.

Suri, Jeremi. *Power and Protest: Global Revolution and the Rise of Détente.* Cambridge, MA: Harvard University Press, 2005.

Sweig, Julia E. *Friendly Fire: Losing Friends and Making Enemies in the Anti-American Century.* NY: Public Affairs, 2006.

Szabo, Stephen F. *The Successor Generation: International Perspectives of Postwar Europeans.* London: Butterworth & Co., 1983.

Tamames, Moncho. *La Cultura del Mal. Una guía del antiamericanismo.* Madrid: Espejo de Tinta, 2005.

Temkin, Moshik. *The Sacco-Vanzetti Affair: America on Trial.* New Haven, CT: Yale University Press, 2009.

Tismaneanu, Vladimir. *Promises of 1968: Crisis, Illusion, and Utopia.* Budapest: Central European University, 2011.

Tocqueville, Alexis de. *Democracy in America.* NY: Library of America, 2004 [1835].

Tomlinson, John. *Cultural Imperialism.* London: Continuum, 1991.

Toscano, F., and James Hiester. *Anti-Yankee Feelings in Latin America: An Anthology of Latin American Writings from Colonial to Modern Times in Their Historical Perspectives.* Washington, DC: University Press of America, 1982.

Troche, Alexander. *"Berlin wird am Mekong verteidigt": Die Ostasienpolitik der Bundesrepublik in China, Taiwan und Süd-Vietnam 1954–1966.* Düsseldorf: Droste Verlag, 2001.

Trollope, Frances. *Domestic Manners of the Americans.* NY: Penguin, 1997 [1832].

United States Strategic Bombing Survey: Summary Report (European War). Washington, DC: U.S. Government Printing Office, 1945.

Vaïsse, Maurice. *La grandeur: Politique étrangère du général de Gaulle, 1958–1969.* Paris: Fayard, 1998.

Varon, Jeremy. *Bringing the War Home: The Weather Underground, the Red Army Faction, and Revolutionary Violence in the Sixties and Seventies.* Berkeley and Los Angeles: University of California Press, 2004.

Vicuña, Carlos. *La Tiranía en Chile.* Santiago: LOM Editorial, 2002 [1928].

Vollnhals, Clemens, ed. *Hitler: Reden, Schriften, Anordnungen. Die Wiedergründung der NSDAP, Februar 1925-Juni 1926.* Munich: K.G. Saur, 1992.

Wagnleitner, Reinhold. *Coca-colonization and the Cold War: the Cultural Mission of the United States in Austria after the Second World War.* Chapel Hill: University of North Carolina Press, 1994.

Wall, Irwin M. *France, the United States, and the Algerian War.* Berkeley and Los Angeles: University of California Press, 2001.

———. *The United States and the Making of Postwar France, 1945–1954.* NY: Cambridge University Press, 1991.

Watson, Bruce. *Sacco and Vanzetti: The Men, the Murders, and the Judgment of Mankind.* NY: Viking, 2007.

Weidermann, Volker. *Lichtjahre. Eine kurze Geschichte der deutschen Literatur von 1945 bis heute.* Cologne: Kiepenheuer & Witsch, 2006.

Weinberg, Gerhard L., ed. *Hitler's Second Book: The Unpublished Sequel to Mein Kampf.* NY: Enigma Books, 2003.

Weiner, Tim. *Legacy of Ashes: The History of the CIA.* NY: Random House, 2008.

Werth, Alexander. *De Gaulle: A Political Biography.* NY: Simon and Schuster, 1966.

Wilkinson, Richard, and Kate Pickett. *The Spirit Level: Why Greater Equality Makes Societies Stronger.* NY: Bloomsbury Press, 2009.

Williams, William Appleman. *The Tragedy of American Diplomacy.* NY: Dell, 1962.

Wittner, Lawrence S. *Toward Nuclear Abolition: A History of the World Nuclear Disarmament Movement, 1971-Present.* Stanford, CA: Stanford University Press, 2003.

Wood, Gordon S. *The Americanization of Benjamin Franklin.* NY: Penguin, 2004.

Woodward, C. Vann. *The Old World's New World.* NY: Oxford University Press, 1991.

Wright, Lawrence. *The Looming Tower: Al-Qaeda and the Road to 9/11.* NY: Knopf, 2006.

Zweig, Stefan. *Die Welt von Gestern: Erinnerungen eines Europäers.* Frankfurt: Fischer, 1982 [1943].

Selected Articles (Others appear in the footnotes.)

Aron, Raymond. "Reflections on American Diplomacy." *Daedalus* 91:4 (Fall 1962): 717–32.

Bemis, Samuel Flagg. "'America' and 'Americans'." *Yale Review* 57 (1968): 326.

Berg, Manfred. "Das Problem des 20. Jahrhunderts: die internationale Geschichte und die Transformation der Rassenfrage in den USA." In *Deutschland und die USA in der Internationalen Geschichte des 20. Jahrhunderts*, edited by Manfred Berg and Philipp Gassert, 171–92. Stuttgart: Franz Steiner Verlag, 2004.

Bevir, Mark. "Begriffsgeschichte." *History and Theory* 39:2 (May 2000): 273–84.

Boschetti, Anna. "Sartre and the Age of the American Novel." In *Situating Sartre in Twentieth-Century Thought and Culture*, edited by Jean-François Fourny and Charles D. Minahen, 71–92. NY: Palgrave Macmillan, 1997.

"British Opinions of America." *American Quarterly Review* 20:40 (December 1836): 405.

Buchanan, William. "How Others See Us." *Annals of the American Academy of Political and Social Sciences* 295 (September 1954): 1–12.

"Capt. Basil Hall's *Travels in North America.*" *The Westminster Review* 11:22 (October 1829): 447.

Carrigan, William D., and Clive Webb. "The Lynching of Persons of Mexican Origin or Descent in the United States, 1848 to 1928." *Journal of Social History* 37:2 (Winter 2003): 411–38.

Césari, Laurent. "Que reste-t-il de l'influence politique française en indochine (1954–1966)?" In *Du conflit d'Indochine aux conflits indochinois*, edited by Pierre Brocheux, 21–36. Paris: Éditions Complexe, 2000.

Cogan, Charles. "Lost Opportunity or Mission Impossible: De Gaulle's Initiatives in China and Vietnam, 1963–1964." *French Politics & Society* 13:1 (1995): 54–77.

Cole, Juan. "Anti-Americanism: It's the Policies." *American Historical Review* 111:4 (October 2006): 1120–29.

Confino, Michael. "Solzhenitsyn, the West, and the New Russian Nationalism." *Journal of Contemporary History* 26 (1991): 611–36.

Costigliola, Frank C. "The Failed Design: Kennedy, de Gaulle, and the Struggle for Europe." *Diplomatic History* 8:3 (Summer 1984): 227–51.

Crespi, Leo P. "The Influence of Military Government Sponsorship in German Opinion Polling." *International Journal of Opinion and Attitude Research* (1950): 151–78.

Davis, Belinda. "The City as Theater of Protest: West Berlin and West Germany, 1962–1983." In *The Spaces of the Modern City: Imaginaries, Politics, and Everyday Life*, edited by Gyan Prakash and Kevin M. Kruse, 247–74. Princeton: Princeton UP, 2008.

———. "What's Left? Popular and Democratic Political Participation in Postwar Europe." *American Historical Review* 113:2 (April 2008): 363–90.

De Corcelle, Francisque. "De L'escalavage aux Etats-Unis." *Revue des deux mondes* 4:6 (1836): 227–46.

Devillers, Philippe. "Le Général de Gaulle et l'Asie." In *De Gaulle et le tiers Monde*, edited by Institut Charles de Gaulle, 299–327. Paris: Pédone, 1984.

Dunn, W.E. "The Post-War Attitude of Hispanic America toward the United States." *Hispanic American Historical Review* 3:2 (1920): 177–83.

Eaton, Joseph. "From Anglophile to Nationalist: Robert Walsh's *An Appeal from the Judgments of Great Britain.*" *Pennsylvania Magazine of History and Biography* 132:2 (April 2008): 141–72.

Erskine, Hazel. "The Polls: World Opinion of U.S. Racial Problems." *Public Opinion Quarterly* 32 (1968): 299–312.

Espinosa, Aurelio M. "The Term Latin America." *Hispania* 1:3 (September 1918): 135–43.

Friedman, Max Paul. "Anti-Americanism and U.S. Foreign Relations." *Diplomatic History* 32:4 (2008): 497–514.

———. "Beyond 'Voting with their Feet': Toward a Conceptual History of 'America' in European Migrant Sending Communities, 1860s to 1914." *Journal of Social History* 40:3 (Spring 2007): 557–75.

———. "Fracas in Caracas: Latin American Diplomatic Resistance to United States Intervention in Guatemala in 1954." *Diplomacy & Statecraft* 21:4 (2010): 669–89.

———. "Of Sartre, Race, and Rabies: 'Anti-Americanism' and the Transatlantic Politics of Intellectual Engagement." *Atlantic Studies* 8:3 (2011): 361–77.

Gienow-Hecht, Jessica C.E. "Always Blame the Americans: Anti-Americanism in Europe in the Twentieth Century." *American Historical Review* 111:4 (October 2006): 1067–91.

Gjerde, Jon. "'Here in America There Is Neither King nor Tyrant': European Encounters with Race, 'Freedom,' and their European Pasts." *Journal of the Early Republic* 19 (1999): 673–90.

Gleijeses, Piero. "Juan Jose Arévalo and the Caribbean Legion." *Journal of Latin American Studies* 21:1 (February 1989): 133–45.

———. "The Limits of Sympathy: The United States and the Independence of Spanish America." *Journal of Latin American Studies* 24:3 (October 1992): 481–505.

Goedde, Petra. "Macht im Spiegel der Geschlechter- und Rassenbeziehungen: US-Soldaten und die deutsche Bevölkerung." In *Die USA und Deutschland im Zeitalter des Kalten Krieges 1945–1968*, edited by Detlef Junker, 785–94. Stuttgart: DVA, 2001.

Grandin, Greg. "Your Americanism and Mine: Americanism and Anti-Americanism in the Americas." *American Historical Review* 111:4 (October 2006): 1042–66.

Gunda, Béla. "America in Hungarian Folk Tradition." *The Journal of American Folklore* 83:330 (1970): 406–16.

Hodgson, Geoffrey. "Anti-Americanism and American Exceptionalism." *Journal of Transatlantic Studies* 2:1 (2004): 27–38.

Hoffmann, Stanley. "The Will to Grandeur: de Gaulle as Political Artist." *Daedalus* (Summer 1968): 829–87.

Holder, Calvin B. "Racism toward Black African Diplomats during the Kennedy Administration." *Journal of Black Studies* 14:1 (September 1983): 31–48.

Hove, Mark T. "The Arbenz Factor: Salvador Allende, U.S.-Chilean Relations, and the 1954 U.S. Intervention in Guatemala." *Diplomatic History* 31:4 (September 2007): 623–63.

Imhoff, Gérard. "Der Amerikanismus der zwanziger Jahre oder die Versuchung einer alternativen Weltbildes." *Revue d'Allemagne* 22 (1990): 427–37.

Jarausch, Konrad H. "Mißverständnis Amerika: Antiamerikanismus als Projektion." In *Antiamerikanismus im 20. Jahrhundert: Studie zu Ost- und Mitteleuropa*, edited by Jan C. Behrends, et al., 34–49. Bonn: Dietz, 2005.

Joffe, Josef. "Dissecting Anti-Isms." *The American Interest* 1:4 (Summer 2006).

Kern, Louis. "'Slavery Recedes but the Prejudice to which It Has Given Birth Is Immovable': Beaumont and Tocqueville Confront Racism and Slavery in Ante-Bellum America and Orléanist France." In *National Stereotypes in Perspective: Americans in France, Frenchmen in America*, edited by William L. Chew, 143–86. Rodopi, 2001.

Kirk, John M. "José Martí and the United States: A Further Interpretation." *Journal of Latin American Studies* 9:2 (November 1977): 275–90.

Krastev, Ivan. "The Anti-American Century?" *Journal of Democracy* 15:2 (April 2004): 5–16.

Kremp, Werner. "Von der Höhe sozialisitischer Kultur zur neuen Macht auf dem Weltschachbrett: Sozialdemokratische Amerikabilder 1890–1914." In *Zwei Wege in die Moderne: Aspekte der deutsch-amerikanischen Beziehungen 1900–1918*, edited by Ragnhild Fiebig-von-Hase and Jürgen Heideking, 119–27. Trier: Wissenschaftlicher Verlag, 1998.

Lange, Wigand. "Antiamerikanismus und Zensur im Kabarett der Besatzungszeit 1945–49." *Frankfurter Hefte* 39 (1984): 55–61.

Lettau, Reinhard. "Täglicher Faschismus. Eine Zeitungs-Collage." *Kursbuch* 22 (December 1970): 1–44.

Makdisi, Ussama. "'Anti-Americanism' in the Arab World: An Interpretation of a Brief History." *Journal of American History* 89:2 (September 2002): 538–56.

Markovits, Andrei S. "Anti-Americanism and the Struggle for a West-German Identity." In *The Federal Republic of Germany at Forty*, edited by Peter H. Merkl, 35–54. NY: New York University Press, 1989.

———. "European Anti-Americanism (and Anti-Semitism): Ever Present Though Always Denied." Harvard University Gunzburg Center for European Studies Working Paper Series, 2003.

Mausbach, Wilfried. "Auschwitz and Vietnam: West German Protest Against America's War During the 1960s." In *America, the Vietnam War, and the World: Comparative and International Perspectives*, edited by Andreas W. Daum, Lloyd C. Gardner, and Wilfried Mausbach, 279–98. NY: Cambridge University Press, 2003.

McGirr, Lisa. "The Passion of Sacco and Vanzetti: A Global History." *Journal of American History* 93:4 (March 2007): 1085–115.

McPherson, Alan L. "Myths of Anti-Americanism: The Case of Latin America." *Brown Journal of World Affairs* 10:2 (Winter/Spring 2004): 141–52.

Mechtersheimer, Alfred. "Antiamerikanisch – weshalb eigentlich nicht? Von der Pflicht, dem weltweit verheerenden Einfluss der USA zu widerstehen." In *Der Krieg der Köpfe. Vom Golfkrieg zur neuen Weltordnung*, edited by Helmut Thielen, 105–19. Bad Honnef: Horlemann, 1991.

Meers, Sharon I. "The British Connection: How the United States Covered Its Tracks in the 1954 Coup in Guatemala." *Diplomatic History* 16 (Summer 1992): 409–28.

Mohr, George. "Die amerikanische Opposition gegen den Krieg in Vietnam." *Kursbuch* 6 (1966): 5–39.

Morton, Adam David. "The Social Function of Carlos Fuentes: A Critical Intellectual or in the Shadow of the State?" *Bulletin of Latin American Research* 22 (January 2003): 27–51.

Mueller, Harald, and Thomas Risse-Kappen. "Origins of Estrangement: The Peace Movement and the Changed Image of America in West Germany." *International Security* 12:1 (Summer 1987): 52–88.

Muhlen, Norbert. "America and American Occupation in German Eyes." *Annals of the American Academy of Political and Social Science* 295 (September 1954): 52–61.

Myrdal, Gunnar. "America and Vietnam." *Transition* 33 (October-November 1967): 15–18.

Niebuhr, Reinhold. "Why They Dislike Us." *The New Leader* 37:15 (April 1954): 3.

Nuti, Leopoldo. "The Center-Left Government in Italy and the Escalation of the Vietnam War." In *America, the Vietnam War, and the World: Comparative and International Perspectives*, edited by Andreas W. Daum, Lloyd C. Gardner, and Wilfried Mausbach, 259–78. NY: Cambridge University Press, 2003.

O'Connor, Brendon, and Martin Griffiths. "Making Sense of Anti-Americanism." In *The Rise of Anti-Americanism*, edited by Brendon O'Connor and Martin Griffiths, 1. NY: Routledge, 2006.

Pérez, Louis A., Jr. "Incurring a Debt of Gratitude: 1898 and the Moral Sources of United States Hegemony in Cuba." *American Historical Review* 104:2 (April 1999): 356–98.

Perry, Edward. "Anti-American Propaganda in Hispanic America." *Hispanic American Historical Review* 3:1 (1920): 17–40.

Peter, Klaus. "Supermacht USA. Hans Magnus Enzensberger über Amerika, Politik und Verbrechen." In *Amerika in der deutschen Literatur*, edited by Sigrid Bauschinger, Horst Denkler, and Wilfried Malsch, 368–81. Stuttgart: Reclam, 1975.

Pocock, J.G.A. "Verbalizing a Political Act: Toward a Politics of Speech." In *Language and Politics*, edited by Michael Shapiro, 38–39. NY: NYU Press, 1984.

Portelli, Alessandro. "The Centre Cannot Hold: Music as Political Communication in Post-War Italy." In *The Art of Persuasion: Political Communication in Italy from 1945 to the 1990s*, edited by Luciano Cheles and Lucio Sponza, 258–77. Manchester: Manchester University Press, 2001.

Raithel, Thomas. "'Amerika' als Herausforderung in Deutschland und Frankreich in den 1920er Jahren." In *Deutschland – Frankreich – Nordamerika: Transfers, Imaginationen, Beziehungen*, edited by Chantal Metzger and Hartmut Kaelble, 90. Stuttgart: Franz Steiner Verlag, 2006.

Reuband, Karl-Heinz. "Antiamerikanismus – ein deutsches Problem?" *S&F (Sicherheit und Frieden)* 3:1 (1985): 46–52.

Rigoulot, Pierre. "American Justice as a Pretext for Anti-Americanism." *Human Rights Review* 4:3 (April 2003): 55–62.

Röhrich, Lutz. "Auswandererschicksal im Lied." In *Der große Aufbruch. Studien zur Amerikaauswanderung*, edited by Peter Assion, 71–108. Marburg: Jonas Verlag, 1985.

Romano, Renee. "No Diplomatic Immunity: African Diplomats, the State Department, and Civil Rights, 1961–1964." *Journal of American History* 87:2 (September 2000): 546–79.

Rose, Arnold M. "Anti-Americanism in France." *Antioch Review* 12:4 (Winter 1952): 468–84.

Scholtyseck, Joachim. "Anti-Amerikanismus in der deutschen Geschichte." *Historisch-politische Mitteilungen* 10 (2003): 23–42.

Schoonover, Thomas D. "A United States Dilemma: Economic Opportunity and Anti-Americanism in El Salvador, 1901–1911." *Pacific Historical Review* 58 (November 1989): 403–28.

Schulz, Kristina. "Studentische Bewegungen und Protestkampagnen." In *Die sozialen Bewegungen in Deutschland seit 1945*, edited by Roland Roth and Dieter Riucht, 418–46. Frankfurt: Campus Verlag, 2008.

Schwann, Gesine. "Das deutsche Amerikabild seit der Weimarer Republik." *Aus Politik und Zeitgeschichte* 26 (June 1986): 3–15.

Skinner, Quentin. "Rhetoric and Conceptual Change." *Finnish Yearbook of Political Thought* 3 (1999): 60–73.

Spiro, Herbert J. "Anti-Americanism in Western Europe." *Annals of the American Academy of Political Science* (May 1988): 124.

Steiman, Lionel B. "The Eclipse of Humanism: Zweig between the Wars." *Modern Austrian Literature* 14:3/4 (1981): 147–93.

Stokes, William S. "Cultural Anti-Americanism in Latin America." In *Issues and Conflicts: Studies in Twentieth Century American Diplomacy*, edited by George L. Anderson, 315–38. Lawrence: University of Kansas Press, 1959.

Suri, Jeremi. "The Rise and Fall of an International Counterculture, 1960-1975." *American Historical Review* 114:1 (February 2009): 45–68.

Turner, Frederick C. "Anti-Americanism in Mexico, 1910–1913." *Hispanic American Historical Review* 47:4 (November 1967): 502–18.

Wagner, Wolfgang. "Das Amerikabild der Europäer." In *Amerika und Westeuropa. Gegenwarts- und Zukunftsprobleme*, edited by Karl Kaiser and Hans-Peter Schwarz, 20. Stuttgart: Belser, 1977.

Wall, Irwin M. "From Anti-Americanism to Francophobia: The Saga of French and American Intellectuals." *French Historical Studies* 18:4 (Autumn 1994): 1083–100.

Walser, Martin. "Praktiker, Weltfremde und Vietnam." *Kursbuch* 9 (1967): 168–76.

Wright, Gordon. "Blurred and Distorted Images: France Viewed from the American Shore, 1880–1990." *French American Review* 61:2 (1990): 22.

Wunderlich, Werner. "Das Schlaraffenland in der deutschen Sprache und Literatur. Bibliographischer Überblick und Forschungsstand." *Fabula* 27 (1986): 54–75.

Young, John. "Great Britain's Latin American Dilemma: The Foreign Office and the Overthrow of 'Communist' Guatemala, June 1954." *International History Review* 8 (November 1986): 573–92.

Zahniser, Marvin R., and W. Michael Weis. "A Diplomatic Pearl Harbor? Richard Nixon's Goodwill Mission to Latin America in 1958." *Diplomatic History* 13:2 (April 1989): 163–90.

About the Author

Max Paul Friedman is an historian of U.S. foreign relations at American University in Washington, D.C. After receiving his Ph.D. from the University of California at Berkeley, he held a Woodrow Wilson Postdoctoral Fellowship, an Alexander von Humboldt Foundation Fellowship, and taught at the University of Colorado at Boulder, Florida State University, and the University of Cologne. His first book, *Nazis and Good Neighbors: The United States Campaign against the Germans of Latin America in World War II* (Cambridge University Press, 2003), won the Herbert Hoover Prize in U.S. History and the A.B. Thomas Prize in Latin American Studies. The Society for Historians of American Foreign Relations awarded him the Bernath Article Prize and the Bernath Lecture Prize for his scholarship, which has appeared in *Atlantic Studies, Diplomacy & Statecraft, Diplomatic History, German Life and Letters, Holocaust and Genocide Studies, Journal of American Studies, Journal of Social History, Modern Intellectual History, Oral History Review, Procesos: revista ecuatoriana de historia, Revue française d'études américaines*, and *The Americas: A Quarterly Review of Inter-American Cultural History*, among others. He is coeditor, with Padraic Kenney, of *Partisan Histories: The Past in Contemporary Global Politics* (Palgrave Macmillan, 2005).

Index

99 Luftballons, 216

Abrams, Elliot, 218
Acheson, Dean, 131, 159, 166, 234
Action Française, 75
Adams, John, 21
Adams, John Quincy, 24, 25, 42
Adenauer, Konrad, 195, 213
Adorno, Theodor W., 73, 203, 205
Afghanistan, 92, 149, 220, 225, 228, 230, 232, 236
Africa, 46, 109
  and de Gaulle, 160
  decolonization, 160
  diplomats in the U.S., 108
  migrants to the U.S., 59
  support for March on Washington (1963), 109
African Americans, 7–8, 9, 54, 107–109, 111, 232. *See also* Little Rock Crisis. *See also* jazz, 9–10, 11, 68. *See also* United States: racism in. *See also* slavery
  blood donations, 112
  in Germany, 94
  newspapers, 35, 147
Alamán, Lucas, 42
Alaya, Muhammad, Mufti, 91
Albania, 144
Albert, Heinrich Christoph, 29
Albertz, Heinrich, 194
Algeria, 4, 6, 69, 111, 115, 160, 165, 177, 179, 184, 192
  Sacco and Vanzetti protests, 76
  U.S. support for, 106
  War of independence, 208, 229

Alien and Sedition Acts, 22
Allen, George V., 101
Alliance for Progress, 151–152, 154
Alphand, Hervé, 164, 165, 166–167, 175, 177
al-Qaeda, 8, 225–226, 228–229, 232–233, 234
Alsop, Joseph, 106
Alterman, Eric, 226
America First, 55
American Alliance of Labor and Democracy, 54
American Anti-Slavery Society, 251
American Bar Association, 80
American Civil War, 25, 35, 60
American exceptionalism, 7, 46, 51, 69–70, 90, 133, 227, 238
American Federation of Labor, 54, 131
American Legion, 55–56, 81, 171, 192
American Notes, 31, 32–33, 39
American Red Cross, 112
American Revolution, 21–22, 29, 41, 60
Americanization, 59–61, 72–74
  Europe, 190, 195
  Mexico, 126
  West Germany, 17, 201, 205, 207, 211
anarchism, 75, 76, 77–78, 80
Anders, Günther, 196
Anderson, Marian, 156
Anderson, Richard M., 192
Anderson, Sherwood, 121
Anglophobia, 2, 91
Antarctica, 65
Anti-Kommunism in Latin America, 151
anti-Semitism, 11–12, 23, 55, 71, 72, 75, 80, 111, 202

Arabs, 226, 232–234
  and Guatemala coups, 143
  Arab Spring, 234
  Bay of Pigs, 149
  hajj, 91
  nationalism, 69, 91, 149, 229
  relations with U.S., 90
  September 11, 2001, attacks of, 224
  World War I, 69
Araujo, Manuel Enrique, 66
Arbenz Guzmán, Jacobo, 129–132, 135, 140,
  142, 144–145, 151, 153
Arendt, Hannah, 81, 114
Arévalo, Juan José, 15, 129, 130–131,
  151–155
Argentina, 43, 78
  and Guatemala coups, 137–138, 144
  anti-Argentinism, 2
  Bay of Pigs, 150
  immigration, 46
  Sacco and Vanzetti protests, 76
Ariel, 43–44
Aron, Raymond, 90, 117, 129, 167, 170, 203
Asia, 4, 91–92, 160, 167, 183, 186, 227,
  239
  and Guatemala coups, 15
  anti-Asianism, 202
  decolonization, 109, 160
  immigration, 59
Atlantic Crossings, 59
Aubrac, Raymond, 188
Auschwitz, 197, 202, 206
Austin, Stephen, 65
Australia, 46, 76, 163, 225
Austria, 14, 43, 58, 71, 73, 100, 121, 144,
  184, 216
  and Mexico, 64
  Anschluß, 200
  Sacco and Vanzetti protests, 76
Austria-Hungary, 46

Baader, Andreas, 209
Bacon, Francis, 8
Bailey, Thomas A., 135
Baker, Russell, 169
Bakunin, Mikhail, 77
Baldwin, James, 211
Ball, George, 156, 159, 161, 170, 185,
  203
Baring, Arnulf, 197
Barnes, Fred, 229
Barthes, Roland, 3
Bassler, Hilmar, 201

Batista, Fulgencio, 128, 132, 149
Baudissin, Graf Adelbert von, 38
Bebel, August, 75
Belgium, 76, 100, 116, 209, 215
  and Vietnam War protests, 191
  anti-Belgianism, 209
Belize, 132
Bell, John O., 152, 154–155
Bemis, Samuel Flagg, 40
Bergen, Peter, 232
Berlin, 80, 98, 109, 159, 177, 236, 240
  and Iraq, 226
  and Vietnam War, 183, 191, 193–194, 195,
    201, 205, 207, 208–209, 213
  Berlin Airlift, 91, 98, 213
  Berlin Wall, 209
  Kennedy speech (1963), 106, 219, 225
  Sacco and Vanzetti protests, 76
  September 11, 2001, attacks of, 224
Berlusconi, Silvio, 2
Berman, Russell, 3, 227, 238
Bernays, Edward, 101
Betancourt, Rómulo, 146, 149, 153–154, 155
Bhutto, Zulfikar Ali, 234
Bidault, Georges, 164
Biermann, Wolf, 222
Bilbao, Francisco, 14, 20, 42–43, 44
Bill Haley and the Comets, 195
bin Laden, Osama, 225, 231, 232–233
Bin Sultan, Bandar, Prince, 233
Black Americans. *See* African Americans
Bloch, Ernst, 195
Blunt, Roy, 230
Boeters, Gustav, 84
Bohan, Merwin L., 64
Bohlen, Charles, 159, 166, 167, 172, 184,
  187
Bohrer, Karl-Heinz, 197
Boizet, Jacques, 179
Bolívar, Simón, 40–41
Bolivarian Society, 40
Bolivia, 43, 134, 136, 138, 149
Böll, Heinrich, 6, 195, 210
Bond, Christopher S., 227
Bonneau, Gabriel, 132
Bonnet, Henri, 141
Borah, William H., 76
Börne, Ludwig, 30
Boss Tweed, 80
Boutmy, Émile, 59
Bowles, Chester, 149
Brandenburg Gate, 225, 236
Brando, Marlon, 211

Brandt, Willy, 183, 213
Brazil, 11, 46, 73, 78, 138
  and Guatemala coups, 144
  anti-Brazilianism, 2
  Bay of Pigs, 150
Brecht, Bertolt, 199, 202
Brel, Jacques, 195
Brissot de Warville, Jean-Pierre, 29
British Guiana, 130
British Institute of Public Opinion (BIPO),
  95
Brockdorff, Alexander Graf von, 75
Brooke, Rupert, 38
Brooks, David, 218
Brown, George, 194
Brown-Waite, Ginny, 230
Bruce, David, 211
Bruno, Giordano, 29
Buchanan, William, 119
Buchhorn, Henrik, 226
Büchner, Georg, 30
Buffon, Comte de, 3
Bundy, McGeorge, 161, 171, 176, 181
Burma, 143, 145
Burns, Robert, 119
Burt, Richard, 220
Bush, George H. W., 217, 221
Bush, George W., 1, 8, 11, 224, 228–229, 234,
  236–237
  Presidential administration, 3, 225, 226,
    227, 229, 235, 237

Caccia, Harold, 181
Caldwell, Erskine, 111
Cambodia, 160, 178, 179, 184, 186–187
Camden, Earl of, 21
Camus, Albert, 115, 142
Canada, 1, 24, 32, 37, 46, 109, 143, 180, 229,
  239
  Bay of Pigs, 149
  Quebec independence, 172
  Sacco and Vanzetti protests, 76
Candler, Isaac, 34, 38–39
Cantril, Hadley, 95, 119
Cardozo, Benjamin, 79
Carías, Tiburcio, 129
Carlucci, Frank C., 215
Carlyle, Thomas, 26
Carnegie Corporation, 119
Carranza, Venustiano, 63–64
Carstens, Karl, 182
Carter, Jimmy, 214, 217, 219
Cartier, Raymond, 106

Casey, Richard, 163
Castañeda, Jorge, 228
Castillo Armas, Carlos, 140, 141, 143, 145,
  151
Castillo Arriola, Eduardo, 140
Castro, Fidel, 22, 111, 130, 147–150, 160
Catholic Church, 7, 40, 41–42, 53, 57, 116,
  123, 133, 144
Central Intelligence Agency (CIA), 4, 119,
  211, 219
  and France, 113, 169, 170
  and Great Britain, 31
  and Guatemala coups, 15, 128–131, 134,
    145, 147, 152, 153, 154–155
  and Middle East, 225, 232, 233
  and Nicaragua, 218
  Suez Canal Crisis, 106
Césaire, Aimé, 112
Ceylon, 143
Chamberlain, Houston Stewart, 71
Chamberlain, Neville, 196
Chamberlin, Wendy, 234
Chamorro, Pedro Joaquín, 67
Chamoun, Camille, 162
Charterhouse of Parma, The, 26
Chávez, Hugo, 233
Chechnya, 233
Chevallier, R.M.B., 132, 144
Chiang Kai-Shek. *See* Jiang Jieshi
Chiddick, John, 110
Chile, 42–43, 130, 138, 153, 168
  and Guatemala coups, 132–133, 134, 136,
    143–144
China, 11, 12, 47, 77, 224, 227
  and Cambodia, 186
  and Vietnam War, 167, 174, 175, 176,
    179–180, 184–185, 187, 189, 190, 193
  anti-Sinism, 12
  diplomatic recognition of, 159, 167–168,
    184
  immigration, 46, 48
  nuclear weapons, 163
  split with Soviet Union, 160, 167, 240
  Taiwan Strait Crisis, 163
Chirac, Jacques, 4, 228–229, 231
Churchill, Winston, 141, 142, 170, 230
CIA. *See* Central Intelligence Agency
Civil Rights Act of 1964, 109
Clay, Henry, 25
Cleary Gottlieb, law firm, 185
Clemenceau, Georges, 70
Clinton, Bill, 226, 237
Clinton, Hillary, 226

Coca-Cola, 103, 113, 201, 209
Cockburn, George, 39
Cohn, Roy, 121
Cohn-Bendit, Daniel, 207–208
Cold War
    détente, 159–160, 182, 183, 188, 190,
        213–214, 221
    end of, 17, 221–222
    U-2 spy plane controversy, 166
Cole, Juan, 234
Colombani, Jean-Marie, 225
Colombia, 145
    10th Inter-American Conference, 136–137
    Bay of Pigs, 149
    secession of Panama, 67, 125
Commager, Henry Steele, 118–119
Committee on Public Information, 54
communism, 8, 212, 240
    and France, 178, 184
    and immigration, 53
    and independence movements, 240
    and Jews, 55
    and Latin America, 15, 123, 126, 139–140,
        168
    and Southeast Asia, 186, 188, 207
    and U.S. civil rights, 85, 107, 108
    and Vietnam, 185
    Bolshevik Revolution. See Soviet Union:
        Bolshevik Revolution
    collapse of, 221–222
    in Latin America, 151
    independence movements, 92, 160
    Sacco and Vanzetti protests, 76, 78
    U.S. views of, 17, 54–55, 87–90, 99, 156,
        211, 240
    views of Soviet Union, 77, 98
    views of U.S., 75, 77, 81, 97, 104
Communist International, 78
Communist Party USA, 55, 75, 85, 89
Confederate States of America, 35
Confédération Générale du Travail (CGT),
    77
Congo, 160, 206
Congrès des Ecrivains et Artistes Noirs,
    112
Congress for Cultural Freedom, 112
Connally, John, 169
Continental Congress, 21
Coolidge, Calvin, 71, 79, 83
Cooper, James Fenimore, 23
Cooperative for American Remittances to
    Europe (CARE), 98
Corrigan, Robert F., 154

Cortines, Adolfo Ruiz, 127
Costa Rica, 136, 143, 146, 154
Costigliola, Frank, 163
Coughlin, Charles, 55
Council for Democracy, 55
Council on Foreign Relations, 227
Courtade, Pierre, 103
Couve de Murville, Maurice, 164, 175–176,
    182, 184
Creel, George, 54
Crespi, Leo P., 96–98, 99, 101
Crèvecoeur, J. Hector St. John de, 29, 45
Crosnier, Charles, 85
Cuba, 41, 44, 56, 114, 128, 160, 205
    26th of July Movement, 148
    and communism, 77, 148, 149, 206
    and Guatemala coups, 132, 144
    and Vietnam War protests, 190
    Bay of Pigs, 130, 147, 148–151, 158,
        239
    Cuban Missile Crisis, 165–167
    Cuban Revolution, 111, 129, 147
    Cuban war of independence, 44, 57
    House of Representatives, 57
    Operation Mongoose, 151
    Sacco and Vanzetti protests, 76
    U.S. occupation of, 67, 68, 75
Cuban Electric Company, 136
Cummings, Alan, 192
Cunningham, Duke, 229
Curie, Marie, 79
Czechoslovakia, 78, 115, 117, 132, 144,
    212

D'Souza, Dinesh, 226, 229
Darío, Rubén, 67–68
Daud, Mohammad, 91–92
Davies, Harold, 194
Dawes Plan, 74–75
Dawes, Charles G., 74
de Beaumont, Gustave, 34
de Beauvoir, Simone, 111, 113–114, 118
de Chastellux, Marquis François-Jean, 29
de Corcelle, Francisque, 34
de Gaulle, Charles, 231
    and China (PRC), 167–168
    and John F. Kennedy, 158, 165, 167, 174,
        228
    and Latin America, 160, 168, 191
    and Soviet Union, 159–160, 170, 174
    and U.S. monetary policy, 168–169
    and Vietnam War, 172–189, 191, 192–193,
        212, 228, 229

Cambodia speech, 186–187
Cuban Missile Crisis, 165–166
decolonization, 160–161
European Unity, 159–160
independence within NATO, 159, 165, 171, 172
nuclear weapons, 159, 164–165
on U.S. hegemony, 169–171
restoration of French power, 159–161, 162
U.S. images of, 16, 157–159, 173, 176, 177–178
U-2 spy plane controversy, 166
Vietnam War, 5, 16, 158
World War II, 175
de Madariaga, Salvador, 40
de Massot, Pierre, 103
de Pauw, Cornelius, 3
de Zavala, Lorenzo, 124
Declaration of Independence, 148
Defense Department, 119, 234
Denmark, 22, 100, 143, 144, 196, 224, 239
Deutsches Institut für Volksumfragen (DIVO), 96, 107
Dewey, John, 121
Dickens, Charles, 14, 19, 20, 31–34, 35, 38–39, 231
Dillon, Douglas, 116
Diner, Dan, 8, 93, 196, 222
Disney, Walt, 14, 72
Dodd, Thomas, 147
Dollar Diplomacy, 68, 75
Domestic Manners of the Americans, 31, 32
Dominican Republic, 128
U.S. occupation of (1916–1924), 68, 75, 142
U.S. occupation of (1965), 191, 199
Dondero, George A., 121
Dos Passos, John, 79, 111
Douglass, Frederick, 35
Dow Chemical, 74
Dowd, Maureen, 226
Dreiser, Theodore, 121
Dresden, bombing of, 196, 222
Dreyfus Affair, 76, 79–81, 116
Dreyfus, Alfred, 14, 80
Du Bois, W.E.B., 85, 121
Du Pont Chemicals, 74
Duden, Gottfried, 29
Duhamel, Georges, 82, 85
Dulles, Allen, 106, 140, 143–144

Dulles, John Foster, 123, 133, 135–137, 139, 140–141, 143–145, 150, 152, 154, 162–163
Dunn, W.E., 64
Dunne, Finley Peter, 37
Durant, Henry, 95
Dutschke, Rudi, 207, 209, 210
Dylan, Bob, 205

East Germany, 200, 208–209, 210, 213
Easter March movement, 214
Eastern Europe, 89, 101, 114, 160, 221
Eastern State Penitentiary, 32
Ecuador, 43, 76, 134
Eden, Anthony, 132, 141
Edmondson, Robert Edward, 55
Egypt, 69, 106, 109, 149, 179, 231–232, 234
Suez Canal Crisis, 165, 177
Einem, Carl von, 75
Einstein, Albert, 79
Eisenhower, Dwight D., 104–105, 119–120, 161
and 10th Inter-American Conference, 134–136
and Cuba, 147, 148
and France, 158
and Guatemala, 131, 152
and Latin America, 143–144, 145–146
and Mexico, 128
and Middle East, 91
General of the Army, 88, 157
Little Rock Crisis, 107, 118
nuclear weapons, 163–164
Presidential administration, 16, 91, 101, 104, 107, 109, 119, 127, 130, 132, 134–135, 136, 144, 148
Suez Canal Crisis, 106, 165, 177
Taiwan Strait Crisis, 162–163
U-2 spy plane controversy, 166
El Salvador, 66
Elias, Norbert, 39
Éluard, Paul, 102
Emerson, Ralph Waldo, 26, 37
EMNID-Institut, 96
Engels, Friedrich, 61
environmentalism, 7, 11, 190, 210, 214, 215
Enzensberger, Hans Magnus, 6, 195, 205–206, 222
Erhard, Ludwig, 168, 182
Erler, Fritz, 183
Estrada, Pedro, 146
Etherington-Smith, Gordon, 180
eugenics, 59, 84

Europe
  Americans in, 25, 68, 98, 104–106
  and Guatemala coups, 15, 132, 141, 143
  and Obama, 236–237
  and Vietnam War, 16, 190–200, 211
  and War of 1898, 56–58
  Bay of Pigs, 149–150
  communism, 89–90, 93, 98, 99
  Cuban Missile Crisis, 166
  Cuban Revolution, 148
  immigration, 28, 45–51, 59, 239
  imperialism in Latin America, 42, 65
  Iraq, U.S. invasion and occupation of,
    226–228
  Left, 8–9, 17, 60–61, 111, 118
  modernity, 11
  monetary policy, 168–169
  nuclear weapons, 17, 214–216
  pacifism, 216
  racism, 59, 107–108
  Right, 8–9, 59, 68, 82
  Sacco and Vanzetti protests, 79
  September 11, 2001, attacks of, 224
  U.S. culture, 17, 26, 27, 68, 82–83, 195. *See
    also* Americanization
  U.S. economic competition, 58, 68, 70, 96
  U.S. hegemony, 170
  U.S. racism, 7
  unity, 159–160
  views of U.S., 8, 19–20, 26–40, 45–51, 70,
    82, 83, 95–101
  women, 190
  World War II, 92–93
European Defense Community, 159
Evans, Rowland, 191
Everard, T.J., 176
Everest, Robert, 39
Ewing, Samuel, 24

Faisal, Emir, 69
Fall, Bernard, 16, 177, 179, 186–187
Falwell, Jerry, 226
Fanon, Frantz, 112
fascism, 8, 17, 113, 191, 209
  in the U.S., 114, 116, 204, 206, 222
Faubus, Orville, 107
Faulkner, William, 105, 111, 156
Faure, Edgar, 167
Fearon, Henry Bradshaw, 38
Federación Obrera Regional Argentina
    (FORA), 77
Federal Bureau of Investigation (FBI), 108,
    229

Federal Republic of Germany (FRG). *See* West
    Germany
Federal Trade Commission, 136
Federalist Party, 22, 24
Federation of Chilean Students, 22
Ferguson, Niall, 227
Fernández Vanga, Epifanio, 58
Figueres, José, 143, 146
Finland, 100, 184, 215, 224
Fischer, Joschka, 222
Fitzjohn, William H., 108
Five Points, NY, 32
Fletcher, Frank F., 124
Ford Foundation, 119
Ford Motor Company, 74
Ford, Henry, 14, 72, 86
Formosa, 143, 184
  Taiwan Strait Crisis, 163
France, 56. *See also* Chirac, Jacques. *See also*
    de Gaulle, Charles. *See also* Dreyfus
    Affair. *See also* Paris
  American Cultural Center, 191
  Americans in, 68, 81
  and Algeria, 4, 6, 69, 75, 90, 110, 141, 165,
    177, 184, 192, 208, 229
  and American Revolution, 41
  and China, 159–160
  and Germany, 8, 99, 159
  and Guatemala coups, 140–142, 145
  and Indochina, 5, 69, 110, 115, 120, 172,
    178, 179, 185
  and Mexico, 43, 63, 64
  and the Holocaust, 6
  and Vietnam War, 16, 158, 160, 167–168,
    172–173, 194
  and Vietnam War protests, 191–193, 196,
    207, 212
  and War of 1898, 58
  anti-Gallicism, 4–5, 21, 80, 100, 102,
    158–159, 165, 230
  Bay of Pigs, 149
  colonialism, 69, 97, 110, 111
  communism, 22, 81, 90, 102–104, 118,
    121
  Fourth Republic, 105
  French Revolution, 30
  German occupation zone, 98
  immigration, 46
  Iraq, U.S. invasion and occupation of,
    225–226, 228–231
  Left, 36, 39, 105, 192
  modernity, 106
  negritude movement, 110

nuclear weapons, 215, 216
Parti Communiste Français (PCF), 90,
    102–107, 110, 114–115, 117, 161
Pastry War, 64
quasi-war with U.S., 21–22
racism, 6, 110
Rassemblement Démocratique
    Révolutionnaire (RDR), 115
Right, 36, 39, 75, 105
Sacco and Vanzetti protests, 76, 78,
    79
September 11, 2001, attacks of,
    224–225
slavery, 34
Suez Canal Crisis, 165, 177, 239
Taiwan Strait Crisis, 163
U.S. culture, 26, 195
U.S. military bases in, 91
Vichy government, 22, 102, 159,
    230
views of U.S., 15, 28–29, 73, 75, 90,
    105–106, 116, 235, 236
women, 102, 117, 126
World War I, 70–71, 230
World War I reparations, 74
World War II, 92, 230
France, Anatole, 79
Franco, Francisco, 156
Frankfurt, 204, 205, 207
Frankfurt School, 73, 203. *See also* Adorno,
    Theodor; Horkheimer, Max; Marcuse,
    Herbert
Frankfurter, Felix, 79
Franklin, Benjamin, 21, 26, 29
Free Speech Movement, 207
Freedom Fries, 4, 53, 229
Freeman, Charles M., 61
Freeman, Joseph, 75
Freemasons, 22
Frei, Eduardo, 168
Frémont, John C., 25
Fried, Erich, 198–200
Fuentes, Carlos, 6, 129, 156
Fulbright, William J., 2, 146, 207
Fuqua, Carl J., 108

Gaitskell, Hugh, 100
Galeano, Eduardo, 125
Galileo, 29
Galleani, Luigi, 77–78
Gallienne, Willfred, 132
Gallup Poll, 107
Gallup, George H., 95

Garraud, Jean-Marie, 176
Gavin, James, 174
Gee, Jack, 192
Geier Sturzflug, 216
General Electric, 74
General Motors, 74
Gerbi, Antonello, 20
Germany, 39, 75, 86, 177, 235, 239. *See also*
    Nazis, West Germany, East Germany
    and France, 80, 98–99, 102, 171
    and Guatemala coups, 15
    and Latin America, 43
    and Mexico, 62
    and War of 1898, 58
    Anschluß, 200
    anti-Germanism, 2, 53
    Christian Democratic Union (CDU),
        183
    Cold War rearmament, 106
    eugenics, 84
    former Nazis in, 6, 17, 93–94, 195–202,
        205
    immigration, 61
    intellectual views of U.S., 6, 8, 17, 29–31,
        37–38, 60–61
    Iraq, Gulf War (1991), 222–223
    Iraq, U.S. invasion and occupation of, 225,
        226, 228, 229
    modernity, 98
    New Wave music, 216
    postwar occupation, 93–95
    Right, 75, 85
    Sacco and Vanzetti protests, 76
    September 11, 2001, attacks of, 224
    Social Democratic Party (SPD), 61, 72, 75,
        183, 214
    U.S. investment in, 71, 74
    U.S. military bases in, 91
    views of U.S., 8, 47–50, 236
    Weimar Republic, 71–75, 83, 85–86, 197,
        201
    women, 93–95, 99, 190
    World War I, 53, 68, 70, 71, 93
    World War I reparations, 74–75
    World War II, 87, 88, 93, 98,
        102–103, 131, 133, 196, 201, 203,
        204, 205, 213
    Young Germany movement, 30, 61
Gershwin, George, 121
Gerstäcker, Friedrich, 29
Gilded Age, 27, 239
Ginsberg, Allen, 211
Glucksmann, André, 214

Goebbels, Joseph, 36
Goethe, Johann Wolfgang von, 30
Goldfinger, 169
Goldwater, Barry, 147
Gollwitzer, Helmut, 195, 202, 210
Goluchowski, Agenor, 58
Gómez, Máximo, 57
Gompers, Samuel, 54
Good Neighbor policy, 130, 131, 134, 137,
    143
Gorbachev, Mikhail, 221
Government Accountability Office, 227
Gowen, Franklin G., 134
Gramsci, Antonio, 170
Grass, Günter, 6
Grayson, George W., 64
Great Britain, 73. *See also* American
    Revolution. *See also* War of 1812
  American colonies, 21
  and Americanization, 60
  and Cambodia, 186
  and China (PRC), 167
  and Dreyfus Affair, 80–81
  and France, 9, 164, 185
  and George W. Bush, 228, 235
  and Guatemala coups, 15, 132, 133–134,
      140–142, 144, 155
  and Honduras, 132
  and India, 69
  and Latin America, 41, 43
  and Mexico, 62, 63, 64
  and Middle East, 69, 141
  and U.S. monetary policy, 169
  and U.S. policy in Europe, 100–101
  and Vietnam War, 16, 158, 173,
      175, 176, 180–182, 183–184,
      194
  and Vietnam War protests, 192, 194,
      211–212
  Bay of Pigs, 148–149, 150
  Beirut Crisis, 162
  communism, 90, 121
  eugenics, 84
  German occupation zone, 98
  imperialism, 90–91
  Iraq, U.S. invasion and occupation of, 225,
      226, 228
  Labor Party, 100, 142, 150
  nuclear weapons, 215–216
  Sacco and Vanzetti protests, 76, 78
  Suez Canal Crisis, 177, 239
  Taiwan Strait Crisis, 163
  Tories, 150

U.S. civil rights, 109
U.S. economic competition, 22, 58
views of U.S., 14, 26–28, 31–34, 37, 38–39,
    55–56, 77
World War I, 53, 70
World War I reparations, 74
World War II, 92, 103, 200, 230
Great Depression, 65
Greece, 46, 121, 133, 143, 144, 210
Grenada, 221
Guatemala, 145, 152, 154
  1954 coup, 15, 129–147, 151–152
  1963 coup, 16, 151–156, 239
  Agrarian Reform Law, 129
  communism, 15, 130–131, 140, 152,
      153
  women, 129
  World War II, 133
Guevara, Che, 130
Guilaine, Louis, 75
Gulf War (1991). *See* Iraq, Gulf War (1991)
Gulf War (2003–2011). *See* Iraq: U.S. invasion
    and occupation of
Gutzkow, Karl, 30

Habermas, Jürgen, 195, 197, 201–202, 204,
    210, 222
Hagerty, James C., 132
Haig, Alexander M., 215
Haiti, 41, 68, 75, 142
Halfeld, Adolf, 73, 85
Hall, Basil, 38
Hall, William Cornelius, 193
Hammett, Dashiell, 121
Hanoi, 175, 179, 180, 187
Hanson, Victor Davis, 3, 45
Harriman, Averell, 160, 187–188
Haseler, Stephen, 8, 28, 162
Hastert, Dennis, 229
Hauck, Johannes, 49–50
Haushofer, Karl, 75
Hawaii, 56
Haymarket Riot, 60
Hegghammer, Thomas, 232
Heine, Heinrich, 8, 14, 20, 23, 31
Helgoland, 182
Helms, Jesse, 8
Helms, Richard, 153
Hemingway, Ernest, 111, 121, 148
Herder, Johann Gottfried, 29
Herf, Jeffrey, 72
Herrick, Myron, 78
Hillis, Newell Dwight, 53

Hitler, Adolf, 121, 199–200, 207, 210
  analogies to, 36, 144, 147, 185, 196, 222
  views of U.S., 14, 71–72, 86
  World War II, 102, 186
Ho Chi Minh, 69, 176, 178, 179, 181, 187,
    196, 209
Hoffman, Clare Eugene, 55
Holland, 43
Holland, Henry, 143
Hollander, Paul, 3, 7, 10–11, 36, 45, 203,
    215, 221–222, 227
Hollywood, 9, 12, 66, 72, 82–83, 85–86, 89,
    113, 232
Holocaust, 6, 12, 92, 200, 208
Home, Lord (Alec Douglas-Home), 180
Honduras, 129, 132, 134, 135, 140
Hook, Sidney, 112
Hoover, Herbert, 70
Hoover, J. Edgar, 110
Hoppenot, Henri, 140
Horkheimer, Max, 11–12, 73, 203–205
Horowitz, David, 226
Hose, Sam, 85
House Un-American Activities Committee
    (HUAC), 88, 114, 116, 121
Huerta, Victoriano, 124
Hughes, Charles Evans, 53
Hughes, Thomas L., 146
Humboldt, Alexander von, 39
Humphrey, Hubert, 171, 190–194, 211
Hungary, 3, 50–51, 76, 99, 107, 117, 199, 224
Huret, Jules, 85
Hussein, Saddam, 222, 225, 227–228, 238
Huyssen, Andreas, 207

Ibáñez, Carlos, 22
immigration, 9, 11, 25, 45–51, 59, 61, 73,
    212
  as pro-Americanism, 20, 28, 45
  immigrant views of America, 20, 30, 47–51,
    239
  opposition to, 14, 23, 53, 54, 55, 72. *See
    also* Sacco and Vanzetti
  return migration, 46
imperialism, 69, 75, 92, 96
India, 46, 69, 143, 170, 183, 184, 236
Indochina. *See also* France: and Indochina. *See
    also* Vietnam
Indonesia, 90, 143, 179
Iniciativa de la América, 43
Institut Français d'Opinion Publique (IFOP),
    95, 103, 107
Institut für Demoskopie (IfD), 96

Inter-American Conference, 64
  10th, 135–139
  6th, 137
  7th, 137
  8th, 137
International Monetary Fund, 177
International Workers of the World (IWW),
    77
Iran, 91, 206, 208–209, 218, 228, 237
  September 11, 2001, attacks of, 224
Iran-Contra affair, 218
Iraq, 69, 91, 106, 222, 240
  Gulf War (1991), 222–223
  September 11, 2001, attacks of, 224
  U.S. invasion and occupation of, 4–5, 12,
    17, 25, 228–229, 230, 236, 239
Ireland, 23, 46, 215
Islam, 91, 225, 226, 228, 231–234
Israel, 12, 90–91, 109, 222, 228
  and Guatemala coups, 143
  Palestinian conflict, 111
  Suez Canal Crisis, 177
  U.S. support of, 54, 232
Istituto Italiano dell'Opinione Pubblica, 107
Italy, 4, 100–101, 239
  and de Gaulle, 169–171
  and Guatemala coups, 15, 139, 143,
    144
  and Vietnam War, 190–191, 194
  anti-Italianism, 2, 22
  Bay of Pigs, 150
  communism, 89, 121, 191
  immigration, 46, 47–48, 54, 75–76
  Iraq, U.S. invasion and occupation of, 225,
    228
  nuclear weapons, 215, 216
  Partito Comunista Italiano (PCI), 89
  Sacco and Vanzetti protests, 76, 78
  U.S. culture, 195
  views of U.S., 96, 116, 237
  women, 126
  World War II, 191
Iturriaga, José, 124–125, 126–127, 142
Izcoa Díaz, Evaristo, 57

J'accuse, 80, 116
Jackson, C.D., 119
Jackson, William H., 119
Jakarta, 236
Jamaica, 109
James, Daniel, 144
James, Henry, 28
James, William, 80

Jansen, Josef, 182
Japan, 69, 163, 170
  and Guatemala coups, 143, 144
  immigration, 48, 50
  nuclear weapons, 90
  Sacco and Vanzetti protests, 76, 78
  World War II, 56, 87, 88, 102
Jara, Aníbal, 134
Jarausch, Konrad, 222
Jay, John, 21
jazz, 103–104, 111, 197, 231
Jefferson, Thomas, 21, 24, 41
Jews, 73–74, 89. *See also* Dreyfus Affair. *See
    also* anti-Semitism
  and Nazi Germany, 86, 200, 203, 207
  and the Rosenberg trial, 116
  anti-Zionists, 12
  conspiracy theories about, 9, 11–12, 22, 55,
    68, 71–72, 73, 75
  immigration, 46
  Iraq War, 222
  Zionists, 12, 54
Jiang Jieshi, 156, 163
Jim Crow, 84–85, 108
Jiménez de Aréchaga, Justino, 138
Johnson, Lyndon B., 211
  analogies to Hitler, 196–197
  and de Gaulle, 159, 184
  and Vietnam War, 181–183, 184, 185, 188,
    203, 205, 212
  Presidential administration, 16, 179, 181,
    193
Joint Chiefs of Staff, 163, 176
Joliot-Curie, Frédéric, 102
Jones, T.K., 215
Jordan, 162
Joseph, Franz M., 119
Joxe, Louis, 184
Judeophobia. *See* anti-Semitism
Justice Department, 54, 132

Kafka, Franz, 83
Kagan, Robert, 216, 227
Kalisher, Peter, 193
Kashani, Sayyed Abolqasem, Mullah, 91
Kästner, Erich, 195
Kautsky, Karl, 61
Kayser, Rudolf, 74
Kennan, George, 100, 207
Kennedy, Jacqueline, 158, 167
Kennedy, John F., 200
  and Algeria, 165
  and China (PRC), 168

  and de Gaulle, 158–159, 161, 168, 184
  and Germany, 198
  and Guatemala coups, 153–156
  and Latin America, 146, 151
  and Vietnam War, 174–176, 177
  Bay of Pigs, 149–150
  Berlin speech (1963), 106, 219, 225
  civil rights movement, 109
  Cuban Missile Crisis, 165–166
  death of, 167, 175, 197, 228
  nuclear weapons, 164
  Presidential administration, 15, 16, 109,
    148, 150–151, 152, 156, 158, 172, 175,
    179
Kennedy, Robert F., 187, 197, 207
Kent, Sherman, 155
Khrushchev, Nikita, 150, 151, 165, 166
Kilcullen, David, 233
King, Martin Luther, Jr., 8, 109, 197,
    206–207
Kipling, Rudyard, 38
Kissinger, Henry, 92, 162, 169, 187–188
Klee, Eugen, 131, 132
Klein Reidel, Federico, 132–133, 143
Knight, Frances, 105
Know-Nothing Party, 53
Koran, 232
Korea, 69, 177, 178
Korean War, 121, 136
Koselleck, Reinhardt, 7
Krastev, Ivan, 5
Kraus, Karl, 72
Krause, Peter, 5, 222
Krauthammer, Charles, 226
Ku Klux Klan, 55, 76, 85, 114
Kuisel, Richard, 6, 161

La América en peligro, 42, 43
La Fontaine, Jean de, 116
Laboulaye, Édouard-René Lefèbvre de, 29
Lafayette, Marquis de, 34
Lalouette, Roger, 179
Lambelin, Roger, 75
Lamprecht, Karl, 37
Lang, Fritz, 117
Lansing, Robert, 69
Laos, 174, 178, 180
Larmon, Sigurd, 119
Last of the Mohicans, The, 23
Latin America, 9, 20, 39, 120, 239
  and Guatemala coups, 15, 129–147,
    151–156
  Big Stick diplomacy, 131, 143

immigration, 59
Left, 75, 123
modernity, 44, 67–68
Right, 123
U.S. hegemony, 170
U.S. intervention in, 8, 13, 15–16, 137–139
U.S. support of dictators, 8, 91, 146, 151, 156, 234
U.S. view as "hot-blooded", 15, 41, 57, 62
views of U.S., 7, 39–45, 58, 68, 156
Wars of Independence, 41
Lawrence, T.E., 69
Le Pen, Jean-Marie, 22
Leacock, Stephen, 37
League of Nations, 54
League of the Rights of Man, 79
Lebanon, 11, 91, 145
Bay of Pigs, 149
Beirut Crisis, 162, 163
Lee, Spike, 226
Lee, Walter G., 114
Lenin, Vladimir, 69, 77
Leninism, 152
Lenschau, Thomas, 58
Lettau, Reinhard, 194, 206
Lévi-Strauss, Claude, 3
Lévy, Bernard-Henri, 117
Lewis, Anthony, 218
Lewis, Flora, 126
Lewis, Sinclair, 83
liberty cabbage, 53
Libya, 91
Liebknecht, Wilhelm, 61
Liliuokalani, Queen, 56
Limbaugh, Rush, 237
Lincoln Memorial, 109
Lincoln, Abraham, 8, 25, 53, 84, 156
Lindbergh, Charles, 81
Lippmann, Walter, 95, 145, 162, 176, 185
Lithuania, 76, 78
Little Rock Crisis, 106–108, 118, 146, 147
Lloyd, Selwyn, 163
Lodge, Henry Cabot, 140–141, 182, 184–185, 186
López Mateos, Adolfo, 128
Louis XVI, 26, 28
Lowenthal, Richard, 208
Luce, Henry, 211
Luxemburg, Rosa, 207
Lynd, Helen Merrell, 83
Lynd, Robert, 83
Lyon, Cecil B., 166

Macmillan, Harold, 148, 162–163
Madison, James, 24
Presidential administration, 41
Magill, Samuel E., 61–62
Magnien, Bernard, 22
Magoon, Charles, 57
Mailer, Norman, 121
Main Street, 83
Makins, Roger, 141
Malaysia, 144, 181
Malraux, André, 175
Malta, 69
Manac'h, Etienne, 175, 178, 188, 212
Mann, Thomas, 79
Mansfield, Mike, 184
March on Washington (1963), 109
Marcos, Ferdinand, 217
Marcus, John T., 105
Marcuse, Herbert, 203–204
Markle, Bob, 35
Markovits, Andrei, 5, 36, 45
Marshall Plan, 97, 118, 121, 213
Marshall, George Catlett, 121
Martí, José, 9, 44–45, 57, 143
Martin Chuzzlewit, 31–32
Martin, Edwin, 153, 154–155
Martin, Joseph W., Jr., 89
Martin, Josiah, 21
Marx, Karl, 60–61, 77, 82
Marxism, 110, 114–115, 118, 152, 203, 207
Mathews, Shailer, 54
Maurras, Charles, 22, 73, 75
Mausbach, Wilfried, 196
Maximilian I, 64
May, Karl, 72
McCain, John, 179
McCann-Erickson, 120
McCarthy, Joseph, 89, 114, 116, 118, 121–122
McCarthy, Mary, 113–114
McCarthyism, 15, 89–90, 118, 120–121, 143, 146, 204, 240
McCormick, Robert, 89
McGhie, J.I., 180
McGirr, Lisa, 81
McNamara, Robert, 5, 117, 188–189, 203
McPherson, Alan, 6
Mead, Walter Russell, 170
Mein Kampf, 72
Meinhof, Ulrike, 209
Mejía Godoy, Carlos, 218

Melville, Herman, 156
Mendès-France, Pierre, 185
Menzies, Robert, 163
Mexico, 43, 152, 154
  and France, 168
  and Guatemala coups, 132, 134, 144,
    155
  and Pancho Villa, 62–63, 65
  and Vietnam War protests, 196
  anti-Mexicanism, 2, 42, 65–66, 127, 128
  Bay of Pigs, 149
  braceros, 127
  Inter-American Conference, 10th, 135,
    137–138, 139
  Juan Crow restrictions in U.S., 65
  Mexican American War, 13, 25, 43, 62,
    64–65
  Mexican Revolution, 14, 61, 62, 64, 66,
    132
  migrant workers in U.S., 65–66, 127–128
  National Museum of Interventions, 64–65
  Operation Wetback, 128
  Pastry War, 64
  Sacco and Vanzetti protests, 76
  U.S. criticism of, 6, 41, 42, 61–66, 126,
    127
  U.S. racism, 65–66
  Veracruz, U.S. occupation of, 62, 65, 124,
    142, 149
  views of U.S., 42, 123–128, 156, 228
  women, 126
Meyer, Armin H., 91
Middle East, 91, 162, 210, 232
  and democracy, 8, 233
  and Guatemala coups, 15
  immigration, 46
  Jewish immigration, 90–91
  protests of U.S. policy, 11
Middleton, Drew, 101
Mier, Fray Servando Teresa de, 124
Miller, Arthur, 121, 156, 211
Minor, Harold, 91
Missouri Compromise, 34
Molotov, Vyacheslav, 144
Monroe Doctrine, 41–42, 67
Monroe, James, 38, 42
  Presidential administration, 41
Mora, José A., 136
Morals of Manners, 38
More, Thomas, 8
Morgenthau, Henry, 93
Morocco, 120, 149
Morris, Gouverneur, 21
Morse, Wayne, 207

Mundt, Karl, 89
Musharraf, Pervez, 234
Muslim Brotherhood, 231
Mutual Security Agency, 90
Myrdal, Gunnar, 112, 212–213

Napoleon Bonaparte, 24
Napoleon III, 43, 64
Nasser, Gamal Abdel, 106, 149, 177
National Association for the Advancement of
  Colored People (NAACP), 108
National Automobile Chamber of Commerce,
  63
National Liberation Front (NLF), 179
National Press Club, 226
National Red Cross, 79
National Security Council (NSC), 124,
  125–126, 131, 134, 137, 145–146, 147,
  159, 164
National Socialism. *See* Nazis.
Native Americans, 32, 207
Nazis, 2, 23, 230. *See also* Holocaust
  analogies to, 36, 56, 195–196, 204, 206
  in France, 102
  in West Germany. *See* Germany: former
    Nazis in
  Jewish refugees, 203, 208
  modernity, 72
  resistance to, 6, 210
  views of the U.S., 71–73, 83, 85–86
Nearing, Scott, 75
Nena, 216
Nenni, Pietro, 191, 194
Netherlands, 76, 90, 92, 97, 100, 109, 144
New Atlantis, 8
New Deal, 130, 131
New Left, 17, 203, 206, 210
New Zealand, 163, 225
Ngo Dinh Diem, 156, 174–175, 176, 178–180
Nguyen Cao Ky, 199–200
Niagara Falls, 32
Nicaragua, 43, 128, 138
  Banco Nacional, 68
  Sandinistas, 67, 218
  U.S. occupation of, 66–68, 75, 130, 142
Niebuhr, Reinhold, 92, 106, 116, 121, 170,
  241
Niemöller, Martin, 195
Nixon, Richard, 145, 146–147, 156, 169,
  206
  Presidential administration, 169
Nobel Committee, 237
Nolting, Frederick, 175
Noriega Morales, Manuel, 154

North Atlantic Treaty Organization (NATO), 150, 162, 164, 171, 172, 201, 214, 215, 225
North Korea, 228
North, Oliver, 218
Norway, 39, 46, 100, 109, 144, 149
Novak, Robert, 191
nuclear weapons, 88, 151, 159, 163–166, 195
  opposition to, 17, 90, 214–216, 219, 221, 240

O'Connor, Brendon, 5
O'Neill, Eugene, 156
O'Shaughnessy, Nelson, 63
Obama, Barack, 236–238
Obregón, Álvaro, 63
Office of the Military Government, United States (OMGUS), 96
Ohnesorg, Benno, 208
Operation PBSUCCESS, 134
Operations Coordinating Board (OCB), 119
Organisation de l'Armée Secrète (OAS), 111
Organization of American States (OAS), 132, 140–141
Overstreet, Harry Allen, 55

Pacto del Caribe, 152
Padilla, Heberto, 111
Pakistan, 149, 183, 213, 234, 236
Palestine, 54, 69, 111, 225, 233
  Jewish immigration, 90–91
  Palestinian guerrillas, 210
Palme, Olof, 212
Palmer Raids, 78
Palmer, A. Mitchell, 78
Panama, 67, 125, 138
  Panama Canal, 142, 176
Pan-American Highway, 136
Paraguay, 43, 76
Paris, 7, 176, 179, 230. *See also* Vietnam War: Paris Peace Conference. *See also* World War I: Paris Peace Conference
  Americanization in, 195
  Americans in, 24, 69–71, 81, 106, 112, 158, 161, 164, 165–166, 174, 178, 185, 187, 226
  and Vietnam War protests, 191, 192–193, 196, 207, 211
  communism, 116, 121
  criticism of U.S. racism, 111, 112, 117
  jazz, 104

nuclear weapons, 215, 216
  protest of U.S racism, 84
  Sacco and Vanzetti protests, 76, 78, 79, 80
  September 11, 2001, attacks of, 224
  U.S.-Soviet Summit (1960), 166
  World War II, 117
Parkhurst, Henry Clinton, 62
Parry, Hugh J., 97
Patterson, Robert, 226
Paz, Octavio, 65
Pearson, Drew, 114
People's Republic of China. *See* China
Peralta Azurdia, Enrique, 152, 154–155
Pérez Jiménez, Marcos, 136, 146
Perruche, Georges, 179
Perry, Edward, 64
Pershing Missile, protests, 214, 216, 222–223
Pershing, John J., 62, 65
Peru, 43, 136, 145, 154
Pétain, Phillippe, 22
Petraeus, David, 179
Peurifoy, John, 133, 140
Pew Global Attitudes Project, 234
Peyrefitte, Alain de, 170, 174
Pham Van Dong, 187
Philippines, 56, 144, 217
  U.S. occupation of, 35, 68, 80
Phipps, H.B., 63
Picasso, Pablo, 102
Pipes, Daniel, 45
Piscator, Erwin, 202
Platt Amendment, 57
Platt, Rutherford H., Jr., 64
Pocock, J.G.A., 6
Poe, Edgar Allan, 156
Poffenberger, Albert T., 83
Poinsett, Joel Roberts, 42
Poland, 11, 78, 92, 220
Polk, James, 124
  Presidential administration, 25
Pollock, Jackson, 121
Portales, Diego, 42
Portugal, 76, 78, 202, 236
Powell, Colin, 179
Prager, Max, 58
Pratt, Mary Louise, 39
Presley, Elvis, 195
Prohibition, 72, 76
Protocols of the Elders of Zion, 23
Proudhon, Pierre-Joseph, 77
Psychological Strategy Board (PSB), 91, 119, 128–129, 159
Public Broadcasting Services (PBS), 55

Puerto Rico, 44, 56, 57–58, 151
    U.S. annexation of, 67
Pullman Railway Strike, 60
Puritans, 22
Pye, Lucian, 7

Quai d'Orsay, 165, 172, 175, 179
Quakers, 26
Queen Victoria, 80
Quemoy and Matsu. *See* Formosa: Taiwan
    Strait Crisis
Quintanilla, Luis, 132
Qutb, Sayyid, 231–232

Rabe, Stephen, 130
Race or Nation, 54
Radu, Michael, 40
Ramirez, Luis, 66
Rankin, John, 114
Rathenau, Walther, 83
Reagan, Ronald, 215, 216–219, 220–221,
    235, 236
    Presidential administration, 17, 220, 221
Red Army Faction (RAF), 209–210
Redmond, Bernard, 193
Remorino, Jerónimo, 138
Renan, Ernest, 29
Rentoul, Robert Reid, 84
Republican Party, 88, 152
Respectful Prostitute, The, 111
Ressam, Ahmed, 229
Reston, James, 174
Revel, Jean-François, 8, 36
Rhodes, Cecil, 60
Richter, Ann, 226
Rivera, Diego, 79, 143
Rivers, Mendel, 171, 230
Robert du Gardier, Roger, 165
Robertson, Pat, 226
Robeson, Paul, 112
Rockefeller Foundation, 119
Rodgers, Daniel, 59
Rodó, José Enrique, 9, 43–44
Rodríguez, Antonio, 63
Roger, Philippe, 3, 103, 105, 161, 231
Rolland, Romain, 73, 79
Romania, 76
Romualdi, Serafino, 131
Roosevelt Corollary, 67
Roosevelt, Franklin D., 11, 88, 130, 131, 148,
    156, 158
    Presidential administration, 137
Roosevelt, Theodore, 53, 55, 67–68
Roper, Elmo, 95

Rose, Arnold M., 105
Rosenberg, Alfred, 83, 85
Rosenberg, Ethel, 116, 117
Rosenberg, Julius, 116, 117
Rosier, Clarence, 108
Rostow, Walt, 159
Roth, Philip, 211
Rubin, Barry, 5, 40, 64, 125
Rubin, Judith Colp, 5, 40, 64, 125
Rubinstein, Alvin Z., 64
Rubottom, Roy, 145–146
Rumsfeld, Donald, 228, 234
Rusk, Dean, 108–109, 161, 165, 171,
    175–176, 179, 188, 196
Ruskin, John, 27
Russell, Bertrand, 31, 36, 76, 212
Russia, 31, 43. *See also* Soviet Union
    anti-Russianism, 2, 21, 23. *See also* Soviet
        Union: anti-Russianism
    immigration, 46
September 11, 2001, attacks of, 224
Rutherford, Janet, 226

Sacco, Nicola, 14, 75–81
Said, Edward, 233
Saigon, 172, 175, 180, 182–183, 186
Sainteny, Jean, 187–188
Sala, G. A., 38
Salazar, António de Oliveira, 156
Salomon, Alice, 85–86
Sandino, Augusto, 66, 67
Saragat, Giuseppe, 170
Sartre, Jean-Paul, 6, 15, 87, 204, 231
    and Vietnam War, 110–111, 117, 212
    communism, 110, 111–112, 114–115
    criticism of U.S. racism, 109–113
    Soviet Union, 114–118
Saudi Arabia, 91, 120, 233
Sauter, Samuel Friedrich, 49
Scheuer, Michael, 232
Schiller, Friedrich, 210
Schine, David, 121
Schlamm, William S., 211
Schlegelberger, Guenther, 183
Schlesinger, Arthur M., Jr., 149, 150
Schleyer, Hanns-Martin, 210
Schmidt, Helmut, 214
Schröder, Gerhard, 182
Schwan, Gesine, 223
Schweitzer, Daniel, 22
Scopes Monkey Trial, 76
Scott, Winfield, 124
Scottsboro, 111
Second Sex, The, 111

Sedgwick, Catharine Maria, 38
Sée, Paul, 58
Senghor, Leopold, 112
September 11, 2001, attacks of, 1, 3, 12, 17, 224–226, 228, 231, 233
Serge, Victor, 115
Shafarevich, Igor, 23
Shah of Iran, 208–209
Shahn, Ben, 79
Shark and the Sardines, The, 151, 153, 154
Shaw, George Bernard, 14, 52, 55–56, 79
Shell Oil, 134
Siegfried, André, 73
Sierra Leone, 108
Sieve, Harold, 192
Sihanouk, Norodom, 160, 178, 184
Sinclair, Upton, 79
sit-ins, 108, 205, 207
Skinner, Quentin, 6
Slansky, Rudolf, 115
slavery, 8, 25, 27, 30, 32, 33–35, 43
Smith, Lamar, 114
Smith, Sydney, 27
Smith, Walter Bedell, 127, 136
Smithsonian, National Museum of American History, 64
Social Science Research Council, 119
Social Security Program, 89
socialism, 9, 14, 54, 61, 68, 71, 72, 75, 81, 116, 133, 213, 239
Société Africaine de Culture, 112
Sombart, Werner, 61, 83
Somoza, Anastasio, 128, 218
Soustelle, Jacques, 142
South Africa, 76, 109, 206, 217–218
South America. *See* Latin America
South Korea, 143, 170
Southeast Asia. *See* Vietnam
Soviet Union. *See also* Russia
    and China (PRC), 160, 163, 167, 240
    and France, 114–115, 117–118, 159–160, 170
    and Guatemala, 130, 131, 132, 133
    and Guatemala coups, 140, 142, 146
    and Latin America, 123–125, 132
    and Mexico, 123–125, 128
    and Vietnam War, 69, 174–175, 176, 181, 184, 190, 194
    anti-Russianism, 97–98, 100, 124, 125
    anti-Sovietism, 2
    Bay of Pigs, 148, 149–150
    Berlin Airlift, 213
    Bolshevik Revolution, 54, 61, 123

    collapse of, 222
    Cuban Missile Crisis, 165–166
    Eastern Europe, 101
    European views of, 89–90, 97–98, 101, 103, 114–118, 163, 170–204, 214, 217
    German occupation zone, 93, 95, 98
    German women, mass rape of, 93, 99
    gulags, 115, 204
    invasion of Afghanistan, 220, 225, 232–233
    invasion of Czechoslovakia, 117, 212
    invasion of Hungary, 107, 117, 199
    KGB, 221
    nuclear weapons, 151, 164, 165, 214–215
    relations with U.S., 13, 61, 87–90, 100, 101, 118, 215, 216, 219, 221, 227
    Sacco and Vanzetti protests, 77–78
    World War II, 92–93, 94, 102–103, 117
Sow, Malick, 108
Sozialistischer Deutscher Studentenbund (SDS), 195, 204, 209
Spain, 57–58, 109. *See also* War of 1898
    and Mexico, 63–64
    Cuban war of independence, 44
    Iraq, U.S. invasion and occupation of, 225, 226
    nuclear weapons, 215
    Sacco and Vanzetti protests, 76, 78
    Spanish Empire, 40–41
Spanish American War, 142. *See* War of 1898
Speaight, Robert, 141, 144
Spengler, Oswald, 83
Spirit of the Times, The, 33, 39
Springsteen, Bruce, 226
Stalin, Josef, 115
Stalinism, 111, 114–115
Stamp Act, 21
State Department, 90, 119
    and Cuba, 147, 148
    and Europe, 93, 119, 121
    and France, 159, 176, 178, 187
    and Guatemala, 131, 133–134, 144, 145–146, 151–153, 154–155
    and Iraq, 227
    and Latin America, 64, 124, 127, 129
    and Mexico, 6, 62, 156
    and Muslims, 90–92
    Bureau of Intelligence and Research (INR), 107, 146, 151–152, 159
    civil rights movements, 107–109
    Latin America Policy Committee (LAPC), 152
Stead, William T., 60

Steinbeck, John, 111
Stendhal, 26, 29
Stil, André, 103
Stoddard, Lothrop, 62
Stoetzel, Jean, 95
Stokes, William S., 127
Street without Joy, 179
Student Non-Violent Coordinating
    Committee, 207
Students for a Democratic Society (SDS), 195
Suez Canal Crisis, 106, 149, 177, 239
Sullivan, Marianna, 173–174
Sweden, 100, 112, 143, 144
    and Vietnam War, 212–213
    anti-Swedism, 39
    nuclear weapons, 216
    Sacco and Vanzetti protests, 76
Swedish Association of the Blind, 80
Switzerland, 43, 61, 76, 78, 166
Syria, 69

Taft, William Howard, 68, 75
Taiwan. See Formosa
Taliban, 225, 230, 233, 234, 237
Talleyrand-Périgord, Charles Maurice de, 26,
    29, 37
Tardieu, André, 70
Tarnow, Fritz, 72
Taylor, Maxwell, 175, 178, 180, 183
Taylorism, 9
Tello, Manuel, 132
Tempest, The, 9, 44
Thailand, 140, 144
Thomas, Norman, 213
Thompson, Robert, 181
Thompson, Waddy, 65
Thomson, David, 83
Thoreau, Henry David, 83, 207
Thorez, Maurice, 115
Thorkelson, Jacob, 55
Tintenfisch, 206
Tito, Josip, 160, 176
Tocqueville, Alexis de, 34, 36–37, 39, 239
Torres, Leticia, 142
Treitschke, Heinrich von, 30
Trial, The, 83
Trollope, Frances, 14, 20, 31–32, 37, 38, 231
Trujillo, Rafael, 128
Truman Doctrine, 88
Truman, Harry, 88, 108, 118, 121, 131,
    159
    Presidential administration, 15, 93
Tunisia, 234

Turgot, Anne-Robert-Jacques, 28
Turkey, 143
Twain, Mark, 32, 35–36, 80, 84
Tyler, John, 65
Tyler, William, 168

U Thant, 184
ul-Haq, Zia, 234
und Vietnam und, 198
Unda Murillo, Jesús, 154
United Fruit Company (UFCO), 130–131
United Nations, 119, 120, 131, 140–141, 165,
    222, 228
United States
    accusations of imperialism, 56–58
    and Vietnam War, U.S. protests, 192, 194,
        196, 206, 211
    annexation of Texas, 25, 41–43, 124
    anti-French expressions, 4–5, 53, 80–81,
        229–230
    anti-German expressions, 53
    anti-imperialists, 35, 56
    cession of Florida, 41
    civil disobedience, 17
    civil rights movements, 204
    Export-Import Bank, 136
    German occupation zone, 94–95, 96,
        98
    lynching, 65, 84–85, 114, 117
    modernity, 2, 5, 7, 10–11, 19, 52, 67–68,
        72, 76–77, 79, 120, 220, 234
    monetary policy, 168–169
    nativism, 23, 55
    nuclear weapons protests, 215
    racism, 6, 15, 17, 72, 84–86, 104, 106–110,
        111–113, 127, 147, 205, 207, 232
    rape in Germany, 98
    relations with Muslims, 91, 224–226, 228,
        231–234, 236
    women in, 7, 9, 11, 50–51, 55, 85–86, 126,
        171
    World War II, 103, 112, 121, 127
United States Congress, 1, 56, 101
    and Guatemala coups, 146
    anti-French expressions, 4–5, 157, 229–230
    communism, 90
    Cuban Revolution, 147
    House Armed Services Committee, 171
    House Committee on Foreign Affairs, 136
    House of Representatives, 22, 38, 221
    House Select Committee on Communist
        Aggression, 140
    immigration, 55

Iraq, U.S. invasion and occupation of, 227, 238
sanctions on South Africa, 218
Senate Banking Committee, 136
Senate Foreign Relations Committee, 89, 131, 134
United States High Commission for Germany (HICOG), 96–97, 99
United States Information Agency (USIA), 15, 96, 101, 107, 109, 116, 119–120, 121, 144, 213
Uruguay, 44, 76
and Guatemala coups, 136, 138–139, 143
Bay of Pigs, 149
USSR. *See* Soviet Union
utopia, 49–50, 61, 74, 208, 239
Utopia, 8

Vailland, Roger, 103
Vanzetti, Bartolomeo, 14, 75–81
Venezuela, 40, 43, 145–146, 233
and Guatemala coups, 135, 136, 143, 147, 153–154
Bay of Pigs, 149
Versailles, 69
Vietnam, 140, 177, 194
and Guatemala coups, 143
communism, 160, 189, 240
Geneva accords (1954), 180, 184
National Liberation Front (NLF), 212
nationalism, 160, 172, 176, 180, 240
neutralization, 173, 175–176, 180–181, 182–183, 184
North Vietnam, 175, 176, 178, 179–181, 194, 212
South Vietnam, 174, 176, 178–181, 201
Viet Cong, 183, 207
Vietnam War, 106, 168, 216, 235, 239
escalation, 158, 172, 174–176, 180–181, 184–186, 202, 228
Gulf of Tonkin incident, 185, 205
Haiphong Harbor, 209
Mekong River, 183, 201
Operation Rolling Thunder, 185
Paris Peace Conference, 178, 188
Villa, Pancho, 62, 65
Voice of America, 118, 120, 234
Volkssturm, 205
Voltaire, 116
von Wendland, Yorck Alexander Freiherr, 182
Vonnegut, Kurt, 226

Walker, William, 43, 67
Wall Street, 9, 68
Walser, Martin, 206–207
Walsh, Robert, 24–25, 31
Walter, Francis E., 116
Walters, Vernon, 161, 166
War of 1812, 13, 22, 24–25, 132, 226
War of 1898, 44, 52, 56–58, 67, 68
Washington, George, 34, 41, 67, 79, 191, 196
Watergate, 219
Webb-Pomerene Act, 82
Weiss, Peter, 202
Welles, Sumner, 91
Wells, H.G., 79
West Bank, 12, 225, 240
West Germany, 7, 121. *See also* Germany
and de Gaulle, 159, 168
and Guatemala coups, 131–132, 142, 144
and Soviet Union, 89, 93, 98–100
and Vietnam War, 16, 158, 173, 180, 181–183, 190
and Vietnam War protests, 17, 191, 202–210, 214, 222–223
Bay of Pigs, 149
Christian Democratic Union, 142, 150, 200–201
communism, 89, 93, 121, 142, 201–202
Emergency Laws, 209
former Nazis in. *See* Germany: former Nazis in
German Bundestag, 220
Green Party, 190, 215, 222
Kommune, 209
Left, 190, 196, 197, 201, 202, 206, 207–208
nuclear weapons, 17, 164, 195, 214–216
Ostpolitik, 213–214
pacifism, 205, 216
radicals, 197, 200, 208, 209–211
Right, 201, 202
Social Democratic Party (SPD), 150, 195, 201, 213
U.S. civil rights, 109
U.S. culture, 195, 197, 201, 205
U.S. military in, 201, 214
views of U.S., 98–100, 116
Westbindung, 213
women, 214–215
West Point Military Academy, 32, 179
Western Europe. *See* Europe
Westrick, Ludger, 182
Whig Party, 25

White, William Allen, 79, 84
White, William S., 186
Whitman, Ann, 145
Whitman, Walt, 67, 205, 206
Wilcox, Robert W., 56
Wilde, Oscar, 38
Wiley, Alexander, 134
Wilhelm II, 71
Will, George, 230
Wilson, Harold, 181, 194
Wilson, Joe, 238
Wilson, Woodrow, 53, 62, 68–71, 74,
    178
  Presidential administration, 63
Winton, George Beverly, 62
Wood, Alice, 54
Woodward, C. Vann, 27, 45, 47
World Association for Public Opinion
    Research, 96
World Congress of Peace, 115
World Trade Center, 1993 attack, 229
World War I, 81, 82, 201
  growth of U.S. influence, 68, 70, 77
  immigration, 45, 53

Paris Peace Conference, 68–69, 71, 178
  U.S. domestic intolerance, 53–54
  U.S. entry, 53, 70, 186
  war debts, 70–71, 74–75
World War II, 119, 185, 196, 230
  end of, 87–88
  propaganda, 87, 93
  U.S. entry, 186
Wright, Frances, 23
Wright, Frank Lloyd, 121
Wright, Richard, 112
Würzburg, bombing of, 196

Yalta Conference, 89
Ydígoras Fuentes, Miguel, 152–155
Young Plan, 74
Yugoslavia, 121, 160, 189

Zaghlul, Saad, 69
Zakaria, Fareed, 228
Zelaya López, José Santos, 66
Zola, Emile, 80, 115, 116
Zoot Suit Riots, 65
Zweig, Stefan, 14, 73–74